Man and His Fictions

AN INTRODUCTION TO FICTION-MAKING,
ITS FORMS AND USES

For Adam M. Parry

Professor of Classics, Yale University

1928–1971

. . . but Grimes . . . was of the immortals. He was a life force. Sentenced to death in Flanders, he popped up in Wales; drowned in Wales, he emerged in South America; engulfed in the dark mystery of Egdon Mire, he would rise again somewhere at sometime, shaking from his limbs the musty integuments of the tomb. Surely he had followed in the Bacchic train of distant Arcady, and played on the reeds of myth by forgotten streams, and taught the childish satyrs the art of love? Had he not suffered unscathed the fearful dooms of all the offended gods of all the histories, fire, brimstone, and yawning earthquakes, plague and pestilence? Had he not stood, like the Pompeian sentry, while the Citadels of the Plain fell to ruin about his ears? Had he not, like some grease-caked Channel swimmer, breasted the waves of the Deluge? Had he not moved unseen when darkness covered the waters?

Evelyn Waugh, *Decline and Fall*

Man and His Fictions

AN INTRODUCTION TO FICTION-MAKING, ITS FORMS AND USES

Alvin B. Kernan
Peter Brooks
J. Michael Holquist

Yale University

HARCOURT BRACE JOVANOVICH, INC.
New York / Chicago / San Francisco / Atlanta

© 1973 by Harcourt Brace Jovanovich, Inc.

ISBN: 0-15-554716-X

Library of Congress Catalog Card Number: 72-92769

Printed in the United States of America

GIFT

Copyrights and Acknowledgments

For permission to use the selections reprinted in this book, the authors are grateful to the following publishers and copyright holders:

ATHENEUM PUBLISHERS, INC. For "Idea" from *Types of Shape* by John Hollander. Copyright © 1969 by John Hollander. Appeared originally in *Massachusetts Review;* and for "Adam's Task" from *The Night Mirror* by John Hollander. Copyright © 1970 by John Hollander. Appeared originally in *New American Review*. Both reprinted by permission of Atheneum Publishers.

BATTEN, BARTON, DURSTINE & OSBORN, INC. For the Pepsi-Cola jingle. Reprinted by permission of Batten, Barton, Durstine & Osborn, Inc.

CALDER AND BOYARS LTD. For "The Dressmaker's Dummy" and "In the Corridors of the Metro" from *Snapshots* by Alain Robbe-Grillet, translated by Bruce Marrissette; and for excerpts from *For A New Novel* by Alain Robbe-Grillet, translated by Richard Howard. Reprinted by permission of Calder and Boyars Ltd.

JONATHAN CAPE LTD. For "Soap Powders and Detergents" from *Mythologies* by Roland Barthes, translated by Annette Lavers. Reprinted by permission of Jonathan Cape Ltd.

COLLINS-KNOWLTON-WING, INC. For *The Stronger* by August Strindberg from *Six Plays of Strindberg*, translated by Elizabeth Sprigge. Copyright © 1955, by Elizabeth Sprigge. Reprinted by permission of Collings-Knowlton-Wing, Inc.

CROWN PUBLISHER, INC. For selections reprinted from *Superman*. Edited by E. Nelson Bridwell. © 1939 Detective Comics, Inc. Renewed 1966 by National Periodical Publications, Inc. © 1971 National Periodical Publications, Inc. Used by permission of Crown Publishers, Inc.

J. M. DENT & SONS LTD. For *The Heart of Darkness* by Joseph Conrad. Reprinted by permission of J. M. Dent & Sons Ltd. and the Trustees for the Joseph Conrad Estate.

DOUBLEDAY & COMPANY, INC. . For "Frame Tale" © 1963, 1966, 1968, 1969 by John Barth from *Lost in the Funhouse* by John Barth; and for an excerpt from *Homer, The Odyssey* translated by Robert Fitzgerald, copyright © 1961 by Robert Fitzgerald. Both reprinted by permission of Doubleday & Company, Inc.

E. P. DUTTON & CO. INC. For "Diary of a Madman" by Nikolai Gogol, translated by Priscilla Meyer. Copyright © 1973 by Priscilla Meyer. From the forthcoming publication by E. P. Dutton & Co., Inc. entitled *Gogol and Dostoevsky: A Problem in Literary Evolution* by permission of Priscilla Meyer and E. P. Dutton & Co., Inc.

FABER AND FABER LIMITED For "The Hippopotamus" from *Collected Poems 1909–1962* by T. S. Eliot. Reprinted by permission of Faber and Faber Limited.

FALSTAFF BREWING CORPORATION For the Ballantine beer jingle. Reprinted by permission of Falstaff Brewing Corporation.

GROVE PRESS, INC. For "The Theater of Cruelty" from *The Theater and Its Double* by Antonin Artaud, translated by Mary C. Richards. Copyright © 1960 by John Calder (Publishers); for "The Garden of Forking Paths" from *Ficciones* by Jorge Luis Borges, translated by Helen Temple and Ruthven Todd. Copyright © 1962 by Grove Press, Inc. Translated from the Spanish © 1956 by Emecé Editores, S.A., Buenos Aires; for "The Dressmaker's Dummy" and "In the Corridors of the Metro" from *Snapshots* by Alain Robbe-Grillet, translated by Bruce Marrissette. Copyright © 1968 by Grove Press, Inc.; and for excerpts from *For a New Novel* by Alain Robbe-Grillet, translated by Richard Howard. Copyright © 1965 by Grove Press. All reprinted by permission of Grove Press, Inc.

HARCOURT BRACE JOVANOVICH, INC. For "The Hippopotamus" from *Collected Poems 1909–1962* by T. S. Eliot, copyright, 1936, by Harcourt Brace Jovanovich, Inc.; copyright © 1963, 1964, by T. S. Eliot. Reprinted by permission of the publishers.

HARPER & ROW, PUBLISHERS, INCORPORATED For an excerpt abridged from pp. 54–80

Contents

III. BEGINNINGS, MIDDLES, AND ENDS: PUTTING THINGS TOGETHER

IV. SHAPING A SELF

Introduction

Literature and Fiction

The word "Literature," which basically means "the written word," has during the last two hundred years or so become the generic term for all imaginative writing, prose and poetry, considered to be of the highest quality. "The best that has been thought and said" is the way Matthew Arnold described and defended this body of writing, which in his view had replaced religion as the highest manifestation of the human spirit in its drive toward perfection, toward "sweetness and light." This conception of Literature has led to the establishment of a body of canonical works, constantly edited by scholars and interpreted by critics, which make up the course of literary study in schools and universities. We all know very well which works are included in Literature and which excluded—*King Lear* is in, *Tarzan* is out—and the table of contents of any anthology of World Literature, such as *From Homer to T. S. Eliot* or *From "Job" to "Waiting for Godot,"* provides a good outline of the canon. The distinction between subliterature and Literature is by now thoroughly institutionalized, not only in the course of study in the schools but in the libraries and the courts as well. The decision of the Library of Congress to reclassify the works of Ernest Hemingway as "Literature" rather than fiction was thoroughly debated, and its instrumentation required changing a great many call numbers and catalogue cards. A decision by a judge that a particular book is Literature or Art, not pornography, will, though the contents remain the same, mean the difference between publication and suppression, prosperity and jail.

Just what distinguishes Literature from that kind of writing which is not Literature is not entirely clear, and this is indeed one of the questions which this book asks you to consider. Certainly popularity is not the answer. *Gone with the Wind* has been far better known and loved in our time than a more awesome book dealing with the Civil War,

William Faulkner's *Absalom, Absalom;* but Faulkner is Literature while Margaret Mitchell is not. Popularity and easy comprehension almost seem to be signs that a work is not true Literature, while neglect and difficulty are taken as the marks of true genius. But this distinction is too easy, and the reviewers, scholars, critics, teachers, and men of letters who make decisions about what is Literature and what is only entertainment offer a variety of solid reasons for their judgments. Beyond the obvious test that a work has endured and been revered by the best minds over a long period of time, as has, say, Homer's *Iliad* or Vergil's *Aeneid,* these judges apply such other tests as quality of characterization ("Are the characters profound, consistent within themselves, believable?"); power and truthfulness of the theme ("Does the work deal with subjects of enduring and universal concern to man, and does it give voice to opposing points of view so that we feel that the fullness of truth in all its conflicting variety has been presented?"); and effectiveness of style ("Are the words well chosen, the parts adjusted artfully to one another, the individual pieces structured in such a way as to create a harmonious whole?"). More scrupulous critics get down to finer details of technique such as the management of meter and rhyme (or lack of it) in poetry, the selection of forceful metaphors, and the skillful handling of point of view.

Such tests as these, never capable of scientifically precise application, rest in turn on more general theories about the nature of Art and Literature which have become dominant in the nineteenth and twentieth centuries. There was a time when imaginative writing was thought to perform quite simple tasks: it imitated reality (the mimetic theory), it instructed and taught correct moral conduct (the didactic theory), and it delighted and amused (the ludic theory). But in the last two hundred years or so, when science and history have presented themselves as alternative and superior ways of performing at least the first two of these traditional functions, philosophers and poets have sought and elaborated more transcendental justifications. Myth critics have seen Literature as preserving deep within itself primal rites and ancient stories going back to the beginnings of the human race and containing fundamental truths about man and nature. Aestheticians have found in Art the manifestation of abstract beauty and idealized form, far superior to anything to be found in nature. A related group of theoreticians, who might be called "second-world critics," have seen Art as poesis, the construction of an idealized world, the product of the imagination, more lovely in its workings and in its form than the actual world. Psychoanalytic critics have sought and found in Art the mysterious energies of the id, the configurations of the "collective unconscious," the illogicality of dreams, and the strange images and grammar of preconscious thought.

Different as such theories may seem to be, they share a tendency to isolate Literature from familiar life. Literature in these views expresses the eternal, plunges to the depths of the self, returns to the primal

2

mysteries of the human race, creates ideal beauty, and, like Keats'
Grecian urn, hard, perfect in form, and removed from time, remains
always

> . . . a friend to man, to whom thou say'st,
> "Beauty is truth, truth beauty,"—that is all
> Ye know on earth, and all ye need to know.

As Literature became the principal means by which man gave voice
and form to his "immortal longings," expressed powers more urgent,
authentic, and perfect than the drab and debasing "reality" of an industrial society and a world defined by scientific rationalism, so the poet
became a prophet and visionary, heavy of countenance and sunken of
eye, as befits one who communicates with the deep mysteries of the self
and ponders the energies of the cosmos. Works of visual art, carrying
part of the immense burden of man's spiritual life, of his humanity, became rare objects of great price (literally as well as figuratively), almost
sacred things, to be placed in museums where they stand isolated in their
radiant perfection. Something of the same kind has happened in the
study of Literature, and the classroom has become in some ways the
literary museum, even at times the secular church, in which these so
potent objects, the great writings of the past, the highest reaches of the
human imagination, are displayed and interpreted. And the effect
achieved in the classroom or library is sometimes unfortunately close to
that in the museum. If a crucifix becomes Art by being stripped from the
church where it was a part of a complex effort to deal with human suffering; or a portrait is transformed by being removed to a bare museum
wall from the gallery of a great house where it manifested the continuity
of the past with the present; so plays and poetry often become Literature
by being separated from the needs which created them and the societies
and men who used them.

The concepts of Art and Literature tend to focus our attention, as
does a museum, on isolated objects, on the created thing, the painting,
statue, poem, or novel; and we have all profited enormously from looking
long and hard at these works and trying to understand what they are
and what they mean, in and of themselves. But by now many have come
to feel that this close, fine focus of the term Literature is too cramped
and narrow, cutting great writing off from the urgent world of our
immediate lives, from a consideration of the social reality out of which
it emerges, from the larger context of the extensive world of analogous
fiction-making. We need a word other than Literature, with its highly
specialized meaning and its inbuilt presumptions, a word which shifts
the emphasis somewhat from the isolated written work to the faculty of
mind which makes the work and to the large general category of human
activities to which it belongs. No single word quite achieves this effect,
but "fiction" comes the closest.

3

In common usage "fiction" most often means popular novels of a fairly low order, entertainment like detective stories, westerns, spy thrillers, and romances. But the word still derives much of its meaning, and draws most of its strength, from its Latin root (*fingere, fictum*), which means to shape, form, invent, pretend. The replacement of the word "Literature" with the word "fiction," then, immediately opens for our consideration the very large area of things which are made by man, the full range of his fictions, and places Literature *within* this greatly extended context. At the same time our attention is shifted from the written word and the printed book—the solid, set object—to that strange but not unfamiliar activity, apparently peculiar to man, of employing a variety of media, clay, colors, metals, sounds, and movements, as well as words, to construct fictitious realities. Seen from this perspective, Literature loses a good deal of its mystery, but gains significance by taking its place as "first among equals," a crucial part of man's fictions.

How Large Is the World of Fiction?

As we have been using the word, "fiction" can apply to everything that man makes, to tools, machinery, buildings, legal systems, and daydreams, as well as to stories, poems, and plays. Such a wide range of meaning is not a disadvantage in the long run, for it serves to remind us how completely man lives in a man-made or man-arranged world, in a culture, and how closely connected stories and poems are to man's central business, the shaping of things to his own ideas and purposes. To see that the elaboration of a systematic philosophy, the design of an automobile, and the telling of a story are different manifestations of the same instinct to construct fictions may be a bit startling, but it does have the value of breaking down absolute divisions between things based on the *kind* of thing made and substituting a unity centering on the act and purpose of making.

We need, however, to limit the meaning of the word "fiction" somewhat, and we propose, in this book at least, to consider as fictions primarily those works which are openly or tacitly accepted by creator or audience as not being *literally* true. In other words, fictions will here be defined as works in which the feigning and pretense are understood for what they are and acknowledged by formulas such as "once upon a time," rituals such as the raising of the curtain in a theater or the darkening of the lights in a movie house, and words such as "it was like a dream." Understood in this way, fiction would not include mathematical statements like $c = \pi d$ or rituals like the celebration of the mass when the bread and wine are believed to be actually changed into the body and blood of Christ. Fiction, as we are using the word, would not include, in short, any attempt to imitate reality directly, or to construct a theory or tentative explanation of observed facts, though it should be noted in passing that from the point of view of another mathematics or another religion such concepts as the circumference of a circle and the blood of Christ might be thought of not as realities but as fictions created to project the mind upon the world. Fiction would include, however, forms such as advertising and realistic novels, where there is a pretense of recreating or imitating actual things and people but the pretense is understood as a convention. We need not literally and specifically believe that using a particular brand of soap will make us happy and lead to a prosperous marriage (which is what the ad shows happening) for the "idea" to linger that using that particular soap may indeed improve life in some unspecified way. Similarly, though a realistic novel may claim to "tell it like it is," we all understand that this is not the way it literally is, detail by detail, but that the author has carefully selected details, highlighted some and shadowed others, foreshortened time, and patterned the whole to create a fiction which has, as the formula invariably goes, "no relation to any persons living or dead." The line between reality and fiction—between persons living or dead and "characters"—is not, of course, so easily or absolutely drawn, and the problematic relationship between stories and actuality is perhaps the central issue with which any theory of fiction must deal.

Even with our narrowed definition of fiction as understood pretense, the range of activity on which the word opens is far larger than the world of imaginative writing defined by the more traditional term Literature. Lionel Trilling remarks in "Freud and Literature" that "the mind, as Freud sees it, is in the greater part of its tendency exactly a poetry-making organ." If we substitute the word "fiction" for "poetry," this seems so obvious that we are likely to overlook its significance. It is, strangely enough, always the obvious which escapes us until someone calls our attention to the fact that the Emperor is indeed wearing no clothes—or, more aptly for our argument, *is* wearing them. The clothes in this case are, of course, the innumerable fictions which are a part of our daily lives, not only the novels, plays, poems, and operas which are a part of "high culture," but the songs, television shows, movies, comic strips and comic books; the detective stories, westerns, "true romances," and science fiction novels; the light shows, recorded sounds, rock concerts, amusement parks, and fanciful dress usually consigned to "mass culture." One step further, not a very big step, and we come to the vast area of games: chess and football, poker and horse-racing, playing with dolls and doctor kits, ring-around-the-rosy and crossword puzzles, "dress-up" and costume balls. Because games center on "real" activities such as thinking logically or running, they may not seem at first to belong to the world of fictions, but in fact they set their action off in a make-believe space (a chessboard or a playing field), control it by rules, limit its time, and design its suspense as relentlessly as a novel or movie. Advertising too is a world of fiction-making, composed largely of little dramas centering around automobiles, deodorants, refrigerators, and, above all, soap. And that relatively new business, but old profession, of public relations or "image-making" is trying to make the construction of fictions an exact science. Then there is that large group of fictions that take place exclusively inside rather than outside the head, in the theater of the mind rather than the theater of the world. Daydreams are, of course, only little stories, usually with the dreamer as hero, that we tell ourselves to pass the time or create a fictional world more pleasant, or at least more dramatic, than the fully waking world. With the hallucinations released by drugs and trance, and the deep-dreams of sleep, we pass into a strange area of spontaneous fiction-making in which unwilled fictions create themselves out of the depths of the mind. Here too we encounter neurotic or psychotic delusions of being followed or persecuted, of being two persons, of being unable to breathe or forced to vomit, fictions shaped by the mind but assumed to be reality by the sufferer.

The selections which make up this book were chosen to illustrate, as far as possible, the great range of man's fictions and thus to force consideration not only of the variety of uses to which man puts the power of fiction-making, but of its pervasiveness in our lives.

What Fictions Do and How They Do It

It has recently been estimated that large parts of our sleep are spent dreaming. If we add to this the time spent watching television, going to the movies, playing games, reading, and daydreaming, then it is clear that a very large portion of our lives is passed within fictions of our own or another's making. Understanding fictions, which occupy more of our time than eating or participating in politics or making a living, then becomes a crucial part of knowing ourselves, and learning what work fictions do and how they do it becomes as important as understanding the economy or exploring the workings of government.

The selections in this book are chosen to ask, though not necessarily to answer, a number of very simple but very basic questions: Why do men construct fictions? What are the consequences of their fictions? What are the dangers of fiction? Are some fictions better than others, and what is meant by "better"? How does fiction relate to reality? Do fictions have any characteristic features or patterns, and do such patterns help to explain how fictions work and why they are useful to us?

6

The selections which raise these questions and offer at least partial or provisional answers are necessarily limited in number and length by the size of our book; and the fact that it is a *book* restricts us to those fictions which can be printed. But this book is not intended primarily as an entire course in itself—though it can be used in this way—but rather as the spine or armature around which a larger, more extensive course in man's fictions can be constructed by teachers and students. Cervantes' *Don Quixote* is probably the supreme treatment of the relationship of fiction to reality and its attendant values and dangers, while a movie like *Blow-Up* is a vivid and powerful visual demonstration of what plot is and how it works. For different reasons neither of these fictions could be included here, but material of this kind can be quite naturally and easily used in an actual course dealing with man's fictions. The type of course suggested by this textbook will, in fact, only succeed if the teachers and students who use it extend its concept of "fiction" to the great expanse of fictions which are so large a part of our environment. This means constantly going out into the larger world and pulling additional fictions into the directional field set up in these pages.

It may well be objected that despite the shift of emphasis from Literature to fiction, the majority of the selections printed here are drawn from Literature and could easily be included in any standard collection. This is true, and in reply it could be argued that it is necessary to begin any new approach slowly and cautiously, and that it is not our intention to deny the importance of great literature but only to place it in a larger, more truly humanistic context, to see it as a crucial part of the full life of man in his encounter and attempt to deal with himself and his world by means of fictions. It is also necessary to add that one of the things which makes Literature so central to the world of fictions also makes it particularly useful for our purposes in this book: its self-consciousness. That is, where the usual fiction, the soap opera or the love story, simply goes ahead and does its work without asking itself why and how it is doing it, some of the most intriguing fictions—most frequently of the kind called Literature—while performing their function also query themselves, ask why men tell stories, what a story is, and how fiction relates to reality. That is, they question their own value even as they demonstrate it, and in this way they become simultaneously fiction and critical theory.

It is this type of self-conscious writing which makes up the bulk of our selections, doing double-duty as an instance of fiction and as the skeptical questioner of fiction. Story-tellers, for example, have always been fascinated with their own art, and the ancient practice of including story-tellers and stories within the larger story always asks implicitly why men tell stories and with what effect. And with these largest and most fundamental of questions we begin, with Shahrazad telling stories of such fascination and suspense that the King allows her to live for a thousand nights in order to hear her next story, until on night one-thousand-and-one his heart softens, he breaks his vow to use a woman once and then kill

7

her, he marries Shahrazad, and they live happily ever after. Turn your TV to another "Mission Impossible" and you will still find men creating fictions to save their lives, as Saturday night after Saturday night Mr. Phelps and his experts, the actor and the electronic technician, create fictional substitutes for reality, the inside of a submarine within an old warehouse, a faked telephone call, or a mockup of a prison, in order to prevent atomic warfare and defeat the totalitarian baddies. The basic plot formula of "Mission Impossible," as basic as it is to *The Thousand Nights and a Night,* is the familiar irony that men create fictions in order to reveal "truths."

But the power to create fictions is a dangerous power, like the magic to which it is so often compared; and men have long recognized that its effects can be destructive as well as helpful. Some idea of the long history of the attacks on fiction-making, extending from Plato to the modern controversy over violence on television, is presented in the introduction to "Stories That Should Not Be Told." Philosophers and critics who attack fictions usually attack them as lies, as statements of untruth to be avoided in favor of historical and scientific statements of what is true. But some writers have been aware that the dangers of fiction are of a more subtle kind, and some of the materials in this section raise complex questions about how the writer's motivation affects the nature and value of his fictions, whether there are stories which should not be told, whether the effect of certain fictions is not so harmful as to call into doubt their usefulness. Sooner or later all such questions lead us to the even more complicated issue of how fictions relate to the "real" and the "true." The selections in "Fact or Symbol?: The Relationship of Fiction to Reality" are chosen not only to offer further answers to why men create fictions, but also to raise the question of how these fictions relate to and interact with what is perceived as reality. Here too, particularly in Conrad's *Heart of Darkness,* the baffling nature of "reality" is presented and we are asked to consider whether we can indeed ever come near this unknown darkness within ourselves and our world except through the approximations and obliquities of fiction.

Up to this point fiction has been considered only as a product of the human mind, a substitute for the directly perceived world, and a tool for performing certain kinds of necessary work. But the question of how fictions perform this work inevitably arises. More precisely, we want to ask: What constants are there in fiction? How do they regularly arrange and correlate their materials to make them more satisfactory and useful to the human mind? The shift in questions is a shift in focus to the internal workings of fictions. It is no longer enough to know that the King was fascinated by Shahrazad's stories, we now want to know why and how these particular stories had this effect on him. In trying to phrase and answer such questions as these we get a great deal closer not only to the details of fiction—to traditional rhetoric and poetics—but to the human mind, for if men prefer one pattern or arrangement of events to

8

another, then we may reasonably infer that these patterns tell us something about the construction of the mind, about its habitual directions and intentions.

Once again, however, the emphasis falls not so much on the created thing as on the action that characteristically creates this kind of thing and the ends sought. Parts II, III, and IV, "Encountering Things," "Beginnings, Middles, and Ends," and "Shaping a Self," are designed not primarily to direct attention to the usual components of fiction in and of themselves but to ask questions about what kind of work these components, in their many variant forms, are used for. Thus, for example, in "Encountering Things" the stress is not on metaphor as a technical rhetorical device but on the human need to create metaphor, the need to bring objects into relation with consciousness, to make the objective world cease to be "other" from man, to give it meaning and warmth. In the various ways suggested in the different sections of Part II, a fragmented and alien world of things is illuminated and claimed by being "humanized" in various ways.

Similarly, in "Beginnings, Middles, and Ends" the stress falls not on particular plots or types of stories (genres) so much as it does on what all plots and types of stories try to do: to confer "totality" or structure on a number of objects and events that would not otherwise be related to one another or have a definite start and end. There are no beginnings and no endings in the world's time, only an endless flow out of the eternity of the past and into the eternity of the future. But men, by creating such calendrical fictions as A.U.C. (*ab urbe condita,* from the founding of the city of Rome in 753 B.C.), or historical eras like "The Classical Age" or "The Modern Period," or plots like "Once upon a time . . . . and they lived happily ever after," remove a segment of time from the great flux and confer wholeness upon it by giving it a beginning, middle, and end as absolute as that of the individual life beginning with birth and ending with death.

If the vastness and shapelessness of the process we call time are unacceptable to the human mind, so also is the undifferentiated mass of "stuff"—animal, vegetable, and mineral—out of which man as a distinct species, then individuals, emerge into identity for a time, and to which they return in death (unless fame or an afterlife preserves them as individuals). This emergence, this process of separation and identification, is dramatized in various creation stories: God, like a potter at his wheel, making man from clay, and then making Eve from Adam's rib. This struggle of emergence from nature is enacted in stone in some of the figures Michelangelo carved on the Medici tomb, where fully human faces and torsos struggle upward and outward from the rough blocks of marble in which the rest of their bodies seem imprisoned, not yet released, or perhaps not yet created, by the fiction-making of the sculptor. The chisel with which man carves himself, the potter's wheel on which man creates himself, is another fiction, his conception of self,

9

of identity, of character, of individuality. The final part of this book, "Shaping a Self," deals with the ways in which such fictions as role, character, hero, and personality have been used to separate man from the flux of existence, define him, structure his being, and endow it with purpose and meaning.

The theory of fiction implicit in the selections in this book is essentially a dramatic one. Fictions are not treated as exact imitations of reality or mere amusements but as direct attempts to grapple with and transform an alien, or at least a highly problematical, world. Fiction-making is thus an active force, constantly locked in struggle with the opacity and density of things, the endlessness of time, and the undifferentiated continuum of being. Shahrazad telling story after story until at last death is defeated and the real world becomes as wonderful as her stories, this is the model that explains most of the fictions printed here, though all do not end in so complete a triumph as Shahrazad's. She carries her stories to a conclusion that all fictions strive toward but few ever quite succeed in reaching. She lives out what it is that we are trying to do in all our fictions: humanize the world by giving it the shape and meaning that the mind conceives, not that which the world dictates. Though her story seems marvelous, because there is something marvelous about the power to create fictions, there is, at the same time, nothing mysterious or unlikely about what she does. We live in a world composed largely of our fictions, ranging from our dreams to our systems of government and our cosmologies, and we create and use new fictions every day in an attempt to order our lives and make them happier and more meaningful. Nothing can be more important than understanding a power so pervasive as this, so functional in our lives, and so filled with potential for perverting or furthering life.

Alvin B. Kernan

I.
The Story-Teller

Why Men Tell Stories: The Uses and Values of Fiction

Behind our present-day sophisticated conceptions of author, poet, novelist, and playwright there is an older and simpler profession, that of the teller of tales. Every society has a place and a need for these men who tell their stories aloud in public places (not in the silence and privacy in which we read novels) and tell stories that are not of their own invention but are retellings of familiar "twice-told tales" and rearrangements of traditional materials. Such stories emphasize action rather than character and motivation, and the wisdom they convey is as public as the place of recitation and the fund of stories. That is, they do not question the values of the culture of which they are so important a part but rather reinforce them, prove once again the usefulness of the traditional relationship between men and women, between subject and ruler; the traditional values of courage on the field, honor in dealing with other men, good sense in the raising of children. Sir Richard Burton, the translator of *The Thousand Nights and a Night*, provides us with a vivid picture of the story-teller practicing his ancient craft:

I found the Rawi active on Sundays and Thursdays, the market-days. The favourite place was the "Soko de barra," or large bazaar, outside the town, whose condition is that of Suez and Bayrut half a century ago. It is a foul slope; now slippery with viscous mud, then powdery with fetid dust, dotted with graves and decaying tombs, unclean booths, gargottes and tattered tents, and frequented by women, mere bundles of unclean rags, and by men wearing the haik or burnus, a Franciscan frock, tending their squatting camels and chaffering over cattle for Gibraltar beef-eaters. Here the market-people form a ring about the reciter, a stalwart man affecting little raiment besides a broad waist-belt into which his lower chiffons are tucked, and noticeable only for his shock hair, wild eyes, broad grin, and generally disreputable aspect. He usually handles a short stick; and, when drummer and piper are absent, he carries a tiny tom-tom shaped like an hour-glass, upon which he taps the periods. This Scealuidhe, as the Irish call him, opens the drama with extempore prayer, proving that he and the audience are good Moslems: He speaks slowly and with emphasis, varying the diction with breaks of animation, abundant action, and the most comical grimace: he advances, retires, and wheels about, illustrating every point with pantomime; and his features, voice, and gestures are so expressive that even Europeans who cannot understand a word of Arabic divine the meaning of his tale. The audience stands breathless and motionless, surprising strangers by the ingenuousness and freshness of feeling hidden under their hard and savage exterior. The performance usually ends with the embryo actor going round for alms and flourishing in air every silver bit, the usual honorarium being a few "f'lus," that marvellous money of Barbary, big coppers worth one-twelfth of a penny.*

The effect of such story-tellers on their audience is remarkable, as we can all testify. Again we can go to Burton for a description of how his own hearers reacted when he read to them the stories that he in his travels was translating from *The Thousand Nights and a Night*:

> And then a shift of scene. As the giant grey shadow rises slowly in the East and the vagueness of evening waxes wan in the West and night comes on without a shade of gloaming, and, as it were, with a single stride, and Earth looks old, and pallid, and cold, alt, kalt, and ungestalt [old, cold, and formless], the spectre of her former self, the camp forgathers. The Shaykhs and "white-beards" of the tribe gravely take their places, sitting with outspread skirts like hillocks on the plain, as the Arabs say, around the campfire, whilst I reward their hospitality and secure its continuance by reading or reciting a few pages of their favourite tales. The women and children stand motionless as silhouettes outside the ring; and all are breathless with attention; they seem to drink in the words with eyes and mouth as well as with ears. The most fantastic flights of fancy, the wildest improbabilities, the most impossible of impossibilities, appear to them utterly natural, mere matters of everyday occurrence. They enter thoroughly into each phase of feeling touched upon by the author: they take a personal pride in the chivalrous nature and knightly prowess of Taj al-Muluk; they are touched with tenderness by the self-sacrificing love of Azizah; their mouths water as they hear of heaps of untold gold given away in largesse like clay by the mighty Harun al-Rashid—Aaron the Orthodox: they chuckle with delight every time a Kazi or a Fakir (a judge or a reverend) is scurvily entreated by some Pantagruelist of the Wilderness; and despite their normal solemnity and impassibility, all roar with laughter, sometimes rolling upon the ground till the reader's gravity is sorely tried, at the tales of the garrulous Barber, and of Ali with the Kurdish Sharper. To this magnetising mood the sole exception is when a Badawi of superior accomplishments, who sometimes says his prayers,

---

* From "Terminal Essay."

ejaculates a startling "Astagh-faru'llah"—I pray Allah's pardon!—for listening, not to Carlyle's "downright lies," but to light mention of the sex whose name is never heard amongst the nobility of the Desert.

Nor was it only in Arabia that the immortal Nights did me such notable service: I found the wildlings of Somali-land equally amenable to its discipline; no one was deaf to the charm, and the two women-cooks of my caravan, on its way to Harar, were incontinently dubbed by my men "Shahrazad" and "Dinazad." *

It is not so easy for twentieth-century Western man, skeptical and rationalistic as he is, to respond with the unselfconscious delight of the Bedouin to these wonderful stories. We tend to question why and for what purpose men tell stories, while in primitive societies the necessity and value of fiction seem to be taken for granted. Among the most ancient societies, fictions were apparently understood as sympathetic magic. That is, because words and images were taken not as words representing things but as part of the things themselves, to manipulate the signs was to manipulate the things. To possess a lock of your enemy's hair was to possess him, and any harm done to the hair was done to the man. To enact or tell a story about a successful hunt was to ensure the success of the actual hunt.

We are not entirely free of such beliefs—consider how you would feel if someone told a story in which you died—and their remnants are found in stories like "The Rocking-Horse Winner," where the rocking horse in the nursery somehow becomes the real horse in the real race. At the present time a theatrical group, The Living Theater, enacts revolution on stage, takes it down into the auditorium and among the audience, and expects the audience then to carry it out into the streets and make it the new reality. In practice this new "fictional" reality has usually encountered another reality in the form of the police at the first corner.

But most of the traditional functions of fiction are less bizarre than this use of fiction as magic. The traditional stories of many peoples do such humble work as putting in memorable form the paths to the best waterholes and hunting grounds, or the right way to sacrifice an animal, or the most pleasurable ways of making love. Fictions seem, in fact, to lend themselves to a great variety of uses and are regularly put to work in primitive societies, and perhaps our own, to do whatever work is deemed necessary for the well-being of the people. Certain stories, for example, tell about the origin of the clans that make up a tribe, associate them with particular duties such as making axes or telling stories, and thus justify and order efficiently these activities. Other stories provide continuity with the past and a sense of the oneness and unity of the group by keeping alive the memory of ancient heroes and providing genealogies of the important families, as do the lengthy Polynesian epic poems that tell exactly who was in which canoe on the long voyage to

* From "Translator's Foreword."

their island home. Still other stories recount the deeds of heroes and villains, or even of animals, in such a way as to teach and reinforce desirable conduct, those ways of acting which are believed to further the prosperity and continuity of the tribe. The *Iliad,* for example, praises courage in battle, steadfastness, and cleverness; while the stories of the Hopi, a more passive and peaceful people than the Mycenean Greeks, emphasize adjustment and agreement. The most important stories, however, are the sacred stories or myths that provide a charter for a people's possession of their land and a warrant for their whole way of life. These are stories about the gods and their relationship to man, about the beginning and the organization of the cosmos, and about the birth of the ancestors of the tribe out of the land on which a people live. Such stories, of course, are thought of not as fictions but as revealed truths of the way things are, providing orientation in the universe and the basic value system that controls the most crucial areas of life—birth, passage into adulthood, marriage and procreation, death.

There are traces of all these uses of fiction in our literature: the *Aeneid* lists the noble Roman families whose ancestors were in Aeneas' ships when he journeyed from Troy to Latium; *Sir Gawain and the Green Knight* tells us precisely how to kill and carve up a deer; and Milton's *Paradise Lost* justifies the ways of God to man. But by and large we now leave these older uses of fiction to other methods: we coerce nature with science, not word magic; the best water supply is located and maintained by an engineer; we get our views of the cosmos from astronomers; and our relationship to the gods is defined by theologians and philosophers. But this reassignment of traditional duties elsewhere has not interfered with the production of fictions; in fact we create more of them than ever, and we are faced with the unavoidable question of just what uses these fictions have in our own society. What necessary work do they perform for us?

Many answers have been proposed to this question, a number of which were discussed earlier, in the Introduction: that our fictions imitate reality and delight us with that imitation; that they are pure wish fulfillment, creating a world and plot in which our desires are satisfied; that they are manifestations of man's absolute sense of beauty and order; that they are class apologetics—the simple Marxist view—in which certain economic and social practices are justified; and that they are expressions of the primal energies and unconscious drives that are repressed in ordinary life—the psychoanalytic view. All of these answers are true to at least some degree, and it is important to remember that the fiction-making power seems to have no narrowly determined function, as do the beating of the heart or the sexual urge, but is rather a power, like the ability to think, that can be put to many uses. What we need to understand, however, are not all the many varied uses which fictions can serve, but rather their most basic functions, and their most basic dangers.

Because no convention of story-telling is more honored than the practice of including the telling of a story within the story told, the true subject of many tales becomes the telling of stories, as in the old joke about story-telling:

> It was a dark and stormy night. The Captain and his men were sitting around the campfire. One of the men said, "Captain, tell us a story." And the Captain began, "It was a dark and stormy night. The Captain and his men were sitting around the campfire. One of the men said, 'Captain, tell us a story.' And the Captain began. . . ."

This amusing example scarcely exaggerates the situation in *The Thousand Nights and a Night,* where we find Burton "telling" us the story of Shahrazad telling the King a story of Sindbad the Seaman telling Sindbad the Landsman a story. At times the story that Sindbad the Seaman tells even includes himself when younger telling stories to others. In other selections, "The Rocking-Horse Winner" and "The Case of Miss Lucy R.," there are also internal fictions, not stories in these latter cases but fantasies, which are fictions of a nonliterary kind.

The inclusion of stories within stories and fictions within fictions provides us with a convenient way of pursuing our basic questions: Why do men create fictions and with what results? Each of the following stories offers a dramatized answer to these questions, beginning with the most simple answer and moving to the most complex. No explanation of the use of fictions in our society is more common than the view that they simply amuse, that is, that they drive away boredom; and this is what literally happens in Saki's (H. H. Munro, 1870–1916) little story "The Open Window," where the young girl gets rid of a pompous bore by telling a story. But "The Open Window" ends with her beginning another, more fantastic story for which the motivation is not nearly so clear, and we are left with the possibility that the power to invent stories is a more mysterious force than it previously seemed.

This leads us directly on into the more complex fictional world of *The Thousand Nights and a Night,* where Shahrazad tells her stories for the more heroic end of saving her life, and not only succeeds in this but also manages through her story-telling to bring the kingdom itself to the same happy conclusion at which her many stories have arrived again and again. Fictions are capable of transforming reality, the story seems to be saying. We tell stories in order to live, in order to defeat death, in order to overcome despair. For all its seeming simplicity and obviousness, *The Thousand Nights and a Night* is extraordinarily subtle when looked at closely and curiously, and you will want to examine why the King became disillusioned with life and decided to use women once and then kill them; the ways in which the interior stories parallel and duplicate endlessly, like the decorative motifs of Islam, the story of Shahrazad; and the many different occasions on which stories are told in the interior stories. Not all of the interior stories, of course, prominently fea-

15

ture story-telling. But in the struggle with death and slavery that is central to them all, some form of human inventiveness and cleverness, some art or fiction, plays a crucial part. To see how Sindbad's tricks and stratagems for staying alive perform the same function as Shahrazad's story-telling is to come closer to understanding what fictions are and how they work.

In *The Thousand Nights and a Night* the uses of fiction are solid and obvious, but when we come to Borges' story "Tlön, Uqbar, Orbis Tertius," the reasons for creating fictions are not so clear. Men seem to create fictional worlds within fictional worlds out of some more obscure motives, covering their tracks as they go by hiding their fictions in rare editions of encyclopedias. Fictions are hard to find here, or at least hard to distinguish, and difficult to understand, and the clues must be looked for carefully in small details, such as the encyclopedia, and in the nature of the strange worlds of Uqbar and Tlön. Only gradually do we begin to perceive that these are "mirror worlds," duplicates in opposite of our own world, idealist rather than materialist in philosophy, emphasizing verbs rather than nouns in language, and all fitted together in the most cunning fashion to elaborate through many forms a central governing idea. And only gradually do we begin to see that as strange as these worlds are, they are no stranger than our own, that our own conception of reality or "world view" is as much a fiction as that of Tlön, articulated in the same manner and assembled for the same purpose. Understood properly, "Tlön, Uqbar, Orbis Tertius" makes the largest claims for fiction of any work included in this book, and offers the most subtle explanation of the nature and uses of fiction.

The Open Window

Saki

"My aunt will be down presently, Mr. Nuttel," said a very self-possessed young lady of fifteen; "in the meantime you must try and put up with me."

Framton Nuttel endeavoured to say the correct something which should duly flatter the niece of the moment without unduly discounting the aunt that was to come. Privately he doubted more than ever whether these formal visits on a succession of total strangers would do much towards helping the nerve cure which he was supposed to be undergoing.

"I know how it will be," his sister had said when he was preparing to migrate to this rural retreat; "you will bury yourself down there and not speak to a living soul, and your nerves will be worse than ever for moping. I shall just give you letters of introduction to all the people I know there. Some of them, as far as I can remember, were quite nice."

Framton wondered whether Mrs. Sappleton, the lady to whom he was presenting one of the letters of introduction, came into the nice division.

"Do you know many of the people round here?" asked the niece, when she judged that they had had sufficient silent communion.

"Hardly a soul," said Framton. "My sister was staying here, at the rectory, you know, some four years ago, and she gave me letters of introduction to some of the people here."

He made the last statement in a tone of distinct regret.

"Then you know practically nothing about my aunt?" pursued the self-possessed young lady.

"Only her name and address," admitted the caller. He was wondering whether Mrs. Sappleton was in the married or widowed state. An undefinable something about the room seemed to suggest masculine habitation.

"Her great tragedy happened just three years ago," said the child; "that would be since your sister's time."

"Her tragedy?" asked Framton; somehow in this restful country spot tragedies seemed out of place.

"You may wonder why we keep that window wide open on an October afternoon," said the niece, indicating a large French window that opened on to a lawn.

"It is quite warm for the time of the year," said Framton; "but has that window got anything to do with the tragedy?"

"Out through that window, three years ago to a day, her husband and her two young brothers went off for their day's shooting. They never came back. In crossing the moor to their favourite snipe-shooting ground they were all three engulfed in a treacherous piece of bog. It had been that dreadful wet summer, you know, and places that were safe in other years gave way suddenly without warning. Their bodies were never recovered. That was the dreadful part of it." Here the child's voice lost its self-possessed note and became falteringly human. "Poor aunt always thinks that they will come back some day, they and the little brown spaniel that was lost with them, and walk in at that window just as they used to do. That is why the window is kept open every evening till it is quite dusk. Poor dear aunt, she has often told me how they went out, her husband with his white waterproof coat over his arm, and Ronnie, her youngest brother, singing, 'Bertie, why do you bound?' as he always did to tease her, because she said it got on her nerves. Do you know, sometimes on still, quiet evenings like this, I almost get a creepy feeling that they will all walk in through that window—"

She broke off with a little shudder. It was a relief to Framton when the aunt bustled into the room with a whirl of apologies for being late in making her appearance.

"I hope Vera has been amusing you?" she said.

"She has been very interesting," said Framton.

"I hope you don't mind the open window," said Mrs. Sappleton briskly; "my husband and brothers will be home directly from shooting, and they always come in this way. They've been out for snipe in the marshes today, so they'll make a fine mess over my poor carpets. So like you men-folk, isn't it?"

She rattled on cheerfully about the shooting and the scarcity of birds, and the prospects for duck in the winter. To Framton it was all purely horrible. He made a desperate but only partially successful effort to turn the talk on to a less ghastly topic; he was conscious that his hostess was giving him only a fragment of her attention, and her eyes were constantly straying past him to the open window and the lawn beyond. It was certainly an unfortunate coincidence that he should have paid his visit on this tragic anniversary.

"The doctors agree in ordering me complete rest, an absence of mental excitement, and avoidance of anything in the nature of violent physical exercise," announced Framton, who laboured under the tolerably wide-spread delusion that total strangers and chance acquaintances are hungry for the least detail of one's ailments and infirmities, their cause and cure. "On the matter of diet they are not so much in agreement," he continued.

"No?" said Mrs. Sappleton, in a voice which only replaced a yawn at the last moment. Then she suddenly brightened into alert attention— but not to what Framton was saying.

"Here they are at last!" she cried. "Just in time for tea, and don't they look as if they were muddy up to the eyes!"

Framton shivered slightly and turned towards the niece with a look intended to convey sympathetic comprehension. The child was staring out through the open window with dazed horror in her eyes. In a chill shock of nameless fear Framton swung round in his seat and looked in the same direction.

In the deepening twilight three figures were walking across the lawn towards the window; they all carried guns under their arms, and one of them was additionally burdened with a white coat hung over his shoulders. A tired brown spaniel kept close at their heels. Noiselessly they neared the house, and then a hoarse young voice chanted out of the dusk: "I said, Bertie, why do you bound?"

Framton grabbed wildly at his stick and hat; the hall-door, the gravel-drive, and the front gate were dimly noted stages in his headlong retreat. A cyclist coming along the road had to run into the hedge to avoid imminent collision.

"Here we are, my dear," said the bearer of the white mackintosh, coming in through the window; "fairly muddy, but most of it's dry. Who was that who bolted out as we came up?"

"A most extraordinary man, a Mr. Nuttel," said Mrs. Sappleton; "could only talk about his illnesses, and dashed off without a word of good-bye or apology when you arrived. One would think he had seen a ghost."

"I expect it was the spaniel," said the niece calmly; "he told me he had a horror of dogs. He was once hunted into a cemetery somewhere on the banks of the Ganges by a pack of pariah dogs, and had to spend the night in a newly dug grave with the creatures snarling and grinning and foaming just above him. Enough to make any one lose their nerve."

Romance at short notice was her speciality.

FROM The Thousand Nights and a Night

Translated by Sir Richard Burton

The author of *The Thousand Nights and a Night* is, as Sir Richard Burton remarks, "unknown for the best reason; there never was one." The frame story of the disillusioned kings and Shahrazad telling stories to save her life is of great antiquity and Persian in origin. This original story apparently contained few internal stories, but over the centuries, as the tale of Shahrazad gradually became the common property of Islam, the framework became an enclosing form or gathering place for hundreds of the most popular stories of the Arab world. There have probably never been a full one-thousand-and-one stories, since the majority occupy more than one night in the telling, but the range in time and space of the stories we do have is enormous. They come from ancient Indian folklore, from the caliphate of Baghdad, the deserts of Arabia, the battlegrounds of the crusaders, and the streets of Cairo and Alexandria. There are beast fables, tales of marvelous adventure, love stories, chronicles of historical events and palace intrigues, fantastic visions, low comedies involving a great deal of explicit sex, and moral exempla. Here are such wonderful characters as Shahrazad the story-teller, Sindbad the Sailor, the Caliph Harun al-Rashid, and Al-a-din and his wondrous lamp. Probably none of the stories comes down to us in its original form, for all of them have been told and retold many times, and each retelling adds, changes, brings up to date. Though some of the tales are of later date, *The Thousand Nights and a Night* reached something like its present form in the thirteenth century, and the text from which most modern versions derive was assembled in Cairo in the late eighteenth century. Its history, then, is something like that of those other wonderful collections, the *Iliad,* the *Odyssey,* the *Metamorphoses,* the *Decameron,* the *Canterbury Tales,* the Hindu *Katha Sarit Sagara,* and even to a degree Dante's *Divine Comedy,* in all of which a number of traditional stories passed down through long periods of time were at last assembled under the pressure of a great idea into a composite picture of the values and history of a people.

The translation of Sir Richard Burton (1821–90), the British civil

19

servant, Orientalist, philologist, explorer, and linguist appeared in 1885–86. But Burton had worked on it for many years during his travels and his consular service, and its magical effect on him during those difficult times is another testimony to its worth, and another dramatization of its central theme: that an unacceptable reality can be changed by man's power to create fictions.

> This work, laborious as it may appear, has been to me a labour of love, an unfailing source of solace and satisfaction. During my long years of official exile to the luxuriant and deadly deserts of Africa, Eastern and Western, and to the dull and dreary half-clearings of South America, it proved itself a talisman against ennui and despondency. . . . From my dull and commonplace and "respectable" surrounding, the Jinn bore me off at once to the land of my predilection, Arabia, a region so familiar to my mind that even when I cast my first glance at the scene, it seemed a reminiscence of some by-gone metempsychic life in the far distant Past. Again I stood under the diaphanous skies, in air glorious as aether, whose every breath causes men's spirits to bubble like sparkling wine. Once more I saw the evening star hanging like a golden lamp from the pure front of the western firmament; and the after-glow transfiguring and transforming as by magic, the gazelle-brown and tawny-clay tints and the homely and rugged features of the scene into a fairy-land lit with a light which never shines on other soils or seas.*

There is a legend that anyone who reads through all *The Thousand Nights and a Night* will die soon after, and so rather than expose anyone to this risk we print here only a small portion of the total: the frame story of Shahrazad and several stories she tells about the adventures of Sindbad the Sailor. These stories are among the oldest and the best in the book, and in their enormous variety and wealth of detail they provide a very good sense of the tone of the whole. They also are sufficient to clarify the way in which the basic plot, repeated in hundreds of variant forms, unifies the extraordinary diversity and immense detail of the stories. That plot is given its most basic and comprehensive form in the frame story of Shahrazad confronting death by telling stories, where by the skillful management of suspense and the other arts of the fiction-maker, she at last rescues life from death, giving birth to three children and marrying the king. Again and again in *The Nights,* life triumphs over the threat of death by means of art or fiction, and so frequently does the saving art take the form of telling stories—Sindbad the Landsman is saved from a death of poverty and toil by wandering into that garden of marvels where he hears the stories of Sindbad the Sailor—that it is impossible to avoid the conclusion that this is a book more about telling stories than anything else. But just as in these stories death takes many other forms than literal death—slavery, for example, or poverty, or tedium —so does the saving fiction take other forms than story-telling. Like

---

* From "Translator's Foreword."

20

Shahrazad, Sindbad also faces death, death from great serpents and huge prehistoric birds, death from the sea and from devils, death from being entombed alive. Sometimes he aids his survival by telling stories; but his life-saving fictions are mostly manifestations of other forms of human skill and creativity: the invention of wine, or the contrivance of sticks that prevents the serpent from swallowing him. Each of these "fictions," by virtue of their functioning in the basic plot in the same way that story-telling does elsewhere, comes to be a part of that extensive field of activity which we have called fiction-making, the construction of those things which *are not* until man thinks them and makes them, of which stories are perhaps the most perfect and absolute form.

■

Verily the works and words of those gone before us have become instances and examples to men of our modern day, that folk may view what admonishing chances befel other folk and may therefrom take warning; and that they may peruse the annals of antique peoples and all that hath betided them, and be thereby ruled and restrained:—Praise, therefore, be to Him who hath made the histories of the Past an admonition unto the Present! Now of such instances are the tales called "A Thousand Nights and a Night," together with their far-famed legends and wonders. Therein it is related . . . that, in tide of yore and in time long gone before, there was a King of the Kings of the Banu Sasán in the Islands of India and China, a Lord of armies and guards and servants and dependents. He left only two sons, one in the prime of manhood and the other yet a youth, while both were Knights and Braves, albeit the elder was a doughtier horseman than the younger. So he succeeded to the empire; when he ruled the land and lorded it over his lieges with justice so exemplary that he was beloved by all the peoples of his capital and of his kingdom. His name was King Shahryar, and he made his younger brother, called Shah Zaman, Lord of Samarcand in Barbarian-land. These two ceased not to abide in their several kingdoms and the law was ever carried out in their dominions; and each ruled his own realm with equity and fair-dealing to his subjects, in extreme solace and enjoyment; and this condition continually endured for a score of years. But at the end of the twentieth twelvemonth the elder King yearned for a sight of his younger brother and felt that he must look upon him once more. So he took counsel with his Wazir about visiting him, but the Minister, finding the project unadvisable, recommended that a letter be written and a present be sent under his charge to the younger brother with an invitation to visit the elder. Having accepted this advice the King forthwith bade prepare handsome gifts, such as horses with saddles of gem-encrusted gold; Mamelukes, or white slaves; beautiful handmaids, high-breasted virgins, and splendid stuffs and costly. He then wrote a letter to Shah Zaman expressing his warm love and strong wish to see him, ending with these words, "We therefore hope of the favour and affection of the beloved brother that he will condescend to bestir himself and turn his face uswards. Furthermore we have sent our Wazir to make all ordinance for the march, and our one and only desire is to see thee ere we die; but if thou delay or disappoint us we shall not survive the blow. Wherewith peace be upon thee!" Then King Shahryar, having sealed the missive and given it to the Wazir with the offerings aforementioned, commanded him to shorten his skirts and strain his strength and make all expedition in going and returning. "Hearkening and obedience!" quoth the Minister, who fell to making ready without stay and packed up his loads and prepared all his requisites without delay. This occupied him three days, and on the dawn of the fourth he took leave of his King and marched right away, over desert and hill-way, stony waste and pleasant lea without halting by night or by day. But whenever he entered a realm whose ruler was subject to his Suzerain, where he was greeted with magnificent gifts of gold and silver and all manner of presents fair and rare, he would tarry there three days, the term of the guest-rite; and, when he left on the fourth, he would be honourably escorted for a whole day's march. As soon as the Wazir drew near Shah Zaman's court in Samarcand he despatched to report his arrival one of his high officials, who presented himself before the King; and, kissing ground between his hands, delivered his message. Hereupon the King commanded sundry of his Grandees and Lords of his land to fare forth and meet his brother's Wazir at the distance of a full day's journey; which they did, greeting him respectfully and wishing him all prosperity and forming an escort and a procession. When he entered the city he proceeded straightway to the palace, where he presented himself in the royal presence; and, after kissing ground and praying for the King's health and happiness and for victory over all his foes, he informed him that his brother was yearning to see him, and prayed for the pleasure of a visit. He then delivered the letter which Shah Zaman took from his hand and read: it contained sundry hints and allusions which required thought; but, when the King had fully comprehended its import, he said, "I hear and I obey the commands of the beloved brother!" adding to the Wazir, "But we will not march till after the third day's hospitality." He appointed for the Minister fitting quarters in the palace; and, pitching tents for the troops, rationed them with whatever they might require of meat and drink and other necessaries. On the fourth day he made ready for wayfare and got together sumptuous presents befitting his elder brother's majesty, and established his chief Wazir viceroy of the land during his absence. Then he caused his tents and camels and mules to be brought forth and encamped, with their bales and loads, attendants and guards, within sight of the city, in readiness to set out next morning for his brother's capital. But when the night was half spent he bethought him that he had forgotten in his palace somewhat which he should have brought with him, so he returned privily and entered his apartments, where he found the Queen, his wife, asleep on his own carpet-bed, embracing with both arms a black cook of loathsome aspect and foul with kitchen grease and grime. When he saw this the world waxed black before his sight and he said, "If such case happen while I am yet within sight of the city what will be the doings of this damned whore during my long absence at my brother's court?" So he drew his scymitar and, cutting the two into four pieces with a single blow, left them on the carpet and returned presently to his camp without letting anyone know of what had happened. Then he gave orders for immediate departure and set out at once and began his travel; but he could not help thinking over his wife's conduct and he kept ever saying to himself, "How could she do this deed by me? How could she work her own death?" till excessive grief seized him, his colour changed to yellow, his body waxed weak and he was threatened with a dangerous malady, such an one as bringeth men to die. So the Wazir shortened his stages and tarried long at the watering-stations and did his best to solace the King. Now when Shah Zaman drew near the capital of his brother he despatched vaunt-couriers and messengers of glad tidings to announce his arrival, and Shahryar came forth to meet him with his Wazirs and Emirs and Lords and Grandees of his realm; and saluted him and joyed with exceeding joy and caused the city to be decorated in his honour. When, however, the brothers met, the elder could not but see the change of complexion in the younger and questioned him of his case whereto he replied, " 'Tis caused by the travails of travel and wayfare and my case needeth care, for I have suffered from the change of water and air! but Allah be praised for reuniting me with a brother so dear and so rare!" On this wise he dissembled and kept his secret, adding, "O King of the time and Caliph of the tide, only toil and moil have tinged my face yellow with bile and hath made my eyes sink deep in my head." Then the two entered the capital in all honour; and the elder brother lodged the younger in a palace overhanging the pleasure garden, and, after a time, seeing his condition still unchanged, he attributed it to his separation from his country and kingdom. So he let him wend his own ways and asked no questions of him till one day when he again said, "O my brother, I see thou art grown weaker of body and yellower of colour." "O my brother," replied Shah Zaman, "I have an internal wound": still he would not tell him what he had witnessed in his wife. Thereupon Shahryar summoned doctors and surgeons and bade them treat his brother according to the rules of art, which they did for a whole month; but their sherbets and potions naught availed, for he would dwell upon the deed of his wife, and despondency, instead of diminishing, prevailed, and leach-craft treatment utterly failed. One day his elder brother said to him, "I am going forth to hunt and course and to take my pleasure and pastime; maybe this would lighten thy heart." Shah Zaman, however, refused, saying, "O my brother, my soul yearneth for naught of this sort and I entreat thy favour to suffer me tarry quietly in this place, being wholly taken up with my malady." So King Shah Zaman passed his night in the palace and, next morning, when his brother had gone forth, he removed from his room and sat him down at one of the lattice-windows overlooking the pleasure grounds; and there he abode thinking with saddest thought over his wife's betrayal and burning sighs issued from his tortured breast. And as he continued in this case lo! a postern of the palace, which was carefully kept private, swung open and out of it came twenty slave girls surrounding his brother's wife who was wondrous fair, a model of beauty and comeliness and symmetry and perfect loveliness and who paced with the grace of a gazelle which panteth for the cooling stream. Thereupon Shah Zaman drew back from the window, but he kept the bevy in sight espying them from a place whence he could not be espied. They walked under the very lattice and advanced a little way into the garden till they came to a jetting fountain amiddlemost a great basin of water; then they stripped off their clothes and behold, ten of them were women, concubines of the King, and the other ten were white slaves. Then they all paired off, each with each: but the Queen, who was left alone, presently cried out in a loud voice, "Here to me, O my lord Saeed!" and there sprang with a drop-leap from one of the trees a big slobbering blackamoor with rolling eyes which showed the whites, a truly hideous sight. He walked boldly up to her and threw his arms round her neck, while she embraced him as warmly. On like wise did the other slaves with the girls till all had satisfied their passions, and they ceased not from kissing and clipping, and carousing till day began to wane; when the men resumed their disguises and all, except the negro who swarmed up the tree, entered the palace and closed the postern-door as before. Now, when Shah Zaman saw this conduct of his sister-in-law he said in himself, "By Allah, my calamity is lighter than this! My brother is a greater King among the kings than I am, yet this infamy goeth on in his very palace, and his wife is in love with that filthiest of filthy slaves. But this only showeth that they all do it, and that there is no woman but who cuckoldeth her husband; then the curse of Allah upon one and all and upon the fools who lean against them for support or who place the reins of conduct in their hands." So he put away his melancholy and despondency, regret and repine, and allayed his sorrow by constantly repeating those words, adding, " 'Tis my conviction that no man in this world is safe from their malice!" When supper-time came they brought him the trays and he ate with voracious appetite, for he had long refrained from meat, feeling unable to touch any dish however dainty. Then he returned grateful thanks to Almighty Allah, praising Him and blessing Him, and he spent a most restful night, it having been long since he had savoured the sweet food of sleep. Next day he broke his fast heartily and began to recover health and strength, and presently regained excellent condition. His brother came back from the chase ten days after, when he rode out to meet him and they saluted each other; and when King Shahryar looked at King Shah Zaman he saw how the hue of health had returned to him, how his face had waxed ruddy and how he ate with an appetite after his late scanty diet. He wondered much and said, "O my brother, I was so anxious that thou wouldst join me in hunting and chasing, and wouldst take thy pleasure and pastime in my dominion!" He thanked him and excused himself; then the two took horse and rode into the city and, when they were seated at their ease in the palace, the food-trays were set before them and they ate their sufficiency. After the meats were removed and they had washed their hands, King Shahryar turned to his brother and said, "My mind is overcome with wonderment at thy condition. I was desirous to carry thee with me to the chase but I saw thee changed in hue, pale and wan to view, and in sore trouble of mind too. But now Alhamdolillah—glory be to God!—I see thy natural colour hath returned to thy face and that thou art again in the best of case. It was my belief that thy sickness came of severance from thy family and friends, and absence from capital and country, so I refrained from troubling thee with further questions. But now I beseech thee to expound to me the cause of thy complaint and thy change of colour, and to explain the reason of thy recovery and the return to the ruddy hue of health which I am wont to view. So speak out and hide naught!" When Shah Zaman heard this he bowed groundwards awhile his head, then raised it and said, "I will tell thee what caused my complaint and my loss of colour; but excuse my acquainting thee with the cause of its return to me and the reason of my complete recovery: indeed I pray thee not to press me for a reply." Said Shahryar, who was much surprised by these words, "Let me hear first what produced thy pallor and thy poor condition." "Know, then, O my brother," rejoined Shah Zaman, "that when thou sentest thy Wazir with the invitation to place myself between thy hands, I made ready and marched out of my city; but presently I minded me having left behind me in the palace a string of jewels intended as a gift to thee. I returned for it alone and found my wife on my carpet bed and in the arms of a hideous black cook. Accordingly I slew the twain and came to thee, yet my thoughts brooded over this business and I lost my bloom and became weak. But excuse me if I still refuse to tell thee what was the reason of my complexion returning." Shahryar shook his head, marvelling with extreme marvel, and with the fire of wrath flaming up from his heart, he cried, "Indeed, the malice of woman is mighty!" Then he took refuge from them with Allah and said, "In very sooth, O my brother, thou hast escaped many an evil by putting thy wife to death, and right excusable were thy wrath and grief for such mishap which never yet befel crowned King like unto thee. By Allah, had the case been mine, I would not have been satisfied without slaying a thousand women and that way madness lies! But now praise be to Allah who hath tempered to thee thy tribulation, and needs must thou acquaint me with that which so suddenly restored to thee complexion and health, and explain to me what causeth this concealment." "O King of the Age, again I pray thee excuse my so doing!" "Nay, but thou must." "I fear, O my brother, lest the recital cause thee more anger and sorrow than afflicted me." "That were but a better reason," quoth Shahryar, "for telling me the whole history, and I conjure thee by Allah not to keep back aught from me." Thereupon Shah Zaman told him all he had seen, from commencement to conclusion, ending with these words, "When I beheld thy calamity and the treason of thy wife, O my brother, and I reflected that thou art in years my senior and in sovereignty my superior, mine own sorrow was belittled by the comparison, and my mind recovered tone and temper: so throwing off melancholy and despondency, I was able to eat and drink and sleep, and thus I speedily regained health and strength. Such is the truth and the whole truth." When King Shahryar heard this he waxed wroth with exceeding wrath, and rage was like to strangle him; but presently he recovered himself and said, "O my brother, I would not give thee the lie in this matter, but I cannot credit it till I see it with mine own eyes." "An thou wouldst look upon thy calamity," quoth Shah Zaman, "rise at once and make ready again for hunting and coursing, and then hide thyself with me, so shalt thou witness it and thine eyes shall verify it." "True," quoth the King; whereupon he let make proclamation of his intent to travel, and the troops and tents went forth the city, camping within sight, and Shahryar sallied out with them and took seat amidmost his host, bidding the slaves admit no man to him. When night came on he summoned his Wazir and said to him, "Sit thou in my stead and let none wot of my absence till the term of three days." Then the brothers disguised themselves and returned by night with all secrecy to the palace, where they passed the dark hours: and at dawn they seated themselves at the lattice overlooking the pleasure grounds, when presently the Queen and her handmaids came out as before, and passing under the windows made for the fountain. Here they stripped, ten of them being men and ten women, and the King's wife cried out, "Where art thou, O Saeed?" The hideous blackamoor dropped from the tree straightway; and, rushing into her arms without stay or delay, cried out, "I am Sa'ad al-Din Saood!" The lady laughed heartily, and all fell to satisfying themselves and remained so occupied for a couple of hours; then they went into the basin and, after performing the Ghusl, or complete ablution, donned their dresses and retired as they had done before. When King Shahryar saw this infamy of his wife and concubines he became as one distraught and he cried out, "Only in utter solitude can man be safe from the doings of this vile world! By Allah, life is naught but one great wrong." Presently he added, "Do not thwart me, O my brother, in what I propose"; and the other answered, "I will not." So he said, "Let us up as we are and forthright depart hence, for we have no concern with Kingship, and let us overwander Allah's earth, worshipping the Almighty till we find some one to whom the like calamity hath happened; and if we find none then will death be more welcome to us than life." So the two brothers issued from a second private postern of the palace; and they never stinted wayfaring by day and by night, until they reached a tree a-middle of a meadow hard by a spring of sweet water on the shore of the salt sea. Both drank of it and sat down to take their rest; and when an hour of the day had gone by, lo! they heard a mighty roar and uproar in the middle of the main as though the heavens were falling upon the earth; and the sea brake with waves before them, and from it towered a black pillar, which grew and grew till it rose skywards and began making for that meadow. Seeing it, they waxed fearful exceedingly and climbed to the top of the tree, which was a lofty; whence they gazed to see what might be the matter. And behold, it was a Jinni, huge of height and burly of breast and bulk, broad of brow and black of blee bearing on his head a coffer of crystal. He strode to land, wading through the deep, and coming to the tree whereupon were the two Kings, seated himself beneath it. He then set down the coffer on its bottom and out of it drew a casket, with seven padlocks of steel, which he unlocked with seven keys of steel he took from beside his thigh, and out of it a young lady to come was seen, white-skinned and of winsomest mien, of stature fine and thin, and bright as though a moon of the fourteenth night she had been, or the sun raining lively sheen. Even so the poet Utayyah hath excellently said:—

> She rose like the morn as she shone through the night,
>   And she gilded the grove with her gracious sight:
> From her radiance the sun taketh increase, when
>   She unveileth and shameth the moonshine bright.
> Bow down all beings between her hands
>   As she showeth charms with her veil undight.
> And she flooded cities with torrent tears
>   When she flasheth her look of leven-light.

The Jinni seated her under the tree by his side and gazing at her said, "O choicest love of this heart of mine! O dame of noblest line, whom I snatched away on thy bride-night that none might prevent me taking thy first love, and whom none save myself hath loved or hath enjoyed: O my sweetheart! I would lief sleep a little while." He then laid his head upon the lady's thighs, and stretching out his legs which extended down to the sea, slept and snored and snarked like the roll of thunder. Presently she raised her gracious head towards the tree-top and saw the two Kings perched near the summit; then she softly lifted off her lap the Jinni's pate which she was tired of supporting and placed it upon the ground; then standing upright under the tree signed to the Kings, "Come ye down, ye two, and fear naught from this Ifrit." They were in a terrible fright when they found that she had seen them and answered her in the same manner, "Allah upon thee and by thy modesty, O lady, excuse us from coming down!" But she rejoined by saying, "Allah upon you both that ye come down forthright, and if ye come not, I will rouse upon you my husband, this Ifrit, and he shall do you to die by the illest of deaths"; and she continued making signals to them. So, being afraid, they came down to her and she rose before them, and urged them, saying "Do this without stay or delay, otherwise will I arouse and set upon you this Ifrit who shall slay your straightway." They said to her, "O our lady, we conjure thee by Allah, let us off this work, for we are fugitives from such and in extreme dread and terror of this thy husband. How then can we do in such a way as thou desirest?" "Leave this talk: it needs must be so," quoth she, and she swore by Him who raised the skies on high, without prop or pillar, that, if they worked not her will, she would cause them to be slain and cast into the sea. Whereupon out of fear King Shahryar said to King Shah Zaman, "O my brother, do thou what she biddeth thee do"; but he replied, "I will not do it till thou do it before I do." And they began disputing about her. Then quoth she to the twain, "How is it I see you disputing and demurring; if ye do not come forward like men, I will arouse upon you the Ifrit." At this, by reason of their sore dread of the Jinni, both did as she bade them; and she said, "Well done!" She then took from her pocket a purse and drew out a knotted string, whereon were strung five hundred and seventy seal rings, and asked, "Know ye what be these?" They answered her saying, "We know not!" Then quoth she, "These be the signets of five hundred and seventy men who have all embraced me upon the horns of this foul, this foolish, this filthy Ifrit; so give me also your two seal rings, ye pair of brothers." When they had drawn their two rings from their hands and given them to her, she said to them, "Of a truth this Ifrit bore me off on my bride-night, and put me into a casket and set the casket in a coffer and to the coffer he affixed seven strong padlocks of steel and deposited me on the deep bottom of the sea that raves, dashing and clashing with waves; and guarded me so that I might remain chaste and honest, quotha! that none save himself might have connexion with me. But I have embraced as many of my kind as I please, and this wretched Jinni wotteth not that Destiny may not be averted nor hindered by aught, and that whatso woman willeth the same she fulfilleth however man nilleth. Even so saith one of them:—

> Rely not on women;
>   Trust not to their hearts,
> Whose joys and whose sorrows
>   Are hung to their parts!
> Lying love they will swear thee
>   Whence guile ne'er departs;
> Take Yúsuf for sample
>   'Ware sleights and 'ware smarts!
> Iblis ousted Adam
>   (See ye not?) thro' their arts.

And another saith:—

Stint thy blame, man! 'Twill drive to a passion without bound;
  My fault is not so heavy as fault in it hast found.
If true lover I become, then to me there cometh not
  Save what happened unto many in the by-gone stound.
For wonderful is he and right worthy of our praise
  Who from wiles of female wits kept him safe and kept him sound.

28

Hearing these words they marvelled with exceeding marvel, and she went from them to the Ifrit and, taking up his head on her thigh as before, said to them softly, "Now wend your ways and bear yourselves beyond the bounds of his malice." So they fared forth saying either to other, "Allah! Allah!" and, "There be no Majesty and there be no Might save in Allah, the Glorious, the Great; and with Him we seek refuge from women's malice and sleight, for of a truth it hath no mate in might. Consider, O my brother, the ways of this marvellous lady with an Ifrit who is so much more powerful than we are. Now since there hath happened to him a greater mishap than that which befel us and which should bear us abundant consolation, so return we to our countries and capitals, and let us decide never to intermarry with womankind and presently we will show them what will be our action." Thereupon they rode back to the tents of King Shahryar, which they reached on the morning of the third day; and, having mustered the Wazirs and Emirs, the Chamberlains and high officials, he gave a robe of honour to his Viceroy and issued orders for an immediate return to the city. There he sat him upon his throne and sending for the Chief Minister, the father of the two damsels who (Inshallah!) will presently be mentioned, he said, "I command thee to take my wife and smite her to death; for she hath broken her plight and her faith." So he carried her to the place of execution and did her die. Then King Shahryar took brand in hand and repairing to the Serráglio slew all the concubines and their Mamelukes. He also sware himself by a binding oath that whatever wife he married he would abate her virginity at night and slay her next morning to make sure of his honour: "for," said he, "there never was nor is there one chaste woman upon the face of earth." Then Shah Zaman prayed for permission to fare homewards; and he went forth equipped and escorted and travelled till he reached his own country. Meanwhile Shahryar commanded his Wazir to bring him the bride of the night that he might go to her; so he produced a most beautiful girl, the daughter of one of the Emirs and the King went unto her at eventide and when morning dawned he bade his Minister strike off her head; and the Wazir did accordingly for fear of the Sultan. On this wise he continued for the space of three years; marrying a maiden every night and killing her the next morning, till folk raised an outcry against him and cursed him, praying Allah utterly to destroy him and his rule; and women made an uproar and mothers wept and parents fled with their daughters till there remained not in the city a young person of a sufficient age for marriage. Presently the King ordered his Chief Wazir, the same who was charged with the executions, to bring him a virgin as was his wont; and the Minister went forth and searched and found none; so he returned home in sorrow and anxiety fearing for his life from the King. Now he had two daughters, named Shahrazad and Dunyazad,[1] of

---

[1] Shahrazad (Persian) = City-freer; in the older version Scheherazade (probably both from Shírzád = lion-born). Dunyazad = World-freer. . . . [The footnotes in this selection are Sir Richard Burton's.]

whom the elder had perused the books, annals and legends of preceding Kings, and the stories, examples, and instances of by-gone men and things; indeed it was said that she had collected a thousand books of histories relating to antique races and departed rulers. She had perused the works of the poets and knew them by heart; she had studied philosophy and the sciences, arts and accomplishments; and she was pleasant and polite, wise and witty, well read and well bred. Now on that day she said to her father, "Why do I see thee thus changed and laden with cark and care? Concerning this matter quoth one of the poets:—

> Tell whoso hath sorrow
>   Grief never shall last:
> E'en as joy hath no morrow
>   So woe shall go past.

When the Wazir heard from his daughter these words he related to her, from beginning to end, all that had happened between him and the King. Thereupon said she, "By Allah, O my father, how long shall this slaughter of women endure? Shall I tell thee what is in my mind in order to save both sides from destruction?" "Say on, O my daughter," quoth he, and quoth she, "I wish thou wouldst give me in marriage to this King Shahryar; either I shall live or I shall be a ransom for the virgin daughters of Moslems and the cause of their deliverance from his hands and thine." "Allah upon thee!" cried he in wrath exceeding that lacked no feeding, "O scanty of wit, expose not thy life to such peril! How durst thou address me in words so wide from wisdom and unfar from foolishness? Know that one who lacketh experience in worldly matters readily falleth into misfortune; and whoso considereth not the end keepeth not the world to friend, and the vulgar say:—I was lying at mine ease: naught but my officiousness brought me unease." "Needs must thou," she broke in, "make me a doer of this good deed, and let him kill me an he will: I shall only die a ransom for others." "O my daughter," asked he, "and how shall that profit thee when thou shalt have thrown away thy life?" and she answered, "O my father it must be, come of it what will!" The Wazir was again moved to fury and blamed and reproached her, ending with, "In very deed I fear lest the same befal thee which befel the Bull and the Ass with the Husbandman." "And what," asked she, "befel them, O my father?" Whereupon the Wazir [told the tale of the bull and the ass. A rich merchant has the gift from Allah of being able to understand the speech of animals but will die if he ever reveals what he has heard. One day he overhears the bull complaining to the ass of his hard life under the yoke in the fields, whereupon the ass advises the bull to play sick, which he does. The merchant, knowing what is going on, has the ass put in harness to replace the bull, whereupon the ass nearly dies of the hard work and beatings and realizes he must find some way to get the bull to work again.] "And even so, O my daughter," said the Wazir, "thou wilt die for lack of wits; therefore sit thee still and say naught and expose not thy life to such stress; for, by Allah, I offer thee the best advice, which cometh of my affection and kindly solicitude for thee." "O my father," she replied, "needs must I go up to this King and be married to him." Quoth he, "Do not this deed"; and quoth she, "Of a truth I will": whereat he rejoined, "If thou be not silent and bide not still, I will do with thee even what the merchant did with his wife." "And what did he?" asked she. [The Wazir proceeds to tell the rest of the story. The ass tells the bull that he has heard that the merchant has decided to send him, since he is sick and useless, to the slaughterhouse. The bull decides to get well at once, and when the merchant comes to see him the bull snorts, paws, and bellows loudly. The merchant falls on his back and roars with laughter. His wife is consumed with curiosity and wants to know what is so funny, but the merchant cannot tell her lest he die. But she insists, and the merchant loves her so much that he prepares to tell her and die. But then he overhears a cock talking about how he manages his hens with no trouble at all, and taking his advice the merchant simply gives his wife a good beating, which solves all the problems.]

 . . . "And thou also, O my daughter!" continued the Wazir, "unless thou turn from this matter I will do by thee as that trader did to his wife." But she answered him with much decision, "I will never desist, O my father, nor shall this tale change my purpose. Leave such talk and tattle. I will not listen to thy words and, if thou deny me, I will marry myself to him despite the nose of thee. And first I will go up to the King myself and alone, and I will say to him:—I prayed my father to wive me with thee, but he refused, being resolved to disappoint his lord, grudging the like of me to the like of thee." Her father asked, "Must this needs be?" and she answered, "Even so." Hereupon the Wazir, being weary of lamenting and contending, persuading and dissuading her, all to no purpose, went up to King Shahryar and, after blessing him and kissing of ground before him, told him all about his dispute with his daughter from first to last, and how he desired to bring her to him that night. The King wondered with exceeding wonder; for he had made an especial exception of the Wazir's daughter, and said to him, "O most faithful of Counsellors, how is this? Thou wottest that I have sworn by the Raiser of the Heavens that after this night I shall say to thee on the morrow's morning:—Take her and slay her! and, if thou slay her not, I will slay thee in her stead without fail." "Allah guide thee to glory and lengthen thy life, O King of the Age," answered the Wazir, "'tis she who hath so determined: all this have I told her and more; but she will not hearken to me, and she persisteth in passing this coming night with the King's Highness." So Shahryar rejoiced greatly and said, "'Tis well; go get her ready and this night bring her to me." The Wazir returned to his daughter and reported to her the command saying, "Allah make not thy father desolate by thy loss!" But Shahrazad rejoiced with exceeding joy and gat ready all she required and said to her younger sister, Dunyazad,

"Note well what directions I entrust to thee! When I have gone in to the King I will send for thee, and when thou comest to me and seest that he hath had his will of me, do thou say to me:—O my sister, an thou be not sleepy, relate to me some new story, delectable and delightsome, the better to speed our waking hours; and I will tell thee a tale which shall be our deliverance, if so Allah please, and which shall turn the King from his blood-thirsty custom." Dunyazad answered, "With love and gladness." So when it was night their father the Wazir carried Shahrazad to the King, who was gladdened at the sight and asked, "Hast thou brought me my need?" and he answered, "I have." But when the King took her to his bed she wept; which made him ask, "What aileth thee?" She replied, "O King of the Age, I have a younger sister and lief would I take leave of her this night before I see the dawn." So he sent at once for Dunyazad and she came and kissed the ground between his hands, when he permitted her to take her seat near the foot of the couch. Then the King arose and abated his bride's virginity, and the three fell asleep. But when it was midnight Shahrazad awoke and signalled to her sister Dunyazad who sat up and said, "Allah, upon thee, O my sister, recite to us some new story, delightsome and delectable, wherewith to while away the waking hours of our latter night." "With joy and goodly gree," answered Shahrazad, "if this pious and auspicious King permit me." "Tell on," quoth the King who chanced to be sleepless and restless, and therefore was pleased with the prospect of hearing her story. So Shahrazad rejoiced; and thus, on the first night of the Thousand Nights and a Night, she began. . . . [We now move to night five hundred thirty-six and the tales of]

Sindbad The Seaman and Sindbad The Landsman

There lived in the city of Baghdad, during the reign of the Commander of the Faithful, Harun al-Rashid, a man named Sindbad the Hammal, one in poor case who bore burdens on his head for hire. It happened to him one day of great heat that whilst he was carrying a heavy load, he became exceeding weary and sweated profusely; the heat and the weight alike oppressing him. Presently, as he was passing the gate of a merchant's house, before which the ground was swept and watered, and where the air was temperate, he sighted a broad bench beside the door; so he set his load thereon, to take rest and smell the air, ——And Shahrazad perceived the dawn of day and ceased saying her permitted say.

Now when it was the Five Hundred and Thirty-seventh Night,

She said, It hath reached me, O auspicious King, that when the Hammal set his load upon the bench to take rest and smell the air, there came out upon him from the court-door a pleasant breeze and a delicious fragrance. He sat down on the edge of the bench, and at once heard from within the melodious sound of lutes and other stringed instruments, and mirth-exciting voices singing and reciting, together with the song of birds warbling and glorifying Almighty Allah in various tunes and tongues; turtles, mocking-birds, merles, nightingales, cushats and stone-curlews, whereat he marvelled in himself and was moved to mighty joy and solace. Then he went up to the gate and saw within a great flower-garden wherein were pages and black slaves, and such a train of servants and attendants and so forth as is found only with Kings and Sultans; and his nostrils were greeted with the savoury odours of all manner meats rich and delicate, and delicious and generous wines. So he raised his eyes heavenwards and said, "Glory to Thee, O Lord, O Creator and Provider, who providest whomso Thou wilt without count or stint! O mine Holy One, I cry Thee pardon for all sins and turn to Thee repenting of all offences! O Lord, there is no gainsaying Thee in Thine ordinance and Thy dominion, neither wilt Thou be questioned of that Thou dost, for Thou indeed over all things art Almighty! Extolled be Thy perfection: whom Thou wilt Thou makest poor and whom Thou wilt Thou makest rich! Whom Thou wilt Thou exaltest and whom Thou wilt Thou abasest, and there is no god but Thou! How mighty is Thy majesty and how enduring Thy dominion and how excellent Thy government! Verily, Thou favourest whom wilt of Thy servants, whereby the owner of this place abideth in all joyance of life and delighteth himself with pleasant scents and delicious meats and exquisite wines of all kinds. For indeed Thou appointest unto Thy creatures that which Thou wilt and that which Thou hast foreordained unto them; wherefore are some weary and others are at rest and some enjoy fair fortune and affluence, whilst others suffer the extreme of travail and misery, even as I do." And he fell to reciting:—

How many by my labours, that evermore endure,
    All goods of life enjoy and in cooly shade recline?
Each morn that dawns I wake in travail and in woe,
    And strange is my condition and my burden gars me pine:
Many others are in luck and from miseries are free,
    And Fortune never loads them with loads the like o' mine:
They live their happy days in all solace and delight;
    Eat, drink, and dwell in honour 'mid the noble and the digne:
All living things were made of a little drop of sperm,
    Thine origin is mine and my provenance is thine;
Yet the difference and distance 'twixt the twain of us are far
    As the difference of savour 'twixt vinegar and wine:
But at Thee, O God All-wise! I venture not to rail
    Whose ordinance is just and whose justice cannot fail.

When Sindbad the Porter had made an end of reciting his verses, he bore up his burden and was about to fare on, when there came forth to him from the gate a little foot-page, fair of face and shapely of shape and dainty of dress who caught him by the hand, saying, "Come in and speak with my lord, for he calleth for thee." The Porter would have excused himself to the page, but the lad would take no refusal; so he left his load with the doorkeeper in the vestibule and followed the boy into the house, which he found to be a goodly mansion, radiant and full of majesty, till he brought him to a grand sitting-room wherein he saw a company of nobles and great lords, seated at tables garnished with all manner of flowers and sweet-scented herbs, besides great plenty of dainty viands and fruits dried and fresh and confections and wines of the choicest vintages. There also were instruments of music and mirth, and lovely slave-girls playing and singing. All the company was ranged according to rank, and in the highest place sat a man of worshipful and noble aspect, whose beard-sides hoariness had stricken; and he was stately of stature and fair of favour, agreeable of aspect and full of gravity and dignity and majesty. So Sindbad the Porter was confounded at that which he beheld and said in himself, "By Allah, this must be either a piece of Paradise or some King's palace!" Then he saluted the company with much respect, praying for their prosperity and kissing ground before them, stood with his head bowed down in humble attitude.——And Shahrazad perceived the dawn of day and ceased to say her permitted say.

Now when it was the Five Hundred and Thirty-eighth Night,

She said, It hath reached me, O auspicious King, that Sindbad the Porter, after kissing ground between their hands, stood with his head bowed down in humble attitude. The master of the house bade him draw near and be seated and bespoke him kindly, bidding him welcome. Then he set before him various kinds of viands, rich and delicate and delicious, and the Porter, after saying his Bismillah, fell to and ate his fill, after which he exclaimed, "Praised be Allah whatso be our case!" and washing his hands, returned thanks to the company for his entertainment. Quoth the host, "Thou art welcome and thy day is a blessed. But what are thy name and calling?" Quoth the other, "O my lord, my name is Sindbad the Hammal, and I carry folk's goods on my head for hire." The house-master smiled and rejoined, "Know, O Porter, that thy name is even as mine, for I am Sindbad the Seaman; and now, O Porter, I would have thee let me hear the couplets thou recitedst at the gate anon." The Porter was abashed and replied, "Allah upon thee! Excuse me, for toil and travail and lack of luck when the hand is empty teach a man ill manners and boorish ways." Said the host, "Be not ashamed; thou art become my brother; but repeat to me the verses, for they pleased me whenas I heard thee recite them at the gate." Hereupon the Porter repeated the couplets and they delighted the merchant, who said to him:—Know, O Hammal, that my story is a wonderful one, and thou shalt hear all that befell me and all I underwent ere I rose to this state of prosperity and became the lord of this place wherein thou seest me; for I came not to this high estate save after travail sore and perils galore, and how much toil and trouble have I not suffered in days of yore! I have made seven voyages, by each of which hangeth a marvellous tale, such as confoundeth the reason, and all this came to pass by doom of fortune and fate; for from what destiny doth write there is neither refuge nor flight. Know, then, good my lords (continued he) that I am about to relate the

First Voyage of Sindbad Hight The Seaman

My father was a merchant, one of the notables of my native place, a moneyed man and ample of means, who died whilst I was yet a child, leaving me much wealth in money and lands and farmhouses. When I grew up I laid hands on the whole and ate of the best and drank freely and wore rich clothes and lived lavishly, companioning and consorting with youths of my own age, and considering that this course of life would continue for ever and ken no change. Thus did I for a long time, but at last I awoke from my heedlessness, and returning to my senses, I found my wealth had become unwealth and my condition ill-conditioned, and all I once hent had left my hand. And recovering my reason I was stricken with dismay and confusion and bethought me of a saying of our lord Solomon, son of David (upon whom be the Peace!), which I had heard aforetime from my father, "Three things are better than other three; the day of death is better than the day of birth, a live dog is better than a dead lion, and the grave is better than want." Then I got together my remains of estates and property and sold all, even my clothes, for three thousand dirhams, with which I resolved to travel to foreign parts . . . . So taking heart I bought me goods, merchandise and all needed for a voyage and, impatient to be at sea, I embarked, with a company of merchants, on board a ship bound for Bassorah. There we again embarked and sailed many days and nights, and we passed from isle to isle and sea to sea and shore to shore, buying and selling and bartering everywhere the ship touched, and continued our course till we came to an island as it were a garth of the gardens of Paradise. Here the captain cast anchor and making fast to the shore, put out the landing planks. So all on board landed and made furnaces and lighting fires therein, busied themselves in various ways, some cooking and some washing, whilst other some walked about the island for solace, and the crew fell to eating and drinking and playing and sporting. I was one of the walkers but, as we were thus engaged, behold the master, who was standing on the gunwale, cried out to us at the top of his voice, saying, "Ho there! passengers, run for your lives and hasten back to the ship and leave your gear and save yourselves from destruction, Allah preserve you! For this island whereon ye stand is no true island, but a great fish stationary a-middlemost of the sea, whereon the sand hath settled and trees have sprung up of old time, so that it is become like unto an island; but, when ye lighted fires on it, it felt the heat and moved; and in a moment it will sink with you into the sea and ye will all be drowned. So leave your gear and seek your safety ere ye die";———And Shahrazad perceived the dawn of day and ceased saying her permitted say.

She said, It hath reached me, O auspicious King, that when the ship-master cried to the passengers, "Leave your gear and seek safety, ere ye die"; all who heard him left gear and goods, clothes washed and un-washed, fire-pots and brass cooking-pots, and fled back to the ship for their lives, and some reached it while others (amongst whom was I) did not, for suddenly the island shook and sank into the abysses of the deep, with all that were thereon, and the dashing sea surged over it with clash-ing waves. I sank with the others down, down into the deep, but Al-mighty Allah preserved me from drowning and threw in my way a great wooden tub of those that had served the ship's company for tubbing. I gripped it for the sweetness of life and, bestriding it like one riding, paddled with my feet like oars, whilst the waves tossed me as in sport right and left. Meanwhile, the captain made sail and departed with those who had reached the ship, regardless of the drowning and the drowned; and I ceased not following the vessel with my eyes, till she was hid from sight and I made sure of death. Darkness closed in upon me while in this plight, and the winds and waves bore me on all that night and the next day, till the tub brought to with me under the lee of a lofty island, with trees overhanging the tide. I caught hold of a branch and by its aid clambered up on to the land . . . .

[After several other adventures, occupying three more nights of tell-ing, Sindbad recovers his lost goods and returns safely to Baghdad.] This, then, is the story of my first voyage, and to-morrow, Inshallah! I will tell you the tale of the second of my seven voyages. (Saith he who telleth the tale), Then Sindbad the Seaman made Sindbad the Lands-man sup with him and bade give him an hundred gold pieces, saying, "Thou has cheered us with thy company this day." The Porter thanked him and taking the gift, went his way, pondering that which he had heard and marvelling mightily at what things betide mankind. He passed the night in his own place, and with early morning repaired to the abode of Sindbad the Seaman, who received him with honour and seated him by his side. As soon as the rest of the company was assembled, he set meat and drink before them and when they had well eaten and drunken and were merry and in cheerful case, he took up his discourse and re-counted to them in these words the narrative of

The Second Voyage of Sindbad The Seaman

Know, O my brother, that I was living a most comfortable and en-joyable life, in all solace and delight, as I told you yesterday,———And Shahrazad perceived the dawn of day and ceased saying her permitted say.

She continued, It hath reached me, O auspicious King, that when Sindbad
the Seaman's guests were all gathered together he thus bespake them:—I
was living a most enjoyable life until one day my mind became possessed
with the thought of travelling about the world of men, and seeing their
cities and islands; and a longing seized me to traffic and to make money
by trade. Upon this resolve I took a great store of cash and buying goods
and gear fit for travel, bound them up in bales. Then I went down to the
river-bank, where I found a noble ship and brand-new about to sail,
equipped with sails of fine cloth and well manned and provided; so I
took passage in her, with a number of other merchants, and after embark-
ing our goods we weighed anchor the same day. Right fair was our
voyage and we sailed from place to place and from isle to isle; and
whenever we anchored we met a crowd of merchants and notables and
customers, and we took to buying and selling and bartering. At last
Destiny brought us to an island, fair and verdant, in trees abundant,
with yellow-ripe fruits luxuriant, and flowers fragrant and birds warbling
soft descant; and streams chrystalline and radiant; but no sign of man
showed to the descrier, no, not a blower of the fire. The captain made
fast with us to this island, and the merchants and sailors landed and
walked about, enjoying the shade of the trees and the song of the birds,
that chanted the praises of the One, the Victorious, and marvelling at
the works of the Omnipotent King. I landed with the rest; and, sitting
down by a spring of sweet water that welled up among the trees, took
out some vivers I had with me and ate of that which Allah Almighty
had allotted unto me. And so sweet was the zephyr and so fragrant were
the flowers, that presently I waxed drowsy and, lying down in that place,
was soon drowned in sleep. When I awoke, I found myself alone, for
the ship had sailed and left me behind, nor had one of the merchants or
sailors bethought himself of me. I searched the island right and left, but
found neither man nor Jinn, whereat I was beyond measure troubled
and my gall was like to burst for stress of chagrin and anguish and concern, because I was left quite alone, without aught of worldly gear or
meat or drink, weary and heart-broken. So I gave myself up for lost and
said, "Not always doth the crock escape the shock. I was saved the first
time by finding one who brought me from the desert island to an inhabited place, but now there is no hope for me." Then I fell to weeping
and wailing and gave myself up to an access of rage, blaming myself for
having again ventured upon the perils and hardships of voyage, whenas I
was at my ease in mine own house in mine own land, taking my pleasure
with good meat and good drink and good clothes and lacking nothing,
neither money nor goods. And I repented me of having left Baghdad, and
this the more after all the travails and dangers I had undergone in my
first voyage, wherein I had so narrowly escaped destruction, and exclaimed, "Verily we are Allah's and unto Him we are returning!" I was

indeed even as one mad and Jinn-struck and presently I rose and walked about the island, right and left and every whither, unable for trouble to sit or tarry in any one place. Then I climbed a tall tree and looked in all directions, but saw nothing save sky and sea and trees and birds and isles and sands. However, after a while my eager glances fell upon some great white thing, afar off in the interior of the island; so I came down from the tree and made for that which I had seen; and behold, it was a huge white dome rising high in air and of vast compass. I walked all around it, but found no door thereto, nor could I muster strength or nimbleness to climb it by reason of its exceeding smoothness and slipperiness. So I marked the spot where I stood and went round about the dome to measure its circumference, which I found fifty good paces. And as I stood, casting about how to gain an entrance, the day being near its fall and the sun being near the horizon, behold, the sun was suddenly hidden from me and the air became dull and dark. Methought a cloud had come over the sun, but it was the season of summer; so I marvelled at this and lifting my head looked steadfastly at the sky, when I saw the cloud was none other than an enormous bird, of gigantic girth and inordinately wide of wing which, as it flew through the air, veiled the sun and hid it from the island. At this sight my wonder redoubled and I remembered a story——And Shahrazad perceived the dawn of day and ceased to say her permitted say.

Now when it was the Five Hundred and Forty-fourth Night,

She said, It hath reached me, O auspicious King, that Sindbad the Seaman continued in these words:—My wonder redoubled and I remembered a story I had heard aforetime of pilgrims and travellers, how in a certain island dwelleth a huge bird, called the "Rukh," which feedest its young on elephants; and I was certified that the dome which caught my sight was none other than a Rukh's egg. As I looked and wondered at the marvellous works of the Almighty, the bird alighted on the dome and brooded over it, with its wings covering it and its legs stretched out behind it on the ground, and in this posture it fell asleep, glory be to Him who sleepeth not! When I saw this, I arose, and unwinding my turband from my head, doubled it and twisted it into a rope, with which I girt my middle and bound my waist fast to the legs of the Rukh, saying in myself, "Peradventure this bird may carry me to a land of cities and inhabitants, and that will be better than abiding in this desert island." I passed the night watching and fearing to sleep, lest the bird should fly away with me unawares; and as soon as the dawn broke and morn shone, the Rukh rose off its egg, and spreading its wings with a great cry, flew up into the air, dragging me with it; nor ceased it to soar and to tower till I thought it had reached the limit of the firmament; after which it descended earthwards, little by little, till it lighted on the top of a high hill. As soon as I found myself on the hard ground, I made haste to unbind myself, quaking for fear of the bird, though it took no heed of me nor even felt me; and, loosing my turband from its feet, I made off with my best speed. Presently, I saw it catch up in its huge claws something from the earth and rise with it high in air, and observing it narrowly I saw it to be a serpent big of bulk and gigantic of girth, wherewith it flew away clean out of sight. I marvelled at this and faring forwards found myself on a peak overlooking a valley, exceeding great and wide and deep, and bounded by vast mountains that spired high in air: none could descry their summits, for the excess of their height, nor was any able to climb up thereto. When I saw this, I blamed myself for that which I had done and said, "Would Heaven I had tarried in the island! It was better than this wild desert; for there I had at least fruits to eat and water to drink, and here are neither trees nor fruits, nor streams. But there is no Majesty and there is no Might save in Allah, the Glorious, the Great! Verily, as often as I am quit of one peril, I fall into a worse danger and a more grievous." However, I took courage and walking along the Wady found that its soil was of diamond, the stone wherewith they pierce minerals and precious stones and porcelain and the onyx, for that it is a dense stone and a dure, whereon neither iron nor hardhead hath effect, neither can we cut off aught therefrom nor break it, save by means of leadstone. Moreover, the valley swarmed with snakes and vipers, each big as a palm tree, that would have made but one gulp of an elephant; and they came out by night, hiding during the day, lest the Rukhs and eagles pounce on them and tear them to pieces, as was their wont, why I wot not. And I repented of what I had done and said, "By Allah, I have made haste to bring destruction upon myself!" The day began to wane as I went along and I looked about for a place where I might pass the night, being in fear of the serpents; and I took no thought of meat and drink in my concern for my life. Presently I caught sight of a cave nearhand with a narrow doorway; so I entered, and seeing a great stone close to the mouth, I rolled it up and stopped the entrance, saying to myself, "I am safe here for the night; and as soon as it is day, I will go forth and see what destiny will do." Then I looked within the cave and saw at the upper end a great serpent brooding on her eggs, at which my flesh quaked and my hair stood on end; but I raised my eyes to Heaven, and committing my case to fate and lot, abode all that night without sleep till daybreak, when I rolled back the stone from the mouth of the cave and went forth, staggering like a drunken man, and giddy with watching and fear and hunger. As in this sore case I walked along the valley, behold, there fell down before me a slaughtered beast; but I saw no one, whereat I marvelled with great marvel, and presently re-membered a story I had heard aforetime of traders and pilgrims and travellers; how the mountains where are the diamonds are full of perils and terrors, nor can any fare through them; but the merchants who traffic in diamonds have a device by which they obtain them, that is to say, they take a sheep and slaughter and skin it and cut it in pieces and cast morsels down from the mountain-tops into the valley-sole, where the meat being fresh and sticky with blood, some of the gems cleave to it. There they leave it till mid-day, when the eagles and vultures swoop down upon it and carry it in their claws to the mountain-summits, whereupon the merchants approach and shout at them and scare them away from the meat. Then they come and, taking the diamonds which they find sticking to it, go their ways with them and leave the meat to the birds and beasts; nor can any come at the diamonds but by this device ——And Shahrazad perceived the dawn of day and ceased saying her permitted say.

Now when it was the Five Hundred and Forty-fifth Night,

She said, It hath reached me, O auspicious King, that Sindbad the Sea-man continued his relation of what befell him in the Mountain of Dia-monds, and informed them that the merchants cannot come at the dia-monds save by the device aforesaid. So when I saw the slaughtered beast fall (he pursued) and bethought me of the story, I went up to it and filled my pockets and shawl-girdle and turband and the folds of my clothes with the choicest diamonds; and as I was thus engaged, down fell before me another great piece of meat. Then with my enrolled tur-band, and lying on my back, I set the bit on my breast so that I was hidden by the meat, which was thus raised above the ground. Hardly had I gripped it, when an eagle swooped down upon the flesh, and seizing it with his talons, flew up with it high in air and me clinging thereto, and ceased not its flight till it alighted on the head of one of the mountains where dropping the carcass he fell to rending it; but, behold, there arose behind him a great noise of shouting and clattering of wood, whereat the bird took fright and flew away. . . .

[Made rich by the diamonds he has brought from the valley, Sind-bad returns once again to Baghdad.]

The Third Voyage of Sindbad The Seaman

As I told you yesterday, I returned from my second voyage overjoyed at my safety and with great increase of wealth, Allah having requited me all that I had wasted and lost, and I abode awhile in Baghdad-city savouring the utmost ease and prosperity and comfort and happiness, till the carnal man was once more seized with longing for travel and diver-sion and adventure, and yearned after traffic and lucre and emolument, for that the human heart is naturally prone to evil. So making up my mind I laid in great plenty of goods suitable for a sea-voyage and re-pairing to Bassorah, went down to the shore and found there a fine ship ready to sail, with a full crew and a numerous company of merchants, men of worth and substance; faith, piety and consideration. I embarked with them and we set sail on the blessing of Allah Almighty and on His aidance and His favour to bring our voyage to a safe and prosperous issue and already we congratulated one another on our good fortune and boon voyage. We fared on from sea to sea and from island to island and city to city, in all delight and contentment, buying and selling wherever we touched, and taking our solace and our pleasure, till one day when, as we sailed athwart the dashing sea, swollen with clashing billows, behold, the master (who stood on the gunwale examining the ocean in all directions) cried out with a great cry, and buffeted his face and pluckt out his beard and rent his raiment, and bade furl the sail and cast the anchors. So we said to him, "O Rais, what is the matter?" "Know, O my brethren (Allah preserve you!), that the wind hath gotten the better of us and hath driven us out of our course into mid-ocean, and destiny, for our ill-luck, hath brought us to the Mountain of the Zughb, a hairy folk like apes, among whom no man ever fell and came forth alive; and my heart presageth that we all be dead men." Hardly had the master made an end of his speech when the apes were upon us. They surrounded the ship on all sides, swarming like locusts and crowding the shore. They were the most frightful of wild creatures, covered with black hair like felt, foul of favour and small of stature, being but four spans high, yellow-eyed and black-faced; none knoweth their language nor what they are, and they shun the company of men. We feared to slay them or strike them or drive them away, because of their inconceivable multitude; lest, if we hurt one, the rest fall on us and slay us, for numbers prevail over courage; so we let them do their will, albeit we feared they would plunder our goods and gear. They swarmed up the cables and gnawed them asunder, and on like wise they did with all the ropes of the ship, so that it fell off from the wind and stranded upon their mountainous coast. Then they laid hands on all the merchants and crew, and landing us on the island, made off with the ship and its cargo and went their ways, we wot not whither. We were thus left on the island, eating of its fruits and pot-herbs and drinking of its streams till, one day, we espied in its midst what seemed an inhabited house. So we made for it as fast as our feet could carry us and behold, it was a castle strong and tall, compassed about with a lofty wall, and having a two-leaved gate of ebony-wood, both of which leaves open stood. We entered and found within a space wide and bare like a great square, round which stood many high doors open thrown, and at the farther end a long bench of stone and braziers, with cooking gear hanging thereon and about it great plenty of bones; but we saw no one and marvelled thereat with exceeding wonder. Then we sat down in the courtyard a little while and presently falling asleep, slept from the forenoon till sundown, when lo! the earth trembled under our feet and the air rumbled with a terrible tone. Then there came down upon us, from the top of the castle, a huge creature in the likeness of a man, black of colour, tall and big of bulk, as he were a great date-tree, with eyes like coals of fire and eye-teeth like boar's tusks and a vast big gape like the mouth of a well. Moreover, he had long loose lips like [a] camel's, hanging down upon his breast, and ears like two Jarms [2] falling over his shoulder-blades and the nails of his

[2] A kind of barge . . . used on the Nile. . . .

hands were like the claws of a lion. When we saw this frightful giant, we were like to faint and every moment increased our fear and terror; and we became as dead men for excess of horror and affright.——And Shahrazad perceived the dawn of day and ceased saying her permitted say.

Now when it was the Five Hundred and Forty-seventh Night,

She said, It hath reached me, O auspicious King, that Sindbad the Seaman continued:—When we saw this frightful giant we were struck with exceeding terror and horror. And after trampling upon the earth, he sat awhile on the bench; then he arose and coming to us seized me by the arm choosing me out from among my comrades the merchants. He took me up in his hand and turning me over felt me, as a butcher feeleth a sheep he is about to slaughter, and I but a little mouthful in his hands; but finding me lean and fleshless for stress of toil and trouble and weariness, let me go and took up another, whom in like manner he turned over and felt and let go; nor did he cease to feel and turn over the rest of us, one after another, till he came to the master of the ship. Now he was a sturdy, stout, broad-shouldered wight, fat and in full vigour; so he pleased the giant, who seized him, as a butcher seizeth a beast, and throwing him down, set his foot on his neck and brake it; after which he fetched a long spit and thrusting it up his backside brought it forth of the crown of his head. Then, lighting a fierce fire, he set over it the spit with the Rais thereon, and turned it over the coals, till the flesh was roasted, when he took the spit off the fire and set it like a Kabáb-stick before him. Then he tare the body, limb from limb, as one jointeth a chicken and, rending the flesh with his nails, fell to eating of it and gnawing the bones, till there was nothing left but some of these, which he threw on one side of the wall. This done, he sat for a while; then he lay down on the stone-bench and fell asleep, snarking and snoring like the gurgling of a lamb or a cow with its throat cut; nor did he awake till morning, when he rose and fared forth and went his ways. As soon as we were certified that he was gone, we began to talk with one another, weeping and bemoaning ourselves for the risk we ran, and saying, "Would Heaven we had been drowned in the sea or that the apes had eaten us! That were better than to be roasted over the coals; by Allah, this is a vile, foul death! But whatso the Lord willeth must come to pass, and there is no Majesty and there is no Might, save in Him, the Glorious, the Great! We shall assuredly perish miserably and none will know of us; as there is no escape for us from this place." Then we arose and roamed about the island, hoping that haply we might find a place to hide us in or a means of flight, for indeed death was a light matter to us, provided we were not roasted over the fire [3] and eaten. However, we could find no hiding-place and the evening overtook us; so, of the excess of our

[3] Fire is forbidden as a punishment amongst Moslems, the idea being that it should be reserved for the next world. Hence the sailors fear the roasting more than the eating: with ours it would probably be the reverse. . . .

42

terror, we returned to the castle and sat down awhile. Presently, the earth trembled under our feet and the black ogre came up to us and turning us over, felt one after other, till he found a man to his liking, whom he took and served as he had done the captain, killing and roasting and eating him: after which he lay down on the bench and slept all night, snarking and snoring like a beast with its throat cut, till daybreak, when he arose and went out as before. Then we drew together and conversed and said one to other, "By Allah, we had better throw ourselves into the sea and be drowned than die roasted; for this is an abominable death!" Quoth one of us, "Hear ye my words! let us cast about to kill him, and be at peace from the grief of him and rid the Moslems of his barbarity and tyranny." Then said I, "Hear me, O my brothers; if there is nothing for it but to slay him, let us carry some of this firewood and planks down to the sea-shore and make us a boat wherein, if we succeed in slaughtering him, we may either embark and let the waters carry us whither Allah willeth, or else abide here till some ship pass, when we will take passage in it. If we fail to kill him, we will embark in the boat and put out to sea; and if we be drowned, we shall at least escape being roasted over a kitchen fire with sliced weasands; whilst, if we escape, we escape, and if we be drowned, we die martyrs." "By Allah," said they all, "this rede is a right"; and we agreed upon this, and set about carrying it out. So we haled down to the beach the pieces of wood which lay about the bench; and, making a boat, moored it to the strand, after which we stowed therein somewhat of victual and returned to the castle. As soon as evening fell the earth trembled under our feet and in came the blackamoor upon us, snarling like a dog about to bite. He came up to us and feeling us and turning us over one by one, took one of us and did with him as he had done before and ate him, after which he lay down on the bench and snored and snorted like thunder. As soon as we were assured that he slept, we arose and, taking two iron spits of those standing there, heated them in the fiercest of the fire, till they were red-hot, like burning coals, when we gripped fast hold of them and going up to the giant, as he lay snoring on the bench, thrust them into his eyes and pressed upon them, all of us, with our united might, so that his eyeballs burst and he became stone blind. Thereupon he cried with a great cry, whereat our hearts trembled, and springing up from the bench, he fell a-groping after us blind-fold. We fled from him, right and left and he saw us not, for his sight was altogether blent; but we were in terrible fear of him and made sure we were dead men despairing of escape. Then he found the door, feeling for it with his hands, and went out roaring aloud; and behold, the earth shook under us, for the noise of his roaring, and we quaked for fear. As he quitted the castle we followed him and betook ourselves to the place where we had moored our boat, saying to one another, "If this accursed abide absent till the going down of the sun and come not to the castle, we shall know that he is dead; and if he come back, we will embark in the boat and paddle till we escape, committing our affair to Allah." But, as we spoke, behold, up came the blackamoor with other two as they were Ghuls, fouler and more frightful than he, with eyes like red-hot coals; which when we saw we hurried into the boat and casting off the moorings paddled away and pushed out to sea. As soon as the ogres caught sight of us, they cried out at us and running down to the sea-shore, fell a-pelting us with rocks, whereof some fell amongst us and others fell into the sea. We paddled with all our might till we were beyond their reach, but the most part of us were slain by the rock-throwing, and the winds and waves sported with us and carried us into the midst of the dashing sea, swollen with billows clashing. We knew not whither we went and my fellows died one after another, till there remained but three, myself and two others.——And Shahrazad perceived the dawn of day and ceased to say her permitted say.

Now when it was the Five Hundred and Forty-eighth Night,

She said, It hath reached me, O auspicious King, that Sindbad the Seaman thus continued:—Most part of us were slain by the rock-throwing and only three of us remained on board the boat, for, as often as one died, we threw him into the sea. We were sore exhausted for stress of hunger, but we took courage and heartened one another and worked for dear life and paddled with main and might, till the winds cast us upon an island, as we were dead men for fatigue and fear and famine. We landed on the island and walked about it for a while, finding that it abounded in trees and streams and birds; and we ate of the fruits and rejoiced in our escape from the black and our deliverance from the perils of the sea; and thus we did till nightfall, when we lay down and fell asleep for excess of fatigue. But we had hardly closed our eyes before we were aroused by a hissing sound, like the sough of wind, and awaking, saw a serpent like a dragon, a seld-seen sight, of monstrous make and belly of enormous bulk which lay in a circle around us. Presently it reared its head and seizing one of my companions, swallowed him up to his shoulders; then it gulped down the rest of him, and we heard his ribs crack in its belly. Whereon it went its way, and we abode in sore amazement and grief for our comrade, and mortal fear for ourselves, saying, "By Allah, this is a marvellous thing! Each kind of death that threateneth us is more terrible than the last. We were rejoicing in our escape from the black ogre and our deliverance from the perils of the sea; but now we have fallen into that which is worse. There is no Majesty and there is no Might save in Allah! By the Almighty, we have escaped from the blackamoor and from drowning: but how shall we escape from this abominable and viperish monster?" Then we walked about the island, eating of its fruits and drinking of its streams till dusk, when we climbed up into a high tree and went to sleep there, I being on the topmost bough. As soon as it was dark night up came the serpent, looking right and left; and, making for the tree whereon we were, climbed up to my comrade and swallowed him down to his shoulders. Then it coiled about the bole with him, whilst I, who could not take my eyes off the sight, heard his bones crack in its belly, and it swallowed him whole, after which it slid down from the tree. When the day broke and the light showed me that the serpent was gone, I came down, as I were a dead man for stress of fear and anguish, and thought to cast myself into the sea and be at rest from the woes of the world; but could not bring myself to this, for verily life is dear. So I took five pieces of wood, broad and long, and bound one crosswise to the soles of my feet and others in like fashion on my right and left sides and over my breast; and the broadest and largest I bound across my head and made them fast with ropes. Then I lay down on the ground on my back, so that I was completely fenced in by the pieces of wood, which enclosed me like a bier. So as soon as it was dark up came the serpent, as usual, and made towards me, but could not get at me to swallow me for the wood that fenced me in. So it wriggled round me on every side, whilst I looked on, like one dead by reason of my terror; and every now and then it would glide away and come back; but as often as it tried to come at me, it was hindered by the pieces of wood wherewith I had bound myself on every side. It ceased not to beset me thus from sundown till dawn, but when the light of day shone upon the beast it made off, in the utmost fury and extreme disappointment. Then I put out my hand and unbound myself, well-nigh down among the dead men for fear and suffering; and went down to the island-shore, whence a ship afar off in the midst of the waves suddenly struck my sight. So I tore off a great branch of a tree and made signs with it to the crew, shouting out the while; which when the ship's company saw they said to one another, "We must stand in and see what this is; peradventure 'tis a man." So they made for the island and presently heard my cries, whereupon they took me on board and questioned me of my case. I told them all my adventures from first to last, whereat they marvelled mightily and covered my shame with some of their clothes. . . .

[Again Sindbad miraculously recovers all his goods—and more—and returns safely to his home.]

The Fourth Voyage of Sindbad The Seaman

[After the usual departure and shipwreck, Sindbad has several adventures and comes at last to a city where he teaches the king a number of crafts, including the making of saddles. In gratitude Sindbad is given a wife, and Shahrazad continues her story on night five hundred fifty-three.]

. . . It hath reached me, O auspicious King, that Sindbad the Seaman continued in these words:—Now after the King my master had married me to this choice wife, he also gave me a great and goodly house standing alone, together with slaves and officers, and assigned me pay and allowances. So I became in all ease and contentment and delight, and forgot everything which had befallen me of weariness and trouble and hardship; for I loved my wife with fondest love and she loved me no less, and we were as one and abode in the utmost comfort of life and in its happiness. And I said in myself, "When I return to my native land I will carry her with me." But whatso is predestined to a man, that needs must be, and none knoweth what shall befall him. We lived thus a great while, till Almighty Allah bereft one of my neighbours of his wife. Now he was a gossip of mine; so hearing the cry of the keeners I went in to condole with him on his loss and found him in very ill plight, full of trouble and weary of soul and mind. I condoled with him and comforted him, saying, "Mourn not for thy wife who hath now found the mercy of Allah; the Lord will surely give thee a better in her stead and thy name shall be great and thy life shall be long in the land, Inshallah!" But he wept bitter tears and replied, "O my friend, how can I marry another wife and how shall Allah replace her to me with a better than she, whenas I have but one day left to live?" "O my brother," said I, "return to thy senses and announce not the glad tidings of thine own death, for thou are well, sound and in good case." "By thy life, O my friend," rejoined he, "to-morrow thou wilt lose me and wilt never see me again till the Day of Resurrection." I asked, "How so?" and he answered, "This very day they bury my wife, and they bury me with her in one tomb; for it is the custom with us, if the wife die first, to bury the husband alive with her and in like manner the wife, if the husband die first; so that neither may enjoy life after losing his or her mate." "By Allah," cried I, "this is a most vile, lewd custom, and not to be endured of any!" Meanwhile, behold, the most part of the townsfolk came in and fell to condoling with my gossip for his wife and for himself. Presently they laid the dead woman out, as was their wont; and, setting her on a bier, carried her and her husband without the city, till they came to a place in the side of a mountain at the end of the island by the sea; and here they raised a great rock and discovered the mouth of a stone-riveted pit or well, leading down into a vast underground cavern that ran beneath the mountain. Into this pit they threw the corpse, then tying a rope of palm-fibres under the husband's armpits, they let him down into the cavern, and with him a great pitcher of fresh water and seven scones by way of viaticum. When he came to the bottom he loosed himself from the rope and they drew it up; and, stopping the mouth of the pit with the great stone, they returned to the city, leaving my friend in the cavern with his dead wife. When I saw this I said to myself, "By Allah, this fashion of death is more grievous than the first!" And I went in to the King and said to him, "O my lord, why do ye bury the quick with the dead?" Quoth he, "It hath been the custom, thou must know, of our forbears and our olden Kings from time immemorial, if the husband die first, to bury his wife with him, and the like with the wife, so we may not sever them, alive or dead." I asked, "O King of the age, if the wife of a foreigner like myself die among you, deal ye with him as with yonder man?" and he answered, "Assuredly, we do with him even as thou hast seen." When I heard this, my gall-bladder was like to burst for the violence of my dismay and concern for myself: my wit became dazed; I felt as if in a vile dungeon; and hated their society; for I went about in fear lest my wife should die before me and they bury me alive with her. However, after a while, I comforted myself, saying, "Haply I shall predecease her, or shall have returned to my own land before she die, for none knoweth which shall go first and which shall go last." Then I applied myself to diverting my mind from this thought with various occupations; but it was not long before my wife sickened and complained and took to her pillow and fared after a few days to the mercy of Allah; and the King and the rest of the folk came, as was their wont, to condole with me and her family, and to console us for her loss and not less to condole with me for myself. Then the women washed her and arraying her in her richest raiment and golden ornaments, necklaces and jewelry, laid her on the bier and bore her to the mountain aforesaid, where they lifted the cover of the pit and cast her in; after which all my intimates and acquaintances and my wife's kith and kin came round me, to farewell me in my lifetime and console me for my own death, whilst I cried out among them, saying, "Almighty Allah never made it lawful to bury the quick with the dead! I am a stranger, not one of your kind; and I cannot abear your custom, and had I known it I never would have wedded among you!" They heard me not and paid no heed to my words, but laying hold of me, bound me by force and let me down into the cavern, with a large gugglet of sweet water and seven cakes of bread, according to their custom. When I came to the bottom, they called out to me to cast myself loose from the cords, but I refused to do so; so they threw them down on me, and closing the mouth of the pit with the stones aforesaid, went their ways.——And Shahrazad perceived the dawn of day and ceased to say her permitted say.

Now when it was the Five Hundred and Fifty-fourth Night,

She said, It hath reached me, O auspicious King, that Sindbad the Seaman continued:—When they left me in the cavern with my dead wife and, closing the mouth of the pit, went their ways, I looked about me and found myself in a vast cave full of dead bodies, that exhaled a fulsome and loathsome smell and the air was heavy with the groans of the dying. Thereupon I fell to blaming myself for what I had done, saying, "By Allah, I deserve all that hath befallen me and all that shall befall me! What curse was upon me to take a wife in this city? There is no Majesty and there is no Might save in Allah, the Glorious, the Great! As often as I say I have escaped from one calamity, I fall into a worse. By Allah, this is an abominable death to die! Would Heaven I had died a decent death and been washed and shrouded like a man and a Moslem. Would I had been drowned at sea or perished in the mountains! It were better than to die this miserable death!" And on such wise I kept blaming my own folly and greed of gain in that black hole, knowing not night

47

from day; and I ceased not to ban the Foul Fiend and to bless the Almighty Friend. Then I threw myself down on the bones of the dead and lay there, imploring Allah's help and, in the violence of my despair, invoking death which came not to me, till the fire of hunger burned my stomach and thirst set my throat aflame, when I sat up and feeling for the bread, ate a morsel and upon it swallowed a mouthful of water. After this, the worst night I ever knew, I arose, and exploring the cavern, found that it extended a long way with hollows in its sides; and its floor was strewn with dead bodies and rotten bones, that had lain there from olden time. So I made myself a place in the cavity of the cavern, afar from the corpses lately thrown down and there slept. I abode thus a long while, till my provision was like to give out; and yet I ate not save once every day or second day; nor did I drink more than an occasional draught, for fear my victual should fail me before my death; and I said to myself, "Eat little and drink little; belike the Lord shall vouchsafe deliverance to thee!" One day, as I sat thus, pondering my case and bethinking me how I should do when my bread and water should be exhausted, behold, the stone that covered the opening was suddenly rolled away and the light streamed down upon me. Quoth I, "I wonder what is the matter: haply they have brought another corpse." Then I espied folk standing about the mouth of the pit, who presently let down a dead man and a live woman, weeping and bemoaning herself, and with her an ampler supply of bread and water than usual. I saw her and she was a beautiful woman; but she saw me not; and they closed up the opening and went away. Then I took the leg-bone of a dead man and, going up to the woman, smote her on the crown of the head; and she cried one cry and fell down in a swoon. I smote her a second and a third time, till she was dead, when I laid hands on her bread and water and found on her great plenty of ornaments and rich apparel, necklaces, jewels and gold trinkets [4]; for it was their custom to bury women in all their finery. I carried the vivers to my sleeping place in the cavern-side and ate and drank of them sparingly, no more than sufficed to keep the life in me, lest the provaunt come speedily to an end and I perish of hunger and thirst. Yet did I never wholly lose hope in Almighty Allah. I abode thus a great while, killing all the live folk they let down into the cavern and taking their provisions of meat and drink; till one day, as I slept, I was awakened by something scratching and burrowing among the bodies in a corner of the cave and said, "What can this be?" fearing wolves or hyænas. So I sprang up and seizing the leg-bone aforesaid, made for the noise. As soon as the thing was ware of me, it fled from me into the inward of the cavern, and lo! it was a wild beast. However, I followed it to the further end, till I saw afar off a point of light not bigger than a star, now appearing and then disappearing. So I made for it, and as I drew near, it grew larger and brighter, till I was certified that it was a crevice in the rock, leading to the open country; and I said to myself,

---

[4] The confession is made with true Eastern sang-froid and probably none of the hearers "disapproved" of the murders which saved the speaker's life.

"There must be some reason for this opening: either it is the mouth of a second pit, such as that by which they let me down, or else it is a natural fissure in the stonery." So I bethought me awhile and nearing the light, found that it came from a breach in the back side of the mountain which the wild beasts had enlarged by burrowing, that they might enter and devour the dead and freely go to and fro. When I saw this, my spirits revived and hope came back to me and I made sure of life, after having died a death. So I went on, as in a dream, and making shift to scramble through the breach, found myself on the slope of a high mountain, over-looking the salt sea and cutting off all access thereto from the island, so that none could come at that part of the breach from the city. I praised my Lord and thanked Him, rejoicing greatly and heartening myself with the prospect of deliverance; then I returned through the crack to the cavern and brought out all the food and water I had saved up and donned some of the dead folk's clothes over my own; after which I gathered together all the collars and necklaces of pearls and jewels, and trinklets of gold and silver set with precious stones, and other ornaments and valuables I could find upon the corpses; and making them into bundles with the grave clothes and raiment of the dead, carried them out to the back of the mountain facing the sea-shore, where I established myself, purposing to wait there till it should please Almighty Allah to send me relief by means of some passing ship. I visited the cavern daily and as often as I found folk buried alive there, I killed them all in-differently, men and women, and took their victual and valuables and transported them to my seat on the sea-shore. Thus I abode a long while.——And Shahrazad perceived the dawn of day and ceased saying her permitted say.

Now when it was the Five Hundred and Fifty-fifth Night,

She said, It hath reached me, O auspicious King, that Sindbad the Sea-man continued:—And after carrying all my victuals and valuables from the cavern to the coast I abode a long while by the sea, pondering my case, till one day I caught sight of a ship passing in the midst of the clashing sea, swollen with dashing billows. So I took a piece of a white shroud I had with me and, tying it to a staff, ran along the sea-shore, making signals therewith and calling to the people in the ship, till they espied me and hearing my shouts, sent a boat to fetch me off. . . .

[Sindbad recovers his goods and returns home in great prosperity to tell his friends of his most recent adventures. But he is drawn to the sea once more and is again shipwrecked.]

Now when it was the Five Hundred and Fifty-seventh Night,

She said, It hath reached me, O auspicious King, that Sindbad the Sea-man continued:—So when I escaped drowning and reached the island which afforded me fruit to eat and water to drink, I returned thanks to the Most High and glorified Him; after which I sat till nightfall, hearing no voice and seeing none inhabitant. Then I lay down, well-nigh dead for travail and trouble and terror, and slept without surcease till morning, when I arose and walked about under the trees till I came to the channel of a draw-well fed by a spring of running water, by which well sat an old man of venerable aspect, girt about with a waist-cloth [5] made of the fibre of palm-fronds. Quoth I to myself, "Haply this Shaykh [6] is of those who were wrecked in the ship and hath made his way to this island." So I drew near to him and saluted him, and he returned my salam by signs, but spoke not; and I said to him, "O nuncle mine, what causeth thee to sit here?" He shook his head and moaned and signed to me with his hand as who should say, "Take me on thy shoulders and carry me to the other side of the well-channel." And quoth I in my mind, "I will deal kindly with him and do what he desireth; it may be I shall win me a reward in Heaven for he may be a paralytic." So I took him on my back and, carrying him to the place whereat he pointed, said to him, "Dismount at thy leisure." But he would not get off my back and wound his legs about my neck. I looked at them and seeing that they were like a buffalo's hide for blackness and roughness, was affrighted and would have cast him off; but he clung to me and gripped my neck with his legs, till I was well-nigh choked, the world grew black in my sight, and I fell senseless to the ground like one dead. But he still kept his seat, and raising his legs drummed with his heels and beat harder than palm-rods my back and shoulders, till he forced me to rise for excess of pain. Then he signed to me with his hand to carry him hither and thither among the trees which bore the best fruits; and if ever I refused to do his bidding or loitered or took my leisure he beat me with his feet more grievously than if I had been beaten with whips. He ceased not to signal with his hand wherever he was minded to go; so I carried him about the island, like a captive slave, and he urined on and bewrayed my shoulders and back, dismounting not night nor day: and whenas he wished to sleep he wound his legs about my neck and leaned back and slept awhile; then arose and beat me, whereupon I sprang up in haste, unable to gainsay him because of the pain he inflicted on me. And, indeed, I blamed myself and sore repented me of having taken compassion on him, and continued in this condition, suffering fatigue not to be described, till I said to myself, "I wrought him a weal and he requited me with my ill. By Allah, never more will I do any man a service so long as I live." And again and again I besought the Most High that I might die, for stress of weariness and misery; and thus I abode a long while, till one day I came with him to a place wherein was abundance of gourds, many of them dry. So I took a great dry gourd, and cutting open the head, scooped out the inside and cleaned it: after which I gathered grapes from a vine which grew hard by, and squeezed them into the gourd till it was full of the juice. Then I stopped up the mouth and set it in the sun, where I left it for some days until it became strong wine, and every

[5] Arab. "Izár," the earliest garb of Eastern man; and, as such preserved in the Meccan pilgrimage. The "waist-cloth" is either tucked in or kept in place by a girdle.
[6] Chief, sheikh. [The editors.]

day I used to drink of it to comfort and sustain me under my fatigue with that froward and obstinate field, and as often as I drink myself drunk I forgot my troubles and took new heart. One day he saw me drinking, and signed to me with his hand, as who should say, "What is that?" Quoth I, "It is an excellent cordial, which cheereth the heart and reviveth the spirits." Then, being heated with wine, I ran and danced with him among the trees, clapping my hands and singing and making merry; and I staggered under him by design. When he saw this, he signed to me to give him the gourd that he might drink, and I feared him and gave it him. So he took it and draining it to the dregs, cast it on the ground, whereupon he grew frolicsome and began to clap hands and jig to and fro on my shoulders, and he made water upon me so copiously that all my dress was drenched. But presently the fumes of the wine rising to his head, he became helplessly drunk and his side-muscles and limbs relaxed, and he swayed to and fro on my back. When I saw that he had lost his senses for drunkenness, I put my hand to his legs and loosing them from my neck, stooped down well-nigh to the ground and threw him at full length.——And Shahrazad perceived the dawn of day and ceased to say her permitted say.

Now when it was the Five Hundred and Fifty-eighth Night,

She said, It hath reached me, O auspicious King, that Sindbad the Seaman continued:—So I threw the devil off my shoulders, hardly crediting my deliverance from him and fearing lest he should shake off his drunkenness and do me a mischief. Then I took up a great stone from among the trees and coming up to him smote him therewith on the head with all my might, and crushed in his skull as he lay dead drunk. Thereupon his flesh and fat and blood being in a pulp, he died and went to his deserts, The Fire, no mercy of Allah be upon him! I then returned, with a heart at ease, to my former station on the sea-shore and abode in that island many days, eating of its fruits and drinking of its waters and keeping a look-out for passing ships, till one day, as I sat on the beach recalling all that had befallen me, and saying, "I wonder if Allah will save me alive and restore me to my home and family and friends!" behold, a ship was making for the island through the dashing sea and clashing waves. Presently it cast anchor and the passengers landed; so I made for them, and when they saw me all hastened up to me and gathering round me, questioned me of my case and how I came thither. I told them all that had betided me, whereat they marvelled with exceeding marvel and said, "He who rode on thy shoulder is called the 'Shaykh al-Bahr' or Old Man of the Sea,[7] and none ever felt his legs on neck and came off alive but thou; and those who die under him he eateth; so praised be

[7] More literally "The Chief of the Sea (-Coast)," Shaykh being here a chief rather than an elder (eoldermann, alderman). . . . Our "old man" of the text may have been suggested by the Koranic commentators on chapt vi. When an Infidel rises from the grave, a hideous figure meets him and says, Why wonderest thou at my loathsomeness? I am thine Evil Deeds: thou didst ride upon me in the world and now I will ride upon thee (suiting the action to the words).

Allah for thy safety!" Then they set somewhat of food before me, whereof I ate my fill, and they gave me somewhat of clothes, wherewith I clad myself anew and covered my nakedness; after which they took me up into the ship. . . .

[The remainder of the fifth voyage, the sixth, and most of the seventh are omitted. Sindbad's final return home follows.]

. . . Then we embarked, I and my wife, with all our moveables, leaving our houses and domains and so forth, and set sail, and ceased not sailing from island to island and from sea to sea, with a fair wind and a favouring, till we arrived at Bassorah safe and sound. I made no stay there, but freighted another vessel and transferring my goods to her, set out forthright for Baghdad-city, where I arrived in safety, and entering my quarter and repairing to my house, forgathered with my family and friends and familiars and laid up my goods in my warehouses. When my people who, reckoning the period of my absence on this my seventh voyage, had found it to be seven and twenty years, and had given up all hope of me, heard of my return, they came to welcome me and to give me joy of my safety; and I related to them all that had befallen me; whereat they marvelled with exceeding marvel. Then I forswore travel and vowed to Allah the Most High I would venture no more by land or sea, for that this seventh and last voyage had surfeited me of travel and adventure; and I thanked the Lord (be He praised and glorified!), and blessed Him for having restored me to my kith and kin and country and home. "Consider, therefore, O Sindbad, O Landsman," continued Sindbad the Seaman, "what sufferings I have undergone and what perils and hardships I have endured before coming to my present state." "Allah upon thee, O my lord!" answered Sindbad the Landsman, "pardon me the wrong I did thee." [8] And they ceased not from friendship and fellowship, abiding in all cheer and pleasures and solace of life, till there came to them the Destroyer of delights and the Sunderer of societies, and the Shatterer of palaces and the Caterer for cemeteries, to wit, the Cup of Death, and glory to be the Living One who dieth not!" [We move now to the end of the tales and the conclusion of night one thousand and one.]

Now during this time Shahrazad had borne the King three boy children: so, when she had made an end of the story of Ma'aruf, she rose to her feet and kissing ground before him, said, "O King of the time and unique one of the age and the tide, I am thine handmaid and these thousand nights and a night have I entertained thee with stories of folk gone before and admonitory instances of the men of yore. May I then make bold to crave a boon of Thy Highness?" He replied, "Ask, O Shahrazad, and it shall be granted to thee." Whereupon she cried out to the nurses and the eunuchs, saying, "Bring me my children." So they

[8] I.e., in envying his wealth, with the risk of the evil eye.

brought them to her in haste, and they were three boy children, one walking, one crawling and one sucking. She took them and setting them before the King, again kissed ground and said, "O King of the Age, these are thy children and I crave that thou release me from the doom of death, as a dole to these infants; for, an thou kill me, they will become motherless and will find none among women to rear them as they should be reared." When the King heard this, he wept and straining the boys to his bosom, said, "By Allah, O Shahrazad, I pardoned thee before the coming of these children, for that I found thee chaste, pure, ingenuous and pious! Allah bless thee and thy father and thy mother and thy root and thy branch! I take the Almighty to witness against me that I exempt thee from aught that can harm thee." So she kissed his hands and feet and rejoiced with exceeding joy, saying, "The Lord make thy life long and increase thee in dignity and majesty!" presently adding, "Thou marvelledst at that which befell thee on the part of women; yet there betided the Kings of the Chosroës before thee greater mishaps and more grievous than that which hath befallen thee, and indeed I have set forth unto thee that which happened to Caliphs and Kings and others with their women, but the relation is longsome, and hearkening groweth tedious, and in this is all-sufficient warning for the man of wits and admonishment for the wise." Then she ceased to speak, and when King Shahryar heard her speech and profited by that which she said, he summoned up his reasoning powers and cleansed his heart and caused his understanding revert, and turned to Allah Almighty and said to himself, "Since there befell the Kings of the Chosroës more than that which hath befallen me, never whilst I live shall I cease to blame myself for the past. As for this Shahrazad, her like is not found in the lands; so praise be to Him Who appointed her a means for delivering His creatures from oppression and slaughter!" Then he arose from his séance and kissed her head, whereat she rejoiced, she and her sister Dunyazad, with exceeding joy. When the morning morrowed the King went forth, and sitting down on the throne of the Kingship, summoned the Lords of his land; whereupon the Chamberlains and Nabobs and Captains of the host went in to him and kissed ground before him. He distinguished the Wazir, Shahrazad's sire, with special favour and bestowed on him a costly and splendid robe of honour, and entreated him with the utmost kindness, and said to him, "Allah protect thee for that thou gavest me to wife thy noble daughter, who hath been the means of my repentance from slaying the daughters of folk. Indeed, I have found her pure and pious, chaste and ingenuous, and Allah hath vouchsafed me by her three boy children; wherefore praised be He for His passing favour." Then he bestowed robes of honour upon his Wazirs and Emirs and Chief Officers and he set forth to them briefly that which had betided him with Shahrazad, and how he had turned from his former ways and repented him of what he had done, and purposed to take the Wazir's daughter Shahrazad to wife, and let draw up the marriage-contract with her. When those who were present heard this, they kissed ground before him and blessed him and his betrothed Shahrazad, and the Wazir thanked her.

．　．　．

In due time King Shahryar summoned chroniclers and copyists, and bade them write all that had betided him with his wife, first and last; so they wrote this and named it *The Stories of the Thousand Nights and a Night.* The book came to thirty volumes and these the King laid up in his treasury. And the two brothers abode with their wives in all pleasance and solace of life and its delights, for that indeed Allah the Most High had changed their annoy into joy; and on this wise they continued till there took them the Destroyer of delights and the Severer of societies, the Desolator of dwelling-places, and Garnerer of grave-yards, and they were translated to the ruth of Almighty Allah; their houses fell waste and their palaces lay in ruins, and the Kings inherited their riches. Then there reigned after them a wise ruler, who was just, keen-witted and accomplished, and loved tales and legends, especially those which chronicle the doings of Sovrans and Sultans, and he found in the treasury these marvellous stories and wondrous histories, contained in the thirty volumes aforesaid. So he read in them a first book and a second and a third and so on to the last of them, and each book astounded and delighted him more than that which preceded it, till he came to the end of them. Then he admired whatso he had read therein of description and discourse and rare traits and anecdotes and moral instances and reminiscences, and bade the folk copy them and dispread them over all lands and climes; wherefore their report was bruited abroad and the people named them *The marvels and wonders of the Thousand Nights and a Night.* This is all that hath come down to us of the origin of this book, and Allah is All-knowing. So Glory be to Him Whom the shifts of Time waste not away, nor doth aught of chance or change affect His sway: Whom one case diverteth not from other case, and Who is sole in the attributes of perfect grace. And prayer and the Peace be upon the Lord's Pontiff and Chosen One among His creatures, our Lord MOHAMMED the Prince of mankind through whom we supplicate Him for a goodly and a godly

FINIS.

Tlön.Uqbar.OrbisTertius

Jorge Luis Borges

Translated by James E. Irby

Jorge Luis Borges was born near Buenos Aires in 1899 and has lived his life in Argentina, except for the period between 1914 and 1921, when his family traveled in Europe and he himself attended school in Geneva. His paternal grandmother was English and both he and his father were fluent in English nearly as early as in Spanish. Borges himself tells with amusement of first reading Cervantes in an English translation and then thinking when he came to read the original Spanish that the latter was a poor translation of the English. This incident undoubtedly was the basis for the story "Pierre Menard, Author of the Quixote," and its subjectivity and reverse point of view are characteristic of all his fiction. Borges' life has been, at least as he describes it, outwardly uneventful. Upon his return from Europe he was closely associated with the Ultraist movement in poetry and earned a considerable reputation as a poet, essayist, and literary critic. He spent some years as a cataloguer in a branch library in the outskirts of Buenos Aires and eventually, as his fame grew, became Director of the Argentine National Library and a professor of English literature at the university. He began writing his stories—preferring this form to the novel because of its shortness and precision—in the 1930's, but these remarkable works became famous outside Argentina only in the 1960's.

If the events of Borges' life are in his view somewhat pale, flat, even unreal, that life has been lived at the same time with extraordinary intensity within a world of fictions, *Ficciones* or *Labyrinths* as he himself calls some of his writings. His intense experiences within this fictional world began early in the quietness of his father's large library and have expanded throughout his long life to a knowledge of the books of many languages, to philosophy and history, and to the erudite lore of many places and times. This fascination with fictions is reflected in the strange events described in "Tlön, Uqbar, Orbis Tertius," where men invent the country of Uqbar to provide a base for the subsequent invention of Tlön, which will eventually become a third world, Orbis Tertius. This situation of story within story within story is much the same as that of *The Thousand Nights and a Night*, and after a reference to Islam, Borges' story-teller informs us that Volume XI of *A First Encyclopaedia of Tlön*, which falls into his hands, contains 1001 pages. But the story of Tlön is a stranger story than any Shahrazad tells. For one thing there are no real people in it, and for another its setting is not the living one in which a beautiful young girl tells stories to a cruel king in his rich palace, but the dry abstract form of an encyclopedia, that compendious reduction of all the world to perfect stillness and abstract order. And the motive behind the construction of the fiction of Tlön is not the vital one of a young girl desperately trying to save her life, but rather, insofar as we can puzzle it out, a combination of the desire of certain idealistic philosophers to create a perfectly ordered world out of their own heads and the nihilism and hatred of God of the American millionaire, Ezra Buckley.

How strange! How odd! And then we begin to note that Tlön is really no stranger or odder than the world in which we live; its geometry, philosophy, and language no more arbitrary than our own. There is still another step in the process of discovery—a step that brings us to the possibility that Tlön is not another world at all but the dehumanized, abstract, godless world that modern man is still in the process of constructing for himself. Following the gradually accumulating clues that bring us to this conclusion brings us also to a paradox concerning the uses and values of fiction. The fiction *of* Tlön as conceived by the philosophers and propagated with Buckley's money is both ridiculous in some ways and deadly to life; but, on the other hand, the fiction *about* Tlön as conceived and told by Borges is both delightful and life-enhancing, in that it allows us to see and understand the dangers of certain abstract, rationalistic methods of thinking. To perceive the differences between these two fictions is the key not only to Borges' paradox but to a most important awareness of the ways in which fictions can be used and misused.

∎

I

I owe the discovery of Uqbar to the conjunction of a mirror and an encyclopedia. The mirror troubled the depths of a corridor in a country house on Gaona Street in Ramos Mejía; the encyclopedia is fallaciously called *The Anglo-American Cyclopaedia* (New York, 1917) and is a literal but delinquent reprint of the *Encyclopaedia Britannica* of 1902. The event took place some five years ago. Bioy Casares had had dinner with me that evening and we became lengthily engaged in a vast polemic concerning the composition of a novel in the first person, whose narrator would omit or disfigure the facts and indulge in various contradictions which would permit a few readers—very few readers—to perceive an atrocious or banal reality. From the remote depths of the corridor, the mirror spied upon us. We discovered (such a discovery is inevitable in the late hours of the night) that mirrors have something monstrous about them. Then Bioy Casares recalled that one of the heresiarchs of Uqbar had declared that mirrors and copulation are abominable, because they increase the number of men. I asked him the

origin of this memorable observation and he answered that it was reproduced in *The Anglo-American Cyclopaedia,* in its article on Uqbar.
The house (which we had rented furnished) had a set of this work.
On the last pages of Volume XLVI we found an article on Upsala; on
the first pages of Volume XLVII, one on Ural-Altaic Languages, but not
a word about Uqbar. Bioy, a bit taken aback, consulted the volumes of
the index. In vain he exhausted all of the imaginable spellings: Ukbar,
Ucbar, Ooqbar, Ookbar, Oukbahr . . . Before leaving, he told me that
it was a region of Iraq or of Asia Minor. I must confess that I agreed
with some discomfort. I conjectured that this undocumented country and
its anonymous heresiarch were a fiction devised by Bioy's modesty in
order to justify a statement. The fruitless examination of one of Justus
Perthes' atlases fortified my doubt.

The following day, Bioy called me from Buenos Aires. He told me
he had before him the article on Uqbar, in Volume XLVI of the encyclopedia. The heresiarch's name was not forthcoming, but there was a note
on his doctrine, formulated in words almost identical to those he had
repeated, though perhaps literarily inferior. He had recalled: *Copulation
and mirrors are abominable.* The text of the encyclopedia said: *For one
of those gnostics, the visible universe was an illusion or (more precisely)
a sophism. Mirrors and fatherhood are abominable because they multiply
and disseminate that universe.* I told him, in all truthfulness, that I should
like to see that article. A few days later he brought it. This surprised me,
since the scrupulous cartographical indices of Ritter's *Erdkunde* were
plentifully ignorant of the name Uqbar.

The tome Bioy brought was, in fact, Volume XLVI of the *Anglo-
American Cyclopaedia.* On the half-title page and the spine, the alphabetical marking (Tor-Ups) was that of our copy, but, instead of 917,
it contained 921 pages. These four additional pages made up the article
on Uqbar, which (as the reader will have noticed) was not indicated by
the alphabetical marking. We later determined that there was no other
difference between the volumes. Both of them (as I believe I have
indicated) are reprints of the tenth *Encyclopaedia Britannica.* Bioy had
acquired his copy at some sale or other.

We read the article with some care. The passage recalled by Bioy
was perhaps the only surprising one. The rest of it seemed very plausible,
quite in keeping with the general tone of the work and (as is natural) a
bit boring. Reading it over again, we discovered beneath its rigorous
prose a fundamental vagueness. Of the fourteen names which figured in
the geographical part, we only recognized three—Khorasan, Armenia,
Erzerum—interpolated in the text in an ambiguous way. Of the historical
names, only one: the impostor magician Smerdis, invoked more as a
metaphor. The note seemed to fix the boundaries of Uqbar, but its nebulous reference points were rivers and craters and mountain ranges of that
same region. We read, for example, that the lowlands of Tsai Khaldun
and the Axa Delta marked the southern frontier and that on the islands

of the delta wild horses procreate. All this, on the first part of page 918. In the historical section (page 920) we learned that as a result of the religious persecutions of the thirteenth century, the orthodox believers sought refuge on these islands, where to this day their obelisks remain and where it is not uncommon to unearth their stone mirrors. The section on Language and Literature was brief. Only one trait is worthy of recollection: it noted that the literature of Uqbar was one of fantasy and that its epics and legends never referred to reality, but to the two imaginary regions of Mlejnas and Tlön . . . The bibliography enumerated four volumes which we have not yet found, though the third—Silas Haslam: *History of the Land Called Uqbar*, 1874—figures in the catalogues of Bernard Quaritch's bookshop.[1] The first, *Lesbare und lesenswerthe Bemerkungen über das Land Ukkbar in Klein-Asien*, dates from 1641 and is the work of Johannes Valentinus Andreä. This fact is significant; a few years later, I came upon that name in the unsuspected pages of De Quincey (*Writings*, Volume XIII) and learned that it belonged to a German theologian who, in the early seventeenth century, described the imaginary community of Rosae Crucis—a community that others founded later, in imitation of what he had prefigured.

That night we visited the National Library. In vain we exhausted atlases, catalogues, annuals of geographical societies, travelers' and historians' memoirs: no one had ever been in Uqbar. Neither did the general index of Bioy's encyclopedia register that name. The following day, Carlos Mastronardi (to whom I had related the matter) noticed the black and gold covers of the *Anglo-American Cyclopaedia* in a bookshop on Corrientes and Talcahuano . . . He entered and examined Volume XLVI. Of course, he did not find the slightest indication of Uqbar.

II

Some limited and waning memory of Herbert Ashe, an engineer of the southern railways, persists in the hotel at Adrogué, amongst the effusive honeysuckles and in the illusory depths of the mirrors. In his lifetime, he suffered from unreality, as do so many Englishmen; once dead, he is not even the ghost he was then. He was tall and listless and his tired rectangular beard had once been red. I understand he was a widower, without children. Every few years he would go to England, to visit (I judge from some photographs he showed us) a sundial and a few oaks. He and my father had entered into one of those close (the adjective is excessive) English friendships that begin by excluding confidences and very soon dispense with dialogue. They used to carry out an exchange of books and newspapers and engage in taciturn chess games . . . I remember him in the hotel corridor, with a mathematics book in his hand, sometimes looking at the irrecoverable colors of the sky. One afternoon, we spoke of the duodecimal system of numbering (in which twelve is

---

[1] Haslam has also published *A General History of Labyrinths*. [The footnotes in this story are, of course, Borges'.]

written as 10). Ashe said that he was converting some kind of tables from the duodecimal to the sexagesimal system (in which sixty is written as 10). He added that the task had been entrusted to him by a Norwegian, in Rio Grande do Sul. We had known him for eight years and he had never mentioned his sojourn in that region . . . We talked of country life, of the *capangas,* of the Brazilian etymology of the word *gaucho* (which some old Uruguayans still pronounce *gaúcho*) and nothing more was said—may God forgive me—of duodecimal functions. In September of 1937 (we were not at the hotel), Herbert Ashe died of a ruptured aneurysm. A few days before, he had received a sealed and certified package from Brazil. It was a book in large octavo. Ashe left it at the bar, where—months later—I found it. I began to leaf through it and experienced an astonished and airy feeling of vertigo which I shall not describe, for this is not the story of my emotions but of Uqbar and Tlön and Orbis Tertius. On one of the nights of Islam called the Night of Nights, the secret doors of heaven open wide and the water in the jars becomes sweeter; if those doors opened, I would not feel what I felt that afternoon. The book was written in English and contained 1001 pages. On the yellow leather back I read these curious words which were repeated on the title page: *A First Encyclopaedia of Tlön. Vol. XI. Hlaer to Jangr.* There was no indication of date or place. On the first page and on a leaf of silk paper that covered one of the color plates there was stamped a blue oval with this inscription: *Orbis Tertius.* Two years before I had discovered, in a volume of a certain pirated encyclopedia, a superficial description of a nonexistent country; now chance afforded me something more precious and arduous. Now I held in my hands a vast methodical fragment of an unknown planet's entire history, with its architecture and its playing cards, with the dread of its mythologies and the murmur of its languages, with its emperors and its seas, with its minerals and its birds and its fish, with its algebra and its fire, with its theological and metaphysical controversy. And all of it articulated, coherent, with no visible doctrinal intent or tone of parody.

In the "Eleventh Volume" which I have mentioned, there are allusions to preceding and succeeding volumes. In an article in the *N. R. F.* which is now classic, Néstor Ibarra has denied the existence of those companion volumes; Ezequiel Martínez Estrada and Drieu La Rochelle have refuted that doubt, perhaps victoriously. The fact is that up to now the most diligent inquiries have been fruitless. In vain we have upended the libraries of the two Americas and of Europe. Alfonso Reyes, tired of these subordinate sleuthing procedures, proposes that we should all undertake the task of reconstructing the many and weighty tomes that are lacking: *ex ungue leonem* [the lion is known by its claw]. He calculates, half in earnest and half jokingly, that a generation of *tlönistas* should be sufficient. This venturesome computation brings us back to the fundamental problem: Who are the inventors of Tlön? The plural is inevitable, because the hypothesis of a lone inventor—an infinite Leibniz laboring away darkly and modestly—has been unanimously discounted. It is conjectured that this brave new world is the work of a secret society of astronomers, biologists, engineers, metaphysicians, poets, chemists, algebraists, moralists, painters, geometers . . . directed by an obscure man of genius. Individuals mastering these diverse disciplines are abundant, but not so those capable of inventiveness and less so those capable of subordinating that inventiveness to a rigorous and systematic plan. This plan is so vast that each writer's contribution is infinitesimal. At first it was believed that Tlön was a mere chaos, an irresponsible license of the imagination; now it is known that it is a cosmos and that the intimate laws which govern it have been formulated, at least provisionally. Let it suffice for me to recall that the apparent contradictions of the Eleventh Volume are the fundamental basis for the proof that the other volumes exist, so lucid and exact is the order observed in it. The popular magazines, with pardonable excess, have spread news of the zoology and topography of Tlön; I think its transparent tigers and towers of blood perhaps do not merit the continued attention of *all* men. I shall venture to request a few minutes to expound its concept of the universe.

Hume noted for all time that Berkeley's arguments did not admit the slightest refutation nor did they cause the slightest conviction. This dictum is entirely correct in its application to the earth, but entirely false in Tlön. The nations of this planet are congenitally idealist. Their language and the derivations of their language—religion, letters, metaphysics—all presuppose idealism. The world for them is not a concourse of objects in space; it is a heterogeneous series of independent acts. It is successive and temporal, not spatial. There are no nouns in Tlön's conjectural *Ursprache*, from which the "present" languages and the dialects are derived: there are impersonal verbs, modified by monosyllabic suffixes (or prefixes) with an adverbial value. For example: there is no word corresponding to the word "moon," but there is a verb which in English would be "to moon" or "to moonate." "The moon rose above the river" is *hlör u fang axaxaxas mlö,* or literally: "upward behind the on-streaming it mooned."

The preceding applies to the languages of the southern hemisphere. In those of the northern hemisphere (on whose *Ursprache* there is very little data in the Eleventh Volume) the prime unit is not the verb, but the monosyllabic adjective. The noun is formed by an accumulation of adjectives. They do not say "moon," but rather "round airy-light on dark" or "pale-orange-of-the-sky" or any other such combination. In the example selected the mass of adjectives refers to a real object, but this is purely fortuitous. The literature of this hemisphere (like Meinong's subsistent world) abounds in ideal objects, which are convoked and dissolved in a moment, according to poetic needs. At times they are determined by mere simultaneity. There are objects composed of two terms, one of visual and another of auditory character: the color of the rising sun and the faraway cry of a bird. There are objects of many terms: the sun and the water on a swimmer's chest, the vague tremulous rose color we see with our eyes closed, the sensation of being carried along by a river and also by sleep. These second-degree objects can be combined with others; through the use of certain abbreviations, the process is practically infinite. There are famous poems made up of one enormous word. This word forms a *poetic object* created by the author. The fact that no one believes in the reality of nouns paradoxically causes their number to be unending. The languages of Tlön's northern hemisphere contain all the nouns of the Indo-European languages—and many others as well.

It is no exaggeration to state that the classic culture of Tlön comprises only one discipline: psychology. All others are subordinated to it. I have said that the men of this planet conceive the universe as a series of mental processes which do not develop in space but successively in time. Spinoza ascribes to his inexhaustible divinity the attributes of extension and thought; no one in Tlön would understand the juxtaposition of the first (which is typical only of certain states) and the second—which is a perfect synonym of the cosmos. In other words, they do not conceive that the spatial persists in time. The perception of a cloud of smoke on the horizon and then of the burning field and then of the half-extinguished cigarette that produced the blaze is considered an example of association of ideas.

This monism or complete idealism invalidates all science. If we explain (or judge) a fact, we connect it with another; such linking, in Tlön, is a later state of the subject which cannot affect or illuminate the previous state. Every mental state is irreducible: the mere fact of naming it—i.e., of classifying it—implies a falsification. From which it can be deduced that there are no sciences on Tlön, not even reasoning. The paradoxical truth is that they do exist, and in almost uncountable number. The same thing happens with philosophies as happens with nouns in the northern hemisphere. The fact that every philosophy is by definition a dialectical game, a *Philosophie des Als Ob* [Philosophy of As If], has caused them to multiply. There is an abundance of incredible systems of pleasing design or sensational type. The metaphysicians of Tlön do not seek for the truth or even for verisimilitude, but rather for the astounding. They judge that metaphysics is a branch of fantastic literature. They know that a system is nothing more than the subordination of all aspects of the universe to any one such aspect. Even the phrase "all aspects" is rejectable, for it supposes the impossible addition of the present and of all past moments. Neither is it licit to use the plural "past moments," since it supposes another impossible operation . . . One of the schools of Tlön goes so far as to negate time: it reasons that the present is indefinite, that the future has no reality other than as a present hope, that the past has no reality other than as a present memory.[2] Another school

---

[2] Russell (*The Analysis of Mind*, 1921, page 159) supposes that the planet has been created a few minutes ago, furnished with a humanity that "remembers" an illusory past.

declares that *all time* has already transpired and that our life is only the crepuscular and no doubt falsified and mutilated memory or reflection of an irrecoverable process. Another, that the history of the universe—and in it our lives and the most tenuous detail of our lives—is the scripture produced by a subordinate god in order to communicate with a demon. Another, that the universe is comparable to those cryptographs in which not all the symbols are valid and that only what happens every three hundred nights is true. Another, that while we sleep here, we are awake elsewhere and that in this way every man is two men.

Amongst the doctrines of Tlön, none has merited the scandalous reception accorded to materialism. Some thinkers have formulated it with less clarity than fervor, as one might put forth a paradox. In order to facilitate the comprehension of this inconceivable thesis, a heresiarch of the eleventh century [3] devised the sophism of the nine copper coins, whose scandalous renown is in Tlön equivalent to that of the Eleatic paradoxes. There are many versions of this "specious reasoning," which vary the number of coins and the number of discoveries; the following is the most common:

On Tuesday, X crosses a deserted road and loses nine copper coins. On Thursday, Y finds in the road four coins, somewhat rusted by Wednesday's rain. On Friday, Z discovers three coins in the road. On Friday morning, X finds two coins in the corridor of his house. The heresiarch would deduce from this story the reality—i.e., the continuity—of the nine coins which were recovered. *It is absurd* (he affirmed) *to imagine that four of the coins have not existed between Tuesday and Thursday, three between Tuesday and Friday afternoon, two between Tuesday and Friday morning. It is logical to think that they have existed—at least in some secret way, hidden from the comprehension of men—at every moment of those three periods.*

The language of Tlön resists the formulation of this paradox; most people did not even understand it. The defenders of common sense at first did no more than negate the veracity of the anecdote. They repeated that it was a verbal fallacy, based on the rash application of two neologisms not authorized by usage and alien to all rigorous thought: the verbs "find" and "lose," which beg the question, because they presuppose the identity of the first and of the last nine coins. They recalled that all nouns (man, coin, Thursday, Wednesday, rain) have only a metaphorical value. They denounced the treacherous circumstance "somewhat rusted by Wednesday's rain," which presupposes what is trying to be demonstrated: the persistence of the four coins from Tuesday to Thursday. They explained that *equality* is one thing and *identity* another, and formulated a kind of *reductio ad absurdum*: the hypothetical case of nine men who on nine successive nights suffer a severe pain. Would it not be ridiculous

[3] A century, according to the duodecimal system, signifies a period of a hundred and forty-four years.

—they questioned—to pretend that this pain is one and the same? [4] They said that the heresiarch was prompted only by the blasphemous intention of attributing the divine category of *being* to some simple coins and that at times he negated plurality and at other times did not. They argued: if equality implies identity, one would also have to admit that the nine coins are one.

Unbelievably, these refutations were not definitive. A hundred years after the problem was stated, a thinker no less brilliant than the heresiarch but of orthodox tradition formulated a very daring hypothesis. This happy conjecture affirmed that there is only one subject, that this indivisible subject is every being in the universe and that these beings are the organs and masks of the divinity. X is Y and is Z. Z discovers three coins because he remembers that X lost them; X finds two in the corridor because he remembers that the others have been found . . . The Eleventh Volume suggests that three prime reasons determined the complete victory of this idealist pantheism. The first, its repudiation of solipsism; the second, the possibility of preserving the psychological basis of the sciences; the third, the possibility of preserving the cult of the gods. Schopenhauer (the passionate and lucid Schopenhauer) formulates a very similar doctrine in the first volume of *Parerga und Paralipomena*.

The geometry of Tlön comprises two somewhat different disciplines: the visual and the tactile. The latter corresponds to our own geometry and is subordinated to the first. The basis of visual geometry is the surface, not the point. This geometry disregards parallel lines and declares that man in his movement modifies the forms which surround him. The basis of its arithmetic is the notion of indefinite numbers. They emphasize the importance of the concepts of greater and lesser, which our mathematicians symbolize as $>$ and $<$. They maintain that the operation of counting modifies quantities and converts them from indefinite into definite sums. The fact that several individuals who count the same quantity should obtain the same result is, for the psychologists, an example of association of ideas or of a good exercise of memory. We already know that in Tlön the subject of knowledge is one and eternal.

In literary practices the idea of a single subject is also all-powerful. It is uncommon for books to be signed. The concept of plagiarism does not exist: it has been established that all works are the creation of one author, who is atemporal and anonymous. The critics often invent authors: they select two dissimilar works—the *Tao Te Ching* and the *1001 Nights*, say—attribute them to the same writer and then determine most scrupulously the psychology of this interesting *homme de lettres* . . .

---

[4] Today, one of the churches of Tlön Platonically maintains that a certain pain, a certain greenish tint of yellow, a certain temperature, a certain sound, are the only reality. All men, in the vertiginous moment of coitus, are the same man. All men who repeat a line from Shakespeare *are* William Shakespeare.

Their books are also different. Works of fiction contain a single plot, with all its imaginable permutations. Those of a philosophical nature invariably include both the thesis and the antithesis, the rigorous pro and con of a doctrine. A book which does not contain its counterbook is considered incomplete.

Centuries and centuries of idealism have not failed to influence reality. In the most ancient regions of Tlön, the duplication of lost objects is not infrequent. Two persons look for a pencil; the first finds it and says nothing; the second finds a second pencil, no less real, but closer to his expectations. These secondary objects are called *hrönir* and are, though awkward in form, somewhat longer. Until recently, the *hrönir* were the accidental products of distraction and forgetfulness. It seems unbelievable that their methodical production dates back scarcely a hundred years, but this is what the Eleventh Volume tells us. The first efforts were unsuccessful. However, the *modus operandi* merits description. The director of one of the state prisons told his inmates that there were certain tombs in an ancient river bed and promised freedom to whoever might make an important discovery. During the months preceding the excavation the inmates were shown photographs of what they were to find. This first effort proved that expectation and anxiety can be inhibitory; a week's work with pick and shovel did not manage to unearth anything in the way of a *hrön* except a rusty wheel of a period posterior to the experiment. But this was kept in secret and the process was repeated later in four schools. In three of them the failure was almost complete; in the fourth (whose director died accidentally during the first excavations) the students unearthed—or produced—a gold mask, an archaic sword, two or three clay urns and the moldy and mutilated torso of a king whose chest bore an inscription which it has not yet been possible to decipher. Thus was discovered the unreliability of witnesses who knew of the experimental nature of the search . . . Mass investigations produce contradictory objects; now individual and almost improvised jobs are preferred. The methodical fabrication of *hrönir* (says the Eleventh Volume) has performed prodigious services for archaeologists. It has made possible the interrogation and even the modification of the past, which is now no less plastic and docile than the future. Curiously, the *hrönir* of second and third degree—the *hrönir* derived from another *hrön*, those derived from the *hrön* of a *hrön*—exaggerate the aberrations of the initial one; those of fifth degree are almost uniform; those of ninth degree become confused with those of the second; in those of the eleventh there is a purity of line not found in the original. The process is cyclical: the *hrön* of twelfth degree begins to fall off in quality. Stranger and more pure than any *hrön* is, at times, the *ur*: the object produced through suggestion, educed by hope. The great golden mask I have mentioned is an illustrious example.

Things become duplicated in Tlön; they also tend to become effaced and lose their details when they are forgotten. A classic example is the doorway which survived so long as it was visited by a beggar and disappeared at his death. At times some birds, a horse, have saved the ruins of an amphitheater.

Postscript (1947). I reproduce the preceding article just as it appeared in the *Anthology of Fantastic Literature* (1940), with no omission other than that of a few metaphors and a kind of sarcastic summary which now seems frivolous. So many things have happened since then . . . I shall do no more than recall them here.

In March of 1941 a letter written by Gunnar Erfjord was discovered in a book by Hinton which had belonged to Herbert Ashe. The envelope bore a cancellation from Ouro Preto; the letter completely elucidated the mystery of Tlön. Its text corroborated the hypotheses of Martínez Estrada. One night in Lucerne or in London, in the early seventeenth century, the splendid history has its beginning. A secret and benevolent society (amongst whose members were Dalgarno and later George Berkeley) arose to invent a country. Its vague initial program included "hermetic studies," philanthropy and the cabala. From this first period dates the curious book by Andreä. After a few years of secret conclaves and premature syntheses it was understood that one generation was not sufficient to give articulate form to a country. They resolved that each of the masters should elect a disciple who would continue his work. This hereditary arrangement prevailed; after an interval of two centuries the persecuted fraternity sprang up again in America. In 1824, in Memphis (Tennessee), one of its affiliates conferred with the ascetic millionaire Ezra Buckley. The latter, somewhat disdainfully, let him speak—and laughed at the plan's modest scope. He told the agent that in America it was absurd to invent a country and proposed the invention of a planet. To this gigantic idea he added another, a product of his nihilism [5]: that of keeping the enormous enterprise secret. At that time the twenty volumes of the *Encyclopaedia Britannica* were circulating in the United States; Buckley suggested that a methodical encyclopedia of the imaginary planet be written. He was to leave them his mountains of gold, his navigable rivers, his pasture lands roamed by cattle and buffalo, his Negroes, his brothels and his dollars, on one condition: "The work will make no pact with the impostor Jesus Christ." Buckley did not believe in God, but he wanted to demonstrate to this nonexistent God that mortal man was capable of conceiving a world. Buckley was poisoned in Baton Rouge in 1828; in 1914 the society delivered to its collaborators, some three hundred in number, the last volume of the First Encyclopedia of Tlön. The edition was a secret one; its forty volumes (the vastest undertaking ever carried out by man) would be the basis for another more detailed edition, written not in English but in one of the languages of Tlön. This revision of an illusory world, was called, provisionally, *Orbis Tertius* and one of its modest demiurgi was Herbert Ashe, whether

[5] Buckley was a freethinker, a fatalist and a defender of slavery.

65

as an agent of Gunnar Erfjord or as an affiliate, I do not know. His having received a copy of the Eleventh Volume would seem to favor the latter assumption. But what about the others?

In 1942 events became more intense. I recall one of the first of these with particular clarity and it seems that I perceived then something of its premonitory character. It happened in an apartment on Laprida Street, facing a high and light balcony which looked out toward the sunset. Princess Faucigny Lucinge had received her silverware from Poitiers. From the vast depths of a box embellished with foreign stamps, delicate immobile objects emerged: silver from Utrecht and Paris covered with hard heraldic fauna, and a samovar. Amongst them—with the perceptible and tenuous tremor of a sleeping bird—a compass vibrated mysteriously. The Princess did not recognize it. Its blue needle longed for magnetic north; its metal case was concave in shape; the letters around its edge corresponded to one of the alphabets of Tlön. Such was the first intrusion of this fantastic world into the world of reality.

I am still troubled by a stroke of chance which made me the witness of the second intrusion as well. It happened some months later, at a country store owned by a Brazilian in Cuchilla Negra. Amorim and I were returning from Sant' Anna. The River Tacuarembó had flooded and we were obliged to sample (and endure) the proprietor's rudimentary hospitality. He provided us with some creaking cots in a large room cluttered with barrels and hides. We went to bed, but were kept from sleeping until dawn by the drunken ravings of an unseen neighbor, who intermingled inextricable insults with snatches of *milongas*—or rather with snatches of the same *milonga*. As might be supposed, we attributed this insistent uproar to the store owner's fiery cane liquor. By daybreak, the man was dead in the hallway. The roughness of his voice had deceived us: he was only a youth. In his delirium a few coins had fallen from his belt, along with a cone of bright metal, the size of a die. In vain a boy tried to pick up this cone. A man was scarcely able to raise it from the ground. I held it in my hand for a few minutes; I remember that its weight was intolerable and that after it was removed, the feeling of oppressiveness remained. I also remember the exact circle it pressed into my palm. This sensation of a very small and at the same time extremely heavy object produced a disagreeable impression of repugnance and fear. One of the local men suggested we throw it into the swollen river; Amorim acquired it for a few pesos. No one knew anything about the dead man, except that "he came from the border." These small, very hard cones (made from a metal which is not of this world) are images of the divinity in certain regions of Tlön.

Here I bring the personal part of my narrative to a close. The rest is in the memory (if not in the hopes or fears) of all my readers. Let it suffice for me to recall or mention the following facts, with a mere brevity of words which the reflective recollection of all will enrich or amplify. Around 1944, a person doing research for the newspaper *The American* (of Nashville, Tennessee) brought to light in a Memphis library the forty volumes of the First Encyclopedia of Tlön. Even today there is a controversy over whether this discovery was accidental or whether it was permitted by the directors of the still nebulous *Orbis Tertius*. The latter is most likely. Some of the incredible aspects of the Eleventh Volume (for example, the multiplication of the *hrönir*) have been eliminated or attenuated in the Memphis copies; it is reasonable to imagine that these omissions follow the plan of exhibiting a world which is not too incompatible with the real world. The dissemination of objects from Tlön over different countries would complement this plan . . .[6] The fact is that the international press infinitely proclaimed the "find." Manuals, anthologies, summaries, literal versions, authorized re-editions and pirated editions of the Greatest Work of Man flooded and still flood the earth. Almost immediately, reality yielded on more than one account. The truth is that it longed to yield. Ten years ago any symmetry with a semblance of order—dialectical materialism, anti-Semitism, Nazism—was sufficient to entrance the minds of men. How could one do other than submit to Tlön, to the minute and vast evidence of an orderly planet? It is useless to answer that reality is also orderly. Perhaps it is, but in accordance with divine laws—I translate: inhuman laws—which we never quite grasp. Tlön is surely a labyrinth, but it is a labyrinth devised by men, a labyrinth destined to be deciphered by men.

The contact and the habit of Tlön have disintegrated this world. Enchanted by its rigor, humanity forgets over and again that it is a rigor of chess masters, not of angels. Already the schools have been invaded by the (conjectural) "primitive language" of Tlön; already the teaching of its harmonious history (filled with moving episodes) has wiped out the one which governed in my childhood; already a fictitious past occupies in our memories the place of another, a past of which we know nothing with certainty—not even that it is false. Numismatology, pharmacology and archaeology have been reformed. I understand that biology and mathematics also await their avatars . . . A scattered dynasty of solitary men has changed the face of the world. Their task continues. If our forecasts are not in error, a hundred years from now someone will discover the hundred volumes of the Second Encyclopedia of Tlön.

Then English and French and mere Spanish will disappear from the globe. The world will be Tlön. I pay no attention to all this and go on revising, in the still days at the Adrogué hotel, an uncertain Quevedian translation (which I do not intend to publish) of Browne's *Urn Burial*.

[6] There remains, of course, the problem of the *material* of some objects.

Stories That
Should Not Be Told:
Dangerous Fictions

At the end of "Tlön, Uqbar, Orbis Tertius," Borges recounts wryly the way in which the fiction of Tlön swept the world once it was made public: "Almost immediately, reality yielded on more than one account. The truth is that it longed to yield." And then he adds with considerable sharpness, "Ten years ago any symmetry with a semblance of order—dialectical materialism, anti-Semitism, Nazism—was sufficient to entrance the minds of men. How could one do other than submit to Tlön, to the minute and vast evidence of an orderly planet? It is useless to answer that reality is also orderly. Perhaps it is, but in accordance with divine laws—I translate: inhuman laws—which we never quite grasp."

In the stories we have read so far the creation of fictions has been treated as a good and useful thing, but there is a long tradition of suspecting these "symmetries with a semblance of order." In *The Republic* (Chapters 9 and 10) Socrates banishes the poets from his ideal state because they tell lies about the gods, sometimes picturing them as brutal and amoral when they must in fact be good and perfect, and because at other times they are only too truthful about men, representing some heroes as violent and treacherous, and thus encouraging others to act in the same way. Only "convenient fictions" will be allowed in Socrates' republic, and these must be carefully guarded by the rulers of the state and designed in such a way as to instruct men in useful ways of thought and right conduct. The Church Fathers, the early great Christian theologians, hotly contested the value of secular literature, the pagan writings of the City of Man, and defended the absolute value of the sacred writings of the City of God, the books of the Bible through which God spoke His truths. The more radical of the Protestant reformers in the sixteenth and seventeenth centuries forbad and destroyed the "images" in the churches. Stained glass, statues, and paintings were, along with elaborate ceremonies, considered mere fictions that interfered with a true knowledge of God and His mysteries, which could only be truly known in the depths of the individual soul and in the revealed truths to be found in the Bible. In the eighteenth and nineteenth centuries, and on into the twentieth, attacks on fiction, such as Thomas Love Peacock's *The Four Ages of Poetry*, have been made not in the name of the revealed truths of religion but in the name of the experimental truths of science. Fictions are no longer graven images but vulgar errors or, at best, inspired guesses made by prescientific man. The old stories are now treated as but crude attempts to know and state the truths about man and nature that such sciences as psychology, sociology, and biology offer us in a precise language and subject to experimental verification.

It seems obvious that the major attacks on fiction-making have come from men and movements which believe they are in possession of an absolute truth or a method for finding that truth. If you know for certain by means of philosophy, religion, or science what reality truly is, then you will be skeptical about the possibility of there being any value in man's "unreal" fictions, stories, images, and make-believes.

But beneath these large-scale philosophic attacks on the value of fictions, there has also been a persistent, tough-minded suspicion about some very real dangers of fictions at an immediately practical level. There are always in every society some stories that cannot be told—though this view is now being disputed in some circles that favor absolute freedom, and in recent years we have come a long way toward testing this view.

Stories that explicitly describe certain sexual acts, pornography, have been taboo in Western society until the last few years; and fictions telling damaging lies about individuals or institutions, libels, are forbidden in most societies. Also, there continues to be more and more concern about the effect upon American society of the enormous amount of advertising to which we are all exposed. Many believe that the fictions we call advertisements are a corrupting influence, public lies told for the sake of profit by hucksters who have phony values, are cynical about the intelligence and character of people, and are spokesmen for the crudest kind of materialism. The dangers of the raw violence and lack of concern for human life found in many movies, comic books, and television programs, particularly the animated cartoons viewed chiefly by children, have been a continuous subject of debate. The arguments against this public violence were persuasively presented by Dr. Frederic Wertham in his book *Seduction of the Innocent* (1953), but his views are called into question by an experiment described in *Television and Aggression, An Experimental Field Study* (1971) by Seymour Feshbach and Robert D. Singer. For a six-week period Feshbach and Singer controlled the television viewing of two groups of boys from a number of schools. One group watched only programs with high aggressive content, while the other watched only programs with low aggressive content. An attempt was then made to measure the aggressive behavior of the two groups, and it was found that the boys who had watched the programs with high aggressive content were significantly less aggressive in their conduct. With all the doubts one may have about such matters as our ability to measure aggression accurately, the experiment still serves to remind us that we really know very little about how fictions actually affect their audience. A fiction containing a great deal of violence may not stimulate us to actual violence but may rather satisfy the desire for violence. In this view, sex crimes would not be triggered by pornography but inhibited by it, and the fictions of any society should represent the exact opposite of the values and conduct the society intends to teach. This has not been, however, the view of most societies, and fictions have traditionally been designed as a kind of compromise between illicit and acceptable conduct, satisfying the desire for the illicit by showing it in action but casting it as the villain and punishing it, while featuring the acceptable as the hero and depicting its ultimate triumph over wickedness.

Despite our increasing worries about the dangers of fictions as their number and influence increase in our technological society, a strong belief also persists (largely derived from the nineteenth-century tradition that Art and Literature are the purest expressions of the human soul) that *all* kinds of fiction are good. We are therefore inclined to believe automatically that any exercise of the power of censorship is bad because it limits freedom and stifles the creative impulse. The reader may say to himself that he does not believe in censorship of any kind, that no subject is taboo. But is this really so? Did you perhaps wonder in reading the particularly unpleasant passage about the black slave in the introductory frame story to *The Thousand Nights and a Night* whether at this time and in these circumstances in the United States it might not be better to suppress such a painful fiction? It is there in the manuscript and it presumably reflects accurately the historical attitude, a mixture of hatred and fear, of the Arabs toward the Africans they traded and bought into slavery. But might it not be better considered one of the many subjects that society has agreed to be improper and harmful fictions? Writers and artists have themselves known that there are such things as destructive fictions, and the selections that follow are chosen to present a range of the perceived dangers. It is most important that you look very carefully and with open eyes at these works, trying to understand why some fictions might be dangerous, rather than falling back on the fixed, preformed attitude that all censorship is wrong and all fiction good.

The most obvious danger of fiction-making is that this power may be misused to tell malicious and damaging lies of the kind that Jim Kendall tells and stages with such catastrophic results in Ring Lardner's (1885–1933) "Haircut." There can be saving lies like the one Marlow tells Kurtz's "Intended" in *Heart of Darkness*—that Kurtz died with her name on his lips—but there always seems to be a potential for disaster in fictions that are believed to be literally true. Who would have thought that

Doc Stair's commonplace metaphor (a simple fictional form) that "anybody that would do a thing like that ought not to be let live" would be taken literally by Paul Dickson, the village simpleton, and lead to the blast of the shotgun and the corpse of Jim Kendall?

The trial of the two Soviet writers Sinyavsky and Daniel in Moscow in February 1966 offers an example of other dangers of fiction. Sinyavsky and Daniel had published abroad certain of their works that were believed by the Soviet authorities to be critical of Russia and therefore harmful to the state. The main defense of the two writers was that their work was Art or Literature and therefore not to be judged by any practical effects that it might unintentionally have. And so in a strange way the courtroom was transformed into a class in literature with Sinyavsky and Daniel as the teachers, staking their freedom and perhaps their lives on their ability to persuade the court of some fundamental facts about the fictive nature of Literature: that the views of the author are not identical with the views expressed by his characters, that fictions are to be understood not literally but symbolically, and that the aim of a story is universal truth about human nature rather than a literal description of particular men, times, and places. From the point of view of Sinyavsky and Daniel the dangers of fiction were that their stories would be misread and misinterpreted. But the judges were unconvinced by their literary argument, and from their point of view Sinyavsky and Daniel were hypocrites who, while pretending to write only fictions, had attacked the Soviet Union by showing it in these stories to be ridiculous, brutal, and murderous. Furthermore, these stories had been published abroad, thus demonstrating that the authors intended them to be used as anti-Soviet propaganda. No one, of course, dared raise at the trial the possibility that the Soviet Union might actually be as bad as the judges believed Sinyavsky and Daniel had portrayed it in their stories, and therefore the question of the right of fiction to tell the truth, no matter how painful or harmful, did not come up. But this possibility lurks always in the background, and in order fully to understand the arguments for censorship made in "The Examination of Yuli Daniel," you must consider whether you yourselves would not wish to place some limitations on the telling of truth or the invention of fictions.

The final story in this section, D. H. Lawrence's (1885–1930) "The Rocking-Horse Winner," is a strange tale that can be read in many ways. Psychoanalytic critics, for example, have seen in it the expression of a desperate love of a small boy for a cold and indifferent mother, in which the rocking-horse is a fictional substitute for the mother. Other critics have seen the rocking-horse as a "magical" fiction used to predict the future and make the family rich. However you interpret the rocking-horse, and perhaps no certainty is possible about it, it is the key to the story; and it is, of course, a fiction that the boy in his desperate loneliness and need substitutes for a missing reality. For a time the replacement works: Paul breaks through into the future, foresees what will happen, and makes a great deal of money by betting on the races. But the fiction does not nourish him, he sickens, and in one last climactic effort to control the future by means of his fiction he rides his rocking-horse on into death. There is a fine British movie of "The Rocking-Horse Winner" in which the head of the horse at once promises enormous power and menaces with a demonic energy. This mixture of the power to save and the power to kill is the force that must be managed by anyone who rides the horse Pegasus, the winged steed symbolizing poetic inspiration, the power to create fiction.

Haircut

Ring Lardner

I got another barber that comes over from Carterville and helps me out Saturdays, but the rest of the time I can get along all right alone. You can see for yourself that this ain't no New York City and besides that, the most of the boys works all day and don't have no leisure to drop in here and get themselves prettied up.

You're a newcomer, ain't you? I thought I hadn't seen you round before. I hope you like it good enough to stay. As I say, we ain't no New York City or Chicago, but we have pretty good times. Not as good, though, since Jim Kendall got killed. When he was alive, him and Hod Meyers used to keep this town in an uproar. I bet they was more laughin' done here than any town its size in America.

Jim was comical, and Hod was pretty near a match for him. Since Jim's gone, Hod tries to hold his end up just the same as ever, but it's tough goin' when you ain't got nobody to kind of work with.

They used to be plenty fun in here Saturdays. This place is jam-packed Saturdays, from four o'clock on. Jim and Hod would show up right after their supper, round six o'clock. Jim would set himself down in that big chair, nearest the blue spittoon. Whoever had been settin' in that chair, why they'd get up when Jim come in and give it to him.

You'd of thought it was a reserved seat like they have sometimes in a theayter. Hod would generally always stand or walk up and down, or some Saturdays, of course, he'd be settin' in this chair part of the time, gettin' a haircut.

Well, Jim would set there a w'ile without openin' his mouth only to spit, and then finally he'd say to me, "Whitey,"—my right name, that is, my right first name, is Dick, but everybody round here calls me Whitey —Jim would say, "Whitey, your nose looks like a rosebud tonight. You must of been drinkin' some of your aw de cologne."

So I'd say, "No, Jim, but you look like you'd been drinkin' somethin' of that kind or somethin' worse."

Jim would have to laugh at that, but then he'd speak up and say, "No, I ain't had nothin' to drink, but that ain't sayin' I wouldn't like somethin'. I wouldn't even mind if it was wood alcohol."

Then Hod Meyers would say, "Neither would your wife." That would set everybody to laughin' because Jim and his wife wasn't on very good terms. She'd of divorced him only they wasn't no chance to get alimony and she didn't have no way to take care of herself and the kids. She couldn't never understand Jim. He *was* kind of rough, but a good fella at heart.

Him and Hod had all kinds of sport with Milt Sheppard. I don't suppose you've seen Milt. Well, he's got an Adam's apple that looks more like a mushmelon. So I'd be shavin' Milt and when I'd start to shave down here on his neck, Hod would holler, "Hey, Whitey, wait a minute! Before you cut into it, let's make up a pool and see who can guess closest to the number of seeds."

And Jim would say, "If Milt hadn't of been so hoggish, he'd of ordered a half a cantaloupe instead of a whole one and it might not of stuck in his throat."

All the boys would roar at this and Milt himself would force a smile, though the joke was on him. Jim certainly was a card!

There's his shavin' mug, settin' on the shelf, right next to Charley Vail's. "Charles M. Vail." That's the druggist. He comes in regular for his shave, three times a week. And Jim's is the cup next to Charley's. "James H. Kendall." Jim won't need no shavin' mug no more, but I'll leave it there just the same for old time's sake. Jim certainly was a character!

Years ago, Jim used to travel for a canned goods concern over in Carterville. They sold canned goods. Jim had the whole northern half of the State and was on the road five days out of every week. He'd drop in here Saturdays and tell his experiences for that week. It was rich.

I guess he paid more attention to playin' jokes than makin' sales. Finally the concern let him out and he come right home here and told everybody he'd been fired instead of sayin' he'd resigned like most fellas would of.

It was a Saturday and the shop was full and Jim got up out of that chair and says, "Gentlemen, I got an important announcement to make. I been fired from my job."

Well, they asked him if he was in earnest and he said he was and nobody could think of nothin' to say till Jim finally broke the ice himself. He says, "I been sellin' canned goods and now I'm canned goods myself."

You see, the concern he'd been workin' for was a factory that made canned goods. Over in Carterville. And now Jim said he was canned himself. He was certainly a card!

Jim had a great trick that he used to play w'ile he was travelin'. For instance, he'd be ridin' on a train and they'd come to some little town like, well, like, we'll say, like Benton. Jim would look out the train window and read the signs on the stores.

For instance, they'd be a sign, "Henry Smith, Dry Goods." Well, Jim would write down the name and the name of the town and when he got to wherever he was goin' he'd mail back a postal card to Henry Smith at Benton and not sign no name to it, but he'd write on the card, well, somethin' like "Ask your wife about that book agent that spent the afternoon last week," or "Ask your Missus who kept her from gettin' lonesome the last time you was in Carterville." And he'd sign the card, "A Friend."

Of course, he never knew what really come of none of these jokes, but he could picture what *probably* happened and that was enough.

Jim didn't work very steady after he lost his position with the Carterville people. What he did earn, doin' odd jobs round town, why he spent pretty near all of it on gin and his family might of starved if the stores hadn't of carried them along. Jim's wife tried her hand at dressmakin', but they ain't nobody goin' to get rich makin' dresses in this town.

As I say, she'd of divorced Jim, only she seen that she couldn't support herself and the kids and she was always hopin' that some day Jim would cut out his habits and give her more than two or three dollars a week.

They was a time when she would go to whoever he was workin' for and ask them to give her his wages, but after she done this once or twice, he beat her to it by borrowin' most of his pay in advance. He told it all round town, how he had outfoxed his Missus. He certainly was a caution!

But he wasn't satisfied with just outwittin' her. He was sore the way she had acted, tryin' to grab off his pay. And he made up his mind he'd get even. Well, he waited till Evans's Circus was advertised to come to town. Then he told his wife and two kiddies that he was goin' to take them to the circus. The day of the circus, he told them he would get the tickets and meet them outside the entrance to the tent.

Well, he didn't have no intentions of bein' there or buyin' tickets or nothin'. He got full of gin and laid round Wright's poolroom all day. His wife and the kids waited and waited and of course he didn't show up. His wife didn't have a dime with her, or nowhere else, I guess. So she finally had to tell the kids it was all off and they cried like they wasn't never goin' to stop.

Well, it seems, w'ile they was cryin', Doc Stair came along and he asked what was the matter, but Mrs. Kendall was stubborn and wouldn't tell him, but the kids told him and he insisted on takin' them and their mother in the show. Jim found this out afterwards and it was one reason why he had it in for Doc Stair.

Doc Stair come here about a year and a half ago. He's a mighty handsome young fella and his clothes always look like he has them made to order. He goes to Detroit two or three times a year and w'ile he's there he must have a tailor take his measure and then make him a suit to order. They cost pretty near twice as much, but they fit a whole lot better than if you just bought them in a store.

74

For a w'ile everybody was wonderin' why a young doctor like Doc Stair should come to a town like this where we already got old Doc Gamble and Doc Foote that's both been here for years and all the practice in town was always divided between the two of them.

Then they was a story got round that Doc Stair's gal had throwed him over, a gal up in the Northern Peninsula somewheres, and the reason he come here was to hide himself away and forget it. He said himself that he thought they wasn't nothin' like general practice in a place like ours to fit a man to be a good all round doctor. And that's why he'd came.

Anyways, it wasn't long before he was makin' enough to live on, though they tell me that he never dunned nobody for what they owed him, and the folks here certainly has got the owin' habit, even in my business. If I had all that was comin' to me for just shaves alone, I could go to Carterville and put up at the Mercer for a week and see a different picture every night. For instance, they's old George Purdy—but I guess I shouldn't ought to be gossipin'.

Well, last year, our coroner died, died of the flu. Ken Beatty, that was his name. He was the coroner. So they had to choose another man to be coroner in his place and they picked Doc Stair. He laughed at first and said he didn't want it, but they made him take it. It ain't no job that anybody would fight for and what a man makes out of it in a year would just about buy seeds for their garden. Doc's the kind, though, that can't say no to nothin' if you keep at him long enough.

But I was goin' to tell you about a poor boy we got here in town— Paul Dickson. He fell out of a tree when he was about ten years old. Lit on his head and it done somethin' to him and he ain't never been right. No harm in him, but just silly. Jim Kendall used to call him cuckoo; that's a name Jim had for anybody that was off their head, only he called people's head their bean. That was another of his gags, callin' head bean and callin' crazy people cuckoo. Only poor Paul ain't crazy, but just silly.

You can imagine that Jim used to have all kinds of fun with Paul. He'd send him to the White Front Garage for a left-handed monkey wrench. Of course they ain't no such a thing as a left-handed monkey wrench.

And once we had a kind of a fair here and they was a baseball game between the fats and the leans and before the game started Jim called Paul over and sent him way down to Schrader's hardware store to get a key for the pitcher's box.

They wasn't nothin' in the way of gags that Jim couldn't think up, when he put his mind to it.

Poor Paul was always kind of suspicious of people, maybe on account of how Jim had kept foolin' him. Paul wouldn't have much to do with anybody only his own mother and Doc Stair and a girl here in town named Julie Gregg. That is, she ain't a girl no more, but pretty near thirty or over.

When Doc first come to town, Paul seemed to feel like here was a real friend and he hung round Doc's office most of the w'ile; the only time he wasn't there was when he'd go home to eat or sleep or when he seen Julie Gregg doin' her shoppin'.

When he looked out Doc's window and seen her, he'd run downstairs and join her and tag along with her to the different stores. The poor boy was crazy about Julie and she always treated him mighty nice and made him feel like he was welcome, though of course it wasn't nothin' but pity on her side.

Doc done all he could to improve Paul's mind and he told me once that he really thought the boy was gettin' better, that they was times when he was as bright and sensible as anybody else.

But I was goin' to tell you about Julie Gregg. Old Man Gregg was in the lumber business, but got to drinkin' and lost the most of his money and when he died, he didn't leave nothin' but the house and just enough insurance for the girl to skimp along on.

Her mother was a kind of a half invalid and didn't hardly ever leave the house. Julie wanted to sell the place and move somewheres else after the old man died, but the mother said she was born here and would die here. It was tough on Julie, as the young people round this town—well, she's too good for them.

She's been away to school and Chicago and New York and different places and they ain't no subject she can't talk on, where you take the rest of the young folks here and you mention anything to them outside of Gloria Swanson or Tommy Meighan and they think you're delirious. Did you see Gloria in Wages of Virtue? You missed somethin'!

Well, Doc Stair hadn't been here more than a week when he come in one day to get shaved and I recognized who he was as he had been pointed out to me, so I told him about my old lady. She's been ailin' for a couple years and either Doc Gamble or Doc Foote, neither one, seemed to be helpin' her. So he said he would come out and see her, but if she was able to get out herself, it would be better to bring her to his office where he could make a completer examination.

So I took her to his office and w'ile I was waitin' for her in the reception room, in come Julie Gregg. When somebody comes in Doc Stair's office, they's a bell that rings in his inside office so as he can tell they's somebody to see him.

So he left my old lady inside and come out to the front office and that's the first time him and Julie met and I guess it was what they call love at first sight. But it wasn't fifty-fifty. This young fella was the slickest lookin' fella she'd ever seen in this town and she went wild over him. To him she was just a young lady that wanted to see the doctor.

She'd came on about the same business I had. Her mother had been doctorin' for years with Doc Gamble and Doc Foote and without no results. So she'd heard they was a new doc in town and decided to give him a try. He promised to call and see her mother that same day.

I said a minute ago that it was love at first sight on her part. I'm not only judgin' by how she acted afterwards but how she looked at him that first day in his office. I ain't no mind reader, but it was wrote all over her face that she was gone.

Now Jim Kendall, besides bein' a jokesmith and a pretty good drinker, well, Jim was quite a lady-killer. I guess he run pretty wild durin' the time he was on the road for them Carterville people, and besides that, he'd had a couple little affairs of the heart right here in town. As I say, his wife could of divorced him, only she couldn't.

But Jim was like the majority of men, and women, too, I guess. He wanted what he couldn't get. He wanted Julie Gregg and worked his head off tryin' to land her. Only he'd of said bean instead of head.

Well, Jim's habits and his jokes didn't appeal to Julie and of course he was a married man, so he didn't have no more chance than, well, than a rabbit. That's an expression of Jim's himself. When somebody didn't have no chance to get elected or somethin', Jim would always say they didn't have no more chance than a rabbit.

He didn't make no bones about how he felt. Right in here, more than once, in front of the whole crowd, he said he was stuck on Julie and anybody that could get her for him was welcome to his house and his wife and kids included. But she wouldn't have nothin' to do with him; wouldn't even speak to him on the street. He finally seen he wasn't gettin' nowheres with his usual line so he decided to try the rough stuff. He went right up to her house one evenin' and when she opened the door he forced his way in and grabbed her. But she broke loose and before he could stop her, she run in the next room and locked the door and phoned to Joe Barnes. Joe's the marshal. Jim could hear who she was phonin' to and he beat it before Joe got there.

Joe was an old friend of Julie's pa. Joe went to Jim the next day and told him what would happen if he ever done it again.

I don't know how the news of this little affair leaked out. Chances is that Joe Barnes told his wife and she told somebody else's wife and they told their husband. Anyways, it did leak out and Hod Meyers had the nerve to kid Jim about it, right here in this shop. Jim didn't deny nothin' and kind of laughed it off and said for us all to wait; that lots of people had tried to make a monkey out of him, but he always got even.

Meanw'ile everybody in town was wise to Julie's bein' wild mad over the Doc. I don't suppose she had any idear how her face changed when him and her was together; of course she couldn't of, or she'd of kept away from him. And she didn't know that we was all noticin' how many times she made excuses to go up to his office or pass it on the other side of the street and look up in his window to see if he was there. I felt sorry for her and so did most other people.

Hod Meyers kept rubbin' it into Jim about how the Doc had cut him out. Jim didn't pay no attention to the kiddin' and you could see he was plannin' one of his jokes.

One trick Jim had was the knack of changin' his voice. He could make you think he was a girl talkin' and he could mimic any man's voice. To show you how good he was along this line, I'll tell you the joke he played on me once.

You know, in most towns of any size, when a man is dead and needs a shave, why the barber that shaves him soaks him five dollars for the job; that is, he don't soak *him,* but whoever ordered the shave. I just charge three dollars because personally I don't mind much shavin' a dead person. They lay a whole lot stiller than live customers. The only thing is that you don't feel like talkin' to them and you get kind of lonesome.

Well, about the coldest day we ever had here, two years ago last winter, the phone rung at the house w'ile I was home to dinner and I answered the phone and it was a woman's voice and she said she was Mrs. John Scott and her husband was dead and would I come out and shave him.

Old John had always been a good customer of mine. But they live seven miles out in the country, on the Streeter road. Still I didn't see how I could say no.

So I said I would be there, but would have to come in a jitney and it might cost three or four dollars besides the price of the shave. So she, or the voice, it said that was all right, so I got Frank Abbott to drive me out to the place and when I got there, who should open the door but old John himself! He wasn't no more dead than, well, than a rabbit.

It didn't take no private detective to figure out who had played me this little joke. Nobody could of thought it up but Jim Kendall. He certainly was a card!

I tell you this incident just to show you how he could disguise his voice and make you believe it was somebody else talkin'. I'd of swore it was Mrs. Scott had called me. Anyways, some woman.

Well, Jim waited till he had Doc Stair's voice down pat; then he went after revenge.

He called Julie up on a night when he knew Doc was over in Carterville. She never questioned but what it was Doc's voice. Jim said he must see her that night; he couldn't wait no longer to tell her somethin'. She was all excited and told him to come to the house. But he said he was expectin' an important long distance call and wouldn't she please forget her manners for once and come to his office. He said they couldn't nothin' hurt her and nobody would see her and he just *must* talk to her a little w'ile. Well, poor Julie fell for it.

Doc always keeps a night light in his office, so it looked to Julie like they was somebody there.

Meanw'ile Jim Kendall had went to Wright's poolroom, where they was a whole gang amusin' themselves. The most of them had drank plenty of gin, and they was a rough bunch even when sober. They was always strong for Jim's jokes and when he told them to come with him and see some fun they give up their card games and pool games and followed along.

Doc's office is on the second floor. Right outside his door they's a flight of stairs leadin' to the floor above. Jim and his gang hid in the dark behind these stairs.

Well, Julie come up to Doc's door and rung the bell and they was nothin' doin'. She rung it again and she rung it seven or eight times. Then she tried the door and found it locked. Then Jim made some kind of a noise and she heard it and waited a minute, and then she says, "Is that you, Ralph?" Ralph is Doc's first name.

They was no answer and it must of came to her all of a sudden that she'd been bunked. She pretty near fell downstairs and the whole gang after her. They chased her all the way home, hollerin', "Is that you, Ralph?" and "Oh, Ralphie, dear, is that you?" Jim says he couldn't holler it himself, as he was laughin' too hard.

Poor Julie! She didn't show up here on Main Street for a long, long time afterward.

And of course Jim and his gang told everybody in town, everybody but Doc Stair. They was scared to tell him, and he might of never knowed only for Paul Dickson. The poor cuckoo, as Jim called him, he was here in the shop one night when Jim was still gloatin' yet over what he'd done to Julie. And Paul took in as much of it as he could understand and he run to Doc with the story.

It's a cinch Doc went up in the air and swore he'd make Jim suffer. But it was a kind of a delicate thing, because if it got out that he had beat Jim up, Julie was bound to hear of it and then she'd know that Doc knew and of course knowin' that he knew would make it worse for her than ever. He was goin' to do somethin', but it took a lot of figurin'.

Well, it was a couple days later when Jim was here in the shop again, and so was the cuckoo. Jim was goin' duck-shootin' the next day and had came in lookin' for Hod Meyers to go with him. I happened to know that Hod had went over to Carterville and wouldn't be home till the end of the week. So Jim said he hated to go alone and he guessed he would call it off. Then poor Paul spoke up and said if Jim would take him he would go along. Jim thought a w'ile and then he said, well, he guessed a half-wit was better than nothin'.

I suppose he was plottin' to get Paul out in the boat and play some joke on him, like pushin' him in the water. Anyways, he said Paul could go. He asked him had he ever shot a duck and Paul said no, he'd never even had a gun in his hands. So Jim said he could set in the boat and watch him and if he behaved himself, he might lend him his gun for a couple of shots. They made a date to meet in the mornin' and that's the last I seen of Jim alive.

Next mornin', I hadn't been open more than ten minutes when Doc Stair come in. He looked kind of nervous. He asked me had I seen Paul Dickson. I said no, but I knew where he was, out duck-shootin' with Jim Kendall. So Doc says that's what he had heard, and he couldn't understand it because Paul had told him he wouldn't never have no more to do with Jim as long as he lived.

He said Paul had told him about the joke Jim had played on Julie.

He said Paul had asked him what he thought of the joke and the Doc had told him that anybody that would do a thing like that ought not to be let live.

I said it had been a kind of a raw thing, but Jim just couldn't resist no kind of a joke, no matter how raw. I said I thought he was all right at heart, but just bubblin' over with mischief. Doc turned and walked out.

At noon he got a phone call from old John Scott. The lake where Jim and Paul had went shootin' is on John's place. Paul had came runnin' up to the house a few minutes before and said they'd been an accident. Jim had shot a few ducks and then give the gun to Paul and told him to try his luck. Paul hadn't never handled a gun and he was nervous. He was shakin' so hard that he couldn't control the gun. He let fire and Jim sunk back in the boat, dead.

Doc Stair, bein' the coroner, jumped in Frank Abbott's flivver and rushed out to Scott's farm. Paul and old John was down on the shore of the lake. Paul had rowed the boat to shore, but they'd left the body in it, waitin' for Doc to come.

Doc examined the body and said they might as well fetch it back to town. They was no use leavin' it there or callin' a jury, as it was a plain case of accidental shootin'.

Personally I wouldn't never leave a person shoot a gun in the same boat I was in unless I was sure they knew somethin' about guns. Jim was a sucker to leave a new beginner have his gun, let alone a half-wit. It probably served Jim right, what he got. But still we miss him round here. He certainly was a card!

Comb it wet or dry?

The Examination of Yuli Daniel

Translated and edited by Max Hayward

In February 1966, in Moscow, Andrei Sinyavsky, who used the pen name Abram Tertz, and Yuli Daniel, who used the pen name Nikolai Arzhak, were brought to trial under Article 70 of the Soviet Criminal Code for slandering and subverting the state. Sinyavsky, born in 1925, was a scholar and staff member at the Gorky Institute of World Literature and was well known as an editor of the poems of Boris Pasternak and as an author. Yuli Daniel, also born in 1925, served in the army during the Second World War and earned his living primarily as a translator of poetry. The two men were friends and shared a political position that supported the revolution and the communist state but was sharply critical of the Stalinist period and of the dreadful sufferings the Russian people had been forced to endure. In the late 1950's and early 1960's both had sent abroad a number of their essays and stories, and these works had been printed in Europe and America and praised by certain anti-Soviet critics. It was the contention of the state that Sinyavsky and Daniel had intended in these writings to attack the Soviet Union and give aid to its enemies; but the writers, contrary to usual practice, chose not to plead guilty to the charges and thus obtained the courtroom as a forum in which to defend their conception of literature. A secret transcript of the trial was made, by what means is not known, and the following portions of the examination of Daniel are taken from the published transcript *On Trial, The Soviet State versus "Abram Tertz" and "Nikolai Arzhak."*

The stories that were alleged to be defamatory and harmful to the state are translated in *Dissonant Voices in Soviet Literature* (New York: Pantheon, 1964), and the reader may well wish to read them there at first hand. A brief summary of the most important stories referred to in the trial will provide a sufficient background for reading the following selection. The most important Daniel story, "This Is Moscow Speaking," deals with a public announcement that August 10, 1960, will be "Public Murder Day," when all citizens above the age of sixteen will be allowed between 6:00 A.M. and midnight to kill other persons, with the exception of certain officials. The response is rather confused, with fierce pogroms in some places and little activity in others. The hero of the story is outraged by the brutality of the government and the indifference of the people, and he decides to kill the leaders; but then he remembers the dreadful carnage of the last war and what death is actually like, and decides to kill no one. "Hands" is about the trembling hands of an old member of the secret police. After the revolution he was ordered to kill a number of priests with a machine gun, but "as a joke" his friends had put blanks in the gun, and as he fired an old priest continued to move toward him with his hands raised. "The Man from Minap" is a fantasy about a man who finds that he can control the sex of the children he begets. If he thinks of Karl Marx during the sexual act the child will be a boy; if he thinks of Klara Zetkin, a prominent German communist, the child will be a girl. The story obviously spoofs the official belief in the absolute power of communism and "correct thought" to control events. "Atonement" is set in the period after Khrushchev's attack on Stalin, when political pressure eased. A man is suspected of having betrayed a number of people during the bad Stalinist years and is gradually driven insane by the hatred directed toward him, a hatred that grows out of a general bad conscience and the knowledge that no one had done anything to help the victims or prevent the atrocities.

Despite the eloquence with which Sinyavsky and Daniel defended themselves and the cause of literature, the verdict was "guilty." Sinyavsky was sentenced to seven years in a labor camp and Daniel to five years. Although the Soviet government has refused to change its

81

position and the two writers went to prison, the outcry against the trial has been widespread, and even the communist parties and papers of western Europe have attacked the trial and the sentence.

In the excerpt below, after a discussion of the royalties Daniel had earned from foreign printings of his works, the prosecutor turns to the stories themselves.

■

PROSECUTOR: And now, Daniel, will you explain the ideology of *This Is Moscow Speaking?*

DANIEL: For me there is a difference between content and ideology. First, I want to tell how and why this story was written. The idea was suggested by a friend. I was attracted by the notion that in describing an imaginary Public Murder Day I could shed light on the psychology and behavior of people. The plot itself, a Public Murder Day, was what gave this particular story its political coloring. I must mention my own political position, leaving aside the literary aim I had set myself. In 1960–61, when I was writing this story, I—and not only I, but any person who thought seriously about the situation in our country— was convinced that a new cult of personality was about to be established. Stalin had not been dead all that long. We all remembered well what were called "violations of socialist legality." And again I saw all the symptoms: there was again one man who knew everything, again one person was being exalted, again one person was dictating his will to agricultural experts, artists, diplomats and writers. Again we saw one single name in the newspapers and on posters, and every utterance of this person, however crude or trivial, was again being held up to us as a revelation, as the quintessence of wisdom. . . .

JUDGE: And so, in fear of a restoration of the cult of personality in our country, you decided to turn to the publishers Harper & Row in Washington?

DANIEL: I am not talking now about why I sent the story abroad, but about why I wrote it.

JUDGE: Go ahead.

DANIEL: Well, seeing all this happen and remembering the horrors of the purges and violations of legality under Stalin, I concluded—and I am a pessimist by nature—that the terrible days of Stalin's cult could come back. And, as you may recall, in those days things happened that were far more terrible than anything in my story. Remember the mass purges, the deportation and annihilation of entire peoples. What I wrote was child's play by comparison. . . .

JUDGE: I understand, of course, that the author's narrative and words spoken by his characters are two different things. But here is what you wrote in *This Is Moscow Speaking*. (*He quotes the conversation with Volodya Margulis, including the passage, "But, do they expect to gain from this Decree?" etc.*)

DANIEL: You are quite right in saying that the attitude of the author is not always identical with that of his characters. And the hero of my story objects to the words you have quoted. He says, "We must stand up for the Soviet regime." So the passage you have just read is quite clear.

JUDGE: Is that the same hero who fires his tommy gun "from the hip"?

DANIEL: That's right. And I'll explain this too. The idea of the story is, briefly, that a human being should remain a human being, no matter in what circumstances he may find himself, no matter under what pressure and from what quarter. He should remain true to himself, to himself alone, and have nothing to do with anything that his conscience rejects, that goes against his human instinct. . . . Now about this passage with the words "from the hip." The indictment describes it as a call to settle accounts with the party leaders and the government. It is true that my hero is speaking about the leaders; he mentions them because he remembers the mass persecutions and feels that those who are guilty should bear responsibility. But at this point the indictment breaks off the quotation. The book does not stop there, nor even does this particular soliloquy of my hero stop there. He recalls scenes of killing and slaughter that he· saw in the war. And this mental image fills him with revulsion. The indictment obviously gives a tendentious interpretation to this passage. After all, the same hero says further on: "I want to kill no one." How can any reader then say this character wants to kill? It should be clear to everyone that he does not.

JUDGE: But you are by-passing the main point. Your hero is allowed to kill by decree of the Soviet Government. In other words, we have a bad government, and a good character who does not want to kill anyone except the government?

DANIEL: That does not follow from the story. The hero says "no one." No one means no one.

JUDGE: But you do have such a decree in the story?

DANIEL: Yes.

PROSECUTOR: I would like to ask Daniel to read the epigraph to Chapter 4.

JUDGE: I don't see any need for reading unprintable language in this courtroom.

PROSECUTOR: I still would like permission to read the epigraph, with cuts, without the bad language.[1]

JUDGE: Go ahead, but without the bad language.

PROSECUTOR: (*reading*): "I hate them so much I have spasms, I scream, I tremble. Oh, if only all these —— could be collected and destroyed at once!" Well, Daniel, how do you explain this epigraph?

DANIEL: It's an epigraph to the hero's thoughts. . . . (*Laughter in the courtroom. Daniel looks around nervously.*)

PROSECUTOR: Who is it that you hate so? Who do you want to destroy?

DANIEL: Who are you talking to? To me or to my hero, or to someone else?

PROSECUTOR: Who is your positive hero?[2] Who expresses your point of view in the story?

DANIEL: I have already told you once before in our preliminary talk that the story has no entirely positive hero and that there doesn't have to be one.

PROSECUTOR: We had no preliminary talk. But who expresses the author's point of view? Where does it come in?

DANIEL: The characters do convey the author's attitudes, but only in part. No single character is identical with the author. Maybe it's bad literature, but it is literature, and it doesn't divide everything into black and white.

PROSECUTOR: I would like to read out the findings of Glavlit[3] about Arzhak's story: "*This Is Moscow Speaking* is a monstrous lampoon." . . . (*There follows an assessment of the story that agrees completely with the indictment, except that the Glavlit report finds that the story also has an element of anti-Semitism.*) Do you agree with this assessment, Daniel?

DANIEL: Certainly not. The report says that I express my ideas through "the mouths of my characters." That is a naïve

[1] The "bad language" omitted is the Russian word for "whores." (The quotation is on p. 277 of *Dissonant Voices*.) [The footnotes in this selection are Hayward's.]

[2] In the language of Soviet literary criticism the characters (referred to as "heroes") of novels and plays, etc., are divided into "positive" and "negative." It is implicit in the official doctrine of "socialist realism" that "positive" heroes should set a good example in their public and private lives, and that they should triumph over the "negative" characters, at least morally. In the last years of Stalin's life the rigid enforcement of this requirement resulted in a standard plot in which an inevitable "happy ending" was preceded by a "conflict" between the "negative" and "positive" characters.

[3] "Glavlit," a portmanteau word derived from: "*glavnoye upravlenie po delam literatury i izdatelstv*" (Chief Directorate on Matters of Literature and Publishing Houses), is the Soviet censorship agency originally set up by decree of the Council of People's Commissars in 1922. It is rarely referred to in public, but all works appearing in print in the Soviet Union have to be submitted to it. . . .

accusation, to put it mildly. That way you can accuse any Soviet writer of being anti-Soviet. Just take the White Guards in the works of Lavrenev, Sholokhov, Leonov—[4]

PROSECUTOR: (*interrupting*): Have the Western press comparisons of you with Dostoyevsky gone to your head so much that you now compare yourself with leading Soviet writers?

DANIEL: I am not comparing myself with anyone. All I mean is that it is not what characters say but the author's own attitude toward what they say that is important.

PROSECUTOR: In the preliminary investigation didn't you say you were in partial agreement with the Glavlit findings?

DANIEL: That is true, but only with the bare facts as given there.

PROSECUTOR: (*reading from the Glavlit report*): "In the author's view, the Soviet people blindly follow the party leadership." How would you judge your story in the light of this?

DANIEL: I didn't mean to say anything so harsh. To some extent I agree with the idea that the political initiative of the masses . . . I don't believe in it very much. I consider the masses politically passive.

PROSECUTOR: In other words, if a "Public Murder Day" were proclaimed, you would expect everyone simply to rush off to kill as they were told?

DANIEL: No, I don't say that in the story. The "Public Murder Day" is a literary device, chosen as a way of studying people's reactions.

JUDGE: There is something I want to clear up. Just imagine a communal apartment where Ivanova is having a quarrel with Sidorova.[5] If Ivanova were to write that there is a certain lady who is making life difficult for another lady, then it would be an innuendo, a figure of speech. But if she were to write that Sidorova was throwing garbage into her soup, then we would have something like a libel, slander or something else subject to legal proceedings. You were, after all, writing about the Soviet Government, not about ancient Babylon, but about a specific government that proclaimed a "Public Murder Day," and you name the date—August 10, 1960. Is that a device or outright slander?

DANIEL: Let me just use your example. If Ivanova were to write that Sidorova literally flies about on a broomstick or turns

---

[4] Boris Lavrenev (1891–1959), Mikhail Sholokhov (born 1905), and Leonid Leonov (born 1899) are "classical" Soviet writers who had White Guardist characters in novels dealing with the Civil War. The portrayal of "counterrevolutionaries" in Soviet literature in the first years after the Revolution (e.g., in Leonov's *Badgers*, 1925) was often remarkably detached. The hero of Sholokhov's *And Quiet Flows the Don*, Grigori Melekhov, actually serves the White Guardist cause for considerable periods during the Civil War.

[5] Sidorova and Ivanova are common Russian surnames in the feminine form.

herself into an animal, that would be a literary device, not slander. I took an obviously fantastic situation.

JUDGE: But here is what B. Filippov wrote: "Can we say that what Arzhak describes is all that far removed from reality?" So, you see, Daniel, it is not just a literary device, is it?

DANIEL: It is a literary device.

PROSECUTOR: Daniel, do you deny that the "Public Murder Day" supposedly proclaimed by the Soviet Government is in fact slander?

DANIEL: I hold that slander is something you can make people believe, at least theoretically. (*Laughter in the courtroom.*)

JUDGE: I want to clear this up. (*Reading from the law code:*) "Slander is the spreading of information known to be false and defamatory." That is the legal side of it.

DANIEL: What about imaginary situations, then?

JUDGE: I will go back to my example. If Ivanova were to assert that Sidorova did something that Sidorova did not in fact do, then lawyers would call such a statement slander.

PROSECUTOR: You have slandered ordinary Soviet people. Just look how Soviet people supposedly react to the proclamation of "Public Murder Day." (*He reads excerpts.*) These are supposed to be educated people. How can that be anything but slander? Take your conversation with Margulis—

DANIEL: (*interrupting*): That's not my conversation, it's my hero talking.

PROSECUTOR: But isn't that slander on the Soviet people?

DANIEL: In that case Mayakovsky's *Bathhouse* and *Bedbug* would also be slander on the Soviet people. Didn't Mayakovsky slander Pierre Skripkin?

PROSECUTOR: Let's not talk about that. Just show me a single Soviet person in your story who seems like a real Soviet person. Just look at the picture you give of our intellectuals!

DANIEL: You talk about Soviet intellectuals as if they were all worthy of admiration.

PROSECUTOR: Just show me one person who is portrayed in a good light. (*He reads excerpt.*) Isn't that slander on the Soviet people, on the Soviet Government?

DANIEL: Even the statutes of the Writers Union don't require writers to write only about noble, intelligent and good people. Why should I be obliged to write about good people in a work of satire? Satirists from Aristophanes to Gogol—

PROSECUTOR: Your head has been turned!

DANIEL: May I make a statement? I am a writer. I cannot avoid referring to the history of literature, to the experience of

86

other writers. That does not mean I put myself on a par with them. I don't, either as regards wisdom or talent. I wish the prosecutor would stop saying that I do.

PROSECUTOR: In your story you mention *Izvestia* and *Literature and Life,* you mention the writers Bezymensky and Mikhalkov. You slander the entire Soviet press, all Soviet writers. What is it if not slander on the Soviet press?

DANIEL: No, it is not slander on the Soviet press. I was alluding to individual writers, timeservers. It is a parody of the hackneyed style, the clichés that we often find in our papers.

PROSECUTOR: I expected that answer, and I am going back to the passage about *Izvestia.* It says that "as usual, the paper printed an editorial calling for observance of 'Public Murder Day,' " etc. As usual! Isn't that slander on the entire Soviet press?

DANIEL: It's a gibe at the style of newspaper articles.

PROSECUTOR: Now, at last, you are speaking with your real voice.

JUDGE: There is no need for remarks that do not advance the case.

DANIEL: I always speak with my real voice.

PROSECUTOR: You write that the people are anti-Semitic and just waiting to start a pogrom. You compare its mood with what led to Babi Yar.[6] But there the killers were Fascists. Isn't it blasphemous to compare our entire people with the Fascists?

DANIEL: It does not follow from the passage that the entire Soviet people is anti-Semitic; all that follows is that a few individuals are so inclined. I was talking about certain people, without mentioning names, who might want to settle private accounts; I said there might be a few examples of such scum. Nothing more than this can be read into the text.

PROSECUTOR: A few individuals or the entire people—we will see right away. (*He reads a passage describing how Georgians killed Armenians, Armenians killed Georgians, and in Central Asia everyone killed Russians.*) Isn't that slander on the entire Soviet people?

DANIEL: No. It is not slander on the entire Soviet people.

PROSECUTOR: And you say that all this happens under the direction of the Central Committee. Isn't that slander?

DANIEL: You keep forgetting that the starting point for all this is an imaginary situation, not something that actually happened. (*Laughter in courtroom.*)

· · ·

[6] A ravine in Kiev where the Germans massacred thousands of Jews in 1941. In his famous poem Evgeny Evtushenko complained that no monument had been put up there. The prosecutor's reference is to a passage on p. 273 of *Dissonant Voices.*

PROSECUTOR: Why did you write works that could be interpreted as anti-Soviet?

DANIEL: Are you asking about them all or about any one in particular?

PROSECUTOR: You can tell us about any one of them.

DANIEL: I'll talk about "Hands." I know I don't have the right to put questions to the court. But can the prosecution point to a single sentence, a single word, a single syllable that could be interpreted as anti-Soviet? This story is a literary version of an actual event that was recounted to me. There is nothing in the story to justify the charges against me. The indictment contradicts itself when it talks about this story. The indictment contends that the Soviet regime has never used force. But such a point of view is not scientific, it is not Marxist, it is not Leninist. According to Lenin, revolution is coercion, and the state is coercive, and [in a revolutionary state there is] coercion of the minority by the majority. The indictment charges that I wrote: "The Soviet regime used violence against the Soviet people." There is nothing along these lines in the story, which is about the execution of counterrevolutionaries. There is nothing in the story to suggest that this calls for retribution. It cannot be interpreted as in the indictment. Now, about "The Man from Minap." I don't like this story; it is poorly written, crude, and in bad taste, but it contains nothing anti-Soviet. It is a satire, a caricature, an extravaganza; all this is in the tradition of satiric writing. Why is the portrayal of ten bad persons passed off by the prosecution as a portrayal of the whole of Soviet society? The characters of a satirical work are always negative, and the positive hero is always a conventional figure in such writings. There is no basis for saying that the story is directed against the morals and ethics of Soviety society. Why did I write it? Among my friends there are many scientists, and one of them told me about the fuss over Bashyan and Lepeshinskaya [7] (I don't equate these two names) and that such sensational affairs have done harm to our science. The story dealt with that scandal and not with the branch of science in question. Glavlit evidently feels I should have glorified the events that I satirize.

---

[7] Olga Lepeshinskaya (1871–1963) was a Soviet biologist who, like Lysenko, became notorious in the last years of Stalin's life for her attacks on genetics and strident advocacy of her own dubious theories. In 1950 she received the Stalin prize for what was claimed to be "a great discovery in biology." This consisted in a claim that there were noncellular forms of life. One of her most active supporters was G. M. Boshyan (misspelled Bashyan in the transcript). . . .

The prosecutor and Daniel have a long argument about the "scientific theories" mentioned in the Glavlit report.

The judge reads a passage from the report describing the story as a libel on "certain scientific theories."

JUDGE: Daniel, were you attacking Bashyan in this story?

DANIEL: No, I was attacking the practice of making sensational publicity about scientific discoveries.

JUDGE: And if that is the main point of the story, why does your character Volodya think about Karl Marx and Klara Zetkin at such an inappropriate time and in such a situation?

DANIEL: That can be explained by the haste with which the story was written (*Disapproving murmur and coarse laughter in the courtroom.*)

JUDGE: Your story "Hands" is about the distant past. Why did you send this story abroad instead of, say, "Escape"?

DANIEL: I wanted what I had written to be printed. I am convinced that there is nothing anti-Soviet in my works. But I know that our editors and publishers think that there are certain forbidden themes which should not be dealt with in literature. There are a number of topics on which writers do not write, or publishers do not publish them. The subject of "Hands" is a taboo one which is passed over in silence. It is about a kind of work which is bloody and difficult, but necessary. The hero of the story is a worker who later serves in the Cheka. And because of this work his hands tremble. (*Summarizes the story.*)

JUDGE: But why did you send this one abroad first?

DANIEL: Because I could assume that this story would not be published here: it is about a forbidden subject that has not been dealt with in our literature since the 1930's. . . .

JUDGE: But why this, and not "Escape" or some translations? It is written in a gruesome style. (*Reads a passage.*) But that's not the point. Why was the subject of the shooting of the priests so important to you at this time? Why did you have to bring the subject up again at this time? The *émigrés* made a lot of fuss about Tikhon.[8] Does this have anything to do with literature?

DANIEL: But the hero does not know why he is executing people.

JUDGE: (*reads a passage, then says*): It is obvious that they would love to publish this abroad.

DANIEL: I had no political purpose when I wrote this story. (*Laughter in the courtroom.*)

. . .

[8] Tikhon was the first Patriarch of the Russian Orthodox Church. . . . Many priests (like those executed in Daniel's story) suffered because of their support of him. . . .

PROSECUTOR: You wrote things which, upon your own admission, could be interpreted as anti-Soviet. You did this over a long period of time. You knew how these things were interpreted in the West. Let us hear how you yourself would describe your conduct.

DANIEL: I've always thought and I continue to think that my books were not anti-Soviet and that I put no anti-Soviet meaning into them, since I did not criticize or make fun of the basic principles of our life. I do not equate individuals with the social system as such, or the government with the state, or a certain period with the Soviet epoch as a whole. The state may exist for centuries but a government is often short-lived and frequently inglorious. As regards my attitude to their publication abroad, this is another matter—I regret it. Until my arrest I could only guess at the reaction to my works in the West. During the investigation I understood that my works had been interpreted there as being attacks not on individual persons but on the system, not as attacks on a certain period but as attacks on the cause as a whole. None of my things is anti-Soviet in its basic idea—you cannot say that it is anti-Soviet to suggest that a man should always remain human, even if he finds himself in a situation like that of the "Public Murder Day."

JUDGE: Even in the monstrous situation involving the Supreme Soviet of the U.S.S.R.?

DANIEL: Yes, and I do not regard that as anti-Soviet.

JUDGE: And you sent these literary figments of your imagination abroad?

DANIEL: That I regret.

JUDGE: Your inventions involve one political idea after another. (*Repeats passages already quoted in the indictment.*)

DANIEL: Our literature and press are silent about the things on which I write. But literature is entitled to deal with any period and any question. I feel that there should be no prohibited subjects in the life of society.

PROSECUTOR: But you took the year 1960. You thought up this decree!

. . .

KISENISHSKY: Tell us how you got the idea for the story "Atonement."

DANIEL: In recent years we have often heard about people being exposed as slanderers whose denunciations landed innocent people in jail. I wanted to show a rather different situation—how a man must feel if he has been falsely accused of doing something as terrible as this. This was something that actually happened to somebody I knew well. That's how the idea of the story came to me. The indictment says that the underlying notion of the story is that everybody is to blame for the cult of personality and the mass persecutions. I agree with this interpretation, but not with the word "slanderous" used to describe the story. I feel that every member of society is responsible for what happens in society. And I make no exception for myself. I wrote that "everybody is to blame" because there has been no reply to the question of who is to blame. Nobody has ever publicly stated who was to blame for these crimes, and I will never believe that three men—Stalin, Beria and Ryumin—could alone do such terrible things to the whole country. But nobody has yet replied to the question as to who is guilty.

KISENISHSKY: When did you last send a manuscript abroad and why did you stop sending them?

DANIEL: In 1963.

KISENISHSKY: Give us the main facts about your life.

DANIEL: I was born in 1925. I went straight from school to the front line; during the war I fought on the second Ukrainian and third Byelorussian fronts. After being severely wounded, I was demobilized and received a pension as a war invalid. In 1946 I entered Kharkov University, and then transferred to the Moscow Province Teachers Training College, from which I was graduated. Then I taught for two years at a school in Lyudinovo. After that I taught for four years in Moscow.

SOKOLOV: (*people's assessor*): Obviously you must have foreseen the impact of the publication of your manuscripts. What did you think it would be?

DANIEL: If I had foreseen such an impact, I would not have sent my manuscripts abroad.

JUDGE: But you must have foreseen their political effect?

DANIEL: I did not think about how my works would be judged from a political point of view. I thought only in terms of how they would be judged from the point of view of their literary qualities or failings.

JUDGE: Then why did you have all these political details—that monstrous decree, the execution of a priest because of Tikhon, and the Institute of Scientific Profanation?

DANIEL: In *This Is Moscow Speaking* all these details are part and parcel of the fantastic plot of the story.

JUDGE: All the people in it are moral degenerates—surely this has a political purpose, and has nothing to do with the plot. Why, for what reason, did you have all this? Wasn't it in order to create a certain impression?

DANIEL: It was not part of my intention to depict good people.

91

The colors are laid on rather thick in my story, but I was not trying to portray good people. I was showing how bad people might behave in an imaginary situation.

JUDGE: In the situation resulting from that decree of the Supreme Soviet!

DANIEL: I've already said that I would regard any excesses as possible if the cult of personality were to return.

PROSECUTOR: You say that you didn't think about politics. But what about this sentence here, for example, in your story *This Is Moscow Speaking:* "Anyway, to tell the truth, to be printed abroad, by anti-Soviet publishers is not so good"? What are we to make of this?

DANIEL: It means exactly what it says—it's not very nice. I repeat once more that I've already said what I think about the ethical side of the matter.

JUDGE: Are there any points which you would like to make to the court?

DANIEL: Yes. The Prosecution constantly equates the author with his characters. This is particularly impermissible if the characters in question, to put it mildly, are not quite right in the head. For instance in "Atonement" the main character has gone out of his mind and it is he who shouts: "Our prisons are within us!"

JUDGE: (*interrupts*): He only goes mad a page further on.

DANIEL: No. On the next page he is already in a mental hospital. Another thing—quotations are always given without any reference to the state of the characters who utter them. One has gone out of his mind, another is an alcoholic.

JUDGE: All your intellectuals are drunkards.

DANIEL: I beg you, in the first place, not to quote out of context, and, in the second place, to take account of the condition of the characters. And if I have overdone things here and there, this should not be put down to my being an anti-Soviet, but to my lack of literary skill. (*Laughter in the courtroom.*)

The Rocking-Horse Winner

D. H. Lawrence

There was a woman who was beautiful, who started with all the advantages, yet she had no luck. She married for love, and the love turned to dust. She had bonny children, yet she felt they had been thrust upon her, and she could not love them. They looked at her coldly, as if they were finding fault with her. And hurriedly she felt she must cover up some fault in herself. Yet what it was that she must cover up she never knew. Nevertheless, when her children were present, she always felt the centre of her heart go hard. This troubled her, and in her manner she was all the more gentle and anxious for her children, as if she loved them very much. Only she herself knew that at the centre of her heart was a hard little place that could not feel love, no, not for anybody. Everybody else said of her: "She is such a good mother. She adores her children." Only she herself, and her children themselves, knew it was not so. They read it in each other's eyes.

There were a boy and two little girls. They lived in a pleasant house, with a garden, and they had discreet servants, and felt themselves superior to anyone in the neighbourhood.

Although they lived in style, they felt always an anxiety in the house. There was never enough money. The mother had a small income, and the father had a small income, but not nearly enough for the social position which they had to keep up. The father went in to town to some office. But though he had good prospects, these prospects never materialised. There was always the grinding sense of the shortage of money, though the style was always kept up.

At last the mother said, "I will see if *I* can't make something." But she did not know where to begin. She racked her brains, and tried this thing and the other, but could not find anything successful. The failure made deep lines come into her face. Her children were growing up, they would have to go to school. There must be more money, there must be more money. The father, who was always very handsome and expensive in his tastes, seemed as if he never *would* be able to do anything worth doing. And the mother, who had a great belief in herself, did not succeed any better, and her tastes were just as expensive.

And so the house came to be haunted by the unspoken phrase: *There must be more money! There must be more money!* The children could hear it all the time, though nobody said it aloud. They heard it at Christmas, when the expensive and splendid toys filled the nursery. Behind the shining modern rocking-horse, behind the smart doll's-house, a voice would start whispering: "There *must* be more money! There *must* be more money!" And the children would stop playing, to listen for a moment. They would look into each other's eyes, to see if they had all heard. And each one saw in the eyes of the other two that they too had heard. "There *must* be more money! There *must* be more money!"

It came whispering from the springs of the still-swaying rocking-horse, and even the horse, bending his wooden, champing head, heard it. The big doll, sitting so pink and smirking in her new pram, could hear it quite plainly, and seemed to be smirking all the more self-consciously because of it. The foolish puppy, too, that took the place of the teddy-bear, he was looking so extraordinarily foolish for no other reason but that he heard the secret whisper all over the house: "There *must* be more money!"

93

Yet nobody ever said it aloud. The whisper was everywhere, and therefore no one spoke it. Just as no one ever says: "We are breathing!" in spite of the fact that breath is coming and going all the time.

"Mother," said the boy Paul one day, "why don't we keep a car of our own? Why do we always use uncle's, or else a taxi?"

"Because we're the poor members of the family," said the mother.

"But why *are* we, mother?"

"Well,—I suppose," she said slowly and bitterly, "it's because your father has no luck."

The boy was silent for some time.

"Is luck money, mother?" he asked, rather timidly.

"No, Paul. Not quite. It's what causes you to have money."

"Oh!" said Paul vaguely. "I thought when Uncle Oscar said *filthy lucker*, it meant money."

"*Filthy lucre* does mean money," said the mother. "But it's lucre, not luck."

"Oh!" said the boy. "Then what *is* luck, mother?"

"It's what causes you to have money. If you're lucky you have money. That's why it's better to be born lucky than rich. If you're rich, you may lose your money. But if you're lucky, you will always get more money."

"Oh! Will you? And is father not lucky?"

"Very unlucky, I should say," she said bitterly.

The boy watched her with unsure eyes.

"Why?" he asked.

"I don't know. Nobody ever knows why one person is lucky and another unlucky."

"Don't they? Nobody at all? Does *nobody* know?"

"Perhaps God. But He never tells."

"He ought to, then. And aren't you lucky either, mother?"

"I can't be, if I married an unlucky husband."

"But by yourself, aren't you?"

"I used to think I was, before I married. Now I think I am very unlucky indeed."

"Why?"

"Well—never mind! Perhaps I'm not really," she said.

The child looked at her, to see if she meant it. But he saw, by the lines of her mouth, that she was only trying to hide something from him.

"Well, anyhow," he said stoutly, "I'm a lucky person."

"Why?" said his mother, with a sudden laugh.

He stared at her. He didn't even know why he had said it.

"God told me," he asserted, brazening it out.

"I hope He did, dear!" she said, again with a laugh, but rather bitter.

"He did, mother!"

"Excellent!" said the mother, using one of her husband's exclamations.

The boy saw she did not believe him; or rather, that she paid no attention to his assertion. This angered him somewhere, and made him want to compel her attention.

He went off by himself, vaguely, in a childish way, seeking for the clue to "luck." Absorbed, taking no heed of other people, he went about with a sort of stealth, seeking inwardly for luck. He wanted luck, he wanted it, he wanted it. When the two girls were playing dolls in the nursery, he would sit on his big rocking-horse, charging madly into space, with a frenzy that made the little girls peer at him uneasily. Wildly the horse careered, the waving dark hair of the boy tossed, his eyes had a strange glare in them. The little girls dared not speak to him.

When he had ridden to the end of his mad little journey, he climbed down and stood in front of his rocking-horse, staring fixedly into its lowered face. Its red mouth was slightly open, its big eye was wide and glassy-bright.

"Now!" he would silently command the snorting steed. "Now, take me to where there is luck! Now take me!"

And he would slash the horse in the neck with the little whip he had asked Uncle Oscar for. He *knew* the horse could take him to where there was luck, if only he forced it. So he would mount again, and start on his furious ride, hoping at last to get there. He knew he could get there.

"You'll break your horse, Paul!" said the nurse.

"He's always riding like that! I wish he'd leave off!" said his elder sister Joan.

But he only glared down on them in silence. Nurse gave him up. She could make nothing of him. Anyhow he was growing beyond her.

One day his mother and his Uncle Oscar came in when he was on one of his furious rides. He did not speak to them.

"Hallo, you young jockey! Riding a winner?" said his uncle.

"Aren't you growing too big for a rocking-horse? You're not a very little boy any longer, you know," said his mother.

But Paul only gave a blue glare from his big, rather close-set eyes. He would speak to nobody when he was in full tilt. His mother watched him with an anxious expression on her face.

At last he suddenly stopped forcing his horse into the mechanical gallop, and slid down.

"Well, I got there!" he announced fiercely, his blue eyes still flaring, and his sturdy long legs straddling apart.

"Where did you get to?" asked his mother.

"Where I wanted to go," he flared back at her.

"That's right, son!" said Uncle Oscar. "Don't you stop till you get there. What's the horse's name?"

"He doesn't have a name," said the boy.

"Gets on without all right?" asked the uncle.

"Well, he has different names. He was called Sansovino last week."

"Sansovino, eh? Won the Ascot. How did you know his name?"

"He always talks about horse-races with Bassett," said Joan.

The uncle was delighted to find that his small nephew was posted with all the racing news. Bassett, the young gardener, who had been wounded in the left foot in the war and had got his present job through

Oscar Cresswell, whose batman he had been, was a perfect blade of the "turf." He lived in the racing events, and the small boy lived with him.

Oscar Cresswell got it all from Bassett.

"Master Paul comes and asks me, so I can't do more than tell him, sir," said Bassett, his face terribly serious, as if he were speaking of religious matters.

"And does he ever put anything on a horse he fancies?"

"Well—I don't want to give him away—he's a young sport, a fine sport, sir. Would you mind asking him himself? He sort of takes a pleasure in it, and perhaps he'd feel I was giving him away, sir, if you don't mind."

Bassett was serious as a church.

The uncle went back to his nephew, and took him off for a ride in the car.

"Say, Paul, old man, do you ever put anything on a horse?" the uncle asked.

The boy watched the handsome man closely.

"Why, do you think I oughtn't to?" he parried.

"Not a bit of it! I thought perhaps you might give me a tip for the Lincoln."

The car sped on into the country, going down to Uncle Oscar's place in Hampshire.

"Honour bright?" said the nephew.

"Honour bright, son!" said the uncle.

"Well, then, Daffodil."

"Daffodil! I doubt it, sonny. What about Mirza?"

"I only know the winner," said the boy. "That's Daffodil."

"Daffodil, eh?"

There was a pause. Daffodil was an obscure horse comparatively.

"Uncle!"

"Yes, son?"

"You won't let it go any further, will you? I promised Bassett."

"Bassett be damned, old man! What's he got to do with it?"

"We're partners. We've been partners from the first. Uncle, he lent me my first five shillings, which I lost. I promised him, honour bright, it was only between me and him; only you gave me that ten-shilling note I started winning with, so I thought you were lucky. You won't let it go any further, will you?"

The boy gazed at his uncle from those big, hot, blue eyes, set rather close together. The uncle stirred and laughed uneasily.

"Right you are, son! I'll keep your tip private. Daffodil, eh? How much are you putting on him?"

"All except twenty pounds," said the boy. "I keep that in reserve."

The uncle thought it a good joke.

"You keep twenty pounds in reserve, do you, you young romancer? What are you betting, then?"

"I'm betting three hundred," said the boy gravely. "But it's between you and me, Uncle Oscar! Honour bright?"

The uncle burst into a roar of laughter.

"It's between you and me all right, you young Nat Gould," he said, laughing. "But where's your three hundred?"

"Bassett keeps it for me. We're partners."

"You are, are you! And what is Bassett putting on Daffodil?"

"He won't go quite as high as I do, I expect. Perhaps he'll go a hundred and fifty."

"What, pennies?" laughed the uncle.

"Pounds," said the child, with a surprised look at his uncle. "Bassett keeps a bigger reserve than I do."

Between wonder and amusement Uncle Oscar was silent. He pursued the matter no further, but he determined to take his nephew with him to the Lincoln races.

"Now, son," he said, "I'm putting twenty on Mirza, and I'll put five for you on any horse you fancy. What's your pick?"

"Daffodil, uncle."

"No, not the fiver on Daffodil!"

"I should if it was my own fiver," said the child.

"Good! Good! Right you are! A fiver for me and a fiver for you on Daffodil."

The child had never been to a race-meeting before, and his eyes were blue fire. He pursed his mouth tight, and watched. A Frenchman just in front had put his money on Lancelot. Wild with excitement, he flayed his arms up and down, yelling *Lancelot! Lancelot!* in his French accent.

Daffodil came in first, Lancelot second, Mirza third. The child, flushed and with eyes blazing, was curiously serene. His uncle brought him four five-pound notes, four to one.

"What am I to do with these?" he cried, waving them before the boy's eyes.

"I suppose we'll talk to Bassett," said the boy. "I expect I have fifteen hundred now; and twenty in reserve; and this twenty."

His uncle studied him for some moments.

"Look here, son!" he said. "You're not serious about Bassett and that fifteen hundred, are you?"

"Yes, I am. But it's between you and me, uncle. Honour bright!"

"Honour bright all right, son! But I must talk to Bassett."

"If you'd like to be a partner, uncle, with Bassett and me, we could all be partners. Only, you'd have to promise, honour bright, not to let it go beyond us three. Bassett and I are lucky, and you must be lucky, because it was your ten shillings I started winning with. . . ."

Uncle Oscar took both Bassett and Paul into Richmond Park for an afternoon, and there they talked.

"It's like this, you see, sir," Bassett said. "Master Paul would get me talking about racing events, spinning yarns, you know, sir. And he was always keen on knowing if I'd made or if I'd lost. It's about a year since, now, that I put five shillings on Blush of Dawn for him: and we lost. Then the luck turned, with that ten shillings he had from you: that we put on Singhalese. And since that time, it's been pretty steady, all things considering. What do you say, Master Paul?"

"We're all right when we're sure," said Paul. "It's when we're not quite sure that we go down."

"Oh, but we're careful then," said Bassett.

"But when are you *sure?*" smiled Uncle Oscar.

"It's Master Paul, sir," said Bassett, in a secret, religious voice. "It's as if he had it from heaven. Like Daffodil, now, for the Lincoln. That was as sure as eggs."

"Did you put anything on Daffodil?" asked Oscar Cresswell.

"Yes, sir. I made my bit."

"And my nephew?"

Bassett was obstinately silent, looking at Paul.

"I made twelve hundred, didn't I, Bassett? I told uncle I was putting three hundred on Daffodil."

"That's right," said Bassett, nodding.

"But where's the money?" asked the uncle.

"I keep it safe locked up, sir. Master Paul he can have it any minute he likes to ask for it."

"What, fifteen hundred pounds?"

"And twenty! And *forty*, that is, with the twenty he made on the course."

"It's amazing!" said the uncle.

"If Master Paul offers you to be partners, sir, I would, if I were you: if you'll excuse me," said Bassett.

Oscar Cresswell thought about it.

"I'll see the money," he said.

They drove home again, and, sure enough, Bassett came round to the garden-house with fifteen hundred pounds in notes. The twenty pounds reserve was left with Joe Glee, in the Turf Commission deposit.

"You see, it's all right, uncle, when I'm *sure!* Then we go strong, for all we're worth. Don't we, Bassett?"

"We do that, Master Paul."

"And when are you sure?" said the uncle, laughing.

"Oh, well, sometimes I'm *absolutely* sure, like about Daffodil," said the boy; "and sometimes I have an idea; and sometimes I haven't even an idea, have I, Bassett? Then we're careful, because we mostly go down."

"You do, do you! And when you're sure, like about Daffodil, what makes you sure, sonny?"

"Oh, well, I don't know," said the boy uneasily. "I'm sure, you know, uncle; that's all."

"It's as if he had it from heaven, sir," Bassett reiterated.

"I should say so!" said the uncle.

But he became a partner. And when the Leger was coming on, Paul was "sure" about Lively Spark, which was a quite inconsiderable horse. The boy insisted on putting a thousand on the horse, Bassett went for five hundred, and Oscar Cresswell two hundred. Lively Spark came in first, and the betting had been ten to one against him. Paul had made ten thousand.

"You see," he said, "I was absolutely sure of him."

Even Oscar Cresswell had cleared two thousand.

"Look here, son," he said, "this sort of thing makes me nervous."

"It needn't, uncle! Perhaps I shan't be sure again for a long time."

"But what are you going to do with your money?" asked the uncle.

"Of course," said the boy, "I started it for mother. She said she had no luck, because father is unlucky, so I thought if I was lucky, it might stop whispering."

"What might stop whispering?"

"Our house. I *hate* our house for whispering."

"What does it whisper?"

"Why—why"—the boy fidgeted—"why, I don't know. But it's always short of money, you know, uncle."

"I know it, son, I know it."

"You know people send mother writs, don't you, uncle?"

"I'm afraid I do," said the uncle.

"And then the house whispers, like people laughing at you behind your back. It's awful, that is! I thought if I was lucky—"

"You might stop it," added the uncle.

The boy watched him with big blue eyes, that had an uncanny cold fire in them, and he said never a word.

"Well, then!" said the uncle. "What are we doing?"

"I shouldn't like mother to know I was lucky," said the boy.

"Why not, son?"

"She'd stop me."

"I don't think she would."

"Oh!"—and the boy writhed in an odd way—"I *don't* want her to know, uncle."

"All right, son! We'll manage it without her knowing."

They managed it very easily. Paul, at the other's suggestion, handed over five thousand pounds to his uncle, who deposited it with the family lawyer, who was then to inform Paul's mother that a relative had put five thousand pounds into his hands, which sum was to be paid out a thousand pounds at a time, on the mother's birthday, for the next five years.

"So she'll have a birthday present of a thousand pounds for five successive years," said Uncle Oscar. "I hope it won't make it all the harder for her later."

Paul's mother had her birthday in November. The house had been "whispering" worse than ever lately, and, even in spite of his luck, Paul could not bear up against it. He was very anxious to see the effect of the birthday letter, telling his mother about the thousand pounds.

When there were no visitors, Paul now took his meals with his parents, as he was beyond the nursery control. His mother went into town nearly every day. She had discovered that she had an odd knack of sketching furs and dress materials, so she worked secretly in the studio of a friend who was the chief "artist" for the leading drapers. She drew the figures of ladies in furs and ladies in silk and sequins for the newspaper advertisements. This young woman artist earned several thousand pounds a year, but Paul's mother only made several hundreds, and she was again dissatisfied. She so wanted to be first in something, and she did not succeed, even in making sketches for drapery advertisements.

She was down to breakfast on the morning of her birthday. Paul watched her face as she read her letters. He knew the lawyer's letter. As his mother read it, her face hardened and became more expressionless. Then a cold, determined look came on her mouth. She hid the letter under the pile of others, and said not a word about it.

"Didn't you have anything nice in the post for your birthday, mother?" said Paul.

"Quite moderately nice," she said, her voice cold and absent.

She went away to town without saying more.

But in the afternoon Uncle Oscar appeared. He said Paul's mother had had a long interview with the lawyer, asking if the whole five thousand could not be advanced at once, as she was in debt.

"What do you think, uncle?" said the boy.

"I leave it to you, son."

"Oh, let her have it, then! We can get some more with the other," said the boy.

"A bird in the hand is worth two in the bush, laddie!" said Uncle Oscar.

"But I'm sure to *know* for the Grand National; or the Lincolnshire; or else the Derby. I'm sure to know for *one* of them," said Paul.

So Uncle Oscar signed the agreement, and Paul's mother touched the whole five thousand. Then something very curious happened. The voices in the house suddenly went mad, like a chorus of frogs on a spring evening. There were certain new furnishings, and Paul had a tutor. He was *really* going to Eton, his father's school, in the following autumn. There were flowers in the winter, and a blossoming of the luxury Paul's mother had been used to. And yet the voices in the house, behind the sprays of mimosa and almond-blossom, and from under the piles of iridescent cushions, simply trilled and screamed in a sort of ecstasy: "There *must* be more money! Oh-h-h; there *must* be more money. Oh, now, now-w! Now-w-w—there *must* be more money!—more than ever! More than ever!"

It frightened Paul terribly. He studied away at his Latin and Greek with his tutors. But his intense hours were spent with Bassett. The Grand National had gone by: he had not "known," and had lost a hundred pounds. Summer was at hand. He was in agony for the Lincoln. But even for the Lincoln he didn't "know," and he lost fifty pounds. He became wild-eyed and strange, as if something were going to explode in him.

"Let it alone, son! Don't you bother about it!" urged Uncle Oscar. But it was as if the boy couldn't really hear what his uncle was saying.

"I've got to know for the Derby! I've got to know for the Derby!" the child reiterated, his big blue eyes blazing with a sort of madness.

His mother noticed how overwrought he was.

"You'd better go to the seaside. Wouldn't you like to go now to the seaside, instead of waiting? I think you'd better," she said, looking down at him anxiously, her heart curiously heavy because of him.

But the child lifted his uncanny blue eyes.

"I couldn't possibly go before the Derby, mother!" he said. "I couldn't possibly!"

"Why not?" she said, her voice becoming heavy when she was opposed. "Why not? You can still go from the seaside to see the Derby with your Uncle Oscar, if that's what you wish. No need for you to wait here. Besides, I think you care too much about these races. It's a bad sign. My family has been a gambling family, and you won't know till you grow up how much damage it has done. But it has done damage. I shall have to send Bassett away, and ask Uncle Oscar not to talk racing to you, unless you promise to be reasonable about it: go away to the seaside and forget it. You're all nerves!"

"I'll do what you like, mother, so long as you don't send me away till after the Derby," the boy said.

"Send you away from where? Just from this house?"

"Yes," he said, gazing at her.

"Why, you curious child, what makes you care about this house so much, suddenly? I never knew you loved it."

He gazed at her without speaking. He had a secret within a secret, something he had not divulged, even to Bassett or to his Uncle Oscar.

But his mother, after standing undecided and a little bit sullen for some moments, said:

"Very well, then! Don't go to the seaside till after the Derby, if you don't wish it. But promise me you won't let your nerves go to pieces. Promise you won't think so much about horse-racing and *events*, as you call them!"

"Oh, no," said the boy casually. "I won't think much about them, mother. You needn't worry. I wouldn't worry, mother, if I were you."

"If you were me and I were you," said his mother, "I wonder what we *should* do!"

"But you know you needn't worry, mother, don't you?" the boy repeated.

"I should be awfully glad to know it," she said wearily.

"Oh, well, you *can*, you know. I mean, you *ought* to know you needn't worry," he insisted.

"Ought I? Then I'll see about it," she said.

Paul's secret of secrets was his wooden horse, that which had no name. Since he was emancipated from a nurse and a nursery-governess, he had had his rocking-horse removed to his own bedroom at the top of the house.

"Surely, you're too big for a rocking-horse!" his mother had remonstrated.

"Well, you see, mother, till I can have a *real* horse, I like to have *some* sort of animal about," had been his quaint answer.

"Do you feel he keeps you company?" she laughed.

"Oh, yes! He's very good, he always keeps me company, when I'm there," said Paul.

So the horse, rather shabby, stood in an arrested prance in the boy's bedroom.

The Derby was drawing near, and the boy grew more and more tense. He hardly heard what was spoken to him, he was very frail, and his eyes were really uncanny. His mother had sudden strange seizures of uneasiness about him. Sometimes, for half-an-hour, she would feel a sudden anxiety about him that was almost anguish. She wanted to rush to him at once, and know he was safe.

Two nights before the Derby, she was at a big party in town, when one of her rushes of anxiety about her boy, her first-born, gripped her heart till she could hardly speak. She fought with the feeling, might and main, for she believed in commonsense. But it was too strong. She had to leave the dance and go downstairs to telephone to the country. The children's nursery-governess was terribly surprised and startled at being rung up in the night.

"Are the children all right, Miss Wilmot?"

"Oh, yes, they are quite all right."

"Master Paul? Is he all right?"

"He went to bed as right as a trivet. Shall I run up and look at him?"

"No," said Paul's mother reluctantly. "No! Don't trouble. It's all right. Don't sit up. We shall be home fairly soon." She did not want her son's privacy intruded upon.

"Very good," said the governess.

It was about one o'clock when Paul's mother and father drove up to their house. All was still. Paul's mother went to her room and slipped off her white fur cloak. She had told her maid not to wait up for her. She heard her husband downstairs, mixing a whiskey-and-soda.

And then, because of the strange anxiety at her heart, she stole upstairs to her son's room. Noiselessly she went along the upper corridor. Was there a faint noise? What was it?

She stood, with arrested muscles, outside his door, listening. There was a strange, heavy, and yet not loud noise. Her heart stood still. It was a soundless noise, yet rushing and powerful. Something huge, in violent, hushed motion. What was it? What in God's name was it? She ought to know. She felt that she knew the noise. She knew what it was.

Yet she could not place it. She couldn't say what it was. And on and on it went, like a madness.

Softly, frozen with anxiety and fear, she turned the door-handle.

The room was dark. Yet in the space near the window, she heard and saw something plunging to and fro. She gazed in fear and amazement.

Then suddenly she switched on the light, and saw her son, in his green pajamas, madly surging on the rocking-horse. The blaze of light suddenly lit him up, as he urged the wooden horse, and lit her up, as she stood, blonde, in her dress of pale green and crystal, in the doorway.

"Paul!" she cried. "Whatever are you doing?"

"It's Malabar!" he screamed, in a powerful, strange voice. "It's Malabar!"

His eyes blazed at her for one strange and senseless second, as he ceased urging his wooden horse. Then he fell with a crash to the ground, and she, all her tormented motherhood flooding upon her, rushed to gather him up.

But he was unconscious, and unconscious he remained, with some brain-fever. He talked and tossed, and his mother sat stonily by his side.

"Malabar! It's Malabar! Bassett, Bassett, I *know*! It's Malabar!"

So the child cried, trying to get up and urge the rocking-horse that gave him his inspiration.

"What does he mean by Malabar?" asked the heart-frozen mother.

"I don't know," said the father stonily.

"What does he mean by Malabar?" she asked her brother Oscar.

"It's one of the horses running for the Derby," was the answer.

And, in spite of himself, Oscar Cresswell spoke to Bassett, and himself put a thousand on Malabar: at fourteen to one.

The third day of the illness was critical: they were waiting for a change. The boy, with his rather long, curly hair, was tossing ceaselessly on the pillow. He neither slept nor regained consciousness, and his eyes were like blue stones. His mother sat, feeling her heart had gone, turned actually into a stone.

In the evening, Oscar Cresswell did not come, but Bassett sent a message, saying could he come up for one moment, just one moment? Paul's mother was very angry at the intrusion, but on second thought she agreed. The boy was the same. Perhaps Bassett might bring him to consciousness.

The gardener, a shortish fellow with a little brown moustache, and sharp little brown eyes, tiptoed into the room, touched his imaginary cap to Paul's mother, and stole to the bedside, staring with glittering, smallish eyes at the tossing, dying child.

"Master Paul!" he whispered. "Master Paul! Malabar came in first all right, a clean win. I did as you told me. You've made over seventy thousand pounds, you have; you've got over eighty thousand. Malabar came in all right, Master Paul."

"Malabar! Malabar! Did I say Malabar, mother? Did I say Malabar? Do you think I'm lucky, mother? I knew Malabar, didn't I? Over eighty thousand pounds! I call that lucky, don't you, mother? Over eighty thousand pounds! I knew, didn't I know I knew? Malabar came in all right. If I ride my horse till I'm sure, then I tell you, Bassett, you can go as high as you like. Did you go for all you were worth, Bassett?"

"I went a thousand on it, Master Paul."

"I never told you, mother, that if I can ride my horse, and *get there*, then I'm absolutely sure—oh, absolutely! Mother, did I ever tell you? I *am* lucky!"

"No, you never did," said the mother.

But the boy died in the night.

And even as he lay dead, his mother heard her brother's voice saying to her: "My God, Hester, you're eighty-odd thousand to the good, and a poor devil of a son to the bad. But, poor devil, poor devil, he's best gone out of a life where he rides his rocking-horse to find a winner."

Fact or Symbol?
The Relationship
of Fiction to Reality

Again and again throughout this book the question arises: What is the relationship of the images and stories that man constructs out of his own mind to the given reality of the world, the way things are no matter how man thinks of them and represents them? This question is of crucial importance to an understanding of fictions because the answer ultimately determines our judgments about the value of fictions in general and the superiority of some fictions over others.

There are two absolute ways to approach the problem. The first is to take the subjective position upon which the whole fictitious world of Borges' Tlön is structured. In the Tlönish view of things, everything that man sees, thinks, and says is a fiction. The concept of reality itself is only an agreed-upon fiction because man's means of perceiving and reporting —his senses, his logic, and his language—create reality. In this view the seer makes what is seen, and mathematics and science are only more abstract, systematic fictions than *The Thousand Nights and a Night*. (There is, however, a more moderate subjectivity which accepts the separate existence of things and events outside our minds, but contends that we can never know them as they truly are in themselves because we can observe them only through our own instruments of perception and our own cultural preconceptions. Our attempts to describe this external reality can at best only be an approximation of the truth.) Writers have long been acutely aware of this problem and many of their works explore it deeply. For example, in Borges' short story, "The Library of Babel," an infinite library contains every possible combination of letters, every book that can be written. Here every book has its opposite and every convincing proof its equally convincing disproof. All writings are fictions and can only be judged by the standards of fiction itself. The question becomes not how "true" a story is in relation to reality, which does not exist, but how true it is to itself. Is it consistent internally? Is it shapely and beautiful?

The equally radical opposing view is the more familiar objective or materialist position which assumes that things do exist independently of the perceiver and that there is therefore an absolute truth which can be known, at least partially. In this philosophy a statement or fiction is judged by the degree to which it approximates truth, and scientific and historical statements are to be preferred to fictions. Fictions are admissible only if they convey information about the way things actually are, and realistic fiction is, of course, always superior to the fantastic. In a modified form something like this is probably what most men and most writers have always believed to be the function of fiction: to tell the truth in an indirect, not a literal, fashion about what men and life are like. This view of fiction is regularly dramatized in Western literature, which persistently turns on the encounter of man's dreams with an overriding reality. For all his greatness as a man, Oedipus discovers that he cannot escape his fate, the oracle's prediction that he will kill his father and marry his mother; and for all Hamlet's desire to understand his world and escape his destiny, he is swept into a bloody revenge plot that is not of his own making. This failure of the mind to impress itself upon the real world, and the subsequent need for adjustment to reality, has been one of the constant themes of modern literature.

These then are the two extreme positions on the relation of fiction to reality: on the one hand the subjective belief that the only things we can know or say are fictions, and on the other hand the view that reality is knowable but that it is so different from our fictions that there can be no, or very little, correlation between the two. But there is a third view, more pragmatic than philosophically exact, which assumes that reality and fiction mesh in some important way and that the degree to which they mesh is crucial. The selections in this section focus on situations where mind and reality confront each other in a fundamental way.

In Freud's case report "Miss Lucy R." from his early book *Studies on Hysteria* (1895), written with Josef Breuer, we come very close to the most primary form of fiction-making, the tendency of the mind to create symbolic substitutes for reality. In this case the symbol or fiction is nasal rather than verbal, the smell of burned pastry and then cigar smoke. Since Lucy R. smells these odors when they are not actually present, the fictions are in the first instance pure inventions, the pretense that things exist which in fact do not. She is therefore considered sick, a mild neurotic. She herself finds this fiction which does not seem to correspond to reality intolerable, so she goes to the doctor for help. Help consists in discovering that the smells of burned pastry and cigar smoke do in fact correspond to a psychic reality, not a physical reality. The smells were originally part of larger scenes that they have come to represent in the same way that in the trope "synecdoche" the part stands for the whole—that is, fifty sails for fifty ships, or fifty swords for fifty soldiers. To the patient's mind the imagined smells are functional, though not entirely satisfactory, because they ease the pain of reality and permit her to be aware of past events that are too distressing to be thought of as they actually occurred. The smell of cigar smoke is bearable, the memory of her employer's lack of feeling for her is not. Fictions function for Miss Lucy R. as they do so often for all of us in fairy tales and romance, which take an unpleasant reality and transform it in such a way to make it at least bearable, perhaps even enjoyable.

But to the psychoanalyst, probing like a detective for clues and uncovering truth below truth, the odors—though no longer absolute lies since they correspond in an indirect and abbreviated way to reality—are still unsatisfactory fictions because they mask reality and prevent Lucy R. from seeing what actually took place. Her cure is effected only when the fictions disappear altogether: she stops smelling cigar smoke when it is not present, and she faces directly the plain truth that her employer never loved her and never will. For a determined realist, such as Freud seems to be here, health would seem to consist of ridding oneself of all fictions whatsoever and living entirely with things as they actually are, though Freud understands better than perhaps anyone else that the human mind works and the personality functions by a continuing substitution of fictions for realities.

It is impossible, however, not to notice that that "reality" which Freud considers so superior to fiction itself has some distinctly fictional characteristics. Take, for example, the case report itself, which seems so matter-of-fact and clinical in tone. The reality of the therapy was not, however, so beautifully clear and cleanly "plotted," as Freud tells us:

> I will now relate the history of this analysis. It could have occurred under more favorable conditions, but as a matter of fact what should have taken place in one session was extended over a number of them. She could only visit me during my office hours, during which I could devote to her but little of my time. One single conversation had to be extended for over a week as her duties did not permit her to come to me often from such a distance, so that the conversation was frequently broken off and resumed at the next session.

Yet this is not the way the rest of the report reads, and we are left with the inescapable conclusion that in order to state the truth about Miss Lucy R., Freud carefully selected his materials and arranged them in an artful if not a fictional manner. The therapy itself also proceeds in a manner remarkably similar to the way fictions are seen to work in the remainder of this book. Analysis begins with an isolated, seemingly impenetrable event, the smells, and the cure is achieved by probing the patient's memory, giving the smells a context, and then providing them with a plot—a beginning, a middle, and an end. Only when the neurotic symptom is handled in the manner of a complex fiction does it become acceptable as truth, and so it would seem that if fictions can obscure truth, they can also reveal it. Those who wish to explore these matters further in Freud will find other case studies in *Studies on Hysteria* of great interest, particularly that of "Katherina." There are longer and more complex studies of a similar nature, such as "The Wolf Man" or the fascinating "Case of Doctor Schreber." Freud's method of therapy and his investigation of the mind proceed always through the exploration of fictions of various kinds, dreams, daydreams, slips of the tongue and pen, totemism, and many forms of compulsive behavior and other neurotic symptoms. Thus, any of his works from *The Interpretation of Dreams* to *The Future of an Illusion* may be studied with great profit as an analysis of fiction—its origins, its functions, its values, and its dangers.

Freud was, as many writers have pointed out, trained in nineteenth-century Vienna as a laboratory scientist, a neurologist to be specific, and he shared the views of that laboratory tradition about truth and reality. But truth and reality may be more problematical, and their relationship to fiction therefore more uncertain. The title of Joseph Conrad's *Heart of Darkness* suggests very nicely this problematical quality of the truth at the center of things. The exploration of the heart of darkness that the story-teller Marlow relates takes place on many levels simultaneously. It is a fictional realization of the nineteenth-century desire to penetrate all the mysterious places of the world and fill out the maps of such unknown areas as the Congo. It is also an exposure of the greed, brutality, and inefficiency that lie at the heart of commercialism and imperialism, most specifically that of the Belgian exploitation of central Africa, but by implication of all the idealistic shams man uses to cover a primary ineradicable selfishness and stupidity. On another level, Marlow's journey, proceeding stage by stage from the sea through the outer and inner stations to the head of navigation, is also a journey into the depths of the self. In this it resembles Freud's and Miss Lucy R.'s exploration of her mind. When the psychoanalyst arrives at his goal he finds, however, not a heart of darkness but a scene of great clarity and a sad but definite realization that a hoped-for love does not and cannot exist. But when Marlow arrives at his goal he finds darkness in the heart of that strange man Kurtz, the signs of some abominable rites, and a tribe of mysterious savages. It is important to notice how vague and mysterious this place and these people are. Just what Kurtz did is not certain, things are seen from a distance, words are spoken but not understood. In other words, when we come face to face with reality it is not ever easy to describe, and its meaning is much more difficult to come by than the scientist or analyst might think. If reality, and particularly the reality of our own natures, is this elusive and ambiguous, then a fiction may be a better, even a more accurate, technique for dealing with it than the crisp, clear prose of the case report with its precise scientific references to "rhinitis" and "caries of the ethmoid." At least Conrad seems to think so, for he approaches the heart of darkness through the story teller, Marlow, as if stories were the only way of getting at the "truth." And even the story cannot be too precise and sure of its meaning if it is to capture something of reality:

> The yarns of seamen have a direct simplicity, the whole meaning of which lies within the shell of a cracked nut. But Marlow was not typical (if his propensity to spin yarns be excepted), and to him the meaning of an episode was not inside like a kernel but outside, enveloping the tale which brought it out only as a glow brings out a haze, in the likeness of one of these misty halos that sometimes are made visible by the spectral illumination of moonshine.

The Case of Miss Lucy R.

Sigmund Freud

Translated by A. A. Brill

The events reported in "The Case of Miss Lucy R." emerged in the course of Freud's treatment of a young woman in Vienna in 1892–93, and appeared in print in *Studies on Hysteria* (Vienna, 1895), a volume jointly authored by Dr. Josef Breuer and Dr. Sigmund Freud (1856–1939). Breuer was an older colleague of Freud's who had worked with hysterics—we would now more likely say "neurotics"—and had discovered, almost by accident, that under hypnosis one of his patients was able to recall the circumstances in which his symptoms originated, and that recalling this knowledge to consciousness effected a cure. The basics of the psychoanalytic theory are here in this discovery: that neurosis is related to unremembered prior events, that these events are not forgotten but suppressed and can be recalled under the right circumstances, and that conscious awareness of them either alleviates the symptoms or causes them to disappear. It was on this foundation that Freud was to erect a complete theory of the dynamics of the human mind. In the 1890's he began using hypnotism as a method for stimulating the patients' memory but soon abandoned it in favor of free association.

No special knowledge of psychoanalysis is needed to understand "The Case of Miss Lucy R.," for Freud is here at the very beginning of his work and feeling his way very carefully toward the construction of a theory. The emphasis is therefore on the facts: Lucy R. smells certain odors when they are not present, she is able to remember that these odors are connected with earlier painful events, the odors disappear.

This is an excellent place to begin an understanding of Freudian theory, but from the point of view of this book "The Case of Miss Lucy R." serves as a primer to the study of fictions and their relation to reality. We have here a fiction in its plainest form, a delusion that certain smells are present when they are not, and yet that fiction turns out to relate to reality in a curious way. Furthermore, the first fiction, the smell of burned pastry, is a fictional substitute for a second fiction, the smell of cigar smoke. You will wish to ask yourself why the mind constructed these fictions one atop the other in the first place, and also why they were unsatisfactory to both patient and analyst.

One short section in which Freud explains his difficulties with hypnotism as a therapeutic method and his shift to the process of free association is deleted.

■

Towards the end of 1892 a friendly colleague recommended to me a young lady whom he had been treating for chronic recurrent purulent rhinitis. It was later found that the obstinacy of her trouble was caused by a caries of the ethmoid.[1] She finally complained of new symptoms which this experienced physician could no longer refer to local affections. She had lost all perception of smell and was almost constantly bothered by one or two subjective sensations of smell. This she found very irksome. In addition to this she was depressed in spirits, weak, and complained of a heavy head, loss of appetite, and an incapacity for work.

This young lady visited me from time to time during my office hours —she was a governess in the family of a factory superintendent living in the suburbs of Vienna. She was an English lady of rather delicate constitution, anemic, and with the exception of her nasal trouble was in good health. Her first statements concurred with those of her physician. She suffered from depression and lassitude, and was tormented by subjective sensations of smell. Of hysterical signs, she showed a quite distinct general analgesia without tactile impairment, the fields of vision showed no narrowing on coarse testing with the hand, the nasal mucous membrane was totally analgesic and reflexless, tactile sensation was absent, and the perception of this organ was abolished for specific as well as for other stimuli, such as ammonia or acetic acid. The purulent nasal catarrh was then in a state of improvement.

On first attempting to understand this case the subjective sensations of smell had to be taken as recurrent hallucinations interpreting persistent hysterical symptoms. The depression was perhaps the affect belonging to the trauma [2] and there must have been an episode during which the present subjective sensations were objective. This episode must have been the trauma, the symbols of which recurred in memory as sensations of smell. Perhaps it would be more correct to consider the recurring hallucinations of smell with the accompanying depression as equivalents of hysterical attacks. The nature of recurrent hallucinations really makes them unfit to take the part of continuous symptoms and this really did not

1 Nasal infection. [All footnotes are by the present editors.]
2 Psychic wound; the result of a painful psychic experience.

occur in this rudimentarily developed case. On the other hand it was absolutely to be expected that the subjective sensations of smell would show such a specialization as to be able to correspond in its origin to a very definite and real object.[3]

This expectation was soon fulfilled, for on being asked what odor troubled her most she stated that it was an odor of burned pastry. I could then assume that the odor of burned pastry really occurred in the traumatic event. It is quite unusual to select sensations of smell as memory symbols of traumas, but it is quite obvious why these were here selected. She was afflicted with purulent rhinitis, hence the nose and its perceptions were in the foreground of her attention. All I knew about the life of the patient was that she took care of two children whose mother died a few years ago from a grave and acute disease.

As a starting point of the analysis I decided to use the "odor of burned pastry." I will now relate the history of this analysis. It could have occurred under move favorable conditions, but as a matter of fact what should have taken place in one session was extended over a number of them. She could only visit me during my office hours, during which I could devote to her but little of my time. One single conversation had to be extended for over a week as her duties did not permit her to come to me often from such a distance, so that the conversation was frequently broken off and resumed at the next session.

On attempting to hypnotize Miss Lucy R. she did not merge into the somnambulic [4] state. I therefore was obliged to forego somnambulism and the analysis was made while she was in a state not perhaps differing much from the normal.

·   ·   ·

My memory helped me out of this embarrassment. I, myself, saw Bernheim adduce proof that the recollections of somnambulism are only manifestly forgotten in the waking state and can be readily reproduced by slight urging accompanied by hand pressure which is supposed to mark another conscious state. He, for instance, imparted to a somnambulist the negative hallucination that he was no more present, and then attempted to make himself noticeable to her by the most manifold and regardless attacks, but was unsuccessful. After the patient was awakened he asked her what he did to her during the time that she thought he was not there. She replied very much astonished, that she knew nothing, but he did not give in, insisting that she would recall everything; and placed his hand on her forehead so that she should recall things, and behold, she finally related all that she did not apparently perceive in the somnam-

---

[3] I.e., the particular nature of the symptoms, the hallucinatory smells, would relate directly to the actual events in which they originated.

[4] Hypnotic.

bulic state and about which she ostensibly knew nothing in the waking state.[5]

This astonishing and instructive experiment was my model. I decided to proceed on the supposition that my patients knew everything that was of any pathogenic [6] significance, and that all that was necessary was to force them to impart it. When I reached a point where to the question "Since when have you this symptom?" or, "Where does it come from?" I received the answer, "I really don't know this," I proceeded as follows: I placed my hand on the patient's forehead or took her head between my hands and said, "Under the pressure of my hand it will come into your mind. In the moment that I stop the pressure you will see something before you, or something will pass through your mind which you must note. It is that which we are seeking. Well, what have you seen or what came into your mind?"

On applying this method for the first time (it was not in the case of Miss Lucy R.) I was surprised to find just what I wanted, and I may say that it has since hardly ever failed me, it always showed me the way to proceed in my investigations and enabled me to conclude all such analyses without somnambulism. Gradually I became so bold that when a patient would answer, "I see nothing," or "Nothing came into my mind," I insisted that it was impossible. They probably had the right thought but did not believe it and repudiated it. I would repeat the procedure as often as they wished, and every time they saw the same thing. Indeed, I was always right; the patients had not as yet learned to let their criticism rest. They repudiated the emerging recollection or fancy because they considered it as a useless intruding disturbance, but after they imparted it, it was always shown that it was the right one. Occasionally after forcing a communication by pressing the head three or four times I got such answer as, "Yes, I was aware of it the first time, but did not wish to say it," or, "I hoped that it would not be this."

By this method it was far more laborious to broaden the alleged narrowed consciousness than by investigating in the somnambulic state, but it made me independent of somnambulism and afforded me an insight into the motives which are frequently decisive for the "forgetting" of recollections. I am in position to assert that this forgetting is often intentional and desired. It is always only manifestly successful.

It appeared to me even more remarkable that apparently long forgotten numbers and dates can be reproduced by a similar process, thus proving an unexpected faithfulness of memory.

The insignificant choice which one has in searching for numbers

[5] Freud is here on the threshold of his theory of the "unconscious," that portion of the mind which remembers events and contains desires that the conscious portion of the mind has purposely forgotten or suppressed because they are "forbidden" or too painful. According to this theory, the mind knows and remembers all that happens, but chooses not to retain all of it in consciousness. Psychoanalysis is in part a technique for bringing these memories out.

[6] Causing sickness.

and dates especially allows us to take to our aid the familiar axiom of the theory of aphasia,[7] namely, that recognition is a slighter accomplishment of memory than spontaneous recollection.

Hence to a patient who is unable to recall in what year, month or day a certain event took place, enumerate the years during which it might have occurred as well as the names of the twelve months and the thirty-one days of the month, and assure him that at the right number or name his eyes will open themselves or that he will feel which number is the correct one. In most cases the patients really decide on a definite date and frequently enough . . . it could be ascertained from existing notes of that time that the date was correctly recognized. At other times and in different patients it was shown from the connection of the recollected facts that the dates thus found were incontestable. A patient, for instance, after a date was found by enumerating for her the dates, remarked, "This is my father's birthday," and added "Of course I expected this episode [about which we spoke] because it was my father's birthday."

I can only slightly touch upon this theme. The conclusion which I wished to draw from all these experiences is that the pathogenic important experiences with all their concomitant circumstances are faithfully retained in memory, even where they seem forgotten, as when the patient seems unable to recall them.

After this long but unavoidable digression I now return to the history of Miss Lucy R. As aforesaid, she did not merge into somnambulism when an attempt was made to hypnotize her, but lay calmly in a degree of mild suggestibility, her eyes constantly closed, the features immobile, the limbs without motion. I asked her whether she remembered on what occasion the smell perception of burned pastry originated. —"Oh, yes, I know it well. It was about two months ago, two days before my birthday. I was with the children (two girls) in the school room playing and teaching them to cook, when a letter just left by the letter carrier was brought in. From its postmark and handwriting I recognized it as one sent to me by my mother from Glasgow and I wished to open it and read it. The children then came running over, pulled the letter out of my hand and exclaimed, 'No you must not read it now, it is probably a congratulatory letter for your birthday and we will keep it for you until then.' While the children were thus playing there was a sudden diffusion of an intense odor. The children forgot the pastry which they were cooking and it became burned. Since then I have been troubled by this odor, it is really always present but is more marked during excitement."

"Do you see this scene distinctly before you?" —"As clearly as I experienced it." —"What was there in it that so excited you?" —"I was touched by the affection which the children displayed towards me."

---

[7] The inability to articulate ideas or speak coherently, as a result of brain damage. Throughout his reports Freud uses terms from physical medicine and gives them psychological meanings. This is in part a result of his own training as a doctor, but also a result of his desire to make psychoanalysis objective and precise.

—"But weren't they always so affectionate?" —"Yes, But I just got the letter from my mother." —"I can't understand in what way the affection of the little ones and the letter from the mother contrasted, a thing which you appear to intimate." —"I had the intention of going to my mother and my heart became heavy at the thought of leaving those dear children." —"What is the matter with your mother? Was she so lonesome that she wanted you, or was she sick just then and you expected some news?" —"No, she is delicate but not really sick, and has a companion with her." —"Why then were you obliged to leave the children?" —"This house had become unbearable to me. The housekeeper, the cook, and the French maid seemed to be under the impression that I was too proud for my position. They united in intriguing against me and told the grandfather of the children all sorts of things about me, and when I complained to both gentlemen I did not receive the support which I expected. I then tendered my resignation to the master (father of the children) but he was very friendly, asking me to reconsider it for two weeks before taking any definite steps. It was while I was in that state of indecision that the incident occurred. I thought that I would leave the house but have remained."—"Aside from the attachment of the children is there anything particular which attracts you to them?" —"Yes, my mother is distantly related to their mother and when the latter was on her death bed I promised her to do my utmost in caring for the children, that I would not forsake them, and be a mother to them, and this promise I broke when offering my resignation."

The analysis of the subjective sensation of smell seemed completed. It was objective and intimately connected with an experience, a small scene, in which contrary affects [8] conflicted, sorrow at forsaking the children, and the mortification which despite all urged her to this decision. Her mother's letter naturally recalled the motives of this decision because she thought of returning to her mother. The conflict of the affects raised this moment to a trauma and the sensation of smell which was connected with it remained as its symbol. The only thing to be explained was the fact that out of all the sensory perceptions of that scene, the perception of smell was selected as the symbol, but I was already prepared to use the chronic nasal affliction as an explanation. On being directly questioned she stated that just at that time she suffered from a severe coryza [9] and could scarcely smell anything but in her excitement she perceived the odor of burned pastry, it penetrated the organically motivated anosmia. [10]

As plausible as this sounded it did not satisfy me; there seemed to be something lacking. There was no acceptable reason wherefore this series of excitements and this conflict of affects should have led to hysteria. Why did it not all remain on a normal psychological basis? In other

[8] Strong, deep-seated feelings; emotions.

[9] Head cold.

[10] The inability to smell, caused by an organic (physical) condition.

114

words, what justified the conversion [11] under discussion? Why did she not recall the scenes themselves instead of the sensations connected with them which she preferred as symbols for her recollection? Such questions might seem superfluous and impertinent when dealing with old hysterias in whom the mechanism of conversion was habitual, but this girl first acquired hysteria through this trauma, or at least through this slight distress.

From the analysis of similar cases I already knew that where hysteria is to be newly acquired one psychic determinant is indispensable; namely, that some presentation [12] must intentionally be repressed from consciousness and excluded from associative elaboration. [13]

In this intentional repression I also find the reason for the conversion of the sum of excitement, [14] be it partial or total. The sum of excitement which is not to enter into psychic association more readily finds the wrong road to bodily innervation. The reason for the repression itself could only be a disagreeable feeling, the incompatibility of one of the repressible ideas with the ruling presentation-mass of the ego. [15] The repressed presentation then avenges itself by becoming pathogenic.

From this I concluded that Miss Lucy R. merged into that moment of hysterical conversion, which must have been under the determinations of that trauma which she intentionally left in the darkness and which she took pains to forget. On considering her attachment for the children and her sensitiveness towards the other persons of the household, there remained but one interpretation which I was bold enough to impart to her. I told her that I did not believe that all these things were simply due to her affection for the children, but that I thought that she was rather in love with her master, perhaps unwittingly, that she really nurtured the hope of taking the place of the mother, and it was for that reason that she became so sensitive towards the servants with whom she had lived peacefully for years. She feared lest they would notice something of her hope and scoff at her.

She answered in her laconic manner: "Yes, I believe it is so." —"But if you knew that you were in love with the master, why did you not tell

[11] The "conversion" of the conflict into the symbol of the smell. Freud is touching here on the mind's general tendency to deal with suppressed material by "converting" it to various other forms, such as imagined odors or dreams.

[12] Prior event, once present to the senses.

[13] I.e., from being associated with other materials in the conscious mind and "elaborated," or pondered, in this larger field of thought.

[14] The affect associated with the suppressed event is now being thought of as an "excitement," or a kind of electrical energy which has been rechanneled.

[15] The idea, somewhat awkwardly expressed here in the English translation, is simply that the repressed idea is painful because it does not square with the ego, the dominant conception of the self held by the conscious mind. For example, a man who thinks of himself as brave might drive out of his conscious and into his unconscious some evidence that he is a coward. The energy of this idea would, however, "convert" itself into some symbolic form and come to consciousness in the way the smells do in the case of Lucy R.

115

me so?" —"But I did not know it, or rather, I did not wish to know it. I wished to crowd it out of my mind, never to think of it, and of late I have been successful."

"Why did you not wish to admit it to yourself? Were you ashamed because you loved a man?" —"O, no, I am not unreasonably prudish; one is certainly not responsible for one's own feelings. I only felt chagrined because it was my employer in whose service I was and in whose house I lived, and toward whom I could not feel as independent as towards another. What is more, I am a poor girl and he is a rich man of a prominent family, and if anybody should have had any inkling about my feelings they would have ridiculed me."

After this I encountered no resistances in elucidating the origin of this affection. She told me that the first years of her life in that house were passed uneventfully. She fulfilled her duties without thinking about unrealizable wishes. One day, however, the serious, and very busy and hitherto very reserved master, engaged her in conversation about the exigencies of rearing the children. He became milder and more cordial than usual, he told her how much he counted on her in the bringing up of his orphaned children, and looked at her rather peculiarly. It was in this moment that she began to love him, and gladly occupied herself with the pleasing hopes which she conceived during the conversation. However, as this was not followed by anything else, and despite her waiting and persevering no other confidential heart-to-heart talk followed, she decided to crowd it out of her mind. She quite agreed with me that the look in connection with the conversation was probably intended for the memory of his deceased wife. She was also perfectly convinced that her love was hopeless.

After this conversation I expected a decided change in her condition but for a time it did not take place. She continued depressed and moody—a course of hydrotherapy which I ordered for her at the same time refreshed her somewhat mornings. The odor of burned pastry did not entirely disappear; though it became rarer and feebler it appeared only, as she said, when she was very much excited.

The continuation of this memory symbol led me to believe that besides the principal scene it represented many smaller side traumas and I therefore investigated everything that might have been in any way connected with the scene of the burned pastry. We thus passed through the theme of family friction, the behavior of the grandfather and others, and with that the sensation of burned odor gradually disappeared. Just then there was a lengthy interruption occasioned by a new nasal affliction which led to the discovery of the caries of the ethmoid.

On her return she informed me that she received many Christmas presents from both gentlemen as well as from the household servants, as if they were trying to appease her and wipe away the recollection of the conflicts of the last months. These frank advances made no impression on her.

116

On questioning her on another occasion about the odor of burned pastry she stated that it had entirely disappeared, but instead she was now bothered by another and similar odor like the smoke of a cigar. This odor really existed before; it was only concealed by the odor of the pastry but now appeared by itself.

I was not very much pleased with the success of my treatment. What occurred here is what a mere symptomatic treatment [16] is generally blamed for, namely, that it removes one symptom only to make room for another. Nevertheless, I immediately set forth to remove this new memory symbol by analysis.

This time I did not know whence this subjective sensation of smell originated, nor on what important occasion it was objective. On being questioned she said, "They constantly smoke at home, I really don't know whether the smell which I feel has any particular significance." I then proposed that she should try to recall things under the pressure of my hands. I have already mentioned that her recollections were plastically vivid, that she was a "visual." Indeed under the pressure of my hands a picture came into her mind—at first only slowly and fragmentarily. It was the dining room of the house in which she waited with the children for the arrival of the gentlemen from the factory for dinner. —"Now we are all at the table, the gentlemen, the French maid, the housekeeper, the children and I. It is the same as usual." —"Just keep on looking at that picture. It will soon become developed and specialized." —"Yes, there is a guest, the chief accountant, an old gentleman who loves the children like his own grandchildren, but he dines with us so frequently that it is nothing unusual." —"Just have patience, keep on looking at the picture, something will certainly happen." —"Nothing happens. We leave the table, the children take leave and go with us up to the second floor as usual." —"Well?" —"It really is something unusual, I now recognize the scene. As the children take leave the chief accountant attempts to kiss them, but my master jumps up and shouts at him, 'Don't kiss the children!' I then experienced a stitch in the heart, and as the gentlemen were smoking, this odor remained in my memory."

This, therefore, was the second, deeper seated scene causing the trauma and leaving the memory symbol. But why was this scene so effective? I then asked her which scene happened first, this one or the one with the burned pastry? —"The last scene happened first by almost two months." —"Why did you feel the stitch at the father's interference? The reproof was not meant for you."—"It was really not right to rebuke an old gentleman in such mannner who was a dear friend and a guest, it could have been said quietly." —"Then you were really affected by your master's impetuosity? Were you perhaps ashamed of him, or have you thought, 'If he could become so impetuous to an old friend guest over such a trifle, how would he act towards me if I were his wife?'" —"No, that is not it."

[16] I.e., a treatment which cures only the symptoms of a disease and does not work on the root causes of the symptoms.

117

—"But still it was about his impetuosity?" —"Yes, about the kissing of the children, he never liked that." Under the pressure of my hands there emerged a still older scene which was the real effective trauma and which bestowed on the scene with the chief accountant the traumatic effectivity.

A few months before a lady friend visited the house and on leaving kissed both children on the lips. The father, who was present, controlled himself and said nothing to the lady, but when she left he was very angry at the unfortunate governess. He said that he held her responsible for this kissing; that it was her duty not to tolerate it; that she was neglecting her duties in allowing such things, and that if it ever happened again he would entrust the education of his children to some one else. This occurred while she believed herself loved and waited for a repetition of that serious and friendly talk. This episode shattered all her hopes. She thought: "If he can upbraid and threaten me on account of such a trifle, of which I am entirely innocent, I must have been mistaken, he never entertained any tenderer feelings towards me, else he would have been considerate." —It was evidently this painful scene that came to her as the father reprimanded the chief accountant for attempting to kiss the children.

On being visited by Miss Lucy R. two days after the last analysis I had to ask her what pleasant things happened to her. She looked as though transformed, she smiled and held her head aloft. For a moment I thought that after all I probably mistook the conditions and that the governess of the children had now become the bride of the master. But she soon dissipated all my suppositions, saying, "Nothing new happened. You really do not know me. You have always seen me while I was sick and depressed. I am otherwise always cheerful. On awakening yesterday morning my burden was gone and since then I feel well." [17] —"What do you think of your chances in the house?"—"I am perfectly clear about that. I know that I have none, and I am not going to be unhappy about it." —"Will you now be able to get along with the others in the house?" —"I believe so, because most of the trouble was due to my sensitiveness." —"Do you still love the master?"—"Certainly I love him, but that does not bother me much. One can think and feel as one wishes."

I now examined her nose and found that the pain and the reflex sensations had almost completely reappeared. She could distinguish odors, but she was uncertain when they were very intense. What part the nasal trouble played in the anosmia I must leave undecided.

The whole treatment extended over a period of nine weeks. Four months later I accidentally met the patient at one of our summer resorts— she was cheerful and stated that her health continued to be good.

---

[17] In Freud's view, cure is accomplished when the symbolic or "converted" forms of the traumatic event are penetrated and the real event concealed behind the symbol is brought to consciousness. Thus knowing and facing reality is health, and "fictionalizing" it, as we would say, is sickness. Freud did not, it should be noted, equate health with happiness.

Heart of Darkness

Joseph Conrad

Born Josef Teodor Konrad Nalecz Korzeniowski, Conrad (1857–1924) was the son of aristocratic Polish parents who died when he was quite young. He went to sea when he was sixteen, and worked for over twenty years in the merchant marine, making his way up to master. He learned English during this time, and when in 1889 he started writing his first novel, *Almayer's Folly,* he was already a distinguished prose stylist in his adopted language. In 1890 he took, for reasons which he himself scarcely understood, the command of a small steamer on the Congo. His experiences there had a profound effect upon him psychologically, as well as destroying his health, and the short novel *Heart of Darkness* published in 1902 grew out of what he saw and learned in the Congo. He spent the remainder of his life in England.

■

I

The *Nellie,* a cruising yawl, swung to her anchor without a flutter of the sails, and was at rest. The flood had made, the wind was nearly calm, and being bound down the river, the only thing for it was to come to and wait for the turn of the tide.

The sea-reach of the Thames stretched before us like the beginning of an interminable waterway. In the offing the sea and the sky were welded together without a joint, and in the luminous space the tanned sails of the barges drifting up with the tide seemed to stand still in red clusters of canvas sharply peaked, with gleams of varnished sprits. A haze rested on the low shores that ran out to sea in vanishing flatness. The air was dark above Gravesend, and farther back still seemed condensed into a mournful gloom, brooding motionless over the biggest, and the greatest, town on earth.

The Director of Companies was our captain and our host. We four affectionately watched his back as he stood in the bows looking to seaward. On the whole river there was nothing that looked half so nautical. He resembled a pilot, which to a seaman is trustworthiness personified. It was difficult to realize his work was not out there in the luminous estuary, but behind him, within the brooding gloom.

Between us there was, as I have already said somewhere, the bond of the sea. Besides holding our hearts together through long periods of separation, it had the effect of making us tolerant of each other's yarns— and even convictions. The Lawyer—the best of old fellows—had, because of his many years and many virtues, the only cushion on deck, and was lying on the only rug. The Accountant had brought out already a box of dominoes, and was toying architecturally with the bones. Marlow sat cross-legged right aft, leaning against the mizzenmast. He had sunken cheeks, a yellow complexion, a straight back, an ascetic aspect, and, with his arms dropped, the palms of hands outwards, resembled an idol. The Director, satisfied the anchor had good hold, made his way aft and sat down amongst us. We exchanged a few words lazily. Afterwards there was silence on board the yacht. For some reason or other we did not begin that game of dominoes. We felt meditative, and fit for nothing but placid staring. The day was ending in a serenity of still and exquisite brilliance. The water shone pacifically; the sky, without a speck, was a benign immensity of unstained light; the very mist on the Essex marsh was like a gauzy and radiant fabric, hung from the wooded rises inland, and draping the low shores in diaphanous folds. Only the gloom to the west, brooding over the upper reaches, became more sombre every minute, as if angered by the approach of the sun.

And at last, in its curved and imperceptible fall, the sun sank low, and from glowing white changed to a dull red without rays and without heat, as if about to go out suddenly, striken to death by the touch of that gloom brooding over a crowd of men.

Forthwith a change came over the waters, and the serenity became less brilliant but more profound. The old river in its broad reach rested unruffled at the decline of day, after ages of good service done to the race that peopled its banks, spread out in the tranquil dignity of a waterway leading to the uttermost ends of the earth. We looked at the venerable stream not in the vivid flush of a short day that comes and departs for ever, but in the august light of abiding memories. And indeed nothing is easier for a man who has, as the phrase goes, "followed the sea" with reverence and affection, than to evoke the great spirit of the past upon the lower reaches of the Thames. The tidal current runs to and fro in its unceasing service, crowded with memories of men and ships it had borne to the rest of home or to the battles of the sea. It had known and served all the men of whom the nation is proud, from Sir Francis Drake to Sir John Franklin, knights all, titled and untitled—the great knights-errant of the sea. It had borne all the ships whose names are like jewels flashing in the night of time, from the *Golden Hind* returning with her round flanks full of treasure, to be visited by the Queen's Highness and thus pass out of the gigantic tale, to the *Erebus* and *Terror*, bound on other conquests —and that never returned. It had known the ships and the men. They had sailed from Deptford, from Greenwich, from Erith—the adventurers and the settlers; kings' ships and the ships of men on 'Change; captains, admirals, the dark "interlopers" of the Eastern trade, and the commissioned "generals" of East India fleets. Hunters for gold or pursuers of fame, they all had gone out on that stream, bearing the sword, and often the torch, messengers of the might within the land, bearers of a spark from the sacred fire. What greatness had not floated on the ebb of that river into the mystery of an unknown earth! . . . The dreams of men, the seed of commonwealths, the germs of empires.

The sun set; the dusk fell on the stream, and lights began to appear along the shore. The Chapman lighthouse, a three-legged thing erect on a mud-flat, shone strongly. Lights of ships moved in the fairway—a great stir of lights going up and going down. And farther west on the upper reaches the place of the monstrous town was still marked ominously on the sky, a brooding gloom in sunshine, a lurid glare under the stars.

"And this also," said Marlow suddenly, "has been one of the dark places of the earth."

He was the only man of us who still "followed the sea." The worst that could be said of him was that he did not represent his class. He was a seaman, but he was a wanderer, too, while most seamen lead, if one may so express it, a sedentary life. Their minds are of the stay-at-home order, and their home is always with them—the ship; and so is their country—the sea. One ship is very much like another, and the sea is always the same. In the immutability of their surroundings the foreign shores, the foreign faces, the changing immensity of life, glide past, veiled not by a sense of mystery but by a slightly disdainful ignorance; for there is nothing mysterious to a seaman unless it be the sea itself, which is the mistress of his existence and as inscrutable as Destiny. For the rest, after his hours of work, a casual stroll or a casual spree on shore suffices to unfold for him the secret of a whole continent, and generally he finds the secret not worth knowing. The yarns of seamen have a direct simplicity, the whole meaning of which lies within the shell of a cracked nut. But Marlow was not typical (if his propensity to spin yarns be excepted), and to him the meaning of an episode was not inside like a kernel but outside, enveloping the tale which brought it out only as a glow brings out a haze, in the likeness of one of these misty halos that sometimes are made visible by the spectral illumination of moonshine.

His remark did not seem at all surprising. It was just like Marlow. It was accepted in silence. No one took the trouble to grunt even; and presently he said, very slow—

"I was thinking of very old times, when the Romans first came here, nineteen hundred years ago—the other day. . . . Light came out of this river since—you say Knights? Yes; but it is like a running blaze on a plain, like a flash of lightning in the clouds. We live in the flicker—may it last as long as the old earth keeps rolling! But darkness was here yesterday. Imagine the feelings of a commander of a fine—what d'ye call 'em? —trireme in the Mediterranean, ordered suddenly to the north run overland across the Gauls in a hurry; put in charge of one of these craft the legionaries—a wonderful lot of handy men they must have been, too —used to build, apparently by the hundred, in a month or two, if we may believe what we read. Imagine him here—the very end of the world, a sea the colour of lead, a sky the colour of smoke, a kind of ship about as rigid as a concertina—and going up this river with stores, or orders, or what you like. Sand-banks, marshes, forests, savages,—precious little to eat fit for a civilized man, nothing but Thames water to drink. No Falernian wine here, no going ashore. Here and there a military camp lost in a wilderness, like a needle in a bundle of hay—cold, fog, tempests, disease, exile, and death—death skulking in the air, in the water, in the bush. They must have been dying like flies here. Oh, yes—he did it. Did it very well, too, no doubt, and without thinking much about it either, except afterwards to brag of what he had gone through in his time, perhaps. They were men enough to face the darkness. And perhaps he was cheered by keeping his eye on a chance of promotion to the fleet at Ravenna by and by, if he had good friends in Rome and survived the awful climate. Or think of a decent young citizen in a toga—perhaps too much dice, you know—coming out here in the train of some prefect, or tax-gatherer, or trader even, to mend his fortunes. Land in a swamp, march through the woods, and in some inland post feel the savagery, the utter savagery, had closed round him—all that mysterious life of the wilderness that stirs in the forest, in the jungles, in the hearts of wild men. There's no initiation either into such mysteries. He has to live in the midst of the incomprehensible, which is also detestable. And it has a fascination, too, that goes to work upon him. The fascination of the abomination—you know, imagine the growing regrets, the longing to escape, the powerless disgust, the surrender, the hate."

He paused.

"Mind," he began again, lifting one arm from the elbow, the palm of the hand outwards, so that, with his legs folded before him, he had the pose of a Buddha preaching in European clothes and without a lotus-flower—"Mind, none of us would feel exactly like this. What saves us is efficiency—the devotion to efficiency. But these chaps were not much account, really. They were no colonists; their administration was merely a squeeze, and nothing more, I suspect. They were conquerors, and for that you want only brute force—nothing to boast of, when you have it, since your strength is just an accident arising from the weakness of others. They grabbed what they could get for the sake of what was to be got. It was just robbery with violence, aggravated murder on a great scale, and men going at it blind—as is very proper for those who tackle a darkness. The conquest of the earth, which mostly means the taking it away from those who have a different complexion or slightly flatter noses than ourselves, is not a pretty thing when you look into it too much. What redeems it is the idea only. An idea at the back of it; not a sentimental pretence but an idea; and an unselfish belief in the idea—something you can set up, and bow down before, and offer a sacrifice to. . . ."

He broke off. Flames glided in the river, small green flames, red flames, white flames, pursuing, overtaking, joining, crossing each other—then separating slowly or hastily. The traffic of the great city went on in the deepening night upon the sleepless river. We looked on, waiting patiently—there was nothing else to do till the end of the flood; but it was only after a long silence, when he said, in a hesitating voice, "I suppose you fellows remember I did once turn fresh-water sailor for a bit," that we knew we were fated, before the ebb began to run, to hear about one of Marlow's inconclusive experiences.

"I don't want to bother you much with what happened to me personally," he began, showing in this remark the weakness of many tellers of tales who seem so often unaware of what their audience would best like to hear; "yet to understand the effect of it on me you ought to know how I got out there, what I saw, how I went up that river to the place where I first met the poor chap. It was the farthest point of navigation and the culminating point of my experience. It seemed somehow to throw a kind of light on everything about me—and into my thoughts. It was sombre enough, too—and pitiful—not extraordinary in any way—not very clear either. No, not very clear. And yet it seemed to throw a kind of light.

"I had then, as you remember, just returned to London after a lot of Indian Ocean, Pacific, China Seas—a regular dose of the East—six years or so, and I was loafing about, hindering you fellows in your work and invading your homes, just as though I had got a heavenly mission to civilize you. It was very fine for a time, but after a bit I did get tired of resting. Then I began to look for a ship—I should think the hardest work on earth. But the ships wouldn't even look at me. And I got tired of that game, too.

"Now when I was a little chap I had a passion for maps. I would look for hours at South America, or Africa, or Australia, and lose myself in all the glories of exploration. At that time there were many blank spaces on the earth, and when I saw one that looked particularly inviting on a map (but they all look that) I would put my finger on it and say, 'When I grow up I will go there.' The North Pole was one of these places, I remember. Well, I haven't been there yet, and shall not try now. The glamour's off. Other places were scattered about the Equator, and in every sort of latitude all over the two hemispheres. I have been in some of them, and . . . well, we won't talk about that. But there was one yet—the biggest, the most blank, so to speak—that I had a hankering after.

"True, by this time it was not a blank space any more. It had got filled since my boyhood with rivers and lakes and names. It had ceased to be a blank space of delightful mystery—a white patch for a boy to dream gloriously over. It had become a place of darkness. But there was in it one river especially, a mighty big river, that you could see on the map, resembling an immense snake uncoiled, with its head in the sea, its body at rest curving afar over a vast country, and its tail lost in the depths of the land. And as I looked at the map of it in a ship-window, it fascinated me as a snake would a bird—a silly little bird. Then I remembered there was a big concern, a Company for trade on that river. Dash it all! I thought to myself, they can't trade without using some kind of craft on that lot of fresh water—steamboats! Why shouldn't I try to get charge of one? I went on along Fleet Street, but could not shake off the idea. The snake had charmed me.

"You understand it was a Continental concern, that Trading society; but I have a lot of relations living on the Continent, because it's cheap and not so nasty as it looks, they say.

"I am sorry to own I began to worry them. This was already a fresh departure for me. I was not used to get things that way, you know. I always went my own road and on my own legs where I had a mind to go. I wouldn't have believed it of myself; but, then—you see—I felt somehow I must get there by hook and by crook. So I worried them. The men said 'My dear fellow,' and did nothing. Then—would you believe it?—I tried the women. I, Charlie Marlow, set the women to work—to get a job. Heavens! Well, you see, the notion drove me. I had an aunt, a dear enthusiastic soul. She wrote: 'It will be delightful. I am ready to do anything, anything for you. It is a glorious idea. I know the wife of a very high personage in the Administration, and also a man who has lots of influence with,' etc., etc. She was determined to make no end of fuss to get me appointed skipper of a river steamboat, if such was my fancy.

"I got my appointment—of course; and I got it very quick. It appears the Company had received news that one of their captains had been killed in a scuffle with the natives. This was my chance, and it made me the more anxious to go. It was only months and months afterwards, when I made the attempt to recover what was left of the body, that I heard the original quarrel arose from a misunderstanding about some hens. Yes, two black hens. Fresleven—that was the fellow's name, a Dane—thought himself wronged somehow in the bargain, so he went ashore and started to hammer the chief of the village with a stick. Oh, it didn't surprise me in the least to hear this, and at the same time to be told that Fresleven was the gentlest, quietest creature that ever walked on two legs. No doubt he was; but he had been a couple of years already out there engaged in the noble cause, you know, and he probably felt the need at last of asserting his self-respect in some way. Therefore he whacked the old nigger mercilessly, while a big crowd of his people watched him, thunderstruck, till some man—I was told the chief's son—in desperation at hearing the old chap yell, made a tentative jab with a spear at the white man—and of course it went quite easy between the shoulder-blades. Then the whole population cleared into the forest, expecting all kinds of calamities to happen, while, on the other hand, the steamer Fresleven commanded left also in a bad panic, in charge of the engineer, I believe. Afterwards nobody seemed to trouble much about Fresleven's remains, till I got out and stepped into his shoes. I couldn't let it rest, though; but when an opportunity offered at last to meet my predecessor, the grass growing through his ribs was tall enough to hide his bones. They were all there. The supernatural being had not been touched after he fell. And the village was deserted, the huts gaped black, rotting, all askew within the fallen enclosures. A calamity had come to it, sure enough. The people had vanished. Mad terror had scattered them, men, women, and children, through the bush, and they had never returned. What became of the hens I don't know either. I should think the cause of progress got them, anyhow. However, through this glorious affair I got my appointment, before I had fairly begun to hope for it.

"I flew around like mad to get ready, and before forty-eight hours I was crossing the Channel to show myself to my employers, and sign the contract. In a very few hours I arrived in a city that always makes me think of a whited sepulchre. Prejudice no doubt. I had no difficulty in finding the Company's offices. It was the biggest thing in the town, and everybody I met was full of it. They were going to run an over-sea empire, and make no end of coin by trade.

"A narrow and deserted street in deep shadow, high houses, innumerable windows with venetian blinds, a dead silence, grass sprouting between the stones, imposing carriage archways right and left, immense double doors standing ponderously ajar. I slipped through one of these cracks, went up a swept and ungarnished staircase, as arid as a desert, and opened the first door I came to. Two women, one fat and the other slim, sat on straw-bottomed chairs, knitting black wool. The slim one got up and walked straight at me—still knitting with downcast eyes—and only just as I began to think of getting out of her way, as you would for a somnambulist, stood still, and looked up. Her dress was as plain as an umbrella-cover, and she turned round without a word and preceded me into a waiting-room. I gave my name, and looked about. Deal table in the middle, plain chairs all round the walls, on one end a large shining map, marked with all the colours of a rainbow. There was a vast amount of red—good to see at any time, because one knows that some real work is done in there, a deuce of a lot of blue, a little green, smears of orange, and, on the East Coast, a purple patch, to show where the jolly pioneers of progress drink the jolly lager-beer. However, I wasn't going into any of these. I was going into the yellow. Dead in the centre. And the river was there—fascinating—deadly—like a snake. Ough! A door opened, a white-haired secretarial head, but wearing a compassionate expression, appeared, and a skinny forefinger beckoned me into the sanctuary. Its light was dim, and a heavy writing-desk squatted in the middle. From behind that structure came out an impression of pale plumpness in a frock-coat. The great man himself. He was five feet six, I should judge, and had his grip on the handle-end of ever so many millions. He shook hands, I fancy, murmured vaguely, was satisfied with my French. *Bon voyage.*

"In about forty-five seconds I found myself again in the waiting-room with the compassionate secretary, who, full of desolation and sympathy, made me sign some document. I believe I undertook amongst other things not to disclose any trade secrets. Well, I am not going to.

125

"I began to feel slightly uneasy. You know I am not used to such ceremonies, and there was something ominous in the atmosphere. It was just as though I had been let into some conspiracy—I don't know—something not quite right; and I was glad to get out. In the outer room the two women knitted black wool feverishly. People were arriving, and the younger one was walking back and forth introducing them. The old one sat on her chair. Her flat cloth slippers were propped up on a foot-warmer, and a cat reposed on her lap. She wore a starched white affair on her head, had a wart on one cheek, and silver-rimmed spectacles hung on the tip of her nose. She glanced at me above the glasses. The swift and indifferent placidity of that look troubled me. Two youths with foolish and cheery countenances were being piloted over, and she threw at them the same quick glance of unconcerned wisdom. She seemed to know all about them and about me, too. An eerie feeling came over me. She seemed uncanny and fateful. Often far away there I thought of these two, guarding the door of Darkness, knitting black wool as for a warm pall, one introducing, introducing continuously to the unknown, the other scrutinizing the cheery and foolish faces with unconcerned old eyes. *Ave!* Old knitter of black wool. *Morituri te salutant.* Not many of those she looked at ever saw her again—not half, by a long way.

There was yet a visit to the doctor. 'A simple formality,' assured me the secretary, with an air of taking an immense part in all my sorrows. Accordingly a young chap wearing his hat over the left eyebrow, some clerk I suppose—there must have been clerks in the business, though the house was as still as a house in a city of the dead—came from somewhere up-stairs, and led me forth. He was shabby and careless, with ink-stains on the sleeves of his jacket, and his cravat was large and billowy, under a chin shaped like the toe of an old boot. It was a little too early for the doctor, so I proposed a drink, and thereupon he developed a vein of joviality. As we sat over our vermouths he glorified the Company's business, and by and by I expressed casually my surprise at him not going out there. He became very cool and collected all at once. 'I am not such a fool as I look, quoth Plato to his disciples,' he said sententiously, emptied his glass with great resolution, and we rose.

"The old doctor felt my pulse, evidently thinking of something else the while. 'Good, good for there,' he mumbled, and then with a certain eagerness asked me whether I would let him measure my head. Rather surprised, I said Yes, when he produced a thing like calipers and got the dimensions back and front and every way, taking notes carefully. He was an unshaven little man in a threadbare coat like a gaberdine, with feet in slippers, and I thought him a harmless fool. 'I always ask leave, in the interests of science, to measure the crania of those going out there,' he said. 'And when they come back, too?' I asked. 'Oh, I never see them,' he remarked; 'and, moreover, the changes take place inside, you know.' He smiled, as if at some quiet joke. 'So you are going out there. Famous. Interesting, too.' He gave me a searching glance, and made another note.

126

'Ever any madness in your family?' he asked, in a matter-of-fact tone. I felt very annoyed. 'Is that question in the interests of science, too?' 'It would be,' he said, without taking notice of my irritation, 'interesting for science to watch the mental changes of individuals, on the spot, but . . .' 'Are you an alienist?' I interrupted. 'Every doctor should be—a little,' answered that original, imperturbably. 'I have a little theory which you messieurs who go out there must help me to prove. This is my share in the advantages my country shall reap from the possession of such a magnificent dependency. The mere wealth I leave to others. Pardon my questions, but you are the first Englishman coming under my observation . . .' I hastened to assure him I was not in the least typical. 'If I were,' said I, 'I wouldn't be talking like this with you.' 'What you say is rather profound, and probably erroneous,' he said, with a laugh. 'Avoid irritation more than exposure to the sun. Adieu. In the tropics one must before everything keep calm.' . . . He lifted a warning forefinger . . . 'Du calme, du calme, Adieu.'

"One thing more remained to do—say good-bye to my excellent aunt. I found her triumphant. I had a cup of tea—the last decent cup of tea for many days—and in a room that most soothingly looked just as you would expect a lady's drawing-room to look, we had a long quiet chat by the fireside. In the course of these confidences it became quite plain to me I had been represented to the wife of the high dignitary, and goodness knows to how many more people besides, as an exceptional and gifted creature—a piece of good fortune for the Company—a man you don't get hold of every day. Good heavens! and I was going to take charge of a two-penny-half-penny river-steamboat with a penny whistle attached! It appeared, however, I was also one of the Workers, with a capital—you know. Something like an emissary of light, something like a lower sort of apostle. There had been a lot of such rot let loose in print and talk just about that time, and the excellent woman, living right in the rush of all that humbug, got carried off her feet. She talked about 'weaning those ignorant millions from their horrid ways,' till, upon my word, she made me quite uncomfortable. I ventured to hint that the Company was run for profit.

" 'You forget, dear Charlie, that the labourer is worthy of his hire,' she said, brightly. It's queer how out of touch with truth women are. They live in a world of their own, and there has never been anything like it, and never can be. It is too beautiful altogether, and if they were to set it up it would go to pieces before the first sunset. Some confounded fact we men have been living contentedly with ever since the day of creation would start up and knock the whole thing over.

"After this I got embraced, told to wear flannel, be sure to write often, and so on—and I left. In the street—I don't know why—a queer feeling came to me that I was an imposter. Odd thing that I, who used to clear out for any part of the world at twenty-four hours' notice, with less thought than most men give to the crossing of a street, had a moment—I won't say of hesitation, but of startled pause, before this commonplace affair. The best way I can explain it to you is by saying that, for a second or two, I felt as though, instead of going to the centre of a continent, 1 were about to set off for the centre of the earth.

"I left in a French steamer, and she called in every blamed port they have out there, for, as far as I could see, the sole purpose of landing soldiers and custom-house officers. I watched the coast. Watching a coast as it slips by the ship is like thinking about an enigma. There it is before you—smiling, frowning, inviting, grand, mean, insipid, or savage, and always mute with an air of whispering, 'Come and find out.' This one was almost featureless, as if still in the making, with an aspect of monotonous grimness. The edge of a colossal jungle, so dark-green as to be almost black, fringed with white surf, ran straight, like a ruled line, far, far away along a blue sea whose glitter was blurred by a creeping mist. The sun was fierce, the land seemed to glisten and drip with steam. Here and there greyish-whitish specks showed up clustered inside the white surf, with a flag flying above them perhaps. Settlements some centuries old, and still no bigger than pinheads on the untouched expanse of their background. We pounded along, stopped, landed soldiers; went on, landed custom-house clerks to levy toll in what looked like a God-forsaken wilderness, with a tin shed and a flag-pole lost in it; landed more soldiers—to take care of the custom-house clerks, presumably. Some, I heard, got drowned in the surf; but whether they did or not, nobody seemed particularly to care. They were just flung out there, and on we went. Every day the coast looked the same, as though we had not moved; but we passed various places—trading places—with names like Gran' Bassam, Little Popo; names that seemed to belong to some sordid farce acted in front of a sinister back-cloth. The idleness of a passenger, my isolation amongst all these men with whom I had no point of contact, the oily and languid sea, the uniform sombreness of the coast, seemed to keep me away from the truth of things, within the toil of a mournful and senseless delusion. The voice of the surf heard now and then was a positive pleasure, like the speech of a brother. It was something natural, that had its reason, that had a meaning. Now and then a boat from the shore gave one a momentary contact with reality. It was paddled by black fellows. You could see from afar the white of their eyeballs glistening. They shouted, sang; their bodies streamed with perspiration; they had faces like grotesque masks—these chaps; but they had bone, muscle, a wild vitality, an intense energy of movement, that was as natural and true as the surf along their coast. They wanted no excuse for being there. They were a great comfort to look at. For a time I would feel I belonged still to a world of straightforward facts; but the feeling would not last long. Something would turn up to scare it away. Once, I remember, we came upon a man-of-war anchored off the coast. There wasn't even a shed there, and she was shelling the bush. It appears the French had one of their wars going on thereabouts. Her ensign dropped limp like a rag; the muzzles of the long six-inch guns stuck out all over the low hull; the greasy, slimy swell swung her up lazily and let her down, swaying her thin masts. In the empty immensity of earth, sky, and water, there she was, incomprehensible, firing into a continent. Pop, would go one of the six-inch guns; a small flame would dart and vanish, a little white smoke would disappear, a tiny projectile would give a feeble screech—and nothing happened. Nothing could happen. There was a touch of insanity in the proceeding, a sense of lugubrious drollery in the sight; and it was not dissipated by somebody on board assuring me earnestly there was a camp of natives—he called them enemies!—hidden out of sight somewhere.

"We gave her her letters (I heard the men in that lonely ship were dying of fever at the rate of three a day) and went on. We called at some more places with farcical names, where the merry dance of death and trade goes on in a still and earthy atmosphere as of an overheated catacomb; all along the formless coast bordered by dangerous surf, as if Nature herself had tried to ward off intruders; in and out of rivers, streams of death in life, whose banks were rotting into mud, whose waters, thickened into slime, invaded the contorted mangroves, that seemed to writhe at us in the extremity of an impotent despair. Nowhere did we stop long enough to get a particularized impression, but the general sense of vague and oppressive wonder grew upon me. It was like a weary pilgrimage amongst hints for nightmares.

"It was upward of thirty days before I saw the mouth of the big river. We anchored off the seat of the government. But my work would not begin till some two hundred miles farther on. So as soon as I could I made a start for a place thirty miles higher up.

"I had my passage on a little sea-going steamer. Her captain was a Swede, and knowing me for a seaman, invited me on the bridge. He was a young man, lean, fair, and morose, with lanky hair and a shuffling gait. As we left the miserable little wharf, he tossed his head contemptuously at the shore. 'Been living there?' he asked. I said, 'Yes.' 'Fine lot these government chaps—are they not?' he went on, speaking English with great precision and considerable bitterness. 'It is funny what some people will do for a few francs a month. I wonder what becomes of that kind when it goes upcountry?' I said to him I expected to see that soon. 'So-o-o!' he exclaimed. He shuffled athwart, keeping one eye ahead vigilantly. 'Don't be too sure,' he continued. 'The other day I took up a man who hanged himself on the road. He was a Swede, too.' 'Hanged himself! Why, in God's name?' I cried. He kept on looking out watchfully. 'Who knows? The sun too much for him, or the country perhaps.'

At last we opened a reach. A rocky cliff appeared, mounds of turned-up earth by the shore, houses on a hill, others with iron roofs, amongst a waste of excavations, or hanging to the declivity. A continuous noise of the rapids above hovered over this scene of inhabited devastation. A lot of people, mostly black and naked, moved about like ants. A jetty pro-

129

jected into the river. A blinding sunlight drowned all this at times in a sudden recrudescence of glare. 'There's your Company's station,' said the Swede, pointing to three wooden barrack-like structures on the rocky slope. 'I will send your things up. Four boxes did you say? So. Farewell.'

"I came upon a boiler wallowing in the grass, then found a path leading up the hill. It turned aside for the boulders, and also for an undersized railway-truck lying there on its back with its wheels in the air. One was off. The thing looked as dead as the carcass of some animal. I came upon more pieces of decaying machinery, a stack of rusty rails. To the left a clump of trees made a shady spot, where dark things seemed to stir feebly. I blinked, the path was steep. A horn tooted to the right, and I saw the black people run. A heavy and dull detonation shook the ground, a puff of smoke came out of the cliff, and that was all. No change appeared on the face of the rock. They were building a railway. The cliff was not in the way or anything; but this objectless blasting was all the work going on.

"A slight clinking behind me made me turn my head. Six black men advanced in a file, toiling up the path. They walked erect and slow, balancing small baskets full of earth on their heads, and the clink kept time with their footsteps. Black rags were wound round their loins, and the short ends behind waggled to and fro like tails. I could see every rib, the joints of their limbs were like knots in a rope; each had an iron collar on his neck, and all were connected together with a chain whose bights swung between them, rhythmically clinking. Another report from the cliff made me think suddenly of that ship of war I had seen firing into a continent. It was the same kind of ominous voice; but these men could by no stretch of imagination be called enemies. They were called criminals, and the outraged law, like the bursting shells, had come to them, an insoluble mystery from the sea. All their meagre breasts panted together, the violently dilated nostrils quivered, the eyes stared stonily uphill. They passed me within six inches, without a glance, with that complete, death-like indifference of unhappy savages. Behind this raw matter one of the reclaimed, the product of the new forces at work, strolled despondently, carrying a rifle by its middle. He had a uniform jacket with one button off, and seeing a white man on the path, hoisted his weapon to his shoulder with alacrity. This was simple prudence, white men being so much alike at a distance that he could not tell who I might be. He was speedily reassured, and with a large, white, rascally grin, and a glance at his charge, seemed to take me into partnership in his exalted trust. After all, I also was a part of the great cause of these high and just proceedings.

"Instead of going up, I turned and descended to the left. My idea was to let that chain-gang get out of sight before I climbed the hill. You know I am not particularly tender; I've had to strike and to fend off. I've had to resist and to attack sometimes—that's only one way of resisting—without counting the exact cost, according to the demands of such sort of life as I had blundered into. I've seen the devil of violence, and the devil of greed, and the devil of hot desire; but, by all the stars! these were strong, lusty, red-eyed devils, that swayed and drove men—men, I tell you. But as I stood on the hillside, I foresaw that in the blinding sunshine of that land I would become acquainted with a flabby, pretending, weak-eyed devil of a rapacious and pitiless folly. How insidious he could be, too, I was only to find out several months later and a thousand miles farther. For a moment I stood appalled, as though by a warning. Finally I descended the hill, obliquely, towards the trees I had seen.

"I avoided a vast artificial hole somebody had been digging on the slope, the purpose of which I found it impossible to divine. It wasn't a quarry or a sandpit, anyhow. It was just a hole. It might have been connected with the philanthropic desire of giving the criminals something to do. I don't know. Then I nearly fell into a very narrow ravine, almost no more than a scar in the hillside. I discovered that a lot of imported drainage-pipes for the settlement had been tumbled in there. There wasn't one that was not broken. It was a wanton smash-up. At last I got under the trees. My purpose was to stroll into the shade for a moment; but no sooner within than it seemed to me I had stepped into the gloomy circle of some Inferno. The rapids were near, and an uninterrupted, uniform, headlong, rushing noise filled the mournful stillness of the grove, where not a breath stirred, not a leaf moved, with a mysterious sound—as though the tearing pace of the launched earth had suddenly become audible.

"Black shapes crouched, lay, sat between the trees leaning against the trunks, clinging to the earth, half coming out, half effaced within the dim light, in all the attitudes of pain, abandonment, and despair. Another mine on the cliff went off, followed by a slight shudder of the soil under my feet. The work was going on. The work! And this was the place where some of the helpers had withdrawn to die.

They were dying slowly—it was very clear. They were not enemies, they were not criminals, they were nothing earthly now—nothing but black shadows of disease and starvation, lying confusedly in the greenish gloom. Brought from all the recesses of the coast in all the legality of time contracts, lost in uncongenial surroundings, fed on unfamiliar food, they sickened, became inefficient, and were then allowed to crawl away and rest. These moribund shapes were free as air—and nearly as thin. I began to distinguish the gleam of the eyes under the trees. Then, glancing down, I saw a face near my hand. The black bones reclined at full length with one shoulder against the tree, and slowly the eyelids rose and the sunken eyes looked up at me, enormous and vacant, a kind of blind, white flicker in the depths of the orbs, which died out slowly. The man seemed young —almost a boy—but you know with them it's hard to tell. I found nothing else to do but to offer him one of my good Swede's ship's biscuits I had in my pocket. The fingers closed slowly on it and held—there was no other movement and no other glance. He had tied a bit of white worsted round his neck—Why? Where did he get it? Was it a badge—an ornament—a charm—a propitiatory act? Was there any idea at all connected with it? It looked startling round his black neck, this bit of white thread from beyond the seas.

"Near the same tree two more bundles of acute angles sat with their legs drawn up. One, with his chin propped on his knees, stared at nothing, in an intolerable and appalling manner: his brother phantom rested its forehead, as if overcome with a great weariness; and all about others were scattered in every pose of contorted collapse, as in some picture of a massacre or a pestilence. While I stood horror-struck, one of these creatures rose to his hands and knees, and went off on all-fours towards the river to drink. He lapped out of his hand, then sat up in the sunlight, crossing his shins in front of him, and after a time let his woolly head fall on his breastbone.

"I didn't want any more loitering in the shade, and I made haste towards the station. When near the buildings I met a white man, in such an unexpected elegance of getup that in the first moment I took him for a sort of vision. I saw a high starched collar, white cuffs, a light alpaca jacket, snowy trousers, a clean necktie, and varnished boots. No hat. Hair parted, brushed, oiled, under a green-lined parasol held in a big white hand. He was amazing, and had a penholder behind his ear.

"I shook hands with this miracle, and I learned he was the Company's chief accountant, and that all the bookkeeping was done at this station. He had come out for a moment, he said, 'to get a breath of fresh air.' The expression sounded wonderfully odd, with its suggestion of sedentary desk-life. I wouldn't have mentioned the fellow to you at all, only it was from his lips that I first heard the name of the man who is so indissolubly connected with the memories of that time. Moreover, I respected the fellow. Yes; I respected his collars, his vast cuffs, his brushed hair. His appearance was certainly that of a hairdresser's dummy; but in the great demoralization of the land he kept up his appearance. That's backbone. His starched collars and got-up shirt-fronts were achievements of character. He had been out nearly three years; and later, I could not help asking him how he managed to sport such linen. He had just the faintest blush, and said modestly, 'I've been teaching one of the native women about the station. It was difficult. She had a distaste for the work.' Thus this man had verily accomplished something. And he was devoted to his books, which were in apple-pie order.

"Everything else in the station was in a muddle—heads, things, buildings. Strings of dusty niggers with splay feet arrived and departed; a stream of manufactured goods, rubbishy cottons, beads, and brass-wire set into the depths of darkness, and in return came a precious trickle of ivory.

"I had to wait in the station for ten days—an eternity. I lived in a hut in the yard, but to be out of the chaos I would sometimes get into the accountant's office. It was built of horizontal planks, and so badly put together that, as he bent over his high desk, he was barred from neck to heels with narrow strips of sunlight. There was no need to open the big shutter to see. It was hot there, too; big flies buzzed fiendishly, and did not sting, but stabbed. I sat generally on the floor, while, of faultless appearance (and even slightly scented), perching on a high stool, he wrote, he wrote. Sometimes he stood up for exercise. When a truckle-bed with a sick man (some invalid agent from upcountry) was put in there, he exhibited a gentle annoyance. 'The groans of this sick person,' he said, 'distract my attention. And without that it is extremely difficult to guard against clerical errors in this climate.'

"One day he remarked, without lifting his head, 'In the interior you will no doubt meet Mr. Kurtz.' On my asking who Mr. Kurtz was, he said he was a first-class agent; and seeing my disappointment at this information, he added slowly, laying down his pen, 'He is a very remarkable person.' Further questions elicited from him that Mr. Kurtz was at present in charge of a trading-post, a very important one, in the true ivory-country, at the very bottom of there. Sends in as much ivory as all the others put together . . .' He began to write again. The sick man was too ill to groan. The flies buzzed in a great peace.

"Suddenly there was a growing murmur of voices and a great tramping of feet. A caravan had come in. A violent babble of uncouth sounds burst out on the other side of the planks. All the carriers were speaking together, and in the midst of the uproar the lamentable voice of the chief agent was heard 'giving it up' tearfully for the twentieth time that day. . . . He rose slowly. 'What a frightful row,' he said. He crossed the room gently to look at the sick man, and returning, said to me, 'He does not hear.' 'What! Dead?' I asked, startled. 'No, not yet,' he answered, with great composure. Then, alluding with a toss of the head to the tumult in the station-yard, 'When one has got to make correct entries, one comes to hate those savages—hate them to death.' He remained thoughtful for a moment. 'When you see Mr. Kurtz' he went on, 'tell him from me that everything here'—he glanced at the deck—'is very satisfactory. I don't like to write to him—with those messengers of ours you never know who may get hold of your letter—at that Central Station.' He stared at me for a moment with his mild bulging eyes. 'Oho, he will go far, very far,' he began again. 'He will be a somebody in the Administration before long. They, above—the Council in Europe, you know—mean him to be.'

"He turned to his work. The noise outside had ceased, and presently in going out I stopped at the door. In the steady buzz of flies the homeward-bound agent was lying flushed and insensible; the other, bent over his books, was making correct entries of perfectly correct transactions; and fifty feet below the doorstep I could see the still treetops of the grove of death.

"Next day I left that station at last, with a caravan of sixty men, for a two-hundred-mile tramp.

"No use telling you much about that. Paths, paths, everywhere; a stamped-in network of paths spreading over the empty land, through the long grass, through burnt grass, through thickets, down and up chilly ravines, up and down stony hills ablaze with heat; and a solitude, a solitude, nobody, not a hut. The population had cleared out a long time ago. Well, if a lot of mysterious niggers armed with all kinds of fearful weapons suddenly took to travelling on the road between Deal and Gravesend, catching the yokels right and left to carry loads for them, I fancy every farm and cottage thereabouts would get empty very soon. Only here the dwellings were gone, too. Still I passed through several abandoned villages. There's something pathetically childish in the ruins of grass walls. Day after day, with the stamp and shuffle of sixty pairs of bare feet behind me, each pair under a 60-lb. load. Camp, cook, sleep, strike camp, march. Now and then a carrier dead in harness, at rest in the long grass near the path, with an empty water-gourd and his long staff lying by his side. A great silence around and above. Perhaps on some quiet night the tremor of far-off drums, sinking, swelling, a tremor vast, faint; a sound weird, appealing, suggestive, and wild—and perhaps with as profound a meaning as the sound of bells in a Christian country. Once a white man in an unbuttoned uniform, camping on the path with an armed escort of lank Zanzibaris, very hospitable and festive—not to say drunk. Was looking after the upkeep of the road, he declared. Can't say I saw any road or any upkeep, unless the body of a middle-aged negro, with a bullet-hole in the forehead, upon which I absolutely stumbled three miles farther on, may be considered as a permanent improvement. I had a white companion, too, not a bad chap, but rather too fleshy and with the exasperating habit of fainting on the hot hillsides, miles away from the least bit of shade and water. Annoying, you know, to hold your own coat like a parasol over a man's head while he is coming to. I couldn't help asking him once what he meant by coming there at all. 'To make money, of course. What do you think?' he said, scornfully. Then he got fever, and had to be carried in a hammock slung under a pole. As he weighed sixteen stone I had no end of rows with the carriers. They jibbed, ran away, sneaked off with their loads in the night—quite a mutiny. So, one evening, I made a speech in English with gestures, not one of which was lost to the sixty pairs of eyes before me, and the next morning I started the hammock off in front all right. An hour afterwards I came upon the whole concern wrecked in a bush—man, hammock, groans, blankets, horrors. The heavy pole had skinned his poor nose. He was very anxious for me to kill somebody, but there wasn't the shadow of a carrier near. I remembered the old doctor—'It would be interesting for science to watch the mental changes of individuals, on the spot.' I felt I was becoming scientifically interesting. However, all that is to no purpose. On the fifteenth day I came in sight of the big river again, and hobbled into the Central Station. It was on a back water surrounded by scrub and forest, with a pretty border of smelly mud on one side, and on the three others enclosed by a crazy fence of rushes. A neglected gap was all the gate it had, and the first glance at the place was enough to let you see the flabby devil was running that show. White men with long staves in their hands appeared languidly from amongst the buildings, strolling up to take a look at me, and then retired out of sight somewhere. One of them, a stout, excitable chap with black moustaches, informed me with great volubility and many digressions, as soon as I told him who I was, that my steamer was at the bottom of the river. I was thunderstruck. What, how, why? Oh, it was 'all right.' The 'manager hmself' was there. All quite correct. 'Everybody had behaved splendidly! Splendidly!'—'you must,' he said in agitation, 'go and see the general manager at once. He is waiting!'

"I did not see the real significance of that wreck at once. I fancy I see it now, but I am not sure—not at all. Certainly the affair was too stupid—when I think of it—to be altogether natural. Still . . . But at the moment it presented itself simply as a confounded nuisance. The steamer was sunk. They had started two days before in a sudden hurry up the river with the manager on board, in charge of some volunteer skipper, and before they had been out there three hours they tore the bottom out of her on stones, and she sank near the south bank. I asked myself what I was to do there, now my boat was lost. As a matter of fact, I had plenty to do in fishing my command out of the river. I had set about it the very next day. That, and the repairs when I brought the pieces to the station, took some months.

"My first interview with the manager was curious. He did not ask me to sit down after my twenty-mile walk that morning. He was commonplace in complexion, in feature, in manners, and in voice. He was of middle size and of ordinary build. His eyes, of the usual blue, were perhaps remarkably cold, and he certainly could make his glance fall on one as trenchant and heavy as an axe. But even at these times the rest of his person seemed to disclaim the intention. Otherwise there was only an indefinable, faint expression of his lips, something stealthy—a smile—not a smile—I remember it, but I can't explain. It was unconscious, this smile was, though just after he had said something it got intensified for an instant. It came at the end of his speeches like a seal applied on the words to make the meaning of the commonest phrase appear absolutely inscrutable. He was a common trader, from his youth up employed in these parts—nothing more. He was obeyed, yet he inspired neither love nor fear, nor even respect. He inspired uneasiness. That was it! Uneasiness. Not a definite mistrust—just uneasiness—nothing more. You have no idea how effective such a . . . a . . . faculty can be. He had no genius for organizing, for initiative, or for order even. That was evident in such things as the deplorable state of the station. He had no learning, and no intelligence. His position had come to him—why? Perhaps because he was never ill . . . He had served three terms of three years out there . . . Because triumphant health in the general rout of constitutions is a kind of power in itself. When he went home on leave he rioted on a large scale—pompously. Jack ashore—with a difference—in externals only. This one could gather from his casual talk. He originated nothing, he could keep the routine going—that's all. But he was great. He was great by this little thing that it was impossible to tell what could control such a man. He never gave that secret away. Perhaps there was nothing within him. Such a suspicion made one pause—for out there there were no external checks. Once when various tropical diseases had laid low almost every 'agent' in the station, he was heard to say, 'Men who come out here should have no entrails.' He sealed the utterance with that smile of his, as though it had been a door opening into a darkness he had in his keeping. You fancied you had seen things—but the seal was on. When annoyed at mealtimes by the constant quarrels of the white men about precedence, he ordered an immense round table to be made, for which a special house had to be built. This was the station's mess-room. Where he sat was the first place—the rest were nowhere. One felt this to be his unalterable conviction. He was neither civil nor uncivil. He was quiet. He allowed his 'boy'—an overfed young negro from the coast—to treat the white men, under his very eyes, with provoking insolence.

"He began to speak as soon as he saw me. I had been very long on the road. He could not wait. Had to start without me. The up-river stations had to be relieved. There had been so many delays already that he did not know who was dead and who was alive, and how they got on— and so on, and so on. He paid no attention to my explanation, and, playing with a stick of sealing-wax, repeated several times that the situation was 'very grave, very grave.' There were rumours that a very important station was in jeopardy, and its chief, Mr. Kurtz, was ill. Hoped it was not true. Mr. Kurtz was . . . I felt weary and irritable. Hang Kurtz, I thought. I interrupted him by saying I had heard of Mr. Kurtz on the coast. 'Ah! So they talk of him down there,' he murmured to himself. Then he began again, assuring me Mr. Kurtz was the best agent he had, an exceptional man, of the greatest importance to the Company; therefore I could understand his anxiety. He was, he said, 'very, very uneasy.' Certainly he fidgeted on his chair a good deal, exclaimed, 'Ah, Mr. Kurtz!' broke the stick of sealing-wax and seemed dumfounded by the accident. Next thing he wanted to know 'how long it would take to' . . . I interrupted him again. Being hungry, you know, and kept on my feet too, I was getting savage. 'How can I tell?' I said. 'I haven't even seen the wreck yet—some months, no doubt.' All this talk seemed to me so futile. 'Some months,' he said. 'Well, let us say three months before we can make a start. Yes. That ought to do the affair.' I flung out of his hut (he lived all alone in a clay hut with a sort of verandah) muttering to myself my opinion of him. He was a chattering idiot. Afterwards I took it back when it was borne in upon me startlingly with what extreme nicety he had estimated the time requisite for the 'affair.'

"I went to work the next day, turning, so to speak, my back on that station. In that way only it seemed to me I could keep my hold on the redeeming facts of life. Still, one must look about sometimes; and then I saw this station, these men strolling aimlessly about in the sunshine of the yard. I asked myself sometimes what it all meant. They wandered here and there with their absurd long staves in their hands, like a lot of faithless pilgrims bewitched inside a rotten fence. The word 'ivory' rang in the air, was whispered, was sighed. You would think they were praying to it. A taint of imbecile rapacity blew through it all, like a whiff from some corpse. By Jove! I've never seen anything so unreal in my life. And outside, the silent wilderness surrounding this cleared speck on the earth struck me as something great and invincible, like evil or truth, waiting patiently for the passing away of this fantastic invasion.

"Oh, these months! Well, never mind. Various things happened. One evening a grass shed full of calico, cotton prints, beads, and I don't know what else, burst into a blaze so suddenly that you would have thought the earth had opened to let an avenging fire consume all that trash. I was smoking my pipe quietly by my dismantled steamer, and saw them all cutting capers in the light, with their arms lifted high, when the stout man with moustaches came tearing down to the river, a tin pail in his hand, assured me that everybody was 'behaving splendidly, splendidly,' dipped about a quart of water and tore back again. I noticed there was a hole in the bottom of his pail.

"I strolled up. There was no hurry. You see the thing had gone off like a box of matches. It had been hopeless from the very first. The flame had leaped high, driven everybody back, lighted up everything—and collapsed. The shed was already a heap of embers glowing fiercely. A nigger was being beaten near by. They said he had caused the fire in some way; be that as it may, he was screeching most horribly. I saw him, later, for several days, sitting in a bit of shade looking very sick and trying to recover himself: afterwards he arose and went out—and the wilderness without a sound took him into its bosom again. As I approached the glow from the dark I found myself at the back of two men, talking. I heard the name of Kurtz pronounced, then the words, "take advantage of this unfortunate accident.' One of the men was the manager. I wished him a good evening. 'Did you ever see anything like it—eh? it is incredible,' he said, and walked off. The other man remained. He was a first-class agent, young, gentlemanly, a bit reserved, with a forked little beard and a hooked nose. He was stand-offish with the other agents, and they on their side said he was the manager's spy upon them. As to me, I had hardly ever spoken to him before. We got into talk, and by and by we strolled away from the hissing ruins. Then he asked me to his room, which was in the main building of the station. He struck a match, and I perceived that this young aristocrat had not only a silver-mounted dressing-case but also a whole candle all to himself. Just at that time the manager was the only man supposed to have any right to candles. Native mats covered the clay walls; a collection of spears, assegais, shields, knives was hung up in trophies. The business intrusted to this fellow was the making of bricks—so I had been informed; but there wasn't a fragment of a brick anywhere in the station, and he could not make bricks without something, I don't know what— straw maybe. Anyway, it could not be found there and as it was not likely to be sent from Europe, it did not appear clear to me what he was waiting for. An act of special creation perhaps. However, they were all waiting—all the sixteen or twenty pilgrims of them—for something; and upon my word it did not seem an uncongenial occupation, from the way they took it, though the only thing that ever came to them was disease— as far as I could see. They beguiled the time by backbiting and in- triguing against each other in a foolish kind of way. There was an air of plotting about that station, but nothing came of it, of course. It was as unreal as everything else—as the philanthropic pretence of the whole concern, as their talk, as their government, as their show of work. The only real feeling was a desire to get appointed to a trading-post where ivory was to be had, so that they could earn percentages. They intrigued and slandered and hated each other only on that account—but as to effectually lifting a little finger—oh, no. By heavens! there is something after all in the world allowing one man to steal a horse while another must not look at a halter. Steal a horse straight out. Very well. He has done it. Perhaps he can ride. But there is a way of looking at a halter that would provoke the most charitable of saints into a kick.

"I had no idea why he wanted to be sociable, but as we chatted in there it suddenly occurred to me the fellow was trying to get at some- thing—in fact, pumping me. He alluded constantly to Europe, to the people I was supposed to know there—putting leading questions as to my acquaintances in the sepulchral city, and so on. His little eyes glit- tered like mica discs—with curiosity—though he tried to keep up a bit of superciliousness. At first I was astonished, but very soon I became aw- fully curious to see what he would find out from me. I couldn't possibly imagine what I had in me to make it worth his while. It was very pretty to see how he baffled himself, for in truth my body was full only of chills, and my head had nothing in it but that wretched steamboat business. It was evident he took me for a perfectly shameless prevaricator. At last he got angry, and, to conceal a movement of furious annoyance, he yawned. I rose. Then I noticed a small sketch in oils, on a panel, repre- senting a woman, draped and blindfolded, carrying a lighted torch. The background was sombre—almost black. The movement of the woman was stately, and the effect of the torchlight on the face was sinister.

"It arrested me, and he stood by civilly, holding an empty half-pint champagne bottle (medical comforts) with the candle stuck in it. To my question he said Mr. Kurtz had painted this—in this very station more than a year ago—while waiting for means to go to his trading-post. 'Tell me, pray,' said I, 'who is this Mr. Kurtz?'

" 'The chief of the Inner Station,' he answered in a short tone, looking away. 'Much obliged,' I said, laughing. 'And you are the brickmaker of the Central Station. Every one knows that.' He was silent for a while.

'He is a prodigy,' he said at last. 'He is an emissary of pity and science and progress, and devil knows what else. We want,' he began to declaim suddenly, 'for the guidance of the cause intrusted to us by Europe, so to speak, higher intelligence, wide sympathies, a singleness of purpose.' 'Who says that?' I asked. 'Lots of them,' he replied. 'Some even write that; and so *he* comes here, a special being, as you ought to know.' 'Why ought I to know?' I interrupted, really surprised. He paid no attention. 'Yes. Today he is chief of the best station, next year he will be assistant-manager, two years more and . . . but I daresay you know what he will be in two years' time. You are of the new gang—the gang of virtue. The same people who sent him specially also recommended you. Oh, don't say no. I've my own eyes to trust.' Light dawned upon me. My dear aunt's influential acquaintances were producing an unexpected effect upon that young man. I nearly burst into a laugh. 'Do you read the Company's confidential correspondence?' I asked. He hadn't a word to say. It was great fun. 'When Mr. Kurtz,' I continued, severely, 'is General Manager, you won't have the opportunity.'

"He blew the candle out suddenly, and we went outside. The moon had risen. Black figures strolled about listlessly, pouring water on the glow, whence proceeded a sound of hissing; steam ascended in the moonlight, the beaten nigger groaned somewhere. 'What a row the brute makes!' said the indefatigable man with the moustaches, appearing near us. 'Serve him right. Transgression—punishment—bang! Pitiless, pitiless. That's the only way. This will prevent all conflagrations for the future. I was just telling the manager . . .' He noticed my companion, and became crestfallen all at once. 'Not in bed yet,' he said, with a kind of servile heartiness; 'it's so natural. Ha! Danger—agitation.' He vanished. I went on to the riverside, and the other followed me. I heard a scathing murmur at my ear, 'Heap of muffs—go to.' The pilgrims could be seen in knots gesticulating, discussing. Several had still their staves in their hands. I verily believe they took these sticks to bed with them. Beyond the fence the forest stood up spectrally in the moonlight, and through the dim stir, through the faint sounds of that lamentable courtyard, the silence of the land went home to one's very heart—it's mystery, its greatness, the amazing reality of its concealed life. The hurt nigger moaned feebly somewhere near by, and then fetched a deep sigh that made me mend my pace away from there. I felt a hand introducing itself under my arm. 'My dear sir,' said the fellow, 'I don't want to be misunderstood, and especially by you, who will see Mr. Kurtz long before I can have that pleasure. I wouldn't like him to get a false idea of my disposition. . . .'

"I let him run on, this papier-maché Mephistopheles, and it seemed to me that if I tried I could poke my forefinger through him, and would find nothing inside but a little loose dirt, maybe. He, don't you see, had been planning to be assistant-manager by and by under the present man, and I could see that the coming of that Kurtz had upset them both not a little. He talked precipitately, and I did not try to stop him. I had my shoulders against the wreck of my steamer, hauled up on the slope like a carcass of some big river animal. The smell of mud, of primeval mud, by Jove! was in my nostrils, the high stillness of primeval forest was before my eyes; there were shiny patches on the black creek. The moon had spread over everything a thin layer of silver—over the rank grass, over the mud, upon the wall of matted vegetation standing higher than the wall of a temple, over the great river I could see through a sombre gap glittering, glittering, as it flowed broadly by without a murmur. All this was great, expectant, mute, while the man jabbered about himself. I wondered whether the stillness on the face of the immensity looking at us two were meant as an appeal or as a menace. What were we who had strayed in here? Could we handle that dumb thing, or would it handle us? I felt how big, how confoundedly big, was that thing that couldn't talk, and perhaps was deaf as well. What was in there? I could see a little ivory coming out from there, and I had heard Mr. Kurtz was in there. I had heard enough about it, too—God knows! Yet somehow it didn't bring any image with it—no more than if I had been told an angel or a field was in there. I believed it in the same way one of you might believe there are inhabitants in the planet Mars. I knew once a Scotch sailmaker who was certain, dead sure, there were people in Mars. If you asked him for some idea how they looked and behaved, he would get shy and mutter something about 'walking on all-fours.' If you as much as smiled, he would—though a man of sixty—offer to fight you. I would not have gone so far as to fight for Kurtz, but I went for him near enough to lie. You know I hate, detest, and can't bear a lie, not because I am straighter than the rest of us, but simply because it appalls me. There is a taint of death, a flavour of mortality in lies—which is exactly what I hate and detest in the world—what I want to forget. It makes me miserable and sick, like biting something rotten would do. Temperament, I suppose. Well, I went near enough to it by letting the young fool there believe anything he liked to imagine as to my influence in Europe. I became in an instant as much of a pretence as the rest of the bewitched pilgrims. This simply because I had a notion it somehow would be of help to that Kurtz whom at the time I did not see—you understand. He was just a word for me. I did not see the man in the name any more than you do. Do you see him? Do you see the story? Do you see anything? It seems to me I am trying to tell you a dream—making a vain attempt, because no relation of a dream can convey the dream-sensation, that commingling of absurdity, surprise, and bewilderment in a tremor of struggling revolt, that notion of being captured by the incredible which is of the very essence of dreams. . . ."

He was silent for a while.

". . . No, it is impossible; it is impossible to convey the life-sensation of any given epoch of one's existence—that which makes its truth, its meaning—its subtle and penetrating essence. It is impossible. We live, as we dream—alone. . . ."

140

He paused again as if reflecting, then added:

"Of course in this you fellows see more than I could then. You see me, whom you know. . . ."

It had become so pitch dark that we listeners could hardly see one another. For a long time already he, sitting apart, had been no more to us than a voice. There was not a word from anybody. The others might have been asleep, but I was awake. I listened, I listened on the watch for the sentence, for the word, that would give me the clue to the faint uneasiness inspired by his narrative that seemed to shape itself without human lips in the heavy night-air of the river.

". . . Yes—I let him run on," Marlow began again, "and think what he pleased about the powers that were behind me. I did! And there was nothing behind me! There was nothing but that wretched, old, mangled steamboat I was leaning against, while he talked fluently about 'the necessity for every man to get on.' 'And when one comes out here, you conceive, it is not to gaze at the moon.' Mr. Kurtz was a 'universal genius,' but even a genius would find it easier to work with 'adequate tools—intelligent men.' He did not make bricks—why, there was a physical impossibility in the way—as I was well aware; and if he did secretarial work for the manager, it was because 'no sensible man rejects wantonly the confidence of his superiors.' Did I see it? I saw it. What more did I want? What I really wanted was rivets, by heaven! Rivets. To get on with the work—to stop the hole. Rivets I wanted. There were cases of them down at the coast—cases—piled up—burst—split! You kicked a loose rivet at every second step in that station-yard on the hillside. Rivets had rolled into the grove of death. You could fill your pockets with rivets for the trouble of stooping down—and there wasn't one rivet to be found where it was wanted. We had plates that would do, but nothing to fasten them with. And every week the messenger, a lone negro, letter-bag on shoulder and staff in hand, left our station for the coast. And several times a week a coast caravan came in with trade goods—ghastly glazed calico that made you shudder only to look at it, glass beads value about a penny a quart, confounded spotted cotton handkerchiefs. And no rivets. Three carriers could have brought all that was wanted to set that steamboat afloat.

"He was becoming confidential now, but I fancy my unresponsive attitude must have exasperated him at last, for he judged it necessary to inform me he feared neither God nor devil, let alone any mere man. I said I could see that very well, but what I wanted was a certain quantity of rivets—and rivets were what really Mr. Kurtz wanted, if he had only known it. Now letters went to the coast every week. . . . 'My dear sir,' he cried, ' I write from dictation.' I demanded rivets. There was a way—for an intelligent man. He changed his manner; became very cold, and suddenly began to talk about a hippopotamus; wondered whether sleeping on board the steamer (I stuck to my salvage night and day) I wasn't disturbed. There was an old hippo that had the bad habit of getting out on the bank and roaming at night over the station grounds.

The pilgrims used to turn out in a body and empty every rifle they could lay hands on at him. Some even had sat up o' nights for him. All this energy was wasted, though. 'That animal has a charmed life,' he said; 'but you can say this only of brutes in this country. No man—you apprehend me?—no man here bears a charmed life.' He stood there for a moment in the moonlight with his delicate hooked nose set a little askew, and his mica eyes glittering without a wink, then, with a curt Goodnight, he strode off. I could see he was disturbed and considerably puzzled, which made me feel more hopeful than I had been for days. It was a great comfort to turn from that chap to my influential friend, the battered, twisted, ruined, tin-pot steamboat. I clambered on board. She rang under my feet like an empty Huntley & Palmer biscuit-tin kicked along a gutter; she was nothing so solid in make, and rather less pretty in shape, but I had expended enough hard work on her to make me love her. No influential friend would have served me better. She had given me a chance to come out a bit—to find out what I could do. No, I don't like work. I had rather laze about and think of all the fine things that can be done. I don't like work—no man does—but I like what is in the work—the chance to find yourself. Your own reality—for yourself, not for others— what no other man can ever know. They can only see the mere show, and never can tell what it really means.

"I was not surprised to see somebody sitting aft, on the deck, with his legs dangling over the mud. You see I rather chummed with the few mechanics there were in that station, whom the other pilgrims naturally despised—on account of their imperfect manners, I suppose. This was the foreman—a boiler-maker by trade—a good worker. He was a lank, bony, yellow-faced man, with big intense eyes. His aspect was worried, and his head was as bald as the palm of my hand; but his hair in falling seemed to have stuck to his chin, and had prospered in the new locality, for his beard hung down to his waist. He was a widower with six young children (he had left them in charge of a sister of his to come out there), and the passion of his life was pigeon-flying. He was an enthusiast and a connoisseur. He would rave about pigeons. After work hours he used sometimes to come over from his hut for a talk about his children and his pigeons; at work, when he had to crawl in the mud under the bottom of the steamboat, he would tie up that beard of his in a kind of white serviette he brought for the purpose. It had loops to go over his ears. In the evening he could be seen squatted on the bank rinsing that wrapper in the creek with great care, then spreading it solemnly on a bush to dry.

"I slapped him on the back and shouted, 'We shall have rivets!' He scrambled to his feet exclaiming, 'No! Rivets!' as though he couldn't believe his ears. Then in a low voice, 'You . . . eh?' I don't know why we behaved like lunatics. I put my finger to the side of my nose and nodded mysteriously. 'Good for you!' he cried, snapped his fingers above his head, lifting one foot. I tried a jig. We capered on the iron deck. A frightful clatter came out of that hulk, and the virgin forest on the other bank of the creek sent it back in a thundering roll upon the sleeping station. It must have made some of the pilgrims sit up in their hovels. A dark figure obscured the lighted doorway of the manager's hut, vanished, then, a second or so after, the doorway itself vanished, too. We stopped, and the silence driven away by the stamping of our feet flowed back again from the recesses of the land. The great wall of vegetation, an exuberant and entangled mass of trunks, branches, leaves, boughs, festoons, motionless in the moonlight, was like a rioting invasion of soundless life, a rolling wave of plants, piled up, crested, ready to topple over the creek, to sweep every little man of us out of his little existence. And it moved not. A deadened burst of mighty splashes and snorts reached us from afar, as though an ichthyosaurus had been taking a bath of glitter in the great river. 'After all,' said the boiler-maker in a reasonable tone, 'why shouldn't we get the rivets?' Why not, indeed! I did not know of any reason why we shouldn't. 'They'll come in three weeks,' I said, confidently.

"But they didn't. Instead of rivets there came an invasion, an infliction, a visitation. It came in sections during the next three weeks, each section headed by a donkey carrying a white man in new clothes and tan shoes, bowing from that elevation right and left to the impressed pilgrims. A quarrelsome band of footsore sulky niggers trod on the heels of the donkey; a lot of tents, campstools, tin boxes, white cases, brown bales would be shot down in the court-yard, and the air of mystery would deepen a little over the muddle of the station. Five such instalments came, with their absurd air of disorderly flight with the loot of innumerable outfit shops and provision stores, that, one would think, they were lugging, after a raid, into the wilderness for equitable division. It was an inextricable mess of things decent in themselves but that human folly made look like the spoils of thieving.

"This devoted band called itself the Eldorado Exploring Expedition, and I believe they were sworn to secrecy. Their talk, however, was the talk of sordid buccaneers: it was reckless without hardihood, greedy without audacity, and cruel without courage; there was not an atom of foresight or of serious intention in the whole batch of them, and they did not seem aware these things are wanted for the work of the world. To tear treasure out of the bowels of the land was their desire, with no more moral purpose at the back of it than there is in burglars breaking into a safe. Who paid the expenses of the noble enterprise I don't know; but the uncle of our manager was leader of that lot.

"In exterior he resembled a butcher in a poor neighbourhood, and his eyes had a look of sleepy cunning. He carried his fat paunch with ostentation on his short legs, and during the time his gang infested the station spoke to no one but his nephew. You could see these two roaming about all day long with their heads close together in an everlasting confab.

143

"I had given up worrying myself about the rivets. One's capacity for that kind of folly is more limited than you would suppose. I said Hang! —and let things slide. I had plenty of time for meditation, and now and then I would give some thought to Kurtz. I wasn't very interested in him. No. Still, I was curious to see whether this man, who had come out equipped with moral ideas of some sort, would climb to the top after all and how he would set about his work when there."

II

"One evening as I was lying flat on the deck of my steamboat, I heard voices approaching—and there were the nephew and the uncle strolling along the bank. I laid my head on my arm again, and had nearly lost myself in a doze, when somebody said in my ear, as it were: 'I am as harmless as a little child, but I don't like to be dictated to. Am I the manager—or am I not? I was ordered to send him there. It's incredible.'. . . I became aware that the two were standing on the shore alongside the forepart of the steamboat, just below my head. I did not move; it did not occur to me to move: I was sleepy. 'It *is* unpleasant,' grunted the uncle. 'He has asked the Administration to be sent there,' said the other, 'with the idea of showing what he could do; and I was instructed accordingly. Look at the influence that man must have. Is it not frightful?' They both agreed it was frightful, then made several bizarre remarks: 'Make rain and fine weather—one man—the Council— by the nose'—bits of absurd sentences that got the better of my drowsiness, so that I had pretty near the whole of my wits about me when the uncle said, 'The climate may do away with this difficulty for you. Is he alone there?' 'Yes,' answered the manager; 'he sent his assistant down the river with a note to me in these terms: "Clear this poor devil out of the country, and don't bother sending more of that sort. I had rather be alone than have the kind of men you can dispose of with me." It was more than a year ago. Can you imagine such impudence!' 'Anything since then?' asked the other hoarsely. 'Ivory,' jerked the nephew; 'lots of it— prime sort—lots—most annoying, from him.' 'And with that?' questioned the heavy rumble. 'Invoice,' was the reply fired out, so to speak. Then silence. They had been talking about Kurtz.

"I was broad awake by this time, but, lying perfectly at ease, re- mained still, having no inducement to change my position. 'How did that ivory come all this way?' growled the elder man, who seemed very vexed. The other explained that it had come with a fleet of canoes in charge of an English half-caste clerk Kurtz had with him; that Kurtz had apparently intended to return himself, the station being by that time bare of goods and stores, but after coming three hundred miles, had suddenly decided to go back, which he started to do alone in a small dugout with four paddlers, leaving the half-caste to continue down the river with the ivory. The two fellows there seemed astounded at anybody attempting such a thing. They were at a loss for an adequate motive. As to me, I seemed to see Kurtz for the first time. It was a distinct glimpse: the dugout, four paddling savages, and the lone white man turning his back suddenly on the headquarters, on relief, on thoughts of home— perhaps; setting his face towards the depths of the wilderness, towards his empty and desolate station. I did not know the motive. Perhaps he was just simply a fine fellow who stuck to his work for its own sake. His name, you understand, had not been pronounced once. He was 'that man.' The half-caste, who, as far as I could see, had conducted a difficult trip with great prudence and pluck, was invariably alluded to as 'that scoundrel.' The 'scoundrel' had reported that the 'man' had been very ill—had recovered imperfectly. . . . The two below me moved away then a few paces, and strolled back and forth at some little distance. I heard: 'Military post—doctor—two hundred miles—quite alone now— unavoidable delays—nine months—no news—strange rumours.' They approached again, just as the manager was saying, 'No one, as far as I know, unless a species of wandering trader—a pestilential fellow, snapping ivory from the natives.' Who was it they were talking about now? I gathered in snatches that this was some man supposed to be in Kurtz's district, and of whom the manager did not approve. 'We will not be free from unfair competition till one of these fellows is hanged for an example,' he said. 'Certainly,' grunted the other; 'get him hanged! Why not? Anything—anything can be done in this country. That's what I say; nobody here, you understand, *here*, can endanger your position. And why? You stand the climate—you outlast them all. The danger is in Europe; but there before I left I took care to——' They moved off and whispered, then their voices rose again. 'The extraordinary series of delays is not my fault. I did my best.' The fat man sighed. 'Very sad.' 'And the pestiferous absurdity of his talk,' continued the other; 'he bothered me enough when he was here. "Each station should be like a beacon on the road towards better things, a centre for trade of course, but also for humanizing, improving, instructing." Conceive you—that ass! And he wants to be manager! No, it's——' Here he got choked by excessive indignation, and I lifted my head the least bit. I was surprised to see how near they were—right under me. I could have spat upon their hats. They were looking on the ground, absorbed in thought. The manager was switching his leg with a slender twig: his sagacious relative lifted his head. 'You have been well since you came out this time?' he asked. The other gave a start. 'Who? I? Oh! Like a charm—like a charm. But the rest—oh, my goodness! All sick. They die so quick, too, that I haven't the time to send them out of the country—it's incredible!' 'H'm. Just so,' grunted the uncle. 'Ah! my boy, trust to this—I say, trust to this.' I saw him extend his short flipper of an arm for a gesture that took in the forest, the creek, the mud, the river—seemed to beckon with a dishonouring flourish before the sunlit face of the land a treacherous appeal to the lurking death, to the hidden evil, to the profound darkness of its heart. It was so startling that I leaped to my feet and looked back at the edge of the forest, as though I had expected an answer of some sort to that black display of confidence. You know the foolish notions that come to one sometimes. The high stillness confronted these two figures with its ominous patience, waiting for the passing away of a fantastic invasion.

"They swore aloud together—out of sheer fright, I believe—then pretending not to know anything of my existence, turned back to the station. The sun was low; and leaning forward side by side, they seemed to be tugging painfully uphill their two ridiculous shadows of unequal length, that trailed behind them slowly over the tall grass without bending a single blade.

"In a few days the Eldorado Expedition went into the patient wilderness, that closed upon it as the sea closes over a diver. Long afterwards the news came that all the donkeys were dead. I know nothing as to the fate of the less valuable animals. They, no doubt, like the rest of us, found what they deserved. I did not inquire. I was then rather excited at the prospect of meeting Kurtz very soon. When I say very soon I mean it comparatively. It was just two months from the day we left the creek when we came to the bank below Kurtz's station.

"Going up that river was like travelling back to the earliest beginnings of the world, when vegetation rioted on the earth and the big trees were kings. An empty stream, a great silence, an impenetrable forest. The air was warm, thick, heavy, sluggish. There was no joy in the brilliance of sunshine. The long stretches of the waterway ran on, deserted, into the gloom of over-shadowed distances. On silvery sand-banks hippos and alligators sunned themselves side by side. The broadening waters flowed through a mob of wooded islands; you lost your way on that river as you would in a desert, and butted all day long against shoals, trying to find the channel, till you thought yourself bewitched and cut off for ever from everything you had known once—somewhere— far away—in another existence perhaps. There were moments when one's past came back to one, as it will sometimes when you have not a moment to spare to yourself; but it came in the shape of an unrestful and noisy dream, remembered with wonder amongst the overwhelming realities of this strange world of plants, and water, and silence. And this stillness of life did not in the least resemble a peace. It was the stillness of an implacable force brooding over an inscrutable intention. It looked at you with a vengeful aspect. I got used to it afterwards; I did not see it any more; I had no time. I had to keep guessing at the channel; I had to discern, mostly by inspiration, the signs of hidden banks; I watched for sunken stones; I was learning to clap my teeth smartly before my heart flew out, when I shaved by a fluke some infernal sly old snag that would have ripped the life out of the tin-pot steamboat and drowned all the pilgrims; I had to keep a lookout for the signs of dead wood we could cut up in the night for next day's steaming. When you have to attend to things of that sort, to the mere incidents of the surface, the reality—

the reality, I tell you—fades. The inner truth is hidden—luckily, luckily. But I felt it all the same; I felt often its mysterious stillness watching me at my monkey tricks, just as it watches you fellows performing on your respective tight-ropes for—what is it? half-a-crown a tumble——"

"Try to be civil, Marlow," growled a voice, and I knew there was at least one listener awake besides myself.

"I beg your pardon. I forgot the heartache which makes up the rest of the price. And indeed what does the price matter, if the trick be well done? You do your tricks very well. And I didn't do badly either, since I managed not to sink that steamboat on my first trip. It's a wonder to me yet. Imagine a blindfolded man set to drive a van over a bad road. I sweated and shivered over that business considerably, I can tell you. After all, for a seaman, to scrape the bottom of the thing that's supposed to float all the time under his care is the unpardonable sin. No one may know of it, but you never forget the thump—eh? A blow on the very heart. You remember it, you dream of it, you wake up at night and think of it—years after—and go hot and cold all over. I don't pretend to say that steamboat floated all the time. More than once she had to wade for a bit, with twenty cannibals splashing around and pushing. We had enlisted some of these chaps on the way for a crew. Fine fellows—cannibals—in their place. They were men one could work with, and I am grateful to them. And, after all, they did not eat each other before my face: they had brought along a provision of hippo-meat which went rotten, and made the mystery of the wilderness stink in my nostrils. Phoo! I can sniff it now. I had the manager on board and three or four pilgrims with their staves—all complete. Sometimes we came upon a station close by the bank, clinging to the skirts of the unknown, and the white men rushing out of a tumble-down hovel, with great gestures of joy and surprise and welcome, seemed very strange—had the appearance of being held there captive by a spell. The word ivory would ring in the air for a while—and on we went again into the silence, along empty reaches, round the still bends, between the high walls of our winding way, reverberating in hollow claps the ponderous beat of the stern-wheel. Trees, trees, millions of trees, massive, immense, running up high; and at their foot, hugging the bank against the stream, crept the little be-grimed steamboat, like a sluggish beetle crawling on the floor of a lofty portico. It made you feel very small, very lost, and yet it was not alto-gether depressing, that feeling. After all, if you were small, the grimy beetle crawled on—which was just what you wanted it to do. Where the pilgrims imagined it crawled to I don't know. To some place where they expected to get something. I bet! For me it crawled towards Kurtz—exclusively; but when the steam-pipes started leaking we crawled very slow. The reaches opened before us and closed behind, as if the forest had stepped leisurely across the water to bar the way for our return. We penetrated deeper and deeper into the heart of darkness. It was very quiet there. At night sometimes the roll of drums behind the curtain of trees would run up the river and remain sustained faintly, as if hovering in the air high over our heads, till the first break of day. Whether it meant war, peace, or prayer we could not tell. The dawns were heralded by the descent of a chill stillness; the wood-cutters slept, their fires burned low; the snapping of a twig would make you start. We were wanderers on a prehistoric earth, on an earth that wore the aspect of an unknown planet. We could have fancied ourselves the first of men taking possession of an accursed inheritance, to be subdued at the cost of profound anguish and of excessive toil. But suddenly, as we struggled round a bend, there would be a glimpse of rush walls, of peaked grass-roofs, a burst of yells, a whirl of black limbs, a mass of hands clapping, of feet stamping, of bodies swaying, of eyes rolling, under the droop of heavy and motionless foliage. The steamer toiled along slowly on the edge of a black and incomprehensible frenzy. The prehistoric man was cursing us, praying to us, welcoming us—who could tell? We were cut off from the comprehension of our surroundings; we glided past like phantoms, wondering and secretly appalled, as sane men would be before an enthusiastic outbreak in a madhouse. We could not understand because we were too far and could not remember because we were travelling in the night of first ages, of those ages that are gone, leaving hardly a sign— and no memories.

"The earth seemed unearthly. We are accustomed to look upon the shackled form of a conquered monster, but there—there you could look at a thing monstrous and free. It was unearthly, and the men were—— No, they were not inhuman. Well, you know, that was the worst of it—this suspicion of their not being inhuman. It would come slowly to one. They howled and leaped, and spun, and made horrid faces; but what thrilled you was just the thought of their humanity—like yours—the thought of your remote kinship with this wild and passionate uproar. Ugly. Yes, it was ugly enough; but if you were man enough you would admit to yourself that there was in you just the faintest trace of a response to the terrible frankness of that noise, a dim suspicion of there being a meaning in it which you—you so remote from the night of first ages—could comprehend. And why not? The mind of man is capable of anything— because everything is in it, all the past as well as all the future. What was there after all? fear, sorrow, devotion, valour, rage—who can tell?— but truth—truth stripped of its cloak of time. Let the fool gape and shudder—the man knows, and can look on without a wink. But he must at least be as much of a man as these on the shore. He must meet that truth with his own true stuff—with his own inborn strength. Principles won't do. Acquisitions, clothes, pretty rags—rags that would fly off at the first good shake. No; you want a deliberate belief. An appeal to me in this fiendish row—is there? Very well; I hear; I admit, but I have a voice, too, and for good or evil mine is the speech that cannot be silenced. Of course, a fool, what with sheer fright and fine sentiments, is always safe. Who's that grunting? You wonder I didn't go ashore for a howl and a dance? Well, no—I didn't. Fine sentiments, you say? Fine sentiments, be hanged! I had no time. I had to mess about with white-lead and strips of woolen blanket helping to put bandages on those leaky steampipes— I tell you. I had to watch the steering, and circumvent those snags, and get the tin-pot along by hook or by crook. There was surface-truth enough in these things to save a wiser man. And between whiles I had to look after the savage who was fireman. He was an improved specimen; he could fire up a vertical boiler. He was there below me, and, upon my word, to look at him was as edifying as seeing a dog in a parody of breeches and a feather hat, walking on his hind-legs. A few months of training had done for that really fine chap. He squinted at the steam-gauge and at the water-gauge with an evident effort of intrepidity— and he had filed teeth, too, the poor devil, and the wool of his pate shaved into queer patterns, and three ornamental scars on each of his cheeks. He ought to have been clapping his hands and stamping his feet on the bank, instead of which he was hard at work, a thrall to strange witchcraft, full of improving knowledge. He was useful because he had been instructed; and what he knew was this—that should the water in that transparent thing disappear, the evil spirit inside the boiler would get angry through the greatness of his thirst, and take a terrible vengeance. So he sweated and watched the glass fearfully (with an impromptu charm, made of rags, tied to his arm, and a piece of polished bone, as big as a watch, stuck flatways through his lower lip), while the wooded banks slipped past us slowly, the short noise was left behind, the interminable miles of silence—and we crept on, towards Kurtz. But the snags were thick, the water was treacherous and shallow, the boiler seemed indeed to have a sulky devil in it, and thus neither that fireman nor I had any time to peer into our creepy thoughts.

"Some fifty miles below the Inner Station we came upon a hut of reeds, an inclined and melancholy pole, with the unrecognizable tatters of what had been a flag of some sort flying from it, and a neatly stacked woodpile. This was unexpected. We came to the bank, and on the stack of firewood found a flat piece of board with some faded pencil-writing on it. When deciphered it said: 'Wood for you. Hurry up. Approach cautiously.' There was a signature, but it was illegible—not Kurtz—a much longer word. 'Hurry up,' Where? Up the river? 'Approach cautiously.' We had not done so. But the warning could not have been meant for the place where it could be only found after approach. Something was wrong above. But what—and how much? That was the question. We commented adversely upon the imbecility of that telegraphic style. The bush around said nothing, and would not let us look very far either. A torn curtain of red twill hung in the doorway of the hut, and flapped sadly in our faces. The dwelling was dismantled; but we could see a white man had lived there not very long ago. There remained a rude table—a plank on two posts; a heap of rubbish reposed in a dark corner, and by the door I picked up a book. It had lost its covers, and the pages had been thumbed into a state of extremely dirty softness; but the back had been lovingly stitched afresh with white cotton thread, which looked clean yet. It was an extraordinary find. Its title was, *An Inquiry into some Points of Seamanship,* by a man Towser, Towson—some such name— Master in his Majesty's Navy. The matter looked dreary reading enough, with illustrative diagrams and repulsive tables of figures, and the copy was sixty years old. I handled this amazing antiquity with the greatest possible tenderness, lest it should dissolve in my hands. Within, Towson or Towser was inquiring earnestly into the breaking strain of ships' chains and tackle, and other such matters. Not a very enthralling book; but at the first glance you could see there a singleness of intention, an honest concern for the right way of going to work, which made these humble pages, thought out so many years ago, luminous with another than a professional light. The simple old sailor, with his talk of chains and purchases, made me forget the jungle and the pilgrims in a delicious sensation of having come upon something unmistakably real. Such a book being there was wonderful enough but still more astounding were the notes pencilled in the margin, and plainly referring to the text. I couldn't believe my eyes! They were in cipher! Yes, it looked like cipher. Fancy a man lugging with him a book of that description into this no- where and studying it—and making notes—in cipher at that! It was an extravagant mystery.

"I had been dimly aware for some time of a worrying noise, and when I lifted my eyes I saw the woodpile was gone, and the manager, aided by all the pilgrims, was shouting at me from the riverside. I slipped the book into my pocket. I assure you to leave off reading was like tearing myself away from the shelter of an old and solid friendship.

"I started the lame engine ahead. 'It must be this miserable trader— this intruder,' exclaimed the manager, looking back malevolently at the place we had left. 'He must be English,' I said. 'It will not save him from getting into trouble if he is not careful,' muttered the manager darkly. I observed with assumed innocence that no man was safe from trouble in this world.

"The current was more rapid now, the steamer seemed at her last gasp, the stern-wheel flopped languidly, and I caught myself listening on tiptoe for the next beat of the boat, for in sober truth I expected the wretched thing to give up every moment. It was like watching the last flickers of a life. But still we crawled. Sometimes I would pick out a tree a little way ahead to measure our progress towards Kurtz by, but I lost it invariably before we got abreast. To keep the eyes so long on one thing was too much for human patience. The manager displayed a beautiful resignation. I fretted and fumed and took to arguing with myself whether or no I would talk openly with Kurtz; but before I could come to any conclusion it occurred to me that my speech or my silence, indeed any action of mine, would be a mere futility. What did it matter what any one knew or ignored? What did it matter who was

150

manager? One gets sometimes such a flash of insight. The essentials of this affair lay deep under the surface, beyond my reach, and beyond my power of meddling.

"Towards the evening of the second day we judged ourselves about eight miles from Kurtz's station. I wanted to push on; but the manager looked grave, and told me the navigation up there was so dangerous that it would be advisable, the sun being very low already, to wait where we were till next morning. Moreover, he pointed out that if the warning to approach cautiously were to be followed, we must approach in day-light—not at dusk or in the dark. This was sensible enough. Eight miles meant nearly three hours' steaming for us, and I could also see suspicious ripples at the upper end of the reach. Nevertheless, I was annoyed beyond expression at the delay, and most unreasonably, too, since one night more could not matter much after so many months. As we had plenty of wood, and caution was the word, I brought up in the middle of the stream. The reach was narrow, straight, with high sides like a railway cutting. The dusk came gliding into it long before the sun had set. The current ran smooth and swift, but a dumb immobility sat on the banks. The living trees, lashed together by the creepers and every living bush of the undergrowth, might have been changed into stone, even to the slenderest twig, to the lightest leaf. It was not sleep—it seemed unnatural, like a state of trance. Not the faintest sound of any kind could be heard. You looked on amazed, and began to suspect yourself of being deaf—then the night came suddenly, and struck you blind as well. About three in the morning some large fish leaped, and the loud splash made me jump as though a gun had been fired. When the sun rose there was a white fog, very warm and clammy, and more blinding than the night. It did not shift or drive; it was just there, standing all round you like something solid. At eight or nine, perhaps, it lifted as a shutter lifts. We had a glimpse of the towering multitude of trees, of the immense matted jungle, with the blazing little ball of the sun hanging over it—all perfectly still—and then the white shutter came down again, smoothly, as if sliding in greased grooves. I ordered the chain, which we had begun to heave in, to be paid out again. Before it stopped running with a muffled rattle, a cry, a very loud cry, as of infinite desolation, soared slowly in the opaque air. It ceased. A complaining clamour, modulated in savage discords, filled our ears. The sheer unexpectedness of it made my hair stir under my cap. I don't know how it struck the others: to me it seemed as though the mist itself had screamed, so suddenly, and apparently from all sides at once, did this tumultuous and mournful uproar arise. It culminated in a hurried outbreak of almost intolerably excessive shrieking, which stopped short, leaving us stiffened in a variety of silly attitudes, and obstinately listening to the nearly as appalling and excessive silence. 'Good God! What is the meaning——' stammered at my elbow one of the pilgrims—a little fat man, with sandy hair and red whiskers, who wore sidespring boots, and pink pyjamas tucked into his socks. Two others remained open-mouthed a whole minute, then dashed into the little cabin, to rush out incontinently and stand darting scared glances, with Winchesters at 'ready' in their hands. What we could see was just the steamer we were on, her outlines blurred as though she had been on the point of dissolving, and a misty strip of water, perhaps two feet broad, around her—and that was all. The rest of the world was nowhere, as far as our eyes and ears were concerned. Just nowhere. Gone, disappeared; swept off without leaving a whisper or a shadow behind.

"I went forward, and ordered the chain to be hauled in short, so as to be ready to trip the anchor and move the steamboat at once if necessary. 'Will they attack?' whispered an awed voice. 'We will be all butchered in this fog,' murmured another. The faces twitched with the strain, the hands trembled slightly, the eyes forgot to wink. It was very curious to see the contrast of expressions of the white men and of the black fellows of our crew, who were as much strangers to that part of the river as we, though their homes were only eight hundred miles away. The whites, of course greatly discomposed, had besides a curious look of being painfully shocked by such an outrageous row. The others had an alert, naturally interested expression; but their faces were essentially quiet, even those of the one or two who grinned as they hauled at the chain. Several exchanged short, grunting phrases, which seemed to settle the matter to their satisfaction. Their headman, a young, broad-chested black, severely draped in dark-blue fringed cloths, with fierce nostrils and his hair all done up artfully in oily ringlets, stood near me. 'Aha!' I said, just for good fellowship's sake. 'Catch 'im,' he snapped, with a bloodshot widening of his eyes and a flash of sharp teeth—'catch 'im. Give 'im to us.' 'To you, eh?' I asked; 'what would you do with them?' 'Eat 'im!' he said curtly, and, leaning his elbow on the rail, looked out into the fog in a dignified and profoundly pensive attitude. I would no doubt have been properly horrified, had it not occurred to me that he and his chaps must be very hungry: that they must have been growing increasingly hungry for at least this month past. They had been engaged for six months (I don't think a single one of them had any clear idea of time, as we at the end of countless ages have. They still belonged to the beginnings of time—had no inherited experience to teach them as it were), and of course, as long as there was a piece of paper written over in accordance with some farcical law or other made down the river, it didn't enter anybody's head to trouble how they would live. Certainly they had brought with them some rotten hippo-meat, which couldn't have lasted very long, anyway, even if the pilgrims hadn't, in the midst of a shocking hullabaloo, thrown a considerable quantity of it overboard. It looked like a high-handed proceeding; but it was really a case of legitimate self-defence. You can't breathe dead hippo waking, sleeping, and eating, and at the same time keep your precarious grip on existence. Besides that, they had given them every week three pieces of brass wire, each about nine inches long; and the theory was they were to buy their provisions with that currency in riverside villages. You can see how *that* worked. There were either no villages, or the people were hostile, or the director, who like the rest of us fed out of tins, with an occasional old he-goat thrown in, didn't want to stop the steamer for some more or less recondite reason. So, unless they swallowed the wire itself, or made loops of it to snare the fishes with, I don't see what good their extravagant salary could be to them. I must say it was paid with a regularity worthy of a large and honourable trading company. For the rest, the only thing to eat—though it didn't look eatable in the least—I saw in their possession was a few lumps of some stuff like half-cooked dough, of a dirty lavender colour, they kept wrapped in leaves, and now and then swallowed a piece of, but so small that it seemed done more for the looks of the thing than for any serious purpose of sustenance. Why in the name of all the gnawing devils of hunger they didn't go for us—they were thirty to five—and have a good tuck-in for once, amazes me now when I think of it. They were big powerful men, with not much capacity to weigh the consequences, with courage, with strength, even yet, though their skins were no longer glossy and their muscles no longer hard. And I saw that something restraining, one of those human secrets that baffle probability, had come into play there. I looked at them with a swift quickening of interest—not because it occurred to me I might be eaten by them before very long, though I own to you that just then I perceived—in a new light, as it were—how unwholesome the pilgrims looked, and I hoped, yes, I positively hoped, that my aspect was not so—what shall I say?—so—unappetizing: a touch of fantasic vanity which fitted well with the dream-sensation that pervaded all my days at that time. Perhaps I had a little fever, too. One can't live with one's finger everlastingly on one's pulse. I had often 'a little fever,' or a little touch of other things—the playful paw-strokes of the wilderness, the preliminary trifling before the more serious onslaught which came in due course. Yes; I looked at them as you would on any human being, with a curiosity of their impulses, motives, capacities, weaknesses, when brought to the test of an inexorable physical necessity. Restraint! What possible restraint? Was it superstition, disgust, patience, fear—or some kind of primitive honour? No fear can stand up to hunger, no patience can wear it out, disgust simply does not exist where hunger is; and as to superstition, beliefs, and what you may call principles, they are less than chaff in a breeze. Don't you know the devilry of lingering starvation, its exasperating torment, its black thoughts, its sombre and brooding ferocity? Well, I do. It takes a man all his inborn strength to fight hunger properly. It's really easier to face bereavement, dishonour, and the perdition of one's soul—than this kind of prolonged hunger. Sad, but true. And these chaps, too, had no earthly reason for any kind of scruple. Restraint! I would just as soon have expected restraint from a hyena prowling amongst the corpses of a battlefield. But there was the

153

fact facing me—the fact dazzling, to be seen, like the foam on the depths of the sea, like a ripple on an unfathomable enigma, a mystery greater—when I thought of it—than the curious, inexplicable note of desperate grief in this savage clamour that had swept by us on the river-bank, behind the blind whiteness of the fog.

"Two pilgrims were quarrelling in hurried whispers as to which bank. 'Left.' 'No, no; how can you? Right, right, of course.' 'It is very serious,' said the manager's voice behind me; 'I would be desolated if anything should happen to Mr. Kurtz before we came up.' I looked at him, and had not the slightest doubt he was sincere. He was just the kind of man who would wish to preserve appearances. That was his restraint. But when he muttered something about going on at once, I did not even take the trouble to answer him. I knew, and he knew, that it was impossible. Were we to let go our hold of the bottom, we would be absolutely in the air—in space. We wouldn't be able to tell where we were going to—whether up or down stream, or across—till we fetched against one bank or the other—and then we wouldn't know at first which it was. Of course I made no move. I had no mind for a smash-up. You couldn't imagine a more deadly place for a shipwreck. Whether drowned at once or not, we were sure to perish speedily in one way or another. 'I authorize you to take all the risks,' he said, after a short silence. 'I refuse to take any,' I said shortly; which was just the answer he expected, though its tone might have surprised him. 'Well, I must defer to your judgment. You are captain,' he said with marked civility. I turned my shoulder to him in sign of my appreciation, and looked into the fog. How long would it last? It was the most hopeless lookout. The approach to this Kurtz grubbing for ivory in the wretched bush was beset by as many dangers as though he had been an enchanted princess sleeping in a fabulous castle. 'Will they attack, do you think?' asked the manager, in a confidential tone.

"I did not think they would attack, for several obvious reasons. The thick fog was one. If they left the bank in their canoes they would get lost in it, as we would be if we attempted to move. Still, I had also judged the jungle of both banks quite impenetrable—and yet eyes were in it, eyes that had seen us. The riverside bushes were certainly very thick; but the undergrowth behind was evidently penetrable. However, during the short lift I had seen no canoes anywhere in the reach— certainly not abreast of the steamer. But what made the idea of attack inconceivable to me was the nature of the noise—of the cries we had heard. They had not the fierce character boding immediate hostile intention. Unexpected, wild, and violent as they had been, they had given me an irresistible impression of sorrow. The glimpse of the steamboat had for some reason filled those savages with unrestrained grief. The danger, if any, I expounded, was from our proximity to a great human passion let loose. Even extreme grief may ultimately vent itself in violence—but more generally takes the form of apathy. . . .

"You should have seen the pilgrims stare! They had no heart to grin, or even to revile me: but I believe they thought me gone mad—with fright, maybe. I delivered a regular lecture. My dear boys, it was no good bothering. Keep a lookout? Well, you may guess I watched the fog for the signs of lifting as a cat watches a mouse; but for anything else our eyes were of no more use to us than if we had been buried miles deep in a heap of cotton-wool. It felt like it, too—choking, warm, stifling. Besides, all I said, though it sounded extravagant, was absolutely true to fact. What we afterwards alluded to as an attack was really an attempt at repulse. The action was very far from being aggressive—it was not even defensive, in the usual sense: it was undertaken under the stress of desperation, and in its essence was purely protective.

"It developed itself, I should say, two hours after the fog lifted, and its commencement was at a spot, roughly speaking, about a mile and a half below Kurtz's station. We had just floundered and flopped round a bend, when I saw an islet, a mere grassy hummock of bright green, in the middle of the stream. It was the only thing of the kind; but as we opened the reach more, I perceived it was the head of a long sand-bank, or rather of a chain of shallow patches stretching down the middle of the river. They were discoloured, just awash, and the whole lot was seen just under the water, exactly as a man's backbone is seen running down the middle of his back under the skin. Now, as far as I did see, I could go to the right or to the left of this. I didn't know either channel, of course. The banks looked pretty well alike, the depth appeared the same; but as I had been informed the station was on the west side, I naturally headed for the western passage.

"No sooner had we fairly entered it than I became aware it was much narrower than I had supposed. To the left of us there was the long uninterrupted shoal, and to the right a high, steep bank heavily overgrown with bushes. Above the bush the trees stood in serried ranks. The twigs overhung the current thickly, and from distance to distance a large limb of some tree projected rigidly over the stream. It was then well on in the afternoon, the face of the forest was gloomy, and a broad strip of shadow had already fallen on the water. In this shadow we steamed up—very slowly, as you may imagine. I sheered her well in-shore—the water being deepest near the bank, as the sounding-pole informed me.

"One of my hungry and forbearing friends was sounding in the bows just below me. This steamboat was exactly like a decked scow. On the deck, there were two little teakwood houses, with doors and windows. The boiler was in the fore-end, and the machinery right astern. Over the whole there was a light roof, supported on stanchions. The funnel projected through that roof, and in front of the funnel a small cabin built of light planks served for a pilot-house. It contained a couch, two camp-stools, a loaded Martini-Henry leaning in one corner, a tiny table, and the steering-wheel. It had a wide door in front and a broad shutter at each side. All these were always thrown open, of course. I spent my days perched up there on the extreme fore-end of that roof, before the door. At night I slept, or tried to, on the couch. An athletic black, belonging to some coast tribe and educated by my poor predecessor, was the helmsman. He sported a pair of brass earrings, wore a blue cloth wrapper from the waist to the ankles, and thought all the world of himself. He was the most unstable kind of fool I had ever seen. He steered with no end of a swagger while you were by; but if he lost sight of you, he became instantly the prey of an abject funk, and would let that cripple of a steamboat get the upper hand of him in a minute.

"I was looking down at the sounding-pole, and feeling much annoyed to see at each try a little more of it stick out of that river, when I saw my poleman give up the business suddenly, and stretch himself flat on the deck, without even taking the trouble to haul his pole in. He kept hold of it though, and it trailed in the water. At the same time the fireman, whom I could also see below me, sat down abruptly before his furnace and ducked his head. I was amazed. Then I had to look at the river mighty quick, because there was a snag in the fairway. Sticks, little sticks, were flying about—thick: they were whizzing before my nose, dropping below me, striking behind me against my pilot-house. All this time the river, the shore, the woods, were very quiet—perfectly quiet. I could only hear the heavy splashing thump of the stern-wheel and the patter of these things. We cleared the snag clumsily. Arrows, by Jove! We were being shot at! I stepped in quickly to close the shutter on the land-side. That fool-helmsman, his hands on the spokes, was lifting his knees high, stamping his feet, champing his mouth, like a reined-in horse. Confound him! And we were staggering within ten feet of the bank. I had to lean right out to swing the heavy shutter, and I saw a face amongst the leaves on the level with my own, looking at me very fierce and steady; and then suddenly, as though a veil had been removed from my eyes, I made out, deep in the tangled gloom, naked breasts, arms, legs, glaring eyes—the bush was swarming with human limbs in movement, glistening, of bronze colour. The twigs shook, swayed, and rustled, the arrows flew out of them, and then the shutter came to. 'Steer her straight,' I said to the helmsman. He held his head rigid, face forward; but his eyes rolled, he kept on lifting and setting down his feet gently, his mouth foamed a little. 'Keep quiet!' I said in a fury. I might just as well have ordered a tree not to sway in the wind. I darted out. Below me there was a great scuffle of feet on the iron deck; confused exclamations; a voice screamed, 'Can you turn back?' I caught sight of a V-shaped ripple on the water ahead. What? Another snag! A fusillade burst out under my feet. The pilgrims had opened with their Winchesters, and were simply squirting lead into that bush. A deuce of a lot of smoke came up and drove slowly forward. I swore at it. Now I couldn't see the ripple or the snag either. I stood in the doorway, peering, and the arrows came in swarms. They might have been poisoned, but they looked as though they wouldn't kill a cat. The bush began to howl. Our wood-cutters raised a warlike whoop; the report of a rifle just at my back deafened me. I glanced over my shoulder, and the pilot-house was yet full of noise and smoke when I made a dash at the wheel. The fool-nigger had dropped everything, to throw the shutter open and let off that Martini-Henry. He stood before the wide opening, glaring, and I yelled at him to come back, while I straightened the sudden twist out of that steamboat. There was no room to turn even if I had wanted to, the snag was somewhere very near ahead in that confounded smoke, there was no time to lose, so I just crowded her into the bank—right into the bank, where I knew the water was deep.

"We tore slowly along the overhanging bushes in a whirl of broken twigs and flying leaves. The fusillade below stopped short, as I had foreseen it would when the squirts got empty. I threw my head back to a glinting whizz that traversed the pilot-house, in at one shutter-hole and out at the other. Looking past that mad helmsman, who was shaking the empty rifle and yelling at the shore, I saw vague forms of men running bent double, leaping, gliding, distinct, incomplete, evanescent. Something big appeared in the air before the shutter, the rifle went overboard, and the man stepped back swiftly, looked at me over his shoulder in an extraordinary, profound, familiar manner, and fell upon my feet. The side of his head hit the wheel twice, and the end of what appeared a long cane clattered round and knocked over a little campstool. It looked as though after wrenching that thing from somebody ashore he had lost his balance in the effort. The thin smoke had blown away, we were clear of the snag, and looking ahead I could see that in another hundred yards or so I would be free to sheer off, away from the bank; but my feet felt so very warm and wet that I had to look down. The man had rolled on his back and stared straight up at me; both his hands clutched that cane. It was the shaft of a spear that, either thrown or lunged through the opening, had caught him in the side just below the ribs; the blade had gone in out of sight, after making a frightful gash; my shoes were full; a pool of blood lay very still, gleaming dark-red under the wheel; his eyes shone with an amazing lustre. The fusillade burst out again. He looked at me anxiously, gripping the spear like something precious, with an air of being afraid I would try to take it away from him. I had to make an effort to free my eyes from his gaze and attend to the steering. With one hand I felt above my head for the line of the steam whistle, and jerked out screech after screech hurriedly. The tumult of angry and warlike yells was checked instantly, and then from the depths of the woods went out such a tremulous and prolonged wail of mournful fear and utter despair as may be imagined to follow the flight of the last hope from the earth. There was a great commotion in the bush; the shower of arrows stopped, a few dropping shots rang out sharply—then silence, in which the languid beat of the stern-wheel came plainly to my ears. I put the helm hard a-starboard at the moment when the pilgrim in pink

157

pyjamas, very hot and agitated, appeared in the doorway. 'The manager sends me——' he began in an official tone, and stopped short. 'Good God!' he said, glaring at the wounded man.

"We two whites stood over him, and his lustrous and inquiring glance enveloped us both. I declare it looked as though he would presently put to us some question in an understandable language; but he died without uttering a sound, without moving a limb, without twitching a muscle. Only in the very last moment, as though in response to some sign we could not see, to some whisper we could not hear, he frowned heavily, and that frown gave to his black death-mask an inconceivably sombre, brooding, and menacing expression. The lustre of inquiring glance faded swiftly into vacant glassiness. 'Can you steer?' I asked the agent eagerly. He looked very dubious; but I made a grab at his arm, and he understood at once I meant him to steer whether or no. To tell you the truth, I was morbidly anxious to change my shoes and socks. 'He is dead,' murmured the fellow, immensely impressed. 'No doubt about it,' said I, tugging like mad at the shoe-laces. 'And by the way, I suppose Mr. Kurtz is dead as well by this time.'

"For the moment that was the dominant thought. There was a sense of extreme disappointment, as though I had found out I had been striving after something altogether without a substance. I couldn't have been more disgusted if I had travelled all this way for the sole purpose of talking with Mr. Kurtz. Talking with . . . I flung one shoe overboard, and became aware that that was exactly what I had been looking forward to—a talk with Kurtz. I made the strange discovery that I had never imagined him as doing, you know, but as discoursing. I didn't say to myself, 'Now I will never see him,' or 'Now I will never shake him by the hand,' but, 'Now I will never hear him.' The man presented himself as a voice. Not of course that I did not connect him with some sort of action. Hadn't I been told in all the tones of jealousy and admiration that he had collected, bartered, swindled, or stolen more ivory than all the other agents together? That was not the point. The point was in his being a gifted creature, and that of all his gifts the one that stood out preëminently, that carried with it a sense of real presence, was his ability to talk, his words—the gift of expression, the bewildering, the illuminating, the most exalted and the most contemptible, the pulsating stream of light, or the deceitful flow from the heart of an impenetrable darkness.

"The other shoe went flying unto the devil-god of that river. I thought, 'By Jove! it's all over. We are too late; he has vanished—the gift has vanished, by means of some spear, arrow, or club. I will never hear that chap speak after all'—and my sorrow had a startling extravagance of emotion, even such as I had noticed in the howling sorrow of these savages in the bush. I couldn't have felt more of lonely desolation somehow, had I been robbed of a belief or had missed my destiny in life. . . . Why do you sigh in this beastly way, somebody? Absurd? Well, absurd.

Good Lord! mustn't a man ever—— Here, give me some tobacco." . . .

There was a pause of profound stillness, then a match flared, and Marlow's lean face appeared, worn, hollow, with downward folds and dropped eyelids, with an aspect of concentrated attention; and as he took vigorous draws at his pipe, it seemed to retreat and advance out of the night in the regular flicker of tiny flame. The match went out.

"Absurd!" he cried. "This is the worst of trying to tell. . . . Here you all are, each moored with two good addresses, like a hulk with two anchors, a butcher round one corner, a policeman round another, excellent appetites, and temperature normal—you hear—normal from year's end to year's end. And you say, Absurd! Absurd be—exploded! Absurd! My dear boys, what can you expect from a man who out of sheer nervousness had just flung overboard a pair of new shoes! Now I think of it, it is amazing I did not shed tears. I am, upon the whole, proud of my fortitude. I was cut to the quick at the idea of having lost the inestimable privilege of listening to the gifted Kurtz. Of course I was wrong. The privilege was waiting for me. Oh, yes, I heard more than enough. And I was right, too. A voice. He was very little more than a voice. And I heard—him—it—this voice—other voices—all of them were so little more than voices—and the memory of that time itself lingers around me, impalpable, like a dying vibration of one immense jabber, silly, atrocious, sordid, savage, or simply mean, without any kind of sense. Voices, voices—even the girl herself—now——"

He was silent for a long time.

"I laid the ghost of his gifts at last with a lie," he began, suddenly. "Girl! What? Did I mention a girl? Oh, she is out of it—completely. They—the women I mean—are out of it—should be out of it. We must help them to stay in that beautiful world of their own, lest ours gets worse. Oh, she had to be out of it. You should have heard the disinterred body of Mr. Kurtz saying, 'My Intended.' You would have perceived directly then how completely she was out of it. And the lofty frontal bone of Mr. Kurtz! They say the hair goes on growing sometimes, but this—ah—specimen, was impressively bald. The wilderness had patted him on the head, and, behold, it was like a ball—an ivory ball; it had caressed him, and—lo!—he had withered; it had taken him, loved him, embraced him, got into his veins, consumed his flesh, and sealed his soul to its own by the inconceivable ceremonies of some devilish initiation. He was its spoiled and pampered favourite. Ivory? I should think so. Heaps of it, stacks of it. The old mud shanty was bursting with it. You would think there was not a single tusk left either above or below the ground in the whole country. 'Mostly fossil,' the manager had remarked, disparagingly. It was no more fossil than I am; but they call it fossil when it is dug up. It appears these niggers do bury the tusks sometimes—but evidently they couldn't bury this parcel deep enough to save the gifted Mr. Kurtz from his fate. We filled the steamboat with it, and had to pile a lot on the deck. Thus he could see and enjoy as long as he could see, because the appreciation of this favour had remained with him to the last. You should have heard him say, 'My ivory.' Oh, yes, I heard him. 'My Intended, my ivory, my station, my river, my——' everything belonged to him. It made me hold my breath in expectation of hearing the wilderness burst into a prodigious peal of laughter that would shake the fixed stars in their places. Everything belonged to him—but that was a trifle. The thing was to know what he belonged to, how many powers of darkness claimed him for their own. That was the reflection that made you creepy all over. It was impossible—it was not good for one either—trying to imagine. He had taken a high seat amongst the devils of the land—I mean literally. You can't understand. How could you?—with solid pavement under your feet, surrounded by kind neighbours ready to cheer you or to fall on you, stepping delicately between the butcher and the policeman, in the holy terror of scandal and gallows and lunatic asylums—how can you imagine what particular region of the first ages a man's untrammelled feet may take him into by the way of solitude—utter solitude without a policeman—by the way of silence—utter silence, where no warning voice of a kind neighbour can be heard whispering of public opinion? These little things make all the great difference. When they are gone you must fall back upon your own innate strength, upon your own capacity for faithfulness. Of course you may be too much of a fool to go wrong—too dull even to know you are being assaulted by the powers of darkness. I take it, no fool ever made a bargain for his soul with the devil; the fool is too much of a fool, or the devil too much of a devil—I don't know which. Or you may be such a thunderingly exalted creature as to be altogether deaf and blind to anything but heavenly sights and sounds. Then the earth for you is only a standing place—and whether to be like this is your loss or your gain I won't pretend to say. But most of us are neither one nor the other. The earth for us is a place to live in, where we must put up with sights, with sounds, with smells, too, by Jove!—breathe dead hippo, so to speak, and not be contaminated. And there, don't you see? Your strength comes in, the faith in your ability for the digging of unostentatious holes to bury the stuff in—your power of devotion, not to yourself, but to an obscure, back-breaking business. And that's difficult enough. Mind, I am not trying to excuse or even explain—I am trying to account to myself for—for—Mr. Kurtz—for the shade of Mr. Kurtz. This initiated wraith from the back of Nowhere honoured me with its amazing confidence before it vanished altogether. This was because it could speak English to me. The original Kurtz had been educated partly in England, and—as he was good enough to say himself—his sympathies were in the right place. His mother was half-English, his father was half-French. All Europe contributed to the making of Kurtz; and by and by I learned that, most appropriately, the International Society for the Suppression of Savage Customs had intrusted him with the making of a report, for its future guidance. And he had written it, too. I've seen it. I've read it. It was eloquent, vibrating with eloquence, but too high-strung, I think. Seventeen pages of close writing he had found time for! But this must have been before his—let us say—nerves, went wrong, and caused him to preside at certain midnight dances ending with unspeakable rites, which—as far as I reluctantly gathered from what I heard at various times—were offered up to him—do you understand?—to Mr. Kurtz himself. But it was a beautiful piece of writing. The opening paragraph, however, in the light of later information, strikes me now as ominous. He began with the argument that we whites, from the point of development we had arrived at, 'must necessarily appear to them [savages] in the nature of supernatural beings—we approach them with the might as of a deity,' and so on, and so on. 'By the simple exercise of our will we can exert a power for good practically unbounded,' etc., etc. From that point he soared and took me with him. The peroration was magnificent, though difficult to remember, you know. It gave me the notion of an exotic Immensity ruled by an august Benevolence. It made me tingle with enthusiasm. This was the unbounded power of eloquence—of words—of burning noble words. There were no practical hints to interrupt the magic current of phases, unless a kind of note at the foot of the last page, scrawled evidently much later, in an unsteady hand, may be regarded as the exposition of a method. It was very simple, and at the end of that moving appeal to every altruistic sentiment it blazed at you, luminous and terrifying, like a flash of lightning in a serene sky: 'Exterminate all the brutes!' The curious part was that he had apparently forgotten all about that valuable postscriptum, because, later on, when he in a sense came to himself, he repeatedly entreated me to take good care of 'my pamphlet' (he called it), as it was sure to have in the future a good influence upon his career. I had full information about all these things, and, besides, as it turned out, I was to have the care of his memory. I've done enough for it to give me the indisputable right to lay it, if I choose, for an everlasting rest in the dust-bin of progress, amongst all the sweepings and, figuratively speaking, all the dead cats of civilization. But then, you see, I can't choose. He won't be forgotten. Whatever he was, he was not common. He had the power to charm or frighten rudimentary souls into an aggravated witch-dance in his honour; he could also fill the small souls of the pilgrims with bitter misgivings: he had one devoted friend at least, and he had conquered one soul in the world that was neither rudimentary nor tainted with self-seeking. No; I can't forget him, though I am not prepared to affirm the fellow was exactly worth the life we lost in getting to him. I missed my late helmsman awfully—I missed him even while his body was still lying in the pilot-house. Perhaps you will think it passing strange this regret for a savage who was no more account than a grain of sand in a black Sahara. Well, don't you see, he had done something, he had steered; for months I had him at my back—a help—an instrument. It was a kind of partnership. He steered for me—I had to look after him, I worried about his deficiencies, and thus a subtle bond had been created, of which I only became aware when it was suddenly broken. And the intimate profundity of that look he gave me when he received his hurt remains to this day in my memory—like a claim of distant kinship affirmed in a supreme moment.

"Poor fool! If he had only left that shutter alone. He had no restraint, no restraint—just like Kurtz—a tree swayed by the wind. As soon as I had put on a dry pair of slippers, I dragged him out, after first jerking the spear out of his side, which operation I confess I performed with my eyes shut tight. His heels leaped together over the little doorstep; his shoulders were pressed to my breast; I hugged him from behind desperately. Oh! he was heavy, heavy; heavier than any man on earth, I should imagine. Then without more ado I tipped him overboard. The current snatched him as though he had been a wisp of grass, and I saw the body roll over twice before I lost sight of it for ever. All the pilgrims and the manager were then congregated on the awning-deck about the pilot-house, chattering at each other like a flock of excited magpies, and there was a scandalized murmur at my heartless promptitude. What they wanted to keep that body hanging about for I can't guess. Embalm it, maybe. But I had also heard another, and a very ominous, murmur on the deck below. My friends the woodcutters were likewise scandalized, and with a better show of reason—though I admit that the reason itself was quite inadmissible. Oh, quite! I had made up my mind that if my late helmsman was to be eaten, the fishes alone should have him. He had been a very second-rate helmsman while alive, but now he was dead he might have become a first-class temptation, and possibly cause some startling trouble. Besides, I was anxious to take the wheel, the man in pink pyjamas showing himself a hopeless duffer at the business.

"This I did directly the simple funeral was over. We were going half-speed, keeping right in the middle of the stream, and I listened to the talk about me. They had given up Kurtz, they had given up the station; Kurtz was dead, and the station had been burnt—and so on—and so on. The red-haired pilgrim was beside himself with the thought that at least this poor Kurtz had been properly avenged. 'Say! We must have made a glorious slaughter of them in the bush. Eh? What do you think? Say?' He positively danced, the bloodthirsty little gingery beggar. And he had nearly fainted when he saw the wounded man! I could not help saying, 'You made a glorious lot of smoke, anyhow.' I had seen, from the way the tops of the bushes rustled and flew, that almost all the shots had gone too high. You can't hit anything unless you take aim and fire from the shoulder; but these chaps fired from the hip with their eyes shut. The retreat, I maintained—and I was right—was caused by the screeching of the steam whistle. Upon this they forgot Kurtz, and began to howl at me with indignant protests.

"The manager stood by the wheel murmuring confidentially about the necessity of getting well away down the river before dark at all events, when I saw in the distance a clearing on the riverside and the outlines of some sort of bulding. 'What's this?' I asked. He clapped his hands in wonder. 'The station!' he cried. I edged in at once, still going half-speed.

"Through my glasses I saw the slope of a hill interspersed with rare trees and perfectly free from undergrowth. A long decaying building on the summit was half buried in the high grass; the large holes in the peaked roof gaped black from afar; the jungle and the woods made a background. There was no enclosure or fence of any kind; but there had been one apparently, for near the house half-a-dozen slim posts remained in a row, roughly trimmed, and with their upper ends ornamented with round carved balls. The rails, or whatever there had been between, had disappeared. Of course the forest surrounded all that. The river-bank was clear, and on the waterside I saw a white man under a hat like a cartwheel beckoning persistently with his whole arm. Examining the edge of the forest above and below, I was almost certain I could see movements—human forms gliding here and there. I steamed past prudently, then stopped the engines and let her drift down. The man on the shore began to shout, urging us to land. 'We have been attacked,' screamed the manager. 'I know—I know. It's all right,' yelled back the other, as cheerful as you please. 'Come along. It's all right. I am glad.'

"His aspect reminded me of something I had seen—something funny I had seen somewhere. As I manoeuvered to get alongside, I was asking myself, 'What does this fellow look like?' Suddenly I got it. He looked like a harlequin. His clothes had been made of some stuff that was brown holland probably, but it was covered with patches all over, with bright patches, blue, red, and yellow—patches on the back, patches on the front, patches on elbows, on knees; coloured binding around his jacket, scarlet edging at the bottom of his trousers; and the sunshine made him look extremely gay and wonderfully neat withal, because you could see how beautifully all this patching had been done. A beardless, boyish face, very fair, no features to speak of, nose peeling, little blue eyes, smiles and frowns chasing each other over that open countenance like sunshine and shadow on a wind-swept plain. 'Look out, captain!' he cried; 'there's a snag lodged in here last night.' What! Another snag? I confess I swore shamefully. I had nearly holed my cripple, to finish off that charming trip. The harlequin on the bank turned his little pug-nose up to me. 'You English?' he asked, all smiles. 'Are you?' I shouted from the wheel. The smiles vanished, and he shook his head as if sorry for my disappointment. Then he brightened up. 'Never mind!' he cried encouragingly. 'Are we in time?' I asked. 'He is up there,' he replied, with a toss of the head up the hill, and becoming gloomy all of a sudden. His face was like the autumn sky, overcast one moment and bright the next.

"When the manager, escorted by the pilgrims, all of them armed to the teeth, had gone to the house this chap came on board. 'I say, I don't like this. These natives are in the bush,' I said. He assured me earnestly it was all right. 'They are simple people,' he added; 'well, I am glad you came. It took me all my time to keep them off.' 'But you said it was all right,' I cried. 'Oh, they meant no harm,' he said; and as I stared he corrected himself, 'Not exactly.' Then vivaciously, 'My faith, your pilot-house wants a clean-up!' In the next breath he advised me to keep enough steam on the boiler to blow the whistle in case of any trouble. 'One good screech will do more for you than all your rifles. They are simple people,' he repeated. He rattled away at such a rate he quite overwhelmed me. He seemed to be trying to make up for lots of silence, and actually hinted, laughing, that such was the case. 'Don't you talk with Mr. Kurtz?' I said. 'You don't talk with that man—you listen to him,' he exclaimed with severe exaltation. 'But now——' He waved his arm, and in the twinkling of an eye was in the uttermost depths of despondency. In a moment he came up again with a jump, possessed himself of both my hands, shook them continuously, while he gabbled: 'Brother sailor . . . honour . . . pleasure . . . delight . . . introduce myself . . . Russian . . . son of an arch-priest . . . Government of Tambov . . . What? Tobacco! English tobacco; the excellent English tobacco! Now, that's brotherly. Smoke? Where's a sailor that does not smoke?'

"The pipe soothed him, and gradually I made out he had run away from school, had gone to sea in a Russian ship; ran away again; served some time in English ships; was now reconciled with the arch-priest. He made a point of that. 'But when one is young one must see things, gather experience, ideas; enlarge the mind.' 'Here!' I interrupted. 'You can never tell! Here I met Mr. Kurtz,' he said, youthfully solemn and reproachful. I held my tongue after that. It appears he had persuaded a Dutch trading-house on the coast to fit him out with stores and goods, and had started for the interior with a light heart and no more idea of what would happen to him than a baby. He had been wandering about that river for nearly two years alone, cut off from everybody and everything. 'I am not so young as I look. I am twenty-five,' he said. 'At first old Van Shuyten would tell me to go to the devil,' he narrated with keen enjoyment; 'but I stuck to him, and talked and talked, till at last he got afraid I would talk the hind-leg off his favourite dog, so he gave me some cheap things and a few guns, and told me he hoped he would never see my face again. Good old Dutchman, Van Shuyten. I've sent him one small lot of ivory a year ago, so that he can't call me a little thief when I get back. I hope he got it. And for the rest I don't care. I had some wood stacked for you. That was my old house. Did you see?'

"I gave him Towson's book. He made as though he would kiss me, but restrained himself. 'The only book I had left, and I thought I had lost it,' he said, looking at it ecstatically. 'So many accidents happen to a man going about alone, you know. Canoes get upset sometimes—and sometimes you've got to clear out so quick when the people get angry.' He thumbed the pages. 'You made notes in Russian?' I asked. He nodded. 'I thought they were written in cipher,' I said. He laughed, then became serious. 'I had lots of trouble to keep these people off,' he said. 'Did they want to kill you?' I asked. 'Oh, no!' he cried, and checked himself. 'Why did they attack us?' I pursued. He hesitated, then said shamefacedly, 'They don't want him to go.' 'Don't they?' I said curiously. He nodded a nod full of mystery and wisdom. 'I tell you,' he cried, 'this man has enlarged my mind.' He opened his arms wide, staring at me with his little blue eyes that were perfectly round."

III

"I looked at him, lost in astonishment. There he was before me, in motley, as though he had absconded from a troupe of mimes, enthusiastic, fabulous. His very existence was improbable, inexplicable, and altogether bewildering. He was an insoluble problem. It was inconceivable how he had existed, how he had succeeded in getting so far, how he had managed to remain—why he did not instantly disappear. 'I went a little farther,' he said, 'then still a little farther—till I had gone so far that I don't know how I'll ever get back. Never mind. Plenty time. I can manage. You take Kurtz away quick—quick—I tell you.' The glamour of youth enveloped his parti-coloured rags, his destitution, his loneliness, the essential desolation of his futile wanderings. For months—for years—his life hadn't been worth a day's purchase; and there he was gallantly, thoughtlessly alive, to all appearance indestructible solely by the virtue of his few years and of his unreflecting audacity. I was seduced into something like admiration—like envy. Glamour urged him on, glamour kept him unscathed. He surely wanted nothing from the wilderness but space to breathe in and to push on through. His need was to exist, and to move onwards at the greatest possible risk, and with a maximum of privation. If the absolutely pure, uncalculating, unpractical spirit of adventure had ever ruled a human being, it ruled this bepatched youth. I almost envied him the possession of this modest and clear flame. It seemed to have consumed all thought of self so completely, that even while he was talking to you, you forgot that it was he—the man before your eyes—who had gone through these things. I did not envy him his devotion to Kurtz, though. He had not meditated over it. It came to him, and he accepted it with a sort of eager fatalism. I must say that to me it appeared about the most dangerous thing in every way he had come upon so far.

"They had come together unavoidably, like two ships becalmed near each other, and lay rubbing sides at last. I suppose Kurtz wanted an audience, because on a certain occasion, when encamped in the forest, they had talked all night, or more probably Kurtz had talked. 'We talked of everything,' he said, quite transported at the recollection. 'I forgot there was such a thing as sleep. The night did not seem to last an hour. Everything! Everything! . . . Of love, too.' 'Ah, he talked to you of love!' I said, much amused. 'It isn't what you think,' he cried, almost passionately. 'It was in general. He made me see things—things.'

"He threw his arms up. We were on deck at the time, and the headman of my wood-cutters, lounging near by, turned upon him his heavy and glittering eyes. I looked around, and I don't know why, but I assure you that never, never before, did this land, this river, this jungle, the very arch of this blazing sky, appear to me so hopeless and so dark, so impenetrable to human thought, so pitiless to human weakness. 'And, ever since, you have been with him, of course?' I said.

"On the contrary. It appears their intercourse had been very much broken by various causes. He had, as he informed me proudly, managed to nurse Kurtz through two illnesses (he alluded to it as you would to some risky feat), but as a rule Kurtz wandered alone, far in the depths of the forest. 'Very often coming to this station, I had to wait days and days before he would turn up,' he said. 'Ah, it was worth waiting for!— sometimes.' 'What was he doing? exploring or what?' I asked. 'Oh, yes, of course'; he had discovered lots of villages, a lake, too—he did not know exactly in what direction; it was dangerous to inquire too much—but mostly his expeditions had been for ivory. 'But he had no goods to trade with by that time,' I objected. 'There's a good lot of cartridges left even yet,' he answered, looking away. 'To speak plainly, he raided the country,' I said. He nodded. 'Not alone, surely!' He muttered something about the villages round that lake. 'Kurtz got the tribe to follow him, did he?' I suggested. He fidgeted a little. 'They adored him,' he said. The tone of these words was so extraordinary that I looked at him searchingly. It was curious to see his mingled eagerness and reluctance to speak of Kurtz. The man filled his life, occupied his thoughts, swayed his emotions. 'What can you expect?' he burst out; 'he came to them with thunder and lightning, you know—and they had never seen anything like it—and very terrible. He could be very terrible. You can't judge Mr. Kurtz as you would an ordinary man. No, no, no! Now—just to give you an idea—I don't mind telling you, he wanted to shoot me, too, one day—but I don't judge him.' 'Shoot you!' I cried. 'What for?' 'Well, I had a small lot of ivory the chief of that village near my house gave me. You see I used to shoot game for them. Well, he wanted it, and wouldn't hear reason. He declared he would shoot me unless I gave him the ivory and then cleared out of the country, because he could do so, and had a fancy for it, and there was nothing on earth to prevent him killing whom he jolly well pleased. And it was true, too. I gave him the ivory. What did I care! But I didn't clear out. No, no. I couldn't leave him. I had to be careful, of course, till we got friendly again for a time. He had his second illness then. Afterwards I had to keep out of the way; but I didn't mind. He was living for the most part in those villages on the lake. When he came down to the river, sometimes he would take to me, and sometimes it was better for me to be careful. This man suffered too much. He hated all this, and somehow he couldn't get away. When I had a chance I begged him to try and leave while there was time; I offered to go back with him. And he would say yes, and then he would remain; go off on

166

another ivory hunt; disappear for weeks; forget himself amongst these people—forget himself—you know.' 'Why! he's mad,' I said. He protested indignantly. Mr. Kurtz couldn't be mad. If I had heard him talk, only two days ago, I wouldn't dare hint at such a thing. . . . I had taken up my binoculars while we talked, and was looking at the shore, sweeping the limit of the forest at each side and at the back of the house. The consciousness of there being people in that bush, so silent, so quiet—as silent and quiet as the ruined house on the hill—made me uneasy. There was no sign on the face of nature of this amazing tale that was not so much told as suggested to me in desolate exclamations, completed by shrugs, in interrupted phrases, in hints ending in deep sighs. The woods were unmoved, like a mask—heavy, like the closed door of a prison— they looked with their air of hidden knowledge, of patient expectation, of unapproachable silence. The Russian was explaining to me that it was only lately that Mr. Kurtz had come down to the river, bringing along with him all the fighting men of that lake tribe. He had been absent for several months—getting himself adored, I suppose—and had come down unexpectedly, with the intention to all appearance of making a raid either across the river or down stream. Evidently the appetite for more ivory had got the better of the—what shall I say?—less material aspirations. However he had got much worse suddenly. 'I heard he was lying helpless, and so I came up—took my chance,' said the Russian. 'Oh, he is bad, very bad.' I directed my glass to the house. There were no signs of life, but there was the ruined roof, the long mud wall peeping above the grass, with three little square window-holes, no two of the same size; all this brought within reach of my hand, as it were. And then I made a brusque movement, and one of the remaining posts of that vanished fence leaped up in the field of my glass. You remember I told you I had been struck at the distance by certain attempts at ornamentation, rather remarkable in the ruinous aspect of the place. Now I had suddenly a nearer view, and its first result was to make me throw my head back as if before a blow. Then I went carefully from post to post with my glass, and I saw my mistake. These round knobs were not ornamental but symbolic; they were expressive and puzzling, striking and disturbing— food for thought and also for vultures if there had been any looking down from the sky; but at all events for such ants as were industrious enough to ascend the pole. They would have been even more impressive, those heads on the stakes, if their faces had not been turned to the house. Only one, the first I had made out, was facing my way. I was not so shocked as you may think. The start back I had given was really nothing but a movement of surprise. I had expected to see a knob of wood there, you know. I returned deliberately to the first I had seen—and there it was, black, dried, sunken, with closed eyelids—a head that seemed to sleep at the top of that pole, and, with the shrunken dry lips showing a narrow white line of the teeth, was smiling, too, smiling continuously at some endless and jocose dream of that eternal slumber.

167

"I am not disclosing any trade secrets. In fact, the manager said afterwards that Mr. Kurtz's methods had ruined the district. I have no opinion on that point, but I want you clearly to understand that there was nothing exactly profitable in these heads being there. They only showed that Mr. Kurtz lacked restraint in the gratification of his various lusts, that there was something wanting in him—some small matter which, when the pressing need arose, could not be found under his magnificent eloquence. Whether he knew of his deficiency himself I can't say. I think the knowledge came to him at last—only at the very last. But the wilderness had found him out early, and had taken on him a terrible vengeance for the fantastic invasion. I think it had whispered to him things about himself which he did not know, things of which he had no conception till he took counsel with this great solitude—and the whisper had proved irresistibly fascinating. It echoed loudly within him because he was hollow at the core. . . . I put down the glass, and the head that had appeared near enough to be spoken to seemed at once to have leaped away from me into inaccessible distance.

"The admirer of Mr. Kurtz was a bit crestfallen. In a hurried, in-distinct voice he began to assure me he had not dared to take these—say, symbols—down. He was not afraid of the natives; they would not stir till Mr. Kurtz gave the word. His ascendancy was extraordinary. The camps of the people surrounded the place, and the chiefs came every day to see him. They would crawl. . . . 'I don't want to know anything of the ceremonies used when approaching Mr. Kurtz,' I shouted. Curious, this feeling that came over me that such details would be more intolerable than those heads drying on the stakes under Mr. Kurtz's windows. After all, that was only a savage sight, while I seemed at one bound to have been transported into some lightless region of subtle horrors, where pure, uncomplicated savagery was a positive relief, being something that had a right to exist—obviously—in the sunshine. The young man looked at me with surprise. I suppose it did not occur to him that Mr. Kurtz was no idol of mine. He forgot I hadn't heard any of these splendid monologues on, what was it? on love, justice, conduct of life—or what not. If it had come to crawling before Mr. Kurtz, he crawled as much as the veriest savage of them all. I had no idea of the conditions, he said: these heads were the heads of rebels. I shocked him excessively by laughing. Rebels! What would be the next definition I was to hear? There had been enemies, criminals, workers—and these were rebels. Those rebellious heads looked very subdued to me on their sticks. 'You don't know how such a life tries a man like Kurtz,' cried Kurtz's last disciple. 'Well, and you?' I said. 'I! I! I am a simple man. I have no great thoughts. I want nothing from anybody. How can you compare me to . . . ?' His feelings were too much for speech, and suddenly he broke down. 'I don't understand,' he groaned. 'I've been doing my best to keep him alive, and that's enough. I had no hand in all this. I have no abilities. There hasn't been a drop of medicine or a mouthful of invalid food for months here. He was shamefully abandoned. A man like this, with such ideas. Shamefully! Shamefully! I—I—haven't slept for the last ten nights . . .'

"His voice lost itself in the calm of the evening. The long shadows of the forest had slipped downhill while we talked, had gone far beyond the ruined hovel, beyond the symbolic row of stakes. All this was in the gloom, while we down there were yet in the sunshine, and the stretch of the river abreast of the clearing glittered in a still and dazzling splendour, with a murky and overshadowed bend above and below. Not a living soul was seen on the shore. The bushes did not rustle.

"Suddenly round the corner of the house a group of men appeared, as though they had come up from the ground. They waded waist-deep in the grass, in a compact body, bearing an improvised stretcher in their midst. Instantly, in the emptiness of the landscape, a cry arose whose shrillness pierced the still air like a sharp arrow flying straight to the very heart of the land; and, as if by enchantment, streams of human beings—of naked human beings—with spears in their hands, with bows, with shields, with wild glances and savage movements, were poured into the clearing by the dark-faced and pensive forest. The bushes shook, the grass swayed for a time, and then everything stood still in attentive immobility.

" 'Now, if he does not say the right thing to them we are all done for,' said the Russian at my elbow. The knot of men with the stretcher had stopped, too, halfway to the steamer, as if petrified. I saw the man on the stretcher sit up, lank and with an uplifted arm, above the shoulders of the bearers. 'Let us hope that the man who can talk so well of love in general will find some particular reason to spare us this time,' I said. I resented bitterly the absurd danger of our situation, as if to be at the mercy of that atrocious phantom had been a dishonouring necessity. I could not hear a sound, but through my glasses I saw the thin arm extended commandingly, the lower jaw moving, the eyes of that apparition shining darkly far in its bony head that nodded with grotesque jerks. Kurtz—Kurtz—that means short in German—don't it? Well, the name was as true as everything else in his life—and death. He looked at least seven feet long. His covering had fallen off, and his body emerged from it pitiful and appalling as from a winding-sheet. I could see the cage of his ribs all astir, the bones of his arm waving. It was as though an animated image of death carved out of old ivory had been shaking its hand with menaces at a motionless crowd of men made of dark and glittering bronze. I saw him open his mouth wide—it gave him a weirdly voracious aspect, as though he had wanted to swallow all the air, all the earth, all the men before him. A deep voice reached me faintly. He must have been shouting. He fell back suddenly. The stretcher shook as the bearers staggered forward again, and almost at the same time I noticed that the crowd of savages was vanishing without any perceptible movement of retreat, as if the forest that had ejected these beings so suddenly had

169

drawn them in again as the breath is drawn in a long aspiration.

"Some of the pilgrims behind the stretcher carried his arms—two shot-guns, a heavy rifle, and a light revolver-carbine—the thunderbolts of that pitiful Jupiter. The manager bent over him murmuring as he walked beside his head. They laid him down in one of the little cabins— just a room for a bed place and a camp-stool or two, you know. We had brought his belated correspondence, and a lot of torn envelopes and open letters littered his bed. His hand roamed feebly amongst these papers. I was struck by the fire of his eyes and the composed languor of his expression. It was not so much the exhaustion of disease. He did not seem in pain. This shadow looked satiated and calm, as though for the moment it had had its fill of all the emotions.

"He rustled one of the letters, and looking straight in my face said, 'I am glad.' Somebody had been writing to him about me. These special recommendations were turning up again. The volume of tone he emitted without effort, almost without the trouble of moving his lips, amazed me. A voice! a voice! It was grave, profound, vibrating, while the man did not seem capable of a whisper. However, he had enough strength in him—factitious no doubt—to very nearly make an end of us, as you shall hear directly.

"The manager appeared silently in the doorway; I stepped out at once and he drew the curtain after me. The Russian, eyed curiously by the pilgrims, was staring at the shore. I followed the direction of his glance.

"Dark human shapes could be made out in the distance, flitting indistinctly against the gloomy border of the forest, and near the river two bronze figures, leaning on tall spears, stood in the sunlight under fantastic head-dresses of spotted skins, warlike and still in statesque repose. And from right to left along the lighted shore moved a wild and gorgeous apparition of a woman.

"She walked with measured steps, draped in striped and fringed clothes, treading the earth proudly, with a slight jingle and flash of barbarous ornaments. She carried her head high; her hair was done in the shape of a helmet; she had brass leggings to the knee, brass wire gauntlets to the elbow, a crimson spot on her tawny cheek, innumerable necklaces of glass beads on her neck; bizarre things, charms, gifts of witch-men, that hung about her, glittered and trembled at every step. She must have had the value of several elephant tusks upon her. She was savage and superb, wild-eyed and magnificent; there was something ominous and stately in her deliberate progress. And in the hush that had fallen suddenly upon the whole sorrowful land, the immense wilderness, the colossal body of the fecund and mysterious life seemed to look at her, pensive, as though it had been looking at the image of its own tenebrous and passionate soul.

"She came abreast of the steamer, stood still, and faced us. Her long shadow fell to the water's edge. Her face had a tragic and fierce aspect of wild sorrow and of dumb pain mingled with the fear of some struggling, half-shaped resolve. She stood looking at us without a stir, and like the wilderness itself, with an air of brooding over an inscrutable purpose. A whole minute passed, and then she made a step forward. There was a low jingle, a glint of yellow metal, a sway of fringed draperies, and she stopped as if her heart had failed her. The young fellow by my side growled. The pilgrims murmured at my back. She looked at us all as if her life had depended upon the unswerving steadiness of her glance. Suddenly she opened her bared arms and threw them up rigid above her head, as though in an uncontrollable desire to touch the sky, and at the same time the swift shadows darted out on the earth, swept around on the river, gathering the steamer into a shadowy embrace. A formidable silence hung over the scene.

"She turned away slowly, walked on, following the bank, and passed into the bushes to the left. Once only her eyes gleamed back at us in the dusk of the thickets before she disappeared.

" 'If she had offered to come aboard I really think I would have tried to shoot her,' said the man of patches, nervously. 'I have been risking my life every day for the last fortnight to keep her out of the house. She got in one day and kicked up a row about those miserable rags I picked up in the storeroom to mend my clothes with. I wasn't decent. At least it must have been that, for she talked like a fury to Kurtz for an hour, pointing at me now and then. I don't understand the dialect of this tribe. Luckily for me, I fancy Kurtz felt too ill that day to care, or there would have been mischief. I don't understand. . . . No—it's too much for me. Ah, well, it's all over now.'

"At this moment I heard Kurtz's deep voice behind the curtain: 'Save me!—save the ivory, you mean. Don't tell me. Save *me*! Why, I've had to save you. You are interrupting my plans now. Sick! Sick! Not so sick as you would like to believe. Never mind. I'll carry my ideas out yet—I will return. I'll show you what can be done. You with your little peddling notions—you are interfering with me. I will return. I. . . .'

"The manager came out. He did me the honour to take me under the arm and lead me aside. 'He is very low, very low,' he said. He considered it necessary to sigh, but neglected to be consistently sorrowful. 'We have done all we could for him—haven't we? But there is no disguising the fact, Mr. Kurtz has done more harm than good to the Company. He did not see the time was not ripe for vigorous action. Cautiously, cautiously—that's my principle. We must be cautious yet. The district is closed to us for a time. Deplorable! Upon the whole, the trade will suffer. I don't deny there is a remarkable quantity of ivory—mostly fossil. We must save it, at all events—but look how precarious the position is—and why? Because the method is unsound.' 'Do you,' said I, looking at the shore, 'call it "unsound method?"' 'Without doubt,' he exclaimed hotly. 'Don't you?' . . . 'No method at all,' I murmured after a while. 'Exactly,' he exulted. 'I anticipated this. Shows a complete want of

171

judgment. It is my duty to point it out in the proper quarter.' 'Oh,' said I, 'that fellow—what's his name?—the brickmaker, will make a readable report for you.' He appeared confounded for a moment. It seemed to me I had never breathed an atmosphere so vile, and I turned mentally to Kurtz for relief—positively for relief. 'Nevertheless I think Mr. Kurtz is a remarkable man,' I said with emphasis. He started, dropped on me a cold heavy glance, said very quietly, 'he *was*,' and turned his back on me. My hour of favour was over; I found myself lumped along with Kurtz as a partisan of methods for which the time was not ripe: I was unsound! Ah! but it was something to have at least a choice of nightmares.

"I had turned to the wilderness really, not to Mr. Kurtz, who, I was ready to admit, was as good as buried. And for a moment it seemed to me as if I also were buried in a vast grave full of unspeakable secrets. I felt an intolerable weight oppressing my breast, the smell of the damp earth, the unseen presence of victorious corruption, the darkness of an impenetrable night. . . . The Russian tapped me on the shoulder. I heard him mumbling and stammering something about 'brother seaman—couldn't conceal—knowledge of matters that would affect Mr. Kurtz's reputation.' I waited. For him evidently Mr. Kurtz was not in his grave; I suspect that for him Mr. Kurtz was one of the immortals. 'Well!' said I at last, 'speak out. As it happens, I am Mr. Kurtz's friend—in a way.'

"He stated with a good deal of formality that had we not been 'of the same profession,' he would have kept the matter to himself without regard to consequences. 'He suspected there was an active ill-will to-wards him on the part of these white men that——, 'You are right,' I said, remembering a certain conversation I had overheard. 'The manager thinks you ought to be hanged.' He showed a concern at this intelligence which amused me at first. 'I had better get out of the way quietly,' he said earnestly. 'I can do no more for Kurtz now, and they would soon find some excuse. What's to stop them? There's a military post three hundred miles from here.' 'Well, upon my word,' said I, 'perhaps you had better go if you have any friends amongst the savages near by.' 'Plenty,' he said. 'They are simple people—and I want nothing, you know.' He stood biting his lip, then: 'I don't want any harm to happen to these whites here, but of course I was thinking of Mr. Kurtz's reputation —but you are a brother seaman and——' 'All right,' said I, after a time. 'Mr. Kurtz's reputation is safe with me.' I did not know how truly I spoke.

"He informed me, lowering his voice, that it was Kurtz who had ordered the attack to be made on the steamer. 'He hated sometimes the idea of being taken away—and then again. . . . But I don't understand these matters. I am a simple man. He thought it would scare you away—that you would give it up, thinking him dead. I could not stop him. Oh, I had an awful time of it this last month.' 'Very well,' I said. 'He is all right now.' 'Ye-e-es,' he muttered, not very convinced apparently. 'Thanks,' said I; 'I shall keep my eyes open.' 'But quiet—eh?' he urged anxiously. 'It would be awful for his reputation if anybody here——' I promised a complete discretion with great gravity. 'I have a canoe and three black fellows waiting not very far. I am off. Could you give me a few Martini-Henry cartridges?' I could, and did, with proper secrecy. He helped himself, with a wink at me, to a handful of my tobacco. 'Between sailors—you know—good English tobacco.' At the door of the pilot-house he turned round—'I say, haven't you a pair of shoes you could spare?' He raised one leg. 'Look.' The soles were tied with knotted strings sandalwise under his bare feet. I rooted out an old pair, at which he looked with admiration before tucking it under his left arm. One of his pockets (bright red) was bulging with cartridges, from the other (dark blue) peeped 'Towson's Inquiry,' etc., etc. He seemed to think himself excellently well equipped for a renewed encounter with the wilderness. 'Ah! I'll never, never meet such a man again. You ought to have heard him recite poetry—his own, too, it was, he told me. Poetry!' He rolled his eyes at the recollection of these delights. 'Oh, he enlarged my mind!' 'Goodbye,' said I. He shook hands and vanished in the night. Sometimes I ask myself whether I had ever really seen him—whether it was possible to meet such a phenomenon! . . .

"When I woke up shortly after midnight his warning came to my mind with its hint of danger that seemed, in the starred darkness, real enough to make me get up for the purpose of having a look round. On the hill a big fire burned, illuminating fitfully a crooked corner of the station-house. One of the agents with a picket of a few of our blacks, armed for the purpose, was keeping guard over the ivory; but deep within the forest, red gleams that wavered, that seemed to sink and rise from the ground amongst confused columnar shapes of intense blackness, showed the exact position of the camp where Mr. Kurtz's adorers were keeping their uneasy vigil. The monotonous beating of a big drum filled the air with muffled shocks and a lingering vibration. A steady droning sound of many men chanting each to himself some weird incantation came out from the black, flat wall of the woods as the humming of bees comes out of a hive, and had a strange narcotic effect upon my half-awake senses. I believe I dozed off leaning over the rail, till an abrupt burst of yells, an overwhelming outbreak of a pent-up and mysterious frenzy, woke me up in a bewildered wonder. It was cut short all at once, and the low droning went on with an effect of audible and soothing silence. I glanced casually into the little cabin. A light was burning within, but Mr. Kurtz was not there.

"I think I would have raised an outcry if I had believed my eyes. But I didn't believe them at first—the thing seemed so impossible. The fact is I was completely unnerved by a sheer blank fright, pure abstract terror, unconnected with any distinct shape of physical danger. What made this emotion so overpowering was—how shall I define it?—the moral shock I received, as if something altogether monstrous, intolerable to thought and odious to the soul, had been thrust upon me unexpectedly.

This lasted of course the merest fraction of a second, and then the usual sense of commonplace, deadly danger, the possibility of a sudden onslaught and massacre, or something of the kind, which I saw impending, was positively welcome and composing. It pacified me, in fact, so much that I did not raise an alarm.

"There was an agent buttoned up inside an ulster and sleeping on a chair on deck within three feet of me. The yells had not awakened him; he snored very slightly; I left him to his slumbers and leaped ashore. I did not betray Mr. Kurtz—it was ordered I should never betray him— it was written I should be loyal to the nightmare of my choice. I was anxious to deal with this shadow by myself alone—and to this day I don't know why I was so jealous of sharing with any one the peculiar blackness of that experience.

"As soon as I got on the bank I saw a trail—a broad trail through the grass. I remember the exultation with which I said to myself, 'He can't walk—he is crawling on all-fours—I've got him.' The grass was wet with dew. I strode rapidly with clenched fists. I fancy I had some vague notion of falling upon him and giving him a drubbing. I don't know. I had some imbecile thoughts. The knitting old woman with the cat obtruded herself upon my memory as a most improper person to be sitting at the other end of such an affair. I saw a row of pilgrims squirting lead in the air out of Winchesters held to the hip. I thought I would never get back to the steamer, and imagined myself living alone and unarmed in the woods to an advanced age. Such silly things—you know. And I remember I confounded the beat of the drum with the beating of my heart, and was pleased at its calm regularity.

"I kept to the track though—then stopped to listen. The night was very clear; a dark blue space, sparkling with dew and starlight, in which black things stood very still. I thought I could see a kind of motion ahead of me. I was strangely cocksure of everything that night. I actually left the track and ran in a wide semicircle (I verily believe chuckling to myself) so as to get in front of that stir, of that motion I had seen— if indeed I had seen anything. I was circumventing Kurtz as though it had been a boyish game.

"I came upon him, and, if he had not heard me coming, I would have fallen over him, too, but he got up in time. He rose, unsteady, long, pale, indistinct, like a vapour exhaled by the earth, and swayed slightly, misty and silent before me; while at my back the fires loomed between the trees, and the murmur of many voices issued from the forest. I had cut him off cleverly; but when actually confronting him I seemed to come to my senses, I saw the danger in its right proportion. It was by no means over yet. Suppose he began to shout? Though he could hardly stand, there was still plenty of vigour in his voice. 'Go away—hide yourself,' he said, in that profound tone. It was very awful. I glanced back. We were within thirty yards from the nearest fire. A black figure stood up, strode on long black legs, waving long black arms, across the glow.

It had horns—antelope horns, I think—on its head. Some sorcerer, some witch-man, no doubt: it looked fiendlike enough. 'Do you know what you are doing?' I whispered. 'Perfectly,' he answered, raising his voice for that single word: it sounded to me far off and yet loud, like a hail through a speaking-trumpet. 'If he makes a row we are lost,' I thought to myself. This clearly was not a case for fisticuffs, even apart from the very natural aversion I had to beat that Shadow—this wandering and tormented thing. 'You will be lost,' I said—'utterly lost.' One gets sometimes such a flash of inspiration, you know. I did say the right thing, though indeed he could not have been more irretrievably lost than he was at this very moment, when the foundations of our intimacy were being laid—to endure—to endure—even to the end—even beyond.

"'I had immense plans,' he muttered irresolutely. 'Yes,' said I; 'but if you try to shout I'll smash your head with——' There was not a stick or a stone near. 'I will throttle you for good,' I corrected myself. 'I was on the threshold of great things,' he pleaded, in a voice of longing, with a wistfulness of tone that made my blood run cold. 'And now for this stupid scoundrel——' 'Your success in Europe is assured in any case,' I affirmed steadily. I did not want to have the throttling of him, you understand—and indeed it would have been very little use for any practical purpose. I tried to break the spell—the heavy, mute spell of the wilderness—that seemed to draw him to its pitiless breast by the awakening of forgotten and brutal instincts, by the memory of gratified and monstrous passions. This alone, I was convinced, had driven him out to the edge of the forest, to the bush, towards the gleam of fires, the throb of drums, the drone of weird incantations; this alone had beguiled his unlawful soul beyond the bounds of permitted aspirations. And, don't you see, the terror of the position was not in being knocked on the head—though I had a very lively sense of that danger, too—but in this, that I had to deal with a being to whom I could not appeal in the name of anything high or low. I had, even like the niggers, to invoke him—himself—his own exalted and incredible degradation. There was nothing either above or below him, and I knew it. He had kicked himself loose of the earth. Confound the man! he had kicked the very earth to pieces. He was alone, and I before him did not know whether I stood on the ground or floated in the air. I've been telling you what we said—repeating the phrases we pronounced—but what's the good? They were common everyday words—the familiar, vague sounds exchanged on every waking day of life. But what of that? They had behind them, to my mind, the terrific suggestiveness of words heard in dreams, of phrases spoken in nightmares. Soul! If anybody ever struggled with a soul, I am the man. And I wasn't arguing with a lunatic either. Believe me or not, his intelligence was perfectly clear—concentrated, it is true, upon himself with horrible intensity, yet clear; and therein was my only chance—barring, of course, the killing him there and then, which wasn't so good, on account of unavoidable noise. But his soul was mad. Being alone in the wilderness, it had looked within itself, and, by heavens! I tell you, it had gone mad. I had—for my sins, I suppose—to go through the ordeal of looking into it myself. No eloquence could have been so withering to one's belief in mankind as his final burst of sincerity. He struggled with himself, too. I saw it—I heard it. I saw the inconceivable mystery of a soul that knew no restraint, no faith, and no fear, yet struggling blindly with itself. I kept my head pretty well; but when I had him at last stretched on the couch, I wiped my forehead, while my legs shook under me as though I had carried half a ton on my back down that hill. And yet I had only supported him, his bony arm clasped round my neck—and he was not much heavier than a child.

"When next day we left at noon, the crowd, of whose presence behind the curtain of trees I had been acutely conscious all the time, flowed out of the woods again, filled the clearing, covered the slope with a mass of naked, breathing, quivering, bronze bodies. I steamed up a bit, then swung down stream, and two thousand eyes followed the evolutions of the splashing, thumping, fierce river-demon beating the water with its terrible tail and breathing black smoke into the air. In front of the first rank, along the river, three men, plastered with bright red earth from head to foot, strutted to and fro restlessly. When we came abreast again, they faced the river, stamped their feet, nodded their horned heads, swayed their scarlet bodies; they shook towards the fierce river-demon a bunch of black feathers, a mangy skin with a pendent tail—something that looked like a dried gourd; they shouted periodically together strings of amazing words that resembled no sounds of human language; and the deep murmurs of the crowd, interrupted suddenly, were like the responses of some satanic litany.

"We had carried Kurtz into the pilot-house: there was more air there. Lying on the couch, he stared through the open shutter. There was an eddy in the mass of human bodies, and the woman with helmeted head and tawny cheeks rushed out to the very brink of the stream. She put out her hands, shouted something, and all that wild mob took up the shout in a roaring chorus of articulated, rapid, breathless utterance.

" 'Do you understand this?' I asked.

"He kept on looking out past me with fiery, longing eyes, with a mingled expression of wistfulness and hate. He made no answer, but I saw a smile, a smile of indefinable meaning, appearing on his colourless lips that a moment after twitched convulsively. 'Do I not?' he said slowly, gasping, as if the words had been torn out of him by a supernatural power.

"I pulled the string of the whistle, and I did this because I saw the pilgrims on deck getting out their rifles with an air of anticipating a jolly lark. At the sudden screech there was a movement of abject terror through that wedged mass of bodies. 'Don't! don't you frighten them away,' cried some one on deck disconsolately. I pulled the string time

176

after time. They broke and ran, they leaped, they crouched, they swerved, they dodged the flying terror of the sound. The three red chaps had fallen flat, face down on the shore, as though they had been shot dead. Only the barbarous and superb woman did not so much as flinch, and stretched tragically her bare arms after us over the sombre and glittering river.

"And then that imbecile crowd down on the deck started their little fun, and I could see nothing more for smoke.

"The brown current ran swiftly out of the heart of darkness, bearing us down towards the sea with twice the speed of our upward progress; and Kurtz's life was running swiftly, too, ebbing, ebbing out of his heart into the sea of inexorable time. The manager was very placid, he had no vital anxieties now, he took us both in with a comprehensive and satisfied glance: the 'affair' had come off as well as could be wished. I saw the time approaching when I would be left alone of the party of 'unsound method.' The pilgrims looked upon me with disfavour. I was, so to speak, numbered with the dead. It is strange how I accepted this unforeseen partnership, this choice of nightmares forced upon me in the tenebrous land invaded by these mean and greedy phantoms.

"Kurtz discoursed. A voice! a voice! It rang deep to the very last. It survived his strength to hide in the magnificent folds of eloquence the barren darkness of his heart. Oh, he struggled; he struggled! The wastes of his weary brain were haunted by shadowy images now—images of wealth and fame revolving obsequiously round his unextinguishable gift of noble and lofty expression. My Intended, my station, my career, my ideas—these were the subjects for the occasional utterances of elevated sentiments. The shade of the original Kurtz frequented the beside of the hollow sham, whose fate it was to be buried presently in the mould of primeval earth. But both the diabolic love and the unearthly hate of the mysteries it had penetrated fought for the possession of that soul satiated with primitive emotions, avid of lying fame, of sham distinction, of all the appearances of success and power.

"Sometimes he was contemptibly childish. He desired to have kings meet him at railway-stations on his return from some ghastly Nowhere, where he intended to accomplish great things. 'You show them you have in you something that is really profitable, and then there will be no limits to the recognition of your ability,' he would say. 'Of course you must take care of the motives—right motives—always.' The long reaches that were like one and the same reach, monotonous bends that were exactly alike, slipped past the steamer with their multitude of secular trees looking patiently after this grimy fragment of another world, the forerunner of change, of conquest, of trade, of massacres, of blessings. I looked ahead—piloting. 'Close the shutter,' said Kurtz suddenly one day; 'I can't bear to look at this.' I did so. There was a silence. 'Oh, but I will wring your heart yet!' he cried at the invisible wilderness.

177

"We broke down—as I had expected—and had to lie up for repairs at the head of an island. This delay was the first thing that shook Kurtz's confidence. One morning he gave me a packet of papers and a photograph—the lot tied together with a shoe-string. 'Keep this for me,' he said. 'This noxious fool' (meaning the manager) 'is capable of prying into my boxes when I am not looking.' In the afternoon I saw him. He was lying on his back with closed eyes, and I withdrew quietly, but I heard him mutter, 'Live rightly, die, die . . .' I listened. There was nothing more. Was he rehearsing some speech in his sleep, or was it a fragment of a phrase from some newspaper article? He had been writing for the papers and meant to do so again, 'for the furthering of my ideas. It's a duty.'

"His was an impenetrable darkness. I looked at him as you peer down at a man who is lying at the bottom of a precipice where the sun never shines. But I had not much time to give him, because I was helping the engine-driver to take to pieces the leaky cylinders, to straighten a bent connecting-rod, and in other such matters. I lived in an infernal mess of rust, filings, nuts, bolts, spanners, hammers, ratchet-drills— things I abominate, because I don't get on with them. I tended the little forge we fortunately had aboard; I toiled wearily in a wretched scrap-heap—unless I had the shakes too bad to stand.

"One evening coming in with a candle I was startled to hear him say a little tremulously, 'I am lying here in the dark waiting for death.' The light was within a foot of his eyes. I forced myself to murmur, 'Oh, nonsense!' and stood over him as if transfixed.

"Anything approaching the change that came over his features I have never seen before, and hope never to see again. Oh, I wasn't touched. I was fascinated. It was as though a veil had been rent. I saw on that ivory face the expression of sombre pride, of ruthless power, of craven terror—of an intense and hopeless despair. Did he live his life again in every detail of desire, temptation, and surrender during that supreme moment of complete knowledge? He cried in a whisper at some image, at some vision—he cried out twice, a cry that was no more than a breath:

" 'The horror! The horror!'

"I blew the candle out and left the cabin. The pilgrims were dining in the mess-room, and I took my place opposite the manager, who lifted his eyes to give me a questioning glance, which I successfully ignored. He leaned back, serene, with that peculiar smile of his sealing the unexpressed depths of his meanness. A continuous shower of small flies streamed upon the lamp, upon the cloth, upon our hands and faces. Suddenly the manager's boy put his insolent black head in the doorway, and said in a tone of scathing contempt:

" 'Mistah Kurtz—he dead.'

"All the pilgrims rushed out to see. I remained, and went on with my dinner. I believe that I was considered brutally callous. However, I did not eat much. There was a lamp in there—light, don't you know—

178

and outside it was so beastly, beastly dark. I went no more near the remarkable man who had pronounced a judgment upon the adventures of his soul on this earth. The voice was gone. What else had been there? But I am of course aware that next day the pilgrims buried something in a muddy hole.

"And then they very nearly buried me.

"However, as you see, I did not go to join Kurtz there and then. I did not. I remained to dream the nightmare out to the end, and to show my loyalty to Kurtz once more. Destiny. My destiny! Droll thing life is— that mysterious arrangement of merciless logic for a futile purpose. The most you can hope from it is some knowledge of yourself—that comes too late—a crop of unextinguishable regrets. I have wrestled with death. It is the most unexciting contest you can imagine. It takes place in an impalpable greyness, with nothing underfoot, with nothing around, without spectators, without clamour, without glory, without the great desire of victory, without the great fear of defeat, in a sickly atmosphere of tepid scepticism, without much belief in your own right, and still less in that of your adversary. If such is the form of ultimate wisdom, then life is a greater riddle than some of us think it to be. I was within a hair's breadth of the last opportunity for pronouncement, and I found with humiliation that probably I would have nothing to say. This is the reason why I affirm that Kurtz was a remarkable man. He had something to say. He said it. Since I had peeped over the edge myself, I understand better the meaning of his stare, that could not see the flame of the candle, but was wide enough to embrace the whole universe, piercing enough to penetrate all the hearts that beat in the darkness. He had summed up— he had judged. 'The horror!' He was a remarkable man. After all, this was the expression of some sort of belief; it had candour, it had conviction, it had a vibrating note of revolt in its whisper, it had the appalling face of a glimpsed truth—the strange commingling of desire and hate. And it is not my own extremity I remember best—a vision of greyness without form filled with physical pain, and a careless contempt for the evanescence of all things—even of this pain itself. No! It is his extremity that I seem to have lived through. True, he had made that last stride, he had stepped over the edge, while I had been permitted to draw back my hesitating foot. And perhaps in this is the whole difference; perhaps all the wisdom, and all truth, and all sincerity, are just compressed into that inappreciable moment of time in which we step over the threshold of the invisible. Perhaps! I like to think my summing-up would not have been a word of careless contempt. Better his cry— much better. It was an affirmation, a moral victory paid for by innumerable defeats, by abominable terrors, by abominable satisfactions. But it was a victory! That is why I have remained loyal to Kurtz to the last, and even beyond, when a long time after I heard once more, not his own voice, but the echo of his magnificent eloquence thrown to me from a soul as translucently pure as a cliff of crystal.

"No, they did not bury me, though there is a period of time which

I remember mistily, with a shuddering wonder, like a passage through some inconceivable world that had no hope in it and no desire. I found myself back in the sepulchral city resenting the sight of people hurrying through the streets to filch a little money from each other, to devour their infamous cookery, to gulp their unwholesome beer, to dream their insignificant and silly dreams. They trespassed upon my thoughts. They were intruders whose knowledge of life was to me an irritating pretence, because I felt so sure they could not possibly know the things I knew. Their bearing, which was simply the bearing of commonplace individuals going about their business in the assurance of perfect safety, was offensive to me like the outrageous flauntings of folly in the face of a danger it is unable to comprehend. I had no particular desire to enlighten them, but I had some difficulty in restraining myself from laughing in their faces so full of stupid importance. I daresay I was not very well at that time. I tottered about the streets—there were various affairs to settle—grinning bitterly at perfectly respectable persons. I admit my behaviour was inexcusable, but then my temperature was seldom normal in these days. My dear aunt's endeavours to 'nurse up my strength' seemed altogether beside the mark. It was not my strength that wanted nursing, it was my imagination that wanted soothing. I kept the bundle of papers given me by Kurtz, not knowing exactly what to do with it. His mother had died lately, watched over, as I was told, by his Intended. A clean-shaved man, with an official manner and wearing gold-rimmed spectacles, called on me one day and made inquiries, at first circuitous, afterwards suavely pressing, about what he was pleased to denominate certain 'documents.' I was not surprised, because I had had two rows with the manager on the subject out there. I had refused to give up the smallest scrap out of that package, and I took the same attitude with the spectacled man. He became darkly menacing at last, and with much heat argued that the Company had the right to every bit of information about its 'territories.' And said he, 'Mr. Kurtz's knowledge of unexplored regions must have been necessarily extensive and peculiar—owing to his great abilities and to the deplorable circumstances in which he had been placed: therefore——, I assured him Mr. Kurtz's knowledge, however extensive, did not bear upon the problems of commerce or administration. He invoked then the name of science. 'It would be an incalulable loss if,' etc., etc. I offered him the report on the 'Suppression of Savage Customs,' with the postscript torn off. He took it up eagerly, but ended by sniffing at it with an air of contempt. 'This is not what we had a right to expect,' he remarked. 'Expect nothing else,' I said. 'There are only private letters.' He withdrew upon some threat of legal proceedings, and I saw him no more; but another fellow, calling himself Kurtz's cousin, appeared two days later, and was anxious to hear all the details about his dear relative's last moments. Incidentally he gave me to understand that Kurtz had been essentially a great musician. 'There was the making of an immense success,' said the man, who was an organist, I believe, with lank grey hair flowing over a greasy coat-collar. I had no reason to doubt his statement; and to this day I am unable to say what was Kurtz's profession, whether he ever had any—which was the greatest of his talents. I had taken him for a painter who wrote for the papers, or else for a journalist who could paint—but even the cousin (who took snuff during the interview) could not tell me what he had been—exactly. He was a universal genius—on that point I agreed with the old chap, who thereupon blew his nose noisily into a large cotton handkerchief and withdrew in senile agitation, bearing off some family letters and memoranda without importance. Ultimately a journalist anxious to know something of the fate of his 'dear colleague' turned up. This visitor informed me Kurtz's proper sphere ought to have been politics 'on the popular side.' He had furry straight eyebrows, bristly hair cropped short, an eyeglass on a broad ribbon, and, becoming expansive, confessed his opinion that Kurtz really couldn't write a bit—'but heavens! how that man could talk. He electrified large meetings. He had faith—don't you see?—he had the faith. He could get himself to believe anything—anything. He would have been a splendid leader of an extreme party.' 'What party?' I asked. 'Any party,' answered the other. 'He was an—an—extremist.' Did I not think so? I assented. Did I know, he asked, with a sudden flash of curiosity, 'what it was that had induced him to go out there?' 'Yes,' said I, and forthwith handed him the famous Report for publication, if he thought fit. He glanced through it hurriedly, mumbling all the time, judged 'it would do,' and took himself off with this plunder.

"Thus I was left at last with a slim packet of letters and the girl's portait. She struck me as beautiful—I mean she had a beautiful expression. I know that the sunlight can be made to lie, too, yet one felt that no manpulation of light and pose could have conveyed the delicate shade of truthfulness upon those features. She seemed ready to listen without mental reservation, without suspicion, without a thought for herself. I concluded I would go and give her back her portrait and those letters myself. Curiosity? Yes; and also some other feeling perhaps. All that had had been Kurtz's had passed out of my hands: his soul, his body, his station, his plans, his ivory, his career. There remained only his memory and his Intended—and I wanted to give that up, too, to the past, in a way—to surrender personally all that remained of him with me to that oblivion which is the last word of our common fate. I don't defend myself. I had no clear perception of what it was I really wanted. Perhaps it was an impulse of unconscious loyalty, or the fulfilment of one of those ironic necessities that lurk in the facts of human existence. I don't know. I can't tell. But I went.

"I thought his memory was like the other memories of the dead that accumulate in every man's life—a vague impress on the brain of shadows that had fallen on it in their swift and final passage; but before the high and ponderous door, between the tall houses of a street as still and decorous as a well-kept alley in a cemetery, I had a vision of him on the stretcher, opening his mouth voraciously, as if to devour all the earth with all its mankind. He lived then before me; he lived as much as he had ever lived—a shadow insatiable of splendid appearances, of frightful realities; a shadow darker than the shadow of the night, and draped nobly in the folds of a gorgeous eloquence. The vision seemed to enter the house with me—the stretcher, the phantom-bearers, the wild crowd of obedient worshippers, the gloom of the forests, the glitter of the reach between the murky bends, the beat of the drum, regular and muffled like the beating of a heart—the heart of a conquering darkness. It was a moment of triumph for the wilderness, an invading and vengeful rush which, it seemed to me, I would have to keep back alone for the salvation of another soul. And the memory of what I had heard him say afar there, with the horned shapes stirring at my back, in the glow of fires, within the patient woods, those broken phrases came back to me, were heard again in their ominous and terrifying simplicity. I remembered his abject pleading, his abject threats, the colossal scale of his vile desires, the meanness, the torment, the tempestuous anguish of his soul. And later on I seemed to see his collected languid manner, when he said one day, 'This lot of ivory now is really mine. The Company did not pay for it. I collected it myself at a very great personal risk. I am afraid they will try to claim it as theirs though. H'm. It is a difficult case. What do you think I ought to do—resist? Eh? I want no more than justice.' . . . He wanted no more than justice—no more than justice. I rang the bell before a mahogany door on the first floor, and while I waited he seemed to stare at me out of the glassy panel—stare with that wide and immense stare embracing, condemning, loathing all the universe. I seemed to hear the whispered cry, 'The horror! The horror!'

"The dusk was falling. I had to wait in a lofty drawingroom with three long windows from floor to ceiling that were like three luminous and bedraped columns. The bent gilt legs and backs of the furniture shone in indistinct curves. The tall marble fireplace had a cold and monumental whiteness. A grand piano stood massively in a corner; with dark gleams on the flat surfaces like a sombre and polished sarcophagus. A high door opened—closed. I rose.

"She came forward, all in black, with a pale head, floating towards me in the dusk. She was in mourning. It was more than a year since his death, more than a year since the news came; she seemed as though she would remember and mourn forever. She took both my hands in hers and murmured, 'I had heard you were coming.' I noticed she was not very young—I mean not girlish. She had a mature capacity for fidelity, for belief, for suffering. The room seemed to have grown darker, as if all the sad light of the cloudy evening had taken refuge on her forehead. This fair hair, this pale visage, this pure brow, seemed surrounded by an ashy halo from which the dark eyes looked out at me. Their glance was guileless, profound, confident, and trustful. She carried her sorrowful head as though she were proud of that sorrow, as though she would say, 'I—I alone know how to mourn for him as he deserves.' But while we were still shaking hands, such a look of awful desolation came upon her face that I perceived she was one of those creatures that are not the play-things of Time. For her he had died only yesterday. And, by Jove! the impression was so powerful that for me, too, he seemed to have died only yesterday—nay, this very minute. I saw her and him in the same instant of time—his death and her sorrow—I saw her sorrow in the very moment of his death. Do you understand? I saw them together—I heard them together. She had said, with a deep catch of the breath, 'I have survived' while my strained ears seemed to hear distinctly, mingled with her tone of despairing regret, the summing up whisper of his eternal condemnation. I asked myself what I was doing there, with a sensation of panic in my heart as though I had blundered into a place of cruel and absurd mysteries not fit for a human being to behold. She motioned me to a chair. We sat down. I laid the packet gently on the little table, and she put her hand over it. . . . 'You knew him well,' she murmured, after a moment of mourning silence.

" 'Intimacy grows quickly out there,' I said. 'I knew him as well as it is possible for one man to know another.'

" 'And you admired him,' she said. 'It was impossible to know him and not to admire him. Was it?'

" 'He was a remarkable man,' I said, unsteadily. Then before the appealing fixity of her gaze, that seemed to watch for more words on my lips, I went on, 'It was impossible not to——'

" 'Love him,' she finished eagerly, silencing me into an appalled dumbness. 'How true! how true! But when you think that no one knew him so well as I! I had all his noble confidence. I knew him best.'

" 'You knew him best,' I repeated. And perhaps she did. But with every word spoken the room was growing darker, and only her forehead, smooth and white, remained illumined by the unextinguishable light of belief and love.

" 'You were his friend,' she went on. 'His friend,' she repeated, a little louder. 'You must have been, if he had given you this, and sent you to me. I feel I can speak to you—and oh! I must speak. I want you—you who have heard his last words—to know I have been worthy of him. . . . It is not pride. . . . Yes! I am proud to know I understood him better than any one on earth—he told me so himself. And since his mother died I have had no one—no one—to—to——,

"I listened. The darkness deepened. I was not even sure whether he had given me the right bundle. I rather suspect he wanted me to take care of another batch of his papers which, after his death, I saw the manager examining under the lamp. And the girl talked, easing her pain in the certitude of my sympathy; she talked as thirsty men drink. I had heard that her engagement with Kurtz had been disapproved by her people. He wasn't rich enough or something. And indeed I don't know whether he had not been a pauper all his life. He had given me some reason to infer that it was his impatience of comparative poverty that drove him out there.

"'. . . Who was not his friend who had heard him speak once?' she was saying. 'He drew men towards him by what was best in them.' She looked at me with intensity. 'It is the gift of the great,' she went on, and the sound of her low voice seemed to have the accompaniment of all the other sounds, full of mystery, desolation, and sorrow, I had ever heard—the ripple of the river, the soughing of the trees swayed by the wind, the murmurs of the crowds, the faint ring of incomprehensible words cried from afar, the whisper of a voice speaking from beyond the threshold of an eternal darkness. 'But you have heard him! You know!' she cried.

"'Yes, I know,' I said with something like despair in my heart, but bowing my head before the faith that was in her, before that great and saving illusion that shone with an unearthly glow in the darkness, in the triumphant darkness from which I could not have defended her—from which I could not even defend myself.

"'What a loss to me—to us!'—she corrected herself with beautiful generosity; then added in a murmur, 'To the world.' By the last gleams of twilight I could see the glitter of her eyes, full of tears—of tears that would not fall.

"'I have been very happy—very fortunate—very proud,' she went on. 'Too fortunate. Too happy for a little while. And now I am unhappy for —for life.'

"She stood up; her fair hair seemed to catch all the remaining light in a glimmer of gold. I rose, too.

"'And of all this,' she went on mournfully, 'of all his promise, and of all his greatness, of his generous mind, of his noble heart, nothing remains—nothing but a memory. You and I——'

"'We shall always remember him,' I said hastily.

"'No!' she cried. 'It is impossible that all this should be lost—that such a life should be sacrificed to leave nothing—but sorrow. You know what vast plans he had. I knew of them, too—I could not perhaps understand—but others knew of them. Something must remain. His words, at least, have not died.'

"'His words will remain,' I said.

"'And his example,' she whispered to herself. 'Men looked up to him—his goodness shone in every act. His example——'

"'True,' I said; 'his example, too. Yes, his example. I forgot that.'

"'But I do not. I cannot—I cannot believe—not yet. I cannot believe that I shall never see him again, that nobody will see him again, never, never, never.'

"She put out her arms as if after a retreating figure, stretching them back and with clasped pale hands across the fading and narrow sheen of the window. Never see him! I saw him clearly enough then. I shall see this eloquent phantom as long as I live, and I shall see her, too, a tragic and familiar Shade, resembling in this gesture another one, tragic also, and bedecked with powerless charms, stretching bare brown arms over the glitter of the infernal stream, the stream of darkness. She said suddenly very low, 'He died as he lived.'

" 'His end,' said I, with dull anger stirring in me, 'was in every way worthy of his life.'

" 'And I was not with him,' she murmured. My anger subsided before a feeling of infinite pity.

" 'Everything that could be done——' I mumbled.

"Ah, but I believed in him more than any one on earth—more than his own mother, more than—himself. He needed me! Me! I would have treasured every sigh, every word, every sign, every glance.'

"I felt like a chill grip on my chest. 'Don't,' I said, in a muffled voice.

" 'Forgive me. I—I have mourned so long in silence—in silence. . . . You were with him—to the last? I think of his loneliness. Nobody near to understand him as I would have understood. Perhaps no one to hear. . . .'

" 'To the very end,' I said, shakily. 'I heard his very last words. . . .' I stopped in a fright.

" 'Repeat them,' she murmured in a heart-broken tone. 'I want—I want—something—something—to—to live with.'

"I was on the point of crying at her, 'Don't you hear them?' The dusk was repeating them in a persistent whisper all around us, in a whisper that seemed to swell menacingly like the first whisper of a rising wind. 'The horror! The horror!'

" 'His last word—to live with,' she insisted. 'Don't you understand I loved him—I loved him—I loved him!'

"I pulled myself together and spoke slowly.

" 'The last word he pronounced was—your name.'

"I heard a light sigh and then my heart stood still, stopped dead short by an exulting and terrible cry, by the cry of inconceivable triumph and of unspeakable pain. 'I knew it—I was sure!' . . . She knew. She was sure. I heard her weeping; she had hidden her face in her hands. It seemed to me that the house would collapse before I could escape, that the heavens would fall upon my head. But nothing happened. The heavens do not fall for such a trifle. Would they have fallen, I wonder, if I had rendered Kurtz that justice which was his due? Hadn't he said he wanted only justice? But I couldn't. I could not tell her. It would have been too dark—too dark altogether. . . ."

Marlow ceased, and sat apart, indistinct and silent, in the pose of a meditating Buddha. Nobody moved for a time. "We have lost the first of the ebb," said the Director suddenly. I raised my head. The offing was barred by a black bank of clouds, and the tranquil waterway leading to the uttermost ends of the earth flowed sombre under an overcast sky— seemed to lead into the heart of an immense darkness.

II.
Encountering Things: Consciousness in the World

What impels a man to sit down to write? Or, to extend the question, why does man create artifacts, art works that have no evident practical value, no immediate usability—paintings, sculptures, poems, model railroads? The activity he performs in creating any of these things is no doubt a form of play that involves the elaboration of a fiction in the dual sense of the word suggested by *fingere:* something that is both *feigned* and *fabricated*—"made up" in two senses. On the most basic level, this feigning and fabricating, this play of the mind and the hands, no doubt have to do with making sense of experience and the world: we "make up" in order to "make sense of," in order to get a grasp on something that would otherwise be incomprehensible, alien to us, other.

To take the problem in its simplest and most radical form: man is consciousness within a world of nonconsciousness. He is, in fact, defined by his essential difference from the world he inhabits, and his self-consciousness is a product of his awareness of this difference. He constantly uses this "difference" to process the world, in an attempt to understand his place in it, its meaning to him, and his meaning to it. As Wallace Stevens argues in his poem "Notes Toward a Supreme Fiction":

> From this the poem springs: that we live in a place
> That is not our own and, much more, not ourselves
> And hard it is in spite of blazoned days.

The art work is compelled into being from the fact that we are not what we live amidst. Even our daydreams—a more or less continuous process by which consciousness reflects on itself as it moves about in the world—seem to be ways of making the phenomena we encounter *mean* in relation to us, making the world inhabitable for consciousness. The activity

187

of building a model railroad is a more concerted form of the mind's processing of phenomena: the fabricating of miniature models with which the human hand and mind can play would appear to be a way of asserting the control of consciousness over phenomena that, outside the model, are unassimilable, even threatening. In terms of literary fictions, description of the world seems to provide a first location and orientation of man in the world. The very fact of writing about phenomena—the putting into language of the things amidst which man lives—may be a first and basic step in asserting the leverage of the human on the nonhuman and making the world assimilable to consciousness.

The world, said the French poet Paul Claudel, is before us like a text to be deciphered. The statement assumes that the world must mean, must be susceptible to the inquiries of consciousness. It really presupposes a prior decision of consciousness that the world shall mean, and an effort to make it mean: the world of the nonhuman must be made to bear the human imprint, be put into relation with man, who can perhaps best be seen as *Homo signiferens*, the bearer of signs and sense, the creator of systems of signs that are sense-making systems. Man could not live with his self-consciousness were he not a sign-maker and a sense-maker, and this is no doubt one of the chief functions of his fiction-making.

The selections of Part II suggest different kinds of attempts to make the world outside of man signify. The first two sections taken together offer a radical alternative, setting forth what could be regarded as the two poles that define the field of the problem. Alain Robbe-Grillet, in a radical argument, contends that we must refuse the temptation to make the world mean, to find a human imprint on things, and must realize that our common tendency to believe in the "romantic heart of things" has nothing to do with the definition of things themselves, but is rather a product of our need to make the world a mirror of human soulstates. Robbe-Grillet claims that writing should seek to preserve a sense of the otherness and neutrality of the objective world. The second group of texts, in contrast, provides examples of a very basic and very old— conceivably the oldest—way of imprinting the human on the world and thereby making sense of it. This is simply man's *naming* of the world. Adam, giving names to things, understands their use and their essence, and hence begins to understand his own place in the ecosystem. His sense of his difference from what surrounds him—his self-consciousness— gives him the power to name, and by naming he begins to locate his own identity.

The personal effort to find, or to make, the world, especially the natural world, not only identifiable but inhabited by meaning is (as Robbe-Grillet detected) pre-eminently the concern of writers in the Romantic tradition. Standing at the threshold of the nineteenth century, the Romantics were perhaps the first writers to feel themselves living in a universe where the old explanatory myths that made every individual thing part of an all-embracing system of spiritual reality no longer obtained: most notably, Christianity, the organizing spiritual, psychological, and political ideal of Europe for centuries, had lost its cohesive and explanatory force. Hence these writers were forced to re-create the relationships of consciousness to the world without the mediations of any predetermined world view, virtually *ex nihilo*. Their naked confrontation with things and their attempts to talk about them suggest that on the plane of rhetoric the most radical, basic instance of fiction is metaphor: the transference (*meta-pherein:* to transport, carry across) of objects into the sphere of consciousness and signification. For Blake, Wordsworth, Keats, and indeed most subsequent writers, the attempt to come to terms with the objective world is posited on a belief that phenomena are not simply "other," cold and neutral. There must, these writers imply, be some concordance of the order of mind and the order of things. But this concordance is not self-evident: it must be wrested from the confrontation with things, from a personal vision of the objective world. The vision reposes on a metaphor, on the discovery of analogies that permit the movement of transference from the realm of natural things to the realm of spiritual things (and vice versa). The critic and theorist of language I. A. Richards has given a general definition of metaphor as a "transaction between contexts," and here it is the transaction between the context of phenomena and the context of mind which is the central imaginative act. As Wordsworth argues in his famous "Ode: Intimations of Immortality," what counts most for man facing his environment are

> those obstinate questionings
> Of sense and outward things,
> Fallings from us, vanishings;
> Blank misgivings of a Creature
> Moving about in worlds not realised . . .

Vision directed at the world "out there" must strive to "realize" these worlds, to make the obstinate questionings lead to an answer by which the world yields a sense of its interrelationship with man.

The metaphor generated by the confrontation of consciousness with things may lie at the inception of fiction-making. One could in fact legitimately argue that naming itself is metaphor in that it represents a transposition of contexts, the "moving" of an object from the realm of phenomenal existence into the realm of linguistic existence. Naming is a "putting into language" of things, the invention of a system of signs to represent the order of things. For mind to discourse of the world at all, metaphor (still using the term in the broadest sense) must be established. Robbe-Grillet's desire to banish metaphor from his descriptions does not infirm this view: destroying the human imprint on things is probably impossible because the very existence of language itself is so closely linked to the creation of human sense that no text—no organized system of linguistic signs—could fail to register that imprint. It exists in our words *for* things. We may even consider that if the making of sense-giving sign systems is crucial to the survival of consciousness within the world of nonconsciousness, metaphor, this root version of fiction-making, is part of the very definition of man.

The use of metaphor to suggest the "romantic heart of things" has not always been so subtle, serious, and self-aware as in Wordsworth, Blake, or Keats. The effort to create a relationship between mind and the world has more often appeared in facile and sentimentalized versions. It has often become what John Ruskin called "the pathetic fallacy," which is the unconscious projection of human emotion onto things, the assumption that the landscape really does react in accordance with human emotions, that things, we might say, bleed in their romantic hearts. We accept a kind of identity of the objective and subjective worlds, and the two contexts of the metaphor lose all distinction. A certain class of children's literature shows this process in extreme form: how many stories are there in which fire engines, tugboats, steam shovels, and teapots are animized and sentimentalized? These objects shed tears when they are stashed away out of obsolescence and puff up with pride when they emerge from retirement to serve their masters. Another example of such an exploitation of the "romantic heart of things" is the implications of much advertising concerned with manufactured objects: the fictions (written, sung, or pictorial) that surround the objects and create a context for them are not intended to be perceived as fictions independent of the object. The message of the fiction is rather supposed to play back on the object, to endow it with qualities of glamour and desirability, so that the way of life evoked in the fiction becomes part of the object and makes it glow with significance. One version of a world inhabited by meaning is in fact an environment of objects related to consciousness through their simple possessability, through the desire for and possibility of acquisition. This desire, and the charged field that it creates around certain valued objects and the way of life they seem to represent, can also be the main thrust of the plot in many modern fictions, as the story *Gobseck* suggests.

The metaphorical links of consciousness and objects can operate in other ways, especially with those writers whose confrontation of the object is mediated by preassumed systems of relations and significances, and who as a result seem to have little difficulty in reading the world as a decipherable text, usually with an explicit or implicit Christian context. The poetry of metaphysical wit is of this type: thought can be embodied in objective form because the objective world is seen to be consonant with the spiritual, its existence subject to the interpretations of the spirit. Mind can with no difficulty play with things. The predominant modern version of the relationship between mind and things called symbolism resembles this play with things only superficially, and is in fact closer to a development of Romantic metaphor. The metaphorist seems almost arbitrarily to charge certain privileged objects with special meanings—often personal meanings—and these objects are consciously made to shine, to bathe in transcendence, while their simultaneous existence as real, untranscendent objects is also recognized. We are asked to see objects as representing what they cannot in fact embody, as new "words" in a superior language.

In considering the following representative efforts of consciousness to deal with the world of things, those that appear falsifications and those that answer to our own views of reality, it is perhaps well to keep in mind both the "fictionality" of each effort (its version is not "provable") and its necessity: it is through the free play of our fiction-making that we make a home for ourselves in the world. As we learned to name the parts of the body through nursery rhymes like "This little piggy went to market," so we learn the names of things through fictions. Without fictions there would be no names for things.

Looking at Things

Alain Robbe-Grillet (1922–) argues the need to reject totally any human imprint on things. Yet one could ask whether description can ever be wholly neutral, and whether objects can ever be wholly "innocent" when consciousness is regarding and registering them. Rejection of the usual links between mind and things may set up its own form of commerce between the two: in considering the texts from *Snapshots,* "The Dressmaker's Dummy" and "In the Corridors of the Metro," one might think of the remark by a French critic, Jean Ricardou, that "things, marked by the refusal of consciousness, become charged with what consciousness refuses."

The Dressmaker's Dummy

Alain Robbe-Grillet

Translated by Bruce Morrissette

The coffeepot is on the table.

It is a four-legged round table, covered with a waxy oilcloth patterned in red and gray squares against a neutral background of yellowish white that may have been formerly ivory colored—or white. In the center, a square ceramic tile serves as a protective base; its design is entirely hidden, or at least made unrecognizable, by the coffeepot placed upon it.

The coffeepot is made of brown earthenware. It consists of a sphere topped by a cylindrical filter holder with a mushroom-shaped lid. The spout is an S with flattened curves, widening out slightly at the base. The handle has, perhaps, the shape of an ear, or rather of the outer fold of an ear; but it would be a misshapen ear, too circular and lacking a lobe, which would thus resemble a "pitcher handle." The spout, the handle, and the mushroom lid are of a creamy color. The rest is of a very light, smooth brown, and shiny.

There is nothing on the table except the waxy tablecloth, the ceramic base, and the coffeepot.

On the right, in front of the window, stands the dressmaker's dummy.

Behind the table, the space above the mantel holds a large rectangular mirror in which may be seen half of the window (the right half) and, on the left (that is, on the right side of the window), the reflection of the wardrobe with its mirror front. In the wardrobe mirror the window may again be seen, in its entirety now, and unreversed (that is, the right French pane on the right and the left one on the left).

Thus there are, above the mantel, three half-sections of window one after another, with an almost unresolved continuity, and which are, in turn (from left to right): one left section unreversed, one right section unreversed, and one right section reversed. Since the wardrobe stands in the corner of the room and extends to the outer edge of the window, the two right half-sections of the latter are seen separated only by a narrow vertical piece of wardrobe, which might be the wood separating the two French window sections (the right upright edge of the left side joined to the left edge of the right side). The three window sections, above the half-curtains, give a view of the leafless trees in the garden.

In this way, the window takes up the entire surface of the mirror, except for the upper portion, in which can be seen a strip of ceiling and the top of the mirrored wardrobe.

In the mirror above the mantel may be seen two other dressmaker's dummies: one in front of the first window section, the narrowest, at the far left, and the other in front of the third section (the one farthest to the right). Neither one is seen straight on; the one on the right has its right side facing the view; the one on the left, slightly smaller, reveals its left side. But it is difficult to be certain of this on first glance, because the two reflections are facing in the same direction and as a consequence both seem to be turned so that the same side shows—the left side, probably.

The three dummies stand in a line. The middle one, whose size is intermediate between that of the two others, occupies the right side of the mirror, in exactly the same direction as the coffeepot standing on the table.

In the spherical surface of the coffeepot is a shiny, distorted reflection of the window, a sort of four-sided figure whose sides form the arcs of a circle. The line of the wooden uprights between the two window sections widens abruptly at the bottom into a vague spot. This is, no doubt, the shadow of the dressmaker's dummy.

The room is quite bright, since the window is unusually wide, even though it has only two sections.

A good smell of hot coffee rises from the pot on the table.

The dressmaker's dummy is no longer in its accustomed spot: it is normally placed in the corner by the window, opposite the mirrored wardrobe. The wardrobe has been placed in its position to help with the fittings.

The design on the ceramic tile base is the picture of an owl, with two large, somewhat frightening eyes. But, for the moment, it cannot be made out, because of the coffeepot.

In the Corridors of the Metro

Alain Robbe-Grillet

Translated by Bruce Morrissette

The Escalator

A group, motionless, at the bottom of the long iron-gray escalator, whose steps flatten out one after the other, at the level of the top platform, disappearing one by one with a noise of well-oiled machinery, with a heavy regularity nevertheless, and at the same time jerky, that produces an impression of unusual velocity at the place where the steps disappear one after the other beneath the horizontal surface, but which seem on the contrary to be moving extremely slowly, and without any sudden jerks, to the glance which, moving down the successive steps, again discovers at the bottom of the long, rectilinear escalator, as if still at the same spot, the identical group whose posture has not varied even slightly, a motionless group, standing on the bottommost steps, having barely left the bottom platform, has suddenly become frozen for the duration of the mechanical ascent, has come to a stop suddenly, in the midst of its agitation, of its haste, as if the act of stepping on the moving stairs had immediately paralyzed their bodies, one after the other, in poses simultaneously relaxed and stiff, suspended, marking a temporary halt in an interrupted race, while the length of the escalator continues its rise, in a regular, uniform movement, rectilinear, slow, almost imperceptible, obliquely tilted to the line of the vertical bodies.

There are five bodies, occupying three or four adjacent steps, on the left side of the stairs, more or less close to the handrail, which moves along—it also—sharing the same movement now made even less perceptible, even more doubtful, by the form of the handrail, a simple, thick ribbon of black rubber, with an unbroken surface, with two straight edges, on which no identifiable mark allows its speed to be determined, except for the two hands resting on it, about a yard apart, toward the bottom of the narrow, slanting band which everywhere else seems stationary, two hands moving upward regularly, without a jerk, synchronously with the whole system.

The uppermost of these two hands belongs to a man wearing a gray suit, of a gray that seems pale, uncertain, yellowish in the yellow light, standing alone on one step, at the top of the group, his body quite straight, his legs together, his left arm held close to his chest, his left hand holding a newspaper folded twice, over which his face leans in a position that looks somewhat exaggerated, so sharply is his neck bent forward, and whose main effect is to expose clearly, instead of his forehead and nose, the extensive bald area of the top of his head, a large round area of pink, shiny scalp across which runs, glued to the skin, a thin, wavy strand of reddish hair.

But the face suddenly looks up, toward the top of the escalator, displaying the forehead, the nose, the mouth in an expressionless array, and remains thus several moments, longer certainly than would be necessary to be sure that the ascent, still not terminated, allows the reading of the newspaper article to be continued, as the man finally decides may be done, abruptly lowering his head, without his face, again hidden now, having revealed by the slightest sign what kind of interest he might have had in his surroundings, which indeed may not even have been observed by those two wide-open, staring eyes, with their empty look. Where the face was, in the same position as at the outset, the round skull appears, with its bald zone in the middle.

As if the man, in the midst of the reading that he has resumed, suddenly thought of that long, empty stairway, perfectly straight, that he so recently contemplated without seeing, and as if he wished by a sort of reflex, or delayed response, also to look backward, to see whether a similar empty space extended in that direction, he turns around, as abruptly as he had raised his face instants before, and without moving the rest of his body. He can observe thus that four persons are standing behind him, motionless, rising smoothly at the same speed as his own, and he immediately resumes his original position, reading his newspaper. The other passengers have not stirred.

Two steps below, after one empty step, are a woman and a child. The woman is positioned exactly behind the man with the newspaper, but she has not placed her right hand on the rail: her arm hangs beside her body, holding some handbag, or grocery sack, or roundish package whose brown bulk barely extends beyond the man's gray pants on one side, thus preventing its exact nature to be determined. The woman is neither old nor young; her face looks tired. She is wearing a red raincoat and a varicolored scarf knotted under her chin. At her left the child, a boy about ten years old wearing a turtleneck sweater and tight pants of blue denim, stands with his head half hanging down on his shoulder, his face turned upward to the right, toward the woman's profile, or else, slightly in front of it, toward the bare wall, uniformly covered with little rectangular tiles of white ceramic, that passes by with absolute regularity above the handrail, between the woman and the man with the newspaper.

There follow, always at the same speed, against this brilliant, white background cut into innumerable little rectangles, all identical and placed in orderly rows with continuous horizontal joints and alternating vertical joints, two silhouettes of men wearing dark-colored suits, the first standing behind the woman dressed in the red raincoat, two steps lower down, keeping his right hand on the rail, then, after three empty steps, the second, standing behind the child, his head hardly rising higher than the boy's thonged sandals, that is, a little below his knees, marked in the back of the blue pants by a multitude of horizontal wrinkles in the cloth.

And the rigid group continues to rise, the posture of each person remaining as unchanged as his relative position in the group. But, since the man at the top had turned around to look down, the man below him, wondering no doubt about the object of this abnormal attention, turns around also. He sees only the long series of steps leading down, and, at the very bottom of the straight, iron-gray escalator, a motionless group, standing on the bottommost steps, having just left the bottom platform, and which now rises with the same slow, sure movement, and remains constantly at the same, fixed distance.

A Corridor

A not too dense crowd of people in a hurry, all walking at the same speed, is traveling down a corridor that has no side passages, running between two elbow turns whose obtuse arcs completely hide the final exits, and whose walls are adorned, on the right as well as on the left, by identical advertising posters following each other at equal intervals. The posters display a woman's head, almost as high by itself alone as one of the people of normal height who pass in front of it, walking quickly, without a side glance.

This giant face, with its tightly curled blond hair, its eyes surrounded by very long lashes, its red lips, its white teeth, is shown in a three-quarter pose, smiling as it looks at the passers-by hurrying past one after the other, while beside it, on the left, a bottle of carbonated pop, at a forty-five-degree angle, points its opening at the partially opened mouth. The advertising slogan is written in cursive letters, in two lines: the word "even" placed above the bottle, and the word "purer" below, at the bottom of the sign, on a line that slants upward slightly from the horizontal lower edge of the poster.

196

The same words are found in the same place on the following poster, with the same tilted bottle whose contents are ready to spill out, and the same impersonal smile. Then, after an empty space covered with white ceramic tile, the same scene again, frozen at the same moment when the lips approach the top of the bottle held forward and the liquid contents about to gush forth, in front of which the same hurrying crowd passes by without turning a head, moving along toward the next poster.

And the mouths multiply, as do the bottles and the eyes as large as hands in the midst of their long, curving lashes. And, on the other wall of the corridor, the same features are exactly repeated (with this difference, that the directions of the glance and the bottle are reversed), following each other at constant intervals on the other side of the dark silhouettes of the travelers, who continue to move by, in a scattered but uninterrupted order, against the sky-blue background of the posters, between the reddish bottles and the pink faces with their parted lips. But, just before the elbow turn at the end of the straight corridor, the crowd is slowed down by a man who has stopped, about a yard away from the left wall. The man has on a gray suit, somewhat worn from wear, and is holding in his right hand, which hangs down alongside his body, a newspaper folded twice. He is engaged in staring at the wall, in the vicinity of a nose, bigger than his whole face, which is located level with his own eyes.

In spite of the great size of the drawing and the lack of details in its execution, the observer's head is bent forward, as if to see more clearly. The passers-by have to move aside momentarily from their straight trajectory in order to get around this unexpected obstacle; almost all pass behind the man, but some, noticing too late the scrutiny that they are about to interrupt, or not willing to change their course for such a minor matter, or aware of nothing at all, pass between the man and the poster, cutting straight through the glance.

Behind the Automatic Door

The crowd has come to a stop behind a double automatic door, now closed, that prevents access to the station platform. The stairs leading down to this area are completely full of bodies pressed one against the other, so that only the heads are visible, with few spaces between them. All the heads are motionless. The faces are frozen, showing no expression of annoyance, impatience, or hope.

Behind the frizzled expanse of the heads, men's heads for the most part, without hats, with short hair and protruding ears, and which slopes downward following the angle of the stairs, but without allowing the regularity of the steps to be perceived, rises the upper portion of the automatic doors, extending a foot or more above the closest row of heads. The two portions of the doors, closed, allow only a tiny space between, almost imperceptible. They are attached, one on the right and the other on the left, to two very straight, narrow members from which they pivot outward when opened. But, for the time being, these two pivots and the two sections of the automatic doors form a practically continuous wall which blocks all passage, rising from the level of the bottommost step.

The whole door system is painted dark green, each of the two sections bearing a big white sign against a rectangular red background, covering almost the entire width. Only the top line of the sign, "Automatic Door," is higher than the last row of heads, which allow only isolated letters of the next line to be glimpsed among the ears of the crowd.

The tightly packed heads slanting gently down the stair slope, the words "Automatic Door" twice repeated across the corridor, then, above, a horizontal band of dark green lacquer. . . . Still higher, the space is free again, up to the semicircular vault overhead, which connects the ceiling of the stairway to that of the station proper, prolonging the former to its extremity.

In this semicircular opening appears thus a part of the train platform, very small in area, and, higher up on the left, in the form of a segment of a circle subtended by the oblique chord formed by the edge of the platform, an even smaller fragment of one car of the train now stopped alongside the platform.

It is the side of a car made of green sheet-iron, no doubt at the very end of the train, after the last doorway, in front of which the travelers are waiting to push into the interior. Something is probably preventing them from entering as quickly as they would like—passengers getting off, or too many people inside—for they remain almost immobile, as far as one can judge by the thin margin of the crowd lying within the field of view.

The only visible elements, in fact, above the hair of the heads and the inscription at the top of the closed automatic doors, are the shoes and the trouser bottoms of the men waiting to get on the train, cut off below the knee by the circular vault of the ceiling.

The trousers are dark in color. The shoes are black, dusty. From time to time, one of them makes an upward movement, then returns to the floor, having moved forward scarcely half an inch, or not at all, or even having moved slightly backward. The nearby shoes, in front and in back, perform, next, similar movements, whose results are as imperceptible. And everything comes to rest again. Lower down, also motionless, after the band of painted metal bearing the words "Automatic Door," come the heads with their close-cut hair, their protruding ears, their expressionless faces.

198

FROM A Future for the Novel

Alain Robbe-Grillet

Translated by Richard Howard

Even the least conditioned observer is unable to see the world around him through entirely unprejudiced eyes. Not, of course, that I have in mind the naive concern for objectivity which the analysts of the (subjective) soul find it so easy to smile at. Objectivity in the ordinary sense of the word—total impersonality of observation—is all too obviously an illusion. But *freedom* of observation should be possible, and yet it is not. At every moment, a continuous fringe of culture (psychology, ethics, metaphysics, etc.) is added to things, giving them a less alien aspect, one that is more comprehensible, more reassuring. Sometimes the camouflage is complete: a gesture vanishes from our mind, supplanted by the emotions which supposedly produced it, and we remember a landscape as *austere* or *calm* without being able to evoke a single outline, a single determining element. Even if we immediately think, "That's literary," we don't try to react against the thought. We accept the fact that what is *literary* (the word has become pejorative) functions like a grid or screen set with bits of different colored glass that fracture our field of vision into tiny assimilable facets.

And if something resists this systematic appropriation of the visual, if an element of the world breaks the glass, without finding any place in the interpretative screen, we can always make use of our convenient category of "the absurd" in order to absorb this awkward residue.

But the world is neither significant nor absurd. It *is,* quite simply. That, in any case, is the most remarkable thing about it. And suddenly the obviousness of this strikes us with irresistible force. All at once the whole splendid construction collapses; opening our eyes unexpectedly, we have experienced, once too often, the shock of this stubborn reality we were pretending to have mastered. Around us, defying the noisy pack of our animistic or protective adjectives, things *are there.* Their surfaces are distinct and smooth, *intact,* neither suspiciously brilliant nor transparent. All our literature has not yet succeeded in eroding their smallest corner, in flattening their slightest curve.

The countless movie versions of novels that encumber our screens provide an occasion for repeating this curious experiment as often as we like. The cinema, another heir of the psychological and naturalistic tradition, generally has as its sole purpose the transposition of a story into images: it aims exclusively at imposing on the spectator, through the intermediary of some well-chosen scenes, the same meaning the written sentences communicated in their own fashion to the reader. But at any given moment the filmed narrative can drag us out of our interior comfort and into this proffered world with a violence not to be found in the corresponding text, whether novel or scenario.

Anyone can perceive the nature of the change that has occurred. In the initial novel, the objects and gestures forming the very fabric of the plot disappeared completely, leaving behind only their *significations:* the empty chair became only absence or expectation, the hand placed on a shoulder became a sign of friendliness, the bars on the window became only the impossibility of leaving. . . . But in the cinema, one *sees* the chair, the movement of the hand, the shape of the bars. What they signify remains obvious, but instead of monopolizing our attention, it becomes something added, even something in excess, because what affects us, what persists in our memory, what appears as essential and irreducible to vague intellectual concepts are the gestures themselves, the objects, the movements, and the outlines, to which the image has suddenly (and unintentionally) restored their *reality.*

It may seem peculiar that such fragments of crude reality, which the filmed narrative cannot help presenting, strike us so vividly, whereas identical scenes in real life do not suffice to free us of our blindness. As a matter of fact, it is as if the very conventions of the photographic medium (the two dimensions, the black-and-white images, the frame of the screen, the difference of scale between scenes) help free us from our own conventions. The slightly "unaccustomed" aspect of this reproduced world reveals, at the same time, the unaccustomed character of the world that surrounds us: it, too, is unaccustomed insofar as it refuses to conform to our habits of apprehension and to our classification.

Instead of this universe of "signification" (psychological, social, functional), we must try, then, to construct a world both more solid and more immediate. Let it be first of all by their *presence* that objects and gestures establish themselves, and let this presence continue to prevail over whatever explanatory theory that may try to enclose them in a system of references, whether emotional, sociological, Freudian or metaphysical.

In this future universe of the novel, gestures and objects will be *there* before being *something;* and they will still be there afterwards, hard, unalterable, eternally present, mocking their own "meaning," that meaning which vainly tries to reduce them to the role of precarious tools, of a temporary and shameful fabric woven exclusively—and deliberately —by the superior human truth expressed in it, only to cast out this awkward auxiliary into immediate oblivion and darkness.

Henceforth, on the contrary, objects will gradually lose their instability and their secrets, will renounce their pseudo-mystery, that suspect interiority which Roland Barthes has called "the romantic heart of things." No longer will objects be merely the vague reflection of the hero's vague soul, the image of his torments, the shadow of his desires. Or rather, if objects still afford a momentary prop to human passions, they will do so only provisionally, and will accept the tyranny of significations only in appearance—derisively, one might say—the better to show how alien they remain to man.

As for the novel's characters, they may themselves suggest many possible interpretations; they may, according to the preoccupations of each reader, accommodate all kinds of comment—psychological, psychiatric, religious, or political—yet their indifference to these "potentialities" will soon be apparent. Whereas the traditional hero is constantly solicited, caught up, destroyed by these interpretations of the author's, ceaselessly projected into an immaterial and unstable *elsewhere*, always more remote and blurred, the future hero will remain, on the contrary, *there*. It is the commentaries that will be left elsewhere; in the face of his irrefutable presence, they will seem useless, superfluous, even improper.

FROM Nature.Humanism.Tragedy

Alain Robbe-Grillet

Translated by Richard Howard

Is there not, first of all, a certain fraudulence in this word *human* which is always being thrown in our faces? If it is not a word quite devoid of meaning, what meaning does it really have?

It seems that those who use it all the time, those who make it the sole criterion of all praise as of all reproach, identify—deliberately, perhaps—a precise (and limited) reflection on man, his situation in the world, the phenomena of his existence, with a certain anthropocentric atmosphere, vague but imbuing all things, giving the world its so-called *signification,* that is, investing it from within by a more or less disingenuous network of sentiments and thoughts. Simplifying, we can summarize the position of our new inquisitors in two sentences; if I say, "The world is man," I shall always gain absolution; while if I say, "Things are things, and man is only man," I am immediately charged with a crime against humanity.

The crime is the assertion that there exists something in the world which is not man, which makes no sign to him, which has nothing in common with him. The crime, above all, according to this view, is to remark this separation, this distance, without attempting to effect the slightest sublimation of it.

What could be, in other words, an "inhuman" work? How, in particular, could a novel which deals with a man, and follows his steps from page to page, describing only what he does, what he sees, or what he imagines, how could such a novel be accused of turning away from man? And it is not the character himself, let us make that clear at once, who is involved in this judgment. As a "character," as an individual animated by torments and passions, no one will ever reproach him with being inhuman, even if he is a sadistic madman and a criminal—the contrary, it would seem.

But now suppose the eyes of this man rest on things without indulgence, insistently: he sees them, but he refuses to appropriate them, he refuses to maintain any suspect understanding with them, any complicity; he asks nothing of them; toward them he feels neither agreement nor dissent of any kind. He can, perhaps, make them the prop of his passions, as of his sense of sight. But his sense of sight is content to take their measurements; and his passion, similarly, rests on their surface, without attempting to penetrate them since there is nothing inside, without feigning the least appeal since they would not answer.

To condemn, in the name of the human, the novel which deals with such a man is therefore to adopt the *humanist* point of view, according to which it is not enough to show man where he is: it must further be proclaimed that man is everywhere. On the pretext that man can achieve only a subjective knowledge of the world, humanism decides to elect man the justification of everything. A true bridge of souls thrown between man and things, the humanist outlook is preeminently a pledge of solidarity.

In the literary realm, the expression of this solidarity appears chiefly as the investigation, worked up into a system, of analogical relations.

Metaphor, as a matter of fact, is never an innocent figure of speech. To say that the weather is "capricious" or the mountain "majestic," to speak of the "heart" of the forest, of a "pitiless" sun, of a village "huddled" in the valley, is, to a certain degree, to furnish clues as to the things themselves: shape, size, situation, etc. But the choice of an analogical vocabulary, however simple, already does something more than account for purely physical data, and what this *more* is can scarcely be ascribed only to the credit of belles-lettres. The height of the mountain assumes, willy-nilly, a moral value; the heat of the sun becomes the result of an intention. . . . In almost the whole of our contemporary literature, these anthropomorphic analogies are repeated too insistently, too coherently not to reveal an entire metaphysical system.

More or less consciously, the goal for the writers who employ such a terminology can only be to establish a constant relation between the universe and the being who inhabits it. Thus man's sentiments will seem alternately to derive from his contacts with the world and to find in that world their natural correspondence if not their fulfillment.

Metaphor, which is supposed to express only a comparison, without any particular motive, actually introduces a subterranean communication, a movement of sympathy (or of antipathy) which is its true *raison d'être*. For, as comparison, metaphor is almost always a useless comparison which contributes nothing new to the description. What would the village lose by being merely "situated" in the valley? The word "huddled" gives us no complementary information. On the other hand it transports the reader (in the author's wake) into the imagined soul of the village; if I accept the word "huddled," I am no longer entirely a spectator; I myself become the village, for the duration of a sentence, and the valley functions as a cavity into which I aspire to disappear.

Taking this possible adherence as their basis, the defenders of metaphor reply that it thereby possesses an advantage: that of making apparent an element which was not so. Having himself become the village, they say, the reader participates in the latter's situation, hence understands it better. Similarly in the case of the mountain: I shall make it easier to see the mountain by saying it is majestic than by measuring the apparent angle from which my gaze registers its height. . . . And this is true sometimes, but it always involves a more serious reversal: it is precisely this participation which is problematical, since it leads to the notion of a hidden unity.

It must even be added that the gain in descriptive value is here no more than an alibi: the true lovers of metaphor seek only to impose the idea of a communication. If they did not possess the verb "huddle," they would not even mention the position of the village. The height of the mountain would be nothing to them, if it did not offer the moral spectacle of "majesty."

Such a spectacle, for them, never remains entirely *external*. It always implies, more or less, a gift received by man: the things around him are like the fairies in the tale, each of whom brought as a gift to the new-born child one of the traits of his future character. The mountain might thus have first communicated to me the feeling of the majestic—that is what is insinuated. This feeling would then be developed in me and, by a natural growth, engender others: magnificence, prestige, heroism, nobility, pride. In my turn I would refer these to other objects, even those of a lesser size (I would speak of a proud oak, of a vase of noble lines), and the world would become the depository of all my aspirations to greatness, would be both their image and their justification, for all eternity.

The same would be true of every feeling, and in these incessant exchanges, multiplied to infinity, I could no longer discern the origin of anything. Was majesty to be located first within, or around me? The question itself would lose its meaning. Only a sublime communion would remain between the world and me.

Then, with habit, I would easily go much farther. Once the principle of this communion was admitted, I would speak of the melancholy of a landscape, of the indifference of a stone, of the fatuousness of a coal scuttle. These new metaphors no longer furnish appreciable information about the objects subject to my scrutiny, but the world of things has been so thoroughly contaminated by my mind that it is henceforth susceptible of any emotion, of any character trait. I will forget that it is I, I alone, who feels melancholy or suffers solitude; these affective elements will soon be considered as the *profound reality* of the material universe, the sole reality—to all intents and purposes—worthy of engaging my interest in it.

Hence there is much more involved than describing our consciousness by using things as raw material, as one might build a cabin out of logs. To identify in this way my own melancholy with that which I attribute to a landscape, to admit this link as more than superficial, is thereby to acknowledge a certain predestination for my present life: this landscape existed *before* me; if it is really the landscape which is sad, it was *already* sad before me, and this correspondence I experience today between its form and my mood were here waiting for me long before I was born; this melancholy has been fated for me forever. . . .

We see to what point the idea of a human *nature* can be linked to the analogical vocabulary. This nature, common to all men, eternal and inalienable, no longer requires a God to establish it. It is enough to know that Mont Blanc has been waiting for me in the heart of the Alps since the tertiary era, and with it all my notions of greatness and purity!

This nature, moreover, does not merely belong to man, since it constitutes the link between his mind and things: it is, in fact, an essence common to all "creation" that we are asked to believe in. The universe and I now have only one soul, only one secret.

Belief in a *nature* thus reveals itself as the source of all humanism, in the habitual sense of the word. And it is no accident if Nature precisely—mineral, animal, vegetable Nature—is first of all clogged with an anthropomorphic vocabulary. This Nature—mountain, sea, forest, desert, valley—is simultaneously our model and our heart. It is, at the same time, within us and around us. It is neither provisional nor contingent. It encrusts us, judges us, and ensures our salvation.

To reject our so-called "nature" and the vocabulary which perpetuates its myth, to propose objects as purely external and superficial, is not—as has been claimed—to deny man; but it is to reject the "pananthropic" notion contained in traditional humanism, and probably in all humanism. It is no more in the last analysis than to lay claim, quite logically, to my freedom.

Therefore nothing must be neglected in this mopping-up operation. Taking a closer look, we realize that the anthropocentric analogies (mental or visceral) are not the only ones to be arraigned. *All* analogies are just as dangerous. And perhaps the most dangerous ones of all are the most secret, those in which man is not named.

204

Let us give some examples, at random. To discover the shape of a horse in the heavens may, of course, derive from a simple process of description and not be of any consequence. But to speak of the "gallop" of the clouds, or of their "flying mane," is no longer entirely innocent. For if a cloud (or a wave or a hill) possesses a mane, if later on the mane of a stallion "flings arrows," if the arrow . . . etc., the reader of such images will emerge from the universe of forms to find himself plunged into a universe of significations. Between the wave and the horse, he will be tempted to conceive an undifferentiated profundity: passion, pride, power, wildness. . . . The idea of a nature leads infallibly to that of a nature common to all things, that is, a *superior* or *higher* nature. The idea of an interiority always leads to the idea of a transcendence.

And the task extends step by step: from the bow to the horse, from the horse to the wave—and from the sea to love. A common nature, once again, must be the eternal answer to the *single question* of our Greco-Christian civilization; the Sphinx is before me, questions me, I need not even try to understand the terms of the riddle being asked, there is only one answer possible, only one answer to everything: man.

This will not do.

There are *questions,* and *answers.* Man is merely, from his own point of view, the only witness.

Man looks at the world, and the world does not look back at him. Man sees things and discovers, now, that he can escape the metaphysical pact others had once concluded for him, and thereby escape servitude and terror. That he can . . . that he *may,* at least, some day.

He does not thereby refuse all contact with the world; he consents on the contrary to utilize it for material ends: a utensil, *as* a utensil, never possesses "depth"; a utensil is entirely form and matter—and purpose.

Man grasps his hammer (or a stone he has selected) and pounds on a stake he wants to drive into the ground. While he uses it in this way, the hammer (or the stone) is merely form and substance: its weight, the striking surface, the other extremity which allows him to hold it. Afterward, man sets the tool down in front of him; if he no longer needs it, the hammer is no more than a thing among things: outside of his use, it has no signification.

And man today (or tomorrow) no longer experiences this absence of signification as a lack, or as a laceration. Confronting such a void, he henceforth feels no dizziness. His heart no longer needs an abyss in which to lodge.

For if he rejects communion, he also rejects tragedy.

Tragedy may be defined, here, as an attempt to "recover" the distance which exists between man and things as a new value; it would be then a test, an ordeal in which victory would consist in being vanquished. Tragedy therefore appears as the last invention of humanism to permit nothing to escape: since the correspondence between man and things has finally been denounced, the humanist saves his empire by immediately instituting a new form of solidarity, the divorce itself becoming a major path to redemption.

There is still almost a communion, but a *painful* one, perpetually in doubt and always deferred, its effectiveness in proportion to its inaccessible character. Divorce-as-a-form-of-marriage is a trap—and it is a falsification.

We see in effect to what degree such a union is perverted: instead of being the quest for a good, it is now the benediction of an evil. Unhappiness, failure, solitude, guilt, madness—such are the accidents of our existence which we are asked to entertain as the best pledges of our salvation. To entertain, not to accept: it is a matter of feeding them at our expense while continuing to struggle against them. For tragedy involves neither a true acceptance nor a true rejection. It is the sublimation of a difference.

Let us retrace, as an example, the functioning of "solitude." I call out. No one answers me. Instead of concluding that there is no one there—which could be a pure and simple observation, dated and localized in space and time—I decide to act as if there *were* someone there, but someone who, for one reason or another, will not answer. The silence which follows my outcry is henceforth no longer a *true* silence; it is charged with a content, a meaning, a depth, a soul—which immediately sends me back to my own. The distance between my cry, to my own ears, and the mute (perhaps deaf) interlocutor to whom it is addressed becomes an anguish, my hope and my despair, a meaning in my life. Henceforth nothing will matter except this false void and the problems it raises for me. Should I call any longer? Should I shout louder? Should I utter different words? I try once again. . . . Very quickly I realize that no one will answer; but the invisible presence I continue to create by my call obliges me to hurl my wretched cries into the silence forever. Soon the sound they make begins to stupefy me. As though bewitched, I call again . . . and again. My solitude, aggravated, is ultimately transmuted into a superior necessity for my alienated consciousness, a promise of my redemption. And I am obliged, if this redemption is to be fulfilled, to persist until my death, crying out for nothing.

According to the habitual process, my solitude is then no longer an accidental, momentary datum of my existence. It becomes part of me, of the entire world, of all men: it is our nature, once again. It is a solitude forever.

Naming Things

As Robbe-Grillet clearly recognizes, the root of the problem is that man lives in a world of things that are other, not himself, and must find a way to be at home there. First of all, perhaps, he must identify the objects amidst which he lives, for this is part of his self-identification. Such an identification implies that what in rhetoric was once called *nominatio*—the naming and listing of things—is possibly the most basic act of consciousness in the world: the process by which man articulates the world to make it signify, and hence renders it inhabitable.

FROM Genesis

2

And out of the ground the Lord God formed every beast of the field, and every fowl of the air; and brought them unto Adam to see what he would call them: and whatsoever Adam called every living creature, that was the name thereof. And Adam gave names to all cattle, and to the fowl of the air, and to every beast of the field. . . .

FROM **Paradise Lost**

John Milton

(*Adam speaks*)
For Man to tell how human Life began   250
Is hard; for who himself beginning knew?
Desire with thee still longer to converse
Induc'd me. As new wak't from soundest sleep
Soft on the flow'ry herb I found me laid
In Balmy Sweat, which with his Beams the Sun
Soon dri'd, and on the reeking moisture fed.
Straight toward Heav'n my wond'ring Eyes I turn'd,
And gaz'd a while the ample Sky, till rais'd
By quick instinctive motion up I sprung,
As thitherward endeavoring, and upright   260
Stood on my feet; about me round I saw
Hill, Dale, and shady Woods, and sunny Plains,
And liquid Lapse of murmuring Streams; by these,
Creatures that liv'd, and mov'd, and walk'd, or flew,
Birds on the branches warbling; all things smil'd,
With fragrance and with joy my heart o'erflow'd.
Myself I then perus'd, and Limb by Limb
Survey'd, and sometimes went, and sometimes ran
With supple joints, as lively vigor led:·
But who I was, or where, or from what cause,   270
Knew not; to speak I tri'd, and forthwith spake,
My Tongue obey'd and readily could name
Whate'er I saw. Thou Sun, said I, fair Light,
And thou enlight'n'd Earth, so fresh and gay,
Ye Hills and Dales, ye Rivers, Woods, and Plains
And ye that live and move, fair Creatures, tell,
Tell, if ye saw, how came I thus, how here?

Adam's Task

John Hollander

"*And Adam gave names to all cattle, and
to the fowl of the air, and to every
beast of the field . . .*"—Gen. 2:20

Thou, paw-paw-paw; thou, glurd; thou, spotted
   Glurd; thou, whitestap, lurching through
The high-grown brush; thou, pliant-footed,
   Implex; thou, awagabu.

Every burrower, each flier
　　Came for the name he had to give:
Gay, first work, ever to be prior,
　　Not yet sunk to primitive.

Thou, verdle; thou, McFleery's pomma;
　　Thou; thou; thou—three types of grawl;　　　　10
Thou, flisket; thou, kabasch; thou, comma-
　　Eared mashawk; thou, all; thou, all.

Were, in a fire of becoming,
　　Laboring to be burned away,
Then work, half-measuring, half-humming,
　　Would be as serious as play.

Thou, pambler; thou, rivarn; thou, greater
　　Wherret, and thou, lesser one;
Thou, sproal; thou, zant; thou, lily-eater.
　　Naming's over. Day is done.　　　　　　20

Upon a Dead Man's Head

John Skelton

Sent to him from an honourable gentlewoman for a token,
he devised this ghostly meditation in English covenable,
in sentence commendable, lamentable, lacrimable, profitable for a soul.

　　　　Your ugly token
　　　　My mind hath broken
　　　　From worldly lust:
　　　　For I have discust
　　　　We are but dust,
　　　　And die we must.
　　　　　It is general
　　　　To be mortal:
　　　　I have well espied
　　　　No man may him hide　　　　　　10
　　　　From Death hollow-eyed,
　　　　With sinews witherèd,
　　　　With bonès shiverèd,
　　　　With his worm-eaten maw,
　　　　And his ghastly jaw
　　　　Gasping aside,
　　　　Naked of hide,
　　　　Neither flesh nor fell.°

18. *fell:* skin.

Then, by my counsell,
Look that ye spell   20
Well this gospell:
For whereso we dwell
Death will us quell,
And with us mell.°
For all our pampered paunches
There may no fraunchis,°
Nor worldly bliss,
Redeem us from this:
Our days be dated
To be check-mated   30
With draughtès of death
Stopping our breath:
Our eyen sinking,
Our bodies stinking,
Our gummès grinning,
Our soulès brinning.°
To whom, then, shall we sue,
For to have rescue,
But to sweet Jesu
On us then for to rue?   40
O goodly Child
Of Mary mild,
Then be our shield!
That we be not exiled
To the dun dale
Of bootless bale,
Nor to the lake
Of fiendès blake.
But grant us grace
To see thy Face,   50
And to purchase
Thine heavenly place,
And thy palace
Full of solace
Above the sky
That is so high,
Eternally
To behold and see
The Trinitie!
Amen.   60
Myrres vous y.°

24. *mell:* meddle.   26. *fraunchis:* franchise.
36. *brinning:* burning.   61. *Myrres vous y:* Look at yourself there.

Five Nursery Rhymes

Eye winker,
Tom tinker,
Nose smeller,
Mouth eater,
Chin chopper,
Guzzlewopper.

■

This little pig went to market,
This little pig stayed at home,
This little pig had roast beef,
This little pig had none,
And this little pig cried,
Wee-wee-wee-wee-wee,
I can't find my way home.

■

This little pig had a rub-a-dub,
This little pig had a scrub-a-scrub,
This little pig-a-wig ran upstairs,
This little pig-a-wig called out, Bears!
Down came the jar with a loud Slam! Slam!
And this little pig had all the jam.

■

Clap hands, clap hands,
Till father comes home;
For father's got money,
But mother's got none.

■

Clap hands, Daddy comes
With his pocket full of plums,
And a cake for *Johnny*.

FROM THE Odyssey

Homer

Translated by Robert Fitzgerald

A more complex example of the naming process is the identification of an object in terms of a man's life.

■

Upon Penélopê, most worn in love and thought,
Athena cast a glance like a grey sea
lifting her. Now to bring the tough bow out and bring
the iron blades. Now try those dogs at archery
to usher bloody slaughter in.

So moving stairward

the queen took up a fine doorhook of bronze,
ivory-hafted, smooth in her clenched hand,
and led her maids down to a distant room,
a storeroom where the master's treasure lay:
bronze, bar gold, black iron forged and wrought.   10
In this place hung the double-torsion bow
and arrows in a quiver, a great sheaf—
quills of groaning.

In the old time in Lakedaimon

her lord had got these arms from Íphitos,
Eurýtos' son. The two met in Messenia
at Ortílokhos' table, on the day
Odysseus claimed a debt owed by that realm—
sheep stolen by Messenians out of Ithaka
in their long ships, three hundred head, and herdsmen.
Seniors of Ithaka and his father sent him   20
on that far embassy when he was young.
But Íphitos had come there tracking strays,
twelve shy mares, with mule colts yet unweaned.

And a fatal chase they led him over prairies
into the hands of Heraklês. That massive
son of toil and mortal son of Zeus
murdered his guest at wine in his own house—
inhuman, shameless in the sight of heaven—
to keep the mares and colts in his own grange.
Now Íphitos, when he knew Odysseus, gave him   30
the master bowman's arm; for old Eurýtos
had left it on his deathbed to his son.
In fellowship Odysseus gave a lance
and a sharp sword. But Heraklês killed Íphitos

before one friend could play host to the other.
And Lord Odysseus would not take the bow
in the black ships to the great war at Troy.
As a keepsake he put it by:
it served him well at home in Ithaka.

Now the queen reached the storeroom door and halted.   40
Here was an oaken sill, cut long ago
and sanded clean and bedded true. Foursquare
the doorjambs and the shining door were set
by the careful builder. Penélopê untied the strap
around the curving handle, pushed her hook
into the slit, aimed at the bolts inside
and shot them back. Then came a rasping sound
as those bright doors the key had sprung gave way—
a bellow like a bull's vaunt in a meadow—
followed by her light footfall entering   50
over the plank floor. Herb-scented robes
lay there in chests, but the lady's milkwhite arms
went up to lift the bow down from a peg
in its own polished bowcase.

                                                 Now Penélopê
sank down, holding the weapon on her knees,
and drew her husband's great bow out, and sobbed
and bit her lip and let the salt tears flow.
Then back she went to face the crowded hall
tremendous bow in hand, and on her shoulder hung
the quiver spiked with coughing death.   60

Cinderella.
or the Little Glass Slipper

Charles Perrault

    Another, very old way of breaking through the seeming intractability of the world to a system of human significances is the postulate that things are not limited, hard and fixed, but subject to transformations that relate them to people in new and wonderful ways.

■

    Once there was a gentleman who married, for his second wife, the proudest and most haughty woman that was ever seen. She had, by a former husband, two daughters of her own humour, who were, indeed, exactly like her in all things. He had likewise, by another wife, a young daughter, but of unparalleled goodness and sweetness of temper, which she took from her mother, who was the best creature in the world.

No sooner were the ceremonies of the wedding over but the mother-in-law began to show herself in her true colours. She could not bear the good qualities of this pretty girl, and the less because they made her own daughters appear the more odious. She employed her in the meanest work of the house: she scoured the dishes, tables, etc., and rubbed madam's chamber, and those of misses, her daughters; she lay up in a sorry garret, upon a wretched straw bed, while her sisters lay in fine rooms, with floors all inlaid, upon beds of the very newest fashion, and where they had looking-glasses so large that they might see themselves at their full length from head to foot.

The poor girl bore all patiently, and dared not tell her father, who would have rattled her off; for his wife governed him entirely. When she had done her work, she used to go into the chimney-corner, and sit down among cinders and ashes, which made her commonly be called *Cinderwench*; but the youngest, who was not so rude and uncivil as the eldest, called her Cinderella. However, Cinderella, notwithstanding her mean apparel, was a hundred times handsomer than her sisters, though they were always dressed very richly.

It happened that the King's son gave a ball, and invited all persons of fashion to it. Our young misses were also invited, for they cut a very grand figure among the quality. They were mightily delighted at this invitation, and wonderfully busy in choosing out such gowns, petticoats, and head-clothes as might become them. This was a new trouble to Cinderella; for it was she who ironed her sisters' linen, and plaited their ruffles; they talked all day long of nothing but how they should be dressed.

"For my part," said the eldest, "I will wear my red velvet suit with French trimming."

"And I," said the youngest, "shall have my usual petticoat; but then, to make amends for that, I will put on my gold-flowered manteau, and my diamond stomacher, which is far from being the most ordinary one in the world."

They sent for the best tire-woman they could get to make up their head-dresses and adjust their double pinners, and they had their red brushes and patches from Mademoiselle de la Poche.

Cinderella was likewise called up to them to be consulted in all these matters, for she had excellent notions, and advised them always for the best, nay, and offered her services to dress their heads, which they were very willing she should do. As she was doing this, they said to her:

"Cinderella, would you not be glad to go to the ball?"

"Alas!" said she, "you only jeer me; it is not for such as I am to go thither."

"Thou art in the right of it," replied they; "it would make the people laugh to see a Cinderwench at a ball."

Anyone but Cinderella would have dressed their heads awry, but she was very good, and dressed them perfectly well. They were almost two days without eating, so much they were transported with joy. They broke above a dozen of laces in trying to be laced up close, that they might have a fine slender shape, and they were continually at their looking-glass. At last the happy day came; they went to Court, and Cinderella followed them with her eyes as long as she could, and when she had lost sight of them, she fell a-crying.

Her godmother, who saw her all in tears, asked her what was the matter.

"I wish I could—I wish I could—"; she was not able to speak the rest, being interrupted by her tears and sobbing.

This godmother of hers, who was a fairy, said to her, "Thou wishest thou couldst go to the ball; is it not so?"

"Y—es," cried Cinderella, with a great sigh.

"Well," said her godmother, "be but a good girl, and I will contrive that thou shalt go." Then she took her into her chamber, and said to her, "Run into the garden, and bring me a pumpkin."

Cinderella went immediately to gather the finest she could get, and brought it to her godmother, not being able to imagine how this pumpkin could make her go to the ball. Her godmother scooped out all the inside of it, having left nothing but the rind; which done, she struck it with her wand, and the pumpkin was instantly turned into a fine coach, gilded all over with gold.

She then went to look into her mouse-trap, where she found six mice, all alive, and ordered Cinderella to lift up a little the trap-door, when, giving each mouse, as it went out, a little tap with her wand, the mouse was that moment turned into a fine horse, which altogether made a very fine set of six horses of a beautiful mouse-coloured dapple-grey. Being at a loss for a coachman,

"I will go and see," says Cinderella, "if there is never a rat in the rat-trap—we may make a coachman of him."

"Thou art in the right," replied her godmother; "go and look."

Cinderella brought the trap to her, and in it there were three huge rats. The fairy made choice of one of the three which had the largest beard, and, having touched him with her wand, he was turned into a fat, jolly coachman, who had the smartest whiskers eyes ever beheld. After that, she said to her:

"Go again into the garden, and you will find six lizards behind the watering-pot, bring them to me."

She had no sooner done so but her godmother turned them into six footmen, who skipped up immediately behind the coach, with their liveries all bedaubed with gold and silver, and clung as close behind each other as if they had done nothing else their whole lives. The fairy then said to Cinderella:

"Well, you see here an equipage fit to go to the ball with; are you not pleased with it?"

"Oh! yes," cried she; "but must I go thither as I am, in these nasty rags?"

Her godmother only just touched her with her wand, and, at the same instant, her clothes were turned into cloth of gold and silver, all beset with jewels. This done, she gave her a pair of glass slippers, the prettiest in the whole world. Being thus decked out, she got up into her coach; but her godmother, above all things, commanded her not to stay till after midnight, telling her, at the same time, that if she stayed one moment longer, the coach would be a pumpkin again, her horses mice, her coachman a rat, her footmen lizards, and her clothes become just as they were before.

She promised her godmother she would not fail of leaving the ball before midnight; and then away she drives, scarce able to contain herself for joy. The King's son, who was told that a great princess, whom no-body knew, was come, ran out to receive her; he gave her his hand as she alighted out of the coach, and led her into the hall, among all the company. There was immediately a profound silence, they left off dancing, and the violins ceased to play, so attentive was everyone to contemplate the singular beauties of the unknown new-comer. Nothing was then heard but a confused noise of:

"Ha! how handsome she is! Ha! how handsome she is!"

The King himself, old as he was, could not help watching her, and telling the Queen softly that it was a long time since he had seen so beautiful and lovely a creature.

All the ladies were busied in considering her clothes and headdress, that they might have some made next day after the same pattern, provided they could meet with such fine materials and as able hands to make them.

The King's son conducted her to the most honourable seat, and afterwards took her out to dance with him; she danced so very gracefully that they all more and more admired her. A fine collation was served up, whereof the young prince ate not a morsel, so intently was he busied in gazing on her.

She went and sat down by her sisters, showing them a thousand civilities, giving them part of the oranges and citrons which the prince had presented her with, which very much surprised them, for they did not know her. While Cinderella was thus amusing her sisters, she heard the clock strike eleven and three-quarters, whereupon she immediately made a courtesy to the company and hasted away as fast as she could.

Being got home, she ran to seek out her godmother, and, after having thanked her, she said she could not but heartily wish she might go next day to the ball, because the King's son had desired her.

As she was eagerly telling her godmother whatever had passed at the ball, her two sisters knocked at the door, which Cinderella ran and opened.

"How long you have stayed!" cried she, gaping, rubbing her eyes and stretching herself as if she had been just waked out of her sleep; she had not, however, any manner of inclination to sleep since they went from home.

216

"If thou hadst been at the ball," says one of her sisters, "thou wouldst not have been tired with it. There came thither the finest princess, the most beautiful ever was seen with mortal eyes; she showed us a thousand civilities, and gave us oranges and citrons."

Cinderella seemed very indifferent in the matter; indeed, she asked them the name of that princess; but they told her they did not know it, and that the King's son was very uneasy on her account and would give all the world to know who she was. At this Cinderella, smiling, replied:

"She must, then, be very beautiful indeed; how happy you have been! Could not I see her? Ah! dear Miss Charlotte, do lend me your yellow suit of clothes which you wear every day."

"Ay, to be sure!" cried Miss Charlotte; "lend my clothes to such a dirty Cinderwench as thou art! I should be a fool."

Cinderella, indeed, expected well such answer, and was very glad of the refusal; for she would have been sadly put to it if her sister had lent her what she asked for jestingly.

The next day the two sisters were at the ball, and so was Cinderella, but dressed more magnificently than before. The King's son was always by her, and never ceased his compliments and kind speeches to her; to whom all this was so far from being tiresome that she quite forgot what her godmother had recommended to her; so that she, at last, counted the clock striking twelve when she took it to be no more than eleven; she then rose up and fled, as nimble as a deer. The Prince followed, but could not overtake her. She left behind one of her glass slippers, which the Prince took up most carefully. She got home, but quite out of breath, and in her nasty old clothes, having nothing left her of all her finery but one of the little slippers, fellow to that she dropped. The guards at the palace gate were asked:

If they had not seen a princess go out.

Who said: They had seen nobody go out but a young girl, very meanly dressed, and who had more the air of a poor country wench than a gentlewoman.

When the two sisters returned from the ball Cinderella asked them: If they had been well diverted, and if the fine lady had been there.

They told her: Yes, but that she hurried away immediately when it struck twelve, and with so much haste that she dropped one of her little glass slippers, the prettiest in the world, which the King's son had taken up; that he had done nothing but look at her all the time at the ball, and that most certainly he was very much in love with the beautiful person who owned the glass slipper.

What they said was very true; for a few days after the King's son caused it to be proclaimed, by sound of trumpet, that he would marry her whose foot this slipper would just fit. They whom he employed began to try it upon the princesses, then the duchesses and all the Court, but in vain; it was brought to the two sisters, who did all they possibly could to thrust their foot into the slipper, but they could not effect it. Cinderella, who saw all this, and knew her slipper, said to them, laughing:

"Let me see if it will not fit me."

Her sisters burst out a-laughing, and began to banter her. The gentleman who was sent to try the slipper looked earnestly at Cinderella, and, finding her very handsome, said:

It was but just that she should try, and that he had orders to let everyone make trial.

He obliged Cinderella to sit down, and, putting the slipper to her foot, he found it went on very easily, and fitted her as if it had been made of wax. The astonishment her two sisters were in was excessively great, but still abundantly greater when Cinderella pulled out of her pocket the other slipper, and put it on her foot. Thereupon, in came her godmother, who, having touched with her wand Cinderella's clothes, made them richer and more magnificent than any of those she had before.

And now her two sisters found her to be that fine, beautiful lady whom they had seen at the ball. They threw themselves at her feet to beg pardon for all the ill-treatment they had made her undergo. Cinderella took them up, and, as she embraced them, cried:

That she forgave them with all her heart, and desired them always to love her.

She was conducted to the young Prince, dressed as she was; he thought her more charming than ever, and, a few days after, married her. Cinderella, who was no less good than beautiful, gave her two sisters lodgings in the palace, and that very same day matched them with two great lords of the Court.

The Romantic
Heart of Things

Robbe-Grillet speaks of his intention to abolish the "romantic heart of things." That phrase, stripped of the pejorative connotation that Robbe-Grillet would give to it, can serve as a general label for the selections that follow. All these texts provide examples of the metaphors generated from the confrontation of consciousness with things. If those of the first group [1] may suggest basically a process of contemplation of things, and an attempt to understand their significance in relation to human consciousness, those in the second group would seem to include an effort to penetrate the heart of things—which may entail an anguished sense of alienation when man is reminded of his difference from things. The two poems of the third group represent, respectively, an experiment by Wordsworth in the extrapolation of a narrative from the suggestive properties of a thing; and the same poet's most ambitious attempt to describe the evolution of one man's relation to natural things. The fourth group brings us to what are probably examples of the "pathetic fallacy" that results when the natural world is thought of as literally endowed with human emotion, and the metaphorical process is no longer clearly recognized.

[1] Groups are indicated by the number of black squares next to each selection title.

▪ Mock On, Mock On

William Blake

Mock on, Mock on, Voltaire, Rousseau: °
Mock on, Mock on; 'tis all in vain!
You throw the sand against the wind,
And the wind blows it back again.

And every sand becomes a Gem
Reflected in the beams divine;
Blown back they blind the mocking Eye,
But still in Israel's paths they shine.

The Atoms of Democritus
And Newton's Particles of light °   10
Are sand upon the Red sea shore,
Where Israel's tents do shine so bright.

▪ To Autumn

John Keats

Season of mists and mellow fruitfulness,
    Close bosom-friend of the maturing sun;
Conspiring with him how to load and bless
    With fruit the vines that round the thatch-eaves run;
To bend with apples the moss'd cottage-trees,
    And fill all fruit with ripeness to the core;
        To swell the gourd, and plump the hazel shells
With a sweet kernel; to set budding more,
    And still more, later flowers for the bees,
    Until they think warm days will never cease,   10
        For Summer has o'er-brimmed their clammy cells.

Who hath not seen thee oft amid thy store?
    Sometimes whoever seeks abroad may find
Thee sitting careless on a granary floor,
    Thy hair soft-lifted by the winnowing wind;
Or on a half-reap'd furrow sound asleep,
    Drows'd with the fume of poppies, while thy hook
        Spares the next swath and all its twined flowers:

1. *Voltaire, Rousseau:* in Blake's view, two representatives of the skepticism of the Enlightenment.
10. *Atoms . . . light:* The Greek philosopher Democritus claimed that everything was made up of structures of atoms; Newton developed a corpuscular theory of light.

And sometimes like a gleaner thou dost keep
   Steady thy laden head across a brook;   20
   Or by a cider-press, with patient look,
      Thou watchest the last oozings hours by hours.

Where are the songs of Spring? Ay, where are they?
   Think not of them, thou hast thy music too,—
While barred clouds bloom the soft-dying day,
   And touch the stubble-plains with rosy hue;
Then in a wailful choir the small gnats mourn
   Among the river sallows, borne aloft
      Or sinking as the light wind lives or dies;
And full-grown lambs loud bleat from hilly bourn;   30
   Hedge-crickets sing; and now with treble soft
   The red-breast whistles from a garden-croft;
      And gathering swallows twitter in the skies.

▪ I Wandered Lonely as a Cloud

William Wordsworth

I wandered lonely as a cloud
That floats on high o'er vales and hills,
When all at once I saw a crowd,
A host of golden daffodils;
Beside the lake, beneath the trees,
Fluttering and dancing in the breeze.

Continuous as the stars that shine
And twinkle on the milky way,
They stretched in never-ending line
Along the margin of a bay: 10
Ten thousand saw I at a glance,
Tossing their heads in sprightly dance.

The waves beside them danced; but they
Out-did the sparkling waves in glee.
A poet could not but be gay,
In such a jocund company:
I gazed—and gazed—but little thought
What wealth the show to me had brought:

For oft, when on my couch I lie
In vacant or in pensive mood,   20
They flash upon that inward eye
Which is the bliss of solitude;
And then my heart with pleasure fills,
And dances with the daffodils.

▪ The Simplon Pass*

William Wordsworth

—Brook and road
Were fellow travellers in this gloomy Pass,
And with them did we journey several hours
At a slow step. The immeasurable height
Of woods decaying, never to be decayed,
The stationary blasts of waterfalls,
And in the narrow rent, at every turn,
Winds thwarting winds bewildered and forlorn,
The torrents shooting from the clear blue sky,
The rocks that muttered close upon our ears,   10
Black drizzling crags that spake by the wayside
As if a voice were in them, the sick sight
And giddy prospect of the raving stream,
The unfettered clouds and region of the heavens,
Tumult and peace, the darkness and the light—
Were all like workings of one mind, the features
Of the same face, blossoms upon one tree,
Characters of the great Apocalypse,
The types and symbols of Eternity,
Of first, and last, and midst, and without end.   20

▪ ▪ The Lamb

William Blake

Little Lamb, who made thee?
Dost thou know who made thee?
Gave thee life, & bid thee feed
By the stream & o'er the mead;
Gave thee clothing of delight,
Softest clothing, wooly, bright;
Gave thee such a tender voice,
Making all the vales rejoice?
Little Lamb, who made thee?
Dost thou know who made thee?   10

Little Lamb, I'll tell thee
Little Lamb, I'll tell thee:

* A pass through the Alps between Italy and Switzerland.

He is callèd by thy name,
For he calls himself a Lamb.
He is meek, & he is mild;
He became a little child.
I a child, & thou a lamb,
We are callèd by his name.
    Little Lamb, God bless thee!
    Little Lamb, God bless thee!   20

■ ■ The Tyger

William Blake

Tyger! Tyger! burning bright
In the forests of the night,
What immortal hand or eye
Could frame thy fearful symmetry?

In what distant deeps or skies
Burnt the fire of thine eyes?
On what wings dare he aspire?
What the hand dare seize the fire?

And what shoulder, & what art,
Could twist the sinews of thy heart?   10
And when thy heart began to beat,
What dread hand? & what dread feet?

What the hammer? what the chain?
In what furnace was thy brain?
What the anvil? what dread grasp
Dare its deadly terrors clasp?

When the stars threw down their spears,
And water'd heaven with their tears,
Did he smile his work to see?
Did he who made the Lamb make thee?   20

Tyger! Tyger! burning bright
In the forests of the night,
What immortal hand or eye,
Dare frame thy fearful symmetry?

■ ■ On Seeing the Elgin Marbles

John Keats

My spirit is too weak—mortality
Weighs heavily on me like unwilling sleep,
And each imagined pinnacle and steep
Of godlike hardship, tells me I must die
Like a sick Eagle looking at the sky.
Yet 'tis a gentle luxury to weep
That I have not the cloudy winds to keep,
Fresh for the opening of the morning's eye.
Such dim-conceivèd glories of the brain
Bring round the heart an undescribable feud;   10
So do these wonders a most dizzy pain,
That mingles Grecian grandeur with the rude
Wasting of old Time—with a billowy main—
A sun—a shadow of a magnitude.

■ ■ Ode on a Grecian Urn

John Keats

Thou still unravish'd bride of quietness,
    Thou foster-child of silence and slow time,
Sylvan historian, who canst thus express
    A flowery tale more sweetly than our rhyme:
What leaf-fring'd legend haunts about thy shape
    Of deities or mortals, or of both,
        In Tempe or the dales of Arcady?
What men or gods are these? What maidens loth?
    What mad pursuit? What struggle to escape?
        What pipes and timbrels? What wild ecstasy?   10

Heard melodies are sweet, but those unheard
    Are sweeter; therefore, ye soft pipes, play on;
Not to the sensual ear, but, more endear'd,
    Pipe to the spirit ditties of no tone:
Fair youth, beneath the trees, thou canst not leave
    Thy song, nor ever can those trees be bare;
        Bold Lover, never, never canst thou kiss
Though winning near the goal—yet, do not grieve;
    She cannot fade, though thou hast not thy bliss,
        For ever wilt thou love, and she be fair!   20

Ah, happy, happy boughs! that cannot shed
  Your leaves, nor ever bid the Spring adieu;
And, happy melodist, unwearied,
  For ever piping songs for ever new;
More happy love! more happy, happy love!
  For ever warm and still to be enjoy'd,
    For ever panting, and for ever young;
All breathing human passion far above,
  That leaves a heart high-sorrowful and cloy'd,
    A burning forehead, and a parching tongue.   30

Who are these coming to the sacrifice?
  To what green altar, O mysterious priest,
Lead'st thou that heifer lowing at the skies,
  And all her silken flanks with garlands dressed?
What little town by river or sea shore,
  Or mountain-built with peaceful citadel,
    Is emptied of this folk, this pious morn?
And, little town, thy streets for evermore
  Will silent be; and not a soul to tell
    Why thou art desolate, can e'er return.   40

O Attic shape! Fair attitude! with brede
  Of marble men and maidens overwrought
With forest branches and the trodden weed;
  Thou, silent form, dost tease us out of thought
As doth eternity: Cold Pastoral!
  When old age shall this generation waste,
    Thou shalt remain, in midst of other woe
Than ours, a friend to man, to whom thou say'st,
  "Beauty is truth, truth beauty,"—that is all
    Ye know on earth, and all ye need to know.   50

▪ ▪ ▪ The Thorn

William Wordsworth

Wordsworth writes: "Arose out of my observing, on the ridge of Quantock Hill, on a stormy day, a thorn which I had often past, in calm and bright weather, without noticing it. I said to myself, 'Cannot I by some invention do as much to make this thorn permanently an impressive object as the storm has made it to my eyes at this moment?' I began the poem accordingly, and composed it with great rapidity."

▪

"There is a Thorn—it looks so old,
  In truth, you'd find it hard to say

How it could ever have been young,
It looks so old and grey.
Not higher than a two years' child
It stands erect, this aged Thorn;
No leaves it has, no prickly points;
It is a mass of knotted joints,
A wretched thing forlorn.
It stands erect, and like a stone   10
With lichens is it overgrown.

"Like rock or stone, it is o'ergrown,
With lichens to the very top,
And hung with heavy tufts of moss,
A melancholy crop:
Up from the earth these mosses creep,
And this poor Thorn they clasp it round
So close, you'd say that they are bent
With plain and manifest intent
To drag it to the ground;   20
And all have joined in one endeavour
To bury this poor Thorn for ever.

"High on a mountain's highest ridge,
Where oft the stormy winter gale
Cuts like a scythe, while through the clouds
It sweeps from vale to vale;
Not five yards from the mountain path,
This Thorn you on your left espy;
And to the left, three yards beyond,
You see a little muddy pond   30
Of water—never dry,
Though but of compass small, and bare
To thirsty suns and parching air.

"And, close beside this aged Thorn,
There is a fresh and lovely sight,
A beauteous heap, a hill of moss,
Just half a foot in height.
All lovely colours there you see,
All colours that were ever seen;
And mossy network too is there,   40
As if by hand of lady fair
The work had woven been;
And cups, the darlings of the eye,
So deep is their vermilion dye.

"Ah me! what lovely tints are there
Of olive green and scarlet bright,
In spikes, in branches, and in stars,
Green, red, and pearly white!

This heap of earth o'ergrown with moss,
Which close beside the Thorn you see,   50
So fresh in all its beauteous dyes,
Is like an infant's grave in size,
As like as like can be:
But never, never any where,
An infant's grave was half so fair.

"Now would you see this aged Thorn,
This pond, and beauteous hill of moss,
You must take care and choose your time
The mountain when to cross.
For oft there sits between the heap,   60
So like an infant's grave in size,
And that same pond of which I spoke,
A Woman in a scarlet cloak,
And to herself she cries,
'Oh misery! oh misery!
Oh woe is me! oh misery!'

"At all times of the day and night
This wretched Woman thither goes;
And she is known to every star,
And every wind that blows;   70
And there, beside the Thorn, she sits
When the blue daylight's in the skies,
And when the whirlwind's on the hill,
Or frosty air is keen and still,
And to herself she cries,
'Oh misery! oh misery!
Oh woe is me! oh misery!' "

"Now wherefore, thus, by day and night,
In rain, in tempest, and in snow,
Thus to the dreary mountain-top   80
Does this poor Woman go?
And why sits she beside the Thorn
When the blue daylight's in the sky
Or when the whirlwind's on the hill,
Or frosty air is keen and still,
And wherefore does she cry?—
O wherefore? wherefore? tell me why
Does she repeat that doleful cry?"

"I cannot tell; I wish I could;
For the true reason no one knows: 90
But would you gladly view the spot,
The spot to which she goes;
The hillock like an infant's grave,
The pond—and Thorn, so old and grey;

227

Pass by her door—'tis seldom shut—
And if you see her in her hut—
Then to the spot away!
I never heard of such as dare
Approach the spot when she is there."

"But wherefore to the mountain-top   100
Can this unhappy Woman go,
Whatever star is in the skies,
Whatever wind may blow?"
"Full twenty years are past and gone
Since she (her name is Martha Ray)
Gave with a maiden's true good-will
Her company to Stephen Hill;
And she was blithe and gay,
While friends and kindred all approved
Of him whom tenderly she loved.   110

"And they had fixed the wedding day,
The morning that must wed them both;
But Stephen to another Maid
Had sworn another oath;
And, with this other Maid, to church
Unthinking Stephen went—
Poor Martha! on that woeful day
A pang of pitiless dismay
Into her soul was sent;
A fire was kindled in her breast,   120
Which might not burn itself to rest.

"They say, full six months after this,
While yet the summer leaves were green,
She to the mountain-top would go,
And there was often seen.
What could she seek?—or wish to hide?
Her state to any eye was plain;
She was with child, and she was mad;
Yet often was she sober sad
From her exceeding pain.   130
O guilty Father—would that death
Had saved him from that breach of faith!

"Sad case for such a brain to hold
Communion with a stirring child!
Sad case, as you may think, for one
Who had a brain so wild!
Last Christmas-eve we talked of this,
And grey-haired Wilfred of the glen
Held that the unborn infant wrought

228

About its mother's heart, and brought   140
Her senses back again:
And, when at last her time drew near,
Her looks were calm, her senses clear.

"More know I not, I wish I did,
And it should all be told to you;
For what became of this poor child
No mortal ever knew;
Nay—if a child to her was born
No earthly tongue could ever tell;
And if 'twas born alive or dead,   150
Far less could this with proof be said;
But some remember well,
That Martha Ray about this time
Would up the mountain often climb.

"And all that winter, when at night
The wind blew from the mountain-peak,
'Twas worth your while, though in the dark,
The churchyard path to seek:
For many a time and oft were heard
Cries coming from the mountain head: 160
Some plainly living voices were;
And others, I've heard many swear,
Were voices of the dead:
I cannot think, whate'er they say,
They had to do with Martha Ray.

"But that she goes to this old Thorn,
The Thorn which I described to you,
And there sits in a scarlet cloak,
I will be sworn is true.
For one day with my telescope,   170
To view the ocean wide and bright,
When to this country first I came,
Ere I had heard of Martha's name,
I climbed the mountain's height:—
A storm came on, and I could see
No object higher than my knee.

" 'Twas mist and rain, and storm and rain:
No screen, no fence could I discover;
And then the wind! in sooth, it was
A wind full ten times over.   180
I looked around, I thought I saw
A jutting crag,—and off I ran,
Head-foremost, through the driving rain,
The shelter of the crag to gain;

And, as I am a man,
Instead of jutting crag, I found
A Woman seated on the ground.

"I did not speak—I saw her face;
Her face!—it was enough for me;
I turned about and heard her cry,   190
'Oh misery! oh misery!'
And there she sits, until the moon
Through half the clear blue sky will go;
And, when the little breezes make
The waters of the pond to shake,
As all the country know,
She shudders, and you hear her cry,
'Oh misery! oh misery!' "

"But what's the Thorn? and what the pond?
And what the hill of moss to her?   200
And what the creeping breeze that comes
The little pond to stir?"
"I cannot tell; but some will say
She hanged her baby on the tree;
Some say she drowned it in the pond,
Which is a little step beyond:
But all and each agree,
The little Babe was buried there,
Beneath that hill of moss so fair.

"I've heard, the moss is spotted red   210
With drops of that poor infant's blood;
But kill a new-born infant thus,
I do not think she could!
Some say if to the pond you go,
And fix on it a steady view,
The shadow of a babe you trace,
A baby and a baby's face,
And that it looks at you;
Whene'er you look on it, 'tis plain
The baby looks at you again.   220

"And some had sworn an oath that she
Should be to public justice brought;
And for the little infant's bones
With spades they would have sought.
But instantly the hill of moss
Before their eyes began to stir!
And, for full fifty yards around,
The grass—it shook upon the ground!
Yet all do still aver

The little Babe lies buried there,   230
Beneath that hill of moss so fair.

"I cannot tell how this may be,
But plain it is the Thorn is bound
With heavy tufts of moss that strive
To drag it to the ground;
And this I know, full many a time,
When she was on the mountain high,
By day, and in the silent night,
When all the stars shone clear and bright,
That I have heard her cry,   240
'Oh misery! oh misery!
Oh woe is me! oh misery!' "

▪ ▪ ▪ Ode: Intimations of Immortality from Recollections of Early Childhood

William Wordsworth

I

There was a time when meadow, grove, and stream,
The earth, and every common sight,
      To me did seem
      Apparelled in celestial light,
The glory and the freshness of a dream.
It is not now as it hath been of yore;—
      Turn wheresoe'er I may,
         By night or day,
The things which I have seen I now can see no more.

II

      The Rainbow comes and goes,   10
      And lovely is the Rose;
      The Moon doth with delight
Look round her when the heavens are bare;
      Waters on a starry night
      Are beautiful and fair;
   The sunshine is a glorious birth;
   But yet I know, where'er I go,
That there hath past away a glory from the earth.

III

Now, while the birds thus sing a joyous song,
   And while the young lambs bound   20
      As to the tabor's sound,
To me alone there came a thought of grief:
A timely utterance gave that thought relief,
      And I again am strong:
The cataracts blow their trumpets from the steep;
No more shall grief of mine the season wrong;
I hear the Echoes through the mountains throng,
The Winds come to me from the fields of sleep,
      And all the earth is gay;
         Land and sea   30
    Give themselves up to jollity,
      And with the heart of May
   Doth every Beast keep holiday;—
     Thou Child of Joy,
Shout round me, let me hear thy shouts, thou
     happy Shepherd-boy!

IV

Ye blessed Creatures, I have heard the call
   Ye to each other make; I see
The heavens laugh with you in your jubilee;
   My heart is at your festival,
    My head hath its coronal,
The fulness of your bliss, I feel—I feel it all.   40
     Oh evil day! if I were sullen
     While Earth herself is adorning,
       This sweet May-morning,
     And the Children are culling
       On every side,
    In a thousand valleys far and wide,
    Fresh flowers; while the sun shines warm,
And the Babe leaps up on his Mother's arm:—
   I hear, I hear, with joy I hear!   50
   —But there's a Tree, of many, one,
A single Field which I have looked upon,
Both of them speak of something that is gone;
     The Pansy at my feet
     Doth the same tale repeat:
Whither is fled the visionary gleam?
Where is it now, the glory and the dream?

V

Our birth is but a sleep and a forgetting:
The Soul that rises with us, our life's Star,
     Hath had elsewhere its setting,   60
     And cometh from afar:

232

Not in entire forgetfulness,
 And not in utter nakedness,
But trailing clouds of glory do we come
 From God, who is our home:
Heaven lies about us in our infancy!
Shades of the prison-house begin to close
 Upon the growing Boy,
But He beholds the light, and whence it flows,
 He sees it in his joy;   70
The Youth, who daily farther from the east
 Must travel, still is Nature's Priest,
 And by the vision splendid
 Is on his way attended;
At length the Man perceives it die away,
And fade into the light of common day.

     VI

Earth fills her lap with pleasures of her own;
Yearnings she hath in her own natural kind,
And, even with something of a Mother's mind,
 And no unworthy aim,   80
 The homely Nurse doth all she can
To make her Foster-child, her Inmate Man,
 Forget the glories he hath known,
And that imperial palace whence he came.

     VII

Behold the Child among his new-born blisses,
A six years' Darling of a pigmy size!
See, where 'mid work of his own hand he lies,
Fretted by sallies of his mother's kisses,
With light upon him from his father's eyes!
See, at his feet, some little plan or chart,   90
Some fragment from his dream of human life,
Shaped by himself with newly-learnèd art;
 A wedding or a festival,
 A mourning or a funeral;
  And this hath now his heart,
 And unto this he frames his song:
  Then will he fit his tongue
To dialogues of business, love, or strife;
 But it will not be long
 Ere this be thrown aside,   100
 And with new joy and pride
The little Actor cons another part;
Filling from time to time his "humorous stage"
With all the Persons, down to palsied Age,
That Life brings with her in her equipage;
 As if his whole vocation
 Were endless imitation.

VIII

Thou, whose exterior semblance doth belie
     Thy Soul's immensity;
Thou best Philosopher, who yet dost keep   110
Thy heritage, thou Eye among the blind,
That, deaf and silent, read'st the eternal deep,
Haunted for ever by the eternal mind,—
     Mighty Prophet! Seer blest!
     On whom those truths do rest,
Which we are toiling all our lives to find,
In darkness lost, the darkness of the grave;
Thou, over whom thy Immortality
Broods like the Day, a Master o'er a Slave,
A Presence which is not to be put by;   120
     To whom the grave
Is but a lonely bed without the sense or sight
     Of day or the warm light,
A place of thought where we in waiting lie;
Thou little Child, yet glorious in the might
Of heaven-born freedom on thy being's height,
Why with such earnest pains dost thou provoke
The years to bring the inevitable yoke,
Thus blindly with thy blessedness at strife?
Full soon thy Soul shall have her earthly freight,   130
And custom lie upon thee with a weight,
Heavy as frost, and deep almost as life!

IX

     O joy! that in our embers
     Is something that doth live,
     That nature yet remembers
     What was so fugitive!
The thought of our past years in me doth breed
Perpetual benediction: not indeed
For that which is most worthy to be blest—
Delight and liberty, the simple creed   140
Of Childhood, whether busy or at rest,
With new-fledged hope still fluttering in his breast:—
     Not for these I raise
     The song of thanks and praise;
     But for those obstinate questionings
     Of sense and outward things,
     Fallings from us, vanishings;
     Blank misgivings of a Creature
Moving about in worlds not realised,
High instincts before which our mortal Nature   150
Did tremble like a guilty Thing surprised:
     But for those first affections,
     Those shadowy recollections,

Which, be they what they may,
Are yet the fountain-light of all our day,
Are yet a master-light of all our seeing;
    Uphold us, cherish, and have power to make
Our noisy years seem moments in the being
Of the eternal Silence: truths that wake,
      To perish never: 160
Which neither listlessness, nor mad endeavour,
      Nor Man nor Boy,
Nor all that is at enmity with joy,
Can utterly abolish or destroy!
    Hence in a season of calm weather
      Though inland far we be,
Our Souls have sight of that immortal sea
      Which brought us hither,
      Can in a moment travel thither,
And see the Children sport upon the shore,   170
And hear the mighty waters rolling evermore.

        X

Then sing, ye Birds, sing, sing a joyous song!
    And let the young Lambs bound
    As to the tabor's sound!
We in thought will join your throng,
    Ye that pipe and ye that play,
    Ye that through your hearts to-day
    Feel the gladness of the May!
What though the radiance which was once so bright
Be now for ever taken from my sight,   180
    Though nothing can bring back the hour
Of splendour in the grass, of glory in the flower;
    We will grieve not, rather find
    Strength in what remains behind;
    In the primal sympathy
    Which having been must ever be;
    In the soothing thoughts that spring
    Out of human suffering;
    In the faith that looks through death,
In years that bring the philosophic mind.   190

        XI

And O, ye Fountains, Meadows, Hills, and Groves,
Forebode not any severing of our loves!
Yet in my heart of hearts I feel your might;
I only have relinquished one delight
To live beneath your more habitual sway.
I love the Brooks which down their channels fret,
Even more than when I tripped lightly as they;
The innocent brightness of a new-born Day
    Is lovely yet;

The Clouds that gather round the setting sun
Do take a sober colouring from an eye
That hath kept watch o'er man's mortality;
Another race hath been, and other palms are won.
Thanks to the human heart by which we live,
Thanks to its tenderness, its joys, and fears,
To me the meanest flower that blows can give
Thoughts that do often lie too deep for tears.

▪ ▪ ▪ ▪ Break.Break.Break

Alfred, Lord Tennyson

Break, break, break,
　　On thy cold gray stones, O Sea!
And I would that my tongue could utter
　　The thoughts that arise in me.

O well for the fisherman's boy,
　　That he shouts with his sister at play!
O well for the sailor lad,
　　That he sings in his boat on the bay!

And the stately ships go on
　　To their haven under the hill;
But O for the touch of a vanished hand,
　　And the sound of a voice that is still!

Break, break, break,
　　At the foot of thy crags, O Sea!
But the tender grace of a day that is dead
　　Will never come back to me.

▪ ▪ ▪ ▪ The Tea-Pot

Hans Christian Andersen

There was a proud tea-pot, proud of its porcelain, proud of its long spout, proud of its broad handle; it had something both before and behind, the spout before and the handle behind, and it talked about it; but it did not talk about its lid; that was cracked, it was riveted, it had a defect, and one does not willingly talk of one's defects; others do that sufficiently. The cups, the cream-pot, and the sugar-basin, the whole of the tea-service would remember more about the frailty of the lid and talk about it, than about the good handle and the splendid spout; the tea-pot knew that.

"I know them!" it said to itself, "I know also my defect and I admit it; therein lies my humility, my modesty; we all have defects, but one has also merits. The cups have a handle, the sugar-basin a lid, I have both of these and another thing besides, which they never have, I have a spout, and that makes me the queen of the tea-table. To the sugar-basin and the cream-pot it is granted to be the servants of sweet taste, but I am the giver, the ruler of all; I disseminate blessing among thirsty humanity; in my inside the Chinese leaves are prepared in the boiling, tasteless water."

The tea-pot said all this in its undaunted youth. It stood on the table laid for tea, and it was lifted by the finest hand; but the finest hand was clumsy, the tea-pot fell, the spout broke off, the handle broke off, the lid is not worth talking about, for enough has been said about it. The tea-pot lay in a faint on the floor; the boiling water ran out of it. That was a hard blow it got, and the hardest of all was that they laughed; they laughed at it, and not at the awkward hand.

"I shall never get that experience out of my mind," said the tea-pot, when it afterwards related its career to itself, "I was called an invalid and set in a corner, and the day after, presented to a woman who begged kitchen-refuse. I came down into poverty, stood speechless both out and in; but there, as I stood, my better life began; one is one thing, and becomes something quite different. Earth was put into me; for a tea-pot, that is the same as to be buried, but in the earth was put a bulb; who laid it there, who gave it, I know not, but given it was, a compensation for the Chinese leaves and the boiling water, a compensation for the broken-off handle and spout. And the bulb lay in the earth, the bulb lay in me, it became my heart, my living heart, and such a thing I had never had before. There was life in me, there was strength and vigour. The pulse beat, the bulb sprouted, it was bursting with thoughts and feelings; then it broke out in flower; I saw it, I carried it, I forgot myself in its loveliness; it is a blessed thing to forget oneself in others! It did not thank me; it did not think about me: it was admired and praised. I was so glad about it; how glad must it have been then! One day I heard it said that it deserved a better pot. They broke me through the middle; it was frightfully painful; but the flower was put in a better pot, and I was thrown out into the yard; I lie there like an old potsherd,—but I have the remembrance, that I cannot lose."

237

The Desire for Things

The phrase "the romantic heart of things" may be taken to mean in part the process by which objects are invested by consciousness with interest, glamour, desirability—the process that Wordsworth consciously engages in with "The Thorn" and that Keats struggles with in "On Seeing the Elgin Marbles" and "Ode on a Grecian Urn." This process surrounds us in the contemporary landscape, where man-made objects are proposed to our possession, and we are solicited virtually to define ourselves through the things we acquire. Industrialism, with its mass production of new objects, inevitably created a new form of fiction-making to give these new objects the attributes of glamour and desirability, and to persuade us that acquiring them will make us enter the world of the fiction.

Advertisements

Pepsi-Cola [1]

There's a whole new way of livin'
Pepsi helps supply the drive
It's got a lot to give to those who like to live
'Cause Pepsi helps 'em come alive
It's the Pepsi generation comin' at ya, goin' strong
Put yourself behind a Pepsi, if you're livin', you belong
You've got a lot to live and Pepsi's got a lot to give
You've got a lot to live and Pepsi's got a lot to give.

Ballantine

To be crisp a beer must be icily light,
Smooth and delicious, precisely right,
Lively golden, crystally clear,
The crisp refresher, Ballantine,
     Ballantine beer.

Vita

Make your day a little bit brighter;
Have a little pickled herring by Vita.

[1] Reprinted with permission of PepsiCo, Inc. Copyright, 1969, PepsiCo, Inc.

239

IT'S
NO
FAIRY
TALE

THAT
THE
QUEEN
OF
ENGLAND
CHOSE
AYNSLEY

photos: Pesin

AND
THE
PRESIDENT'S
DAUGHTER

TOOK
WATERFORD
AS HER
ONE
AND ONLY.

It's one third of your life. Spend it dreaming in Wamsutta.
LUSTERCALE

Soap-Powders and Detergents

Roland Barthes

Translated by Annette Lavers

The first World Detergent Congress (Paris, September 1954) had the effect of authorizing the world to yield to *Omo* euphoria: not only do detergents have no harmful effect on the skin, but they can even perhaps save miners from silicosis. These products have been in the last few years the object of such massive advertising that they now belong to a region of French daily life which the various types of psycho-analysis would do well to pay some attention to if they wish to keep up to date. One could then usefully contrast the psycho-analysis of purifying fluids (chlorinated, for example) with that of soap-powders (*Lux, Persil*) or that of detergents (*Omo*). The relations between the evil and the cure, between dirt and a given product, are very different in each case.

Chlorinated fluids, for instance, have always been experienced as a sort of liquid fire, the action of which must be carefully estimated, otherwise the object itself would be affected, "burnt." The implicit legend of this type of product rests on the idea of a violent, abrasive modification of matter: the connotations are of a chemical or mutilating type: the product "kills" the dirt. Powders, on the contrary, are separating agents: their ideal role is to liberate the object from its circumstantial imperfection: dirt is "forced out" and no longer killed; in the *Omo* imagery, dirt is a diminutive enemy, stunted and black, which takes to its heels from the fine immaculate linen at the sole threat of the judgment of *Omo*. Products based on chlorine and ammonia are without doubt the representatives of a kind of absolute fire, a saviour but a blind one. Powders, on the contrary, are selective, they push, they drive dirt through the texture of the object, their function is keeping public order not making war. This distinction has ethnographic correlatives: the chemical fluid is an extension of the washerwoman's movements when she beats the clothes, while powders rather replace those of the housewife pressing and rolling the washing against a sloping board.

But even in the category of powders, one must in addition oppose against advertisements based on psychology those based on psycho-analysis (I use this word without reference to any specific school). "*Persil* Whiteness," for instance, bases its prestige on the evidence of a result; it calls into play vanity, a social concern with appearances, by offering for comparison two objects, one of which is *whiter than* the other. Advertisements for *Omo* also indicate the effect of the product (and in superlative fashion, incidentally), but they chiefly reveal its mode of action; in doing so, they involve the consumer in a kind of direct experience of the substance, make him the accomplice of a liberation rather than the mere beneficiary of a result; matter here is endowed with value-bearing states.

Omo uses two of these, which are rather novel in the category of detergents: the deep and the foamy. To say that *Omo* cleans in depth (see the Cinéma-Publicité advertisement) is to assume that linen is deep, which no one had previously thought, and this unquestionably results in exalting it, by establishing it as an object favourable to those obscure tendencies to enfold and caress which are found in every human body. As for foam, it is well known that it signifies luxury. To begin with, it appears to lack any usefulness; then, its abundant, easy, almost infinite proliferation allows one to suppose there is in the substance from which it issues a vigorous germ, a healthy and powerful essence, a great wealth of active elements in a small original volume. Finally, it gratifies in the consumer a tendency to imagine matter as something airy, with which contact is effected in a mode both light and vertical, which is sought after like that of happiness either in the gustatory category (foie gras, entremets, wines), in that of clothing (muslin, tulle), or that of soaps (film-star in her bath). Foam can even be the sign of a certain spirituality, inasmuch as the spirit has the reputation of being able to make something out of nothing, a large surface of effects out of a small volume of causes (creams have a very different "psycho-analytical" meaning, of a soothing kind: they suppress wrinkles, pain, smarting, etc.). What matters is the art of having disguised the abrasive function of the detergent under the delicious image of a substance at once deep and airy which can govern the molecular order of the material without damaging it. A euphoria, incidentally, which must not make us forget that there is one plane on which *Persil* and *Omo* are one and the same: the plane of the Anglo-Dutch trust *Unilever*.

Gobseck

Honoré de Balzac

Translated by Katherine Prescott Wormeley

Gobseck, by Honoré de Balzac (1799–1850), was written at the dawn of the modern industrial and capitalist era, and the usurer Gobseck (who is sometimes called a "capitalist") represents what may be a particularly modern obsession with things as wealth and tokens of exchange (though it is perhaps less the obsession than the awareness that is modern). The story suggests in a multiplicity of ways how life can turn on the desire for possession, how acquisition is self-definition, and possession is power. It also shows how literary plots can themselves be generated out of the desire for possession and entire narratives constructed around particularly potent objects.

■

At eleven o'clock one evening, during the winter of 1829–1830, two persons who were not members of the family were still seated in the salon of the Vicomtesse de Grandlieu. One of them, a young and very good-looking man, took leave on hearing the clock strike the hour. When the sound of his carriage-wheels echoed from the courtyard, the viscountess, seeing no one present but her brother and a family friend who were finishing their game of piquet, went up to her daughter as she stood before the fireplace, apparently examining a fire-screen of shaded procelain while she listened to the sound of the same wheels in a manner to justify the mother's anxiety.

"Camille, if you continue to behave toward that young Comte de Restaud as you have done this evening, you will oblige me to close my doors to him. Listen to me, my child; if you have confidence in my affection, let me guide you in life. At seventeen years of age, a girl is unable to judge of either the future, or the past, or of certain social considerations. I shall make only one remark to you: Monsieur de Restaud has a mother who would squander millions, — a woman ill-born, a Demoiselle Goriot, who, in her youth, caused people to talk about her. She behaved so badly to her father that she does not deserve to have so good a son. The young count adores her, and stands by her with a filial piety which is worthy of all praise; he also takes the utmost care of his brother and sister. However admirable such conduct may be," continued the viscountess, in a pointed manner, "so long as the mother lives, all parents would fear to trust the future and the fortune of a daughter to young Restaud."

"I have overheard a few words which make me desirous of intervening between you and Mademoiselle de Grandlieu," said the friend of the family, suddenly. "I've won, Monsieur le comte," he said, turning to his adversary. "I leave you now and rush to the succor of your niece."

"This is what is called having lawyer's ears," cried the viscountess. "My dear Derville, how could you overhear what I was saying in a low voice to Camille?"

"I saw your look and understood it," replied Derville, sitting down on a sofa at the corner of the fireplace.

The uncle took a seat beside his niece, and Madame de Grandlieu placed herself on a low chair between her daughter and Derville.

"It is high time, Madame la vicomtesse, that I should tell you a little tale which will modify the opinion you have formed as to the fortunes of Comte Ernest de Restaud."

"A tale!" cried Camille. "Begin it, quick! monsieur."

Derville cast a look at Madame de Grandlieu which signified that the story he was about to tell would interest her.

244

The Vicomtesse de Grandlieu, by her fortune and the antiquity of her name, was one of the most distinguished women of the faubourg Saint-Germain, and it may not seem natural that a Parisian lawyer should speak to her familiarly, and treat her in a manner so apparently cavalier; but the phenomenon is easily explained. Madame de Grandlieu, who returned to France with the royal family, came to reside in Paris, where she lived, at first, on a stipend granted by Louis XVIII. from the Civil List, — a situation that was quite intolerable. Derville, the lawyer, chanced to discover certain legal blunders in the sale which the Republic had made of the hôtel de Grandlieu, and he asserted that it ought to be restored to the viscountess. He undertook the case for a certain fee, and won it. Encouraged by this success, he sued a fraternity of monks, and harassed them legally, until he obtained the restitution of the forest of Liceney. He also recovered a number of shares in the Orléans canal, and certain parcels of real estate with which the Emperor had endowed a few public institutions.

In this way the fortune of Madame de Grandlieu, restored to her by the care and ability of the young lawyer, amounted to an income of sixty thousand francs a year, before the law of indemnity (which restored to her enormous sums of money) had been passed. A man of the highest honor, learned, modest, and excellent company, he became, henceforth, the "friend of the family." Though his conduct to Madame de Grandlieu had won him the respect and the business of the best houses of the faubourg Saint-Germain, he never profited by that favor as a more ambitious man would have done. He resisted the proposals of the viscountess to sell his practice and enter the magistracy, a career in which, thanks to her influence, he would certainly have obtained a very rapid advancement. With the exception of the hôtel de Grandlieu, where he sometimes passed an evening, he never went into society unless to keep up his connections. It was fortunate for him that his talents had been brought to light by his devotion to the interests of Madame de Grandlieu, otherwise he would have run the risk of losing his practice altogether. Derville had not the soul of a pettifogger.

Ever since Comte Ernest de Restaud had been received in Madame de Grandlieu's salon and Derville had discovered Camille's sympathy for the young man, he had become as assiduous in his own visits as any dandy of the Chaussée-d'Antin newly admitted to the circles of the noble faubourg. A few days before the evening on which our story opens, he was standing near Camille at a ball when he said to her, motioning to the young count: —

"Isn't it a pity that young fellow hasn't two or three millions?"

"Do you call it a pity? I don't think so," she answered. "Monsieur de Restaud has great talent, he is well-educated, and the minister with whom he is placed thinks highly of him. I have no doubt he will become a very remarkable man. Such a *young fellow* will find all the fortune he wants whenever he comes to power."

"Yes, but suppose he were rich now?"

"Suppose he were rich?" echoed Camille, coloring. "Oh! then all the girls in society would be quarrelling for him," she added, with a nod at the quadrilles.

"And then, perhaps," said the lawyer, slyly, "Mademoiselle de Grandlieu would not be the only one on whom his eyes would turn. Why do you blush? You have a liking for him, haven't you? Come, tell me."

Camille rose hastily.

"She loves him," thought Derville.

Since that evening Camille had shown the lawyer very unusual attentions, perceiving that he approved of her inclination for the young count. Until then, although she was not ignorant of the many obligations of her family to Derville, she had always shown him more courtesy than real friendship, more civility than feeling; her manners, and also the tone of her voice, had let him know the distance that conventions placed between them. Gratitude is a debt which children will not always accept as part of their inheritance.

"This affair," said Derville to the viscountess, on the evening when our story opens, "recalls to me the only romantic circumstances of my life — You are laughing already," he said, interrupting himself, "at the idea of a lawyer talking of romance. But I have been twenty-five years of age as well as others; and by that time of life I had already seen very strange things. I shall begin by telling you about a personage whom you can never know, — a usurer. Imagine vividly that pale, wan visage, to which I wish the Academy would allow me to apply the word 'moon-faced'; it looked like tarnished silver. My usurer's hair was flat, carefully combed, and sandy-gray in color. The features of his face, impassible as that of Talleyrand, had apparently been cast in iron. His little eyes, yellow as those of a weasel, had scarcely any lashes and seemed to fear the light; but the peak of an old cap protected them. His pointed nose was so pockmarked about the tip that you might have compared it to a gimlet. He had the thin lips of those little old men and alchemists painted by Rembrandt or Metzu. The man spoke low, in a gentle voice, and was never angry. His age was a problem: it was impossible to say whether he was old before his time, or whether he so spared his youth that it lasted him forever.

"All things in his room were clean and shabby, resembling, from the green cover of the desk to the bedside carpet, the frigid sanctum of old maids who spend their days in rubbing their furniture. In winter, the embers on his hearth, buried beneath a heap of ashes, smoked, but never blazed. His actions, from the hour of his rising to his evening fits of coughing, were subjected to the regularity of clock-work. He was in some respects an automaton, whom sleep wound up. If you touch a beetle crossing a piece of paper, it will stop and feign to be dead; just so this man would interrupt his speech if a carriage passed, in order not to force his voice. Imitating Fontenelle, he economized the vital movement and concentrated all human sentiments upon the I. Consequently, his life flowed on without producing more noise than the sand of an ancient hour-glass. Occasionally, his victims made great outcries, and were furious; after which a dead silence fell, as in kitchens after a duck's neck is wrung.

"Towards evening the man-of-notes became an ordinary mortal; his metals were transformed into a human heart. If he was satisfied with his day he rubbed his hands, and from the chinks and wrinkles of his face a vapor of gayety exhaled, — for it is impossible to otherwise describe the silent play of his muscles, where a sensation, like the noiseless laugh of Leather-Stocking, seemed to lie. In his moments of greatest joy his words were always monosyllabic, and the expression of his countenance invariably negative.

"Such was the neighbor whom chance bestowed upon me at a house where I was living, in the rue des Grès, when I was still a second clerk and had only just finished my third year in the Law-school. This house, which has no courtyard, is damp and gloomy. The rooms get no light except from the street. The cloistral arrangement which divides the building into rooms of equal size, with no issue but a long corridor lighted from above, shows that the house was formerly part of a convent. At this sad aspect the gayety of even a dashing young blood would die away as he entered the usurer's abode. The man and his house resembled each other, like the rock and its barnacle.

"The only being with whom he held communication, socially speaking, was myself. He came to my room, sometimes, to ask for tinder, or to borrow a book or a newspaper, and at night he allowed me to enter his cell, where we talked if he happened to be good-humored. These marks of confidence were the results of four years' vicinity and my virtuous conduct, which, for want of money, very closely resembled his own. Had he relations, or friends? Was he rich or poor? No one could have answered those questions. During these years I never saw any money in his possession. His wealth was no doubt in the cellars of the Bank of France. He collected his notes himself, racing through Paris on legs as sinewy as those of a deer. He was a martyr to his caution. One day, by accident, he showed a bit of gold: a double napoleon made its escape, heaven knows how! through his waistcoat pocket; another tenant, who was following him up the staircase, picked it up and gave it to him.

" 'That is not mine,' he answered, with a gesture of surprise. 'Do you suppose that I have money? Should I live as I do if I were rich?'

"In the mornings he made his own coffee on a tin heater which always stood in the dingy corner of his fireplace. His dinner was brought from a cookshop. Our old portress went up at a fixed hour and put his room in order. And, to cap all, by a singularity which Sterne would have called predestination, the man was named Gobseck.

"Later, when I manged his affairs, I discovered that when we first knew each other he was sixty-six years old. He was born about 1740, in the suburbs of Antwerp, of a Dutchman and a Jewess; his name was Jean-

Esther van Gobseck. You remember, of course, how all Paris was excited about the murder of a woman called *La belle Hollandaise?* When I chanced to speak of it to my neighbor, he said, without expressing the slightest interest or surprise: —

" 'That was my great-niece.'

"He made no other comment on the death of his only known heir, the granddaughter of his sister. From the newspapers I learned that *La belle Hollandaise* was called Sarah van Gobseck. When I asked him by what strange chance his great-niece bore his name, he replied, with a smile: —

" 'The women of our family never marry.'

"This singular man had always refused, through four generations, to know, or even see, a single female member of his family. He abhorred his heirs, and could not conceive that his wealth would ever be possessed by others, even after his death. His mother had despatched him as cabin-boy, when ten years old, to the Dutch possessions in India, where he had lived as he could for twenty years. The wrinkles of his yellow forehead covered the secrets of horrible events, awful terrors, unhoped-for luck, romantic disappointment, and infinite joys; also there were signs of hunger endured, love trodden underfoot, fortune compromised, lost, and refound, life many a time in danger, and saved, perhaps, by sudden decisions, the urgency for which excuses cruelty. He had known Monsieur de Lally, Admiral Simeuse, Monsieur de Kergarouët, Monsieur d'Estaing, the Bailli de Suffren, Monsieur de Portenduère, Lord Cornwallis, Lord Hastings, the father of Tippu Sahib, and Tippu Sahib himself; for this Savoyard, who had served the King of Delhi, and contributed not a little to found the power of the Mahrattas, had done business with him. He also had dealings with Victor Hughes, and several other famous corsairs, for he lived for a long time on the island of Saint Thomas. He had attempted so many things in quest of fortune that he even tried to discover the gold of that tribe of savages so celebrated near Buenos Ayres. He was not a stranger to any of the great events of the war of American Independence. But when he spoke of India or America, which he never did with others, and rarely with me, he seemed to think he had committed an indiscretion, and regretted it.

"If humanity, if social fellowship, are a religion, he must be considered an atheist. Though I set myself to examine him, I must admit, to my confusion, that up to the very last moment his heart was impenetrable to me. I sometimes asked myself to what sex he belonged. If all usurers resemble him, I believe they form a neutral species. Was he faithful to the religion of his mother, and did he look upon all Christians as his prey? Had he made himself a Catholic, a Mohammedan, a Brahman, a Lutheran? I never knew his religious opinions, but he seemed to me more indifferent than sceptical.

"One evening I entered the room of this man transmuted to gold, whom his victims (he called them clients) addressed either in jest or satire as 'Papa Gobseck.' I found him in his armchair, motionless as a statue, his eyes fixed on the mantel of the fireplace, on which he seemed to be scanning memoranda of accounts. A smoky lamp cast out a gleam which, far from coloring his face, brought out its pallor. He looked at me silently, and pointed to the chair which awaited me. 'Of what is this strange being thinking?' I said to myself. 'Does he know that God exists? that there are feelings, women, happiness?' I pitied him as I pity a sick man. And yet I also understood that he possessed by thought the earth he had travelled over, dug into, weighed, sifted, and worked.

" 'Good-evening, papa Gobseck,' I said.

"He turned his head in my direction, his thick black eyebrows slightly contracting; in him that peculiar movement was equivalent to the gayest smile of a Southerner.

" 'You seem as gloomy,' I continued, 'as you were the day you heard of the bankruptcy of that publisher whose cleverness you have always admired, though you were made its 'victim.'

" 'Victim?' he said, in a surprised tone.

" 'Didn't he, in order to obtain his certificate of insolvency, pay up your account with notes subject to the settlement in bankruptcy, and when the business was re-established didn't those notes come under the reduction named in that settlement?'

" 'He was shrewd,' replied the old man, 'but I nipped him back.'

" 'Perhaps you hold a few protested notes? — this is the thirtieth of the month, you know.'

"I had never before mentioned money to him. He raised his eyes to me, satirically; then, in his softest voice, the tones of which were like the sounds a pupil draws from his flute when he has no mouthpiece, he said: —

" 'I am amusing myself.'

" 'Then you do *find* amusement sometimes?'

" 'Do you think there are no poets but those who scribble verses?' he asked, shrugging his shoulders, and casting a look of pity on me.

" 'Poesy in that head!' I thought to myself; for at that time I knew nothing of his life.

" 'What existence is there as brilliant as mine?' he continued, and his eyes brightened. 'You are young; you have the ideas of your blood; you see faces of women in your embers, I see nothing but coals in mine. You believe in everything, I believe in nothing. Keep your illusions, if you can. I am going to reckon up life to you. Whether you travel about the world, or whether you stay in your chimney-corner with a wife, there comes an age when life is nothing more than a habit, practised in some preferred spot. Happiness then consists in the exercise of our faculties applied to real objects. Outside of those two precepts all else is false. My principles have varied like those of other men; I have changed with each latitude in which I lived. What Europe admires, Asia punishes. A vice in Paris is a necessity after you pass the Azores. Nothing is a fixed fact here below;

conventions alone exist, and those are modified by climate. To one who has flung himself forcibly into every social mould, convictions and moralities are nothing more than words without weight. There remains within us but the one true sentiment which Nature implanted there; namely, the instinct of preservation. In European societies this instinct is called *self-interest*. If you had lived as long as I have, you would know that there is but one material thing the value of which is sufficiently certain to be worth a man's while to care for it. That thing is — GOLD. Gold represents all human forces. I have travelled; I have seen in all lands plains and mountains: plains are tiresome, mountains fatiguing; hence, places and regions signify nothing. As for customs and morals, man is the same everywhere; everywhere the struggle between wealth and poverty exists; everywhere it is inevitable. Better, therefore, to be the one to take advantage, than the one to be taken advantage of. Everywhere you will find muscular folk who work their way, and lymphatic folk who fret and worry. Everywhere pleasures are the same; for all emotions are exhausted, and nothing survives of them but the single sentiment of *vanity*. Vanity is always I. Vanity is never truly satisfied except by floods of gold. Desires need time, or physical means, or care. Well! gold contains all those things in the germ, and will give them in reality. None but fools or sick men can find pleasure in playing cards every night to see if they can win a few francs. None but fools can spend their time in asking each other what happens, and whether Madame So-and-so occupies her sofa alone or in company, or whether she has more blood than lymph, more ardor than virtue. None but dupes can think themselves useful to their fellow-men, by laying down political principles to govern events which are still unforeseen. None but ninnies can like to go through the same routine, pacing up and down like animals in a cage; dressing for others, eating for others, glorifying themselves about a horse or a carriage which their neighbor can't copy for at least three days! Isn't that the life of your Parisians, reduced to a few sentences? Let us look at life on a higher plane. There, happiness consists either in strong emotions which wear out life, or in regular occupations worked, as it were, by mechanism at stated times. Above these forms of happiness there exists the curiosity (said to be noble) of knowing the secrets of Nature, or of producing a certain imitation of her effects. Isn't that, in two words, art or knowledge, passion or tranquillity? Well! all human passions, heightened by the play of social interests, parade before me, who live in tranquillity. As for your scientific curiosity, — a sort of combat in which man is always worsted! — I substitute for that a penetration into the secret springs that move humanity. In a word, I possess the world without fatigue, and the world has not the slightest hold upon me. Listen to me,' he continued. 'I will tell you the events of my morning, and you can judge by them of my pleasures.'

"He rose, went to the door and bolted it, drew a curtain of old tapestry, the brass rings grinding on the rod, and sat down again.

" 'This morning,' he said, 'I had only two notes to collect; the others

I had given last evening to clients in place of ready money. So much made, you know! for in discounting them I deduct the cost of collection, taking forty sous for a street cab. A pretty thing it would be if a client made me cross all Paris for six francs discount, — I, who am under bonds to no one! — I, who pay no more than seven francs in taxes! Well, the first note, for a thousand francs, presented by a young man, a dashing fellow, with a spangled waistcoat, eyeglass, tilbury, English horse, etc., was signed by one of the prettiest women in Paris, married to a rich man, — a count. Why should this countess have signed that note (void in law but excellent in fact)? For such poor women fear the scandal which a protested note would cause in their homes; they'll even sell themselves rather than not take up the note. I wanted to know the secret value of that paper. Was it folly, imprudence, love, or charity? The second note, also for a thousand francs, signed "Jenny Malvaut," was presented to me by a linen-draper in a fair way to be ruined. No person having credit at the Bank ever comes to me; the first step taken from my door to my desk means despair, bankruptcy on the verge of discovery, and, above all, the refusal of aid from many bankers. That's how it is that I see none but stags at bay, hunted by the pack of their creditors. The countess lived in the rue du Helder, and Jenny in the rue Montmartre. How many conjectures came into my mind as I went from here this morning! If those two women were not ready to pay, they would receive me with more respect than if I had been their own father. What grimaces that countess would play off upon me in place of her thousand francs! She'd pretend to be cordial, and speak in the coaxing voice such women reserve for holders of notes; she'd shower cajoling words upon me, perhaps implore me, and I —'

"Here the old man cast his eye upon me.

" 'and I — immovable!' he went on. 'I am there as an Avenger; I appear as Remorse. But enough of such fancies. I got there.

" ' "Madame la còmtesse is still in bed," said the lady's-maid.

" ' "When will she be visible?"

" ' "At noon."

" ' "Is Madame la comtesse ill?"

" ' "No, monsieur, but she did not return from a ball till three in the morning."

" ' "My name is Gobseck; tell her my name, and say I shall return at noon."

" 'And off I went, signing my presence on the carpet that covered the stairs. I like to muddy the floors of rich men, not from petty meanness, but to let them feel the claws of necessity. Reached the rue Montmartre, found a shabby sort of house, pushed open the *porte-cochère*, and saw a damp, dark courtyard, where the sun never penetrates. The porter's lodge was dingy, the glass of the window looked like the sleeve of a wadded dressing-gown worn too long; it was greasy, cracked, and discolored.

" ' "Mademoiselle Jenny Malvaut?"

" ' "She's out; but if you have come about a note, the money is here."

" ' "I'll come back," I said.

" 'The moment I heard the porter had the money I wanted to know that girl. I felt sure she was pretty. I spent the morning looking at the engravings displayed on the boulevard. Then, as twelve o'clock sounded, I entered the salon which adjoins the bedroom of Madame la comtesse.

" ' "Madame has just this moment rung for me," said the maid. "I don't think she will see you yet."

" ' "I'll wait," I answered, seating myself in an armchair.

" 'I heard the blinds open in madame's room; then the maid came hurrying in, and said to me: —

" ' "Come in, monsieur."

" 'By the softness of her voice I knew very well her mistress was not ready to pay. What a beautiful woman I then saw! She had flung a camel's-hair shawl round her shoulders so hastily that her shape could be guessed in all its nudity. She wore a nightgown trimmed with frills as white as snow, which showed an annual expense of over two thousand francs for washing. Her black hair fell in heavy curls from a silk handkerchief, carelessly knotted round her head after the Creole fashion. Her bed was the picture of disorder, caused, no doubt, by troubled sleep. A painter would have paid a good deal to have stood a few moments in the midst of this scene. Under draperies voluptuously looped up were pillows on a down quilt of sky-blue silk, the lace of their trimming showing to advantage on that azure background. On a bear's skin, stretched between the carved lion's paws of the mahogany bedstead, lay white satin shoes, tossed off with the carelessness that comes of the fatigue of a ball. On a chair was a rumpled gown, the sleeves touching the floor. Stockings which a breath of wind might have blown away were twisted round the legs of a chair. A fan of value, half-opened, glittered on the chimney-piece. The drawers of the bureau were open. Flowers, diamonds, gloves, a bouquet, a belt, were thrown here and there about the room. I breathed a vague odor of perfumes. All was luxury and disorder, beauty without harmony. Already for this woman, or for her lover, poverty, crouching beneath these riches, raised its head and made them feel its sharpened teeth. The tired face of the countess was in keeping with that room strewn with the fragments of a fête. Those scattered gewgaws were pitiful; collected on her person the night before, they had brought her adoration. These vestiges of love, blasted by remorse, that image of a life of dissipation, of luxury, of tumult, betrayed the efforts of Tantalus to grasp eluding pleasures. A few red spots on the young woman's face showed the delicacy of her skin; but her features seemed swollen, and the brown circle beneath her eyes was more marked than was natural. Still, nature was too vigorous within her to let these indications of a life of folly injure her beauty. Her eyes sparkled. Like an Herodias of Leonardo da Vinci (I've sold those pictures), she was magnificent in life and vigor; there was nothing paltry in her form or in her features; she inspired love, and she seemed to me to be stronger than love. She pleased me. It is long since my heart has beaten. I was paid! I'd give a thousand francs any day for a sensation that recalled to me my youth.

" ' "Monsieur," she said, pointing to a chair, "will you have the kindness to wait for your money?"

" ' "Until to-morrow, at noon, madame," I replied, folding the note I had presented to her. "I have no legal right to protest until then." In my own mind, I was saying to myself: "Pay for your luxury, pay for your name, pay for your pleasures, pay for the monopoly you enjoy! To secure their property rights the rich have invented courts and judges and the guillotine, — candles, in which poor ignorant creatures fly and singe themselves. But for you, who sleep in silk and satin, there's something else: there's remorse, grinding of teeth behind those smiles of yours, jaws of fantastic lions opening to craunch you!"

" ' "A protest!" she cried, looking me in the face; "you can't mean it! Would you have so little consideration for me?"

" ' "If the king himself owed me money, madame, and did not pay it, I'd summons him even quicker than another debtor."

" 'At this moment some one knocked at the door.

" ' "I am not visible," said the countess, imperiously.

" ' "Anastasie, I want to see you very much."

" ' "Not just now, dear," she answered, in a milder voice, but not a kind one.

" ' "What nonsense! I hear you talking to some one," said a man, who could be, of course, none other than the count, as he entered the room.

" 'The countess looked at me; I understood her, and from that moment she became my slave. There was a time in my life, young man, when I might, perhaps, have been fool enough not to protest. In 1763, at Pondicherry, I forgave a woman who swindled me finely. I deserved it; why did I ever trust her!

" ' "What does monsieur want?" said the count.

" 'I saw that woman tremble from head to foot; the white and satiny skin of her throat grew rough and turned, as they say, to goose-flesh. As for me, I laughed inwardly, without a muscle of my face quivering.

" ' "Monsieur is one of my tradesmen," she said.

" 'The count turned his back upon me. I pulled the note half out of my pocket. Seeing that inexorable action, the young woman came close up to me and offered me a diamond ring.

" ' "Take it, and go!" she said.

" 'That was simply an exchange of properties. I bowed, gave her the note, and left the room. The diamond was worth fully twelve hundred francs. In the courtyard I found a swarm of valets, brushing their liveries, blacking their boots, or cleaning the sumptuous equipages. "That," I said to myself, "is what brings these people to me. That's what drives them to steal millions decently, to betray their country. Not to soil his boots by going afoot, the great lord — or he who imitates the lord — takes, once for all, a bath of mud!" I was thinking all that, when the great gates opened, and in drove the cabriolet of the young man who had brought me the note.

" " "Monsieur," I said to him as he got out, "here are two hundred francs, which I beg you to return to Madame la comtesse; and you will please say to her that I hold at her disposition the article she placed in my hands this morning."

" 'He took the two hundred francs with a sarcastic smile, which seemed to say: "Ha! she has paid! so much the better!" I read upon that young man's face the future of the countess. The pretty, fair youth, a gambler without emotion, will ruin himself, ruin her, ruin her husband, ruin her children, spend their dowries, and cause greater devastation through salons than a battery of grape-shot through a regiment. Then I went to the rue Montmartre to find Mademoiselle Jenny Malvaut. I climbed up a steep little staircase. When I reached the fifth floor, I entered a small apartment of two rooms only, where all was as clean and bright as a new ducat. I couldn't see the slightest trace of dust on the furniture of the first room, where I was received by Mademoiselle Jenny, a true Parisian young woman, very simply dressed; head fresh and elegant, prepossessing manner, chestnut hair, well-combed, raised in two puffs upon the temples, which gave a look of mischief to the eyes, that were clear as crystals. The daylight, coming through little curtains hanging at the windows, threw a soft reflection on her modest face. Round her were numerous bits of linen, cut in shapes which showed me her regular occupation; it was evidently that of a seamstress. She sat there like the genius of solitude. When I presented the note I said that I had not found her at home that morning.

" " "But," she said, "the money was with the porter."

" 'I pretended not to hear.

" " "Mademoiselle goes out early, it seems?"

" " "I seldom go out at all; but if one works at night one must take a bath in the daytime."

" 'I looked at her. With one glance I could guess the truth about her. Here was a girl condemned to toil by poverty, belonging, no doubt, to a family of honest farmers; for I noticed a certain ruddiness in her face peculiar to those who are born in the country. I can't tell you what air of virtue it was that breathed from her features, but I seemed to have entered an atmosphere of sincerity and innocence; my lungs were freshened. Poor child! she believed in something! Her simple bedstead of painted wood was surmounted by a crucifix wreathed by two branches of box. I was half-touched. I felt disposed to offer her money at twelve per cent, only to enable her to purchase some good business. "But," I said to myself, "I daresay there's some little cousin who would get money on her signature and eat up all she has." So I went away, being on my guard against such generous ideas, for I've often had occasion to notice that when benevolence does not injure the benefactor it is sure to destroy the person benefited. When you came in I was thinking what a good little wife Jenny Malvaut would make. I compared her pure and solitary life with that of the countess, who, with one foot over the precipice, is about to roll down into the gulf of vice!

" 'Well!' he continued, after a moment of profound silence, during which I examined him, 'do you now think there is no enjoyment in penetrating thus to the inner folds of the human heart, in espousing the life of others, and seeing that life bared before me? Sights forever varied! — hideous sores, mortal sorrows, scenes of love, miseries which the waters of the Seine await, joys of youth leading to the scaffold, despairing laughter, sumptuous festivals! Yesterday, a tragedy, — some good father of a family smothers himself with charcoal because he cannot feed his children. To-morrow, a comedy, — a young man trying to play me the scene of Monsieur Dimanche,[1] varied to suit the times. You have heard the eloquence of our modern preachers vaunted; I've occasionally wasted my time listening to them; they have sometimes made me change my opinion, but my conduct, — as some one, I forget who, says, — never! Well, those good priests, and your Mirabeau and Vergniaud and others are stutterers compared with my orators. Often a young girl in love, an old merchant on the downhill to bankruptcy, a mother trying to hide her son's crime, an artist without food, a great man on the decline of his popularity, who, for want of money, is about to lose the fruit of his efforts, — such beings have made me shudder by the power of their words. Those splendid actors play for me only, but they do not deceive me. My glance is like that of God; it enters the heart. Nothing is hidden from me. Nothing is denied to him who opens and closes the mouth of the sack. I am rich enough to buy the consciences of those who manage the ministers of the nation, — be they ushers or mistresses: isn't that power? I can have beautiful women and tender caresses: isn't that love? Power and pleasure, — don't those two things sum up the whole of your social order? There's a dozen of us such as that in Paris; silent, unknown kings, the arbiters of your destinies. Isn't life itself a machine to which money imparts motion? Know this: means are confounded with results; you will never attain to separating the soul from the senses, spirit from matter. Gold is the spirituality of your present social being. Bound by one and the same interest, we — that dozen men — meet together one day in every week, at the café Thémis, near the Pont Neuf. There we reveal the mysteries of finance. No apparent wealth can mislead us; we possess the secrets of all families. We keep a species of *black book*, in which are recorded most important notes on the public credit, on the Bank, on commerce. Casuists of the Bourse, we form an Inquisition where the most indifferent actions of men of any fortune are judged and analyzed, and our judgment is

---

[1] A scene in Molière's *Don Juan* in which Don Juan, through fast talking, gets the better of a troublesome creditor. The play is printed in Part IV. [The footnotes to this text are by the present editors.]

always true. One of us watches over the judiciary body; another, the financial body; a third, the administrative body; a fourth, the commercial body. As for me, I keep an eye on eldest sons, on artists, men of fashion, gamblers, — the most stirring part of Paris. Every one whom we severally deal with tells us his neighbor's secrets: betrayed passions and bruised vanities are garrulous; vices, vengeances, disappointments are the best police force in the world. My brethren, like myself, have enjoyed all things, are sated with all things, and have come to love power and money solely for power and money themselves. Here,' he added, pointing to his cold and barren room, 'the fiery lover, insulted by a look, and drawing his sabre at a word, kneels and prays to me with clasped hands. Here the proudest merchant, here the woman vain of her beauty, here the dashing soldier, pray, one and all, with tears of rage or anguish in their eyes. Here the most celebrated artists, here the writer whose name is promised to posterity, pray, likewise. Here, too,' he added, laying his hand upon his forehead, 'are the scales in which are weighed the inheritances and the dividends of all Paris. Do you think *now* that there are no enjoyments beneath this livid mask whose immobility has so often amazed you?' he said, turning toward me his wan face, which seemed to smell of money.

"I returned home stupefied. That shrunken old man grew larger; he had changed, before my very eyes, into some fantastic image personifying the power of gold. Life, men, filled me with horror. 'Are all things to be measured by money?' I asked myself. I remember that I did not go to sleep that night till very late. Mounds of gold rose up around me. The beautiful countess filled my thoughts. I confess, to my shame, that her image completely eclipsed that of the simple and chaste creature doomed to toil and to obscurity. But on the morrow, through the mists of waking, the gentle Jenny appeared to me in all her beauty, and I thought of her alone."

"Will you have a glass of *eau sucrée*," said the viscountess, interrupting Derville.

"Gladly," he replied.

"But I don't see, in all this, anything that concerns us," said Madame de Grandlieu, ringing the bell.

"Sardanapalus!" exclaimed Derville, launching his favorite oath. "I am going to wake up Mademoiselle Camille presently by showing her that her happiness has depended, until recently, on papa Gobseck. But the old man is now dead, at the age of eighty-nine, and the Comte de Restaud will soon come into possession of a noble fortune. This needs some explanation. As for Jenny Malvaut, you know her; she is now my wife."

"Poor boy!" exclaimed the viscountess, "he would tell that before a score of people, with his usual frankness."

"Yes, I'd shout it to the universe," said the lawyer.

"Drink your water, my poor Derville. You'll never be anything but the happiest and the best of men."

"I left you in the rue du Helder, with a countess," cried the uncle, waking from a doze. "What did you do there?"

"A few days after my conversation with the old Dutchman," resumed Derville, "I took my licentiate's degree and became, soon after, a barrister. The confidence the old miser had in me increased greatly. He consulted me, gratuitously, on the ticklish affairs in which he embarked after obtaining certain data, — affairs which, to practical minds, would have seemed very dangerous. That man, over whom no human being could have gained any power, listened to my counsels with a sort of respect. It is true that they usually helped him. At last, on the day when I was made head-clerk of the office in which I had worked three years, I left the house in the rue des Grès, and went to live with my patron, who gave me board and lodging, and one hundred and twenty francs a month. That was a fine day for me! When I said good-bye to the old usurer, he expressed neither friendship nor regret; he did not ask me to come and see him; he merely gave me one of those glances which seemed to reveal in him the gift of second-sight. At the end of a week, however, I received a visit from him; he brought me a rather difficult affair, — a dispossession case, — and he continued his gratuitous consultations with as much freedom as if he paid me. At the end of the second year, from 1818 to 1819, my patron — a man of pleasure, and very extravagant — became involved, and was forced to sell his practice. Although at that time a lawyer's practice had not acquired the exorbitant value it now possesses, my patron almost gave away his in asking no more than one hundred and fifty thousand francs for it. An active, intelligent, and well-trained lawyer might live respectably, pay the interest on that sum, and free himself of the debt in ten years, could he only inspire confidence in some one who would lend him the purchase-money. I, the seventh son of a small bourgeois of Noyon, did not possess one penny, and I knew but one capitalist; namely, papa Gobseck. A daring thought, and some strange gleam of hope, gave me courage to go to him. Accordingly, one evening, I slowly walked to the rue des Grès. My heart beat violently as I knocked at the door of that gloomy house. I remembered what the old miser had told me in former days, when I was far, indeed, from imagining the violence of the agony which began on the threshold of that door. I was now about to pray to him like the rest! 'No, no!' I said to myself, 'an honest man should keep his dignity under all circumstances; no fortune is worth a meanness; I'll make myself as stiff as he.' Since my departure, papa Gobseck had hired my room, in order to have no other neighbor; he had also put a little grated peep-hole into the middle of his door, which he did not open till he recognized my face.

" 'Well!' he said, in his fluty little voice, 'so your patron sells his practice.'

" 'How did you know that? He has not mentioned it to a soul but me.'

"The lips of the old man drew toward the corners of his mouth precisely like curtains, and that mute smile was accompanied by a frigid glance.

" 'It needed that fact to bring you here to me,' he said, in a dry tone, and after a pause, during which I remained somewhat confounded.

" 'Listen to me, Monsieur Gobseck,' I said, with as much calmness as I was able to muster in presence of that old man, who fixed upon me his impassible eyes, the clear flame of which disturbed me.

"He made a gesture as if to say, 'Speak.'

" 'I know how difficult it is to move you. I should waste my eloquence in trying to make you see the position of a clerk without a penny, whose only hope is in you, and who has no other heart in the world but yours in which his future is understood. Let us drop the question of heart; business is business, and not romance or sentimentality. Here are the facts: My patron's practice brings him about twenty thousand francs a year, but in my hands I think it would bring forty thousand. He wants to sell it for one hundred and fifty thousand. I feel, here,' I continued, striking my forehead, 'that if you will lend me the purchase-money I can pay it off in ten years.'

" 'That's talking,' replied papa Gobseck, stretching out his hand and pressing mine. 'Never, since I have been in business,' he went on, 'has any one declared more plainly the object of his visit. Security?' he said, looking me over from head to foot. 'Naught' — adding, after a pause, 'How old are you?'

" 'Twenty-five in a few days,' I replied; 'except for that I couldn't purchase.'

" 'True.'

" 'Well?'

" 'Possibly I may do it.'

" 'There's no time to lose; I am likely to have competitors who will put up the price.'

" 'Bring me the certificate of your birth to-morrow morning, and we'll talk the matter over. I'll think of it.'

"The next day, by eight o'clock, I was in the old man's room. He took the official paper, put on his spectacles, coughed, spat, wrapped his big coat round him, and read the extracts from the register of the mayor's office carefully. Then he turned the paper and re-turned it, looked at me, coughed again, wriggled in his chair, and said, finally: —

" 'This is a matter we will try to arrange.' I quivered. 'I get fifty per cent for my money,' he continued; 'sometimes one hundred, two hundred, even five hundred per cent.' I turned pale at these words. 'But, in consideration of our acquaintance, I shall content myself with twelve and a half per cent interest per —' He hesitated. 'Well, yes! for your sake I will be satisfied with thirteen per cent per annum. Will that suit you?'

" 'Yes,' I replied.

" 'But if it is too much," he said, 'speak out, Grotius' [2] (he often called

_____

[2] Hugo Grotius (1583–1645), a famous Dutch jurist, author of *De jure belli et pacis*.

258

me Grotius in fun). 'In asking you thirteen per cent I ply my trade; consider whether you can pay it. I don't like a man who hobnobs to everything. Is it too much?'

" 'No,' I said, 'I can meet it by rather more privation.'

" '*Parbleu!*' he cried, casting his malicious, oblique glance upon me; 'make your clients pay it.'

" 'No, by all the devils!' I cried; 'it will be I who pay it. I'd cut my hand off sooner than fleece others.'

" 'Fiddle!' said papa Gobseck.

" 'Besides, a lawyer's fees go by tariff,' I continued.

" 'They don't,' he said. 'Not for negotiations, suits for recovery of funds, compromises. You can make thousands of francs, according to the interests involved, out of your conferences, trips, drafts of deeds, memoranda, and other verbiage. You'll have to learn that sort of thing. I shall recommend you as the cleverest and most knowing of lawyers; I'll send you such a lot of such cases that all your brother-lawyers will burst with jealousy. Werbrust, Palma, Gigonnet, my friends, shall give you all their dispossession cases, — and God knows how many they are! You'll thus have two practices, — the one you buy, and the one I make for you. You ought to give me fifteen per cent, at least, for my hundred and fifty thousand francs.'

" 'So be it, but not a penny more,' I said, with the firmness of a man who will grant nothing further.

"Papa Gobseck relented at this, and seemed pleased with me.

" 'I'll pay the price to your patron myself,' he said, 'so as to secure myself a solid hold on the security.'

" 'Oh! yes, take all the security you want.'

" 'Also, you must give me fifteen bills of exchange, acceptances in blank, for ten thousand francs each.'

" 'Provided that double value be distinctly recorded — '

" 'No!' cried Gobseck, interrupting me. 'Why do you want me to have more confidence in you than you have in me?' I kept silence. 'And also,' he went on, in a good-humored tone, 'you will do all my business without asking fees, as long as I live; is that agreed to?'

" 'Yes, provided there is no further demand made.'

" 'Right!' he said. '*Ah ça!*' added the little old man, after a momentary pause, his face taking, but with difficulty, an air of good-humor, 'you'll allow me to go and see you sometimes?'

" 'It will always give me pleasure.'

" 'Yes, but when? In the mornings it would be impossible; you have your business and I have mine.'

" 'Come in the evening.'

" 'Oh, no!' he said hastily; 'you ought to go into society and meet your clients; I, too, I have my friends at the café.'

" 'His friends!' thought I. 'Well, then,' I said, 'why not take the dinner-hour?'

"'That's it,' said Gobseck. 'After the Bourse, about five o'clock. You'll see me every Wednesday and Saturday. We talk of our affairs like a couple of friends. Ha! ha! I can be gay sometimes. Give me the wing of a partridge and a glass of champagne, and we'll *talk*. I know many things that can be told in these days; things which will teach you to know men and, above all, women.'

"'So be it for the partridge and the champagne,' I said.

"'Don't be extravagant, or you'll lose my confidence. Get an old woman-servant, — only one, mind; don't set up an establishment. I shall come and see you to look after your health. I've capital invested on your head, he! he! and I ought to keep informed about you. Come back this evening, and bring your patron.'

"'Might I be informed, if there is no indiscretion in asking,' I said to the old man when we reached the threshold of his door, 'of what possible importance the certificate of my birth could be in this affair?'

"Jean-Esther van Gobseck shrugged his shoulders, smiled maliciously, and replied: 'How foolish youth is! Know this, my learned barrister, — you *must* know it to keep from being cheated, — before the age of thirty honesty and talent are still a sort of mortgage to be taken on a man. After that age he is not to be trusted.'

"So saying, he shut the door.

"Three months later I became a barrister, and soon after I had the great good-fortune, madame, of being chosen to undertake the business concerning the restitution of your property. The winning of that suit made me known. In spite of the enormous interest I paid Gobseck, I was able, in five years, to pay off my indebtedness. I married Jenny Malvaut, whom I love sincerely. The likeness between our two lives, our toil, our successes, increased the tie between us. Jenny's uncle, a rich farmer, died, leaving her seventy thousand francs, which helped to pay off my debt. Since that day my life has been nothing but happiness and prosperity — no need, therefore, to say more about myself; nothing is so intolerably dull as a happy man. Let us go back to our personages. About a year after I bought my practice, I was enticed, almost against my will, to a bachelor's breakfast. The party was the result of a wager lost by one of my legal friends to a young man then much in vogue in the world of fashion. Monsieur Maxime de Trailles, the flower of dandyism in those days, enjoyed a great reputation — "

"And still enjoys it," said the Comte de Born, interrupting Derville. "No man wears a coat with more style or drives a tandem better than he. Maxime has the art of playing cards, and eating and drinking with more grace than the rest of the world put together. He knows what is what in horses, hats, and pictures. The women dote upon him. He always spends a hundred thousand francs a year, though no one ever heard of his owning property or a single coupon of interest. A type of the knight-errant of salons, boudoirs, and the boulevards, — an amphibious species, half-man, half-woman, — Comte Maxime de Trailles is a singular being, good *at* everything and good *for* nothing, feared and despised, knowing most things, yet ignorant at bottom, just as capable of doing a benefit as of committing a crime, sometimes base, sometimes noble, more covered with mud than stained with blood, having anxieties but no remorse, caring more for digestion than for thought, feigning passions and feeling none. He's a brilliant ring that might connect the galleys with the highest society. Maxime de Trailles is a man who belongs to that eminently intelligent class from which sprang Mirabeau, Pitt, Richelieu, but which more frequently supplies the world with Comtes de Horn, Fouquier-Tinvilles, and Coignards." [3]

"Well!" resumed Derville, after listening to these remarks of Madame de Grandlieu's brother. "I had heard a great deal of that personage from poor Père Goriot, who was one of my clients; but I had always avoided, when I met him in society, the dangerous honor of his acquaintance. However, my friend urged me so strongly to go to his breakfast that I could not escape doing so without being accused of austerity. You can hardly conceive of a bachelor's breakfast, madame. It is a magnificent show of the greatest rarities, — the luxury of a miser who is sumptuous for one day only. On entering, one is struck by the order that reigns on a table so dazzling with silver and glass and damasked linen. Life is there in its flower; the young men are so graceful, so smiling, they speak low, they resemble the newly wedded, — all seems virgin about them. Two hours later you would think that same room was a battlefield after the battle. On all sides broken glasses, twisted and soiled napkins; dishes half-eaten, and repugnant to the eye; shouts that split the ears, sarcastic toasts, a fire of epigrams, malignant jests, purple faces, eyes inflamed, no longer capable of expression, — involuntary confidences which tell all! In the midst of this infernal racket, some break bottles, others troll songs, they challenge each other, they kiss or fight; an odious smell arises of a hundred odors, shouts on a hundred tones; no one knows what he eats, or what he drinks, or what he says; some are sad, others garrulous; one man is monomaniacal, and repeats the same word like a clock with the striker going; another man wants to command the riot, and the wisest propose an orgy. If any man entered the room in his senses he would think it a Bacchanalian revel. It was in the midst of such a tumult as this that Monsieur de Trailles attempted to insinuate himself into my good graces. I had preserved my senses pretty well, for I was on my guard. As for him, though he affected to be decently drunk, he was perfectly cool, and full of his own projects. I can't say how it was done, but by the time we left Grignon's that evening, at nine o'clock, he had completely bewitched me, and I had promised to take him, the next day, to papa Gobseck. The words honor, virtue, countess, honest woman, adored woman, misery,

---

[3] After the list of three famous statesmen, Balzac gives three historical villains: the Comte de Horn was an assassin, Fouquier-Tinville a public prosecutor during the Reign of Terror (in the French Revolution), Coignard an escaped convict who made good as an army officer, then was recognized and sent back to prison.

despair, shone, thanks to his gilded language, like magic through his talk. When I awoke the next morning, and tried to remember what I had done the day before, I had much difficulty in putting my ideas together. However, it seemed to me that the daughter of one of my clients was in danger of losing her reputation and the respect and love of her husband, if she could not obtain some fifty thousand francs that morning. She had debts: losses at cards, coachmaker's bill, money lost I knew not how. My fascinating friend had assured me that she was rich enough to repair, by a few years of economy, the damage she was about to do to her fortune. Not until morning did I perceive the insistency of my new friend; and I certainly had no idea of the importance it was for papa Gobseck to make peace with this dandy. Just as I was getting out of bed Monsieur de Trailles came to see me.

" 'Monsieur le comte,' I said, after the usual compliments had passed, 'I do not see that you need my introduction in presenting yourself to van Gobseck, the most polite and harmless of all capitalists. He'll give you the money if he has it, or, rather, if you can present him with sufficient security.'

" 'Monsieur,' he replied, 'I have no wish whatever to force you into doing me a service, even though you may have promised it.'

" 'Sardanapalus!' I said to myself; 'shall I let this man think I go back on my word?'

" 'I had the honor to tell you yesterday,' he continued, 'that I have quarrelled, most inopportunely, with papa Gobseck. Now, as there is no other money-lender in Paris who can fork out at once, and the first of the month too, a hundred thousand francs, I begged you to make my peace with him. But let us say no more about it.'

"Monsieur de Trailles looked at me with an air that was politely insulting, and prepared to leave the room.

" 'I am ready to take you to him,' I said.

"When we reached the rue des Grès the dandy looked about him with an attention and an air of anxiety which surprised me. His face became livid, reddened and turned yellow in turn, and drops of sweat stood on his forehead as he saw the door of Gobseck's house. Just as we got out of his cabriolet, a hackney-coach entered the rue des Grès. The falcon eye of the young man enabled him, no doubt, to distinguish a woman in the depths of that vehicle. An expression of almost savage joy brightened his face; he called to a little urchin who was passing, and gave him his horse to hold. We went up at once to the money-lender.

" 'Monsieur Gobseck,' I said, 'I bring you one of my intimate friends (whom I distrust as I do the devil,' I added in his ear). 'To oblige me, I am sure you will restore him to your good graces (at the usual cost), and you will get him out of his present trouble (if you choose).'

"Monsieur de Trailles bowed to the usurer, sat down, and assumed, as if to listen to him, a courtier-like attitude, the graceful lowliness of which would have fascinated you. But my Gobseck sat still on his chair, at the corner of his fire, motionless, impassible. He looked like the statue of Voltaire seen at night under the peristyle of the Théâtre-Français. He slightly lifted, by way of bow, the shabby cap with which he covered his head, and the small amount of yellow skull he thus exhibited completed his resemblance to that marble statue.

" 'I have no money except for my clients,' he said.

" 'That means that you are very angry with me for going elsewhere to ruin myself?' said the count, laughing.

" 'Ruin yourself!' said Gobseck, in a sarcastic tone.

" 'Do you mean that a man can't be ruined if he owns nothing? I defy you to find in all Paris a finer capital than *this*,' cried the dandy, rising, and twirling round upon his heels.

"This buffoonery, which was partly serious, had no power to move Gobseck.

" 'Am I not the intimate friend of Ronquerolles, de Marsay, Franchessini, the two Vandenesses, Ajuda-Pinto, — in short, all the young bloods in Paris? At cards I'm the ally of a prince and an ambassador whom you know. I have my revenues in London, at Carlsbad, Baden, Bath, Spa. Don't you think *that* the most brilliant of industries?'

" 'Surely.'

" 'You make a sponge of me, *mordieu!* you encourage me to swell out in the great world only to squeeze me at a crisis. But all you money-lenders are sponges too, and death will squeeze you.'

" 'Possibly.'

" 'Without spendthrifts what would become of you? We are one, like body and soul.'

" 'True.'

" 'Come, shake hands, old papa Gobseck, and show your magnanimity."

" 'You have come to me,' said Gobseck, coldly, 'because Girard, Palma, Werbrust, and Gigonnet have their bellies full of your notes, which they are offering everywhere at fifty per cent loss. Now as they probably only gave you one-half of their face value, those notes are not worth twenty-five francs on the hundred. No, I thank you! Could I, with any decency,' continued Gobseck, 'lend a single penny to a man who owes thirty thousand francs, and doesn't possess a farthing? You lost ten thousand francs night before last at Baron de Nucingen's ball.'

" 'Monsieur,' replied the count, with rare impudence, looking at the old man haughtily, 'my doings are none of your business. He whose notes are not due owes nothing.'

" 'True.'

" 'My notes will be paid.'

" 'Possibly.'

" 'The question between us reduces itself, at this moment, to whether I present you sufficient security for the sum I wish to borrow.'

" 'Right.'

"The noise of a carriage stopping before the door echoed through the room.

" 'I will now fetch something that will probably satisfy you,' said Monsieur de Trailles, rising, and turning to leave the room.

" 'Oh my son!' cried Gobseck, rising too, and stretching out his arms to me as soon as the young man had disappeared, 'if he only brings me good security, you have saved my life! I should have died! Werbrust and Gigonnet meant to play me a trick. Thanks to you, I shall have a good laugh to-night at their expense.'

"The old man's joy had something frightful about it. It was the sole moment of expansion or feeling I ever saw in him. Rapid and fleeting as it was, that joy will never pass from my memory.

" 'Do me the pleasure to stay here,' he said. 'Though I'm well-armed and sure of my shot, like a man who has hunted tigers and boarded ships to conquer or die, I distrust that elegant scoundrel.'

"He sat down again, this time in an armchair before his desk. His face was once more calm and livid.

" 'Ho! ho!' he said, suddenly turning round to me; 'you are no doubt going to see that handsome creature I once told you about. I hear an aristocratic step in the passage.'

"Sure enough, the young man now returned, leading a lady, in whom I recognized that countess whom Gobseck had once described to me, — a daughter of Père Goriot. The countess did not at first see me, for I was standing back in the recess of a window, my face to the glass. As she entered the damp and gloomy room she cast a look of fear and distrust at Maxime. She was so beautiful that in spite of her faults I pitied her. Some terrible anguish shook her heart; her proud and noble features wore a convulsive expression, scarcely restrained. That young man must by this time have become to her an evil genius. I admired Gobseck, who, four years earlier, had foreseen the fate of these two beings at the time of their first note. 'Probably,' I said to myself, 'that monster with the face of an angel rules her in all possible ways, through vanity, jealousy, pleasure, the triumphs of society.' "

"But," cried Madame de Grandlieu, interrupting Derville, "the very virtues of this woman have been weapons for him; he has made her weep tears of devotion; he has roused in her soul the generosity of our sex; he has abused her tenderness, and sold to her, at a cruel price, her criminal joys."

"I confess to you," said Derville, who did not understand the signs that Madame de Grandlieu was making to him, "that I did not think of the fate of that unhappy creature, so brilliant to the eyes of the world, and so dreadful to those who could read her heart. No, I shuddered with horror as I looked at her slayer, that youth with a brow so pure, a mouth so fresh, a smile so gracious, teeth so white; a man in the semblance of an angel! They stood at this moment before a judge who examined them as an old Dominican of the sixteenth century might have watched the torturing of two Moors in the cellars of the Inquisition.

" 'Monsieur, is there any way of obtaining the value of these diamonds, reserving to myself the right to redeem them?' she said, in a trembling voice, holding out to him a casket.

" 'Yes, madame,' I replied, interposing, and coming forward.

"She looked at me, recognized me, gave a shudder, and then cast upon me that glance which says, in every country, 'Silence!'

" 'The matter you propose,' I continued, 'constitutes an act which we lawyers call sale with right of redemption, — a transaction which consists in yielding and conveying property, either real or personal, for a given time, at the expiration of which the property can be taken back at a previously fixed price.'

"She breathed more easily. Comte Maxime frowned; he thought the usurer would give a smaller sum for the diamonds if subject to this condition. Gobseck, immovable, picked up his magnifier, and silently opened the casket. Were I to live a hundred years I could never forget the picture his face presented to our eyes. His pale cheeks colored; his eyes, in which the glitter of the stones seemed to be reflected, sparkled with unnatural fire. He rose, went to the light, held the diamonds close to his toothless mouth as if he wanted to devour them. He mumbled a few vague words, lifting, one after the other, the bracelets, necklaces, diadems, sprays, — all of which he held to the light to judge of their water, their whiteness and cutting. He took them from the casket, and he laid them back, he played with them to make their fires sparkle, seeming more of a child than an old man, — or, rather, a child and an old man combined.

" 'Fine! they must have been worth three hundred thousand francs before the Revolution. What water! True diamonds of Asia! from Golconda or Visapur! Do you know their value? No, no, Gobseck is the only man in Paris who knows how to appraise them. Under the Empire it would still have cost two hundred thousand francs to collect that set, but now — ' He made a gesture of disgust, and added, 'Now diamonds are losing value every day. Brazil is flooding us with stones, — less white than those of India. Women no longer wear them, except at court. Does madame go to court?'

"While delivering this verdict he was still examining, with indescribable delight, each stone in the casket.

" 'No blemish!' he kept saying, 'One blemish! Here's a flaw — Beautiful stone!'

"His pallid face was so illumined by the light of these stones, that I compared it in my own mind to those old greenish mirrors we find in provincial inns, which receive the reflection of a light without returning it, and give an appearance of apoplexy to the traveller who is bold enough to look into them.

" 'Well?' said the count, striking Gobseck on the shoulder.

"The old child quivered; he laid his toys on the desk, sat down, and became once more a usurer, hard, cold, polished as a marble column.

" 'How much do you want?'

" 'One hundred thousand francs for three years,' replied the count. 'Can we have them?'

" 'Possibly,' answered Gobseck, taking from their mahogany box a pair of scales of inestimable worth for accuracy, — his jewel-case, as it were! He weighed the stones, valuing, at a glance, Heaven knows how! the weight of the settings. During this time the expression on the money-lender's face wavered between joy and sternness. The countess was lost in a stupor, which I noted carefully; she seemed to be measuring the depth of the precipice down which she was falling. There was still some lingering remorse in the soul of that woman; it needed, perhaps, but a single effort, a hand stretched charitably out, to save her. I would try it.

" 'Are these diamonds yours, madame?' I asked, in a clear voice.

" 'Yes, monsieur,' she replied, giving me a haughty glance.

" 'Make out that redemption-deed, meddler,' said Gobseck to me, pointing to his seat at the desk.

" 'Madame is no doubt married?' I continued.

"She bowed her head quickly.

" 'I shall not make out the deed!' I exclaimed.

" 'Why not?' said Gobseck.

" 'Why not?' I echoed, drawing the old man to the window, and speaking in a low voice. 'Because, this woman being *femme couverte*,[4] the deed of redemption would be null, and you could not claim ignorance of a fact proved by the deed itself. You would be obliged to produce the diamonds deposited in your hands, the weight, value, or cutting of which are described in the deed —'

"Gobseck interrupted me by a nod, and then turned to the two sinners.

" 'He is right,' he said. 'The terms are changed — Eighty thousand francs down, and you leave the diamonds with me,' adding, in a muffled tone, 'possession is nine-tenths of the law —'

" 'But —' interposed the young man.

" 'Take it, or leave it,' said Gobseck, giving the casket to the countess. 'I have too many risks to run.'

" 'Madame,' I whispered in her ear, 'you would do better to throw yourself on your husband's mercy.'

"The usurer no doubt guessed my words from the movement of my lips, for he cast a severe look at me. The young man's face became livid. The hesitation of the countess was obvious. The count went closely up to her; and, though he spoke very low, I heard him say: —

" 'Farewell, my Anastasie, be happy! As for me, my troubles will be over to-morrow.'

4 Legally under the control of her husband.

266

" 'Monsieur,' cried the young woman, addressing Gobseck, 'I accept your offer.'

" 'Well, well!' replied the old man, 'it takes a good deal to bring you to terms, fair lady.'

"He drew a check for fifty thousand francs on the Bank of France, and gave it to the countess.

" 'And now,' he said, with a smile like that of Voltaire, 'I shall complete the sum with notes for thirty thousand francs, the soundness of which cannot be questioned. They are as good as gold itself. Monsieur has just said to me: *My notes will be paid.*'

"So saying, he took out and handed to the countess the notes of the young man, protested the night before to several of his brother usurers, who had, no doubt, sold them to Gobseck at a low price, as comparatively worthless. The young man uttered a sort of roar, in the midst of which could be heard the words: 'Old scoundrel!'

"Papa Gobseck did not move one muscle of his face, but he took from a box a pair of pistols, and said, coldly: —

" 'As the insulted party, I fire first.'

" 'Maxime, you owe monsieur an apology,' cried the trembling countess.

" 'I did not intend to offend you,' stammered the young man.

" 'I know that,' replied Gobseck, tranquilly; 'you merely intended not to pay your notes.'

"The countess rose, bowed, and left the room, apparently horrified. Monsieur de Trailles was forced to follow her; but before he did so he turned and said: —

" 'If either of you betray one word of this, I shall have your blood, or you mine.'

" 'Amen!' replied Gobseck, putting away his pistols. 'To risk your blood, you must have some, my lad, and there's nothing but mud in your veins.'

"When the outer door was closed and the two carriages had driven away, Gobseck rose and began to dance about the room, crying out: —

" 'I have the diamonds! I have the diamonds! the fine diamonds! what diamonds! not dear! Ha! ha! ha! Werbrust and Gigonnet, you thought you'd catch old papa Gobseck! *Ego sum papa!* I'm the master of all of you! Paid in full! paid in full! What fools they'll look to-night when I tell 'em the affair over the dominos!'

"This gloomy joy, this ferocity of a savage, excited by the possession of a few white pebbles, made me shudder. I was speechless and stupefied.

" 'Ha! ha! there you are, my boy! We'll dine together. We'll amuse ourselves at your house, for I haven't any home; and those eating-house fellows, with their gravies and sauces and wines, are fit to poison the devil!'

"The expression of my face seemed to bring him back to his usual cold impassibility.

" 'You can't conceive it, can you?' he said, sitting down by the hearth, and putting a tin sauce-pan full of milk on the hob. 'Will you breakfast with me? There may be enough for two.'

" 'Thank you, no,' I replied. 'I never breakfast till twelve o'clock.'

"At that instant hasty steps were heard in the corridor. Some one stopped before Gobseck's door, and rapped upon it several times, with a sort of fury. The usurer looked through the peep-hole before he opened the door, and admitted a man about thirty-five years of age, who had, no doubt, seemed to him inoffensive, in spite of his evident anger. The new-comer, who was simply dressed, looked like the late Duc de Richelieu. It was *the count,* whom you have often met, and who (if you will permit the remark) has the haughty bearing of the statesmen of your faubourg.

" 'Monsieur,' he said to Gobseck, 'my wife has just left this house.'

" 'Possibly.'

" 'Well, monsieur, don't you understand me?'

" 'I have not the honor to know your wife,' replied the usurer. 'Many persons have called here this morning: women, men, girls who looked like young men, and young men who looked like girls. It would be diffi-cult for me to — '

" 'A truce to jesting monsieur; I am talking of the woman who has just left this house.'

" 'How am I to know if she is your wife,' said the usurer, 'inasmuch as I have never before had the advantage of seeing you?'

" 'You are mistaken, Monsieur Gobseck,' said the count, in a tone of the deepest irony. 'We met one morning in my wife's bedroom. You came for the money of a note signed by her, — a note for which she had not received the value.'

" 'It is not my affair to know whether she received its value or not,' replied Gobseck, with a malicious glance at the count. 'I had discounted her note for one of my brethren in business. Besides, monsieur,' he added, not excited or hurried in speech, and slowly pouring some cof-fee into his pan of milk, 'you must permit me to remark, I see no proof that you have any right to make these remonstrances in my house. I came of age in the year sixty-one of the last century.'

" 'Monsieur, you have just bought family diamonds which do not be-long to my wife.'

" 'Without considering myself obliged to let you into the secrets of my business, I must tell you, Monsieur le comte, that if your diamonds have been taken by Madame la comtesse, you should have notified all jewellers by circular letter not to buy them; otherwise, she may sell them piecemeal.'

" 'Monsieur,' cried the count, 'you know my wife.'

" 'Do I?'

" 'She is, in legal phrase, *femme couverte.*'

" 'Possibly.'

" 'She has no legal right to dispose of those diamonds.'

" 'True.'

" 'Well, then, monsieur?'

" 'Well, monsieur, I know your wife; she is *femme couverte*, — that is, under your control; so be it, and she is under other controls as well; but — I — know nothing of — your diamonds. If Madame la comtesse signs notes of hand, she can, no doubt, do other business, — buy diamonds, receive diamonds to sell again. That often happens.'

" 'Adieu, monsieur,' said the count, pale with anger; 'there are courts of justice.'

" 'True.'

" 'Monsieur here,' continued the count, pointing to me, 'must have witnessed the sale.'

" 'Possibly.'

"The count started to leave the room. Suddenly, aware of the seriousness of the affair, I interposed between the belligerent parties.

" 'Monsieur le comte,' I said, 'you are right, and Monsieur Gobseck is not wrong. You could not sue him without bringing your wife into court, and all the odium of this affair would fall on her. I am a barrister, but I owe it to myself, personally, even more than to my official character, to tell you that the diamonds of which you speak were bought by Monsieur Gobseck in my presence; I think, however, that you would do wrong to contest the validity of that sale, the articles of which are never easy to recognize. In equity, you would be right; legally, you would fail. Monsieur Gobseck is too honest a man to deny that this sale has been made to his profit, especially when my conscience and my duty oblige me to declare it. But suppose you bring a suit, Monsieur le comte, the issue would be very doubtful. I advise you, therefore, to compromise with Monsieur Gobseck, who might withdraw of his own good-will, but to whom you would, in any case, be obliged to return the purchase-money. Consent to a deed of redemption in six or eight months, a year even, a period of time which will enable you to pay the sum received by Madame la comtesse, — unless, indeed, you would prefer to buy the diamonds back at once, giving security for the payment.'

"The usurer was sopping his bread in his coffee, and eating his breakfast with quiet indifference; but when I said the word compromise, he looked at me as if to say: —

" 'The scamp! how he profits by my lessons!'

"I returned his look with a glance which he understood perfectly well. The whole affair was doubtful and base; it was necessary to compromise. Gobseck could not take refuge in denial, because I should tell the truth. The count thanked me with a friendly smile. After a discussion, in which Gobseck's cleverness and greed would have put to shame the diplomacy of a congress, I drew up a deed, by which the count admitted having received from the money-lender the sum of eighty-five thousand francs, including interest, on repayment of which sum Gobseck bound himself to return the diamonds.

" 'What hopeless extravagance!' cried the husband, as he signed the deed. 'How is it possible to bridge that yawning gulf?'

" 'Monsieur,' said Gobseck, gravely, 'have you many children?'

"That question made the count quiver as if, like an able surgeon, the usurer had laid his finger suddenly on the seat of a disease. The husband did not answer.

" 'Well!' resumed Gobseck, understanding that painful silence. 'I know your history by heart. That woman is a demon whom, perhaps, you still love; I am not surprised; she moved even me. But you may wish to save your fortune, and secure it to one, or, perhaps, two of your children. Well, cast yourself into the vortex of society, gamble, appear to lose your fortune, and come and see Gobseck frequently. The world will say that I am a Jew, a usurer, a pirate, and have ruined you. I don't care for that! If any one openly insults me I can shoot him; no one handles sword or pistol better than your humble servant; and everybody knows it. But find a friend, if you can, to whom you can make a fictitious sale of your property, — don't you call that, in your legal tongue, making a trust?' he said, turning to me.

"The count seemed entirely absorbed by his own thoughts, and he left us, saying to Gobseck: —

" 'I shall bring you the money to-morrow; have the diamonds ready for me?'

" 'He looks to me as stupid as an honest man,' said Gobseck, when the count had gone.

" 'Say, rather, as stupid as a man who loves passionately.'

" 'The count is to pay you for drawing that deed,' said the old man, as I left him.

"Some days after these scenes, which had initiated me into the terrible mysteries in the lives of fashionable women, I was surprised to see the count enter my own office early one morning.

" 'Monsieur,' he said, 'I have come to consult you on very serious interests, assuring you that I feel the most entire confidence in your character, — as I hope to prove to you. Your conduct towards Madame de Grandlieu is above praise.'

"Thus you see, Madame la vicomtesse," said Derville, interrupting his narrative, "that I have received from you a thousandfold the value of a very simple action. I bowed respectfully, and told him I had done no more than the duty of an honest man.

" 'Well, monsieur,' said the count, 'I have obtained much information about the singular personage to whom you owe your practice. From all I heard I judge that Gobseck belongs to the school of cynical philosophers. What do you think of his honesty?'

" 'Monsieur le comte,' I replied, 'Gobseck is my benefactor — at fifteen per cent,' I added, laughing. 'But that little avarice of his does not justify me in drawing a likeness of him for the benefit of strangers.'

" 'Speak out, monsieur; your frankness cannot injure either Gobseck or yourself. I don't expect to find an angel in a money-lender.'

" 'Papa Gobseck,' I then said, 'is profoundly convinced of one principle, which rules his conduct. According to him, money is merchandise which may, in all security of conscience, be sold cheap or dear, according to circumstances. A capitalist is, in his eyes, a man who enters, by the rate of interest which he claims for his money, as partner by anticipation in all enterprises and all lucrative speculations. Apart from these financial principles and his philosophical observations on human nature, which lead him to behave like a usurer, I am confidently perusaded that, outside of his own particular business, he is the most upright and the most scrupulous man in Paris. There are two men in that man: he is miserly and philosophical; great and petty. If I were to die, leaving children, I should make him their guardian. That, monsieur, is what experience has shown me of Gobseck. I know nothing of his past life. He may have been a pirate; he may have traversed the whole earth, trafficking in diamonds or men, women or state secrets; but I'll swear that no human soul was ever better tried or more powerfully tempered. The day on which I took him the sum which paid off a debt I had incurred to him at fifteen per cent interest, I asked him (not without some oratorical precautions) what motive had led him to make me pay such enormous interest, and why, wishing, as he did, to oblige me, his friend, he had not made the benefit complete. "My son," he replied, "I relieved you of all gratitude by giving you the right to think you owed me nothing; consequently, we are the best friends in the world." That speech, monsieur, will explain the man to you better than any possible words of mine.'

" 'My decision is irrevocably made,' said the count. 'Prepare the necessary deeds to transfer my whole property to Gobseck. I can rely on none but you, monsieur, to draw up the counter-deed, by which he declares that this sale is fictitious, and that he binds himself to place my fortune, administered as he knows how to administer it, in the hands of my eldest son when the lad attains his majority. Now, monsieur, I am compelled to make a statement to you. I dare not keep that deed in my own house. The attachment of my son to his mother makes me fear to tell him of that counter-deed. May I ask you to be its depositary? In case of his death, Gobseck is to make you legatee of my property. All is thus provided for.'

"The count was silent for a few moments, and seemed much agitated.

" 'Pardon me, monsieur,' he went on, 'I suffer terribly; my health causes me the greatest anxiety. Recent troubles have shaken my vital powers cruelly, and necessitate the great step I am now taking.'

" 'Monsieur,' I replied, 'allow me, in the first place, to thank you for the confidence you have in me. But I must justify it by pointing out to you that by this action you disinherit, utterly, your — other children. They bear your name. Were they only the children of a woman once

271

loved, now fallen, they have a right to some means, at least, of existence. I declare to you that I cannot accept the duty with which you honor me, unless their future is secured.'

"These words made the count tremble violently. A few tears came to his eyes, and he pressed my hand.

" 'I did not wholly know you till this moment,' he said; 'you have just given me both pain and pleasure. We will fix the share of those children in the counter-deed.'

"I accompanied him to the door of my office, and it seemed to me that I saw his features relax with satisfaction at the sense that he was doing an act of justice. You see, now, Camille, how young women are led into fatal gulfs. Sometimes a mere dance, an air sung to a piano, a day spent in the country, lead to terrible disasters; vanity, pride, trust in a smile, folly, giddiness, — all lead to it. Shame, Remorse, and Misery are three Furies into whose hands all women fall, infallibly, the moment they pass the limits of —"

"My poor Camille is half-dead with sleep," said the viscountess, interrupting Derville. "Go to bed, my dear; your heart doesn't need such terrifying pictures to keep it pure and virtuous."

Camille de Grandlieu understood her mother, and left the room.

"You went a little too far, my dear Monsieur Derville," said the viscountess. "Lawyers are not mothers of families or preachers."

"But the newspapers tell — "

"My poor Derville!" said Madame de Grandlieu, interrupting him, "I don't know you! Do you suppose that my daughter reads the newspapers? Go on," she said, after a momentary pause.

"Three days later, the deeds were executed by the count, in favor of Gobseck — "

"You can call him the Comte de Restaud, now that my daughter is not here," said the viscountess.

"So be it," said the lawyer. "Well, a long time passed after that scene, and I had not received the counter-deed, which was to have been returned to me for safe-keeping. In Paris, barristers are so hurried along by the current of affairs that they cannot give to their clients' interests any greater attention than clients demand. Nevertheless, one day when Gobseck was dining with me, I remembered to ask him if he knew why I had not heard anything more from Monsieur de Restaud.

" 'There's a very good reason why,' he answered; 'that gentleman is dying. He is one of those tender souls who don't know how to kill grief, and so let grief kill them. Life is a toil, a trade, and people should take the trouble to learn it. When a man knows life, having experienced its pains, his fibre knits, and acquires a certain suppleness which enables him to command his feelings; he makes his nerves into steel springs which bend without breaking. If his stomach is good, a man can live as long as the cedars of Lebanon, which are famous trees.'

" 'Will the count die?'

" 'Possibly. You'll have a juicy affair in that legacy.'

"I looked at my man, and said, in order to sound him, 'Explain to me why the count and I are the only two beings in whom you have taken an interest.'

" 'Because you and he are the only ones who have trusted in me without reservations,' he replied.

"Although this answer induced me to suppose that Gobseck would not take advantage of his position in case the counter-deed was lost, I resolved to go and see the count. After parting from the old man, I went to the rue du Helder, and was shown into a salon where the countess was playing with her children. When she heard my name announced, she rose hastily and came to meet me; then she sat down without a word, and pointed to an armchair near the fire. She put upon her face that impenetrable mask beneath which women of the world know so well how to hide their passions. Griefs had already faded that face; the exquisite lines, which were always its chief merit, alone remained to tell of her beauty.

" 'It is essential, madame,' I said, 'that I should see Monsieur le comte.'

" 'Then you would be more favored than I am,' she said, interrupting me. 'Monsieur de Restaud will see no one; he will scarcely allow the doctor to visit him, and he rejects all attentions, even mine. Such men are so fanciful! they are like children; they don't know what they want.'

" 'Perhaps, like children, they know exactly what they want.'

"The countess colored. I was almost sorry for having made that speech, so worthy of Gobseck.

" 'But,' I continued, to change the conversation, 'Monsieur de Restaud cannot be always alone, I suppose.'

" 'His eldest son is with him,' she said.

"I looked at her; but this time she did not color; she seemed to have strengthened her resolution not to give way.

" 'Let me say, madame, that my request is not indiscreet,' I resumed; 'it is founded on important interests — ' I bit my lips as I said the words, feeling, too late, that I had made a false move. The countess instantly took advantage of my heedlessness.

" 'My interests are not apart from those of my husband,' she said. 'Nothing hinders you from addressing yourself to me.'

" 'The affair which brings me here concerns Monsieur le comte only,' I replied firmly.

" 'I will have him informed of your wish to see him.'

"The polite tone and air she assumed, as she said those words, did not deceive me. I saw plainly she would never let me reach her husband. I talked for a time on indifferent matters, in order to observe her; but, like all women who have formed a plan, she could dissimulate with that rare perfection which, in persons of your sex, Madame la vicomtesse, is, in the highest degree, treacherous. Dare I say it? I began to apprehend the worst of her, — even crime. This impression came from a glimpse into the future, revealed by her gestures, her glance, her manner, and even by the intonations of her voice. I left her —

"And now, madame," continued Derville, after a slight pause, "I must give you a narrative of the scenes which ended this affair, adding certain circumstances which time has revealed to me, and certain details which Gobseck's perspicacity, or my own, have enabled me to divine —

"As soon as the Comte de Restaud appeared to plunge into the pleasures of a gay life, and seemed to squander his money, scenes took place between husband and wife the secret of which was never divulged, although the count found reason to judge more unfavorably than ever of his wife's character. He fell ill from the effects of this shock, and took to his bed; it was then that his aversion to the countess and her two younger children showed itself. He forbade their entrance into his room, and when they attempted to elude this order, their disobedience brought on such dangerous excitement in Monsieur de Restaud that the doctor conjured the countess not to infringe her husband's orders. Madame de Restaud, who by this time had seen the landed estates, the family property, and even the house in which she lived made over, successively, to Gobseck, no doubt understood, in a measure, her husband's real intentions. Monsieur de Trailles, then rather hotly pursued by creditors, was travelling in England. He alone could have made her fully understand the secret precautions which Gobseck had suggested to the count against her. It is said that she resisted affixing her signature, as our laws require, to the sale of lands; nevertheless, the count obtained it in every instance. She appears to have thought that the count was capitalizing his fortune, and placing the total in the hands of some notary, or, possibly, in the Bank. According to her ideas, Monsieur de Restaud must possess a deed of some kind to enable her eldest son to recover a part at least of the landed estate, and this deed was probably now in the count's own custody. She therefore determined to establish a close watch upon her husband's room. Outside of that room she reigned despotically over the household, which she now subjected to the closest watching. She herself remained all day seated in the salon adjoining her husband's bedroom, where she could hear his every word and even his movements. At night, she had a bed made up in the same room; but for most of the time she slept little. The doctor was entirely in her interests. Such devotion seemed admirable. She knew, with the shrewdness natural to treacherous minds, how to explain the repugnance Monsieur de Restaud manifested for her; and she played grief so perfectly that her conduct attained to a sort of celebrity. A few prudes were heard to admit that she redeemed her faults by her present behavior. She herself had constantly before her eyes the poverty that awaited her at the count's death should she lose her presence of mind even for a moment. Consequently, repulsed as she was from the bed of pain on which her husband lay, she drew a magic ring around it. Far from him, but near to him, deprived of her functions, but all powerful, a devoted wife apparently, she sat there, watching for death and fortune, as that insect of the fields, in the depths of the spiral mound he has laboriously thrown up, hearkens to every grain of dust that falls while awaiting his inevitable prey. The severest censors could not deny that the countess was carrying the sentiment of motherhood to an extreme. The death of her father had been, people said, a lesson to her. Adoring her children, she had given them the best and most brilliant of educations; they were too young to understand the immoralities of her life; she had been able to attain her end, and make herself adored by them. I admit that I cannot entirely avoid a sentiment of admiration for this woman, and a feeling of compassion about which Gobseck never ceased to joke me. At this period, the countess, who had recognized, at last, the baseness of Maxime, was expiating, in tears of blood, the faults of her past life. I am sure of this. However odious were the measures which she took to obtain her husband's fortune, they were dictated by maternal affection, and the desire to repair the wrong she had done to her younger children. Each time that Ernest left his father's room, she subjected him to close inquiry on all the count had said and done. The boy lent himself willingly to his mother's wishes, which he attributed to tender feelings, and he often forestalled her questions. My visit was a flash of light to the countess, who believed she saw in me the agent of the count's vengeance; and she instantly determined not to let me see the dying man. I myself, under a strong presentiment of coming evil, was keenly desirous to obtain an interview with Monsieur de Restaud, for I was not without anxiety about the fate of the counter-deed; if it fell into the hands of the countess, she might raise money on it, and the result would be interminable law-suits between herself and Gobseck. I knew the latter well enough to be certain he would never restore the property to the countess, and there were many elements of litigation in the construction of these deeds, the carrying out of which could only be done by me. Anxious to prevent misfortunes before it was too late, I determined to see the countess a second time.

"I have remarked, madame," said Derville to Madame de Grandlieu, in a confidential tone, "that certain moral phenomena exist to which we do not pay sufficient attention in social life. Being by nature an observer, I have carried into the various affairs of self-interest which come into my practice, and in which passions play so vehement a part, a spirit of involuntary analysis. Now, I have always noticed, with ever-recurring surprise, that the secret ideas and intentions of two adversaries are reciprocally divined. We sometimes find, in two enemies, the same lucidity of reasoning, the same power of intellectual sight as there is between two lovers who can read each other's souls. So, when the countess and I were once more in presence of each other, I suddenly understood the cause of her antipathy to me, although she disguised her feelings under the most gracious politeness and amenity. I was the confidant of her husband's affairs, and it was impossible that any woman could avoid hating a man before whom she was forced to blush. On her part, she guessed that, although I was the man to whom her husband gave his confidence, he had not yet given the charge of his property into my hands. Our conversation (which I will spare you) remains in my memory as one of the most perilous struggles in which I have ever been engaged. The countess, gifted by nature with the qualities necessary for the exercise of irresistible seduction, became, in turn, supple, haughty, caressing, confidential; she even went so far as to attempt to rouse my curiosity, and even to excite a sentiment of love in order to master me; but she failed. When I took leave of her I detected, in her eyes, an expression of hate and fury which made me tremble. We parted *enemies*. She would fain have annihilated me, while I felt pity for her, — a feeling which, to certain natures, is the deepest of all insults. That feeling showed itself plainly in the last remarks I made to her. I left, as I believe, an awful terror in her soul, by assuring her that in whatever way she acted she would inevitably be ruined.

" 'If I could only see Monsieur le comte,' I said to her, 'the future of your children —'

" 'I should be at your mercy,' she said, interrupting me with a gesture of disgust.

"The questions between us being declared in so frank and positive a manner, I determined to go forward in my own way, and save that family from the ruin that awaited it. Resolving to commit even legal irregularities, if they were necessary to attain my ends, I made the following preparations: First, I sued the Comte de Restaud for a sum fictitiously due to Gobseck, and obtained a judgment against him. The countess concealed this proceeding; but it gave me the legal right to affix seals to the count's room on his death, which was, of course, my object. Next, I bribed one of the servants of the house, and made him promise to notify me the moment that his master appeared to be dying, were it even in the middle of the night; I did this, in order that I might reach the house suddenly, frighten the countess by threatening to affix the seals instantly, and so get possession of the counter-deed. I heard, afterwards, that this woman was studying the Code while she listened to the moans of her dying husband. What frightful pictures might be made of the souls of those who surround some death-beds, if we could only paint ideas! And money is always the mover of the intrigues there elaborated, the plans there formed, the plots there laid! Let us now turn from these details, irksome, indeed, though they may have enabled you to see the wretchedness of this woman, that of her husband, and the secrets of other homes under like circumstances. For the last two months, the Comte de Restaud, resigned to die, lay alone on his bed, in his own chamber. A mortal disease was slowly sapping both mind and body. A victim to those sick fancies the caprices of which appear inexplicable, he objected to the cleaning of his room, refused all personal cares, and even insisted that no one should make his bed. A sort of apathy took possession of him; the furniture was in disorder, dust and cobwebs lay thick on the delicate ornaments. Formerly choice and luxurious in his tastes, he now seemed to take pleasure in the melancholy spectacle of his room, where the chimney-piece and chairs and tables were encumbered with articles required by illness, — phials, empty or full, and nearly all dirty, soiled linen, broken plates; a warming-pan was before the fire, and a tub, still full of some mineral water. The sentiment of *destruction* was expressed in every detail of this miserable chaos. Death loomed up in things before it invaded the person. The count had a horror of daylight; the outer blinds of the windows were closed, and this enforced darkness added to the gloom of the melancholy place. The sick man was shrunken, but his eyes, in which life appeared to have taken refuge, were still brilliant. The livid whiteness of his face had something horrible about it, increased by the extraordinary length of his hair, which he refused to have cut, so that it now hung in long, straight meshes beside his face. He bore some resemblance to the fanatical hermits of a desert. Grief had extinguished all other human feelings in this man, who was barely fifty years of age, and whom Paris had once known so brilliant and so happy. One morning, about the beginning of December, in the year 1824, he looked at his son Ernest, who was sitting at the foot of his bed, watching him sadly: —

" 'Are you in pain, papa?' asked the lad.

" 'No,' he said, with a frightful smile; 'it is all *here* and *there*,' — he pointed first to his head, and then pressed his fleshless fingers on his heart, with a gesture that made Ernest weep.

" 'Why does not Monsieur Derville come to me?' he said to his valet, whom he thought attached to him, but who was really in the interests of the countess. 'Maurice,' cried the dying man, suddenly sitting up, and seeming to recover his presence of mind, 'I have sent you seven or eight times to my lawyer, within the last fortnight; why doesn't he come? Do you think some one is tricking me? Go and get him instantly, and bring him back with you. If you don't execute my orders, I'll get up myself and go — '

" 'Madame,' said the valet, going into the salon, 'you have heard Monsieur le comte; what am I to do?'

" 'Pretend to go to that lawyer, and then come back and say to Monsieur le comte that his man of business has gone a hundred miles into the country, to try an important case. You can add that he is expected back the last of the week. Sick men always deceive themselves about their state,' she thought; 'he will wait for the lawyer's return.'

"The doctor had that morning told her that the count could scarcely survive the day. When, two hours later, the valet brought back this discouraging message, the count was greatly agitated.

" 'My God! my God!' he repeated many times. 'I have no hope but in thee!'

"He looked at his son for a long while, and said to him, at last, in a feeble voice: —

" 'Ernest, my child, you are very young, but you have a good heart, and you will surely comprehend the sacredness of a promise made to a dying man, — to a father. Do you feel capable of keeping a secret? of burying it in your own breast, so that even your mother shall not suspect it? My son, there is no one but you in this house whom I can trust. You will not betray my confidence?'

" 'No, father.'

" 'Then, Ernest, I shall give you, presently, a sealed package which belongs to Monsieur Derville; you must keep it in such a way that no one can know you have it; you must then manage to leave the house, and throw the package into the post-office box at the end of the street.'

" 'Yes, father.'

" 'Can I rely upon you?'

" 'Yes, father.'

" 'Then kiss me. You make my death less bitter, dear child. In six or seven years you will understand the importance of this secret, — you will then be rewarded for your faithfulness and dexterity, and you will also know, my son, how much I have loved you. Leave me now, for a moment, and watch that no one enters this room.'

"Ernest went out, and found his mother standing in the salon.

" 'Ernest,' she said, 'come here.'

"She sat down, and held her son between her knees, pressing him to her heart, and kissing him.

" 'Ernest,' she said, 'your father has been talking to you.'

" 'Yes, mamma.'

" 'What did he say to you?'

" 'I cannot repeat it, mamma.'

" 'Oh! my dear child,' cried the countess, kissing him with enthusiasm, 'how much pleasure your discretion gives me. Tell the truth, and always be faithful to your word: those are two principles you must never forget.'

" 'Oh! how noble you are, mamma; you were never false, you! — of that I am sure.'

" 'Sometimes, Ernest, I have been false. Yes, I have broken my word under circumstances before which even laws must yield. Listen, my Ernest, you are now old enough and sensible enough to see that your father repulses me, and rejects my care; this is not natural, for you know, my son, how I love him.'

" 'Yes, mamma.'

" 'My poor child,' continued the countess, weeping, 'this misfortune is the result of treacherous insinuations. Wicked people have sought to separate me from your father, in order to satisfy their own cupidity. They want to deprive us of our property and keep it themselves. If your father were well the separation now between us would cease; he would listen to me; you know how good and loving he is; he would recognize his error. But, as it is, his mind is weakened, the prejudice he has taken against me has become a fixed idea, a species of mania, — the effect of his disease. The preference your father shows for you is another proof of the derangement of his faculties. You never noticed before his illness, that he cared less for Pauline and Georges than for you. It is a mere caprice on his part. The tenderness he now feels for you may suggest to him to give you orders to execute. If you do not wish to ruin your family, my dear boy, if you would not see your mother begging her bread like a pauper, you must tell her everything — '

" 'Ah! ah!' cried the count, who, having opened the door, appeared to them suddenly, half naked, already as dry and fleshless as a skeleton. That hollow cry produced a terrible effect upon the countess, who remained motionless, rigid, and half stupefied. Her husband was so gaunt and pale, he looked as if issuing from a grave.

" 'You have steeped my life in misery, and now you seek to embitter my death, to pervert the mind of my son, and make him a vicious man!' cried the count, in a hoarse voice.

"The countess flung herself at the feet of the dying man, whom these last emotions of his waning life made almost hideous, and burst into a torrent of tears.

" 'Mercy! mercy!' she cried.

" 'Have you had pity for me?' he asked. 'I allowed you to squander your own fortune; would you now squander mine, and ruin my son?'

" 'Ah! yes, no pity for me! yes, be inflexible! but the children! Condemn your widow to a convent, and I will obey you; I will expiate my faults by doing all you order; but let the children prosper! the children! the children!'

" 'I have but one child,' replied the count, stretching his fleshless arm, with a despairing gesture, to his son.

" 'Pardon! I repent! I repent!' cried the countess, clasping the cold, damp feet of her husband. Sobs hindered her from speaking; only vague, incoherent words could force their way from her burning throat.

" 'After what you have just said to Ernest do you dare to talk of repentance?' said the dying man, freeing his feet, and throwing over the countess in doing so. 'You shock me,' he added, with an indifference in which there was something awful. 'You were a bad daughter, you have been a bad wife, you will be a bad mother.'

"The unhappy woman fainted as she lay there. The dying man returned to his bed, lay down, and lost consciousness soon after. The priests came to administer the sacraments. He died at midnight, the scene of the morning having exhausted his remaining strength. I reached the house, together with papa Gobseck, half an hour later. Thanks to the excitement that prevailed, we entered the little salon, next to the death-chamber, unnoticed. There we found the three children in tears, between two priests, who were to pass the night with the body. Ernest came to me, and said that his mother wished to be alone, in the count's chamber.

" 'Do not enter,' he said, with an exquisite expression of tone and gesture. 'She is praying.'

"Gobseck laughed, that silent laugh peculiar to him. I was far too moved by the feeling that shone on the boy's young face to share the old man's irony. When Ernest saw us going to the door, he ran to it, and called out: —

" 'Mamma! here are some black men looking for you.'

"Gobseck lifted the child as if he were a feather, and opened the door. What a sight now met our eyes! Frightful disorder reigned in the room. Dishevelled by despair, her eyes flashing, the countess stood erect, speechless, in the midst of clothes, papers, articles of all kinds. Horrible confusion in the presence of death! Hardly had the count expired, before his wife had forced the drawers and the desk. Round her, on the carpet, lay fragments of all kinds, torn papers, portfolios broken open, — all bearing the marks of her daring hands. If, at first, her search had been in vain, something in her attitude and the sort of agitation that possessed her made me think she had ended by discovering the mysterious papers. I turned my eyes to the bed, and, with the instinct that practice in our profession gives me, I divined what had happened. The count's body was rolled to the wall, and lay half across the bed, the nose to the mattress, disdainfully tossed aside, like the envelopes lying on the floor. His inflexible, stiffening limbs gave him an appearance grotesquely horrible. The dying man had no doubt hidden the counter-deed under his pillow, in order to preserve it from danger, while he lived. The countess, baffled in her search, must have divined her husband's thought at last; in fact, it seemed revealed by the convulsive form of his hooked fingers. The pillow was flung upon the ground; the imprint of the wife's foot was still upon it; beside it, and just before her, where she stood, I saw an envelope with many seals, bearing the count's arms. This I picked hastily up, and read a direction, showing that the contents of that envelope had been intended for me. I knew what they were! I looked fixedly at the countess, with the stern intelligence of a judge who examines a guilty person. A fire on the hearth was licking up the remains of the papers. When she saw us enter, the countess had doubtless flung the deed into it, believing (perhaps from its first formal words) that she was destroying a will that deprived her younger children of their property. A tortured conscience, and the involuntary fear inspired by the commission of a crime, had taken from her all power of reflection. Finding herself caught almost in the act, she may have fancied she already felt the branding iron of the galleys. The woman stood there, panting, as she awaited our first words, and looking at us with haggard eyes.

" 'Ah! madame,' I said, taking from the hearth a fragment which the fire had not wholly consumed, 'you have ruined your younger children! These papers secured their property to them.'

"Her mouth stirred, as if she were about to have a paralytic fit.

" 'Hé! hé!' cried Gobseck, whose exclamation had the effect produced by the pushing of a brass candlestick on a bit of marble. After a slight pause, he said to me, calmly: —

" 'Do you want to make Madame la comtesse believe that I am not

280

the sole and legitimate possessor of the property sold to me by Monsieur le comte? This house belongs to me henceforth.'

"The blow of a club applied suddenly to my head could not have caused me greater pain or more surprise. The countess observed the puzzled glance which I cast on the old man.

" 'Monsieur! monsieur!' she said to him; but she could find no other words than those.

" 'Have you a deed of trust?' I said to him.

" 'Possibly.'

" 'Do you intend to take advantage of the crime which madame has committed?'

" 'Precisely.'

"I left the house, leaving the countess sitting by her husband's bedside, weeping hot tears. Gobseck followed me. When we reached the street I turned away from him; but he came to me, and gave me one of those piercing looks with which he sounded hearts, and said, with his fluty voice, in its sharpest tone: —

" 'Do you pretend to judge me?'

"After that I saw but little of him. He let the count's house in Paris, and spent the summers on the Restaud estates in the country, where he played the lord, constructed farms, repaired mills, built roads, and planted trees. I met him one day in the Tuileries gardens.

" 'The countess is living an heroic life,' I said. 'She devotes herself wholly to the education of her children, whom she is bringing up admirably. The eldest is a fine fellow.'

" 'Possibly.'

" 'But,' I said, 'don't you think you ought to help Ernest?'

" 'Help Ernest!' he cried. 'No! Misfortune is our greatest teacher. Misfortune will teach him the value of money, of men, and of women, too. Let him navigate the Parisian sea! When he has learned to be a good pilot it will be soon enough to give him a ship.'

"I left him without further explanation of the meaning of those words. Though Monsieur de Restaud, to whom his mother has no doubt imparted her own repugnance to me, is far, indeed, from taking me for his counsel, I went, two weeks ago, to Gobseck, and told him of Ernest's love for Mademoiselle Camille, and urged him to make ready to accomplish his trust, inasmuch as the young count has almost reached his majority. I found the old man had been confined for a long time to his bed, suffering from a disease which was about to carry him off. He declined to answer until he was able to get up and attend to business, — unwilling, no doubt, to give up a penny while the breath of life was in him; his delay could have no other motive. Finding him very much worse than he thought himself, I stayed with him for some time, and was thus able to observe the progress of a passion which age had converted into a species of mania. In order to have no one in the house he occupied,

281

he had become the sole tenant of it, leaving all the other apartments un-occupied. Nothing was changed in the room in which he lived. The furniture, which I had known so well for sixteen years, seemed to have been kept under glass, so exactly the same was it. His old and faithful portress, married to an old soldier who kept the lodge while she went up to do her master's work, was still his housekeeper, and was now fulfilling the functions of a nurse. Notwithstanding his weak condition, Gobseck still received his clients and his revenues; and he had so carefully simpli-fied his business that a few messages sent by the old soldier were suffi-cient to regulate his external affairs. At the time of the treaty by which France recognized the republic of Hayti, the knowledge possessed by Gobseck of the former fortunes of San Domingo and the colonists, the assigns of whom were claiming indemnity, caused him to be appointed member of the commission instituted to determine these rights, and ad-just the payments due from the Haytian government. Gobseck's genius led him to establish an agency for discounting the claims of the colonists and their heirs and assigns under the names of Werbrust and Gigonnet, with whom he shared all profits without advancing any money, his knowl-edge of these matters constituting his share in the enterprise. This agency was like a distillery, which threw out the claims of ignorant persons, dis-trustful persons, or those whose rights could be contested. As member of the commission, Gobseck negotiated with the large proprietors, who, either to get their claims valued at a high figure, or to have them speedily admitted, offered him gifts in proportion to the sums involved.

"These presents constituted a sort of discount on the sums he could not lay hands on himself; moreover, this agency gave him, at a low price, the claims of petty owners, or timid owners, who preferred an immediate payment, small as the sum might be, to the chance of uncertain payments from the republic. Gobseck was therefore the insatiable boa-constrictor of this great affair. Every morning he received his tribute, and looked it over as the minister of a pacha might have done before deciding to sign a pardon. Gobseck took all things, — from the game-bag of some poor devil, and the pound of candles of a timorous soul, to the plate of the rich, and the gold snuff-boxes of speculators. No one knew what became of these presents made to the old usurer. All things went in to him, nothing came out: —

" 'On the word of an honest woman,' the portress, an old acquain-tance of mine, said to me, 'I believe he swallows 'em! But that don't make him fat, for he's as lank as the pendulum of my clock.'

"Last Monday Gobseck sent the old soldier to fetch me.

" 'Make haste, Monsieur Derville,' said the man as he entered my office; 'the master is going to give in his last account. He's as yellow as a lemon; and he's very impatient to see you. Death has got him; the last rattle growls in his throat.'

"When I entered the chamber of the dying man, I found him on his knees before the fireplace, where, though there was no fire, an enormous heap of ashes lay. Gobseck had crawled to it from his bed, but strength to return had failed him, also the voice with which to call for assistance.

" 'My old friend,' I said, lifting him, and helping him to regain his bed, 'you will take cold; why don't you have a fire?'

" 'I'm not cold,' he answered. 'No fire! no fire! — I'm going I don't know where, boy,' he went on, giving me his last blank, chilling look; 'but it is away from here! I've got the *carphology*,'[5] using a term which made me see how clear and precise his intellect still was. 'I thought my room was full of living gold, and I got up to get some. To whom will mine go? I won't let the government get it. I've made a will; find it, Grotius. The *belle Hollandaise* had a daughter that I saw somewhere; I don't know where — in the rue Vivienne, one evening. I think they call her "La Torpille," — she's pretty; find her, Grotius. You are the executor of my will; take what you want; eat it; there's *pâtés de foie gras,* bags of coffee, sugar, gold spoons. Give the Odiot service to your wife. But who's to have the diamonds? Do you care for them, boy? There's tobacco; sell it in Hamburg; it will bring half as much again. I've got *everything!* and I must leave it all! Come, come, papa Gobseck,' he said to himself, 'no weakness! be yourself.'

"He sat up in bed, his face clearly defined against the pillow like a piece of bronze; he stretched his withered arm and bony hand upon the coverlet, which he grasped as if to hold himself from going. He looked at his hearth, cold as his own metallic eye; and he died with his mind clear, presenting to his portress, the old soldier, and me, an image of those old Romans standing behind the Consuls, such as Lethière has depicted them in his painting of the 'Death of the Sons of Brutus.'

" 'Hasn't he grit, that old Lascar!' said the soldier, in barrack language.

"I still seemed to hear the fantastic enumeration that the dying man had made of his possessions, and my glance, which had followed his, again rested on that heap of ashes, the immense size of which suddenly struck me. I took the tongs, and when I thrust them into the mound, they struck upon a hoard of gold and silver, — no doubt the fruit of his last receipts, which his weakness had prevented him from hiding elsewhere.

" 'Go for the justice-of-peace,' I said, 'and let the seals be put on at once.'

"Moved by Gobseck's last words, and by something the portress had told me, I took the keys of the other apartments, in order to inspect them. In the first room I entered I found the explanation of words I had supposed delirious. Before my eyes were the effects of an avarice in which nought remained but that illogical instinct of hoarding which we see in provincial misers. In the room adjoining that where Gobseck lay were mouldy patties, a mass of eatables of all kinds, shell-fish, and other fish, now rotten, the various stenches of which almost asphyxiated me. Mag-

[5] Also known as floccillation, an aimless plucking at the bedclothes, occurring in the low delirium of fever.

gots and insects swarmed there. These presents, recently made, were lying among boxes of all shapes, chests of tea, bags of coffee. On the fireplace, in a silver soup tureen, were bills of lading of merchandise consigned to him at Havre: bales of cotton, hogsheads of sugar, barrels of rum, coffees, indigos, tobacco, — an absolute bazaar of colonial products! The room was crowded with articles of furniture, silverware, lamps, pictures, vases, books, fine engravings, without frames or rolled up, and curiosities of various descriptions. Possibly this enormous mass of property of all kinds did not come wholly as gifts; part of it may have been taken in pledge for debts unpaid. I saw jewel-cases stamped with armorial bearings, sets of the finest damask, valuable weapons, but all without names. Opening a book, which seemed to me rather out of place, I found in it a number of thousand-franc notes. I resolved, therefore, to examine the most insignificant articles, — to search the floors, the ceilings, the cornices, the walls, and find every fragment of that gold so passionately loved by the old Dutchman, who was worthy, indeed, of Rembrandt's pencil. I have never seen, throughout my legal life, such effects of avarice and originality. When I returned to his own chamber, I found, on his desk, the reason of this progressive heaping up of riches. Under a paper-weight was a correspondence between Gobseck and the merchants to whom, no doubt, he habitually sold his presents. Now whether it was that these dealers were the victims of his astuteness, or that Gobseck wanted too high a price for his provisions and manufactured articles, it was evident that each negotiation was suspended. He had not sold the comestibles to Chevet because Chevet would only take them at a reduction of thirty per cent. Gobseck haggled for a few extra francs, and, meantime, the goods became damaged. As for the silver, he refused to pay the costs of transportation; neither would he make good the wastage on his coffees. In short, every article had given rise to squabbles which revealed in Gobseck the first symptoms of that childishness, that incomprehensible obstinacy which old men fall into whenever a strong passion survives the vigor of their minds. I said to myself, as he had said: —

" 'To whom will all this wealth go?'

"Thinking over the singular information he had given me about his only heiress, I saw that I should be compelled to ransack every questionable house in Paris, in order to cast this enormous fortune at the feet of a bad woman. But — what is of far more importance to us — let me now tell you, that, according to deeds drawn up in due form, Comte Ernest de Restaud will, in a few days, come into possession of a fortune which will enable him to marry Mademoiselle Camille, and also to give a sufficient dowry to his mother, and to portion his brother and sister suitably."

"Well, dear Monsieur Derville, we will think about it," replied Madame de Grandlieu. "Monsieur Ernest ought to be very rich to make a family like ours accept his mother. Remember that my son will one day be Duc de Grandlieu, and will unite the fortunes of the two Grandlieu houses. I wish him to have a brother-in-law to his taste."

"But," said the Comte de Born, "Restaud bears gules, a barre argent, with four inescutcheons or, each charged with a cross sable. It is a very old blazon."

"True," said the viscountess. "Besides, Camille need never see her mother-in-law, who turned the *Res tuta* [6] — the motto of that blazon, brother — to a lie."

"Madame de Beauséant received Madame de Restaud," said the old uncle.

"Yes, but only at her routs," [7] replied the viscountess.

[6] A thing kept safe, preserved.

[7] A large "open house" type of party, therefore not so exclusive as more restricted gatherings.

The Play with Things

One line of development from the metaphor constructed when man's consciousness faces objects seems to give primacy to the objects themselves, which become determinative of man's life, as *Gobseck* demonstrates. Another line of development may stress rather the capacity of mind to play with objects, to make them bend to mind's own processes and arguments, and to give the impression that mind is at home in the world of objects and can use them to embody its meanings. Such an emphasis on the dominance of mind may result from the writer's acceptance of an all-embracing spiritual system that subjects the objective world to the interpretations of spirit, assigns clear priorities, and hence gives the mind the freedom to seek provisional embodiments in objects. This would seem to be the case with the metaphysical wit of Marvell and Donne, who are able to resolve the arguments they have developed by the representation of mental processes through objects, particularly those which man has himself invented to order his knowledge of the physical world. Similarly, to Herbert the physical forms found in the church can be shown to image and represent the divine order.

The poem itself, as some of Herbert's poems demonstrate, can strive toward the status of a thing. The poem's existence as an object, however, is paradoxical, as Shakespeare's Sonnet 65 suggests: its very frailty—ink on paper as compared to brass or marble—is its force; it is only incidentally an object, and its real existence is on another plane. If modern mind has lost the sense of an embracing system that relates the configurations of the objective world to spiritual reality, it continues to be fascinated by the analogies it finds between its mental systems and the order of things, including, as in Pop Art, the mass-produced things of industrial society.

286

The Definition of Love

Andrew Marvell

My Love is of a birth as rare
As 'tis for object strange and high:
It was begotten by despair
Upon Impossibility.

Magnanimous Despair alone
Could show me so divine a thing,
Where feeble Hope could ne'r have flown
But vainly flapt its Tinsel Wing.

And yet I quickly might arrive
Where my extended Soul is fixt   10
But Fate does Iron wedges drive,
And alwaies crouds it self betwixt.

For Fate with jealous Eye does see
Two perfect Loves; nor lets them close:
Their union would her ruine be,
And her Tyrannick pow'r depose.

And therefore her Decrees of Steel
Us as the distant Poles have plac'd,
(Though Loves whole World on us doth wheel)
Not by themselves to be embrac'd.   20

Unless the giddy Heaven fall,
And Earth some new Convulsion tear;
And, us to joyn, the World should all
Be cramp'd into a *Planisphere*.

As Lines so Loves *oblique* may well
Themselves in every Angle greet:
But ours so truly *Paralel*,
Though infinite can never meet.

Therefore the Love which us doth bind,
But Fate so enviously debarrs,   30
Is the Conjunction of the Mind,
And Opposition of the Stars.

A Valediction: Forbidding Mourning

John Donne

As virtuous men passe mildly away,
   And whisper to their soules, to goe,
Whilst some of their sad friends doe say,
   The breath goes now, and some say, no:

So let us melt, and make no noise,
   No teare-floods, nor sigh-tempests move,
T'were prophanation of our joyes
   To tell the layetie our love.

Moving of th'earth brings harmes and feares,
   Men reckon what it did and meant,   10
But trepidation of the spheares,°
   Though greater farre, is innocent.

Dull sublunary lovers love
   (Whose soule is sense) cannot admit
Absence, because it doth remove
   Those things which elemented it.

But we by a love, so much refin'd,
   That our selves know not what it is,
Inter-assured of the mind,
   Care lesse, eyes, lips, and hands to misse.   20

Our two soules therefore, which are one,
   Though I must goe, endure not yet
A breach, but an expansion,
   Like gold to ayery thinnesse beate.

If they be two, they are two so
   As stiffe twin compasses are two,
Thy soule the fixt foot, makes no show
   To move, but doth, if the'other doe.

And though it in the center sit,
   Yet when the other far doth rome,   30
It leanes, and hearkens after it,
   And growes erect, as that comes home.

---

11. *trepidation of the spheares:* oscillation of the heavenly spheres—a theory to explain apparent irregularities in the movements of the planets.

Such wilt thou be to mee, who must
   Like th'other foot, obliquely runne;
Thy firmnes makes my circle just,
   And makes me end, where I begunne.

Sonnet 65

William Shakespeare

Since brass, nor stone, nor earth, nor boundless sea,
But sad mortality o'ersways their power,
How with this rage shall beauty hold a plea,
Whose action is no stronger than a flower?
O! how shall summer's honey breath hold out
Against the wrackful siege of battering days,
When rocks impregnable are not so stout,
Nor gates of steel so strong, but Time decays?
O fearful meditation! where, alack,
Shall Time's best jewel from Time's chest lie hid?   10
Or what strong hand can hold his swift foot back?
Or who his spoil of beauty can forbid?
O! none, unless this miracle have might,
That in black ink my love may still shine bright.

The Hippopotamus

T. S. Eliot

Similiter et omnes revereantur Diaconos, ut mandatum Jesu Christi; et Episcopum, ut Jesum Christum, existentem filium Patris; Presbyteros autem, ut concilium Dei et conjunctionem Apostolorum. Sine his Ecclesia non vocatur; de quibus suadeo vos sic habeo.

S. Ignatii Ad Trallianos. [1]

And when this epistle is read among you, cause that it be read also in the church of the Laodiceans.

The broad-backed hippopotamus
Rests on his belly in the mud;
Although he seems so firm to us
He is merely flesh and blood.

[1] "Let them all revere the Deacons in like manner as a command from Jesus Christ; and the Bishop as the living son of the Father; and the Presbyters also as the council of God and the assembly of the Apostles. Without these there is no church; concerning which I am persuaded and I regard you as thus opined." St. Ignatius to the Trallians.

Flesh and blood is weak and frail,
Susceptible to nervous shock;
While the True Church can never fail
For it is based upon a rock.

The hippo's feeble steps may err
In compassing material ends,   10
While the True Church need never stir
To gather in its dividends.

The 'potamus can never reach
The mango on the mango-tree;
But fruits of pomegranate and peach
Refresh the Church from over sea.

At mating time the hippo's voice
Betrays inflexions hoarse and odd,
But every week we hear rejoice
The Church, at being one with God.   20

The hippopotamus's day
Is passed in sleep: at night he hunts;
God works in a mysterious way—
The Church can sleep and feed at once.

I saw the 'potamus take wing
Ascending from the damp savannas,
And quiring angels round him sing
The praise of God, in loud hosannas.

Blood of the Lamb shall wash him clean
And him shall heavenly arms enfold,   30
Among the saints he shall be seen
Performing on a harp of gold.

He shall be washed as white as snow,
By all the martyr'd virgins kist,
While the True Church remains below
Wrapt in the old miasmal mist.

The Windows

George Herbert

Lord, how can man preach thy eternall word?
      He is a brittle crazie ° glasse:
Yet in thy temple thou dost him afford
      This glorious and transcendent place,
      To be a window, through thy grace.

But when thou dost anneal ° in glasse thy storie,
      Making thy life to shine within
The holy Preachers; then the light and glorie
      More rev'rend grows, & more doth win:
      Which else shows watrish, bleak, & thin.   10

Doctrine and life, colours and light, in one
      When they combine and mingle, bring
A strong regard and aw: but speech alone
      Doth vanish like a flaring thing,
      And in the eare, not conscience ring.

The Church-Floore

George Herbert

Mark you the floore? that square & speckled stone,
      Which looks so firm and strong,
      Is *Patience:*

And th' other black and grave, wherewith each one
      Is checker'd all along,
      Humilitie:

The gentle rising, which on either hand
      Leads to the Quire above,
      Is *Confidence:*

But the sweet cement, which in one sure band   10
      Ties the whole frame, is *Love*
      And *Charitie.*

2. *crazie:* full of cracks.   6. *anneal:* to heat glass in order to color it, as in the making of stained-glass windows.

Hither sometimes Sinne steals, and stains
The marbles neat and curious veins:
But all is cleansed when the marble weeps.
Sometimes Death, puffing at the doore,
Blows all the dust about the floore:
But while he thinks to spoil the room, he sweeps.
Blest be the *Architect*, whose art
Could build so strong in a weak heart.   20

Easter-Wings

George Herbert

Lord, who createdst man in wealth and store,
Though foolishly he lost the same,
Decaying more and more,
Till he became
Most poore:
With thee
O let me rise
As larks, harmoniously,
And sing this day thy victories:
Then shall the fall further the flight in me.   10

My tender age in sorrow did beginne:
And still with sicknesses and shame
Thou didst so punish sinne,
That I became
Most thinne.
With thee
Let me combine
And feel this day thy victorie:
For, if I imp ° my wing on thine,
Affliction shall advance the flight in me.   20

19. *imp:* a term from falconry, meaning to mount extra pinions on a bird's wing.

The Altar

George Herbert

A broken ALTAR, Lord, thy servant reares,
Made of a heart, and cemented with teares:
  Whose parts are as thy hand did frame;
  No workmans tool hath touch'd the same.
        A   HEART   alone
        Is   such a   stone,
        As   nothing   but
        Thy pow'r doth cut.
        Wherefore each part
        Of my hard heart   10
        Meets in this frame,
        To praise thy Name:
  That, if I chance to hold my peace,
  These stones to praise thee may not cease.
O let thy blessed SACRIFICE be mine,
And sanctifie this ALTAR to be thine.

Ana-{ MARY / ARMY }gram

George Herbert

How well her name an *Army* doth present,
In whom the *Lord of Hosts* did pitch his tent!

Idea

(Old Mazda lamp, 50-100-150 W)

John Hollander

On or
off   Either   darkness
unlocked   again   or   feigned
daylight perhaps graded only by
stepped intensities fifty watts apart
In any event no continuities like those
of flickering no nor even of fading Flick
Click and there it is suddenly *Oh yes I see*
Indeed A mind hung brilliantly upon filaments
stung by some untongued brightness opening up
also encloses and the dark unbounded room lit
by bare bulbs collapses into an unhurting box
occupied by furniture now avoidable The dot
of closure menaces the attention which in
the flutter of eyelids can only tremble
like a nervous child lying awake lest
he be aware of the moment a closing
shutter of sleep claps to But a
snapped-off dream disperses
into darkness like gold
becoming mere motes
becoming light If
the eye lies open
to such dust as
sunlight brings
it will never
burn But that
creation make
a visible big
difference in
the way minds
look a shaper
will burn
outwardly
first and
thus once
there was
light

Symbolic Things

Consciousness may not be entirely satisfied by a relationship to things that suggests the play of wit or fancy: objects are used with too great ease, there is no confrontation with their intractability, their hard otherness. Modern consciousness seems often to insist on formulations that simultaneously recognize the autonomy and otherness of the object and permit its use as a personal spiritual token. Mind assigns meanings to certain privileged objects, charging them as symbolic images, always with the awareness that meanings and symbolic values are tenuous, arbitrary, and ambiguous.

In a Station of the Metro

Ezra Pound

The apparition of these faces in the crowd;
Petals on a wet, black bough.

The Jewel Stairs' Grievance

Ezra Pound

The jewelled steps are already quite white with dew,
It is so late that the dew soaks my gauze stockings,
And I let down the crystal curtain
And watch the moon through the clear autumn.

By Rihaku

NOTE: Jewel stairs, therefore a palace. Grievance, therefore there is something to complain of. Gauze stockings, therefore a court lady, not a servant who complains. Clear autumn, therefore he has no excuse on account of weather. Also she has come early, for the dew has not merely whitened the stairs, but has soaked her stockings. The poem is especially prized because she utters no direct reproach. [The note is Pound's.]

Araby

James Joyce

North Richmond Street, being blind, was a quiet street except at the hour when the Christian Brothers' School set the boys free. An uninhabited house of two stories stood at the blind end, detached from its neighbors in a square ground. The other houses of the street, conscious of decent lives within them, gazed at one another with brown imperturbable faces.

The former tenant of our house, a priest, had died in the back drawing-room. Air, musty from having been long enclosed, hung in all the rooms, and the waste room behind the kitchen was littered with old useless papers. Among these I found a few paper-covered books, the pages of which were curled and damp: *The Abbot,* by Walter Scott, *The Devout Communicant* and *The Memoirs of Vidocq.* I liked the last best because its leaves were yellow. The wild garden behind the house contained a central apple-tree and a few straggling bushes under one of which I found the late tenant's rusty bicycle-pump. He had been a very charitable priest; in his will he had left all his money to institutions and the furniture of his house to his sister.

When the short days of winter came dusk fell before we had well eaten our dinners. When we met in the street the houses had grown somber. The space of sky above us was the color of ever-changing violet and towards it the lamps of the street lifted their feeble lanterns. The cold air stung us and we played till our bodies glowed. Our shouts echoed in the silent street. The career of our play brought us through the dark muddy lanes behind the houses where we ran the gauntlet of the rough tribes from the cottages, to the back doors of the dark dripping gardens where odors arose from the ashpits, to the dark odorous stables where a coachman smoothed and combed the horse or shook music from the buckled harness. When we returned to the street light from the kitchen windows had filled the areas. If my uncle was seen turning the corner we hid in the shadow until we had seen him safely housed. Or if Mangan's sister came out on the doorstep to call her brother in to his tea we watched her from our shadow peer up and down the street. We waited to see whether she would remain or go in and, if she remained, we left our shadow and walked up to Mangan's steps resignedly. She was waiting for us, her figure defined by the light from the half-opened door. Her brother always teased her before he obeyed and I stood by the railings looking at her. Her dress swung as she moved her body and the soft rope of her hair tossed from side to side.

Every morning I lay on the floor in the front parlour watching her door. The blind was pulled down to within an inch of the sash so that I could not be seen. When she came out on the doorstep my heart leaped. I ran to the hall, seized my books and followed her. I kept her brown figure always in my eye and, when we came near the point at which our ways diverged, I quickened my pace and passed her. This happened morning after morning. I had never spoken to her, except for a few casual words, and yet her name was like a summons to all my foolish blood.

Her image accompanied me even in places the most hostile to romance. On Saturday evenings when my aunt went marketing I had to go to carry some of the parcels. We walked through the flaring streets, jostled by drunken men and bargaining women, amid the curses of laborers, the shrill litanies of shopboys who stood on guard by the barrels of pigs' cheeks, the nasal chanting of street-singers, who sang a *come-all-you* about O'Donovan Rossa, or a ballad about the troubles in our native land. These noises converged in a single sensation of life for me: I imagined that I bore my chalice safely through a throng of foes. Her name sprang to my lips at moments in strange prayers and praises which I myself did not understand. My eyes were often full of tears (I could not tell why) and at times a flood from my heart seemed to pour itself out into my bosom. I thought little of the future. I did not know whether I would ever speak to her or not or, if I spoke to her, how I could tell her of my confused adoration. But my body was like a harp and her words and gestures were like fingers running upon the wires.

One evening I went into the back drawing-room in which the priest had died. It was a dark rainy evening and there was no sound in the house. Through one of the broken panes I heard the rain impinge upon the earth, the fine incessant needles of water playing in the sodden beds. Some distant lamp or lighted window gleamed below me. I was thankful that I could see so little. All my senses seemed to desire to veil themselves and, feeling that I was about to slip from them, I pressed the palms of my hands together until they trembled, murmuring: "*O love! O love!*" many times.

As last she spoke to me. When she addressed the first words to me I was so confused that I did not know what to answer. She asked me was I going to *Araby*. I forgot whether I answered yes or no. It would be a splendid bazaar, she said she would love to go.

"And why can't you?" I asked.

While she spoke she turned a silver bracelet round and round her wrist. She could not go, she said, because there would be a retreat that week in her convent. Her brother and two other boys were fighting for their caps and I was alone at the railings. She held one of the spikes, bowing her head towards me. The light from the lamp opposite our door caught the white curve of her neck, lit up her hair that rested there and, falling, lit up the hand upon the railing. It fell over one side of her dress and caught the white border of a petticoat, just visible as she stood at ease.

"It's well for you," she said.

"If I go," I said, "I will bring you something."

What innumerable follies laid waste my waking and sleeping thoughts after that evening! I wished to annihilate the tedious intervening days. I chafed against the work of school. At night in my bedroom and by day in the classroom her image came between me and the page I strove to read. The syllables of the word *Araby* were called to me through the silence in which my soul luxuriated and cast an Eastern enchantment over me. I asked for leave to go to the bazaar on Saturday night. My aunt was surprised and hoped it was not some Freemason affair. I answered few questions in class. I watched my master's face pass from amiability to sternness; he hoped I was not beginning to idle. I could not call my wandering thoughts together. I had hardly any patience with the serious work of life which, now that it stood between me and my desire, seemed to me child's play, ugly monotonous child's play.

On Saturday morning I reminded my uncle that I wished to go to the bazaar in the evening. He was fussing at the hallstand, looking for the hat-brush, and answered me curtly:

"Yes, boy, I know."

As he was in the hall I could not go into the front parlour and lie at the window. I left the house in bad humor and walked slowly towards the school. The air was pitilessly raw and already my heart misgave me.

When I came home to dinner my uncle had not yet been home. Still it was early. I sat staring at the clock for some time and, when its ticking began to irritate me, I left the room. I mounted the staircase and gained the upper part of the house. The high cold empty gloomy rooms liberated me and I went from room to room singing. From the front window I saw my companions playing below in the street. Their cries reached me weakened and indistinct and, leaning my forehead against the cool glass, I looked over at the dark house where she lived. I may have stood there for an hour, seeing nothing but the brown-clad figure cast by my imagination, touched discreetly by the lamplight at the curved neck, at the hand upon the railings and at the border below the dress.

When I came downstairs again I found Mrs. Mercer sitting at the fire. She was an old garrulous woman, a pawnbroker's widow, who collected used stamps for some pious purpose. I had to endure the gossip of the tea-table. The meal was prolonged beyond an hour and still my uncle did not come. Mrs. Mercer stood up to go: she was sorry she couldn't wait any longer, but it was after eight o'clock and she did not like to be out late, as the night air was bad for her. When she had gone I began to walk up and down the room, clenching my fists. My aunt said:

"I'm afraid you may put off your bazaar for this night of our Lord."

At nine o'clock I heard my uncle's latchkey in the halldoor. I heard him talking to himself and heard the hallstand rocking when it had received the weight of his overcoat. I could interpret these signs. When he was midway through his dinner I asked him to give me the money to go to the bazaar. He had forgotten.

"The people are in bed and after their first sleep now," he said.

I did not smile. My aunt said to him energetically:

"Can't you give him the money and let him go? You've kept him late enough as it is."

My uncle said he was very sorry he had forgotten. He said he believed in the old saying: "All work and no play makes Jack a dull boy." He asked me where I was going and, when I had told him a second time he asked me did I know *The Arab's Farewell to his Steed*. When I left the kitchen he was about to recite the opening lines of the piece to my aunt.

I held a florin tightly in my hand as I strode down Buckingham Street towards the station. The sight of the streets thronged with buyers and glaring with gas recalled to me the purpose of my journey. I took my seat in a third-class carriage of a deserted train. After an intolerable delay the train moved out of the station slowly. It crept onward among ruinous houses and over the twinkling river. At Westland Row Station a crowd of people pressed to the carriage doors; but the porters moved them back, saying that it was a special train for the bazaar. I remained alone in the bare carriage. In a few minutes the train drew up beside an improvised wooden platform. I passed out on to the road and saw by the lighted dial of a clock that it was ten minutes to ten. In front of me was a large building which displayed the magical name.

I could not find any sixpenny entrance and, fearing that the bazaar would be closed, I passed in quickly through a turnstile, handing a shilling to a weary-looking man. I found myself in a big hall girdled at half its height by a gallery. Nearly all the stalls were closed and the greater part of the hall was in darkness. I recognized a silence like that which pervades a church after a service. I walked into the center of the bazaar timidly. A few people were gathered about the stalls which were still open. Before a curtain, over which the words *Café Chantant* were written in colored lamps, two men were counting money on a salver. I listened to the fall of the coins.

Remembering with difficulty why I had come I went over to one of the stalls and examined porcelain vases and flowered tea-sets. At the door of the stall a young lady was talking and laughing with two young gentlemen. I remarked their English accents and listented vaguely to their conversation.

"O, I never said such a thing!"

"O, but you did!"

"O, but I didn't!"

"Didn't she say that?"

"Yes, I heard her."

"O, there's a . . . fib!"

Observing me the young lady came over and asked me did I wish to buy anything. The tone of her voice was not encouraging; she seemed to have spoken to me out of a sense of duty. I looked humbly at the great jars that stood like Eastern guards at either side of the dark entrance to the stall and murmured:

"No, thank you."

The young lady changed the position of one of the vases and went back to the two young men. They began to talk of the same subject. Once or twice the young lady glanced at me over her shoulder.

I lingered before her stall, though I knew my stay was useless, to make my interest in her wares seem the more real. Then I turned away slowly and walked down the middle of the bazaar. I allowed the two pennies to fall against the sixpence in my pocket. I heard a voice call from one end of the gallery that the light was out. The upper part of the hall was now completely dark.

Gazing up into the darkness I saw myself as a creature driven and derided by vanity; and my eyes burned with anguish and anger.

Meditations in Time of Civil War

William Butler Yeats

I

Ancestral Houses

Surely among a rich man's flowering lawns,
Amid the rustle of his planted hills,
Life overflows without ambitious pains;
And rains down life until the basin spills,

And mounts more dizzy high the more it rains
As though to choose whatever shape it wills
And never stoop to a mechanical
Or servile shape, at others' beck and call.

Mere dreams, mere dreams! Yet Homer had not sung
Had he not found it certain beyond dreams   10
That out of life's own self-delight had sprung
The abounding glittering jet; though now it seems
As if some marvellous empty sea-shell flung
Out of the obscure dark of the rich streams,
And not a fountain, were the symbol which
Shadows the inherited glory of the rich.

Some violent bitter man, some powerful man
Called architect and artist in, that they,
Bitter and violent men, might rear in stone
The sweetness that all longed for night and day,   20
The gentleness none there had ever known;
But when the master's buried mice can play,
And maybe the great-grandson of that house,
For all its bronze and marble, 's but a mouse.

O what if gardens where the peacock strays
With delicate feet upon old terraces,
Or else all Juno from an urn displays
Before the indifferent garden deities;
O what if levelled lawns and gravelled ways
Where slippered Contemplation finds his ease   30
And Childhood a delight for every sense,
But take our greatness with our violence?

What if the glory of escutcheoned doors,
And buildings that a haughtier age designed,
The pacing to and fro on polished floors
Amid great chambers and long galleries, lined
With famous portraits of our ancestors;
What if those things the greatest of mankind
Consider most to magnify, or to bless,
But take our greatness with our bitterness?   40

II

My House

An ancient bridge, and a more ancient tower,
A farmhouse that is sheltered by its wall,
An acre of stony ground,
Where the symbolic rose can break in flower,
Old ragged elms, old thorns innumerable,
The sound of the rain or sound

Of every wind that blows;
The stilted water-hen
Crossing stream again
Scared by the splashing of a dozen cows;   50

A winding stair, a chamber arched with stone,
A grey stone fireplace with an open hearth,
A candle and written page.
Il Penseroso's Platonist toiled on
In some like chamber, shadowing forth
How the daemonic rage
Imagined everything.
Benighted travellers
From markets and from fairs
Have seen his midnight candle glimmering.   60

Two men have founded here. A man-at-arms
Gathered a score of horse and spent his days
In this tumultuous spot,
Where through long wars and sudden night alarms
His dwindling score and he seemed castaways
Forgetting and forgot;
And I, that after me
My bodily heirs may find,
To exalt a lonely mind,
Befitting emblems of adversity.   70

III

My Table

Two heavy trestles, and a board
Where Sato's gift, a changeless sword,°
By pen and paper lies,
That it may moralise
My days out of their aimlessness.
A bit of an embroidered dress
Covers its wooden sheath.
Chaucer had not drawn breath
When it was forged. In Sato's house,
Curved like new moon, moon-luminous,   80
It lay five hundred years.
Yet if no change appears
No moon; only an aching heart
Conceives a changeless work of art.
Our learned men have urged
That when and where 'twas forged
A marvellous accomplishment,
In painting or in pottery, went

72. *Sato's . . . sword:* a Japanese ceremonial sword, the gift to Yeats from a friend.

302

From father unto son
And through the centuries ran   90
And seemed unchanging like the sword.
Soul's beauty being most adored,
Men and their business took
The soul's unchanging look;
For the most rich inheritor,
Knowing that none could pass Heaven's door
That loved inferior art,
Had such an aching heart
That he, although a country's talk
For silken clothes and stately walk,   100
Had waking wits; it seemed
Juno's peacock screamed.°

IV

My Descendants

Having inherited a vigorous mind
From my old fathers, I must nourish dreams
And leave a woman and a man behind
As vigorous of mind, and yet it seems
Life scarce can cast a fragrance on the wind,
Scarce spread a glory to the morning beams,
But the torn petals strew the garden plot;
And there's but common greenness after that.   110

And what if my descendants lose the flower
Through natural declension of the soul,
Through too much business with the passing hour,
Through too much play, or marriage with a fool?
May this laborious stair and this stark tower
Become a roofless ruin that the owl
May build in the cracked masonry and cry
Her desolation to the desolate sky.

The Primum Mobile that fashioned us
Has made the very owls in circles move;   120
And I, that count myself most prosperous,
Seeing that love and friendship are enough,
For an old neighbour's friendship chose the house
And decked and altered it for a girl's love,
And know whatever flourish and decline
These stones remain their monument and mine.

102. *Juno's peacock screamed:* The scream of Juno's peacock apparently symbolizes for Yeats the victory of irrationality.

V

The Road at My Door

An affable Irregular,
A heavily-built Falstaffian man,
Comes cracking jokes of civil war
As though to die by gunshot were   130
The finest play under the sun.

A brown Lieutenant and his men,
Half dressed in national uniform,
Stand at my door, and I complain
Of the foul weather, hail and rain,
A pear-tree broken by the storm.

I count these feathered balls of soot
The moor-hen guides upon the stream,
To silence the envy in my thought;
And turn towards my chamber, caught   140
In the cold snows of a dream.

VI

The Stare's Nest by My Window

The bees build in the crevices
Of loosening masonry, and there
The mother birds bring grubs and flies.
My wall is loosening; honey-bees,
Come build in the empty house of the stare.

We are closed in, and the key is turned
On our uncertainty; somewhere
A man is killed, or a house burned,
Yet no clear fact to be discerned: 150
Come build in the empty house of the stare.

A barricade of stone or of wood;
Some fourteen days of civil war;
Last night they trundled down the road
That dead young soldier in his blood:
Come build in the empty house of the stare.

We had fed the heart on fantasies,
The heart's grown brutal from the fare;
More substance in our enmities
Than in our love; O honey-bees,   160
Come build in the empty house of the stare.

VII

I See Phantoms of Hatred and of the Heart's
Fullness and of the Coming Emptiness

I climb to the tower-top and lean upon broken stone,
A mist that is like blown snow is sweeping over all,
Valley, river, and elms, under the light of a moon
That seems unlike itself, that seems unchangeable,
A glittering sword out of the east. A puff of wind
And those white glimmering fragments of the mist sweep by.
Frenzies bewilder, reveries perturb the mind;
Monstrous familiar images swim to the mind's eye.

'Vengeance upon the murderers,' the cry goes up,   170
'Vengeance for Jacques Molay.' ° In cloud-pale rags, or in lace,
The rage-driven, rage-tormented, and rage-hungry troop,
Trooper belabouring trooper, biting at arm or at face,
Plunges towards nothing, arms and fingers spreading wide
For the embrace of nothing; and I, my wits astray
Because of all that senseless tumult, all but cried
For vengeance on the murderers of Jacques Molay.

Their legs long, delicate and slender, aquamarine their eyes,
Magical unicorns bear ladies on their backs.
The ladies close their musing eyes. No prophecies,   180
Remembered out of Babylonian almanacs,
Have closed the ladies' eyes, their minds are but a pool
Where even longing drowns under its own excess;
Nothing but stillness can remain when hearts are full
Of their own sweetness, bodies of their loveliness.

The cloud-pale unicorns, the eyes of aquamarine,
The quivering half-closed eyelids, the rags of cloud or of lace,
Or eyes that rage has brightened, arms it has made lean,
Give place to an indifferent multitude, give place
To brazen hawks. Nor self-delighting reverie,   190
Nor hate of what's to come, nor pity for what's gone,
Nothing but grip of claw, and the eye's complacency,
The innumerable clanging wings that have put out the moon.

I turn away and shut the door, and on the stair
Wonder how many times I could have proved my worth
In something that all others understand or share;
But O! ambitious heart, had such a proof drawn forth

171. *Jacques Molay:* "A cry for vengeance because of the murder of the Grand
Master of the Templars [Jacques de Molay, burned for witchcraft in 1314] seems to
me a fit symbol for those who labour from hatred, and so for sterility of various
kinds. . . ." [W. B. Y.]

305

A company of friends, a conscience set at ease,
It had but made us pine the more. The abstract joy,
The half-read wisdom of daemonic images,   200
Suffice the ageing man as once the growing boy.

III.

Beginnings, Middles, and Ends: Putting Things Together

In Part II we saw how men strive to make sense of the world, beginning by naming the things in it. In Part III we shall examine some of the ways in which isolated things, once named, are "told": various strategies for arranging things in a meaningful sequence.

Mountains sprawl. But on maps they look very neat. Time as we experience it in our lives is various: when we are happy an hour seems a minute; when we are sad a minute is an hour. But on a clock time is always the same. Men seem to be made uneasy by such apparently natural facts as randomness, eternity, and imprecision, and maps and clocks are just two of the ways in which men impose order on the world. Plot is another; both maps and clocks are a kind of plot. From the history of the universe in cosmology to the history of an individual in psychology, plot is a basic tool by which we explain nature, nations, and ourselves. Like a map, plot is an instrument of discovery. Like a clock, it is a means for measuring movement. Similar to both, plots provide an orientation.

In one way or another—spatially, temporally, logically—all plots have a beginning, a middle, and an end. They differ only in the ways they articulate this sequence and in the relative significance each part of the movement may take on. In logic, for instance, a syllogism not only has the three phases mentioned, it also requires that they be in a linear progression: 1) Socrates is a mortal. 2) All mortals die. 3) Therefore Socrates will die. In this example, 1 and 2 may be reversed, but both are necessary and both must precede 3. Another possible combination is demonstrated by a simple metaphor: Achilles is a lion. The middle of the metaphoric plot, in this example the fierce strength of both Achilles and the lion, is always present, but unlike the middle term of the syllogism, it is implicit, unstated.

Metaphor is but one element of the ancient art of rhetoric, about which Samuel Butler once wrote: "all a rhetorician's rules / Teach nothing but to name his tools." That is, a dictionary of rhetorical terms is really a "grammar of meaning," a series of recipes for making sense. Rhetoric aids the mind in its ceaseless effort to appropriate things to its own realm. It does so by providing various ways to arrange things in sequence so as to convey certain nuances of their relationships to each other. In other words, rhetorical figures are attempts to establish emphasis among two or more things by shifting beginnings, middles, and ends, as in the metaphor. Consider some other examples (it goes without saying that the figures of speech that follow are introduced only as examples of the point we are trying to make): *ploce* is the repetition of the same word in a different sense for the sake of emphasis ("In that great victory, Caesar was *Caesar.*"); *symploce* is the use of the same words at the beginning and the end of successive clauses ("*Spring* clothes the *trees; spring* leads back the birds to the *trees.*"); *anadiplosis* is the use of the same word at the end of one clause and at the beginning of the next ("Still he sought for *fame, fame* that last infirmity of a noble mind."); *epidiplosis* is the use of the same word at the beginning and the end of a sentence ("*Justice* took no note of Joe; and he paid the same tribute to *justice.*"). All these rhetorical devices are simply miniature plots, variations on the semantics of beginning, middle, and end. We need only compare such elementary plots with the involute sequence and complicated actions in a work such as *Paradise Lost,* a Henry James novel, or Marx's *Das Kapital* to see the enormous range of possibilities contained in Aristotle's seemingly simple demand that a plot have a beginning, a middle, and an end.

Most dictionaries give four meanings of "plot": 1) an area marked off on a surface, usually ground; 2) a chart, diagram, or map; 3) the plan of action of a play, novel, short story, etc.; 4) a secret project or scheme, a conspiracy. What all these definitions have in common, their emphasis on borders, is obvious in the first three instances. A conspiracy, too, is defined as a thing set off: it excludes all those not in on the secret. In order to achieve this quality of boundedness, of being marked off, plots work by rules of exclusion; certain things must be left out. What plots leave out, of course, is varying degrees of contingency, the state in which events may occur by chance, accidentally, fortuitously. This is the irrational against which Aristotle inveighs, the messiness of brute nature, of ordinary lived experience, with its confusions, its half-finished sentences, its daily eruptions of the absurd. Plots are a means to cut all that out. In a very real sense plots differentiate themselves as much by the specific nature of what they exclude as they do by the kind of thing they actually incorporate. Thus the plot of tragedy requires that all petty or silly actions be avoided. If, after Hamlet cries "To be or not to be," he should belch, the borders of tragedy would be irreparably breached. It is just this type of border incident that is at the heart of so many modern fictions, suggesting, as we shall see, that plot in our own time is frequently to be explained by the dictionary's fourth meaning, a conspiracy. In Borges and

Barth plot becomes just that, a conspiracy, against previously held conceptions of plot. Marc Saporta's novel *Composition #1* (1962) perhaps represents the extreme of this tendency: the book comes as a carton of unbound, unnumbered pages that the reader is supposed to shuffle from time to time as he would a deck of cards. It is precisely the element of chance, which Aristotle felt must be abjured above all others, that Saporta appeals to for his specific effect.

Saporta's book is more a curious toy than a document in the history of plot morphology, partly because of the author's inability to understand the necessity for *some* thread in a story's carpet, no matter how frayed or difficult to perceive. Perhaps the best answer to the doubts of such unimaginative authors concerning the fecundity of Aristotelian plots is George Herriman's comic strip *Krazy Kat*. It had one basic plot, the eternal triangle. Krazy loved Ignatz Mouse, and Offisa Pup loved Krazy. Ignatz did not love anybody. He would throw a brick at Krazy (who thought this was how the mouse showed he cared), after which he would be jailed by Offisa Pup. This went on—daily—for thirty-five years. Herriman died in 1944, and his art in deploying permutations of this simple story was such that King Features let the strip die with its creator (a most unusual decision in the case of so popular a property).

The need for plots transcends man's thirst for art, grounded, as it seems to be, in the very laws that govern human perception. If we conceive of experience as an ongoing dialectic between mind and nature, two radical possibilities are present: one is that the constructs we put upon the world will become so rigid and hermetic that we will lose contact with reality, evaporate it in our models. The opposite case is also conceivable, that the exterior world, with all its flux and multiplicity, will overwhelm the power of mind to order it. Madness would be the result in either case. Most men succeed in finding a middle way between these two extremes, and they do so by continual experimentation with different plots. Linguistics teaches us that meaning is a function of differences, not similarities: we recognize black not because it is like something else, but because it is not white. More complex acts of recognition require temporal as well as semantic differentiation. For example, ask yourself whether the woman in the illustration on page 310 is putting the celery into the bag or taking it out of the bag. In terms of this drawing alone the question cannot be resolved one way or the other. But now think of the actions that may have preceded the one illustrated. What steps could lead to either of the two possible answers? For instance, the woman might have taken a loaf of bread out of the plastic bag in order that it might be re-used to store the celery in the refrigerator—in which case she is shown, in our picture, definitely putting the celery *into* the bag. Making a temporal sequence on the basis of plausible variables, we have created a plot that solves our problem, that gives meaning to what otherwise is opaque. This is an elementary example of an operation we perform every day of our lives, in hundreds of different ways.

309

Plot, then, is a primal mechanism in fiction-making. If we no longer need stories of the sort mentioned in the Introduction, stories that show where the best water hole may be found or that maintain genealogical ties, we may yet find an existential utility in fictions, particularly those which constitute Literature. Such stories as are found in Greek tragedy, Elizabethan drama, or a Dostoevsky novel have much to tell us about the nature and technique of plots, the importance of which transcends mere aesthetics.

The following texts, at least, have been selected on the basis of such a belief. Aristotle's formula for plots is at once the most economical and widely operative definition available. The creation story from the Bible illustrates one of the oldest ways of organizing complex events: simple chronology. The Edward Lear poem is a tale arranged on the basis of the alphabet, another simple but ubiquitous method for providing a narrative road map. It also is an example of a useful story from our own culture, in that its purpose is clearly to charm children into learning the ABC's. Riddles have in them the fun of guessing a story's ending; each is a miniature detective story. They are simple exercises in the projection of a result from a given situation. More sophisticated examples of the same function may be found in utopias, mathematical formulas, science fiction, governmental decisions based on model "scenarios" developed by the Rand or Hudson institutes, and in theoretical physics.

What such acts of extrapolation suggest is that we often "lie" in order to tell the "truth." That is, we can "know" reality only if we act as if it were the result of a story that in itself may not be true. This is the presupposition that underlies much wisdom literature, such as parables, where a made-up story is told to explain a truth about human nature, or even about the "truest truth," God. The Bible is full of such stories. We have included two examples from *Midrash*, Hebrew Talmudic interpretation, in which, in order to understand the meaning of God's revealed word, the rabbis tell stories that make it knowable. Plot as revelation is even more radically dramatized in the koans of Japanese Zen Buddhism. Whereas *Midrash* seeks to make a holy mystery available to human understanding, the koan attempts the opposite: by demonstrating the limits of normal human understanding it seeks to shock the initiate into a higher mode of perception. It uses words, a plot, to get to a mystery beyond words. Kafka's parable provides a modern example of wisdom literature, where, unlike Christ's parables, the meaning is ambiguous. Somewhat similar to the koan, Kafka's story uses words to get beyond words. *The Hunting of the Snark* is perhaps even more mysterious, an example of pure plot, as divorced from every other element of fiction-making as a story can be without devolving into mere gibberish.

In several of the examples above a basic pattern seems to involve play with a plot's ending. It is for this reason that the detective story, although a relatively new genre as we now conceive it, seems so important for an understanding of plot. It is the most relentlessly *aimed* of all stories, an exercise in teleology, and an example is provided in order to establish the formal properties of the genre. If the narrative presuppositions dramatized in such stories are then applied to a Greek tragedy, it will be clear that they are much older and far more profound than the codification they find in Conan Doyle, Poe, or Agatha Christie.

The Borges story, in the final section of Part III, shows how a new kind of plot may be made by "exploding" an old one (in this case, that of a detective story). And the selection from Sartre voices the suspicion that plots are a trick for limiting man's existential freedom, a prejudice widely held in our own time. And yet, for better or for worse, we seem to need plots. Without them we would be in the predicament dramatized by Samuel Beckett in *The Unnamable* (1959): "What am I to do, what shall I do, what should I do . . . how proceed? By aporia [another rhetorical strategy in which the speaker pretends he is at a loss to organize his thoughts] pure and simple? Or by affirmations and negiations invalidated as uttered?"

311

Ordering the World

FROM THE Poetics

Aristotle

Translated by Ingram Bywater

Aristotle (384–322 B.C.), who studied under Plato, and who later became the tutor of Alexander the Great, is one of the greatest philosophers of all time. The majority of his works that have come down to us (including *The Poetics*) are made up from notes taken by his students. It is no accident that Aristotle should have assigned so important a role to plot in his study of Greek tragedy, for he considered logic the necessary tool for all inquiry—scientific, metaphysical, or aesthetic. Syllogism was the natural sequence of logical thinking. Thus Aristotle's emphasis on beginning, middle, and end in stories is just another aspect of his larger concern for the ordered perception of the world. Scholars continue to debate the meaning of Aristotle's terms, but these arguments need not concern us here. What should be kept in mind is that in the *Poetics* a "beginning" is not just any action, but one that organically leads to another; a "middle" is that which causally continues the action; and an "end" logically concludes it. None of these terms can be understood in isolation from the others.

■

Reserving hexameter poetry and Comedy for consideration hereafter, let us proceed now to the discussion of Tragedy; before doing so, however, we must gather up the definition resulting from what has been said. A tragedy, then, is the imitation of an action that is serious and also, as having magnitude, complete in itself; in language with pleasurable accessories, each kind brought in separately in the parts of the work; in a dramatic, not in a narrative form; with incidents arousing pity and fear, wherewith to accomplish its catharsis of such emotions. Here by "language with pleasurable accessories" I mean that with rhythm and harmony or song superadded; and by "the kinds separately" I mean that some portions are worked out with verse only, and others in turn with song.

I. As they act the stories, it follows that in the first place the Spectacle (or stage-appearance of the actors) must be some part of the whole; and in the second Melody and Diction, these two being the means of their imitation. Here by "Diction" I mean merely this, the composition of the verses; and by "Melody," what is too completely understood to require explanation. But further: the subject represented also is an action; and the action involves agents, who must necessarily have their distinctive qualities both of character and thought, since it is from these that we ascribe certain qualities to their actions. There are in the natural order of things, therefore, two causes, Thought and Character, of their actions, and consequently of their success or failure in their lives. Now the action (that which was done) is represented in the play by the Fable or Plot. The Fable, in our present sense of the term, is simply this, the combination of the incidents, or things done in the story; whereas Character is what makes us ascribe certain moral qualities to the agents; and Thought is shown in all they say when proving a particular point or, it may be, enunciating a general truth. There are six parts consequently of every tragedy, as a whole (that is) of such or such quality, viz. a Fable or Plot, Characters, Diction, Thought, Spectacle, and Melody; two of them arising from the means, one from the manner, and three from the objects of the dramatic imitation; and there is nothing else besides these six. Of these, its formative elements, then, not a few of the dramatists have made due use, as every play, one may say, admits of Spectacle, Character, Fable, Diction, Melody, and Thought.

II. The most important of the six is the combination of the incidents of the story. Tragedy is essentially an imitation not of persons but of action and life, of happiness and misery. All human happiness or misery takes the form of action; the end for which we live is a certain kind of activity, not a quality. Character gives us qualities, but it is in our actions—what we do—that we are happy or the reverse. In a play accordingly they do not act in order to portray the Characters; they include the Characters for the sake of the action. So that it is the action in it, i.e. its Fable or Plot, that is the end and purpose of the tragedy; and the end is everywhere the chief thing. Besides this, a tragedy is impossible without action, but there may be one without Character. The tragedies of most of the moderns are characterless—a defect common among poets of all kinds, and with its counterpart in painting in Zeuxis as compared with Polygnotus; for whereas the latter is strong in character, the work of

Zeuxis is devoid of it. And again: one may string together a series of characteristic speeches of the utmost finish as regards Diction and Thought, and yet fail to produce the true tragic effect; but one will have much better success with a tragedy which, however inferior in these respects, has a Plot, a combination of incidents, in it. And again: the most powerful elements of attraction in Tragedy, the Peripeties [1] and Discoveries, are parts of the Plot. A further proof is in the fact that beginners succeed earlier with the Diction and Characters than with the construction of a story; and the same may be said of nearly all the early dramatists. We maintain, therefore, that the first essential, the life and soul, so to speak, of Tragedy is the Plot; and that the Characters come second—compare the parallel in painting, where the most beautiful colours laid on without order will not give one the same pleasure as a simple black-and-white sketch of a portrait. We maintain that Tragedy is primarily an imitation of action, and that it is mainly for the sake of the action that it imitates the personal agents. Third comes the element of Thought, i.e. the power of saying whatever can be said, or what is appropriate to the occasion. This is what, in the speeches in Tragedy, falls under the arts of Politics and Rhetoric; for the older poets make their personages discourse like statesmen, and the moderns like rhetoricians. One must not confuse it with Character. Character in a play is that which reveals the moral purpose of the agents, i.e. the sort of thing they seek or avoid, where that is not obvious—hence there is no room for Character in a speech on a purely indifferent subject. Thought, on the other hand, is shown in all they say when proving or disproving some particular point, or enunciating some universal proposition. Fourth among the literary elements is the Diction of the personages, i.e., . . . the expression of their thoughts in words, which is practically the same thing with verse as with prose. As for the two remaining parts, the Melody is the greatest of the pleasurable accessories of Tragedy. The Spectacle, though an attraction, is the least artistic of all the parts, and has least to do with the art of poetry. The tragic effect is quite possible without a public performance and actors; and besides, the getting up of the Spectacle is more a matter for the costumier than the poet.

Having thus distinguished the parts, let us now consider the proper construction of the Fable or Plot, as that is at once the first and the most important thing in Tragedy. We have laid it down that a tragedy is an imitation of an action that is complete in itself, as a whole of some magnitude; for a whole may be of no magnitude to speak of. Now a whole is that which has beginning, middle, and end. A beginning is that which is not itself necessarily after anything else, and which has naturally something else after it; an end is that which is naturally after something itself, either as its necessary or usual consequent, and with nothing else after it; and a middle, that which is by nature after one thing and has also another

[1] The reversal of fortune for the protagonist leading either to his fall in tragedy or to his success in comedy.

after it. A well-constructed Plot, therefore, cannot either begin or end at any point one likes; beginning and end in it must be of the forms just described. Again: to be beautiful, a living creature, and every whole made up of parts, must not only present a certain order in its arrangement of parts, but also be of a certain definite magnitude. Beauty is a matter of size and order, and therefore impossible either (1) in a very minute creature, since our perception becomes indistinct as it approaches instantaneity; or (2) in a creature of vast size—one, say, 1,000 miles long —as in that case, instead of the object being seen all at once, the unity and wholeness of it is lost to the beholder. Just in the same way, then, as a beautiful whole made up of parts, or a beautiful living creature, must be of some size, but a size to be taken in by the eye, so a story or Plot must be of some length, but of a length to be taken in by the memory. As for the limit of its length, so far as that is relative to public performances and spectators, it does not fall within the theory of poetry. If they had to perform a hundred tragedies, they would be timed by water-clocks, as they are said to have been at one period. The limit, however, set by the actual nature of the thing is this: the longer the story, consistently with its being comprehensible as a whole, the finer it is by reason of its magnitude. As a rough general formula, "a length which allows of the hero passing by a series of probable or necessary stages from misfortune to happiness, or from happiness to misfortune," may suffice as a limit for the magnitude of the story.

The unity of a Plot does not consist, as some suppose, in its having one man as its subject. An infinity of things befall that one man, some of which it is impossible to reduce to unity; and in like manner there are many actions of one man which cannot be made to form one action. One sees, therefore, the mistake of all the poets who have written a *Heracleid,* a *Theseid,* or similar poems; they suppose that, because Heracles was one man, the story also of Heracles must be one story. Homer, however, evidently understood this point quite well, whether by art or instinct, just in the same way as he excels the rest in every other respect. In writing an *Odyssey,* he did not make the poem cover all that ever befell his hero —it befell him, for instance, to get wounded on Parnassus and also to feign madness at the time of the call to arms, but the two incidents had no necessary or probable connexion with one another—instead of doing that, he took as the subject of the *Odyssey,* as also of the *Iliad,* an action with a Unity of the kind we are describing. The truth is that, just as in the other imitative arts one imitation is always of one thing, so in poetry the story, as an imitation of action, must represent one action, a complete whole, with its several incidents so closely connected that the transposal or withdrawal of any one of them will disjoin and dislocate the whole. For that which makes no perceptible difference by its presence or absence is no real part of the whole.

From what we have said it will be seen that the poet's function is to describe, not the thing that has happened, but a kind of thing that might

315

happen, i.e. what is possible as being probable or necessary. The distinction between historian and poet is not in the one writing prose and the other verse—you might put the work of Herodotus into verse, and it would still be a species of history; it consists really in this, that the one describes the thing that has been, and the other a kind of thing that might be. Hence poetry is something more philosophic and of graver import than history, since its statements are of the nature rather of universals, whereas those of history are singulars. By a universal statement I mean one as to what such or such a kind of man will probably or necessarily say or do—which is the aim of poetry, though it affixes proper names to the characters; by a singular statement, one as to what, say, Alcibiades did or had done to him. In Comedy this has become clear by this time; it is only when their plot is already made up of probable incidents that they give it a basis of proper names, choosing for the purpose any names that may occur to them, instead of writing like the old iambic poets about particular persons. In Tragedy, however, they still adhere to the historic names; and for this reason: what convinces is the possible; now whereas we are not yet sure as to the possibility of that which has not happened, that which has happened is manifestly possible, else it would not have come to pass. Nevertheless even in Tragedy there are some plays with but one or two known names in them, the rest being inventions; and there are some without a single known name, e.g. Agathon's *Antheus,* in which both incidents and names are of the poet's invention; and it is no less delightful on that account. So that one must not aim at a rigid adherence to the traditional stories on which tragedies are based. It would be absurd, in fact, to do so, as even the known stories are only known to a few, though they are a delight none the less to all.

It is evident from the above that the poet must be more the poet of his stories or Plots than of his verses, inasmuch as he is a poet by virtue of the imitative elements in his work, and it is actions that he imitates. And if he should come to take a subject from actual history, he is none the less a poet for that; since some historic occurrences may very well be in the probable and possible order of things; and it is in that aspect of them that he is their poet.

FROM Genesis

The principle of organization here is one of simple chronology, a different act in the drama of creation for each day of the week. This is a widely used principle, from ancient chronicles, with events arranged under the succeeding years or reigns of kings, to modern confessional novels, which often take the form of a diary.

■

1

In the beginning God created the heaven and the earth. And the earth was without form, and void; and darkness was upon the face of the deep. And the spirit of God moved upon the face of the waters. And God said, "Let there be light": and there was light. And God saw the light, that it was good: and God divided the light from the darkness. And God called the light Day, and the darkness he called Night. And the evening and the morning were the first day.

And God said, "Let there be a firmament in the midst of the waters, and let it divide the waters from the waters." And God made the firmament, and divided the waters which were under the firmament from the waters which were above the firmament: and it was so. And God called the firmament Heaven. And the evening and the morning were the second day.

And God said, "Let the waters under the heaven be gathered together unto one place, and let the dry land appear": and it was so. And God called the dry land Earth; and the gathering together of the waters called he Seas: and God saw that it was good. And God said, "Let the earth bring forth grass, the herb yielding seed, and the fruit tree yielding fruit after his kind, whose seed is in itself, upon the earth": and it was so. And the earth brought forth grass, and herb yielding seed after his kind, and the tree yielding fruit, whose seed was in itself, after his kind: and God saw that it was good. And the evening and the morning were the third day.

And God said, "Let there be lights in the firmament of the heaven to divide the day from the night; and let them be for signs, and for seasons, and for days, and years: and let them be for lights in the firmament of the heaven to give light upon the earth": and it was so. And God made two great lights; the greater light to rule the day, and the lesser light to rule the night: he made the stars also. And God set them in the firmament of the heaven to give light upon the earth, and to rule over the day and over the night, and to divide the light from the darkness: and God saw that it was good. And the evening and the morning were the fourth day.

And God said, "Let the waters bring forth abundantly the moving creature that hath life, and fowl that may fly above the earth in the open firmament of heaven." And God created great whales, and every living creature that moveth, which the waters brought forth abundantly, after their kind, and every winged fowl after his kind: and God saw that it was good. And God blessed them, saying, "Be fruitful, and multiply, and fill the waters in the seas, and let fowl multiply in the earth." And the evening and the morning were the fifth day.

And God said, "Let the earth bring forth the living creature after his kind, cattle, and creeping thing, and beast of the earth after his kind": and it was so. And God made the beast of the earth after his kind, and cattle after their kind, and every thing that creepeth upon the earth after his kind: and God saw that it was good. And God said, "Let us make man in our image, after our likeness: and let them have dominion over the fish of the sea, and over the fowl of the air, and over the cattle, and over all the earth, and over every creeping thing that creepeth upon the earth." So God created man in his own image, in the image of God created he him; male and female created he them. And God blessed them, and God said unto them, "Be fruitful, and multiply, and replenish the earth, and subdue it: and have dominion over the fish of the sea, and over the fowl of the air, and over every living thing that moveth upon the earth." And God said, "Behold, I have given you every herb bearing seed, which is upon the face of all the earth, and every tree, in the which is the fruit of a tree yielding seed; to you it shall be for meat. And to every beast of the earth, and to every fowl of the air, and to every thing that creepeth upon the earth, wherein there is life, I have given every green herb for meat": and it was so. And God saw every thing that he had made, and, behold, it was very good. And the evening and the morning were the sixth day.

2

Thus the heavens and the earth were finished, and all the host of them. And on the seventh day God ended his work which he had made; and he rested on the seventh day from all his work which he had made. And God blessed the seventh day, and sanctified it: because that in it he had rested from all his work which God created and made.

Alphabet Poem

Edward Lear

Although known in his own time as an author of travel books and a painter (especially of birds), Edward Lear (1812–88) is best remembered for his nonsense verse, a form in which, together with Lewis Carroll, he rules supreme. In our example the plot is advanced according to the order of the alphabet, without which all but the first and last of the outrageous events would have a purely random sequence. There are several other examples of ABC poems in *Mother Goose*. The trick here consists in using a mechanical or functional progression as the organizing principle for telling a story about people, who are not merely puppets or integers. A common variant is to create a plot according to the rules of a chess game, as in Lewis Carroll's *Through the Looking Glass* or Vladimir Nabokov's novel *The Defense*. An older and more schematic example is the so-called chess morality of medieval times, a little story describing a chess game in which the white pieces (virtues) always defeat the black (vices).

■

A tumbled down, and hurt his Arm, against a bit of wood.
B said, "My Boy, oh, do not cry; it cannot do you good!"
C said, "A Cup of Coffee hot can't do you any harm."
D said, "A Doctor should be fetched, and he would cure the arm."
E said, "An Egg beat up with milk would quickly make him well."
F said, "A Fish, if broiled, might cure, if only by the smell."
G said, "Green Gooseberry, fool, the best of cures I hold."
H said, "His Hat should be kept on, to keep him from the cold."
I said, "Some Ice upon his head will make him better soon."
J said, "Some Jam, if spread on bread, or given in a spoon!"   10
K said, "A Kangaroo is here, — this picture let him see."
L said, "A Lamp pray keep alight, to make some barley tea."
M said, "A Mulberry or two might give him satisfaction."
N said, "Some Nuts, if rolled about, might be a slight attraction."
O said, "An Owl might make him laugh, if only it would wink."
P said, "Some Poetry might be read aloud, to make him think."
Q said, "A Quince I recommend, — a Quince, or else a Quail."
R said, "Some Rats might make him move, if fastened by their tail."
S said, "A Song should now be sung, in hopes to make him laugh!"
T said, "A Turnip might avail, if sliced or cut in half!"   20
U said, "An Urn, with water hot, place underneath his chin!"
V said, "I'll stand upon a chair, and play a Violin!"
W said, "Some Whisky-Whizzgigs fetch, some marbles and a ball!"
X said, "Some double XX ale would be the best of all!"
Y said, "Some Yeast mixed up with salt would make a perfect plaster!"
Z said, "Here is a box of Zinc! Get in, my little master!
         We'll shut you up! We'll nail you down! We will, my little master!
         We think we've all heard quite enough of this your sad disaster!"

Four Riddles

We saw how a metaphor was a plot the middle part of which
was implied. A riddle is a plot the end of which must be guessed. The
riddle is a particularly mysterious kind of question in that it seems to
make no sense unless we know the answer—unlike such questions as
Who was Titus Andronicus? or Where do wallabies live? The answer to
a riddle does two things at once: it not only solves the problem, it makes
the question seem sensible; what was mysterious becomes necessary. It is
this second aspect of riddle answers that seems to explain why in so many
myths extraordinary respect is paid to those who solve riddles. Such figures, by virtue of their ability to get back to the question, to complete
the story, are endowed with magic powers. For example, in certain North
American Indian tales, when the hero solves the riddle, he makes the
sun, whose absence had caused eternal winter, to shine again. When

Oedipus solves the riddle of the Sphinx, he causes the monster that has tormented Thebes to depart. In *The Thousand Nights and a Night*, stories without end ensure life. The opposite happens in myths about riddles, where it is precisely the end of the story (the solution to the puzzle) that defeats death.

■

As round as an apple,
As deep as a pail;
It never cries out
Till it's caught by the tail.   (A bell)

■

There is a creature two-footed, and
also four-footed, and three-footed.
It has one voice. When it goes on
most feet, then it goes most slowly.   (Man)

■

Formed long ago, yet made today,
I'm most enjoyed while others sleep;
What few would like to give away,
Nor any wish to keep.   (A bed)

■

In marble halls as white as milk,
Lined with a skin as soft as silk,
Within a fountain crystal-clear,
A golden apple doth appear.
No doors are there to this stronghold,
Yet thieves break in and steal the gold.   (An egg)

FROM Midrash

These little stories are taken from Hebrew wisdom literature, *Midrash*, originally (during the first five centuries B.C.) an oral tradition of Talmudic interpretation that was put into writing in the first six hundred years A.D. *Midrash* consists primarily of tales that wise men tell in order to explicate a difficult verse. Thus plots are quite explicitly used as a means of cognition; stories are told about stories, and fiction is a means for getting at the holy.

■

Nevertheless

Our masters have taught:
Once the daughter of Nehunia who dug wells for pilgrims fell into a
    deep pit.
They went and told Rabbi Hanina ben Dasa.
The first hour he said to them: She is at ease.
The second hour he said: She is at ease.
The third hour he said: She has come out.
She was asked: Who fetched you up?
She said: A ram happened along, and an old man leading him.
They asked Rabbi Hanina: Are you a prophet?
He said: I am neither a prophet, nor the son of a prophet, but I said to
    myself: Shall that which this righteous man troubles himself with,
    be a stumbling block to his seed?
Rabbi Aha said: Nevertheless, the well digger's son died of thirst.

The Bitter Olive

"And the dove came into him at eventide; and lo in her mouth an olive-
    leaf freshly plucked." (Gen. 8:11)
Whence did she bring it?
Rabbi Bebai said: The gates of the garden of Eden opened; she brought
    it from there.
Rabbi Aibo said: If she brought it from the garden of Eden, ought she not
    to have brought something superior, like cinnamon or balsam?
But with the olive she gave a hint to Noah and said to him:
Master Noah, rather this bitter thing from the hand of the Holy One,
    blessed be he, than a sweet thing from your hand.

Two Koans

The koan has been called "the eye of Zen Buddhism" because
it takes the form of an anecdote about an ancient holy man, a dialogue
between master and monks, or, more usually, a question put forward by a
teacher, and it is used as a means for opening one's mind to the truth of
Zen. It was the invention of teachers who wished to find a short-cut for
their disciples—even if at the beginning a somewhat artificial one—to
satori, the highest state of knowledge in Zen, where a different kind of
thinking obtains. Thus the koan is a story whose purpose is to shock the
hearer into a higher state of perceptual awareness. It is like a riddle in

that its end must be guessed at, but unlike the riddle in that the answer cannot be stated in words. It is also similiar to a syllogism, but the third element of the koan transcends the system of logic operative in the first two propositions. Like *Midrash*, the koan is a story told to get at the highest truth.

■

Master Joshu was asked: "What is the ultimate principle of Buddhism?"
He replied: "The cypress tree in the courtyard."
"You are talking," said another monk, "of an objective symbol."
"No, I am not talking about an objective symbol."
"Then," asked the monk again, "what is the ultimate principle of Budd-
    hism?"
"The cypress tree in the courtyard," again answered Joshu.

■

A clap is the sound of two hands.
What is the sound of one hand?

Leopards in the Temple

Franz Kafka

Translated by Ernst Kaiser and Eithne Wilkins

This is a plot about plots. The movement in this parable by Franz Kafka (1883–1924) from the break into the temple through the drinking from the pitchers to the new ceremony is perhaps the most economical expression of beginning, middle, and end. But the point of the tale concerns an important truth about the nature of stories. Just as the apparently chance intervention of the leopards is made meaningful by its inclusion in the new ritual, so do all attempts at explaining what at first seems strange and incomprehensible require that the disturbing object or event be translated into a familiar pattern by means of a new story. Thomas Kuhn (*The Structure of Scientific Revolutions*, 1962) has argued that essentially the same process is at work in the history of science, where old theories that cannot accomodate new phenomena (leopards in the temple of physics) are modified until they can. E. H. Gombrich (*Art and Illusion*, 1960) puts forward a theory for how we perceive art and the world. As an example he shows a drawing of a rhinoceros made in 1515 by the German master Albrecht Dürer. Dürer was a precise draftsman, but his rhinoceros (based on travelers' tales) looks more like a dragon than

322

the African animal we see today in the zoo. And yet "this half-invented creature served as a model for all renderings of the Rhinoceros, even in natural history books, up to the end of the eighteenth century." Gombrich concludes from this that "the familiar will always remain the likely starting point for the rendering of the unfamiliar." (p. 82)

■

Leopards break into the temple and drink to the dregs what is

in the sacrificial pitchers; this is repeated over and over again; finally it

can be calculated in advance, and it becomes a part of the ceremony.

The Hunting of the Snark

Lewis Carroll

Lewis Carroll (Charles Lutwidge Dodgson, 1832–98) was a professor of mathematics and logic at Christ Church College, Oxford; thus it is not surprising that even the books he wrote primarily for children are dominated by a passion for order. *The Hunting of the Snark* is an exercise in pure morphology; it is a grammar without semantics. The best structural metaphor for the *Snark* is the Butcher's equation in the fifth fit: it is a complicated series of mathematical operations the end of which is the same as the beginning—that is, no matter what number the sequence begins with, that is the number that ends it, and all the action in between is merely process, a pure process that has no other end than itself. The nonsense of the poem is not mere babble, however; otherwise we should not be able to understand it. It employs English syntax and grammar, if not always English vocabulary. Beyond these aids to understanding it, Carroll has supplied a systematic principle of his own, the "rule of three." When the Butcher wants to prove he has heard a jubjub bird, he states three times that he has done so. Now, there will be those who say there is no such thing as a jubjub bird. But in fact—according to the system of the Snark poem—there *is*, and his existence is definitively confirmed through the proof which that system *itself* provides: if a thing is said thrice, it is true. This is of course a parody of the syllogism, which never tells you what you did not already know, but can only reveal what follows from already agreed-upon premises. Carroll's poem is just such a tautology: only the system of its nonsense can give meaning to itself. We understand the *Snark* only because it is always consistent to its unique plot conception.

■

Fit the First

The Landing

"Just the place for a Snark!" the Bellman cried,
　　As he landed his crew with care;
Supporting each man on the top of the tide
　　By a finger entwined in his hair.

"Just the place for a Snark! I have said it twice:
　　That alone should encourage the crew.
Just the place for a Snark! I have said it thrice:
　　What I tell you three times is true."

The crew was complete: it included a Boots—
　　A maker of Bonnets and Hoods—　　　　　　　　　　10
A Barrister, brought to arrange their disputes—
　　And a Broker, to value their goods.

A Billiard-marker, whose skill was immense,
　　Might perhaps have won more than his share—
But a Banker, engaged at enormous expense,
　　Had the whole of their cash in his care.

There was also a Beaver, that paced on the deck,
　　Or would sit making lace in the bow:
And had often (the Bellman said) saved them from wreck
　　Though none of the sailors knew how.　　　　　　　　20

There was one who was famed for the number of things
　　He forgot when he entered the ship:
His umbrella, his watch, all his jewels and rings,
　　And the clothes he had bought for the trip.

He had forty-two boxes, all carefully packed,
　　With his name painted clearly on each:
But, since he omitted to mention the fact,
　　They were all left behind on the beach.

The loss of his clothes hardly mattered, because
　　He had seven coats on when he came,　　　　　　　　30
With three pair of boots—but the worst of it was,
　　He had wholly forgotten his name.

He would answer to "Hi!" or to any loud cry,
　　Such as "Fry me!" or "Fritter my wig!"
To 'What-you-may-call-um!" or "What-was-his-name!"
　　But especially "Thing-um-a-jig!"

324

While, for those who preferred a more forcible word,
    He had different names from these:
His intimate friends called him "Candle-ends,"
    And his enemies "Toasted-cheese."   40

"His form is ungainly—his intellect small—"
    (So the Bellman would often remark)—
"But his courage is perfect! And that, after all,
    Is the thing that one needs with a Snark."

He would joke with hyænas, returning their stare
    With an impudent wag of the head:
And he once went a walk, paw-in-paw, with a bear,
    "Just to keep up its spirits," he said.

He came as a Baker: but owned, when too late—
    And it drove the poor Bellman half-mad—   50
He could only bake Bride-cake—for which, I may state,
    No materials were to be had.

The last of the crew needs especial remark,
    Though he looked an incredible dunce:
He had just one idea—but, that one being "Snark,"
    The good Bellman engaged him at once.

He came as a Butcher: but gravely declared,
    When the ship had been sailing a week,
He could only kill Beavers. The Bellman looked scared,
    And was almost too frightened to speak: 60

But at length he explained, in a tremulous tone,
    There was only one Beaver on board;
And that was a tame one he had of his own,
    Whose death would be deeply deplored.

The Beaver, who happened to hear the remark,
    Protested, with tears in its eyes,
That not even the rapture of hunting the Snark
    Could atone for that dismal surprise!

It strongly advised that the Butcher should be
    Conveyed in a separate ship: 70
But the Bellman declared that would never agree
    With the plans he had made for the trip:

Navigation was always a difficult art,
    Though with only one ship and one bell:
And he feared he must really decline, for his part,
    Undertaking another as well.

325

The Beaver's best course was, no doubt, to procure
    A second-hand dagger-proof coat—
So the Baker advised it—and next, to insure
    Its life in some Office of note: 80

This the Banker suggested, and offered for hire
    (On moderate terms), or for sale,
Two excellent Policies, one Against Fire,
    And one Against Damage From Hail.

Yet still, ever after that sorrowful day,
    Whenever the Butcher was by,
The Beaver kept looking the opposite way,
    And appeared unaccountably shy.

Fit the Second

The Bellman's Speech

The Bellman himself they all praised to the skies—
    Such a carriage, such ease and such grace!   90
Such solemnity, too! One could see he was wise,
    The moment one looked in his face!

He had bought a large map representing the sea,
    Without the least vestige of land:
And the crew were much pleased when they found it to be
    A map they could all understand.

"What's the good of Mercator's North Poles and Equators,
    Tropics, Zones, and Meridian Lines?"
So the Bellman would cry: and the crew would reply
    "They are merely conventional signs!   100

"Other maps are such shapes, with their islands and capes!
    But we've got our brave Captain to thank"
(So the crew would protest) "that he's bought *us* the best—
    A perfect and absolute blank!"

This was charming, no doubt: but they shortly found out
    That the Captain they trusted so well
Had only one notion for crossing the ocean,
    And that was to tingle his bell.

He was thoughtful and grave—but the orders he gave
    Were enough to bewilder a crew.   110
When he cried "Steer to starboard, but keep her head larboard!"
    What on earth was the helmsman to do?

Then the bowsprit got mixed with the rudder sometimes
    A thing, as the Bellman remarked,
That frequently happens in tropical climes,
    When a vessel is, so to speak, "snarked."

But the principal failing occurred in the sailing,
    And the Bellman, perplexed and distressed,
Said he *had* hoped, at least, when the wind blew due East,
    That the ship would *not* travel due West!   120

But the danger was past—they had landed at last,
    With their boxes, portmanteaus, and bags:
Yet at first sight the crew were not pleased with the view
    Which consisted of chasms and crags.

The Bellman perceived that their spirits were low,
    And repeated in musical tone
Some jokes he had kept for a season of woe—
    But the crew would do nothing but groan.

He served out some grog with a liberal hand,
    And bade them sit down on the beach: 130
And they could not but own that their Captain looked grand,
    As he stood and delivered his speech.

"Friends, Romans, and countrymen, lend me your ears!"
    (They were all of them fond of quotations:
So they drank to his health, and they gave him three cheers,
    While he served out additional rations.)

"We have sailed many months, we have sailed many weeks,
    (Four weeks to the month you may mark),
But never as yet ('tis your Captain who speaks)
    Have we caught the least glimpse of a Snark!   140

"We have sailed many weeks, we have sailed many days
    (Seven days to the week I allow),
But a Snark, on the which we might lovingly gaze,
    We have never beheld till now!

"Come, listen, my men, while I tell you again
    The five unmistakable marks
By which you may know, wheresoever you go,
    The warranted genuine Snarks.

"Let us take them in order. The first is the taste,
    Which is meagre and hollow, but crisp: 150
Like a coat that is rather too tight in the waist,
    With a flavour of Will-o-the-wisp.

"Its habit of getting up late you'll agree
   That it carries too far, when I say
That it frequently breakfasts at five-o'clock tea,
   And dines on the following day.

"The third is its slowness in taking a jest.
   Should you happen to venture on one,
It will sigh like a thing that is deeply distressed:
   And it always looks grave at a pun.   160

"The fourth is its fondness for bathing-machines,
   Which it constantly carries about,
And believes that they add to the beauty of scenes—
   A sentiment open to doubt.

"The fifth is ambition. It next will be right
   To describe each particular batch:
Distinguishing those that have feathers, and bite,
   From those that have whiskers, and scratch.

"For, although common Snarks do no manner of harm,
   Yet I feel it my duty to say   170
Some are Boojums—" The Bellman broke off in alarm,
   For the Baker had fainted away.

Fit the Third

The Baker's Tale

They roused him with muffins—they roused him with ice—
   They roused him with mustard and cress—
They roused him with jam and judicious advice—
   They set him conundrums to guess.

When at length he sat up and was able to speak,
   His sad story he offered to tell;
And the Bellman cried "Silence! Not even a shriek!"
   And excitedly tingled his bell.   180

There was silence supreme! Not a shriek, not a scream,
   Scarcely even a howl or a groan,
As the man they called "Ho!" told his story of woe
   In an antediluvian tone.

"My father and mother were honest, though poor—"
   "Skip all that!" cried the Bellman in haste.
"If it once becomes dark, there's no chance of a Snark—
   We have hardly a minute to waste!

328

"I skip forty years," said the Baker, in tears,
    "And proceed without further remark   190
To the day when you took me aboard of your ship
    To help you in hunting the Snark.

"A dear uncle of mine (after whom I was named)
    Remarked, when I bade him farewell—"
"Oh, skip your dear uncle!" the Bellman exclaimed,
    As he angrily tingled his bell.

"He remarked to me then," and that mildest of men,
    " 'If your Snark be a Snark, that is right:
Fetch it home by all means—you may serve it with greens
    And it's handy for striking a light.   200

" 'You may seek it with thimbles—and seek it with care;
    You may hunt it with forks and hope;
You may threaten its life with a railway-share;
    You may charm it with smiles and soap—' "

("That's exactly the method," the Bellman bold
    In a hasty parenthesis cried,
"That's exactly the way I have always been told
    That the capture of Snarks should be tried!")

" 'But oh, beamish nephew, beware of the day,
    If your Snark be a Boojum! For then   210
You will softly and suddenly vanish away,
    And never be met with again!'

"It is this, it is this that oppresses my soul,
    When I think of my uncle's last words:
And my heart is like nothing so much as a bowl
    Brimming over with quivering curds!

"It is this, it is this—" "We have had that before!"
    The Bellman indignantly said.
And the Baker replied "Let me say it once more.
    It is this, it is this that I dread!   220

"I engage with the Snark—every night after dark—
    In a dreamy delirious fight:
I serve it with greens in those shadowy scenes,
    And I use it for striking a light:

"But if ever I meet with a Boojum, that day,
    In a moment (of this I am sure),
I shall softly and suddenly vanish away—
    And the notion I cannot endure!"

Fit the Fourth

The Hunting

The Bellman looked uffish, and wrinkled his brow.
    "If only you'd spoken before!   230
It's excessively awkward to mention it now,
    With the Snark, so to speak, at the door!

"We should all of us grieve, as you well may believe,
    If you never were met with again—
But surely, my man, when the voyage began,
    You might have suggested it then?

"It's excessively awkward to mention it now—
    As I think I've already remarked."
And the man they called "Hi!" replied, with a sigh,
    "I informed you the day we embarked.   240

"You may charge me with murder—or want of sense—
    (We are all of us weak at times):
But the slightest approach to a false pretence
    Was never among my crimes!

"I said it in Hebrew—I said it in Dutch—
    I said it in German and Greek:
But I wholly forgot (and it vexes me much)
    That English is what you speak!"

" 'Tis a pitiful tale," said the Bellman, whose face
    Had grown longer at every word: 250
"But, now that you've stated the whole of your case,
    More debate would be simply absurd.

"The rest of my speech" (he explained to his men)
    "You shall hear when I've leisure to speak it.
But the Snark is at hand, let me tell you again!
    'Tis your glorious duty to seek it!

"To seek it with thimbles, to seek it with care;
    To pursue it with forks and hope;
To threaten its life with a railway-share;
    To charm it with smiles and soap!   260

"For the Snark's a peculiar creature, that won't
    Be caught in a commonplace way.
Do all that you know, and try all that you don't:
    Not a chance must be wasted to-day!

"For England expects—I forbear to proceed:
  'Tis a maxim tremendous, but trite:
And you'd best be unpacking the things that you need
  To rig yourselves out for the fight."

Then the Banker endorsed a blank cheque (which he crossed),
  And changed his loose silver for notes: 270
The Baker with care combed his whiskers and hair,
  And shook the dust out of his coats:

The Boots and the Broker were sharpening a spade—
  Each working the grindstone in turn:
But the Beaver went on making lace, and displayed
  No interest in the concern:

Though the Barrister tried to appeal to its pride,
  And vainly proceeded to cite
A number of cases, in which making laces
  Had been proved an infringement of right.   280

The maker of Bonnets ferociously planned
  A novel arrangement of bows:
While the Billiard-marker with quivering hand
  Was chalking the tip of his nose.

But the Butcher turned nervous, and dressed himself fine,
  With yellow kid gloves and a ruff—
Said he felt it exactly like going to dine,
  Which the Bellman declared was all "stuff."

"Introduce me, now there's a good fellow," he said,
  "If we happen to meet it together!"   290
And the Bellman, sagaciously nodding his head,
  Said "That must depend on the weather."

The Beaver went simply galumphing about,
  At seeing the Butcher so shy:
And even the Baker, though stupid and stout,
  Made an effort to wink with one eye.

"Be a man!" cried the Bellman in wrath, as he heard
  The Butcher beginning to sob.
"Should we meet with a Jubjub, that desperate bird,
  We shall need all our strength for the job!"   300

Fit the Fifth

The Beaver's Lesson

They sought it with thimbles, they sought it with care;
  They pursued it with forks and hope;
They threatened its life with a railway-share;
  They charmed it with smiles and soap.

Then the Butcher contrived an ingenious plan
  For making a separate sally;
And had fixed on a spot unfrequented by man,
  A dismal and desolate valley.

But the very same plan to the Beaver occurred:
  It had chosen the very same place: 310
Yet neither betrayed, by a sign or a word,
  The disgust that appeared in his face.

Each thought he was thinking of nothing but "Snark"
  And the glorious work of the day;
And each tried to pretend that he did not remark
  That the other was going that way.

But the valley grew narrow and narrower still,
  And the evening got darker and colder,
Till (merely from nervousness, not from good will)
  They marched along shoulder to shoulder.   320

Then a scream, shrill and high, rent the shuddering sky
  And they knew that some danger was near:
The Beaver turned pale to the tip of its tail,
  And even the Butcher felt queer.

He thought of his childhood, left far far behind—
  That blissful and innocent state—
The sound so exactly recalled to his mind
  A pencil that squeaks on a slate!

" 'Tis the voice of the Jubjub!" he suddenly cried.
  (This man, that they used to call "Dunce.")   330
"As the Bellman would tell you," he added with pride,
  "I have uttered that sentiment once.

" 'Tis the note of the Jubjub! Keep count, I entreat,
  You will find I have told it you twice.
'Tis the song of the Jubjub! The proof is complete,
  If only I've stated it thrice."

332

The Beaver had counted with scrupulous care,
    Attending to every word:
But it fairly lost heart, and outgrabe in despair,
    When the third repetition occurred.   340

It felt that, in spite of all possible pains,
    It had somehow contrived to lose count,
And the only thing now was to rack its poor brains
    By reckoning up the amount.

"Two added to one—if that could but be done,"
    It said, "with one's fingers and thumbs!"
Recollecting with tears how, in earlier years,
    It had taken no pains with its sums.

"The thing can be done," said the Butcher, "I think.
    The thing must be done, I am sure.   350
The thing shall be done! Bring me paper and ink,
    The best there is time to procure."

The Beaver brought paper, portfolio, pens,
    And ink in unfailing supplies:
While strange creepy creatures came out of their dens
    And watched them with wondering eyes.

So engrossed was the Butcher, he heeded them not,
    As he wrote with a pen in each hand,
And explained all the while in a popular style
    Which the Beaver could well understand.   360

"Taking Three as the subject to reason about—
    A convenient number to state—
We add Seven, and Ten, and then multiply out
    By One Thousand diminished by Eight.

"The result we proceed to divide, as you see,
    By Nine Hundred and Ninety and Two:
Then subtract Seventeen, and the answer must be
    Exactly and perfectly true.

"The method employed I would gladly explain,
    While I have it so clear in my head,   370
If I had but the time and you had but the brain—
    But much yet remains to be said.

"In one moment I've seen what has hitherto been
    Enveloped in absolute mystery,
And without extra charge I will give you at large
    A Lesson in Natural History."

In his genial way he proceeded to say
    (Forgetting all laws of propriety,
And that giving instruction, without introduction,
    Would have caused quite a thrill in Society),   380

"As to temper the Jubjub's a desperate bird,
    Since it lives in perpetual passion:
Its taste in costume is entirely absurd—
    It is ages ahead of the fashion:

"But it knows any friend it has met once before:
    It never will look at a bribe:
And in charity-meetings it stands at the door,
    And collects—though it does not subscribe.

"Its flavour when cooked is more exquisite far
    Than mutton, or oysters, or eggs: 390
(Some think it keeps best in an ivory jar,
    And some, in mahogany kegs)

"You boil it in sawdust: you salt it in glue:
    You condense it with locusts and tape:
Still keeping one principal object in view—
    To preserve its symmetrical shape."

The Butcher would gladly have talked till next day,
    But he felt that the Lesson must end,
And he wept with delight in attempting to say
    He considered the Beaver his friend: 400

While the Beaver confessed, with affectionate looks
    More eloquent even than tears,
It had learned in ten minutes far more than all books
    Would have taught it in seventy years.

They returned hand-in-hand, and the Bellman, unmanned
    (For a moment) with noble emotion,
Said "This amply repays all the wearisome days
    We have spent on the billowy ocean!"

Such friends, as the Beaver and Butcher became,
    Have seldom if ever been known;   410
In winter or summer, 'twas always the same—
    You could never meet either alone.

And when quarrels arose—as one frequently finds
    Quarrels will, spite of every endeavour—
The song of the Jubjub recurred to their minds,
    And cemented their friendship for ever!

Fit the Sixth

The Barrister's Dream

They sought it with thimbles, they sought it with care;
    They pursued it with forks and hope;
They threatened its life with a railway-share;
    They charmed it with smiles and soap.   420

But the Barrister, weary of proving in vain
    That the Beaver's lace-making was wrong,
Fell asleep, and in dreams saw the creature quite plain
    That his fancy had dwelt on so long.

He dreamed that he stood in a shadowy Court,
    Where the Snark, with a glass in its eye,
Dressed in gown, bands, and wig, was defending a pig
    On the charge of deserting its sty.

The Witnesses proved, without error or flaw,
    That the sty was deserted when found: 430
And the Judge kept explaining the state of the law
    In a soft under-current of sound.

The indictment had never been clearly expressed,
    And it seemed that the Snark had begun,
And had spoken three hours, before any one guessed
    What the pig was supposed to have done.

The Jury had each formed a different view
    (Long before the indictment was read),
And they all spoke at once, so that none of them knew
    One word that the others had said.   440

"You must know—" said the Judge: but the Snark exclaimed "Fudge!
    That statute is obsolete quite!
Let me tell you, my friends, the whole question depends
    On an ancient manorial right.

"In the matter of Treason the pig would appear
    To have aided, but scarcely abetted:
While the charge of Insolvency fails, it is clear,
    If you grant the plea 'never indebted.'

"The fact of Desertion I will not dispute:
    But its guilt, as I trust, is removed   450
(So far as relates to the costs of this suit)
    By the Alibi which has been proved.

"My poor client's fate now depends on y̆our votes."
    Here the speaker sat down in his place,
And directed the Judge to refer to his notes
    And briefly to sum up the case.

But the Judge said he never had summed up before;
    So the Snark undertook it instead,
And summed it so well that it came to far more
    Than the Witnesses ever had said!   460

When the verdict was called for, the Jury declined,
    As the word was so puzzling to spell;
But they ventured to hope that the Snark wouldn't mind
    Undertaking that duty as well.

So the Snark found the verdict, although, as it owned,
    It was spent with the toils of the day:
When it said the word "GUILTY!" the Jury all groaned
    And some of them fainted away.

Then the Snark pronounced sentence, the Judge being quite
    Too nervous to utter a word: 470
When it rose to its feet, there was silence like night,
    And the fall of a pin might be heard.

"Transportation for life" was the sentence it gave,
    "And *then* to be fined forty pound."
The Jury all cheered, though the Judge said he feared
    That the phrase was not legally sound.

But their wild exultation was suddenly checked
    When the jailer informed them, with tears,
Such a sentence would have not the slightest effect,
    As the pig had been dead for some years.   480

The Judge left the Court, looking deeply disgusted:
    But the Snark, though a little aghast,
As the lawyer to whom the defence was intrusted,
    Went bellowing on to the last.

Thus the Barrister dreamed, while the bellowing seemed
    To grow every moment more clear:
Till he woke to the knell of a furious bell,
    Which the Bellman rang close at his ear.

Fit the Seventh

The Banker's Fate

They sought it with thimbles, they sought it with care;
    They pursued it with forks and hope;   490
They threatened its life with a railway-share;
    They charmed it with smiles and soap.

And the Banker, inspired with a courage so new
    It was matter for general remark,
Rushed madly ahead and was lost to their view
    In his zeal to discover the Snark.

But while he was seeking with thimbles and care,
    A Bandersnatch swiftly drew nigh
And grabbed at the Banker, who shrieked in despair,
    For he knew it was useless to fly.   500

He offered large discount—he offered a cheque
    (Drawn "to bearer") for seven-pounds-ten:
But the Bandersnatch merely extended its neck
    And grabbed at the Banker again.

Without rest or pause—while those frumious jaws
    Went savagely snapping around—
He skipped and he hopped, and he floundered and flopped,
    Till fainting he fell to the ground.

The Bandersnatch fled as the others appeared
    Led on by that fear-stricken yell: 510
And the Bellman remarked "It is just as I feared!"
    And solemnly tolled on his bell.

He was black in the face, and they scarcely could trace
    The least likeness to what he had been:
While so great was his fright that his waistcoat turned white—
    A wonderful thing to be seen!

To the horror of all who were present that day,
    He uprose in full evening dress,
And with senseless grimaces endeavoured to say
    What his tongue could no longer express.   520

Down he sank in a chair—ran his hands through his hair—
    And chanted in mimsiest tones
Words whose utter inanity proved his insanity,
    While he rattled a couple of bones.

"Leave him here to his fate—it is getting so late!"
   The Bellman exclaimed in a fright.
"We have lost half the day. Any further delay,
   And we sha'n't catch a Snark before night!"

Fit the Eighth

The Vanishing

They sought it with thimbles, they sought it with care;
   They pursued it with forks and hope;   530
They threatened its life with a railway-share;
   They charmed it with smiles and soap.

They shuddered to think that the chase might fail,
   And the Beaver, excited at last,
Went bounding along on the tip of its tail,
   For the daylight was nearly past.

"There is Thingumbob shouting!" the Bellman said.
   "He is shouting like mad, only hark!
He is waving his hands, he is wagging his head,
   He has certainly found a Snark!"   540

They gazed in delight, while the Butcher exclaimed
   "He was always a desperate wag!"
They beheld him—their Baker—their hero unnamed—
   On the top of a neighbouring crag,

Erect and sublime, for one moment of time.
   In the next, that wild figure they saw
(As if stung by a spasm) plunge into a chasm,
   While they waited and listened in awe.

"It's a Snark!" was the sound that first came to their ears,
   And seemed almost too good to be true.   550
Then followed a torrent of laughter and cheers:
   Then the ominous words "It's a Boo—"

Then, silence. Some fancied they heard in the air
   A weary and wandering sigh
That sounded like "—jum!" but the others declare
   It was only a breeze that went by.

338

They hunted till darkness came on, but they found
   Not a button, or feather, or mark,
By which they could tell that they stood on the ground
   Where the Baker had met with the Snark.   560

In the midst of the word he was trying to say,
   In the midst of his laughter and glee,
He had softly and suddenly vanished away—
   For the Snark *was* a Boojum, you see.

Bedrock of Fiction: The Detective Story

The Musgrave Ritual

Arthur Conan Doyle

Poe may have invented the genre of the detective story, but it was Arthur Conan Doyle (1859–1930) who established its universal popularity. Sherlock Holmes has "taken off" from the stories to become an archetypal figure, like Hamlet, Don Quixote, or Tarzan. He is known to millions who never read a line that his creator wrote. Perhaps this is because in a world that is increasingly difficult to understand he represents an optimistic theory of knowledge, the medieval Scholastic principle of *adequatio rei et intellectus:* given enough time the mind of man is adequate to understand everything. There are no mysteries, only puzzles.

Our story is a good example of this principle. At the heart of the tale is a series of questions and answers, explicitly called a *ritual,* something that does not seem to make sense, but is repeated on significant occasions (whenever a Musgrave comes of age) because it has "the saving grace of antiquity." Like all rituals, its significance seems to defy mere reason, and it appears to be a true mystery. But Holmes is a rationalist and does not believe in such things: "It was perfectly obvious to me, on reading the Ritual, that the measurements must refer to some spot to which the rest of the document alluded. . . ." What to others is a ritual is to him only a riddle, and, as we saw in connection with more conventional riddles, the answers to such puzzles endow their questions with common-sense meaning.

Holmes strips away the mystery of the ritual, thanks to his rationalist presuppositions. Insofar as he does so, he represents an essential truth about detective fiction, a truth that explains why as seemingly simple a form of story as this has allusive connections with such complex plots as those found in Greek tragedy or Dostoevsky's novels. For Sherlock, detection is a form of euhemerism. (Euhemerus, a philosopher who flourished about 300 B.C., is generally considered to be the first to propose that the gods originated in legends that grew up around great men in the historical past; thus *euhemerism* is the theory that myths [and their attendant rituals] are based on traditional accounts of real people. In other words, such a view conceives myths to be fictions.) The mysteries that engage most detectives are solvable, reducible to human causes. But such tales contain in them the seed of another possibility: mysteries that are not available to rational solutions, but are nevertheless human.

■

An anomaly which often struck me in the character of my friend Sherlock Holmes was that, although in his methods of thought he was the neatest and most methodical of mankind, and although also he affected a certain quiet primness of dress, he was none the less in his personal habits one of the most untidy men that ever drove a fellow-lodger to distraction. Not that I am in the least conventional in that respect myself. The rough-and-tumble work in Afghanistan, coming on the top of natural Bohemianism of disposition, has made me rather more lax than befits a medical man. But with me there is a limit, and when I find a man who keeps his cigars in the coal-scuttle, his tobacco in the toe end of a Persian slipper, and his unanswered correspondence transfixed by a jack-knife into the very centre of his wooden mantelpiece, then I begin to give myself virtuous airs. I have always held, too, that pistol practice should be distinctly an open-air pastime; and when Holmes, in one of his queer humours, would sit in an armchair with his hair-trigger and a hundred Boxer cartridges and proceed to adorn the opposite wall with a patriotic V. R. done in bullet-pocks, I felt strongly that neither the atmosphere nor the appearance of our room was improved by it.

Our chambers were always full of chemicals and of criminal relics which had a way of wandering into unlikely positions, and of turning up in the butter-dish or in even less desirable places. But his papers were my great crux. He had a horror of destroying documents, especially those which were connected with his past cases, and yet it was only once in every year or two that he would muster energy to docket and arrange them; for, as I have mentioned somewhere in these incoherent memoirs, the outbursts of passionate energy when he performed the remarkable feats with which his name is associated were followed by reactions of lethargy during which he would lie about with his violin and his books, hardly moving save from the sofa to the table. Thus month after month his papers accumulated until every corner of the room was stacked with bundles of manuscript which were on no account to be burned, and which could not be put away save by their owner. One winter's night, as we sat together by the fire, I ventured to suggest to him that, as he had

341

finished pasting extracts into his commonplace book, he might employ the next two hours in making our room a little more habitable. He could not deny the justice of my request, so with a rather rueful face he went off to his bedroom, from which he returned presently pulling a large tin box behind him. This he placed in the middle of the floor, and, squatting down upon a stool in front of it, he threw back the lid. I could see that it was already a third full of bundles of paper tied up with red tape into separate packages.

"There are cases enough here, Watson," said he, looking at me with mischievous eyes. "I think that if you knew all that I had in this box you would ask me to pull some out instead of putting others in."

"These are the records of your early work, then?" I asked. "I have often wished that I had notes of those cases."

"Yes, my boy, these were all done prematurely before my biographer had come to glorify me." He lifted bundle after bundle in a tender, caressing sort of way. "They are not all successes, Watson," said he. "But there are some pretty little problems among them. Here's the record of the Tarleton murders, and the case of Vamberry, the wine merchant, and the adventure of the old Russian woman, and the singular affair of the aluminum crutch, as well as a full account of Ricoletti of the club-foot, and his abominable wife. And here—ah, now this really is something a little *recherché*."

He dived his arm down to the bottom of the chest and brought up a small wooden box with a sliding lid such as children's toys are kept in. From within he produced a crumpled piece of paper, an old-fashioned brass key, a peg of wood with a ball of string attached to it, and three rusty old discs of metal.

"Well, my boy, what do you make of this lot?" he asked, smiling at my expression.

"It is a curious collection."

"Very curious, and the story that hangs round it will strike you as being more curious still."

"These relics have a history, then?"

"So much so that they *are* history."

"What do you mean by that?"

Sherlock Holmes picked them up one by one and laid them along the edge of the table. Then he reseated himself in his chair and looked them over with a gleam of satisfaction in his eyes.

"These," said he, "are all that I have left to remind me of the adventure of the Musgrave Ritual."

I had heard him mention the case more than once, though I had never been able to gather the details. "I should be so glad," said I, "if you would give me an account of it."

"And leave the litter as it is?" he cried mischievously. "Your tidiness won't bear much strain, after all, Watson. But I should be glad that you should add this case to your annals, for there are points in it which make it quite unique in the criminal records of this or, I believe, of any other country. A collection of my trifling achievements would certainly be incomplete which contained no account of this very singular business.

"You may remember how the affair of the *Gloria Scott*, and my conversation with the unhappy man whose fate I told you of, first turned my attention in the direction of the profession which has become my life's work. You see me now when my name has become known far and wide, and when I am generally recognized both by the public and by the official force as being a final court of appeal in doubtful cases. Even when you knew me first, at the time of the affair which you have commemorated in 'A Study in Scarlet,' I had already established a considerable, though not a very lucrative, connection. You can hardly realize, then, how difficult I found it at first, and how long I had to wait before I succeeded in making any headway.

"When I first came up to London I had rooms in Montague Street, just round the corner from the British Museum, and there I waited, filling in my too abundant leisure time by studying all those branches of science which might make me more efficient. Now and again cases came in my way, principally through the introduction of old fellow-students, for during my last years at the university there was a good deal of talk there about myself and my methods. The third of these cases was that of the Musgrave Ritual, and it is to the interest which was aroused by that singular chain of events, and the large issues which proved to be at stake, that I trace my first stride towards the position which I now hold.

"Reginald Musgrave had been in the same college as myself, and I had some slight acquaintance with him. He was not generally popular among the undergraduates, though it always seemed to me that what was set down as pride was really an attempt to cover extreme natural diffidence. In appearance he was a man of an exceedingly aristocratic type, thin, high-nosed, and large-eyed, with languid and yet courtly manners. He was indeed a scion of one of the very oldest families in the kingdom, though his branch was a cadet one which had separated from the northern Musgraves some time in the sixteenth century and had established itself in western Sussex, where the Manor House of Hurlstone is perhaps the oldest inhabited building in the country. Something of his birth-place seemed to cling to the man, and I never looked at his pale, keen face or the poise of his head without associating him with gray archways and mullioned windows and all the venerable wreckage of a feudal keep. Once or twice we drifted into talk, and I can remember that more than once he expressed a keen interest in my methods of observation and inference.

"For four years I had seen nothing of him until one morning he walked into my room in Montague Street. He had changed little, was dressed like a young man of fashion—he was always a bit of a dandy—and preserved the same quiet, suave manner which had formerly distinguished him.

343

" 'How has all gone with you, Musgrave?' I asked after we had cordially shaken hands.

" 'You probably heard of my poor father's death,' said he; 'he was carried off about two years ago. Since then I have of course had the Hurlstone estate to manage, and as I am member for my district as well, my life has been a busy one. But I understand, Holmes, that you are turning to practical ends those powers with which you used to amaze us?'

" 'Yes,' said I, 'I have taken to living by my wits.'

" 'I am delighted to hear it, for your advice at present would be exceedingly valuable to me. We have had some very strange doings at Hurlstone, and the police have been able to throw no light upon the matter. It is really the most extraordinary and inexplicable business.'

"You can imagine with what eagerness I listened to him, Watson, for the very chance for which I had been panting during all those months of inaction seemed to have come within my reach. In my inmost heart I believed that I could succeed where others failed, and now I had the opportunity to test myself.

" 'Pray let me have the details,' I cried.

"Reginald Musgrave sat down opposite to me and lit the cigarette which I had pushed towards him.

" 'You must know,' said he, 'that though I am a bachelor, I have to keep up a considerable staff of servants at Hurlstone, for it is a rambling old place and takes a good deal of looking after. I preserve, too, and in the pheasant months I usually have a house-party, so that it would not do to be short-handed. Altogether there are eight maids, the cook, the butler, two footmen, and a boy. The garden and the stables of course have a separate staff.

" 'Of these servants the one had been longest in our service was Brunton, the butler. He was a young schoolmaster out of place when he was first taken up by my father, but he was a man of great energy and character, and he soon became quite invaluable in the household. He was a well-grown, handsome man, with a splendid forehead, and though he has been with us for twenty years he cannot be more than forty now. With his personal advantages and his extraordinary gifts—for he can speak several languages and play nearly every musical instrument—it is wonderful that he should have been satisfied so long in such a position, but I suppose that he was comfortable and lacked energy to make any change. The butler of Hurlstone is always a thing that is remembered by all who visit us.

" 'But this paragon has one fault. He is a bit of a Don Juan, and you can imagine that for a man like him it is not a very difficult part to play in a quiet country district. When he was married it was all right, but since he has been a widower we have had no end of trouble with him. A few months ago we were in hopes that he was about to settle down again, for he became engaged to Rachel Howells, our second housemaid; but he has thrown her over since then and taken up with Janet Tregellis, the daughter of the head game-keeper. Rachel—who is a very good girl, but of an excitable Welsh temperament—had a sharp touch of brain-fever and goes about the house now—or did until yesterday—like a black-eyed shadow of her former self. That was our first drama at Hurlstone; but a second one came to drive it from our minds, and it was prefaced by the disgrace and dismissal of butler Brunton.

" 'This was how it came about. I have said that the man was intelligent, and this very intelligence has caused his ruin, for it seems to have led to an insatiable curiosity about things which did not in the least concern him. I had no idea of the lengths to which this would carry him until the merest accident opened my eyes to it.

" 'I have said that the house is a rambling one. One day last week— on Thursday night, to be more exact—I found that I could not sleep, having foolishly taken a cup of strong *café noir* after my dinner. After struggling against it until two in the morning, I felt that it was quite hopeless, so I rose and lit the candle with the intention of continuing a novel which I was reading. The book, however, had been left in the billiard-room, so I pulled on my dressing-gown and started off to get it.

" 'In order to reach the billiard-room I had to descend a flight of stairs and then to cross the head of a passage which led to the library and the gun-room. You can imagine my surprise when, as I looked down this corridor, I saw a glimmer of light coming from the open door of the library. I had myself extinguished the lamp and closed the door before coming to bed. Naturally my first thought was of burglars. The corridors at Hurlstone have their walls largely decorated with trophies of old weapons. From one of these I picked a battle-axe, and then, leaving my candle behind me, I crept on tiptoe down the passage and peeped in at the open door.

" 'Brunton, the butler, was in the library. He was sitting, fully dressed, in an easy-chair, with a slip of paper which looked like a map upon his knee, and his forehead sunk forward upon his hand in deep thought. I stood dumb with astonishment, watching him from the darkness. A small taper on the edge of the table shed a feeble light which sufficed to show me that he was fully dressed. Suddenly, as I looked, he rose from his chair, and, walking over to a bureau at the side, he unlocked it and drew out one of the drawers. From this he took a paper, and, returning to his seat, he flattened it out beside the taper on the edge of the table and began to study it with minute attention. My indignation at this calm examination of our family documents overcame me so far that I took a step forward, and Brunton, looking up, saw me standing in the doorway. He sprang to his feet, his face turned livid with fear, and he thrust into his breast the chart-like paper which he had been originally studying.

" ' "So!" said I. "This is how you repay the trust which we have reposed in you. You will leave my service to-morrow."

" 'He bowed with the look of a man who is utterly crushed and slunk past me without a word. The taper was still on the table, and by its light I glanced to see what the paper was which Brunton had taken from the bureau. To my surprise it was nothing of any importance at all, but simply a copy of the questions and answers in the singular old observance called the Musgrave Ritual. It is a sort of ceremony peculiar to our family, which each Musgrave for centuries past has gone through on his coming of age—a thing of private interest, and perhaps of some little importance to the archaeologist, like our own blazonings and charges, but of no practical use whatever.'

" 'We had better come back to the paper afterwards,' said I.

" 'If you think it really necessary,' he answered with some hesitation. 'To continue my statement, however: I relocked the bureau, using the key which Brunton had left, and I had turned to go when I was surprised to find that the butler had returned, and was standing before me.

" ' "Mr. Musgrave, sir," he cried in a voice which was hoarse with emotion, "I can't bear disgrace, sir. I've always been proud above my station in life, and disgrace would kill me. My blood will be on your head, sir—it will, indeed—if you drive me to despair. If you cannot keep me after what has passed, then for God's sake let me give you notice and leave in a month, as if of my own free will. I could stand that, Mr. Musgrave, but not to be cast out before all the folk that I know so well."

" ' "You don't deserve much consideration, Brunton," I answered. "Your conduct has been most infamous. However, as you have been a long time in the family, I have no wish to bring public disgrace upon you. A month, however, is too long. Take yourself away in a week, and give what reason you like for going."

" ' "Only a week, sir?" he cried in a despairing voice. "A fortnight—say at least a fortnight!"

" ' "A week," I repeated, "and you may consider yourself to have been very leniently dealt with."

" 'He crept away, his face sunk upon his breast, like a broken man, while I put out the light and returned to my room.

" 'For two days after this Brunton was most assiduous in his attention to his duties. I made no allusion to what had passed and waited with some curiosity to see how he would cover his disgrace. On the third morning, however, he did not appear, as was his custom, after breakfast to receive my instructions for the day. As I left the dining-room I happened to meet Rachel Howells, the maid. I have told you that she had only recently recovered from an illness and was looking so wretchedly pale and wan that I remonstrated with her for being at work.

" ' "You should be in bed," I said. "Come back to your duties when you are stronger."

" 'She looked at me with so strange an expression that I began to suspect that her brain was affected.

" ' "I am strong enough, Mr. Musgrave," said she.

" ' "We will see what the doctor says," I answered. "You must stop

346

work now, and when you go downstairs just say that I wish to see Brunton."

" ' "The butler is gone," said she.

" ' "Gone! Gone where?"

" ' "He is gone. No one has seen him. He is not in his room. Oh, yes, he is gone, he is gone!" She fell back against the wall with shriek after shriek of laughter, while I, horrified at this sudden hysterical attack, rushed to the bell to summon help. The girl was taken to her room, still screaming and sobbing, while I made inquiries about Brunton. There was no doubt about it that he had disappeared. His bed had not been slept in, he had been seen by no one since he had retired to his room the night before, and yet it was difficult to see how he could have left the house, as both windows and doors were found to be fastened in the morning. His clothes, his watch, and even his money were in his room, but the black suit which he usually wore was missing. His slippers, too, were gone, but his boots were left behind. Where then could butler Brunton have gone in the night, and what could have become of him now?

" 'Of course we searched the house from cellar to garret, but there was no trace of him. It is, as I have said, a labyrinth of an old house, especially the original wing, which is now practically uninhabited; but we ransacked every room and cellar without discovering the least sign of the missing man. It was incredible to me that he could have gone away leaving all his property behind him, and yet where could he be? I called in the local police, but without success. Rain had fallen on the night before, and we examined the lawn and the paths all round the house, but in vain. Matters were in this state, when a new development quite drew our attention away from the original mystery.

" 'For two days Rachel Howells had been so ill, sometimes delirious, sometimes hysterical, that a nurse had been employed to sit up with her at night. On the third night after Brunton's disappearance, the nurse, finding her patient sleeping nicely, had dropped into a nap in the arm-chair, when she woke in the early morning to find the bed empty, the window open, and no signs of the invalid. I was instantly aroused, and, with the two footmen, started off at once in search of the missing girl. It was not difficult to tell the direction which she had taken, for, starting from under her window, we could follow her footmarks easily across the lawn to the edge of the mere, where they vanished close to the gravel path which leads out of the grounds. The lake there is eight feet deep, and you can imagine our feelings when we saw that the trail of the poor demented girl came to an end at the edge of it.

" 'Of course, we had the drags at once and set to work to recover the remains, but no trace of the body could we find. On the other hand, we brought to the surface an object of a most unexpected kind. It was a linen bag which contained within it a mass of old rusted and discoloured metal and several dull-coloured pieces of pebble or glass. This strange find was all that we could get from the mere, and, although we made every possible search and inquiry yesterday, we know nothing of the fate either of Rachel Howells or of Richard Brunton. The county police are at their wit's end, and I have come up to you as a last resource.'

"You can imagine, Watson, with what eagerness I listened to this extraordinary sequence of events, and endeavoured to piece them together, and to devise some common thread upon which they might all hang. The butler was gone. The maid was gone. The maid had loved the butler, but had afterwards had cause to hate him. She was of Welsh blood, fiery and passionate. She had been terribly excited immediately after his disappearance. She had flung into the lake a bag containing some curious contents. These were all factors which had to be taken into consideration, and yet none of them got quite to the heart of the matter. What was the starting-point of this chain of events? There lay the end of this tangled line.

" 'I must see that paper, Musgrave,' said I, 'which this butler of yours thought it worth his while to consult, even at the risk of the loss of his place.'

" 'It is rather an absurd business, this ritual of ours,' he answered. 'But it has at least the saving grace of antiquity to excuse it. I have a copy of the questions and answers here if you care to run your eye over them.'

"He handed me the very paper which I have here, Watson, and this is the strange catechism to which each Musgrave had to submit when he came to man's estate. I will read you the questions and answers as they stand.

" 'Whose was it?'
" 'His who is gone.'
" 'Who shall have it?'
" 'He who will come.'
" 'Where was the sun?'
" 'Over the oak.'
" 'Where was the shadow?'
" 'Under the elm.'
" 'How was it stepped?'
" 'North by ten and by ten, east by five and by five, south by two and by two, west by one and by one, and so under.'
" 'What shall we give for it?'
" 'All that is ours.'
" 'Why should we give it?'
" 'For the sake of the trust.'

" 'The original has no date, but is in the spelling of the middle of the seventeenth century,' remarked Musgrave. 'I am afraid, however, that it can be of little help to you in solving this mystery.'

" 'At least,' said I, 'it gives us another mystery, and one which is even more interesting than the first. It may be that the solution of the one may prove to be the solution of the other. You will excuse me, Musgrave, if I

348

say that your butler appears to me to have been a very clever man, and to have had a clearer insight than ten generations of his masters.'

" 'I hardly follow you,' said Musgrave. 'The paper seems to me to be of no practical importance.'

" 'But to me it seems immensely practical, and I fancy that Brunton took the same view. He had probably seen it before that night on which you caught him.'

" 'It is very possible. We took no pains to hide it.'

" 'He simply wished, I should imagine, to refresh his memory upon that last occasion. He had, as I understand, some sort of map or chart which he was comparing with the manuscript, and which he thrust into his pocket when you appeared.'

" 'That is true. But what could he have to do with this old family custom of ours, and what does this rigmarole mean?'

" 'I don't think that we should have much difficulty in determining that,' said I; 'with your permission we will take the first train down to Sussex and go a little more deeply into the matter upon the spot.'

"The same afternoon saw us both at Hurlstone. Possibly you have seen pictures and read descriptions of the famous old building, so I will confine my account of it to saying that it is built in the shape of an L, the long arm being the more modern portion, and the shorter the ancient nucleus from which the other has developed. Over the low, heavy-lintelled door, in the centre of this old part, is chiselled the date, 1607, but experts are agreed that the beams and stonework are really much older than this. The enormously thick walls and tiny windows of this part had in the last century driven the family into building the new wing, and the old one was used now as a storehouse and a cellar, when it was used at all. A splendid park with fine old timber surrounds the house, and the lake, to which my client had referred, lay close to the avenue, about two hundred yards from the building.

"I was already firmly convinced, Watson, that there were not three separate mysteries here, but one only, and that if I could read the Musgrave Ritual aright I should hold in my hand the clue which would lead me to the truth concerning both the butler Brunton and the maid Howells. To that then I turned all my energies. Why should this servant be so anxious to master this old formula? Evidently because he saw something in it which had escaped all those generations of country squires, and from which he expected some personal advantage. What was it then, and how had it affected his fate?

"It was perfectly obvious to me, on reading the Ritual, that the measurements must refer to some spot to which the rest of the document alluded, and that if we could find that spot we should be in a fair way towards finding what the secret was which the old Musgraves had thought it necessary to embalm in so curious a fashion. There were two guides given us to start with, an oak and an elm. As to the oak there could be no question at all. Right in front of the house, upon the left-hand side of the drive, there stood a patriarch among oaks, one of the most magnificent trees that I have ever seen.

" 'That was there when your Ritual was drawn up,' said I as we drove past it.

" 'It was there at the Norman Conquest in all probability,' he answered. 'It has a girth of twenty-three feet.'

"Here was one of my fixed points secured.

" 'Have you any old elms?' I asked.

" 'There used to be a very old one over yonder, but it was struck by lightning ten years ago, and we cut down the stump.'

" 'You can see where it used to be?'

" 'Oh, yes.'

" 'There are no other elms?'

" 'No old ones, but plenty of beeches.'

" 'I should like to see where it grew.'

"We had driven up in a dog-cart, and my client led me away at once, without our entering the house, to the scar on the lawn where the elm had stood. It was nearly midway between the oak and the house. My investigation seemed to be progressing.

" 'I suppose it is impossible to find out how high the elm was?' I asked.

" 'I can give you it at once. It was sixty-four feet.'

" 'How do you come to know it?' I asked in surprise.

" 'When my old tutor used to give me an exercise in trigonometry, it always took the shape of measuring heights. What I was a lad I worked out every tree and building in the estate.'

"This was an unexpected piece of luck. My data were coming more quickly than I could have reasonably hoped.

" 'Tell me,' I asked, 'did your butler ever ask you such a question?'

"Reginald Musgrave looked at me in astonishment. 'Now that you call it to my mind,' he answered, 'Brunton *did* ask me about the height of the tree some months ago in connection with some little argument with the groom.'

"This was excellent news, Watson, for it showed me that I was on the right road. I looked up at the sun. It was low in the heavens, and I calculated that in less than an hour it would lie just above the topmost branches of the old oak. One condition mentioned in the Ritual would then be fulfilled. And the shadow of the elm must mean the farther end of the shadow, otherwise the trunk would have been chosen as the guide. I had, then, to find where the far end of the shadow would fall when the sun was just clear of the oak."

"That must have been difficult, Holmes, when the elm was no longer there."

"Well, at least I knew that if Brunton could do it, I could also. Besides, there was no real difficulty. I went with Musgrave to his study and whittled myself this peg, to which I tied this long string with a knot at each yard. Then I took two lengths of a fishing-rod, which came to just six feet, and I went back with my client to where the elm had been. The sun was just grazing the top of the oak. I fastened the rod on end, marked out the direction of the shadow, and measured it. It was nine feet in length.

"Of course the calculation now was a simple one. If a rod of six feet threw a shadow of nine, a tree of sixty-four feet would throw one of ninety-six, and the line of the one would of course be the line of the other. I measured out the distance, which brought me almost to the wall of the house, and I thrust a peg into the spot. You can imagine my exultation, Watson, when within two inches of my peg I saw a conical depression in the ground. I knew that it was the mark made by Brunton in his measurements, and that I was still upon his trail.

"From this starting-point I proceeded to step, having first taken the cardinal points by my pocket-compass. Ten steps with each foot took me along parallel with the wall of the house, and again I marked my spot with a peg. Then I carefully paced off five to the east and two to the south. It brought me to the very threshold of the old door. Two steps to the west meant now that I was to go two paces down the stone-flagged passage, and this was the place indicated by the Ritual.

"Never have I felt such a cold chill of disappointment, Watson. For a moment it seemed to me that there must be some radical mistake in my calculations. The setting sun shone full upon the passage floor, and I could see that the old, foot-worn gray stones with which it was paved were firmly cemented together, and had certainly not been moved for many a long year. Brunton had not been at work here. I tapped upon the floor, but it sounded the same all over, and there was no sign of any crack or crevice. But, fortunately, Musgrave, who had begun to appreciate the meaning of my proceedings, and who was now as excited as myself, took out his manuscript to check my calculations.

" 'And under,' he cried. 'You have omitted the "and under." '

"I had thought that it meant that we were to dig, but now, of course, I saw at once that I was wrong. 'There is a cellar under this then?' I cried.

" 'Yes, and as old as the house. Down here, through this door.'

"We went down a winding stone stair, and my companion, striking a match, lit a large lantern which stood on a barrel in the corner. In an instant it was obvious that we had at last come upon the true place, and that we had not been the only people to visit the spot recently.

"It had been used for the storage of wood, but the billets, which had evidently been littered over the floor, were now piled at the sides, so as to leave a clear space in the middle. In this space lay a large and heavy flagstone with a rusted iron ring in the centre to which a thick shepherd's-check muffler was attached.

" 'By jove!' cried my client. 'That's Brunton's muffler. I have seen it on him and could swear to it. What has the villain been doing here?'

"At my suggestion a couple of the county police were summoned to be present, and I then endeavoured to raise the stone by pulling on the cravat. I could only move it slightly, and it was with the aid of one of the constables that I succeeded at last in carrying it to one side. A black hole yawned beneath into which we all peered, while Musgrave, kneeling at the side, pushed down the lantern.

"A small chamber about seven feet deep and four feet square lay open to us. At one side of this was a squat, brass-bound wooden box, the lid of which was hinged upward, with this curious old-fashioned key projecting from the lock. It was furred outside by a thick layer of dust, and damp and worms had eaten through the wood, so that a crop of livid fungi was growing on the inside of it. Several discs of metal, old coins apparently, such as I hold here, were scattered over the bottom of the box, but it contained nothing else.

"At the moment, however, we had no thought for the old chest, for our eyes were riveted upon that which crouched beside it. It was the figure of a man, clad in a suit of black, who squatted down upon his hams with his forehead sunk upon the edge of the box and his two arms thrown out on each side of it. The attitude had drawn all the stagnant blood to the face, and no man could have recognized that distorted liver-coloured countenance; but his height, his dress, and his hair were all sufficient to show my client, when we had drawn the body up, that it was indeed his missing butler. He had been dead some days, but there was no wound or bruise upon his person to show how he had met his dreadful end. When his body had been carried from the cellar we found ourselves still confronted with a problem which was almost as formidable as that with which we had started.

"I confess that so far, Watson, I had been disappointed in my investigation. I had reckoned upon solving the matter when once I had found the place referred to in the Ritual; but now I was there, and was apparently as far as ever from knowing what it was which the family had concealed with such elaborate precautions. It is true that I had thrown a light upon the fate of Brunton, but now I had to ascertain how that fate had come upon him, and what part had been played in the matter by the woman who had disappeared. I sat down upon a keg in the corner and thought the whole matter carefully over.

"You know my methods in such cases, Watson. I put myself in the man's place, and, having first gauged his intelligence, I try to imagine how I should myself have proceeded under the same circumstances. In this case the matter was simplified by Brunton's intelligence being quite first-rate, so that it was unnecessary to make any allowance for the personal equation, as the astronomers have dubbed it. He knew that something valuable was concealed. He had spotted the place. He found that the stone which covered it was just too heavy for a man to move unaided. What would he do next? He could not get help from outside, even if he had someone whom he could trust, without the unbarring of doors and considerable risk of detection. It was better, if he could, to have his helpmate inside the house. But whom could he ask? This girl had been devoted to him. A man always finds it hard to realize that he may have finally lost a woman's love, however badly he may have treated her. He would try by a few attentions to make his peace with the girl Howells, and then would engage her as his accomplice. Together they would come at night to the cellar, and their united force would suffice to raise the stone. So far I could follow their actions as if I had actually seen them.

"But for two of them, and one a woman, it must have been heavy work, the raising of that stone. A burly Sussex policeman and I had found it no light job. What would they do to assist them? Probably what I should have done myself. I rose and examined carefully the different billets of wood which were scattered round the floor. Almost at once I came upon what I expected. One piece, about three feet in length, had a very marked indentation at one end, while several were flattened at the sides as if they had been compressed by some considerable weight. Evidently, as they had dragged the stone up, they had thrust the chunks of wood into the chink until at last when the opening was large enough to crawl through, they would hold it open by a billet placed lengthwise, which might very well become indented at the lower end, since the whole weight of the stone would press it down on to the edge of this other slab. So far I was still on safe ground.

"And now how was I to proceed to reconstruct this midnight drama? Clearly, only one could fit into the hole, and that one was Brunton. The girl must have waited above. Brunton then unlocked the box, handed up the contents presumably—since they were not to be found—and then—and then what happened?

"What smouldering fire of vengeance had suddenly sprung into flame in this passionate Celtic woman's soul when she saw the man who had wronged her—wronged her, perhaps, far more than we suspected—in her power? Was it a chance that the wood had slipped and that the stone had shut Brunton into what had become his sepulchre? Had she only been guilty of silence as to his fate? Or had some sudden blow from her hand dashed the support away and sent the slab crashing down into its place? Be that as it might, I seemed to see that woman's figure still clutching at her treasure trove and flying wildly up the winding stair, with her ears ringing perhaps with the muffled screams from behind her and with the drumming of frenzied hands against the slab of stone which was choking her faithless lover's life out.

"Here was the secret of her blanched face, her shaken nerves, her peals of hysterical laughter on the next morning. But what had been in the box? What had she done with that? Of course, it must have been the old metal and pebbles which my client had dragged from the mere. She had thrown them in there at the first opportunity to remove the last trace of her crime.

"For twenty minutes I had sat motionless, thinking the matter out. Musgrave still stood with a very pale face, swinging his lantern and peering down into the hole.

" 'These are coins of Charles the First,' said he, holding out the few which had been in the box; 'you see we were right in fixing our date for the Ritual.'

" 'We may find something else of Charles the First,' I cried, as the probable meaning of the first two questions of the Ritual broke suddenly upon me. 'Let me see the contents of the bag which you fished from the mere.'

"We ascended to his study, and he laid the débris before me. I could understand his regarding it as of small importance when I looked at it, for the metal was almost black and the stones lustreless and dull. I rubbed one of them on my sleeve, however, and it glowed afterwards like a spark in the dark hollow of my hand. The metal work was in the form of a double ring, but it had been bent and twisted out of its original shape.

" 'You must bear in mind,' said I, 'that the royal party made head in England even after the death of the king, and that when they at last fled they probably left many of their most precious possessions buried behind them, with the intention of returning for them in more peaceful times.'

" 'My ancestor, Sir Ralph Musgrave, was a prominent cavalier and the right-hand man of Charles the Second in his wanderings,' said my friend.

" 'Ah, indeed!' I answered. "Well now, I think that really should give us the last link that we wanted. I must congratulate you on coming into the possession, though in rather a tragic manner, of a relic which is of great intrinsic value, but of even greater importance as a historical curiosity.'

" 'When is it, then?' he gasped in astonishment.

" 'It is nothing less than the ancient crown of the kings of England.'

" 'The crown!'

" 'Precisely. Consider what the Ritual says. How does it run? "Whose was it?" "His who is gone." That was after the execution of Charles. Then, "Who shall have it?" "He who will come." That was Charles the Second, whose advent was already foreseen. There can, I think, be no doubt that this battered and shapeless diadem once encircled the brows of the royal Stuarts.'

" 'And how came it in the pond?'

" 'Ah, that is a question that will take some time to answer.' And with that I sketched out to him the whole long chain of surmise and of proof which I had constructed. The twilight had closed in and the moon was shining brightly in the sky before my narrative was finished.

" 'And how was it then that Charles did not get his crown when he returned?' asked Musgrave, pushing back the relic into its linen bag.

" 'Ah, there you lay your finger upon the one point which we shall probably never be able to clear up. It is likely that the Musgrave who held the secret died in the interval, and by some oversight left this guide to his descendant without explaining the meaning of it. From that day to this it has been handed down from father to son, until at last it came within reach of a man who tore its secret out of it and lost his life in the venture.'

354

"And that's the story of the Musgrave Ritual, Watson. They have the crown down at Hurlstone—though they had some legal bother and a considerable sum to pay before they were allowed to retain it. I am sure that if you mentioned my name they would be happy to show it to you. Of the woman nothing was ever heard, and the probability is that she got away out of England and carried herself and the memory of her crime to some land beyond the seas."

Oedipus the King

Sophocles

Translated by Bernard W. Knox

Aristotle considered this play of Sophocles (496–406 B.C.) the perfect Greek tragedy. It had, in his terms, the best plot. The play is also a significant example of plot understood in the wider sense assumed in the introduction to Part III. Oedipus becomes king of Thebes by solving a riddle, the answer to which is "man." In so doing he defeats the monstrous Sphinx, and it has been suggested that we have here a metaphor for that important stage in human consciousness when man discovered his humanity by overcoming the demons of superstition by whom he had been dominated. A more salient aspect of the puzzle, given our concern with the extensions of literary plot, is that the riddle of the Sphinx contains in it a progression from childhood to old age: man is defined by the beginning, middle, and end of his life. Birth and death, and how we get from one to the other, constitute the riddle at the heart of Sophocles' drama. As the chorus says in the final lines, "Look at Oedipus here, who knew the answer to the famous riddle. . . . On his good fortune all the citizens gazed with envy. Into what a stormy sea of dreadful trouble he has come now. Therefore we must call no man happy while he waits to see his last day. . . ." In other words, a man's life is like a riddle in that it is known only in its conclusion. (Nabokov makes the same point in characteristically modern and debunking terms: "Death is often the point of life's joke."

Oedipus errs in assuming that such a riddle is solvable. He is a detective who is defeated by a mystery greater than his powers to solve it. He solves a crime only to discover that he himself is the criminal (a theme on which many changes are rung in modern fiction, as in Robbe-Grillet's novel *The Erasers* or Borges' tale "Death and the Compass"). Sophocles' tragedy dramatizes the profound implications latent in the "beginning, middle, and end" formula of detective stories. If the truth of Freud's theory of the Oedipus complex is accepted, there is a sense in which we are all the detectives of our own fate.

■

CHARACTERS

OEDIPUS, *King of Thebes*
A PRIEST *of Zeus*
CREON, *brother of Jocasta*
A CHORUS *of Theban citizens*
TIRESIAS, *a blind propet*
JOCASTA, *the queen, wife of Oedipus*
A MESSENGER *from Corinth*
A SHEPHERD
A MESSENGER *from inside the palace*
ANTIGONE ⎫
⎬ *daughters of Oedipus and Jocasta*
ISMENE ⎭

The background is the front wall of a building, with a double door in the center. Steps lead down from the door to stage level. In front of the steps, in the center, a square stone altar.

(*Enter, from the side, a procession of priests and citizens. They carry olive branches which have tufts of wool tied on them. They lay these branches on the altar, then sit on the ground in front of it. The door opens. Enter* OEDIPUS.)

OEDIPUS. My sons! Newest generation of this ancient city of Thebes! Why are you here? Why are you seated there at the altar, with these branches of supplication?

The city is filled with the smoke of burning incense, with hymns to the healing god, with laments for the dead. I did not think it right, my children, to hear reports of this from others. Here I am, myself, world-famous Oedipus.

You, old man, speak up—you are the man to speak for the others. In what mood are you sitting there—in fear or resignation? You may count on me; I am ready to do anything to help. I would be insensitive to pain, if I felt no pity for my people seated here.

PRIEST. Oedipus, ruler of Thebes, you see us here at your altar, men of all ages—some not yet strong enough to fly far from the nest, others heavy with age, priests, of Zeus in my case, and these are picked men from the city's youth. The rest of the Thebans, carrying boughs like us, are sitting in the market place, at the two temples of Athena, and at the prophetic fire of Apollo near the river Ismenus.

You can see for yourself—the city is like a ship rolling dangerously; it has lost the power to right itself and raise its head up out of the waves of death. Thebes is dying. There is a blight on the crops of the land, on the ranging herds of cattle, on the still-born labor of our women. The

356

fever-god swoops down on us, hateful plague, he hounds the city and empties the houses of Thebes. The black god of death is made rich with wailing and funeral laments.

It is not because we regard you as equal to the gods that we sit here in supplication, these children and I; in our judgment you are first of men, both in the normal crises of human life and in relations with the gods.

You came to us once and liberated our city, you freed us from the tribute which we paid that cruel singer, the Sphinx. You did this with no extra knowledge you got from us, you had no training for the task, but, so it is said and we believe, it was with divine support that you restored our city to life. And now, Oedipus, power to whom all men turn, we beg you, all of us here, in supplication—find some relief for us! Perhaps you have heard some divine voice, or have knowledge from some human source. You are a man of experience, the kind whose plans result in effective action. Noblest of men, we beg you, save this city. You must take thought for your reputation. Thebes now calls you its savior because of the energy you displayed once before. Let us not remember your reign as a time when we stood upright only to fall again. Set us firmly on our feet. You brought us good fortune then, with favorable signs from heaven—be now the equal of the man you were. You are king; if you are to rule Thebes, you must have an inhabited city, not a desert waste. A walled city or a ship abandoned, without men living together inside it, is nothing at all.

OEDIPUS. My children, I am filled with pity. I knew what you were longing for when you came here. I know only too well that you are all sick —but sick though you may be, there is not one of you as sick as I. *Your* pain torments each one of you, alone, by himself—but my spirit within me mourns for the city, and myself, and all of you. You see then, I was no dreamer you awoke from sleep. I have wept many tears, as you must know, and in my ceaseless reflection I have followed many paths of thought. My search has found one way to treat our disease— and I have acted already. I have sent Creon, my brother-in-law, to the prophetic oracle of Apollo, to find out by what action or speech, if any, I may rescue Thebes. I am anxious now when I count the days since he left; I wonder what he is doing. He has been away longer than one would expect, longer than he should be. But when he comes, at that moment I would be a vile object if I did not do whatever the god prescribes.

PRIEST. Just as you say these words, these men have signaled to me to announce Creon's arrival.

(*Enter* CREON, *from side.*)

OEDIPUS (*turns to the altar*). O King Apollo! May Creon bring us good fortune and rescue, bright as the expression I see on his face.

PRIEST. I guess that his news is joyful. For on his head is a crown of laurel in bloom.

OEDIPUS. No more guessing—soon we shall know. For he is near enough to hear us now.

(*Raising his voice*) Lord Creon, what statement do you bring us from the god Apollo?

CREON. Good news. For, as I see it, even things hard to bear, if they should turn out right in the end, would be good fortune.

OEDIPUS. What exactly did the god say? *Your* words inspire neither confidence nor fear.

CREON. If you wish to hear my report in the presence of these people (*points to priests*) I am ready. Or shall we go inside?

OEDIPUS. Speak out, before all of us. The sorrows of my people here mean more to me than any fear I may have for my own life.

CREON. Very well. Here is what I was told by the god Apollo. He ordered us, in clear terms, to drive out the thing that defiles this land, which we, he says, have fed and cherished. We must not let it grow so far that it is beyond cure.

OEDIPUS. What is the nature of our misfortune? How are we to rid ourselves of it—by what rites?

CREON. Banishment—or repaying blood with blood. We must atone for a murder which brings this plague-storm on the city.

OEDIPUS. Whose murder? Who is the man whose death Apollo lays to our charge?

CREON. The ruler of this land, my lord, was called Laius. That was before *you* took the helm of state.

OEDIPUS. I know—at least I have heard so. I never saw the man.

CREON. It is to *his* death that Apollo's command clearly refers. We must punish those who killed him—whoever they may be.

OEDIPUS. But where on earth are they? The track of this ancient guilt is hard to detect; how shall we find it now?

CREON. Here in Thebes, Apollo said. What is searched for can be caught. What is neglected escapes.

OEDIPUS. Where did Laius meet his death? In his palace, in the countryside, or on some foreign soil?

CREON. He left Thebes to consult the oracle, so he announced. But he never returned to his home.

OEDIPUS. And no messenger came back? No fellow traveler who saw what happened?

CREON. No, they were all killed—except for one, who ran away in terror. But he could give no clear account of what he saw—except one thing.

OEDIPUS. And what was that? One thing might be the clue to knowledge of many more—if we could get even a slight basis for hope.

CREON. Laius was killed, he said, not by one man, but by a strong and numerous band of robbers.

OEDIPUS. But how could a *robber* reach such a pitch of daring—to kill a king? Unless there had been words—and money—passed between him and someone here in Thebes.

358

CREON. We thought of that, too. But the death of Laius left us helpless and leaderless in our trouble—

OEDIPUS. Trouble? What kind of trouble could be big enough to prevent a full investigation? Your *king* had been killed.

CREON. The Sphinx with her riddling songs forced us to give up the mystery and think about more urgent matters.

OEDIPUS. But I will begin afresh. I will bring it all to light. You have done well, Creon, and Apollo has, too, to show this solicitude for the murdered man. Now you will have *me* on your side, as is only right. I shall be the defender of Thebes, and Apollo's champion, too. I shall rid us of this pollution, not for the sake of a distant relative, but for my own sake. For whoever killed Laius might decide to raise his hand against me. So, acting on behalf of Laius, I benefit myself, too.

(*To priests*) Quickly, my children, as fast as you can, stand up from the steps and take these branches of supplication off the altar.

(*To guards*) One of you summon the people of Thebes here.

I shall leave nothing undone. With God's help we shall prove fortunate—or fall.

PRIEST. My sons, stand up. (*The priests rise.*) King Oedipus has volunteered to do what we came to ask. May Apollo, who sent the message from his oracle, come as our savior, and put an end to the plague.

(*The priests take the olive branches off the altar and exeunt to side.* OEDIPUS *goes back through the palace doors. Enter, from side, the* CHORUS. *They are fifteen dancers, representing old men. They stand for the people of Thebes, whom* OEDIPUS *has just summoned. They chant in unison the following lines, which, in the original Greek, make great use of solemn, traditional formulas of prayer to the gods.*)

CHORUS. Sweet message of Zeus! You have come from Apollo's golden temple to splendid Thebes, bringing us news. My fearful heart is stretched on the rack and shudders in terror.

Hail Apollo, Lord of Delos, healer! I worship and revere you. What new form of atonement will you demand? Or will it be some ancient ceremony, repeated often as the seasons come round? Tell me, daughter of golden Hope, immortal Voice of Apollo.

First I call upon you, immortal Athena, daughter of Zeus. And on your sister Artemis, the protector of this land, who sits in glory on her throne in the market place. And I call on far-shooting Apollo, the archer. Trinity of Defenders against Death, appear to me! If ever in time past, when destruction threatened our city, you kept the flame of pain out of our borders, come now also.

There is no way to count the pains we suffer. All our people are sick. There is no sword of thought which will protect us. The fruits of our famous land do not ripen. Our women cannot ease their labor pains by giving birth. One after another you can see our people speed like winged birds, faster than irresistible fire, to the shore of evening, to death. The city is dying, the deaths cannot be counted. The children lie unburied, unmourned, spreading death. Wives and gray-haired mothers come from all over the city, wailing they come to the altar steps to pray for release from pain and sorrow. The hymn to the Healer flashes out, and with it, accompanied by flutes, the mourning for the dead. Golden daughter of Zeus, Athena, send help and bring us joy.

I pray that the raging War-god, who now without shield and armor hems me in with shouting and burns me, I pray that he may turn back and leave the borders of this land. Let him go to the great sea gulf of the Western ocean or north to the Thracian coasts which give no shelter from the sea. For now, what the night spares, he comes for by day.

Father Zeus, you that in majesty govern the blazing lightning, destroy him beneath your thunderbolt!

Apollo, king and protector! I pray for the arrows from your golden bow—let them be ranged on my side to help me. And with them the flaming torches of Artemis, with which she speeds along the Eastern mountains. And I invoke the god with the golden headdress, who gave this land his name, wine-faced Dionysus, who runs with the maddened girls—let him come to my side, shining with his blazing pine-torch, to fight the god who is without honor among all other gods.

(*The* CHORUS *stays on stage. Enter* OEDIPUS, *from the palace doors. He addresses the* CHORUS—*the people of Thebes.*)

OEDIPUS. You are praying. As for your prayers, if you are willing to hear and accept what I say now and so treat the disease, you will find rescue and relief from distress. I shall make a proclamation, speaking as one who has no connection with this affair, nor with the murder. Even if I had been here at the time, I could not have followed the track very far without some clue. As it is, I became a Theban citizen with you after it happened. So I now proclaim to all of you, citizens of Thebes: whoever among you knows by whose hand Laius son of Labdacus was killed, I order him to reveal the whole truth to me.

If he is afraid to speak up, I order him to speak even against himself, and so escape the indictment, for he will suffer no unpleasant consequence except exile; he can leave Thebes unharmed.

(*Silence while* OEDIPUS *waits for a reply.*)

Secondly, if anyone knows the identity of the murderer, and that he is a foreigner, from another land, let him speak up. I shall make it profitable for him, and he will have my gratitude, too.

(*Pause.*)

But if you keep silent—if someone among you refuses my offer, shielding some relative or friend, or himself—now, listen to what I intend to do in that case. That man, whoever he may be, I banish from this land where I sit on the throne and hold the power; no one shall take him in or speak to him. He is forbidden communion in prayers or offerings to the gods, or in holy water. Everyone is to expel him from their homes as if he were himself the source of infection which Apollo's oracle has just made known to me. That is how I fulfill my obligations as an ally to the god and to the murdered man. As for the murderer himself, I call down a curse on him, whether that unknown figure be one man or one among many. May he drag out an evil death-in-life in misery. And further, I pronounce a curse on myself if the murderer should, with my knowledge, share my house; in that case may I be subject to all the curses I have just called down on these people here. I order you all to obey these commands in full for my sake, for Apollo's sake, and for the sake of this land, withering away in famine, abandoned by heaven.

Even if this action had not been urged by the god, it was not proper for you to have left the matter unsolved—the death of a good man and a king. You should have investigated it. But now I am in command. I hold the office he once held, the wife who once was his is now mine, the mother of my children. Laius and I would be closely connected by children from the same wife, if his line had not met with disaster. But chance swooped down on his life. So I shall fight for him, as if he were my own father. I shall shrink from nothing in my search to find the murderer of Laius, of the royal line of Thebes, stretching back through Labdacus, Polydorus and Cadmus, to ancient Agenor. On those who do not co-operate with these measures I call down this curse in the gods' name: let no crop grow out of the earth for them, their wives bear no children. Rather let them be destroyed by the present plague, or something even worse. But to you people of Thebes who approve of my action I say this: May justice be our ally and all the gods be with us forever!

CHORUS. (*One member of the* CHORUS *speaks for them all.*) You have put me under a curse, King, and under the threat of that curse I shall make my statement. I did not kill Laius and I am not in a position to say who did. This search to find the murderer should have been undertaken by Apollo who sent the message which began it.

OEDIPUS. What you say is just. But to compel the gods to act against their will—no man could do that.

CHORUS LEADER. Then let me make a second suggestion.

OEDIPUS. And a third, if you like—speak up.

CHORUS LEADER. The man who sees most eye to eye with Lord Apollo is Tiresias and from him you might learn most clearly the truth for which you are searching.

OEDIPUS. I did not leave *that* undone either. I have already sent for him, at Creon's suggestion. I have sent for him twice, in fact, and have been wondering for some time why he is not yet here.

CHORUS LEADER. Apart from what he will say, there is nothing but old, faint rumors.

OEDIPUS. What were they? I want to examine every single word.

CHORUS LEADER. Laius was killed, so they say, by some travelers.

OEDIPUS. I heard that, too. Where is the man who saw it?

CHORUS LEADER. If he has any trace of fear in him, he won't stand firm when he hears the curses you have called down on him.

OEDIPUS. If he didn't shrink from the action he won't be frightened by a word.

CHORUS LEADER. But here comes the one who will convict him. These men are bringing the holy prophet of the gods, the only man in whom truth is inborn.

(*Enter* TIRESIAS, *from the side. He has a boy to lead him, and is accompanied by guards.*)

OEDIPUS. Tiresias, you who understand all things—those which can be taught and those which may not be mentioned, things in the heavens and things which walk the earth! You cannot see, but you understand the city's distress, the disease from which it is suffering. You, my lord, are our shield against it, our savior, the only one we have. You may not have heard the news from the messengers. We sent to Apollo and he sent us back this answer: relief from this disease would come to us only if we discovered the identity of the murderers of Laius and then either killed them or banished them from Thebes. Do not begrudge us your knowledge—any voice from the birds or any other way of prophecy you have. Save yourself and this city, save me, from all the infection caused by the dead man. We are in your hands. And the noblest of labors is for a man to help his fellow men with all he has and can do.

TIRESIAS. Wisdom is a dreadful thing when it brings no profit to its possessor. I knew all this well, but forgot. Otherwise I would never have come here.

OEDIPUS. What is the matter? Why this despairing mood?

TIRESIAS. Dismiss me, send me home. That will be the easiest way for both of us to bear our burden.

OEDIPUS. What you propose is unlawful—and unfriendly to this city which raised you. You are withholding information.

TIRESIAS. I do not see that your talking is to the point. And I don't want the same thing to happen to me.

OEDIPUS. If you know something, in God's name, do not turn your back on us. Look. All of us here, on our knees, beseech you.

TIRESIAS. You are all ignorant. I will never reveal my dreadful secrets, or rather, yours.

OEDIPUS. What do you say? You know something? And will not speak? You intend to betray us, do you, and wreck the state?

TIRESIAS. I will not cause pain to myself or to you. Why do you question me? It is useless. You will get nothing from me.

OEDIPUS. You scoundrel! You would enrage a lifeless stone. Will nothing move you? Speak out and make an end of it.

TIRESIAS. You blame my temper, but you are not aware of one *you* live with.

362

OEDIPUS (*to* CHORUS). Who could control his anger listening to talk like this—these insults to Thebes?

TIRESIAS. What is to come will come, even if I shroud it in silence.

OEDIPUS. What is to come, *that* is what you are bound to tell *me*.

TIRESIAS. I will say no more. Do what you like—rage at me in the wildest anger you can muster.

OEDIPUS. I will. I am angry enough to speak out. I understand it all. Listen to me. I think that *you* helped to plan the murder of Laius—yes, and short of actually raising your hand against him you did it. If you weren't blind, I'd say that you alone struck him down.

TIRESIAS. Is that what you say? I charge you now to carry out the articles of the proclamation you made. From now on do not presume to speak to me or to any of these people. *You* are the murderer, *you* are the unholy defilement of this land.

OEDIPUS. Have you no shame? To start up such a story! Do you think you will get away with this?

TIRESIAS. Yes. The truth with all its strength is in me.

OEDIPUS. Who taught you this lesson? You didn't learn it from your prophet's trade.

TIRESIAS. *You* did. I was unwilling to speak but you drove me to it.

OEDIPUS. What was it you said? I want to understand it clearly.

TIRESIAS. Didn't you understand it the first time? Aren't you just trying to trip me up?

OEDIPUS. No, I did not grasp it fully. Repeat your statement.

TIRESIAS. I say that you are the murderer you are searching for.

OEDIPUS. Do you think you can say that twice and not pay for it?

TIRESIAS. Shall I say something more, to make you angrier still?

OEDIPUS. Say what you like. It will all be meaningless.

TIRESIAS. I say that without knowing it you are living in shameful intimacy with your nearest and dearest. You do not see the evil in which you live.

OEDIPUS. Do you think you can go on like this with impunity forever?

TIRESIAS. Yes, if the truth has power.

OEDIPUS. It has, except for you. You have no power or truth. You are blind, your ears and mind as well as eyes.

TIRESIAS. You are a pitiful figure. These reproaches you fling at me, all these people here will fling them at you—and before very long.

OEDIPUS (*contemptuously*). You live your life in one continuous night of darkness. Neither I nor any other man that can see would do you any harm.

TIRESIAS. It is not destiny that I should fall through you. Apollo is enough for that. It is *his* concern.

OEDIPUS. Was it Creon, or you, that invented this story?

TIRESIAS. It is not Creon who harms you—you harm yourself.

OEDIPUS. Wealth, absolute power, skill surpassing skill in the competition of life—what envy is your reward! For the sake of this power which

Thebes entrusted to me—I did not ask for it—to win this power faithful Creon, my friend from the beginning, sneaks up on me treacherously, longing to drive me out. He sets this intriguing magician on me, a lying quack, keen sighted for what he can make, but blind in prophecy.

(To TIRESIAS) Tell me, when were you a true prophet? When the Sphinx chanted her riddle here, did *you* come forward to speak the word that would liberate the people of this town? That riddle was not for anyone who came along to answer—it called for prophetic insight. But you didn't come forward, you offered no answer told you by the birds or the gods. No. *I* came, know-nothing Oedipus. *I* stopped the Sphinx. I answered the riddle with my own intelligence—the birds had nothing to teach me. And now you try to drive me out, you think you will stand beside Creon's throne. I tell you, you will pay in tears for this witch-hunting—you and Creon, the man that organized this conspiracy. If you weren't an old man, you would already have realized, in suffering, what your schemes lead to.

CHORUS LEADER. If we may make a suggestion—both his words and yours, Oedipus, seem to have been spoken in anger. This sort of talk is not what we need—what we must think of is how to solve the problem set by the god's oracle.

TIRESIAS. King though you are, you must treat me as your equal in one respect—the right to reply. That is a power which belongs to me, too. I am not your servant, but Apollo's. I am not inscribed on the records as a dependent of Creon, with no right to speak in person. I can speak, and here is what I have to say. You have mocked at my blindness, but you, who have eyes, cannot see the evil in which you stand; you cannot see where you are living, nor with whom you share your house. Do you even know who your parents are? Without knowing it, you are the enemy of your own flesh and blood, the dead below and the living here above. The double-edged curse of your mother and father, moving on dread feet, shall one day drive you from this land. You see straight now but then you will see darkness. You will scream aloud on that day; there is no place which shall not hear you, no part of Mount Cithaeron here which will not ring in echo, on that day when you know the truth about your wedding, that evil harbor into which you sailed before a fair wind.

There is a multitude of other horrors which you do not even suspect, and they will equate you to yourself and to your own children. There! Now smear me and Creon with your accusations. There is no man alive whose ruin will be more pitiful than yours.

OEDIPUS. Enough! I won't listen to this sort of talk from you. Damn you! My curse on you! Get out of here, quickly. Away from this house, back to where you came from!

TIRESIAS. I would never have come here if you had not summoned me.

OEDIPUS. I didn't know that you were going to speak like a fool—or it would have been a long time before I summoned you to my palace.

TIRESIAS. I am what I am—a fool to you, so it seems, but the parents who brought you into the world thought me sensible enough. (TIRESIAS *turns to go.*)

OEDIPUS. Whom do you mean? Wait! Who is my father?

TIRESIAS. This present day will give you birth and death.

OEDIPUS. Everything you say is the same—riddles, obscurities.

TIRESIAS. Aren't you the best man alive at guessing riddles?

OEDIPUS. Insult me, go on—but that, you will find, is what makes me great.

TIRESIAS. Yet that good fortune was your destruction.

OEDIPUS. What does that matter, if I saved Thebes?

TIRESIAS. I will go, then. Boy, lead me away.

OEDIPUS. Yes, take him away. While you're here you are a hindrance, a nuisance; once out of the way you won't annoy me any more.

TIRESIAS. I am going. But first I will say what I came here to say. I have no fear of you. You cannot destroy me. Listen to me now. The man you are trying to find, with your threatening proclamations, the murderer of Laius, that man is here in Thebes. He is apparently an immigrant of foreign birth, but he will be revealed as a native-born Theban. He will take no pleasure in that revelation. Blind instead of seeing, beggar instead of rich, he will make his way to foreign soil, feeling his way with a stick. He will be revealed as brother and father of the children with whom he now lives, the son and husband of the woman who gave him birth, the murderer and marriage-partner of his father. Go think this out. And if you find that I am wrong, then say I have no skill in prophecy.

(*Exit* TIRESIAS *led by boy to side.* OEDIPUS *goes back into the palace.*)

CHORUS. Who is the man denounced by the prophetic voice from Delphi's cliffs—the man whose bloodstained hands committed a nameless crime? Now is the time for him to run, faster than storm-swift horses. In full armor Apollo son of Zeus leaps upon him, with the fire of the lightning. And in the murderer's track follow dreadful unfailing spirits of vengeance.

The word of Apollo has blazed out from snowy Parnassus for all to see. Track down the unknown murderer by every means. He roams under cover of the wild forest, among caves and rocks, like a wild bull, wretched, cut off from mankind, his feet in pain. He turns his back on the prophecies delivered at the world's center, but they, alive forever, hover round him.

The wise prophet's words have brought me terror and confusion. I cannot agree with him, nor speak against him. I do not know what to say. I waver in hope and fear; I cannot see forward or back. What cause for quarrel was there between Oedipus and Laius? I never heard of one in time past; I know of none now.

I see no reason to attack the great fame of Oedipus in order to avenge the mysterious murder of Laius.

Zeus and Apollo, it is true, understand and know in full the events of man's life. But whether a mere man knows the truth—whether a human prophet knows more than I do—who is to be a fair judge of that? It is true that one man may be wiser than another. But I, for my part, will never join those who blame Oedipus, until I see these charges proved. We all saw how the Sphinx came against him—there his wisdom was proved. In that hour of danger he was the joy of Thebes. Remembering that day, my heart will never judge him guilty of evil action.

(*Enter* CREON, *from side.*)

CREON. Fellow citizens of Thebes, I am here in an angry mood. I hear that King Oedipus brings terrible charges against me. If, in the present dangerous situation, he thinks that I have injured him in any way, by word or deed, let me not live out the rest of my days with such a reputation. The damage done to me by such a report is no simple thing—it is the worst there is—to be called a traitor in the city, by all of you, by my friends.

CHORUS LEADER. This attack on you must have been forced out of him by anger; he lost control of himself.

CREON. Who told him that *I* advised Tiresias to make these false statements?

CHORUS LEADER. That's what was said—but I don't know what the intention was.

CREON. Were his eyes and mind unclouded when he made this charge against me?

CHORUS LEADER. I don't know. It is no use asking *me* about the actions of those who rule Thebes. Here is Oedipus. Look, he is coming out of the palace.

(*Enter* OEDIPUS, *from door.*)

OEDIPUS (*to* CREON). You! What are you doing here? Do you have the face to come to my palace—you who are convicted as my murderer, exposed as a robber attempting to steal my throne? In God's name, tell me, what did you take me for when you made this plot—a coward? Or a fool? Did you think I wouldn't notice this conspiracy of yours creeping up on me in the dark? That once I saw it, I wouldn't defend myself? Don't you see that your plan is foolish—to hunt for a crown without numbers or friends behind you? A crown is won by numbers and money.

CREON. I have a suggestion. You in your turn listen to a reply as long as your speech, and, after you have heard me, *then* judge me.

OEDIPUS. You are a clever speaker, but I am a slow learner—from *you*. I have found you an enemy and a burden to me.

CREON. Just one thing, just listen to what I say.

OEDIPUS. Just one thing, don't try to tell me you are not a traitor.

CREON. Listen, if you think stubbornness deprived of intelligence is a worth-while possession, you are out of your mind.

366

OEDIPUS. Listen, if you think you can injure a close relative and then not pay for it, you are out of your mind.

CREON. All right, that's fair. But at least explain to me what I am supposed to have done.

OEDIPUS. Did you or did you not persuade me that I ought to send for that "holy" prophet?

CREON. Yes, I did, and I am still of the same mind.

OEDIPUS. Well then, how long is it since Laius . . . (*Pause.*)

CREON. Did what? I don't follow your drift.

OEDIPUS. Disappeared, vanished, violently murdered?

CREON. Many years ago; it is a long count back in time.

OEDIPUS. And at that time, was this prophet at his trade?

CREON. Yes, wise as he is now, and honored then as now.

OEDIPUS. Did he mention my name at that time?

CREON. No, at least not in my presence.

OEDIPUS. You investigated the murder of Laius, didn't you?

CREON. We did what we could, of course. But we learned nothing.

OEDIPUS. How was it that this wise prophet did not say all this *then?*

CREON. I don't know. And when I don't understand, *I* keep silent.

OEDIPUS. Here's something you *do* know, and could say, too, if you were a loyal man.

CREON. What do you mean? If I know, I will not refuse to answer.

OEDIPUS. Just this. If he had not come to an agreement with you, Tiresias would never have called the murder of Laius *my* work.

CREON. If that's what he says—you are the one to know. Now I claim my rights from you—answer my questions as I did yours just now.

OEDIPUS. Ask your questions. I shall not be proved a murderer.

CREON. You are married to my sister, are you not?

OEDIPUS. The answer to that question is yes.

CREON. And you rule Thebes jointly and equally with her?

OEDIPUS. She gets from me whatever she wants.

CREON. And I am on an equal basis with the two of you, isn't that right?

OEDIPUS. Yes, it is, and that fact shows what a disloyal friend you are.

CREON. No, not if you look at it rationally, as I am explaining it to you. Consider this point first—do you think anyone would prefer to be supreme ruler and live in fear rather than to sleep soundly at night and still have the same power as the king? I am not the man to long for royalty rather than royal power, and anyone who has any sense agrees with me. As it is now, I have everything I want from you, and nothing to fear; but if I were king, I would have to do many things I have no mind to. How could the throne seem more desirable to me than power and authority which bring me no trouble? I can see clearly—all I want is what is pleasant and profitable at the same time. As it is now, I am greeted by all, everyone salutes me, all those who want something from you play up to me—that's the key to success for them. What makes you think I would give up all this and accept what you have? No, a mind which sees things clearly, as I do, would never turn traitor. I have never been tempted by such an idea, and I would never have put up with anyone who took such action.

You can test the truth of what I say. Go to Delphi and ask for the text of the oracle, to see if I gave you an accurate report. One thing more. If you find that I conspired with the prophet Tiresias, then condemn me to death, not by a single vote, but by a double, yours and mine both. But do not accuse me in isolation, on private, baseless fancy. It is not justice to make the mistake of taking bad men for good, or good for bad. To reject a good friend is the equivalent of throwing away one's own dear life—that's my opinion. Given time you will realize all this without fail: time alone reveals the just man—the unjust you can recognize in one short day.

CHORUS LEADER. That is good advice, my lord, for anyone who wants to avoid mistakes. Quick decisions are not the safest.

OEDIPUS. When a plotter moves against me in speed and secrecy, then I too must be quick to counterplot. If I take my time and wait, then his cause is won, and mine lost.

CREON. What do you want then? Surely you don't mean to banish me from Thebes?

OEDIPUS. Not at all. Death is what I want for you, not exile.

CREON. You give a clear example of what it is to feel hate and envy.

OEDIPUS. You don't believe me, eh? You won't give way?

CREON. No, for I can see you don't know what you are doing.

OEDIPUS. Looking after my own interests.

CREON. And what about mine?

OEDIPUS. You are a born traitor.

CREON. And you don't understand anything.

OEDIPUS. Whether I do or not—I am in power here.

CREON. Not if you rule badly.

OEDIPUS (to CHORUS). Listen to him, Thebes, my city.

CREON. My city, too, not yours alone.

CHORUS LEADER. Stop, my lords. Here comes Jocasta from the house, in the nick of time. With her help, you must compose this quarrel between you.

(Enter JOCASTA, from door.)

JOCASTA. Have you no sense, God help you, raising your voices in strife like this? Have you no sense of shame? The land is plague-stricken and you pursue private quarrels. (To OEDIPUS) You go into the house, and you, too, Creon, inside. Don't make so much trouble over some small annoyance.

CREON. Sister, your husband, Oedipus, claims the right to inflict dreadful punishments on me. He will choose between banishing me from my fatherland and killing me.

OEDIPUS. Exactly, Jocasta, I caught him in a treacherous plot against my life.

CREON. May I never enjoy life, but perish under a curse, if I have done to you any of the things you charge me with.

JOCASTA. In God's name, Oedipus, believe what he says. Show respect for the oath he swore by the gods—do it for my sake and the sake of these people here.

CHORUS. Listen to her, King Oedipus. Think over your decision, take her advice, I beg you.

OEDIPUS. What concession do you want me to make?

CHORUS. Creon was no fool before, and now his oath increases his stature. Respect him.

OEDIPUS. Do you know what you are asking?

CHORUS. Yes, I know.

OEDIPUS. Tell me what it means, then.

CHORUS. This man is your friend—he has sworn an oath—don't throw him out dishonored on the strength of hearsay alone.

OEDIPUS. Understand this. If that is what you are after, you want me to be killed or banished from this land.

CHORUS. No. By the sun, foremost of all the gods! May I perish miserably abandoned by man and God, if any such thought is in my mind. My heart is racked with pain for the dying land of Thebes—must you add new sorrows of your own making to those we already have?

OEDIPUS. Well then, let him go—even if it *does* lead to my death or inglorious banishment. It is *your* piteous speech that rouses my compassion—not what *he* says. As for him, I shall hate him, wherever he goes.

CREON. You show your sulky temper in giving way, just as you did in your ferocious anger. Natures like yours are hardest to bear for their owners—and justly so.

OEDIPUS. Get out, will you? Out!

CREON. I am going. I found you ignorant—but these men think I am right.

(*Exit* CREON *to side.*)

CHORUS (*to* JOCASTA). Lady, why don't you get him into the house quickly?

JOCASTA. I will—when I have found out what happened here.

CHORUS. There was some ignorant talk based on hearsay and some hurt caused by injustice.

JOCASTA. On both sides?

CHORUS. Yes.

JOCASTA. And what did they say?

CHORUS. Enough, that is enough, it seems to me. I speak in the interests of the whole country. Let this matter lie where they left it.

OEDIPUS. You see where your good intentions have brought you. This is the result of turning aside and blunting the edge of my anger.

CHORUS. My king, I said it before, more than once—listen to me. I would be exposed as a madman, useless, brainless, if I were to turn my back on you. You found Thebes laboring in a sea of trouble, you righted her and set her on a fair course. All I wish now is that you should guide us as well as you did then.

JOCASTA. In God's name, explain to me, my lord—what was it made you so angry?

OEDIPUS. I will tell you. I have more respect for you than for these people here. Creon and his conspiracy against me, that's what made me angry.

JOCASTA. Tell me clearly, what was the quarrel between you?

OEDIPUS. He says that *I* am the murderer of Laius.

JOCASTA. On what evidence? His own knowledge, or hearsay?

OEDIPUS. Oh, he keeps his own lips clear of responsibility—he sent a swindling prophet in to speak for him.

JOCASTA. A prophet? In that case, rid your mind of your fear, and listen to me. I can teach you something. There is no human being born that is endowed with prophetic power. I can prove it to you—and in a few words.

A prophecy came to Laius once—I won't say from Apollo himself, but from his priests. It said that Laius was fated to die by the hand of his son, a son to be born to him and to me. Well, Laius, so the story goes, was killed by foreign robbers at a place where three highways meet. As for the son—three days after his birth Laius fastened his ankles together and had him cast away on the pathless mountains.

So, in this case, Apollo did not make the son kill his father or Laius die by his own son's hand, as he had feared. Yet these were the definite statements of the prophetic voices. Don't pay any attention to prophecies. If God seeks or needs anything, he will easily make it clear to us himself.

OEDIPUS. Jocasta, something I heard you say has disturbed me to the soul, unhinged my mind.

JOCASTA. What do you mean? What was it that alarmed you so?

OEDIPUS. I thought I heard you say that Laius was killed at a place where three highways meet.

JOCASTA. Yes, that's what the story was—and still is.

OEDIPUS. Where is the place where this thing happened?

JOCASTA. The country is called Phocis: two roads, one from Delphi and one from Daulia, come together and form one.

OEDIPUS. When did it happen? How long ago?

JOCASTA. We heard the news here in Thebes just before you appeared and became King.

OEDIPUS. O God, what have you planned to do to me?

JOCASTA. What is it, Oedipus, which haunts your spirit so?

OEDIPUS. No questions, not yet. Laius—tell me what he looked like, how old he was.

JOCASTA. He was a big man—his hair had just begun to turn white. And he had more or less the same build as you.

OEDIPUS. O God! I think I have just called down on myself a dreadful curse—not knowing what I did.

370

JOCASTA. What do you mean? To look at you makes me shudder, my lord.

OEDIPUS. I am dreadfully afraid the blind prophet could see. But tell me one more thing that will throw light on this.

JOCASTA. I am afraid. But ask your question; I will answer if I can.

OEDIPUS. Was Laius poorly attended, or did he have a big bodyguard, like a king?

JOCASTA. There were five men in his party. One of them was a herald. And there was one wagon—Laius was riding in it.

OEDIPUS. Oh, it is all clear as daylight now. Who was it told you all this at the time?

JOCASTA. A slave from the royal household. He was the only one who came back.

OEDIPUS. Is he by any chance in the palace now?

JOCASTA. No, he is not. When he came back and saw you ruling in place of Laius, he seized my hand and begged me to send him to work in the country, to the pastures, to the flocks, as far away as I could—out of sight of Thebes. And I sent him. Though he was a slave he deserved this favor from me—and much more.

OEDIPUS. Can I get him back here, in haste?

JOCASTA. It can be done. But why are you so intent on this?

OEDIPUS. I am afraid, Jocasta, that I have said too much—that's why I want to see this man.

JOCASTA. Well, he shall come. But I have a right, it seems to me, to know what it is that torments you so.

OEDIPUS. So you shall. Since I am so full of dreadful expectation, I shall hold nothing back from you. Who else should I speak to, who means more to me than you, in this time of trouble?

My father was Polybus, a Dorian, and my mother Merope, of Corinth. I was regarded as the greatest man in that city until something happened to me quite by chance, a strange thing, but not worth all the attention I paid it. A man at the banquet table, who had had too much to drink, told me, over his wine, that I was not the true son of my father. I was furious, but, hard though it was, I controlled my feelings, for that day at least. On the next day I went to my parents and questioned them. They were enraged against the man who had so taunted me. So I took comfort from their attitude, but still the thing tormented me—for the story spread far and wide. Without telling my parents, I set off on a journey to the oracle of Apollo, at Delphi. Apollo sent me away with my question unanswered but he foretold a dreadful, calamitous future for me—to lie with my mother and beget children men's eyes would not bear the sight of—and to be the killer of the father that gave me life.

When I heard that, I ran away. From that point on I measured the distance to the land of Corinth by the stars. I was running to a place where I would never see that shameful prophecy come true. On my way I came to the place in which you say this king, Laius, met his death.

I will tell you the truth, all of it. As I journeyed on I came near to this triple crossroad and there I was met by a herald and a man riding on a horse-drawn wagon, just as you described it. The driver, and the old man himself, tried to push me off the road. In anger I struck the driver as he tried to crowd me off. When the old man saw me coming past the wheels he aimed at my head with a two-pronged goad, and hit me. I paid him back in full, with interest: in no time at all he was hit by the stick I held in my hand and rolled backwards from the center of the wagon. I killed the whole lot of them.

Now, if this stranger had anything to do with Laius—is there a more unhappy man alive than I? Who could be more hateful to the gods than I am? No foreigner or citizen may take me into his house, no one can talk to me—everyone must expel me from his home. And the man who called down these curses on me was I myself, no one else. With these hands that killed him I defile the dead man's marriage bed. How can I deny that I am vile, utterly unclean? I must be banished from Thebes, and then I may not even see my own parents or set foot on my own fatherland—or else I am doomed to marry my own mother and kill my father Polybus, who brought me up and gave me life. I am the victim of some harsh divinity; what other explanation can there be?

Let it not happen, not that, I beg you, holy majesty of God, may I never see that day! May I disappear from among men without trace before I see such a stain of misfortune come upon me!

CHORUS LEADER. My lord, this makes us tremble. But do not despair—you have still to hear the story from the eyewitness.

OEDIPUS. That's right. That's my hope now, such as it is—to wait for the shepherd.

JOCASTA. Why all this urgency about his coming?

OEDIPUS. I'll tell you. If it turns out that he tells the same story as you— then I, at least, will be cleared of responsibility.

JOCASTA. What was so important in what you heard from me?

OEDIPUS. You said his story was that *several* robbers killed Laius. Well, if he speaks of the same number as you—then I am not the killer. For one could never be equal to many. But if he speaks of one man alone— then clearly the balance tips towards me as the killer.

JOCASTA. You can be sure that his account was made public just as I told it to you; he cannot go back on it, the whole city heard it, not I alone. But, my lord, even if he should depart from his former account in some particular, he still would never make the death of Laius what it was supposed to be—for Apollo said clearly that Laius was to be killed by my son. But that poor infant never killed Laius; it met its own death first. So much for prophecy. For all it can say, I would not, from now on, so much as look to right or left.

372

OEDIPUS. Yes, I agree. But all the same, the shepherd—send someone to fetch him. Do it at once.

JOCASTA. I shall send immediately. And now let us go in. I would not do anything except what pleases you.

(*Exeunt* OEDIPUS *and* JOCASTA *through doors.*)

CHORUS (*chanting in unison*).
May Destiny be with me always;
Let me observe reverence and purity
In word and deed.
Laws that stand above have been established—
Born in the upper air on high;
Their only father is heaven;
No mortal nature, no man gave them birth.
They never forget, or sleep.
In them God is great, and He does not grow old.

The despot is the child of violent pride,
Pride that vainly stuffs itself
With food unseasonable, unfit,
Climbs to the highest rim
And then plunges sheer down into defeat
Where its feet are of no use.
Yet I pray to God to spare that vigor
Which benefits the state.
God is my protector, on Him I shall never cease to call.

The man who goes his way
Overbearing in word and deed,
Who fears no justice,
Honors no temples of the gods—
May an evil destiny seize him
And punish his ill-starred pride.
How shall such a man defend his life
Against God's arrows?
If such deeds as this are honored,
Why should we join the sacred dance and worship?

I shall go no more in reverence to Delphi,
The holy center of the earth,
Nor to any temple in the world,
Unless these prophecies come true,
For all men to point at in wonder.
O Zeus, King of heaven, ruler of all,
If you deserve this name,

Do not let your everlasting power be deceived,
Do not forget.
The old prophecies about Laius are failing,
Men reject them now.
Apollo is without honor everywhere.
The gods are defeated.

(*Enter* JOCASTA, *with branches of olive.*)

JOCASTA (*to* CHORUS). Lords of Thebes, it occurred to me to come to the temples of the gods bearing in my hands these branches and offerings of incense. For Oedipus is distracted with sorrows of all kinds. He does not act like a man in control of his reason, judging the present by the past—he is at the mercy of anyone who speaks to him, especially one who speaks of terrors. I have given him advice, but it does no good. (*Facing the altar*) So I come to you, Lord Apollo, for you are closest to hand. I come in supplication with these emblems of prayer. Deliver us, make us free and clear of defilement. We are all afraid, like passengers on a ship who see their pilot crazed with fear.

(*Enter from side* CORINTHIAN MESSENGER.)

CORINTHIAN MESSENGER (*to* CHORUS). Strangers, can one of you tell me—where is the palace of King Oedipus? Better still, if you know, where is the king himself?

CHORUS LEADER. This is his palace, and he is inside, stranger. This lady is his queen, his wife and mother of his children.

CORINTHIAN MESSENGER. Greetings to the noble wife of Oedipus! May you and all your family be blessed forever.

JOCASTA. The same blessings on you, stranger, for your kind words. But tell us what you want. Why have you come? Have you some news for us?

CORINTHIAN MESSENGER. Good news for your house and your husband, lady.

JOCASTA. What news? Who sent you?

CORINTHIAN MESSENGER. I come from Corinth. My message will bring you joy—no doubt of that—but sorrow, too.

JOCASTA. What is it? How can it work both ways?

CORINTHIAN MESSENGER. The people of Corinth will make Oedipus their king, so I heard there.

JOCASTA. What? Is old Polybus no longer on the throne?

CORINTHIAN MESSENGER. No. He is dead and in his grave.

JOCASTA. What did you say? Polybus is dead? Dead?

CORINTHIAN MESSENGER. Condemn me to death if I am not telling the truth.

JOCASTA (*to servant*). You there, go in quickly and tell your master. O prophecies of the gods, where are you now? Polybus was the man Oedipus feared he might kill—and so avoided him all this time. And now he's dead—a natural death, and not by the hand of Oedipus.

(*Enter* OEDIPUS, *from doors.*)

OEDIPUS. Jocasta, why did you send for me to come out here?

JOCASTA. Listen to what this man says, and see what has become of the holy prophecies of the gods.

OEDIPUS. Who is he? What does he have to say to me?

JOCASTA. He's from Corinth. He came to tell you that your father Polybus is dead and gone.

OEDIPUS. Is this true? Tell me yourself.

CORINTHIAN MESSENGER. If that's what you want to hear first, here it is, a plain statement: Polybus is dead and gone.

OEDIPUS. How? Killed by a traitor, or wasted by disease?

CORINTHIAN MESSENGER. He was old. It did not take much to put him to sleep.

OEDIPUS. By disease, then—that's how he died?

CORINTHIAN MESSENGER. Yes, that, and the length of years he had lived.

OEDIPUS. So! Why then, Jocasta, should we study Apollo's oracle, or gaze at the birds screaming over our heads—those prophets who announced that I would kill my father? He's dead, buried, below ground. And here I am in Thebes—I did not put hand to sword.

Perhaps he died from longing to see me again. That way, it could be said that I was the cause of his death. But there he lies, dead, taking with him all these prophecies I feared—they are worth nothing!

JOCASTA. Is that not what I told you?

OEDIPUS. It is. But I was led astray by fear.

JOCASTA. Now rid your heart of fear forever.

OEDIPUS. No, I must still fear—and who would not?—a marriage with my mother.

JOCASTA. Fear? Why should man fear? His life is governed by the operations of chance. Nothing can be clearly foreseen. The best way to live is by hit and miss, as best you can. Don't be afraid that you may marry your mother. Many a man before you, in dreams, has shared his mother's bed. But to live at ease one must attach no importance to such things.

OEDIPUS. All that you have said would be fine—if my mother were not still alive. But she is, and no matter how good a case you make, I am still a prey to fear.

JOCASTA. But your father's death—that much at least is a great blessing.

OEDIPUS. Yes, I see that. But my mother, as long as she is alive, fills me with fear.

CORINTHIAN MESSENGER. Who is this woman that inspires such fear in you?

OEDIPUS. Merope, old man, the wife of Polybus.

CORINTHIAN MESSENGER. And what is there about her which frightens you?

OEDIPUS. A dreadful prophecy sent by the gods.

CORINTHIAN MESSENGER. Can you tell me what it is? Or is it forbidden for others to know?

OEDIPUS. Yes, I can tell you. Apollo once announced that I am destined to mate with my mother, and shed my father's blood with my own

375

hand. That is why for so many years I have lived far away from Corinth. It has turned out well—but still, there's nothing sweeter than the sight of one's parents.

CORINTHIAN MESSENGER. Is that it? It was in fear of this that you banished yourself from Corinth?

OEDIPUS. Yes. I did not want to be my father's murderer.

CORINTHIAN MESSENGER. My lord, I do not know why I have not already released you from that fear. I came here to bring you good news.

OEDIPUS. If you can do that, you will be handsomely rewarded.

CORINTHIAN MESSENGER. Yes, that was why I came, to bring you home to Corinth, and be rewarded for it.

OEDIPUS. I will never go to the city where my parents live.

CORINTHIAN MESSENGER. My son, it is clear that you don't know what you are doing.

OEDIPUS. What do you mean, old man? In God's name, explain yourself.

CORINTHIAN MESSENGER. You don't know what you are doing, if you are afraid to come home because of *them*.

OEDIPUS. I am afraid that Apollo's prophecy may come true.

CORINTHIAN MESSENGER. That you will be stained with guilt through your parents?

OEDIPUS. Yes, that's it, old man, that's the fear which pursues me always.

CORINTHIAN MESSENGER. In reality, you have nothing to fear.

OEDIPUS. Nothing? How, if I am the son of Polybus and Merope?

CORINTHIAN MESSENGER. Because Polybus was not related to you in any way.

OEDIPUS. What do you mean? Was Polybus not my father?

CORINTHIAN MESSENGER. No more than I am—he was as much your father as I.

OEDIPUS. How can my father be on the same level as you who are nothing to me?

CORINTHIAN MESSENGER. Because he was no more your father than I am.

OEDIPUS. Then why did he call me his son?

CORINTHIAN MESSENGER. He took you from my hands—I gave you to him.

OEDIPUS. Took me from your hands? Then how could he love me so much?

CORINTHIAN MESSENGER. He had been childless, that was why he loved you.

OEDIPUS. *You* gave me to him? Did you . . . buy me? or find me somewhere?

CORINTHIAN MESSENGER. I found you in the shady valleys of Mount Cithaeron.

OEDIPUS. What were you doing there?

CORINTHIAN MESSENGER. Watching over my flocks on the mountainside.

OEDIPUS. A shepherd, were you? A wandering day laborer?

CORINTHIAN MESSENGER. Yes, but at that moment I was your savior.

OEDIPUS. When you picked me us, was I in pain?

CORINTHIAN MESSENGER. Your ankles would bear witness on that point.

376

OEDIPUS. Oh, why do you speak of that old affliction?

CORINTHIAN MESSENGER. You had your ankles pinned together, and I freed you.

OEDIPUS. It is a dreadful mark of shame I have borne since childhood.

CORINTHIAN MESSENGER. From that misfortune comes the name which you still bear.[1]

OEDIPUS. In God's name, who did it? My mother, or my father? Speak.

CORINTHIAN MESSENGER. I don't know. The one who gave you to me is the man to ask, not me.

OEDIPUS. You got me from someone else—you did not find me yourself?

CORINTHIAN MESSENGER. No. Another shepherd gave you to me.

OEDIPUS. Who was he? Do you know? Could you describe him?

CORINTHIAN MESSENGER. I think he belonged to the household of Laius.

OEDIPUS. You mean the man who was once king of this country?

CORINTHIAN MESSENGER. Yes. He was one of the shepherds of Laius.

OEDIPUS. Is he still alive? Can I talk to him?

CORINTHIAN MESSENGER. (to CHORUS). You people who live here would know that better than I.

OEDIPUS (to CHORUS). Is there any one of you people here who knows this shepherd he mentioned? Has anyone seen him in the fields, or here in Thebes?

CHORUS LEADER. I think it is the same man from the fields you wanted to see before. But the queen here, Jocasta, could tell you that.

OEDIPUS. Jocasta, do you remember the man we sent for just now? Is *that* the man he is talking about?

JOCASTA. Why ask who he means? Don't pay any attention to him. Don't even think about what he said—it makes no sense.

OEDIPUS. What? With a clue like this? Give up the search? Fail to solve the mystery of my birth? Never!

JOCASTA. In God's name, if you place any value on your life, don't pursue the search. It is enough that *I* am sick to death.

OEDIPUS. *You* have nothing to be afraid of. Even if my mother turns out to be a slave, and I a slave for three generations back, *your* noble birth will not be called in question.

JOCASTA. Take my advice, I beg you—do not go on with it.

OEDIPUS. Nothing will move me. I *will* find out the whole truth.

JOCASTA. It is good advice I am giving you—I am thinking of you.

OEDIPUS. That "good advice" of yours is trying my patience.

JOCASTA. Ill-fated man. May you never find out who you are!

OEDIPUS (to attendants). One of you go and get that shepherd, bring him here. We will leave *her* to pride herself on her royal birth.

JOCASTA. Unfortunate! That is the only name I can call you by now. I shall not call your name again—ever! (*Exit* JOCASTA *to palace.*)

(*A long silence.*)

---

[1] His name, Oedipus, means, in Greek, "swollen foot." [Translator's note.]

CHORUS. Why has the queen gone, Oedipus, why has she rushed away in such wild grief? I am afraid that from this silence evil will burst out.

OEDIPUS. Burst out what will! I shall know my origin, mean though it be. Jocasta perhaps—she is proud, *like* a woman—feels shame at the low circumstances of my birth. But I count myself the son of Good Chance, the giver of success—I shall not be dishonored. Chance is my mother. My brothers are the months which have made me sometimes small and sometimes great. Such is my lineage and I shall not betray it. I will not give up the search for the truth about my birth. (*Exit* OEDIPUS *to palace.*)

CHORUS (*chanting in unison*).

If I am a true prophet
And see clear in my mind,
Tomorrow at the full moon
Oedipus will honor Mount Cithaeron
As his nurse and mother.
Mount Cithaeron—our king's Theban birthplace!
We shall celebrate it in dance and song—
A place loved by our king.
Lord Apollo, may this find favor in your sight.

Who was it, Oedipus my son, who bore you?
Which of the nymphs that live so long
Was the bride of Pan the mountain god?
Was your mother the bride of Apollo himself?
He loves the upland pastures.
Or was Hermes your father?
Perhaps Dionysus who lives on the mountain peaks
Received you as a welcome gift
From one of the nymphs of Helicon,
His companions in sport.

(*Enter from side the* SHEPHERD, *accompanied by two guards.*)
(*Enter* OEDIPUS, *from doors.*)

OEDIPUS. I never met the man, but, if I may make a guess, I think this man I see is the shepherd we have been looking for all this time. His age corresponds to that of the Corinthian here, and, in any case, the men bringing him are my servants, I recognize them.

(*To* CHORUS LEADER) You have seen the shepherd before, you should know better than I.

CHORUS LEADER. Yes, I recognize him. He was in the household of Laius— a devoted servant, and a shepherd.

OEDIPUS. I question you first—you, the stranger from Corinth. Is this the man you spoke of?

CORINTHIAN MESSENGER. This is the man.

OEDIPUS (*to* SHEPHERD). You, old man, come here. Look me in the face. Answer my questions. Were you a servant of Laius once?

SHEPHERD. I was. A slave. Not bought, though. I was born and reared in the palace.

OEDIPUS. What was your work? How did you earn your living?

SHEPHERD. For most of my life I have followed where the sheep flocks went.

OEDIPUS. And where did you graze your sheep most of the time?

SHEPHERD. Well, there was Mount Cithaeron, and all the country round it.

OEDIPUS. Do you know this man here? Did you ever see him before?

SHEPHERD. Which man do you mean? What would he be doing there?

OEDIPUS. This one, here. Did you ever come across him?

SHEPHERD. I can't say, right away. Give me time. I don't remember.

CORINTHIAN MESSENGER. No wonder he doesn't remember, master. He forgets, but I'll remind him, and make it clear. I am sure he knows very well how the two of us grazed our flocks on Cithaeron—he had two and I only one—we were together three whole summers, from spring until the rising of Arcturus in the fall. When winter came I used to herd my sheep back to their winter huts, and he took his back to the farms belonging to Laius. Do you remember any of this? Isn't that what happened?

SHEPHERD. What you say is true, but it was a long time ago.

CORINTHIAN MESSENGER. Well, then, tell me this. Do you remember giving me a child, a boy, for me to bring up as my own?

SHEPHERD. What are you talking about? Why do you ask that question?

CORINTHIAN MESSENGER. Oedipus here, my good man, Oedipus and that child are one and the same.

SHEPHERD. Damn you! Shut your mouth. Keep quiet!

OEDIPUS. Old man, don't you correct *him*. It is you and your tongue that need correction.

SHEPHERD. What have I done wrong, noble master?

OEDIPUS. You refuse to answer his question about the child.

SHEPHERD. That's because he does not know what he's talking about— he is just wasting your time.

OEDIPUS. If you won't speak willingly, we shall see if pain can make you speak.

(*The guards seize the* SHEPHERD.)

SHEPHERD. In God's name, don't! Don't torture me. I am an old man.

OEDIPUS. One of you twist his arms behind his back, quickly!

SHEPHERD. Oh, God, what for? What more do you want to know?

OEDIPUS. Did you give him the child he asked about?

SHEPHERD. Yes, I did. And I wish I had died that day.

OEDIPUS. You will die now, if you don't give an honest answer.

SHEPHERD. And if I speak, I shall be even worse off.

OEDIPUS (*to guards*). What? More delay?

SHEPHERD. No! No! I said it before—I gave him the child.

OEDIPUS. Where did *you* get it? Was it yours? Or did it belong to someone else?

SHEPHERD. It wasn't mine. Someone gave it to me.

OEDIPUS. Which of these Thebans here? From whose house did it come?

SHEPHERD. In God's name, master, don't ask any more questions.

OEDIPUS. You are a dead man if I have to ask you again.

SHEPHERD. It was a child born in the house of Laius.

OEDIPUS. Was it a slave? Or a member of the royal family?

SHEPHERD. Oh, God, here comes the dreadful truth. And I must speak.

OEDIPUS. And I must hear it. But hear it I will.

SHEPHERD. It was the son of Laius, so I was told. But the lady inside there, your wife, she is the one to tell you.

OEDIPUS. Did *she* give it to you?

SHEPHERD. Yes, my lord, she did.

OEDIPUS. For what purpose?

SHEPHERD. To destroy it.

OEDIPUS. Her own child?

SHEPHERD. She was afraid of dreadful prophecies.

OEDIPUS. What were they?

SHEPHERD. The child would kill its parents, that was the story.

OEDIPUS. Then why did you give it to this old man here?

SHEPHERD. In pity, master. I thought he would take it away to a foreign country—to the place he came from. If you are the man he says you are, you were born the most unfortunate of men.

OEDIPUS. O God! It has all come true. Light, let this be the last time I see you. I stand revealed—born in shame, married in shame, an unnatural murderer. (*Exit* OEDIPUS *into palace.*)

(*Exeunt other at sides.*)

CHORUS.

O generations of mortal men,
I add up the total of your lives
And find it equal to nothing.
What man wins more happiness
Than a mere appearance which quickly fades away?
With your example before me,
Your life, your destiny, miserable Oedipus,
　　　I call no man happy.

Oedipus outranged all others
And won complete prosperity and happiness.
He destroyed the Sphinx, that maiden
With curved claws and riddling songs,
And rose up like a towered wall against death—
Oedipus, savior of our city.
From that time on you were called King,
You were honored above all men,
Ruling over great Thebes.

380

And now—is there a man whose story is more pitiful?
His life is lived in merciless calamity and pain—
A complete reversal from his happy state.
O Oedipus, famous king,
You whom the same great harbor sheltered
As child and father both,
How could the furrows which your father plowed
Bear *you* in silence for so long?

Time, which sees all things, has found you out;
It sits in judgment on the unnatural marriage
Which was both begetter and begot.
      O son of Laius,
I wish I had never seen you.
I weep, like a man wailing for the dead.
      This is the truth:
You returned me to life once
And now you have closed my eyes in darkness.

(*Enter, from the palace, a* MESSENGER.)

MESSENGER. Citizens of Thebes, you who are most honored in this city! What dreadful things you will see and hear! What a cry of sorrow you will raise, if, as true Thebans, you have any feeling for the royal house. Not even the great rivers of Ister and Phasis could wash this house clean of the horrors it hides within. And it will soon expose them to the light of day—horrors deliberately willed, not involuntary. Those calamities we inflict on ourselves are those which cause the most pain.

CHORUS LEADER. The horrors we knew about before were burden enough. What other dreadful news do you bring?

MESSENGER. Here is the thing quickest for me to say and you to hear. Jocasta, our queen, is dead.

CHORUS LEADER. Poor lady. From what cause?

MESSENGER. By her own hand. You are spared the worst of what has happened—you were not there to see it. But as far as my memory serves, you shall hear the full story of that unhappy woman's sufferings.

She came in through the door in a fury of passion and rushed straight towards her marriage bed, tearing at her hair with both hands. Into her bedroom she went, and slammed the doors behind her. She was calling the name of Laius, so long dead, remembering the child she bore to him so long ago—the child by whose hand Laius was to die, and leave her, its mother, to bear monstrous children to her own son. She wailed in mourning for her marriage, in which she had borne double offspring, a husband from her husband and children from her child. And after that—but I do not know exactly how she died. For Oedipus came bursting in, shouting, and so we could not watch Jocasta's suffering to the end; all of us looked at him as he ran to and fro. He rushed from one of us to the other, asking us to give him a sword, to tell him where he could find his wife—no, not his wife, but his mother, his mother and the mother of his children.

It must have been some supernatural being that showed the raving man where she was; it was not one of us. As if led by a guide he threw himself against the doors of her room with a terrible cry; he bent the bolts out of their sockets, and so forced his way into the room. And there we saw Jocasta, hanging, her neck caught in a swinging noose of rope. When Oedipus saw her he gave a deep dreadful cry of sorrow and loosened the rope round her neck. And when the poor woman was lying on the ground—then we saw the most dreadful sight of all. He ripped out the golden pins with which her clothes were fastened, raised them high above his head, and speared the pupils of his eyes. "You will not see," he said, "the horrors I have suffered and done. Be dark forever now—eyes that saw those you should never have seen, and failed to recognize those you longed to see." Murmuring words like these he raised his hands and struck his eyes again, and again. And each time the wounded eyes sent a stream of blood down his chin, no oozing flow but a dark shower of it, thick as a hailstorm.

These are the sorrows which have burst out and overwhelmed them both, man and wife alike. The wealth and happiness they once had was real while it lasted, but now—weeping, destruction, death, shame— name any shape of evil you will, they have them all.

CHORUS. And Oedipus—poor wretched Oedipus—has he now some rest from pain?

MESSENGER. He is shouting, "Open the doors, someone: show me to all the people of Thebes, my father's killer, my mother's"—I cannot repeat his unholy words. He speaks of banishing himself from Thebes, says he will not remain in his house under the curse which he himself pronounced. But he has no strength: he needs someone to guide his steps. The pain is more than he can bear.

But he will show you himself. The bolts of this door are opening. Now you will see a spectacle that even his enemies would pity.

(*Enter* OEDIPUS *from door, blind.*)

CHORUS. O suffering dreadful for mankind to see, most dreadful of all I ever saw. What madness came over you? What unearthly spirit, leaping farther than the mind can conceive, swooped down on your destiny? I pity you. I have many questions to ask you, much I wish to know; my eyes are drawn towards you—but I cannot bear to look. You fill me with horror.

OEDIPUS. Where am I going? Pity me! Where does my voice range to through the air? O spirit, what a leap you made!

CHORUS. To a point of dread, too far for men's ears and eyes.

OEDIPUS. Darkness, dark cloud all around me, enclosing me, unspeakable darkness, irresistible—you came to me on a wind that seemed favorable. Ah, I feel the stab of these sharp pains, and with it the memory of my sorrow.

CHORUS. In such torment it is no wonder that your pain and mourning should be double.

OEDIPUS. My friend! You are by my side still, you alone. You still stay by me, looking after the blind man. I know you are there. I am in the dark, but I can distinguish your voice clearly.

CHORUS. You have done a dreadful thing. How could you bring yourself to put out the light of your eyes? What superhuman power urged you on?

OEDIPUS. It was Apollo, friends, Apollo, who brought to fulfillment all my sufferings. But the hand that struck my eyes was mine and mine alone. What use had I for eyes? Nothing I could see would bring me joy.

CHORUS. It was just as you say.

OEDIPUS. What was there for me to look at, to speak to, to love? What joyful word can I expect to hear, my friends? Take me away, out of this country, quickly, take me away. I am lost, accursed, and hated by the gods beyond all other men.

CHORUS. I am moved to pity by your misfortunes and your understanding of them, too. I wish I had never known you!

OEDIPUS. A curse on the man who freed my feet from the cruel bonds on the mountain, who saved me and rescued me from death. He will get no thanks from me. I might have died then and there; but now I am a source of grief for myself and all who love me.

CHORUS. I wish it had turned out that way, too.

OEDIPUS. I would never have become my father's killer, never have been known to all men as my own mother's husband. Now I am god-forsaken, the son of an accursed marriage, my own father's successor in the marriage bed. If there is any evil worse than the worst that a man can suffer—Oedipus has drawn it for his lot.

CHORUS. I cannot say you made the right decision. You would have been better dead than blind.

OEDIPUS. What I have done was the best thing to do. Don't read me any more lessons, don't give me any more advice. With what eyes could I have faced my father in the house of the dead, or my poor mother? I have done things to them both for which hanging is too small a punishment.

Do you think I longed to look at my children, born the way they were? No, not with these eyes of mine, never! Not this town either, its walls, its holy temples of the gods. From all of this I am cut off, I, the most nobly raised in Thebes, cut off by my own act. It was I who proclaimed that everyone should expel the impious man—the man the gods have now revealed as unholy—and the son of Laius. After I had exposed my own guilt—and what a guilt!—do you think I could have looked at my fellow citizens with steady eyes?

No, no! If there had been some way to block the source of hearing, I would not have held back: I would have isolated my wretched body completely, so as to see and hear nothing at all. If my mind could be put beyond reach of my miseries—that would be my pleasure.

O Cithaeron, why did you receive me? Why did you not take and kill me on the spot, so that I should never reveal my origin to mankind?

O Polybus, and Corinth, and the ancient house I thought was my father's—what a handsome heir you raised up in me, how rotten beneath the surface! For now I am exposed—evil and born in evil.

O three roads in the deep valley, you oak wood and you narrow pass where the three roads meet, you who soaked up my father's blood, spilled by my hand—do you remember me? Do you remember what I did there, and what I did when I came here?

O marriage, marriage! You gave me birth, and then bred up seed from the one you brought into the world. You made an incestuous breed of father, brother, son—bride, wife, mother—all the most shameful things known to man.

But I must not speak of things that should never have been done. Quickly, in God's name, hide me somewhere outside Thebes, kill me. throw me into the sea, where you will never see me again.

Come close to me. I am a man of sorrow, but take courage and touch me. Do not be afraid; do what I ask. The evil is mine; no one but me can bear its weight.

(*Enter* CREON, *from side, with attendants.*)

CHORUS LEADER. Here is Creon. He will listen to your request. Decision and action are up to him, now that he has taken your place as the sole ruler of Thebes.

OEDIPUS. What shall I say to him? What justification, what grounds for trust can I present? In everything I did to him before, I have been proved wrong.

CREON. I have not come to mock you, Oedipus, nor to reproach you for the wrong you did.

(*To attendants*) If you have no respect for the feelings of human beings, at least show reverence for the sunlight which nourishes all men. Do not leave him there in full view, an object of dread and horror which appalls the holy rain and the daylight. Get him into the palace as fast as you can.

(*The attendants move over to* OEDIPUS, *and stand by him until the end of the scene.*)

Only his family should see the family shame; this public spectacle is indecent.

OEDIPUS. In God's name—since you have exceeded my hopes and come in so generous a spirit to one so low—do something for me. I ask it in your interest, not mine.

CREON. What is it you are so anxious to have me do?

OEDIPUS. Banish me from this country as fast as you can—to a place where no man can see me or speak to me.

CREON. You can be sure I would have done so already, but first I wanted to ask the god Apollo what should be done.

OEDIPUS. But his command was clear, every word of it; death for the unholy man, the father-killer.

CREON. That *is* what the oracle said. But all the same, in our situation, it is better to inquire what should be done.

OEDIPUS. Will you consult Apollo about anyone as miserable as I?

CREON. Yes, and this time, I take it, you will believe what the god says.

OEDIPUS. Yes. I command you—and beg you—the woman in the palace, see to her burial. She is your sister, you are the man to do this. As for me, do not condemn this city of my fathers to shelter me within its walls, but let me live on the mountain, on Cithaeron, forever linked with my name, the mountain which my mother and father while they still lived chose as my burial place. Let me die there where they tried to kill me.

And yet I know this—no disease or anything else will destroy me. Otherwise I would never have been saved from death in the first place. I was saved—for some strange and dreadful end.

Well, let my destiny go where it will. As for my children, do not concern yourself about the boys, Creon. They are men; and will always find a way to live, wherever they may be. But my two poor helpless girls, who were always at my table, who shared the same food I ate— take care of them for me.

What I wish for most is this. Let me touch them with these hands, as I weep for my sorrows. Please, my lord! Grant my prayer, generous man! If I could hold them I would think I had them with me, as I did when I could see.

(ANTIGONE *and* ISMENE *are led in from the door by a nurse.*)

What's that? I hear something. Oh, God. It is my daughters, weeping. Creon took pity on me, and sent them to me, my dearest ones, my children. Am I right?

CREON. Yes, you are. I did this for you knowing the joy you always took in them, the joy you feel now.

OEDIPUS. Bless you for it! May you be rewarded for sending them. May God watch over you better than He did over me.

Children, where are you? Come here, come to these hands of mine, your brother's hands, the hands that intervened to make your father's once bright eyes so dim. Blind and thoughtless, I became your father, and your mother was my mother, too. I weep for you—see you I cannot—when I think of your future, the bitter life you will lead, the way men will treat you. What gatherings will you go to, what festivals, without returning home in tears, instead of taking part in the ceremonies?

385

And when you come to the age of marriage, who will take the risk, my daughters, and shoulder the burden of reproach which will be directed at my children—and yours? No reproach is missing. Your father killed his father. He sowed the field from which he himself had sprung, and begot you, his children, at the source of his own being. These are the reproaches you will hear. And who will marry you? There is no one who will do so, children; your destiny is clear—to waste away unmarried, childless.

Creon, you are the only father they have now, for we who brought them into the world are both of us destroyed. Do not abandon them to wander husbandless in poverty: they are your own flesh and blood. Do not make them equal to me and my miserable state, but pity them. They are children, they have no protector but you. Promise me this, noble Creon, touch me with your hand to confirm your promise.

And you, children—if you were old enough to understand, I would have much advice to give you. But as it is, I will tell you what to pray for. Pray that you may find a place where you are allowed to live, and for a life happier than your father's.

CREON. You have wept long enough. Now go inside the house.

OEDIPUS. I must obey, though it gives me no pleasure.

CREON. Yes, everything is good in its proper place and time.

OEDIPUS. I will go in then, but on one condition.

CREON. Tell me what it is. I am listening.

OEDIPUS. You must send me into exile—away from Thebes.

CREON. What you ask for is a gift only Apollo can grant.

OEDIPUS. But I am hateful to the gods above all men.

CREON. In that case, they will grant your request at once.

OEDIPUS. You consent, then?

CREON. It is not my habit to say what I don't mean.

OEDIPUS. Then take me away from here at once.

CREON. Come then, but let go of the children.

OEDIPUS. No, don't take them away from me.

CREON. Don't try to be master in everything. What you once won and held did not stay with you all your life long.

CHORUS.[2] Citizens who dwell in Thebes, look at Oedipus here, who knew the answer to the famous riddle and was a power in the land. On his good fortune all the citizens gazed with envy. Into what a stormy sea of dreadful trouble he has come now. Therefore we must call no man happy while he waits to see his last day, not until he has passed the border of life and death without suffering pain.

---

[2] The translator, sharing the opinion of many authorities, believed the following speech to be an addition to the play made by a later producer, but included the lines for those who wished to use them.

Age of Suspicion: The Failure of Plot

The Garden of Forking Paths

Jorge Luis Borges

Translated by Helen Temple and Ruthven Todd

This story has two plots: that of a well-made detective story with a surprise ending and that of a philosophical parable about the nature of time. By combining the two as he does, Borges raises serious questions about the hyperrational assumptions of all well-made detective fiction: that the mind (the detective) can understand everything (no crime is too complicated). Borges seems to be saying that between heaven and earth there are complexities undreamt of in naive applications of Aristotelian plot.

■

To Victoria Ocampo

In his *A History of the World War* (page 212), Captain Liddell Hart reports that a planned offensive by thirteen British divisions, supported by fourteen hundred artillery pieces, against the German line at Serre-Montauban, scheduled for July 24, 1916, had to be postponed until the morning of the 29th. He comments that torrential rain caused this delay—which lacked any special significance. The following deposition, dictated by, read over, and then signed by Dr. Yu Tsun, former teacher of English at the Tsingtao *Hochschule,* casts unsuspected light upon this event. The first two pages are missing.

* * * * * * * * *

387

. . . and I hung up the phone. Immediately I recollected the voice that had spoken in German. It was that of Captain Richard Madden. Madden, in Viktor Runeberg's office, meant the end of all our work and— though this seemed a secondary matter, *or should have seemed so to me* —of our lives also. His being there meant that Runeberg had been arrested or murdered.[1] Before the sun set on this same day, I ran the same risk. Madden was implacable. Rather, to be more accurate, he was obliged to be implacable. An Irishman in the service of England, a man suspected of equivocal feelings if not of actual treachery, how could he fail to welcome and seize upon this extraordinary piece of luck: the discovery, capture and perhaps the death of two agents of Imperial Germany?

I went up to my bedroom. Absurd though the gesture was, I closed and locked the door. I threw myself down on my narrow iron bed, and waited on my back. The never changing rooftops filled the window, and the hazy six o'clock sun hung in the sky. It seemed incredible that this day, a day without warnings or omens, might be that of my implacable death. In despite of my dead father, in despite of having been a child in one of the symmetrical gardens of Hai Feng, was I to die now?

Then I reflected that all things happen, happen to one, precisely *now*. Century follows century, and things happen only in the present. There are countless men in the air, on land and at sea, and all that really happens happens to me. . . . The almost unbearable memory of Madden's long horseface put an end to these wandering thoughts.

In the midst of my hatred and terror (now that it no longer matters to me to speak of terror, now that I have outwitted Richard Madden, now that my neck hankers for the hangman's noose), I knew that the fast-moving and doubtless happy soldier did not suspect that I possessed the Secret—the name of the exact site of the new British artillery park on the Ancre. A bird streaked across the misty sky and, absently, I turned it into an airplane and then that airplane into many in the skies of France, shattering the artillery park under a rain of bombs. If only my mouth, before it should be silenced by a bullet, could shout this name in such a way that it could be heard in Germany. . . . My voice, my human voice, was weak. How could it reach the ear of the Chief? The ear of that sick and hateful man who knew nothing of Runeberg or of me except that we were in Staffordshire. A man who, sitting in his arid Berlin office, leafed infinitely through newspapers, looking in vain for news from us. I said aloud, "I must flee."

I sat up on the bed, in senseless and perfect silence, as if Madden was already peering at me. Something—perhaps merely a desire to prove

---

[1] A malicious and outlandish statement. In point of fact, Captain Richard Madden had been attacked by the Prussian spy Hans Rabener, alias Viktor Runeberg, who drew an automatic pistol when Madden appeared with orders for the spy's arrest. Madden, in self defense, had inflicted wounds of which the spy later died. —*Note by the manuscript editor.* [The footnotes in this story are Borges'.]

my total penury to myself—made me empty out my pockets. I found just what I knew I was going to find. The American watch, the nickel-plated chain and the square coin, the key ring with the useless but compromising keys to Runeberg's office, the notebook, a letter which I decided to destroy at once (and which I did not destroy), a five shilling piece, two single shillings and some pennies, a red and blue pencil, a handkerchief—and a revolver with a single bullet. Absurdly I held it and weighed it in my hand, to give myself courage. Vaguely I thought that a pistol shot can be heard for a great distance.

In ten minutes I had developed my plan. The telephone directory gave me the name of the one person capable of passing on the information. He lived in a suburb of Fenton, less than half an hour away by train.

I am a timorous man. I can say it now, now that I have brought my incredibly risky plan to an end. It was not easy to bring about, and I know that its execution was terrible. I did not do it for Germany—no! Such a barbarous country is of no importance to me, particularly since it had degraded me by making me become a spy. Furthermore, I knew an Englishman—a modest man—who, for me, is as great as Goethe. I did not speak with him for more than an hour, but during that time, he *was* Goethe.

I carried out my plan because I felt the Chief had some fear of those of my race, of those uncountable forebears whose culmination lies in me. I wished to prove to him that a yellow man could save his armies. Besides, I had to escape the Captain. His hands and voice could, at any moment, knock and beckon at my door.

Silently, I dressed, took leave of myself in the mirror, went down the stairs, sneaked a look at the quiet street, and went out. The station was not far from my house, but I thought it more prudent to take a cab. I told myself that I thus ran less chance of being recognized. The truth is that, in the deserted street, I felt infinitely visible and vulnerable. I recall that I told the driver to stop short of the main entrance. I got out with a painful and deliberate slowness.

I was going to the village of Ashgrove, but took a ticket for a station further on. The train would leave in a few minutes, at eight-fifty. I hurried, for the next would not go until half past nine. There was almost no one on the platform. I walked through the carriages. I remember some farmers, a woman dressed in mourning, a youth deep in Tacitus' Annals and a wounded, happy soldier.

At last the train pulled out. A man I recognized ran furiously, but vainly, the length of the platform. It was Captain Richard Madden. Shattered, trembling, I huddled in the distant corner of the seat, as far as possible from the fearful window.

From utter terror I passed into a state of almost abject happiness. I told myself that the duel had already started and that I had won the first encounter by besting my adversary in his first attack—even if it was only for forty minutes—by an accident of fate. I argued that so small a victory prefigured a total victory. I argued that it was not so trivial, that were it not for the precious accident of the train schedule, I would be in prison or dead. I argued, with no less sophism, that my timorous happiness was proof that I was man enough to bring this adventure to a successful conclusion. From my weakness I drew strength that never left me.

I foresee that man will resign himself each day to new abominations, that soon only soldiers and bandits will be left. To them I offer this advice: *Whosoever would undertake some atrocious enterprise should act as if it were already accomplished, should impose upon himself a future as irrevocable as the past.*

Thus I proceeded, while with the eyes of a man already dead, I contemplated the fluctuations of the day which would probably be my last, and watched the diffuse coming of night.

The train crept along gently, amid ash trees. It slowed down and stopped, almost in the middle of a field. No one called the name of a station. "Ashgrove?" I asked some children on the platform. "Ashgrove," they replied. I got out.

A lamp lit the platform, but the children's faces remained in a shadow. One of them asked me: "Are you going to Dr. Stephen Albert's house?" Without waiting for my answer, another said: "The house is a good distance away but you won't get lost if you take the road to the left and bear to the left at every crossroad." I threw them a coin (my last), went down some stone steps and started along a deserted road. At a slight incline, the road ran downhill. It was a plain dirt way, and overhead the branches of trees intermingled, while a round moon hung low in the sky as if to keep me company.

For a moment I thought that Richard Madden might in some way have divined my desperate intent. At once I realized that this would be impossible. The advice about turning always to the left reminded me that such was the common formula for finding the central courtyard of certain labyrinths. I know something about labyrinths. Not for nothing am I the great-grandson of Ts'ui Pên. He was Governor of Yunnan and gave up temporal power to write a novel with more characters than there are in the *Hung Lou Mêng*, and to create a maze in which all men would lose themselves. He spent thirteen years on these oddly assorted tasks before he was assassinated by a stranger. His novel had no sense to it and nobody ever found his labyrinth.

Under the trees of England I meditated on this lost and perhaps mythical labyrinth. I imagined it untouched and perfect on the secret summit of some mountain; I imagined it drowned under rice paddies or beneath the sea; I imagined it infinite, made not only of eight-sided pavilions and of twisting paths but also of rivers, provinces and kingdoms. . . . I thought of a maze of mazes, of a sinuous, ever growing maze which would take in both past and future and would somehow involve the stars.

Lost in these imaginary illusions I forgot my destiny—that of the

390

hunted. For an undetermined period of time I felt myself cut off from the world, an abstract spectator. The hazy and murmuring countryside, the moon, the decline of the evening, stirred within me. Going down the gently sloping road I could not feel fatigue. The evening was at once intimate and infinite.

The road kept descending and branching off, through meadows misty in the twilight. A high-pitched and almost syllabic music kept coming and going, moving with the breeze, blurred by the leaves and by distance.

I thought that a man might be an enemy of other men, of the differing moments of other men, but never an enemy of a country: not of fireflies, words, gardens, streams, or the West wind.

Meditating thus I arrived at a high, rusty iron gate. Through the railings I could see an avenue bordered with poplar trees and also a kind of summer house or pavilion. Two things dawned on me at once, the first trivial and the second almost incredible: the music came from the pavilion and that music was Chinese. That was why I had accepted it fully, without paying it any attention. I do not remember whether there was a bell, a push-button, or whether I attracted attention by clapping my hands. The stuttering sparks of the music kept on.

But from the end of the avenue, from the main house, a lantern approached; a lantern which alternately, from moment to moment, was crisscrossed or put out by the trunks of the trees; a paper lantern shaped like a drum and colored like the moon. A tall man carried it. I could not see his face for the light blinded me.

He opened the gate and spoke slowly in my language.

"I see that the worthy Hsi P'eng has troubled himself to see to relieving my solitude. No doubt you want to see the garden?"

Recognizing the name of one of our consuls, I replied, somewhat taken aback.

"The garden?"

"The garden of forking paths."

Something stirred in my memory and I said, with incomprehensible assurance:

"The garden of my ancestor, Ts'ui Pên."

"Your ancestor? Your illustrious ancestor? Come in."

The damp path zigzagged like those of my childhood. When we reached the house, we went into a library filled with books from both East and West. I recognized some large volumes bound in yellow silk— manuscripts of the Lost Encyclopedia which was edited by the Third Emperor of the Luminous Dynasty. They had never been printed. A phonograph record was spinning near a bronze phoenix. I remember also a rose-glazed jar and yet another, older by many centuries, of that blue color which our potters copied from the Persians. . . .

Stephen Albert was watching me with a smile on his face. He was, as I have said, remarkably tall. His face was deeply lined and he had

391

gray eyes and a gray beard. There was about him something of the priest, and something of the sailor. Later, he told me he had been a missionary in Tientsin before he "had aspired to become a Sinologist."

We sat down, I upon a large, low divan, he with his back to the window and to a large circular clock. I calculated that my pursuer, Richard Madden, could not arrive in less than an hour. My irrevocable decision could wait.

"A strange destiny," said Stephen Albert, "that of Ts'ui Pên—Governor of his native province, learned in astronomy, in astrology and tireless in the interpretation of the canonical books, a chess player, a famous poet and a calligrapher. Yet he abandoned all to make a book and a labyrinth. He gave up all the pleasures of oppression, justice, of a well-stocked bed, of banquets, and even of erudition, and shut himself up in the Pavilion of the Limpid Sun for thirteen years. At his death, his heirs found only a mess of manuscripts. The family, as you doubtless know, wished to consign them to the fire, but the executor of the estate—a Taoist or a Buddhist monk—insisted on their publication."

"Those of the blood of Ts'ui Pên," I replied, "still curse the memory of that monk. Such a publication was madness. The book is a shapeless mass of contradictory rough drafts. I examined it once upon a time: the hero dies in the third chapter, while in the fourth he is alive. As for that other enterprise of Ts'ui Pên . . . his Labyrinth . . ."

"Here is the Labyrinth," Albert said, pointing to a tall, lacquered writing cabinet.

"An ivory labyrinth?" I exclaimed. "A tiny labyrinth indeed . . . !"

"A symbolic labyrinth," he corrected me. "An invisible labyrinth of time. I, a barbarous Englishman, have been given the key to this transparent mystery. After more than a hundred years most of the details are irrecoverable, lost beyond all recall, but it isn't hard to image what must have happened. At one time, Ts'ui Pên must have said; 'I am going into seclusion to write a book,' and at another, 'I am retiring to construct a maze.' Everyone assumed these were separate activities. No one realized that the book and the labyrinth were one and the same. The Pavilion of the Limpid Sun was set in the middle of an intricate garden. This may have suggested the idea of a physical maze.

"Ts'ui Pên died. In all the vast lands which once belonged to your family, no one could find the labyrinth. The novel's confusion suggested that *it* was the labyrinth. Two circumstances showed me the direct solution to the problem. First, the curious legend that Ts'ui Pên had proposed to create an infinite maze, second, a fragment of a letter which I discovered."

Albert rose. For a few moments he turned his back to me. He opened the top drawer in the high black and gilded writing cabinet. He returned holding in his hand a piece of paper which had once been crimson but which had faded with the passage of time: it was rose colored, tenuous, quadrangular. Ts'ui Pên's calligraphy was justly famous. Eagerly, but without understanding, I read the words which a man of my own blood had written with a small brush: "I leave to various future times, but not to all, my garden of forking paths."

I handed back the sheet of paper in silence. Albert went on:

"Before I discovered this letter, I kept asking myself how a book could be infinite. I could not imagine any other than a cyclic volume, circular. A volume whose last page would be the same as the first and so have the possibility of continuing indefinitely. I recalled, too, the night in the middle of *The Thousand and One Nights* when Queen Scheherezade, through a magical mistake on the part of her copyist, started to tell the story of *The Thousand and One Nights,* with the risk of again arriving at the night upon which she will relate it, and thus on to infinity. I also imagined a Platonic hereditary work, passed on from father to son, to which each individual would add a new chapter or correct, with pious care, the work of his elders.

"These conjectures gave me amusement, but none seemed to have the remotest application to the contradictory chapters of Ts'ui Pên. At this point, I was sent from Oxford the manuscript you have just seen.

"Naturally, my attention was caught by the sentence, 'I leave to various future times, but not to all, my garden of forking paths.' I had no sooner read this, than I understood. *The Garden of Forking Paths* was the chaotic novel itself. The phrase 'to various future times, but not to all' suggested the image of bifurcating in time, not in space. Rereading the whole work confirmed this theory. In all fiction, when a man is faced with alternatives he chooses one at the expense of the others. In the almost unfathomable Ts'ui Pên, he chooses—simultaneously—all of them. He thus *creates* various futures, various times which start others that will in their turn branch out and bifurcate in other times. This is the cause of the contradictions in the novel.

"Fang, let us say, has a secret. A stranger knocks at his door. Fang makes up his mind to kill him. Naturally there are various possible outcomes. Fang can kill the intruder, the intruder can kill Fang, both can be saved, both can die and so on and so on. In Ts'ui Pên's work, all the possible solutions occur, each one being the point of departure for other bifurcations. Sometimes the pathways of this labyrinth converge. For example, you come to this house; but in other possible pasts you are my enemy; in others my friend.

"If you will put up with my atrocious pronunciation, I would like to read you a few pages of your ancestor's work."

His countenance, in the bright circle of lamplight, was certainly that of an ancient, but it shone with something unyielding, even immortal.

With slow precision, he read two versions of the same epic chapter. In the first, an army marches into battle over a desolate mountain pass. The bleak and somber aspect of the rocky landscape made the soldiers feel that life itself was of little value, and so they won the battle easily. In the second, the same army passes through a palace where a banquet is in progress. The splendor of the feast remained a memory throughout the glorious battle, and so victory followed.

With proper veneration I listened to these old tales, although perhaps with less admiration for them in themselves than for the fact that they had been thought out by one of my own blood, and that a man of a distant empire had given them back to me, in the last stage of a desperate adventure, on a Western island. I remember the final words, repeated at the end of each version like a secret command: "Thus the heroes fought, with tranquil heart and bloody sword. They were resigned to killing and to dying."

At that moment I felt within me and around me something invisible and intangible pullulating. It was not the pullulation of two divergent, parallel, and finally converging armies, but an agitation more inaccessible, more intimate, prefigured by them in some way. Stephen Albert continued:

"I do not think that your illustrious ancestor toyed idly with variations. I do not find it believable that he would waste thirteen years laboring over a never ending experiment in rhetoric. In your country the novel is an inferior genre; in Ts'ui Pên's period, it was a despised one. Ts'ui Pên was a fine novelist but he was also a man of letters who, doubtless, considered himself more than a mere novelist. The testimony of his contemporaries attests to this, and certainly the known facts of his life confirm his leanings toward the metaphysical and the mystical. Philosophical conjectures take up the greater part of his novel. I know that of all problems, none disquieted him more, and none concerned him more than the profound one of time. Now then, this is the *only* problem that does not figure in the pages of *The Garden*. He does not even use the word which means *time*. How can these voluntary omissions be explained?"

I proposed various solutions, all of them inadequate. We discussed them. Finally Stephen Albert said: "In a guessing game to which the answer is chess, which word is the only one prohibited?" I thought for a moment and then replied:

"The word is *chess*."

"Precisely," said Albert. "*The Garden of Forking Paths* is an enormous guessing game, or parable, in which the subject is time. The rules of the game forbid the use of the word itself. To eliminate a word completely, to refer to it by means of inept phrases and obvious paraphrases, is perhaps the best way of drawing attention to it. This, then, is the tortuous method of approach preferred by the oblique Ts'ui Pên in every meandering of his interminable novel. I have gone over hundreds of manuscripts, I have corrected errors introduced by careless copyists, I have worked out the plan from this chaos, I have restored, or believe I have restored, the original. I have translated the whole work. I can state categorically that not once has the word *time* been used in the whole book.

"The explanation is obvious. *The Garden of Forking Paths* is a picture, incomplete yet not false, of the universe such as Ts'ui Pên con-

394

ceived it to be. Differing from Newton and Schopenhauer, your ancestor did not think of time as absolute and uniform. He believed in an infinite series of times, in a dizzily growing, ever spreading network of diverging, converging and parallel times. This web of time—the strands of which approach one another, bifurcate, intersect or ignore each other through the centuries—embraces *every* possibility. We do not exist in most of them. In some you exist and not I, while in others I do, and you do not, and in yet others both of us exist. In this one, in which chance has favored me, you have come to my gate. In another, you, crossing the garden, have found me dead. In yet another, I say these very same words, but am an error, a phantom."

"In all of them," I enunciated, with a tremor in my voice. "I deeply appreciate and am grateful to you for the restoration of Ts'ui Pên's garden."

"Not in *all*," he murmured with a smile. "Time is forever dividing itself toward innumerable futures and in one of them I am your enemy."

Once again I sensed the pullulation of which I have already spoken. It seemed to me that the dew-damp garden surrounding the house was infinitely saturated with invisible people. All were Albert and myself, secretive, busy and multiform in other dimensions of time. I lifted my eyes and the short nightmare disappeared. In the black and yellow garden there was only a single man, but this man was as strong as a statue and this man was walking up the path and he was Captain Richard Madden.

"The future exists now," I replied. "But I am your friend. Can I take another look at the letter?"

Albert rose from his seat. He stood up tall as he opened the top drawer of the high writing cabinet. For a moment his back was again turned to me. I had the revolver ready. I fired with the utmost care: Albert fell without a murmur, at once. I swear that his death was instantaneous, as if he had been struck by lightning.

What remains is unreal and unimportant. Madden broke in and arrested me. I have been condemned to hang. Abominably, I have yet triumphed! The secret name of the city to be attacked got through to Berlin. Yesterday it was bombed. I read the news in the same English newspapers which were trying to solve the riddle of the murder of the learned Sinologist Stephen Albert by the unknown Yu Tsun. The Chief, however, had already solved this mystery. He knew that my problem was to shout, with my feeble voice, above the tumult of war, the name of the city called Albert, and that I had no other course open to me than to kill someone of that name. He does not know, for no one can, of my infinite penitence and sickness of the heart.

FROM Nausea

Jean-Paul Sartre

Translated by Lloyd Alexander

Sartre (1905–   ) is a philosopher as well as the author of novels, plays, and short stories. *Nausea* (1938) is his first novel, but it deploys the major concerns that continue to inform all its author's work. Sartre is concerned with the effect of plots (which are here sardonically called adventures) on our lives. How does a projected end vitiate the unique possibility for freedom in the present moment? Must all beginnings become a middle? If so, what principles might ensure the validity of such connections? What glue will serve to hold together the fragments of our lives, give their totality a meaning? As we saw earlier, plots exclude varying degrees of contingency. Therefore the hero of this novel, Roquentin, a poet of contingency, feels they are existential straightjackets.

■

"Have you had many adventures, Monsieur?"

"A few," I answer mechanically, throwing myself back to avoid his tainted breath. Yes. I said that mechanically, without thinking. In fact, I am generally proud of having had so many adventures. But today, I had barely pronounced the words than I was seized with contrition; it seems as though I am lying, that I have never had the slightest adventure in my life, or rather, that I don't even know what the word means any more. At the same time, I am weighed down by the same discouragement I had in Hanoi—four years ago when Mercier pressed me to join him and I stared at a Khmer statuette without answering. And the IDEA is there, this great white mass which so disgusted me then: I hadn't seen if for four years.

"Could I ask you . . ." the Self-Taught Man begins . . .

By Jove! To tell him one of those famous tales. But I won't say another word on the subject.

"There," I say, bending down over his narrow shoulders, putting my finger on a photograph, "there, that's Santillana, the prettiest town in Spain."

"The Santillana of Gil Blas? I didn't believe it existed. Ah, Monsieur, how profitable your conversation is. One can tell you've travelled."

I put out the Self-Taught Man after filling his pockets with post cards, prints and photos. He left enchanted and I switched off the light. I am alone now. Not quite alone. Hovering in front of me is still this idea. It has rolled itself into a ball, it stays there like a large cat; it explains nothing, it does not move, and contents itself with saying no. No, I haven't had any adventures.

I fill my pipe, light it and stretch out on the bed, throwing a coat over my legs. What astonishes me is to feel so sad and exhausted. Even if it were true—that I never had any adventures—what difference would that make to me? First, it seems to be a pure question of words. The business at Meknes, for example, I was thinking about a little while ago: a Moroccan jumped on me and wanted to stab me with an enormous knife. But I hit him just below the temple . . . then he began shouting in Arabic and a swarm of lousy beggars came up and chased us all the way to Souk Attarin. Well, you can call that by any name you like, in any case, it was an event which *happened to* ME.

It is completely dark and I can't tell whether my pipe is lit. A trolley passes: red light on the ceiling. Then a heavy truck which makes the house tremble. It must be six o'clock.

I have never had adventures. Things have happened to me, events, incidents, anything you like. But no adventures. It isn't a question of words; I am beginning to understand. There is something to which I clung more than all the rest—without completely realizing it. It wasn't love. Heaven forbid, not glory, not money. It was . . . I had imagined that at certain times my life could take on a rare and precious quality. There was no need for extraordinary circumstances: all I asked for was a little precision. There is nothing brilliant about my life now: but from time to time, for example, when they play music in the cafés, I look back and tell myself: in old days, in London, Meknes, Tokyo, I have known great moments, I have had adventures. Now I am deprived of this. I have suddenly learned, without any apparent reason, that I have been lying to myself for ten years. And naturally, everything they tell about in books can happen in real life, but not in the same way. It is to this way of happening that I clung so tightly.

The beginnings would have had to be real beginnings. Alas! Now I see so clearly what I wanted. Real beginnings are like a fanfare of trumpets, like the first notes of a jazz tune, cutting short tedium, making for continuity: then you say about these evenings within evenings: "I was out for a walk, it was an evening in May." You walk, the moon has just risen, you feel lazy, vacant, a little empty. And then suddenly you think: "Something has happened." No matter what: a slight rustling in the shadow, a thin silhouette crossing the street. But this paltry event is not like the others: suddenly you see that it is the beginning of a great shape whose outlines are lost in mist and you tell yourself, "Something is beginning."

Something is beginning in order to end: adventure does not let itself be drawn out; it only makes sense when dead. I am drawn, irrevocably, towards this death which is perhaps mine as well. Each instant appears only as part of a sequence. I cling to each instant with all my heart: I know that it is unique, irreplaceable—and yet I would not raise a finger to stop it from being annihilated. This last moment I am spending—in Berlin, in London—in the arms of a woman casually met two days ago— moment I love passionately, woman I may adore—all is going to end, I know it. Soon I shall leave for another country. I shall never rediscover either this woman or this night. I grasp at each second, trying to suck it dry: nothing happens which I do not seize, which I do not fix forever in myself, nothing, neither the fugitive tenderness of those lovely eyes, nor the noises of the street, nor the false dawn of early morning: and even so the minute passes and I do not hold it back, I like to see it pass.

All of a sudden something breaks off sharply. The adventure is over, time resumes its daily routine. I turn; behind me, this beautiful melodious form sinks entirely into the past. It grows smaller, contracts as it declines, and now the end makes one with the beginning. Following this gold spot with my eyes I think I would accept—even if I had to risk death, lose a fortune, a friend—to live it all over again, in the same circumstances, from end to end. But an adventure never returns nor is prolonged.

Yes, it's what I wanted—what I still want. I am so happy when a Negress sings: what summits would I not reach if *my own life* made the subject of the melody.

The idea is still there, unnameable. It waits, peacefully. Now it seems to say:

"Yes? Is *that* what you wanted? Well, that's exactly what you've never had (remember you fooled yourself with words, you called the glitter of travel, the love of women, quarrels, and trinkets adventure) and this is what you'll never have—and no one other than yourself."

But Why? WHY?

Saturday noon:

The Self-Taught Man did not see me come into the reading-room. He was sitting at the end of a table in the back; he had set his book down in front of him but he was not reading. He was smiling at a seedy-looking student who often comes to the library. The student allowed himself to be looked at for a moment, then suddenly stuck his tongue out and made a horrible face. The Self-Taught Man blushed, hurriedly plunged his nose into his book and became absorbed by his reading.

I have reconsidered my thoughts of yesterday. I was completely dry: it made no difference to me whether there had been no adventures. I was only curious to know whether there could *never be any*.

This is what I thought: for the most banal even to become an adventure, you must (and this is enough) begin to recount it. This is what fools people: a man is always a teller of tales, he lives surrounded by his stories and the stories of others, he sees everything that happens to him through them; and he tries to live his own life as if he were telling a story.

But you have to choose: live or tell. For example, when I was in Hamburg, with that Erna girl I didn't trust and who was afraid of me, I led a funny sort of life. But I was in the middle of it, I didn't think about it. And then one evening, in a little café in San Pauli, she left me to go to the ladies' room. I stayed alone, there was a phonograph playing "Blue Skies." I began to tell myself what had happened since I landed. I told myself, "The third evening, as I was going into a dance hall called *La Grotte Bleue*, I noticed a large woman, half seas over. And that woman is the one I am waiting for now, listening to 'Blue Skies,' the woman who is going to come back and sit down at my right and put her arms around my neck." Then I felt violently that I was having an adventure. But Erna came back and sat down beside me, she wound her arms around my neck and I hated her without knowing why. I understand now: one had to begin living again and the adventure was fading out.

Nothing happens while you live. The scenery changes, people come in and go out, that's all. There are no beginnings. Days are tacked on to days without rhyme or reason, an interminable, monotonous addition. From time to time you make a semi-total: you say: I've been travelling for three years, I've been in Bouville for three years. Neither is there any end: you never leave a woman, a friend, a city in one go. And then everything looks alike: Shanghai, Moscow, Algiers, everything is the same after two weeks. There are moments—rarely—when you make a landmark, you realize that you're going with a woman, in some messy business. The time of a flash. After that, the procession starts again, you begin to add up hours and days: Monday, Tuesday, Wednesday. April, May, June. 1924, 1925, 1926.

That's living. But everything changes when you tell about life; it's a change no one notices: the proof is that people talk about true stories. As if there could possibly be true stories; things happen one way and we tell about them in the opposite sense. You seem to start at the beginning: "It was a fine autumn evening in 1922. I was a notary's clerk in Marommes." And in reality you have started at the end. It was there, invisible and present, it is the one which gives to words the pomp and value of a beginning. "I was out walking, I had left the town without realizing it, I was thinking about my money troubles." This sentence, taken simply for what it is, means that the man was absorbed, morose, a hundred leagues from an adventure, exactly in the mood to let things happen without noticing them. But the end is there, transforming everything. For us, the man is already the hero of the story. His moroseness, his money troubles are much more precious than ours, they are all gilded by the light of future passions. And the story goes on in the reverse: instants have stopped piling themselves in a lighthearted way one on top of the other, they are snapped up by the end of the story which draws them and each one of them, in turn, draws out the preceding instant: "It was night, the street was deserted." The phrase is cast out negligently, it seems superfluous; but we do not let ourselves be caught and we put it aside: this is a piece of information whose value we shall subsequently appreciate. And we feel that the hero has lived all the details of this night like annunciations, promises, or even that he lived only those that were promises, blind and deaf to all that did not herald adventure. We forget that the future was not yet there; the man was walking in a night without forethought, a night which offered him a choice of dull rich prizes, and he did not make his choice.

I wanted the moments of my life to follow and order themselves like those of a life remembered. You might as well try and catch time by the tail.

Frame-Tale

John Barth

This story is to the collection of tales (*Lost in the Funhouse*) it precedes what the Shahrazad story is to the other tales in *The Thousand Nights and a Night*. That is why it is called "Frame-Tale." But just as a painting indicates the kind of frame (ornate, simple, large, small, and so forth) that is appropriate to it, so does a story cycle determine the correct narrative for containing itself. The tale of love and magic that surrounds the ancient Arabian cycle is proper not only because its texture and idiom are a key to the same qualities in the other stories; it also motivates them, makes their telling logical. And since the Shahrazad plot has the most definitive conclusion of all the stories, it nicely rounds off a cycle that otherwise might go on forever. Even though the cycle *as a series* raises the possibility of never stopping, the linear—if interrupted—progress of the Shahrazad plot's beginning-middle-end is given priority and can thus contain the threat of an endlessness that would preclude order, or at least the ability of more human beings to see it.

Modern authors, however, find it increasingly difficult to create plots that are ordered, when everything else in the world seems to be so *dis*-ordered. While the attempt to find a literary form adequate to the complexity of modern life has taken many directions, most have in common a suspicion of linear plots. Such plots seem somehow too simple, unrealistic. Thus the frame tale for a modern story cycle will avoid the shapeliness that derives from a happy marriage in the conclusion, such as the Shahrazad story has. But this does not mean that the modern frame tale will necessarily be less well made or less appropriate to the narratives it is designed to contain.

Lost in the Funhouse is a collection of thirteen very complex plots that a fourteenth (our selection) is intended to frame. At first it is difficult to see how one sentence—and an unfinished one, at that—could fulfill this intention, especially in view of the fact that it occurs only at the beginning of the cycle, unlike other, more traditional frame tales, which begin on the first page and end on the last, with the other stories sandwiched in between. But our sentence is not just unfinished—it is endless.

After the page is cut and twisted according to the directions, what you get is a Möbius strip (named after the nineteenth-century German mathematician who invented it), and it, like the circle, is infinite. Thus Barth seems to be saying in the figure as well as in the words of the sentence that whatever tales may follow it are but episodes in the endless story that men have been telling each other since first they acquired language, the story made up of all the other stories that have been told since that ancient time that was "Once upon a."

■

Frame-Tale

Cut on dotted line.
Twist end once and fasten
AB to *ab*, *CD* to *cd*.

(continued)

ONCE UPON A TIME THERE

D

C

A

B

WAS A STORY THAT BEGAN

(*continued*)

IV.
Shaping a Self

"In the beginning God created the Heaven and the Earth." There is a great truth in these words: every genesis is an act of divergence. This, and not that. The process that grows out of such an initial separation is an increasingly more refined series of oppositions that finally, in their totality, define a unique end. Thus, in the Bible, God goes on to separate the waters from the land, night from day, whales in the sea from birds in the air, until he has formed the planet Earth in all its multiple specificity. Astronomers and physicists may be less certain about how our world was born, but most of their theories also begin by assuming a division of matter not totally unlike that captured in the Bible's poetry.

What is true of matter is no less true of consciousness. It too begins in an act (an awareness) of differentiation. Adam is simply the last created of all the animals until he eats the fruit of the tree of knowledge and becomes aware of the distinction between good and evil. The Darwinian view suggests that some apelike creature in the primordial past must have puzzled out one day that he was not a stone or a tree. Human evolution is a history of such discoveries. We are not apes; we are not Cro-Magnons; we are not cavemen at all. The problem in each case was, If I am not *that* kind of thing, what kind *am* I, then? It is in such a question that identity is born. How do I define myself as a particular *something* against an unspecific *everything*?

We can see this definition in later stages of human evolution, which are neatly dramatized in the history of Tarzan. He is just another member of Kerchak's band of apes, remarkable only for his hairlessness, until one day he teaches himself to read: "No longer did he feel shame for his hairless body . . . for now his reason told him that he was of a different race from his wild and hairy companions." Now that he knows what he is *not*, Tarzan's next problem is to know who he is: " 'Look!' he

403

cried, 'Apes of Kerchak. See what Tarzan, the mighty killer, has done. Who else among you has ever killed one of Numa's [the lion's] people? Tarzan is the mightiest amongst you for Tarzan is no ape. Tarzan is - - - -' But here he stopped, for in the language of the anthropoids there was no word for man." [1]

Tarzan can find no way to express his sensed uniqueness so that it will be comprehensible to the others or to himself because no words exist to express this new conception of difference. But even when words are not lacking, as they are for Tarzan, those that are available may not be adequate to the conception of self. In order to understand each other the apes and Tarzan must agree to share their language with each other. But what sets Tarzan apart from the apes is so new and singular that it is not available to the discourse they have in common.

Adam Parry, a distinguished student of Homer, has suggested that Achilles has the same problem in the *Iliad*. Achilles is the greatest of all the heroes before Troy, yet he becomes disillusioned with the restrictive category of hero, sensing that it does not exhaust his uniqueness. He

> is thus the one Homeric hero who does not accept the common language, and feels that it does not correspond to reality. . . . [But] Homer, in fact, has no language, no terms, in which to express this kind of basic disillusionment with society and the external world. . . . Neither Homer, then, in his own person as narrator, nor the characters he dramatizes, can speak any language other than the one which reflects the assumptions of heroic society. [2]

Perhaps the most compelling metaphor for the inability of language to express an essential self is contained in the encounter of anthropologists with the the tribes they seek to study. It is in such confrontations between two distinct cultures that the subtlest questions about relationships between self and society are raised. Claude Lévi-Strauss, a French anthropologist, makes this point eloquently. After a long journey in the wilds of Brazil he finally comes upon the Mundé, a tribe no white man had seen before. He cannot, of course, communicate with them. However, he says,

> even without knowing the language, and although I had no interpreter, I could try to penetrate certain aspects of the natives' thought. . . . And yet, although this adventure was begun with such high enthusiasm, it left me with a feeling of emptiness. . . . I had come upon "my" savages. But alas, they were all *too* savage. . . . They were as close to me as an image seen in a looking-glass: I could touch, but not understand them. [3]

[1] Edgar Rice Burroughs, *Tarzan of the Apes* (New York, 1966; orig. pub. 1912), p. 85.

[2] Adam Parry, "The Language of Achilles," in G. S. Kirk, ed., *The Language and Background of Homer* (Cambridge, 1964), p. 51.

[3] Claude Lévi-Strauss, *Tristes Tropiques*, tr. John Russell (New York, 1965), p. 326.

Are we not all like the anthropologist and "his" savages? Are not the various encounters with others we experience, even in such familiar contexts as home, school, and work, similar to that described above? Our home towns are also Brazils. That is, even when we speak the same language and share the same culture as the others about us, we still feel their inability to define or contain our deepest selves.

Such is the discovery Tarzan and Achilles make: that language is too small a cage to contain them. We have all felt at one time or another the inability of language to express our exact thoughts. How crude is the language of emotion, how many nuances of feeling do we experience between the poles of love and hate for which there are no words? The modern French writer Antonin Artaud once said, "There is no correlation for me between *words* and the exact states of my being. . . . I am the man who has best felt the astounding disorder of his language in its relation to his thought."[4] The distance between words and things, especially the distance between his sense of himself and the ability of language to express that sense, was an obsession with Artaud. Increasingly unable to close this gap, he finally went insane.

We find the imprecision of language most troubling when, as in our examples, we discover that there are no words to express our own uniqueness, our "self." That is why "proper names" are so often felt to be improper when they must stand in for people. If a friend tells us over the phone that he has bought a new desk, we already have a pretty good idea of the desk without having seen it: it will have legs and a flat surface to write on. But what if the same friend tells us he has met someone unfamiliar to us whose name is Bob? What is a "Bob"? In order to know what "Bob" means, we must know the person who gives particular meaning to this name. The person himself is the necessary context here.

But even after we meet Bob, it will be apparent that he is more than his name. And Bob himself will feel that not only is he more than his name, he is also more than all the other categories we use to define people: he is not *just* a man, a son, or a husband, not *just* a student or a baker or a candlestick-maker. Each of these words represents a role, and behind the mask each of these roles provides is a face, a self, that is not expressed by any of them. Consider another example from the *Iliad*: as he sets off for his final battle, Hector, the greatest of the Trojan heroes, bids farewell to his family. His small son is frightened by Hector's helmet, which covers the face. Hector takes it off, and the boy is reassured: he has recognized the specific face of his father, which had been hidden by the mask of the warrior. Just as Hector the father has been subsumed by Hector the hero, so are we all constantly putting on and taking off "uniforms," roles that make us appear similar to everyone else who has assumed the same guise.

Mary Shelley's novel *Frankenstein* (1816) is another parable of identity that has struck deep roots into the popular imagination. It is

[4] *Antonin Artaud Anthology*, ed. Jack Hirschman (San Francisco, 1965), p. 37.

quite literally the story of a man who shapes a self, and the paradox that this self is another accounts for much of the book's power. The scientist, Victor Frankenstein, says, "It was on a dreary night in November that [first] . . . I saw the dull yellow eye of the creature open. . . ." Later the same evening, Frankenstein is awakened: "I beheld the wretch—the miserable monster whom I had created. He held up the curtain of the bed; his eyes . . . were fixed on me. His jaws opened, and he muttered some inarticulate sounds. . . ." [5] Like Tarzan and Achilles, the creature can find no words to express himself—at this point he has no self. He does not even have a role provided by the language of a context-bestowing society such as the band of apes or the company of heroes. Only later and very gradually does he learn to perceive discrete objects. At first the world is for him as it was in Genesis, "without form and void." He says, "I knew and could *distinguish* nothing . . . no distinct ideas occupied my mind, all was confused. I felt light, and hunger, and thirst, and darkness; innumerable sounds rang in my ears, and on all sides various scents saluted me. . . ." [6] But just as the first Adam did, he learns to make further and more complicated distinctions (somewhat like Helen Keller in *The Miracle Worker,* but without anyone else's aid or comfort). He learns to read and to speak. He observes a woodsman's family in their interrelationships and at their daily tasks, learning from them and their books how to be human.

But just as the apes have no concept for man born of woman, men have no concept for a creature born of the charnel house. Thus, when the "monster" finally attempts to enter the circle of the little family, it is only the blind grandfather who "recognizes" him. When the other members of the family return, they see not the inner face of the pathetic creature, but only the mask of the "monster." Blinded by appearances, they flee in terror.

In H. G. Wells' novel *The Invisible Man* (1897) the hero's uniqueness consists in his invisibility, a singularity that occasions fear and misunderstanding in others. Victor Frankenstein's creation has the opposite problem: it is his singular *presence* that cuts him off from others. Finally the creature is forced to become his mask; he "loses face" and turns into a monster, the only concept available in the language of interaction that surrounds him.

What we have been saying about the discrepancy between faces and masks should not suggest that masks as such are a bad thing. We need them in order to live together. If we all insisted on projecting only what was uniquely our own, we would have in the area of identity what happened in the area of language after the Tower of Babel had been constructed. In Lewis Carroll's *Through the Looking Glass* (1872) Humpty Dumpty says "When I use a word . . . it means just what I

[5] Signet Classics Edition (New York, 1965), pp. 56–57.
[6] *Ibid.,* pp. 98–99. Italics ours.

choose it to mean—neither more nor less." If we all insisted on giving words our own meaning, no one else could understand us, and we could understand no one else. The *pathos* of such radical solipsism was a major subject for nineteenth-century, the *danger* of it for twentieth-century fiction. In *Crime and Punishment* (1865) Raskolnikov has a dream in which a plague spreads across Europe: "Men attacked [by the plague] became at once mad and furious. . . . Whole villages, whole towns and peoples went mad from the infection. All were excited and did not understand one another. Each thought that he alone had the truth. . . . Men killed each other in senseless spite . . . all men and all things were involved in destruction." [7] What is amusing in Humpty Dumpty has become sinister in our own time, as can be seen from the very titles of the numberless books that deal with alienation in modern life: Saul Bellow's *Dangling Man* (1944) or *The Victim* (1947); or Sartre's play *No Exit* (1944); the list could be extended indefinitely.

As Erving Goffman, an American sociologist, points out, we need masks to ensure our communality;

> The combined effect of the rule of self-respect and the rule of considerateness is that the person tends to conduct himself during an encounter so as to maintain both his own face [we should say mask] and the face of other participants. . . . This kind of mutual acceptance seems to be a basic structural feature of interaction. . . . It is typically a "working" acceptance, not a "real" one, since it tends to be based not on agreement of candidly expressed, heart-felt evaluations, but upon a willingness to give temporary lip service to judgements with which the participants do not really agree. [8]

Thus human interaction seems to depend on a willing suspension of disbelief—a fiction, in other words. That is, in order to get along with each other we pretend that masks are faces, roles are real. This is something we all have in common, from the most "primitive" to the most "sophisticated" societies. Just as in certain tribes the dancer who wears the mask of a rain god *is,* for the duration of the rain dance, the rain god himself, so when student confronts professor, they are the ideal of their roles to each other for the duration of their no doubt equally ritualistic encounter.

Identity is in this view a continuing and dynamic compromise between what we feel is the essence of ourselves and the essence of the roles we are called upon to assume in encounters with each other and the world. Somewhere in the dialectic between these two essences is located our "character."

The traditional terms critics have used to describe literary characters can thus be understood as referring to various degrees of distance

[7] Modern Library Paperback Edition, tr. Constance Garnett (New York, 1950), pp. 528–29.

[8] *Interaction Ritual* (New York, 1967), p. 11.

between masks and faces, or differing degrees of self-consciousness. For instance, in the ancient world there seems to have been less of a gap between a person and his role than is the case in later history. The dominant figure was the hero, and in epic or tragedy he was defined by the limitations put upon his self-consciousness, as we saw in the example of Achilles. In Greek drama the tragedy more often than not consists in the truth that fate *is* character. Epic heroes wore masklike helmets and tragic heroes were always portrayed by actors wearing real masks; in each instance a metaphor is provided for the primacy of mask over face. A hero, then, *is* his function: there is no distinction between a unique self and a role. That is why when we hear the name of a mythic hero we always think of his story because he is defined by his actions. On the other hand, when we think of figures from later, especially post-Romantic, literature, we think of a distinct person or mood. Thus it is misleading to speak of the role of hero, since it is one that cannot be "played": one either is, or is not, a hero in Homer or Aeschylus. Fate is the basis of character.

The fixity of such characters, their inability to change, is also present in such works as the *Characters* of Theophrastus (d. 287 B.C.), a collection of thirty sketches portraying such types as "the flatterer," "the vain man," and "the superstitious man." Such types differ from heroes in that fate is not character, but character is fate. That is, the type is a human being who is defined by the pre-eminence of one aspect of his personality over all others. Thus, the superstitious man is *always* the superstitious man in everything that he does, and the flatterer is always a flatterer. Theophrastus was a student of Plato's, and it may be said that his types embody the Platonic idea or essence of such categories as vanity and greed. This concept of character was very influential and was reflected in numerous other genres. The Greek New Comedy of the fourth and third centuries B.C. and most of Roman comedy were based on types. In the Renaissance there are descriptions of the perfect courtier, and the drama (again especially the comedy) uses a psychology based on various combinations of the four humors (blood, phlegm, yellow bile, black bile), each of which determined a type: sanguine, phlegmatic, choleric, melancholic. In the Soviet Union "typicalness" is a major tenet of Socialist Realism: the Komsomol organizer represents the ideal of a good Communist; the wavering, weak intellectual is typical of a holdover from a period of bourgeois personalism. Today when we say of someone, "He's quite a character," we usually mean that the person is eccentric because he seems less various than other people, more purely a type of one sort or the other. And when we say "show some character," we mean "be consistent and true to type."

In all the examples above, character is conceived as somehow fixed; there is no distinction made between face and mask. Such conceptions presuppose very little consciousness of a separate and hidden unique self.

408

At the opposite pole would be found those ideas about character based on role-playing, ideas that start by assuming change and multiplicity: one man may play several roles during a day or a lifetime. In this view there is a distance between mask and face, between our basic personality and the various permutations we submit it to in different situations. A mechanic is a patient when he goes to the doctor. But when the doctor brings his car to the mechanic the roles of each are subtly reversed. They are the same men in both encounters, but the differing situations will call for a different version of both the doctor's and the mechanic's "self." We are all existential chameleons.

Of course experience will determine certain roles that are unavailable to us: a quadriplegic cannot play the role of an athlete, for instance. Other roles we exclude by an act of choice: the same quadriplegic, for instance, may be courageous and refuse to play the role of the helpless invalid. Each society provides certain norms of behavior that act as further restraints on what roles may be chosen or how they may be played. Each encounter in a given society is made on the basis of a contract of expectations. If, during the course of a meal at a fine restaurant, one were to slurp his food, avoid conversation, make hearty belches, and then explain that this is how Cossacks used to demonstrate their polite appreciation of good food, he would have broken the contract. One cannot play the role of guest in one culture as he would in another culture. However, society, experience, and choice provide possibilities for combining roles that are various enough to ensure that each man will, as a result of the pattern he achieves out of these, have a distinctive character.

If the drama is the primary genre of character as fate, then the novel is the primary genre of character as a variety of roles interacting with society and circumstances. Ivan Turgenev, for instance, always began a book by conceiving a character and only then imagining what would happen to such a man, what other kind of people he would know, and so on. The novel would then write itself. Novels are about individuals —Tom Jones, Tristram Shandy—not about Oedipus *the King*.

The development of the novel marked a shift in the concept of character. For the Greeks a man was what he did; he was the sum of his public actions, and his private intentions, though taken into account, did not determine his fate. Plot determined character. In the novel actions flow from what a man is, and the focus is on the interplay between inner selves and outer society. Character determines plot. This is, of course, a gross over-simplification, but such a paradigm makes it clear that there is a close relationship between character and plot. And, as we have suggested earlier, this relationship holds true in our lives as well as in books. In Part I, we saw the importance of stories. But the most significant story for any man is that of his own life. In Part II, we saw how mind operates on things. But the thing that mind is most concerned to manipulate is a self. In Part III, we talked about various ways in which mind sought to carve meaningful sequences out of the world's flux. But the sequence that most radically engages the imagination of every man is the beginning, middle, and end of his own life.

Just as there is a gap between mind and things, between mental models of the world and reality itself, between words and objects, there is a space between our inner selves and the various roles we play, between the face and the mask. And in each case character is the fiction that bridges the gap, maintaining the discourse between mind and world. Thus we do in our own lives what authors do in books—we create scenes and characters, and out of them make a story, which when we die will have been our biography. Each man tells the story of his own life. But it is an unrepeatable fiction. Perhaps that is why the dynamics and techniques of the fictions we find in books and in films, in plays and in comic strips, continue to fascinate. They provide on-the-job-training for the authors we must all become in order to be human.

Man's Struggle to Emerge from Nature: The Search for Humanity

In a story by H. G. Wells, "The Island of Dr. Moreau," the vivisectionist Moreau, seeking "to find out the extreme limit of plasticity in a living shape," conducts a number of painful operations on animals in order to make them as much like men as possible. The strange products of his knife, existing somewhere between animal and human, try constantly to realize their human potential. In thick, strange accents they repeat over and over again "The Law" that Moreau has given them:

> The Law
> Not to go on all-fours; *that* is the Law. Are we not Men?
> Not to suck up drink; *that* is the Law. Are we not Men?
> Not to eat flesh or fish; *that* is the Law. Are we not Men?
> Not to claw bark of trees; *that* is the Law. Are we not Men?
> Not to chase other men; *that* is the Law. Are we not Men?

In the end Moreau's creatures fail and revert to animalism, but the attempts of these pitiful things to make themselves into men by denying certain parts of their animal nature dramatize powerfully the efforts of men themselves throughout their history to distinguish man from the other creatures—by denying certain animal activities and, more positively, by seeking to discover and to emphasize some uniquely human characteristics such as speech, thought, tool-making, and art. While the battle would seem to have been won so long ago that men now find it difficult even to think of themselves as a species of animal, the victory has never been so absolute as to obliterate a certain uneasiness. Man has always resembled other animals just a little too closely for comfort, and his physical chemistry does not vary as much as we might like from the laws that seem to govern the rest of matter.

A question so important as this creates intense anxiety so long as it is unresolved, and all events that seem to offer some evidence on this matter generate unusual interest. Thus, still seeking some assurance that man does differ significantly from other animals and from the rest of nature, our own age finds itself extraordinarily curious about "primitive" tribes, such as the Australian Bushmen, where "basic man," stripped of all but the crudest technology, confronts directly the animal and natural world from which he seeks to differentiate himself. The recent movie *Walkabout* is a direct realization of this continuing "identity crisis" of our species. The discovery in the forests of Mindanao of the Tasaday tribe, who have never encountered other men, is front-page news throughout the world because it provides a situation of almost "laboratory purity" in which to see whether man in a state of nature differs much from the animals.

One of the major functions of man's fictions is to face such crucial problems as this and to try to resolve them. We can see fiction doing this work in the first pieces in this section, the various creation stories in which man attempts to distinguish himself in his origins and form from the rest of creation. The same concern, put in a much more sophisticated way, appears in the selections from the *Metamorphoses* of the Roman writer Ovid. Most of Ovid's stories deal with the failure of man to maintain his "humaneness" in a world where there is a constant pressure to reduce men to some object in nature, a bird, a tree, or a river. What is fascinating in Ovid is not so much his pessimism about the possibility of man maintaining his distinction from nature for any great period of time, but the analyses of the nature of the forces, both within man and external to him, that obliterate his humanity. Because the question of man's uniqueness is never settled, our fictions constantly contrive statements of the problem, ranging all the way from comic-book and science-fiction fantasies about the struggle of men with strange monsters and forms of life from other worlds to Shakespeare's *King Lear,* where man tries to discover and preserve the essence of his humanity in the midst of a dreadful situation that threatens to reduce him to "the thing itself . . . a poor, bare, forked animal."

But man as a species has less difficulty in modern times in distinguishing himself from other species than man as an individual has in distinguishing himself from other men. The individual's sense of himself as unique, particular, and not quite like any other man is probably, in terms of evolutionary time, a fairly new concept; but it is of enormous importance to us in a democratic society with a strong emphasis on the rights of the individual. This concept of the individual is under especially heavy pressure today. The enormous growth in the number of men alive at this time threatens to submerge the individual in the tide of humanity, while the increasing complexity of society and its institutions tends to replace the individual with some collective abstraction such as "the man in the gray flannel suit" or "the lonely crowd." At the same time, behavioral psychologists like B. F. Skinner, author of *Walden Two* and *Be-*

412

yond Freedom and Dignity, treat man as a standardized mechanism with a limited number of potentialities that can be engineered by a system of rewards and punishments to achieve any desired social end; propagandists, whether they sell politics or toothpaste, also assume that men in the mass tend to have identical appetites that can be directed towards certain products. Faced with the loss of uniqueness and freedom to some conception of mass or mechanistic man, we respond with a fascinated interest to those boundary situations where the individual self seems in danger of disappearing into mere number and anonymity. François Truffaut's film *The Wild Child* looks carefully at a child raised in the woods without any human contacts in the hope of finding some ineradicable and particular self that is inborn in a man, rather than an identity conferred by a culture. For similar reasons we find ourselves attracted to psychological studies of the "feral child," who seems more savage than human, and the "autistic child," who retreats entirely into himself, scarcely speaking or moving, and refusing to come out into the world and take shape as a character.

As we might expect, a problem so close to ourselves as our identity as particular individuals is also a central subject of our fictions. Western literature has dealt with this question from its beginnings, and the great tragic and epic heros have consistently struggled with such questions as Who am I? and What does it mean to be a man? It is these basic questions which are at the center of such fearful stories as Mary Shelley's *Frankenstein,* discussed earlier, where the strange, sad monster created in the laboratory of the scientist searches desperately for some assurance that in all his strangeness and uniqueness he is still somehow acceptable to other men. But nowhere does the attempt to create the individual self appear more clearly than in the great comic-book heroes such as Superman, Batman, and Captain Marvel. Comic books provide remarkable insights into what men are troubled about simply because they are so crude and direct. In the scenes from *Superman* printed here, for example, the fear of being submerged in the mass of men and the complexity of modern society is perfectly rendered in the figure of the mousy reporter Clark Kent, while the desire to be unique and infinitely powerful is imaged in the marvelous figure of Superman, the child from another, faraway, lost world.

Each of the fictions in this section, different as they are in origin and form, takes place on that most crucial of all frontiers, the dividing line between human nature and the rest of the world, between the individual and the obscurity of the nameless mass.

413

FOUR CREATION STORIES

Almost no type of folk-tale or myth is so universal as the creation story, which explains a people's conception of the origin of man and attempts to distinguish him from the remainder of the world. The details of these stories vary enormously. In some cases man is made out of the blood of the gods, in others out of the clay of the earth, the stones, the minerals, the plants, or some element such as fire. In some stories man is made by a god, in others by animals or natural forces, and in still others he creates himself and springs into being fully grown. The choice of such details and the way they are ordered reveals a great deal about the way the people who create and tell the story think of themselves and their relationship to the rest of the world and the great powers controlling it. But however much the stories may vary, we can sense behind each of them an attempt, by means of a fiction, to deal with the questions, Who and what is man? How did he come to be here? and Why and in what ways is he unlike other things?—in short, What is unique about us as men?

The four creation stories printed here offer a considerable range of answers to these questions. The first, "Eingana the Mother," comes from the Australian bush, and was told in this century to Roland Robinson by the aborigine Rinjeira, of the Djauan tribe. The story is difficult to understand—its terms and frame of reference are not ours—and it seems to speak from a very long time ago and very far away, from what the Australian tribesmen call the "Dreamtime" when the "Ancestors" walked about. The relationship of man and animals is here very close, and the bond is never entirely broken, for such animals as kangaroos and dingos who come forth with man remain his totemic animals, the sacred patrons of his particular clan.

The second story is from an American Indian tribe, the Miwok, and was recorded in the last century. It seems much closer, much more familiar, perhaps because man, although still tied closely to the animal world, is made by the most intelligent part of that world, Coyote. Coyote is a widespread figure in the legends of the American Indians, where he is the trickster, the cunning, clever, scheming fellow who, like man, uses his mind rather than his brawn to solve his problems.

The third story of creation brings us much closer to home; it is the work of the Roman poet Ovid (Publius Ovidius Naso, 43 b.c.–a.d. 18). This story is the opening section of Ovid's *Metamorphoses*, which is discussed in the introduction to the section on transformation stories that

414

follows. Ovid, as is there pointed out, is a pagan poet, and his explanation of the origin and nature of man is essentially that of the pagan, classical world. To his version, and to those of the Australian aborigines and the Miwok Indians, the creation story as it appears in Genesis (the last item in this section) may be compared. It should be noticed that there are two quite different versions of the creation of man, though only one of woman. Biblical scholars explain the duplication as the work of two different writers at different periods of time, which were later conflated when the Old Testament as we know it was assembled from many various writings.

Eingana the Mother

This narrative is mainly an explanation of the first appearance, and nature of, the ancestral being, Eingana. It is a Northern Territory tradition. Eingana is the great earth-mother. She is fertility itself. She is the source of all life, all forms of being.

A significant point is that, in the beginning, Eingana could not give birth in the normal manner. She had to vomit. This recalls the swallowing and vomiting acts of the Greek gods, Cronus and Zeus. Eingana both swallowed and disgorged people alive. The first nature of Eingana appears to recall some primal form of life.

Eingana, pregnant with all forms of life, and in birth travail, had to be speared, the natural opening made, to allow her to give birth. Eingana's travail to give birth here is also the explanation of the sound made by the "bull-roarer" in the Kunapipi ritual.

Eingana is the inexhaustible source of life and spirit. This explanation of her nature shows the aboriginal conception of life and spirit in continuous cycles of birth, death, and re-birth.

When this narrative was given to me, I was on the ceremonial ground of the Kunapipi ritual where initiates, under a ban of silence, and in mute subservience to the tribal elders, were awaiting their ritual birth.

That first time, the creation time, we call Bieingana. The first being we call Eingana. We call Eingana our Mother. Eingana made everything: water, rocks, trees, blackfellows: she made all the birds, flying-foxes, kangaroos and emus. Everything Eingana had inside herself in that first time.

Eingana is snake. She swallowed all the blackfellows. She took them, inside herself, down under the water. Eingana came out, she was big with everything inside her. She came out of Gaieingung, the big water-hole near Bamboo Creek. Eingana was rolling about, every way, on the ground. She was groaning and calling out. She was making a big noise with all the blackfellows, everything, inside her belly.

415

One old-man named Barraiya had been travelling a long way. All the way he had heard Eingana crying out, rolling about and moaning. Barraiya sneaked up. He saw Eingana. He saw the big snake rolling and twisting about, moaning and calling out. Barraiya hooked up his stone-spear. He watched the big snake. He saw where he must spear her. Barraiya speared her underneath, near the anus. All blood came out of that spear-wound and all the blackfellows came out after the blood.

Kandagun the dingo chased after all those blackfellows. He chased after them and split them up into different tribes and languages. When Kandagun chased the blackfellows, some flew away as birds, some bounded away as kangaroos, some raced away as emus, some became flying-foxes, porcupines, snakes, everything, to get away from Kandagun.

That first time, before Barraiya speared Eingana, nothing and no one could be born as they are now. Eingana had to spew everything out of her mouth. Blackfellows had to spew everything. Children could not be born as they are now. That is why Barraiya had to spear Eingana.

The old-man Barraiya had been travelling from the east across to the west. After he speared Eingana, the old-man went back to his place Barraiyawim. There he painted himself on a rock. He turned into the blue-winged kookaburra.

Eingana made the big Boolmoon River, she made the Flying-Fox River and the Roper River. Every river she made. We have water now. That's why we are alive.

Eingana made Bolong the Rainbow-Snake. In the first time when Eingana swallowed blackfellows, she spewed them out and these black-fellows became birds, they became Bonorong the brolga, Janaran the jabiroo, Baruk the diver. Eingana spewed out blackfellows who became Koopoo the kangaroo, Kandagun the dingo, Galwan the goanna, Nabinin-bulgai the flying-fox. All these birds, animals, all these things, Eingana took back. She talked: "I think that all you fellows have to follow me, you have to go my way." Eingana took them all back. She swallowed them again. She let them go in the water as snakes, as Bolong the Rainbow-Snake.

No one can see Eingana. She stays in the middle water. She has a hole there. In the rain-time when the flood-water comes, Eingana stands up out of the middle of the flood-water. Eingana looks out at the country. She lets go all the birds, snakes, animals, children belonging to us; Eingana lets all these things go out of her.

Eingana floats along on the flood-water. She stands up and looks out at the country. She lets every kind of life, belonging to her, go. When the flood-water goes down Eingana goes back to her camp again. She comes back no more. No matter cold weather or hot weather, she does not come out. Next rain-time she comes out and lets go everything that belongs to her: snakes, birds, dingoes, kangaroos, blackfellows, everything.

Eingana keeps hold of a string, a sinew called Toon. This string is joined to the big sinew of any kind of life, behind the heel. Eingana keeps hold of that string all the time. Because we call her mother, you see. When we die Eingana lets that string go. I die. I die forever. My spirit, Malikngor, follows the way of Bolong.

It might be that I die in another place. That one, Malikngor, my spirit goes back to my country, where I was born. Everyone's spirit does this.

Eingana gives back spirit to man and woman all the time. She gives them this spirit in children. Eingana gives spirit a little bit first time to lubra, then more and more. You cannot find this spirit yourself. That one Eingana, or Bolong, has to help you.

If Eingana died, everything would die. There would be no more kangaroos, birds, blackfellows, anything. There would be no more water, everything would die.

The Creation of Man

After the coyote had finished all the work of the world and the inferior creatures, he called a council of them to deliberate on the creation of man. They sat down in an open space in the forest all in a circle, with the lion at the head. On his right sat the grizzly bear, next the cinnamon bear, and so on around according to rank, ending with the little mouse, which sat at the lion's left.

The lion was the first to speak, and he declared he should like to see man created with a mighty voice like himself, wherewith he could frighten all animals. For the rest he would have him well covered with hair, terrible fangs in his claws, strong talons, etc.

The grizzly bear said it was ridiculous to have such a voice as his neighbor, for he was always roaring with it, and scared away the very prey he wished to capture. He said the man ought to have prodigious strength, and move about silently, but very swiftly if necessary, and be able to grip his prey without making a noise.

The buck said the man would, in his way of thinking, look very foolish unless he had a magnificent pair of antlers on his head to fight with. He also thought it very absurd to roar so loudly, and he would pay less attention to a man's throat than he would to his ears and his eyes, for he would have the first like a spider's web, and the second like fire.

The mountain sheep protested he never could see what sense there was in such antlers branching every way only to be caught in the thickets. If the man had horns, mostly rolled up, they would be like a stone on each side of his head, giving it weight and enabling him to butt a great deal harder.

When it came to the coyote's turn to speak, he declared all these were the stupidest speeches he had ever heard, and that he could hardly keep awake while listening to such a pack of noodles and nincompoops. Every one of them wanted to make the man like himself. They might just as well take one of their own cubs and call it a man. As for himself, he knew he was not the best animal that could be made, and he could make one better than himself or any other. Of course the man would have to be like himself in having four legs, five fingers, etc. It was well enough to have a voice like the lion, only the man need not roar all the while with it. The grizzly bear also had some good points, one of which was the shape of his feet, which enabled him easily to stand erect; and he was in favor, therefore, of making the man's feet nearly like the grizzly's. The grizzly, also, was happy in having no tail, for he had learned from his own experience that that organ was only a harbor for fleas. The buck's eyes and ears were pretty good, perhaps better than his own. Then there was the fish, which was naked, and which he envied, because hair was a burden most of the year; and he, therefore, favored a man without hair. His claws ought to be as long as the eagle's, so that he could hold things in them. But after all, with all their separate gifts, they must acknowledge that there was no animal besides himself that had wit enough to supply the man, and he should be obliged, therefore, to make him like himself in that respect also—cunning and crafty.

After the coyote had made an end, the beaver said he never heard such nonsense and twaddle in his life. No tail, indeed! He would make a man with a broad, flat tail, so he could haul mud and sand on it.

The owl said all the animals seemed to have lost their senses, none of them wanted to give the man wings. For himself, he could not see of what use anything on earth could be to himself without wings.

The mole said it was perfect folly to talk about wings, for with them the man would be certain to bump his head against the sky. Besides that, if he had wings and eyes both, he would have his eyes burned out by flying too near the sun; but without eyes he could burrow in the cool, soft earth and be happy.

Last of all the little mouse squeaked out that he would make a man with eyes, of course, so that he could see what he was eating; and as for burrowing in the ground, that was absurd.

So the animals disagreed among themselves, and the council broke up in a row. The coyote flew at the beaver and nipped a piece out of his cheek; the owl jumped on top of the coyote's head and commenced lifting his scalp, and there was a high time. Every animal set to work to make a man according to his own ideas, and taking a lump of earth each one commenced molding it like himself, but the coyote began to make one like he had described in the council. It was so late before they fell to work that nightfall came on before anyone had finished his model, and they all lay down and fell asleep. But the cunning coyote stayed awake and worked hard on his model all night. When all the other animals were sound asleep, he went around and threw water on their models, and so spoiled them. In the morning early he finished his model, and gave

418

it life, long before the others could make new models. And thus it was
that man was made by the coyote.

FROM THE Metamorphoses

Ovid

Translated by Rolfe Humphries

> My intention is to tell of bodies changed
> To different forms; the gods, who made the changes,
> Will help me—or I hope so—with a poem
> That runs from the world's beginning to our own days.

The Creation

> Before the ocean was, or earth, or heaven,
> Nature was all alike, a shapelessness,
> Chaos, so-called, all rude and lumpy matter,
> Nothing but bulk, inert, in whose confusion
> Discordant atoms warred: there was no sun
> To light the universe; there was no moon   10
> With slender silver crescents filling slowly;
> No earth hung balanced in surrounding air;
> No sea reached far along the fringe of shore.
> Land, to be sure, there was, and air, and ocean,
> But land on which no man could stand, and water
> No man could swim in, air no man could breathe,
> Air without light, substance forever changing,
> Forever at war: within a single body
> Heat fought with cold, wet fought with dry, the hard
> Fought with the soft, things having weight contended   20
> With weightless things.
>   Till God, or kindlier Nature,
> Settled all argument, and separated
> Heaven from earth, water from land, our air
> From the high stratosphere, a liberation
> So things evolved, and out of blind confusion
> Found each its place, bound in eternal order.
> The force of fire, that weightless element,
> Leaped up and claimed the highest place in heaven;
> Below it, air; and under them the earth
> Sank with its grosser portions; and the water,   30
> Lowest of all, held up, held in, the land.
>
> Whatever god it was, who out of chaos
> Brought order to the universe, and gave it

Division, subdivision, he molded earth,
In the beginning, into a great globe,
Even on every side, and bade the waters
To spread and rise, under the rushing winds,
Surrounding earth; he added ponds and marshes,
He banked the river-channels, and the waters
Feed earth or run to sea, and that great flood   40
Washes on shores, not banks. He made the plains
Spread wide, the valleys settle, and the forest
Be dressed in leaves; he made the rocky mountains
Rise to full height, and as the vault of Heaven
Has two zones, left and right, and one between them
Hotter than these, the Lord of all Creation
Marked on the earth the same design and pattern.
The torrid zone too hot for men to live in,
The north and south too cold, but in the middle
Varying climate, temperature and season.   50
Above all things the air, lighter than earth,
Lighter than water, heavier than fire,
Towers and spreads; there mist and cloud assemble,
And fearful thunder and lightning and cold winds,
But these, by the Creator's order, held
No general dominion; even as it is,
These brothers brawl and quarrel; though each one
Has his own quarter, still, they come near tearing
The universe apart. Eurus is monarch
Of the lands of dawn, the realms of Araby,   60
The Persian ridges under the rays of morning.
Zephyrus holds the west that glows at sunset,
Boreas, who makes men shiver, holds the north,
Warm Auster governs in the misty southland,
And over them all presides the weightless ether,
Pure without taint of earth.
                                    These boundaries given,
Behold, the stars, long hidden under darkness,
Broke through and shone, all over the spangled heaven,
Their home forever, and the gods lived there,
And shining fish were given the waves for dwelling   70
And beasts the earth, and birds the moving air.

But something else was needed, a finer being,
More capable of mind, a sage, a ruler,
So Man was born, it may be, in God's image,
Or Earth, perhaps, so newly separated
From the old fire of Heaven, still retained
Some seed of the celestial force which fashioned
Gods out of living clay and running water.
All other animals look downward; Man,
Alone, erect, can raise his face toward Heaven.   80

420

FROM Genesis

1

And God said, "Let the earth bring forth the living creature after his kind, cattle, and creeping thing, and beast of the earth after his kind": and it was so. And God made the beast of the earth after his kind, and cattle after their kind, and every thing that creepeth upon the earth after his kind: and God saw that it was good. And God said, "Let us make man in our image, after our likeness: and let them have dominion over the fish of the sea, and over the fowl of the air, and over the cattle, and over all the earth, and over every creeping thing that creepeth upon the earth." So God created man in his own image, in the image of God created he him; male and female created he them. And God blessed them, and God said unto them, "Be fruitful, and multiply, and replenish the earth, and subdue it: and have dominion over the fish of the sea, and over the fowl of the air, and over every living thing that moveth upon the earth." And God said, "Behold, I have given you every herb bearing seed, which is upon the face of all the earth, and every tree, in the which is the fruit of a tree yielding seed; to you it shall be for meat. And to every beast of the earth, and to every fowl of the air, and to every thing that creepeth upon the earth, wherein there is life, I have given every green herb for meat": and it was so. And God saw every thing that he had made, and, behold, it was very good. And the evening and the morning were the sixth day.

2

Thus the heavens and the earth were finished, and all the host of them. And on the seventh day God ended his work which he had made; and he rested on the seventh day from all his work which he had made. And God blessed the seventh day, and sanctified it: because that in it he had rested from all his work which God created and made.

These are the generations of the heavens and of the earth when they were created, in the day that the Lord God made the earth and the heavens, and every plant of the field before it was in the earth, and every herb of the field before it grew: for the Lord God had not caused it to rain upon the earth, and there was not a man to till the ground. But there went up a mist from the earth, and watered the whole face of the ground. And the Lord God formed man of the dust of the ground, and breathed into his nostrils the breath of life; and man became a living soul. And the Lord God planted a garden eastward in Eden; and there he put the man whom he had formed. And out of the ground made the Lord God grow every tree that is pleasant to the sight, and good for food; the tree of life also in the midst of the garden, and the tree of knowledge of good and evil. And a river went out of Eden to water the garden; and from thence it was parted, and became into four heads. The name of the first is Pison: that is it which compasseth the whole land of Havilah, where there is gold; and the gold of that land is good: there is bdellium and the onyx stone. And the name of the second river is Gihon: the same is it that compasseth the whole land of Ethiopia. And the name of the third river is Hiddekel: that is it which goeth toward the east of Assyria. And the fourth river is Euphrates. And the Lord God took the man, and put him into the garden of Eden to dress it and to keep it. And the Lord God commanded the man, saying, "Of every tree of the garden thou mayest freely eat: but of the tree of the knowledge of good and evil, thou shalt not eat of it: for in the day that thou eatest thereof thou shalt surely die."

And the Lord God said, "It is not good that the man should be alone; I will make him an help meet for him." And out of the ground the Lord God formed every beast of the field, and every fowl of the air; and brought them unto Adam to see what he would call them: and whatsoever Adam called every living creature, that was the name thereof. And Adam gave names to all cattle, and to the fowl of the air, and to every beast of the field; but for Adam there was not found an help meet for him. And the Lord God caused a deep sleep to fall upon Adam, and he slept: and he took one of his ribs, and closed up the flesh instead thereof; and the rib, which the Lord God had taken from man, made he a woman, and brought her unto the man. And Adam said, "This is now bone of my bones, and flesh of my flesh: she shall be called Woman, because she was taken out of Man." Therefore shall a man leave his father and mother, and shall cleave unto his wife: and they shall be one flesh. And they were both naked, the man and his wife, and were not ashamed.

THREE STORIES OF TRANSFORMATION

FROM THE Metamorphoses

Ovid

Translated by Rolfe Humphries

Ovid lived and wrote during the period when Augustus was founding and stabilizing the Roman Empire, bringing order out of the political and social chaos of the preceding century, which culminated in the assassination of Julius Caesar in 44 B.C. and the defeat of Mark Antony and Cleopatra at Actium in 31 B.C. Like other famous poets of the time, Vergil and Horace, Ovid in his *Metamorphoses* writes with this political background very much in mind, and his stories are dramatizations of the titanic energies and violent emotions that keep his mythological world as unstable, as constantly changing, as the Roman Republic in its chaotic last years (all this, of course, in contrast to the stable and orderly world of Augustan Rome). But Ovid, who wrote most often of love and apparently had something of a reputation of a sophisticated and elegant trifler, was in the end banished by Augustus from Rome, for somewhat mysterious reasons, and spent the last years of his life in exile among a barbarian people on the shores of the Black Sea.

The reputation of being somehow not quite serious enough, of being more interested in poetry and the skillful telling of a tale than in truth and morality, has clung to Ovid down to the present. But though the manner may be witty and light, it is difficult to think of a more serious theme than that which runs through the many little mythological and semihistorical stories that make up the *Metamorphoses:* the endless process of change involving all things in this world, the desperate attempts of individual men and women to assert their identity in the face of enormous pressures working to reduce them again to animals, to trees and flowers, to streams.

Ovid is a pagan poet, and his poetry reflects some of his world's awareness of how fragile and temporary a thing is identity and the human character. It is always only a step back into nothingness, and the transitions of men into wolves and nymphs into flowing streams in moments of high passion seem not so startling because the distance between man and nature was never very great in the first place. Though Ovid was probably unaware of it, the man-god who was born in Judea during his time was to change all of this by providing a new conception of the individual as a unique soul created by God, responsible for his own thoughts and actions, and free to move not towards Ovidian obliteration in nature but on to eternal life. We look back at Ovid and the pagan world through many centuries of this Christian view of man as an indelible and imperishable soul, but Ovid's stories give us at least some sense of how difficult was man's original identification of himself as distinct from the rest of nature, and how powerful are the forces, both psychological and natural, which resist such attempts to extricate ourselves, both as a species and as individuals, from the great whirl of things.

The Story of Lycaon

This story appears early in the *Metamorphoses* (Book One) and is set in a time when man has barely established himself in the world. His humanity is at this time very much in doubt, and he is prone to sudden, swift, and awful bestialities such as that which overtakes Lycaon. As the story opens Jove is speaking.

"He has indeed been punished.
On that score have no worry. But what he did,
And how he paid, are things that I must tell you.
I had heard the age was desperately wicked,
I had heard, or so I hoped, a lie, a falsehood,
So I came down, as man, from high Olympus,
Wandered about the world. It would take too long
To tell you how widespread was all that evil.
All I had heard was grievous understatement!
I had crossed Maenala, a country bristling   10
With dens of animals, and crossed Cyllene,
And cold Lycaeus' pine woods. Then I came
At evening, with the shadows growing longer,
To an Arcadian palace, where the tyrant
Was anything but royal in his welcome.
I gave a sign that a god had come, and people
Began to worship, and Lycaon mocked them,
Laughed at their prayers, and said: 'Watch me find out
Whether this fellow is a god or mortal,
I can tell quickly, and no doubt about it.'   20
He planned, that night, to kill me while I slumbered;
That was his way to test the truth. Moreover,
And not content with that, he took a hostage,
One sent by the Molossians, cut his throat,
Boiled pieces of his flesh, still warm with life,
Broiled others, and set them before me on the table.
That was enough. I struck, and the bolt of lightning
Blasted the household of that guilty monarch.
He fled in terror, reached the silent fields,
And howled, and tried to speak. No use at all!   30
Foam dripped from his mouth; bloodthirsty still, he turned
Against the sheep, delighting still in slaughter,
And his arms were legs, and his robes were shaggy hair,
Yet he is still Lycaon, the same grayness,
The same fierce face, the same red eyes, a picture
Of bestial savagery. . . ."

The Story of Echo and Narcissus

Echo is a "babbling" nymph who angers Juno by detaining her
in conversation when that goddess is trying to catch Jove in one of his
many amours with earthly women. As punishment Juno decrees that
Echo will forever be a disembodied voice and that that voice will never
be able to begin a conversation but must always echo the last words she
hears. The story, from Book Three, plays the nymph who can live only
in the voice of others against her opposite, the handsome young man,
Narcissus, who lives totally in himself. Neither way works, and both are
swept on to lose themselves in the great process of change, to lose their
human form and be submerged in nature.

And so Tiresias,
Famous through all Aonian towns and cities,
Gave irreproachable answers to all comers
Who sought his guidance. One of the first who tested
The truths he told was a naiad of the river,
Liriope, whom the river-god, Cephisus
Embraced and ravished in his watery dwelling.
In time she bore a child, most beautiful
Even as child, gave him the name Narcissus,
And asked Tiresias if the boy would ever   10
Live to a ripe old age. Tiresias answered:
"Yes, if he never knows himself." How silly
Those words seemed, for how long! But as it happened,
Time proved them true—the way he died, the strangeness
Of his infatuation.
      Now Narcissus
Was sixteen years of age, and could be taken
Either for boy or man; and boys and girls
Both sought his love, but in that slender stripling
Was pride so fierce no boy, no girl, could touch him.
He was out hunting one day, driving deer   20
Into the nets, when a nymph named Echo saw him,
A nymph whose way of talking was peculiar
In that she could not start a conversation
Nor fail to answer other people talking.
Up to this time Echo still had a body,
She was not merely voice. She liked to chatter,
But had no power of speech except the power
To answer in the words she last had heard.
Juno had done this: when she went out looking
For Jove on top of some nymph among the mountains,   30
Echo would stall the goddess off by talking
Until the nymphs had fled. Sooner or later
Juno discovered this and said to Echo:
"The tongue that made a fool of me will shortly
Have shorter use, the voice be brief hereafter."
Those were not idle words; now Echo always
Says the last thing she hears, and nothing further.
She saw Narcissus roaming through the country,
Saw him, and burned, and followed him in secret,
Burning the more she followed, as when sulphur   40
Smeared on the rim of torches, catches fire
When other fire comes near it. Oh, how often
She wanted to come near with coaxing speeches,
Make soft entreaties to him! But her nature
Sternly forbids; the one thing not forbidden
Is to make answers. She is more than ready
For words she can give back. By chance Narcissus
Lost track of his companions, started calling
"Is anybody here?" and "Here!" said Echo.
He looked around in wonderment, called louder   50

425

"Come to me!" "Come to me!" came back the answer.
He looked behind him, and saw no one coming;
"Why do you run from me?" and heard his question
Repeated in the woods. "Let us get together!"
There was nothing Echo would ever say more gladly,
"Let us get together!" And, to help her words,
Out of the woods she came, with arms all ready
To fling around his neck. But he retreated:
"Keep your hands off," he cried, "and do not touch me!
I would die before I give you a chance at me."   60
"I give you a chance at me," and that was all
She ever said thereafter, spurned and hiding,
Ashamed, in the leafy forests, in lonely caverns.
But still her love clings to her and increases
And grows on suffering; she cannot sleep,
She frets and pines, becomes all gaunt and haggard,
Her body dries and shrivels till voice only
And bones remain, and then she is voice only
For the bones are turned to stone. She hides in woods
And no one sees her now along the mountains,   70
But all may hear her, for her voice is living.

She was not the only one on whom Narcissus
Had visited frustration; there were others,
Naiads or Oreads, and young men also
Till finally one rejected youth, in prayer,
Raised up his hands to Heaven: "May Narcissus
Love one day, so, himself, and not win over
The creature whom he loves!" Nemesis heard him,
Goddess of Vengeance, and judged the plea was righteous.
There was a pool, silver with shining water,   80
To which no shepherds came, no goats, no cattle,
Whose glass no bird, no beast, no falling leaf
Had ever troubled. Grass grew all around it,
Green from the nearby water, and with shadow
No sun burned hotly down on. Here Narcissus,
Worn from the heat of hunting, came to rest
Finding the place delightful, and the spring
Refreshing for the thirsty. As he tried
To quench his thirst, inside him, deep within him,
Another thirst was growing, for he saw   90
An image in the pool, and fell in love
With that unbodied hope, and found a substance
In what was only shadow. He looks in wonder,
Charmed by himself, spell-bound, and no more moving
Than any marble statue. Lying prone
He sees his eyes, twin stars, and locks as comely
As those of Bacchus or the god Apollo,
Smooth cheeks, and ivory neck, and the bright beauty
Of countenance, and a flush of color rising

426

In the fair whiteness. Everything attracts him   100
That makes him so attractive. Foolish boy,
He wants himself; the loved becomes the lover,
The seeker sought, the kindler burns. How often
He tries to kiss the image in the water,
Dips in his arms to embrace the boy he sees there,
And finds the boy, himself, elusive always,
Not knowing what he sees, but burning for it,
The same delusion mocking his eyes and teasing.
Why try to catch an always fleeing image,
Poor credulous youngster? What you seek is nowhere,   110
And if you turn away, you will take with you
The boy you love. The vision is only shadow,
Only reflection, lacking any substance.
It comes with you, it stays with you, it goes
Away with you, if you can go away.
No thought of food, no thought of rest, can make him
Forsake the place. Stretched on the grass, in shadow,
He watches, all unsatisfied, that image
Vain and illusive, and he almost drowns
In his own watching eyes. He rises, just a little,   120
Enough to lift his arms in supplication
To the trees around him, crying to the forest:
"What love, whose love, has ever been more cruel?
You woods should know: you have given many lovers
Places to meet and hide in; has there ever,
Through the long centuries, been anyone
Who has pined away as I do? He is charming,
I see him, but the charm and sight escape me.
I love him and I cannot seem to find him!
To make it worse, no sea, no road, no mountain,   130
No city-wall, no gate, no barrier, parts us
But a thin film of water. He is eager
For me to hold him. When my lips go down
To kiss the pool, his rise, he reaches toward me.
You would think that I could touch him—almost nothing
Keeps us apart. Come out, whoever you are!
Why do you tease me so? Where do you go
When I am reaching for you? I am surely
Neither so old or ugly as to scare you,
And nymphs have been in love with me. You promise,   140
I think, some hope with a look of more than friendship.
You reach out arms when I do, and your smile
Follows my smiling; I have seen your tears
When I was tearful; you nod and beckon when I do;
Your lips, it seems, answer when I am talking
Though what you say I cannot hear. I know
The truth at last. He is myself! I feel it,
I know my image now. I burn with love
Of my own self; I start the fire I suffer.

What shall I do? Shall I give or take the asking?   150
What shall I ask for? What I want is with me,
My riches make me poor. If I could only
Escape from my own body! if I could only—
How curious a prayer from any lover—
Be parted from my love! And now my sorrow
Is taking all my strength away; I know
I have not long to live, I shall die early,
And death is not so terrible, since it takes
My trouble from me; I am sorry only
The boy I love must die: we die together."   160
He turned again to the image in the water,
Seeing it blur through tears, and the vision fading,
And as he saw it vanish, he called after:
"Where are you going? Stay: do not desert me,
I love you so. I cannot touch you; let me
Keep looking at you always, and in looking
Nourish my wretched passion!" In his grief
He tore his garment from the upper margin,
Beat his bare breast with hands as pale as marble
And the breast took on a glow, a rosy color,   170
As apples are white and red, sometimes, or grapes
Can be both green and purple. The water clears,
He sees it all once more, and cannot bear it.
As yellow wax dissolves with warmth around it,
As the white frost is gone in morning sunshine,
Narcissus, in the hidden fire of passion,
Wanes slowly, with the ruddy color going,
The strength and hardihood and comeliness,
Fading away, and even the very body
Echo had loved. She was sorry for him now,   180
Though angry still, remembering; you could hear her
Answer "Alas!" in pity, when Narcissus
Cried out "Alas!" You could hear her own hands beating
Her breast when he beat his. "Farewell, dear boy,
Beloved in vain!" were his last words, and Echo
Called the same words to him. His weary head
Sank to the greensward, and death closed the eyes
That once had marveled at their owner's beauty.
And even in Hell, he found a pool to gaze in,
Watching his image in the Stygian water.   190
While in the world above, his naiad sisters
Mourned him, and dryads wept for him, and Echo
Mourned as they did, and wept with them, preparing
The funeral pile, the bier, the brandished torches,
But when they sought his body, they found nothing,
Only a flower with a yellow center
Surrounded with white petals.

428

The Story of Philomela

Tereus, King of Thrace, has married Procne, daughter of the King of Athens, and taken her to his savage land. After Procne gives birth to a son, Itys, she longs to see her sister Philomela, and Tereus goes to fetch her. So begins, in Book Six, one of the most famous stories about the titanic powers of human emotions—fear, lust, revenge, anger—that course through Ovid's world, breaking down all forms of civility and changing man back to beast.

■

The omens, though, were baleful: neither Juno,
Nor Hymen, nor the Graces, blessed the marriage;
The Furies swung, or, maybe, brandished torches
Snatched from a funeral; the Furies lighted
The bridal bed; and above the bridal chamber
Brooded the evil hoot-owl. With such omens
Tereus and Procne married, with such omens
The bride and bridegroom soon were father and mother,
And Thrace rejoiced, and they rejoiced, and offered
Thanks to the gods, making the day of marriage,   10
The day of Itys' birth, both festal days.
People never know, it seems.
                      Five years went by,
And Procne asked a favor of her husband:
"My lord, if any ways of mine have been
A source of satisfaction to my husband,
Let me go see my sister, or let her come
To visit us, with a promise to her father
Of quick return. The sight of my dear sister
Would be the finest present you could give me."
So Tereus promptly had the ship made ready,   20
Sailed off to Athens, landed at Piraeus,
Found Pandion, and they joined hands in greeting
And wished each other well, and Tereus started
To explain the reasons of his coming there,
His wife's request, and the expected promise
Of a stay not over-long, and, as they chatted,
Here Philomela came, in rich apparel,
In richer grace, as lovely as the naiads,
As lovely as the dryads of the woodlands,
As lovely, rather, as they would be, if only   30
They had such clothes as hers, and such a bearing.
And Tereus looked at her, and in that moment
Took fire, as ripe grain burns, or dry leaves burn,
Or hay stored in the hay-mow; and this tribute
She well deserved, but there were other reasons.

429

He was a passionate man, and all the Thracians
Are all too quick at loving; a double fire
Burnt in him, his own passion and his nation's.
So his first impulse was to bribe her guardians,
Corrupt her faithful nurse, or by rich presents,   40
Even if it cost him all his kingdom, win her,
Or take her, and defend what he had taken
By violent war. In that unbridled passion
There was nothing he would not dare, with the flame
      bursting
Out of his breast. Delay, delay! He suffered,
Was all too eager, and when he spoke for Procne
Spoke for himself. Love made him eloquent,
If he went too far, he would lay the blame on Procne,
Saying she wished it so, and he added tears,
As if the tears were shed at her instructions!   50
The hearts of men have such blind darkness in them.
Tereus seems a most devoted husband,
So eager to please Procne, and wins praises,
The secret crime-contriver. Philomela
Is eager to go, wants the same thing, or seems to,
Wheedles her father, and fondles him, and coaxes,
And argues how much good it will do them both,
Her sister and her self (little she knows!)
If she can make the visit. And Tereus, watching,
Sees beyond what he sees: she is in his arms,   60
That is not her father whom her arms go around,
Not her father she is kissing. Everything
Is fuel to his fire. He would like to be
Her father, at that moment; and if he were
He would be as wicked a father as he is husband.
So Pandion says Yes, and Philomela,
Poor girl, is happy, and thanks him; both his daughters,
She thinks, have won; they are losers, both his daughters,
But how was she to know?
                              And the Sun's horses
Swung low to the West, and there was a great banquet,   70
Feasting, and wine in golden cups, then slumber;
And Tereus went to bed, and did not slumber,
In heat for Philomela, thinking of her,
The way she looked, the way she moved, her gestures,
Her visible charms, and what he has not seen,
Or not yet seen, at least he can imagine,
And does, and feeds his fires, and cannot slumber.
And morning came, and the old king and the younger
Shook hands before the leaving, and the older
Spoke through his tears: "Dear son, in all devotion, .   80
Since both the sisters wish it, and since you
Appear to share their wish, I trust her to you.
I beg you, by your honor and our kinship,

430

Protect her with a father's love, and send her
Safe home, as soon as may be, the sweet comfort
Of my declining years. However brief
Her visit, it will seem to me a long one.
And you, my Philomela, if you love me,
Come home to me soon!" And, saying so, he kissed her
With his last plea, and wept, and hands were joined   90
To bind the agreement, and one thing more, he told them,
Give all my love to Procne and to Itys,
And his voice broke, and underneath his sorrow
Foreboding lay.

               And the painted ship went sailing
Over the sea, and Tereus, the savage,
Knew he had won, having, as passenger,
His heart's desire, exults, can wait no more,
Or almost cannot wait, and looks her over
The way an eagle does, who has brought home
To his high nest, hooked by the cruel talons,   100
The prey, still warm, still living, the poor captive
Hopeless before the captor's gloating gaze.

And now the voyage ended, and the vessel
Was worn from travel, and they came stepping down
To their own shores, and Tereus dragged her with him
To the deep woods, to some ramshackle building
Dark in that darkness, and he shut her in there,
Pale, trembling, fearing everything, and asking
Where was her sister? And he told her then
What he was going to do, and straightway did it,   110
Raped her, a virgin, all alone, and calling
For her father, for her sister, but most often
For the great gods. In vain. She shook and trembled
As a frightened lamb which a gray wolf has mangled
And cast aside, poor creature, to a safety
It cannot quite believe. She is like a dove
With her own blood all over her feathers, fearing
The talons that have pierced and left her. Soon
As sense comes back, she tears her loosened hair,
She beats her breast, wild as a woman in mourning,   120
Crying: "O wicked deed! O cruel monster,
Barbarian, savage! Were my father's orders
Nothing to you, his tears, my sister's love,
My own virginity, the bonds of marriage?
Now it is all confused, mixed up; I am
My sister's rival, a second-class wife, and you,
For better and worse, the husband of two women,
Procne my enemy now, at least she should be.
Why not have been my murderer? That crime
Would have been cleaner, have no treachery in it,   130
And I an innocent ghost. If those on high

Behold these things, if there are any gods,
If anything is left, not lost as I am,
What punishment you will pay me, late or soon!
Now that I have no shame, I will proclaim it.
Given the chance, I will go where people are,
Tell everybody; if you shut me here,
I will move the very woods and rocks to pity.
The air of Heaven will hear, and any god,
If there is any god in Heaven, will hear me." 140

The words had their effect. The cruel king
Was moved to a fierce anger, to equal fear;
The double drive of fear and anger drove him
To draw the sword, to catch her by the hair,
To pull the head back, tie the arms behind her,
And Philomela, at the sight of the blade,
Was happy, filled with hope, the thought of death
Most welcome: her throat was ready for the stroke.
But Tereus did not kill her; he seized her tongue
With pincers, though it cried against the outrage, 150
Babbled and made a sound something like *Father*,
Till the sword cut it off. The mangled root
Quivered, the severed tongue along the ground
Lay quivering, making a little murmur,
Jerking and twitching, the way a serpent does
Run over by a wheel, and with its dying movement
Came to its mistress' feet. And even then—
It seems too much to believe—even then, Tereus
Took her, and took her again, the injured body
Still giving satisfaction to his lust. 160

And after that, Tereus went on to Procne,
And Procne asked, of course, about her sister
Asked where she was. And Tereus, with a groan,
Lamented, wept, and told some kind of story,
Saying that she was dead, oh, most convincing
With all his show of sorrow. Therefore Procne
Tore from her shoulders the robe with golden border,
Put on plain black, and built a tomb to honor
The spirit of her sister, and brought gifts
As funeral offerings to the fictive ghost, 170
Mourning a fate that should have been resented
Rather than mourned for.
               And a year went by,
And what of Philomela? Guarded against flight,
Stone blocks around her cottage, no power of speech
To help her tell her wrongs, her grief has taught her
Sharpness of wit, and cunning comes in trouble.
She had a loom to work with, and with purple
On a white background, wove her story in,

432

Her story in and out, and when it was finished,
Gave it to one old woman, with signs and gestures   180
To take it to the queen, so it was taken,
Unrolled and understood. Procne said nothing—
What could she say?—grief choked her utterance,
Passion her sense of outrage. There was no room
For tears, but for confusion only, and vengeance,
But something must be done, and in a hurry.

It was the time when all the Thracian mothers
Held festival for Bacchus, and the night
Shared in their secret; Rhodope by night
Resounded as the brazen cymbals clashed,   190
And so by night the queen went from her palace,
Armed for the rites of Bacchus, in all the dress
Of frenzy, trailing vines for head-dress, deer-skin
Down the left side, and a spear over the shoulder.
So, swiftly through the forest with attendants,
Comrades and worshippers in throngs, and driven
By madness, terrible in rage and anger,
Went Procne, went the Bacchanal, and came
At last to the hidden cottage, came there shrieking,
"Hail, Bacchus!" broke the doors in, found her sister,   200
Dressed her like all the others, hid her face
With ivy-leaves, and dragged her on, and brought her
Home to the palace.
             And when Philomela
Saw where she was, she trembled and grew pale,
As pale as death, and Procne found her a place,
Took off the Bacchic trappings, and uncovered
Her sister's features, white with shame, and took her
Into her arms, but Philomela could not
So much as lift her eyes to face her sister,
Her sister, whom she knew she had wronged. She kept   210
Her gaze on the ground, longing with all her heart
To have the power to call the gods to witness
It was not her fault, but something forced upon her.
She tried to say so with her hand. And Procne,
Burning, could not restrain her wrath; she scolded
Her sister's weeping. "This is no time," she told her,
"For tears, but for the sword, for something stronger
Than sword, if you have any such weapon on you.
I am prepared for any crime, my sister,
To burn the palace, and into the flaming ruin   220
Hurl Tereus, the author of our evils.
I would cut out his tongue, his eyes, cut off
The parts which brought you shame, inflict a thousand
Wounds on his guilty soul. I am prepared
For some great act of boldness, but what it is
I do not know, I wish I did."

The answer

Came to her as her son came in, young Itys.
She looked at him with pitiless eyes; she thought
How like his father he is! That was enough,
She knew, now, what she had to do, all burning   230
With rage inside her, but when the little fellow
Came close and put both arms around his mother,
And kissed her in appealing boyish fashion,
She was moved to tenderness; against her will,
Her eyes filled up with tears, her purpose wavered.
She knew it, and she looked at Philomela,
No more at Itys, then from one to the other,
Saying: "And why should one make pretty speeches,
The other be dumb, and ravished tongue unable
To tell of ravish? Since he calls me mother,   240
Why does she not say Sister? Whose wife are you,
Daughter of Pandion? Will you disgrace him,
Your husband, Tereus? But devotion to him
Is a worse crime." Without more words, a tigress
With a young fawn, she dragged the youngster with her
To a dark corner somewhere in the palace,
And Itys, who seemed to see his doom approaching,
Screamed, and held out his hands, with *Mother, Mother!*
And tried to put his little arms around her
But she, with never a change in her expression,   250
Drove the knife home through breast, through side, one
     wound,
Enough to kill him, but she made another,
Cutting the throat, and they cut up the body
Still living, still keeping something of the spirit,
And part of the flesh leaped in the boiling kettles,
Part hissed on turning skewers, and the room
Dripped blood.

           And this was the feast they served to Tereus,
Who did not know, for the queen made up some story
About a ritual meal, for husbands only,
Which even servants might not watch. High in the chair   260
Sat Tereus, proud, and feasting, almost greedy
On the flesh of his own flesh, and in his darkness
Of mind, he calls: "Bring Itys here!" and Procne
Cannot conceal her cruel joy; she is eager
To be the herald of her bloody murder.
"He has come in," she answers, and he looks
Around, asks where the boy is, asks again,
Keeps calling, and Philomela, with hair all bloody,
Springs at him, and hurls the bloody head of Itys
Full in his father's face. There was no time, ever,   270
When she would rather have had the use of her tongue,
The power to speak, to express her full rejoicing.
With a great cry he turns the table over,

434

Summons the snaky Furies from their valley
Deep in the pit of Styx. Now, if he could,
If he only could, he would open up his belly,
Eject the terrible feast: all he can do
Is weep, call himself the pitiful resting-place
Of his dear son. He draws the sword, pursues them,
Both Pandion's daughters. They went flying from him   280
As if they were on wings. They were on wings!
One flew to the woods, the other to the roof-top,
And even so the red marks of the murder
Stayed on their breasts; the feathers were blood-colored.
Tereus, swift in grief and lust for vengeance,
Himself becomes a bird: a stiff crest rises
Upon his head, and a huge beak juts forward,
Not too unlike a sword. He is the hoopoe,
The bird who looks like war.

The Birth of Superman and The Bridge

Edited by E. Nelson Bridwell

Since the invention of the printing press and movable type, there has been a steadily increasing stream of cheap fiction—romances, stories about crime and criminals, moralized tales about repentant sinners, and depictions of great success in trade and business. This literary underworld has flourished by satisfying the cruder, more direct desires of the reading public for sensational events, titanic heroes who can be admired and condemned at once, and strange, mysterious journeys to extraordinary places. A long line of "pulps" testifies to the durability of this tradition in American life: Buffalo Bill and his cowboys and Indians; *The Police Gazette*, with its detectives and fallen women; *Doc Savage*, with its strange animals and savage tribes; and *G-8 and his Battle Aces* struggling in the skies of France with the demonic devices of the German scientists. But the most popular of these forms of cheap fiction emerged in the late 1930's, in the midst of depression and growing signs of world war, when the first comic books—not comic strips—appeared. The "strips" had already been appearing in newspapers for some forty years, but they were slick, professional, and relatively tame in comparison to the crude drawing and direct explosions of violence—Bam! Zap!—that are the staple of comic books. Words are relatively unimportant in comic books. What matters is the picture, and not the details of the picture, which are always sparse—a slash for a mouth, a dot for an eye—but the symbolic image: the magician in cape and top hat, the superhero bounding over sky-

435

scrapers in a skintight red suit, the masked cowboy riding a great white stallion, the tough detective beating up criminals, and the idealistic explorer of outer space equipped with rockets and rayguns. And the villains are as interesting as the heroes: mad scientists with long hypodermics, polite but devilish orientals, power-mad politicians and gangsters, fiendishly intelligent creatures from other worlds, perverse forms of life.

Mere wish-fulfillment, pop culture, the folk imagination, the sick dreams of a debased society: comic books have been called all these and worse. The charges may be true, but comic books still provide a fascinating case of fiction-making in its most basic form put to its most basic uses. In Superman, the most famous of the comic-book heroes, we have a realization of some of the most fundamental human desires and fantasies: that the individual comes from some world other than this, that his parents are only foster-parents, that he has a strong moral sense, and that, above all, he is a creature of immense power and limitless strength when he chooses to exert it. A pure case of wish fulfillment, it would seem, and interesting as such; but what about Superman's relationship to his alter ego, or double, the mousy, ineffective reporter—he only reports, he doesn't make news—Clark Kent? And what are we to make of Superman's relationship to Lois Lane, whom he loves desperately but hopelessly as Clark Kent, but rejects as Superman? It is a fascinating triangle: Clark Kent loves Lois, but she despises him and loves only Superman, while Superman cares not for her, except as someone to be rescued, though he is Clark Kent. It is, then, not only in the natures of the hero and the antagonist and in the details of the struggle that comic books reveal the imaginative desires and fears of men, but in the complications of relationship, particularly the relationship with another self, as well. If comic-book heroes like Superman reveal our hopes and desires in their most naked forms, they reveal our fears and our complexities also, and show, at least in this particular case, our continuing attempt to individualize ourselves and establish, by means of a fiction once again, our identity as unique persons.

436

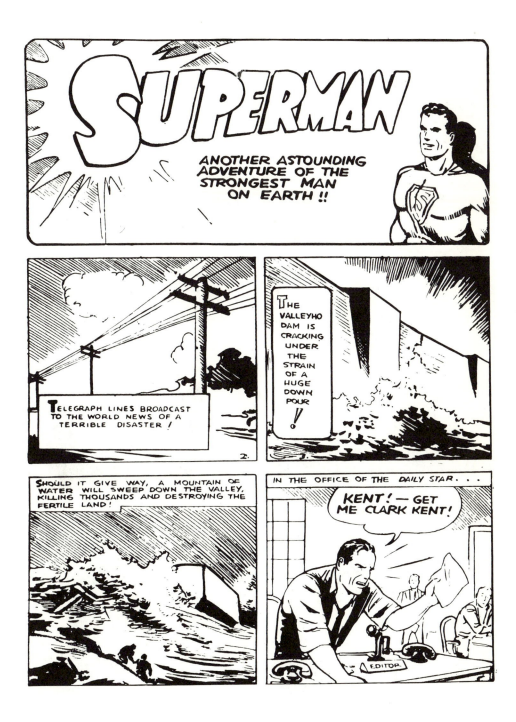

Conceiving the Self

The fictions of the previous section dealt with man's struggle to emerge from nature, to define and preserve a specific conception of "humanness" that could maintain his distinction from everything that surrounds him. Perhaps the majority of our fictions, from all places and ages, concern man as a fully emerged being who faces another problem: the definition of himself as self, as "I" in the world of other human beings who, as individuals or, more forcefully, as the social group, exercise various pressures on this self. These may be pressures to conform to a social standard and code; they may ultimately be pressures that tend to annihilate the individual ego, to make it succumb to the destructive demands of other egos, to the overriding concerns of the social group, or to the needs of some social, political, or metaphysical "higher cause." Such pressures bring varying kinds of response, various definitions by the "self" of its relation to the "other," and to the concerted organization of others known as society, which projects its own image into the individual's consciousness. So much of literature is devoted to these problems that two distinguishable uses of the word "character" tend to merge: a character in literature (that is, the literary figuration of a person) is most often a man who has a sense of his own character (that is, his definition and traits in the psychological or moral sense), and who must test that conception against those proposed by another, or the others.

The fictions in this section can be seen as essentially dramatizing the problems of ego-definition and ego-preservation: the working out of a strong conception of selfhood in relation to the demands of other selves as they are incorporated in social standards and codes. The selections begin with an example from the classical epic: the epic hero is traditionally an instance of a man who has an exceptionally clear conception of himself as a person because the heroic code by which he lives is a

448

clearly defined set of rules or expectations by which society (most immediately, his fellow warriors) tells him what is asked of him and what rewards are normally granted for the performance of certain actions and gestures. At its most basic level, such an ideal defines the hero as the outstanding member of the troop: the best fighter and the biggest landowner, the one who can be counted on for protection, and is rewarded for it by allegiance; the man from whom, in turn, much is expected because much has been given him. But evidently both expectations and rewards can vary greatly from age to age and from one society to another. Throughout his history, man has not ceased to return to the hero and the heroic code in the attempt to redefine the characteristics that elevate a man above others and give him a strong sense of role, function, and self. The medieval code of chivalry, for instance, elaborated the relationship of allegiance and protection in complex and symbolic forms. And during and following the Renaissance, major efforts were made to reinterpret the heroic code, to bend it to the demands of Christian humanism and to the cultivation of social virtues. These efforts inform much of Western literature in the sixteenth, seventeenth, and eighteenth centuries; they are perhaps most notable in the theater, man's most conspicuous mirror for his social self, where typically a "hero" acts out before an audience—the concrete manifestation of society—concerns common to the society.

In a world in which man-to-man combat under the walls of Troy is no longer a possible or desirable determination of heroism, how is man to define his distinct selfhood? If Alexander Pope's eighteenth-century mock-heroic version of Sarpedon's exhortation to Glaukos suggests a subordination of all idiosyncratic self-assertions to the exigencies of social intercourse and the cultivation of those qualities—wit, urbanity, a polite attentiveness to others—that make life in the drawing room possible and pleasant, the implications of Molière's version of the Don Juan figure are more disturbing. Here is a man who has reinterpreted military conquest as erotic conquest and made this the basis of an almost metaphysical quest to affirm the absolute freedom of the individual ego through its subjugation of other egos and its manipulations of social codes. Against the Christian affirmation of the insignificance of the individual's personal claims to freedom and happiness, a great part of the Western tradition has continued to define the self's quest in terms of the will to power.

A significant new moment in the reinterpretation of the self's ways of conceiving, distinguishing, and affirming its nature may come with the Romantic movement and the impulse to total self-expression, the desire to make manifest the whole of one's inner being, with all its needs and desires, and to claim for this inner self the status of arbiter of life, even center of the universe. With the modern emphasis on sincerity, self-expression, individual autonomy—emphases first clearly voiced by Rousseau—we remain close to this tradition, although we have, especially since the Freudian revolution, become less certain of what constitutes the self, more doubtful of its coherence and clarity, more aware of its ruses and role-playings. Yet even when psychology and biology have made more tenuous the definition of self and the concept of character, we still seem to hold fast to a sense of the autonomy and relative definition of character. We probably could not continue to live without this sense; and most of our fictions (despite the precepts of Robbe-Grillet) continue to circle around something we are at least provisionally willing to call "character." If fiction-making responds to our need to re-form reality, it also satisfies our thirst for reality, our desire to know it. We want to know what it is like to be under the skin of another person, and ultimately what it is like to be ourselves. Character, the writing down of self, continues to be primary to our interest in fictions.

■

As he prepares to lead an attack on the fortifications of the Greek camp in Book Twelve of the *Iliad,* Sarpedon, lord of the Lykians and one of the outstanding fighters on the Trojan side, speaks these words of exhortation to his second-in-command, Glaukos. In the translation by Richmond Lattimore, which maintains close fidelity to the Greek, heroism seems to be defined as simply the "biggest deeds expected from the biggest men": wealth, possession, and command should be accompanied by a willingness to lead in combat and to expose oneself to the greatest dangers. In the eighteenth-century translation of the *Iliad* by Alexander Pope (1688–1744), we detect the translator's need to refer this heroism of deed to an underlying moral and social order: "Unless great acts superior merit *prove,* / And *vindicate* the bounteous pow'rs above"; "the first in valour, *as* the first in place"; "Such, they may cry, *deserve* the sov'reign state, / Whom those that envy dare not imitate!" Heroism has been socialized and moralized; command has become identified with aristocracy. Pope's heroic couplets emphasize the series of equations he is establishing between prowess in arms and social rank; and the equivalences implicitly refer to the image of a carefully justified social hierarchy. How does the mock-heroic version of this same speech in *The Rape of the Lock,* in which Clarissa tries to mollify the outraged Belinda, make clearer some of the ethical ideals already latent in Pope's version of the *Iliad?*

FROM THE Iliad

Homer

Translated by Richmond Lattimore

And now he spoke in address to Glaukos, son of Hippolochos:
"Glaukos, why is it you and I are honoured before others   310
with pride of place, the choice meats and the filled wine cups
in Lykia, and all men look on us as if we were immortals,
and we are appointed a great piece of land by the banks of Xanthos,
good land, orchard and vineyard, and ploughland for the planting of
    wheat?
Therefore it is our duty in the forefront of the Lykians
to take our stand, and bear our part of the blazing of battle,
so that a man of the close-armoured Lykians may say of us:
'Indeed, these are no ignoble men who are lords of Lykia,
these kings of ours, who feed upon the fat sheep appointed
and drink the exquisite sweet wine, since indeed there is strength   320
of valour in them, since they fight in the forefront of the Lykians.'
Man, supposing you and I, escaping this battle,
would be able to live on forever, ageless, immortal,
so neither would I myself go on fighting in the foremost
nor would I urge you into the fighting where men win glory.
But now, seeing that the spirits of death stand close about us
in their thousands, no man can turn aside nor escape them,
let us go on and win glory for ourselves, or yield it to others."

FROM THE Iliad

Homer

Translated by Alexander Pope

    Why boast we, Glaucus! our extended reign
Where Xanthus' streams enrich the Lycian plain
Our num'rous herds that range the fruitful field,
And hills where vines their purple harvest yield,
Our foaming bowls with purer nectar crown'd,
Our feasts enhanc'd with music's sprightly sound?
Why on those shores are we with joy survey'd,
Admir'd as heroes, and as gods obey'd?
Unless great acts superior merit prove,
And vindicate the bounteous pow'rs above.   10

'Tis ours, the dignity they give, to grace;
The first in valour, as the first in place;
That when with wond'ring eyes our martial bands
Behold our deeds transcending our commands,
Such, they may cry, deserve the sov'reign state,
Whom those that envy dare not imitate!

Could all our care elude the gloomy grave,
Which claims no less the fearful than the brave,
For lust of fame I should not vainly dare
In fighting fields, nor urge thy soul to war.   20
But since, alas! ignoble age must come,
Disease, and death's inexorable doom,
The life, which others pay, let us bestow,
And give to fame what we to nature owe;
Brave though we fall, and honour'd if we live,
Or let us glory gain, or glory give!

FROM The Rape of the Lock

Alexander Pope

Say why are Beauties praised and honored most,
The wise man's passion, and the vain man's toast?   10
Why decked with all that land and sea afford,
Why Angels called, and Angel-like adored?
Why round our coaches crowd the white-gloved Beaux,
Why bows the side-box from its inmost rows;
How vain are all these glories, all our pains,
Unless good sense preserve what beauty gains:
That men may say, when we the front-box grace:
"Behold the first in virtue as in face!"
Oh! if to dance all night, and dress all day,
Charmed the small-pox, or chased old-age away;   20
Who would not scorn what housewife's cares produce,
Or who would learn one earthly thing of use?
To patch,° nay ogle, might become a Saint,
Nor could it sure be such a sin to paint.
But since, alas! frail beauty must decay,
Curled or uncurled, since Locks will turn to grey;
Since painted, or not painted, all shall fade,
And she who scorns a man, must die a maid;
What then remains but well our power to use,
And keep good-humor still whate'er we lose?   30
And trust me, dear! good-humor can prevail,
When airs, and flights, and screams, and scolding fail.

23. *patch:* to wear beauty patches, or spots, designed to call attention to attractive features.

Beauties in vain their pretty eyes may roll;
Charms strike the sight, but merit wins the soul.

■

The *Pensées* of Blaise Pascal (1623–62)—fragments of an apology for the Christian religion—return often to the literal *vanity* of human self-love: self-love is unjust and contradictory and vain because at the center of man there is a sort of void. Man is incomprehensible to himself, defined by contradictory appetites and characterized by boredom when his appetites are satisfied. He can understand the enigma of his being only through God and sacred history (especially the story of his fall from perfection); and it is only by putting God at the center of his being and directing his self-love toward that principle that man can gain wisdom and understanding.

The libertine created by Molière (Jean-Baptiste Poquelin, 1622–73) is an extreme example of the kind of man whom Pascal is attacking: a man who believes in his own self-sufficiency and has made self-love the cornerstone of his ethics. For Don Juan, libertinism is not merely a matter of erotic conquest and pleasure. The seduction and subjugation of women becomes the means toward realization of a larger desire to know everything by conquering everything, to attain freedom of the self through absolute mastery of others. It is in the logic of his self-conception that Don Juan should deny the existence of any order beyond the human and social, of which he is perfectly the master. The play seems to demonstrate that he may act with impunity within the social realm—there is no one to punish him; he is almost perfectly free—and it is only in a collision with the cosmic order that he is eventually brought down. Many critics have found that this ending, traditional in the Don Juan legend, seems artificial in Molière's drama. If it is indeed contrived, can this be construed as a further comment on the force of Don Juan's philosophy of life?

FROM Pensées

Blaise Pascal

Translated by A. J. Krailsheimer

617

Anyone who does not hate the self-love within him and the instinct which leads him to make himself into a God must be really blind. Who can fail to see that there is nothing so contrary to justice and truth? For it is false that we deserve this position and unjust and impossible to attain it, because everyone demands the same thing. We are thus born into an obviously unjust situation from which we cannot escape but from which we must escape.

However, no [other] religion has observed that this is a sin, that it is innate in us, or that we are obliged to resist it, let alone thought of providing a cure.

597

"The self is hateful. You cover it up, Mitton,[1] but that does not mean that you take it away. So you are still hateful."

"Not so, because by being obliging to everyone as we are, we give them no more cause to hate us."

"True enough if the only hateful thing about the self were the unpleasantness it caused us.

"But if I hate it because it is unjust that it should make itself the centre of everything, I shall go on hating it.

"In a word the self has two characteristics. It is unjust in itself for making itself the centre of everything; it is a nuisance to others in that it tries to subjugate them, for each self is the enemy of all the others and would like to tyrannize them. You take away the nuisance, but not the injustice.

"And thus, you do not make it pleasing to those who hate it for being unjust; you only make it pleasing to unjust people who no longer see it as their enemy. Thus you remain unjust, and can only please unjust people."

688

What is the self?

A man goes to the window to see the people passing by; if I pass by, can I say he went there to see me? No, for he is not thinking of me in particular. But what about a person who loves someone for the sake of her beauty; does he love *her*? No, for smallpox, which will destroy beauty without destroying the person, will put an end to his love for her.

And if someone loves me for my judgement or my memory, do they love me? *me*, myself? No, for I could lose these qualities without losing my self. Where then is this self, if it is neither in the body nor the soul? And how can one love the body or the soul except for the sake of such qualities, which are not what makes up the self, since they are perishable? Would we love the substance of a person's soul, in the abstract, whatever qualities might be in it? That is not possible, and it would be wrong. Therefore we never love anyone, but only qualities.

Let us then stop scoffing at those who win honour through their appointments and offices, for we never love anyone except for borrowed qualities.

[1] Damien Mitton, a worldly free-thinker whom Pascal knew well and with whom he creates an imaginary dialogue here.

Don Juan

Molière

Translated by John Wood

CHARACTERS IN THE PLAY

DON JUAN, *son of Don Luis*
SGANARELLE, *valet to Don Juan*
ELVIRA, *wife of Don Juan*
GUSMAN, *squire to Elvira*
DON CARLOS ⎫ *brothers of Elvira*
DON ALONSO ⎭
DON LUIS, *father of Don Juan*
FRANCISCO, *a poor man*
CHARLOTTE ⎫ *peasant girls*
MATHURINE ⎭
PETER, *a peasant*
STATUE OF THE COMMANDER
LA VIOLETTE ⎫ *servants of Don Juan*
RAGOTIN ⎭
MR DIMANCHE, *a tradesman*
LA RAMÉE, *a ruffian*
Attendants on Don Carlos and Don Alonso
A SPECTRE

The scene is in Sicily.

ACT ONE

SGANARELLE, GUSMAN.

SGANARELLE (*snuff-box in hand*). Aristotle and the philosophers can say what they like, but there's nothing to equal tobacco: it's an honest man's habit, and anyone who can get on without it doesn't deserve to be living at all: it not only clears and enlivens the brain, it's conducive to virtue: a fellow learns from taking it how to comport himself decently. Haven't you noticed how, once a chap starts taking snuff, he behaves politely to everybody, and what a pleasure he takes in offering it right and left wherever he happens to be? He doesn't even wait to be asked or until folk know that they want it! Which just goes to show how it makes for honest and decent behaviour in all those who take it. But enough of that now. Let's come back to what we were talking about. You were saying, my dear Gusman, that Dona Elvira was surprised when we went away, and set out in pursuit of us. She was so much in love with my master, you said, that nothing would do but she must come here to look for us. Shall I tell you, between our two selves, what I think about it? I'm afraid she'll get little return for her love; her journey here will be useless; and you would have done just as well to have stopped where you were.

GUSMAN. But what is the reason? Do tell me, Sganarelle, what makes you take such a gloomy view of the position. Has your master taken you into his confidence? Has he told you that his reason for leaving was a cooling off in his feelings towards us?

SGANARELLE. No, but knowing the lie of the land I have a fair idea of the way things are going, and I could very nearly bet that is what is happening without his having said a word. Of course, I may be wrong, but after all I've had a lot of experience of this sort of thing.

GUSMAN. You mean to say the explanation of Don Juan's unexpected departure is that he is unfaithful to Dona Elvira? You think he could betray her innocent love in this way?

SGANARELLE. No. It's just that he's still young and he hasn't the heart . . .

GUSMAN. But how could a gentleman do such a vile thing?

SGANARELLE. Ay, ay! A lot of difference that makes, his being a gentleman! I can see *that* stopping him from doing anything he wants to do!

GUSMAN. But surely he is bound by the obligations of holy matrimony.

SGANARELLE. Ah, my dear Gusman, believe me, you still don't understand what sort of man Don Juan is.

GUSMAN. No, I certainly don't if he has really betrayed us like that. I just can't understand how, after showing so much affection, after being so very importunate, after all his declarations of love, vows, sighs, tears, passionate letters, protestations, and promises repeated over and over again; in short, after such an overwhelming display of passion and going to the lengths of invading the holy precincts of a convent to carry off Dona Elvira—I repeat I just cannot understand how, after all that, he could find it in his heart to go back on his word.

SGANARELLE. I understand well enough, and if you knew our friend as I do you'd understand that he finds it easy enough. I am not saying his feelings for Dona Elvira have changed. I can't be sure yet. As you know, I left before he did, on his instruction, and he has said nothing to me since he arrived here, but I will say this much as a warning— *inter nos*—that in my master, Don Juan, you see the biggest scoundrel that ever cumbered the earth, a madman, a cur, a devil, a Turk, a heretic who believes neither in Heaven, Hell, nor werewolf: he lives like an animal, like a swine of an Epicurean, a veritable Sardanapalus, shut-

456

ting his ears to every Christian remonstrance, and turning to ridicule everything we believe in. You tell me he has married your mistress— believe me, to satisfy his passion he would have gone further than that, he would have married you as well, ay, and her dog and her cat into the bargain! Marriage means nothing to him. It is his usual method of ensnaring women: he marries 'em left and right, maids or married women, ladies or peasants, shy ones and t'other sort—all come alike to him. If I were to give you the names of all those he has married in one place and another, the list would take till to-night. That surprises you! What I'm saying makes you turn pale, but this is no more than the outline of his character: it would take me much longer to finish the portrait. Let it suffice that the wrath of Heaven is bound to overwhelm him one of these days and that, for my part, I would sooner serve the Devil himself. He's made me witness to so many horrible things that I wish he was—I don't know where! But a nobleman who has given himself over to wickedness is a thing to be dreaded. I am bound to remain with him whether I like it or not: fear serves me for zeal, makes me restrain my feelings and forces me often enough to make a show of approving things that in my heart of hearts I detest. But here he comes —taking a turn in the palace. Let us separate. But just let me say this —I have talked to you frankly and in confidence, and I've opened my mouth pretty freely, but if any word of it were to come to his ears I should declare you had made it all up.   *Exit* GUSMAN.

Enter DON JUAN.

DON JUAN. Who was the man who was talking to you? I thought he looked very much like our friend Gusman, Dona Elvira's man.

SGANARELLE. You are not very far wrong.

DON JUAN. Why! Was it he?

SGANARELLE. Gusman himself.

DON JUAN. And since when has he been in the town?

SGANARELLE. Since yesterday evening.

DON JUAN. And what brings him here?

SGANARELLE. I should have thought you would have had a fair idea of what might be worrying him.

DON JUAN. Our departure, no doubt?

SGANARELLE. The poor fellow is very much upset about it. He was asking me what the reason was.

DON JUAN. And what reply did you give him?

SGANARELLE. I said that you had told me nothing about it.

DON JUAN. Well then, what do you think about it? What is your own view of the matter?

SGANARELLE. I think—without wishing to do you injustice—that you are involved in a new love affair.

DON JUAN. That is what you think, is it?

SGANARELLE. Yes, it is.

DON JUAN. Well, you are quite right. I must confess that someone else has driven all thought of Elvira out of my head.

SGANARELLE. Lord, yes! I know my Don Juan well enough! I know your fancy's a rover, for ever flitting from one entanglement to another; never content to settle down anywhere.

DON JUAN. And do you not think I am right in behaving as I do?

SGANARELLE. Well, master . . .

DON JUAN. Go on, speak out!

SGANARELLE. Of course you are right—if you will have it that way. There's no gainsaying it. But if you'd let me put it my way—it might be a different matter.

DON JUAN. Well, then, I give you leave to speak freely and say what you think.

SGANARELLE. Well, then, master, I tell you frankly I don't like your way of behaving at all. I think it's very wrong to make love left and right the way that you do.

DON JUAN. What! Would you have a man tie himself up to the first woman that captured his fancy, renounce the world for her, and never again look at anyone else? That *is* a fine idea, I must say, to make a virtue of faithfulness, to bury oneself for good and all in one single passion and remain blind ever after to all the other beauties that might catch one's eye! No! Let fools make a virtue of constancy! All beautiful women have a right to our love, and the accident of being the first comer shouldn't rob others of a fair share in our hearts. As for me, beauty delights me wherever I find it and I freely surrender myself to its charms. No matter how far I'm committed—the fact that I am in love with one person shall never make me unjust to the others. I keep an eye for the merits of all of them and render each one the homage, pay each one the tribute that nature enjoins. Come what may, I cannot refuse love to what I find lovable, and so, when a beautiful face is asking for love, if I had ten thousand hearts I would freely bestow every one of them. After all, there is something inexpressibly charming in falling in love and, surely, the whole pleasure lies in the fact that love isn't lasting. How delightful, how entrancing it is to lay siege with a hundred attentions to a young woman's heart; to see, day by day, how one makes slight advances; to pit one's exaltation, one's sighs and one's tears, against the modest reluctance of a heart unwilling to yield; to surmount, step by step, all the little barriers by which she resists; to overcome her proud scruples and bring her at last to consent. But once one succeeds, what else remains? What more can one wish for? All that delights one in passion is over and one can only sink into a tame and slumberous affection—until a new love comes along to awaken desire and offer the charm of new conquests. There is no pleasure to compare with the conquest of beauty, and my ambition is that of all the great conquerors who could never find it in them to set bounds to their ambitions, but must go on for ever from conquest to conquest. Nothing can restrain my impetuous desires. I feel it is in me to love the whole world, and like Alexander still wish for new worlds to conquer.

SGANARELLE. Goodness me! How you do reel it off! Anyone would think you had learned it by heart. You talk like a book.

DON JUAN. And what have you to say about it?

SGANARELLE. What I say is—nay, I don't know what to say! You twist things round so that you seem to be in the right, even when you aren't. I did have some good ideas, but you've muddled me up with your talk. Never mind, another time I'll put my arguments down on paper and then I shall be able to deal with you.

DON JUAN. An excellent idea!

SGANARELLE. But, if I might make use of the liberty you've given me, master, I must say I am very much shocked at the life you are leading.

DON JUAN. Indeed! And what sort of life am I leading?

SGANARELLE. Oh! It's a very good life, only—to see you marrying afresh every month or two as you are doing . . .

DON JUAN. Well, what could be more agreeable?

SGANARELLE. I admit it may be very agreeable—and very amusing. I wouldn't mind doing the same myself if there were no harm in it, but you know, sir, to trifle like that with a holy sacrament and . . .

DON JUAN. Get along with you! That's a matter for Heaven and myself to settle between us without your worrying about it.

SGANARELLE. Upon my word, master, I've always heard tell it was a bad thing to mock at Heaven and that unbelievers came to no good.

DON JUAN. Now then, my dear blockhead, remember what I have told you—I don't like being preached at.

SGANARELLE. I am not referring to you, God forbid! You know what you are doing, you do. If you don't believe in anything, well, you have your own reasons, but there are some silly little fellows who are unbelievers without knowing why; they think it smart to set themselves up as free thinkers. If I had a master like that, I would ask him straight to his face, 'How dare you set yourself up against Heaven as you do? Aren't you afraid to mock at sacred things? What right have you, you little worm, pygmy that you are (I'm talking to the imaginary master), to make a jest of everything that people hold sacred? Do you think because you are a gentleman and wear a fashionable wig, because you have feathers in your hat, and gilt lace on your coat and flame-coloured ribbons (of course, I'm not talking to you)—do you think that you are any the wiser for that, and that you can do as you like and nobody is going to dare to tell you the truth? You take it from me, though I'm only your servant, that sooner or later Heaven punishes the wicked, and those who live evil lives come to bad ends and—'

DON JUAN. Shut up!

SGANARELLE. Why, what's the matter?

DON JUAN. The matter is this. I want you to know that I have fallen in love with a lady and it is her charms that have induced me to come to this town.

SGANARELLE. And aren't you afraid, master, of coming here, where you killed the Commander only six months ago?

DON JUAN. Why should I be afraid? Did I not do the job properly?

SGANARELLE. Oh yes! All fair and proper! He's no cause for complaint!

DON JUAN. Was I not pardoned for that little affair?

SGANARELLE. Yes, but a pardon may not remove the resentment of friends and relations.

DON JUAN. Never mind the disagreeable things that may happen. Let us think of the pleasant ones. The lady I referred to is the most charming creature imaginable. She has just arrived here under the escort of the man she is going to marry. I happened to meet this young couple three or four days before they set out on their journey. I never saw two people so devoted, so completely in love. The manifest tenderness of their mutual affection awakened a like feeling in me. It affected me deeply. My love began in the first place as jealousy. I couldn't bear to see them so happy together; vexation stimulated my desire and I realized what a pleasure it would give me to disturb their mutual understanding and break up an attachment so repugnant to my own susceptibilities, but so far all my efforts have failed and I am driven to my last resort. To-day the future husband intends to take his beloved on the sea and my plans to gratify my passion are laid. Without mentioning it to you I have engaged men and a boat and I expect to carry her off without difficulty.

SGANARELLE. Oh, master!

DON JUAN. What's that?

SGANARELLE. You have done splendidly. You are quite right to do what you are doing. There's nothing in this world like getting what you want.

DON JUAN. Then get ready to come with me. Make yourself responsible for bringing my weapons, so that—Ah! What an inopportune meeting! You rascal! You never told me *she* was here too.

SGANARELLE. Well, master—you never asked me!

DON JUAN. She must be out of her mind not to have changed her clothes and to come to town dressed for the country.

Enter DONA ELVIRA.

DONA ELVIRA. Will you not favour me, Don Juan, with some sign of recognition? Is it too much to hope that you will deign to look at me?

DON JUAN. I confess, madam, that I am surprised. I was not expecting you here.

DONA ELVIRA. Yes, I see that you were not expecting me, and, though you are surprised, it is not in the way that I hoped. Your manner entirely convinces me of what I previously refused to believe. I wonder at my own simplicity, at my soft-hearted reluctance to believe in your duplicity, though you gave me so many proofs of it. Such was my indulgence towards you—no, I confess it now, such was my folly, that I was bent on deceiving myself. I struggled against the evidence of my own eyes, against my own better judgement. In the goodness of my heart I sought excuses for the growing coldness I noticed in you. I invented a thousand reasons to justify your abrupt departure and to acquit you of the faithlessness of which common sense told me you were guilty. The daily warnings of my well-founded suspicions were in vain: I rejected all evidence which counted against you and listened eagerly to a thousand absurd fancies which seemed to indicate that you were not to blame, but your manner just now leaves me no room for doubt, your expression when you first saw me told me more than I ever cared to admit. Nevertheless I should like to hear from your own lips your reasons for leaving me. Speak, Don Juan, I beg you. Let me hear how you will manage to justify yourself.

DON JUAN. Madam, Sganarelle here knows why I came away.

SGANARELLE. Me, master? Excuse me—I know nothing about it.

DONA ELVIRA. Come, speak up Sganarelle. It matters little from whose lips I hear his excuses.

DON JUAN (*signing to* SGANARELLE *to approach*). Come along! Speak to the lady.

SGANARELLE. What d'ye expect me to say?

DONA ELVIRA. Come here, since he will have it so, and explain to me the reasons for so sudden a departure.

DON JUAN. Aren't you going to answer?

SGANARELLE. I can't answer. You're just making a fool of your poor servant.

DON JUAN. Give her an answer, I tell you!

SGANARELLE. Madam—

DONA ELVIRA. Well?

SGANARELLE (*turning to* DON JUAN). Master—

DON JUAN. If you—(*threatening him*).

SGANARELLE. Madam. We left because of Alexander and the other worlds he still had to conquer. (*To* DON JUAN) That's the best I can do, sir.

DONA ELVIRA. Would you be good enough to elucidate these mysteries, Don Juan?

DON JUAN. To tell the truth, madam—

DONA ELVIRA. Come! For a courtier, a man who must be accustomed to this sort of thing, you do give a poor account of yourself. I am sorry to see you so embarrassed. Why don't you take refuge in a gentlemanly effrontery? Why don't you swear that your feelings for me are unchanged, that you still love me more than all the world, and that nothing but death can part us? Can you not say that business of the most pressing importance forced you to leave without an opportunity of informing me, that you are obliged to remain here for a while against your own wishes, and that if only I will return whence I came

I may be assured that you will follow at the earliest possible moment? That you are only too eager to be with me again, and that while you are away from me you suffer the agonies of a body bereft of its soul? Is that not how you should justify yourself instead of letting yourself be put out of countenance as you are?

DON JUAN. Madam, I assure you that I have no gift for dissimulation. I am entirely sincere. I am not going to say that I still have the same feeling for you or that I yearn to be with you again, because the fact is that I came away with the deliberate intention of escaping from you, not for the reasons you imagine, but on grounds of conscience alone. I left because I had come to believe that it would be a sin to live with you longer. My conscience was awakened, madam, and I came to see the error of my ways. I considered how, in order to marry you, I carried you off from the seclusion of a convent, how you yourself broke your vows, and that these are things which God does not forgive. I became a prey to repentance, I came to dread the wrath of Heaven and to realize that our marriage was no more than disguised adultery which must bring down on us a punishment from on high; in short, that I must endeavour to forget you and afford you the opportunity of returning to your former allegiance. Would you oppose so holy a resolution, madam? Would you have me, through loyalty to you, get myself into the bad books of Heaven?

DONA ELVIRA. Ah! Villain. Now I know you for what you are, and, to my misfortune, only when it is too late, when the realization can only bring me to despair! But be assured that your infidelity will not go unpunished, and that the Heaven you mock at will find means to avenge your perfidy to me!

DON JUAN. Ah! Sganarelle, Heaven!

SGANARELLE. Ay, ay, little we care for that! Fellows like us!

DON JUAN. Madam—

DONA ELVIRA. Enough! I will hear no more! Indeed I blame myself for having heard too much already. It is a weakness to allow one's shame to be exposed in this way. In such moments a noble mind should choose its course of action at once. Have no fear that I shall give way to reproaches. No! My anger is not the sort that can find vent in vain words. All its fury is reserved for vengeance. Once again I declare that Heaven will punish you for the wrong you have done me, and if Heaven itself has no terrors for you, then beware, at least, the fury of a woman scorned. *Exit.*

SGANARELLE. If he could but feel some remorse.

DON JUAN (*after a moment's reflection*). Come along, we must consider how to carry out our other little scheme.

SGANARELLE. Ah, what an abominable master I am bound to serve!

ACT TWO

CHARLOTTE, PETER.

CHARLOTTE. Mercy on us, Peter, 'ee be a-come there just in time, then.

PETER. Lor' lumme, yes. Within a hair's breadth o' bein' a-drownded they was, the pair of 'em.

CHARLOTTE. 'Twould be that there squall this morn'n' 'as capsized 'em?

PETER. Lookee, Lottie. I can tell 'ee just 'ow it did come about. 'Twas me as clapped eyes on 'em first in a manner o' speak'n': first to clap eyes on 'em, I be. Down on the beach we was, Fatty Lucas an' me, a-heav'n' clods at each other for a lark we was. A boy for a bit o' lark'n' be Lucas, an' I bain't for miss'n' it neither. A-lark'n' about we was, the way we do be a-lark'n', when I sees someth'n' afar off like, someth'n' a-bobb'n' up an' down in the water like, as seemed to be a-com'n' t'ards us off an' on. I be a-keep'n' an eye on it when all of a sudden I couldn't see noth'n' no more. 'Luke,' says I, 'I reckon yon's fellers a-swimmin' out there.' 'No, indeed,' says 'e, 'see'n' double 'ee be.' 'Not on thy life,' says I, 'them's fellers out there.' 'Not a bit of it,' says 'e. 'A-dazzled by the sunshine 'ee be!' 'No dazzle about it, will 'ee bet on it?' says I. 'Them's two fellers a-swimm'n' this way,' says I. 'Lumme, no!' says 'e, 'I bet they bain't.' 'Will 'ee 'ave a bob on it?' says I. 'Done!' says 'e, 'and there be my money down.' Now I bain't no fool nor yet I bain't a-fancy'n' things neither, so down goes my money, six pennies and two threepenny diddlers. Blow me! bold as if I'd swallowed a whole pint I was, for I be a real venturesome fellow when I be roused like. But I knows well enough what I be about for all that, mind. 'Ardly be the stakes down when I sees the two men plain as daylight. They starts a-making' signs to us for to come out and fetch 'em in. So I ups with the stakes an' 'Quick, Lucas,' says I, 'they be a-call'n' to us to go out an' help 'em.' 'They bain't going to get no 'elp from me,' says 'e. 'Not arter makin' me lose my money,' says 'e. Well then, to be a-cutt'n' it short, such a to-do I did 'ave for to get 'im to come in the boat along o' me. Then we pulls out to 'em, hauls 'em aboard, takes 'em 'ome to a fire, and they strips themselves naked to dry. By 'n' by in comes two more of 'em that had made shift for themselves. When Mathurine comes in, blow me if one of 'em don't start cast'n' sheep's eyes at 'er, and that be just exac'ly 'ow 't all did befall, Lottie.

CHARLOTTE. Did I 'ear 'ee say that one be better-look'n' than t'others, Peter?

PETER. Ay, that'ld be t'maister. A regular gentleman, 'e be—gold lace on his clothes from head to foot. Even his servants be gentlemen, like. Howsumiver 'e'd have been a-drownded right enough, gentleman or no gentleman, if I 'adn't been there.

CHARLOTTE. Ah! Go on with you!

PETER. Lumme! If 't 'adn't ha' been for us 'is number would ha' been up for certain.

CHARLOTTE. Do 'ee think 'e be still there all nakey body, Peter?

PETER. No, no. We seen 'im dressed again. Lor!—I never seen them sort a-dress'n' afore. What a sight of contraptions them courtiers do be a-wear'n'! I'd be lost in 'em, I would—fair amazed I was at the sight o' 'em. 'Pon my word, Lottie, they'm got hair that bain't fast to their heads! Clap it on last thing of all, they do, like a gurt bonnet of flax. They'm got shirts with sleeves thee and me could get lost in. 'Stead o' breeches they'm got aprons as wide as from here to Christmas! 'Stead o' a doublet they'm got a tiny waistcoat, don't come half down the chest like; 'stead o' neck-bands a great neckerchief wi' four great bows o' linen hang'n' down to their middle like. Then they'm got frills at their waists, like, an' great swathes o' lace round their legs, an' to cap all, such a sight o' ribbons, such a sight o' ribbons as be shameful for to see! There bain't no part of 'em, even their shoes, that don't be a-loaded down with 'em. If they was on me, I'd be a-trip'n' over 'em, I would.

CHARLOTTE. 'Pon my word, Peter, I mun go have a look at that.

PETER. Hark 'ee! Just a minute, Lottie, I got someth'n' more to say to 'ee first.

CHARLOTTE. Oh well, then, but tell me quick what it be.

PETER. Look 'ee, Lottie. I been a want'n' for to open my heart to 'ee as the say'n' is. 'Ee knows how I loves 'ee and we be a-goin' for to marry, but Lord, I bain't no ways satisfied with 'ee, like.

CHARLOTTE. Whatever do 'ee mean by that?

PETER. What do I mean by that? I mean 'ee be a terrible vexation to me.

CHARLOTTE. And how do 'ee make that out?

PETER. Lord 'elp me—I believe 'ee don't love me at all.

CHARLOTTE. Ha ha! Be that all?

PETER. Ay, that be all, an' quite enough too it be.

CHARLOTTE. Lor', Peter, 'ee be always a-tell'n' the same tale.

PETER. Ay! I be a-tell'n' the same tale 'cause it be always the same tale for I to be tell'n'. If it war'n't the same tale I wouldn't be a-tell'n' it!

CHARLOTTE. But what mun I do for 'ee? What do 'ee want?

PETER. Lord help me! I want 'ee to love me.

CHARLOTTE. And don't I a-love 'ee?

PETER. No, that 'ee don't! and yet, don't I do all I can to make 'ee? Don't I buy 'ee—no offence, mind—ribbons from all the pedlars that be a-pass'n' by? Don't I be a-break'n' my neck a-clim'n' after birds' nests for 'ee? Don't I make fiddler play for 'ee on thy birthday? An' for all that I may as well be a bang'n' my head against a wall. Look 'ee now, t'ain't no-ways right nor decent not to love them as do be a-lov'n' us.

CHARLOTTE. But indeed I do love 'ee too.

PETER. An' a pretty way o' lov'n' me, indeed!

CHARLOTTE. How do 'ee want me to love 'ee?

PETER. I want 'ee to love me proper like, same as other folks do be a-lov'n'.

CHARLOTTE. Don't I love 'ee proper like?

PETER. No, that 'ee don't. When a maid do love proper 'tis plain for to be seen—there be a thousand ways of show'n' it for them that do love whole-hearted like. Look 'ee now, that fat Thomasina, she be fair daft about young Robin. She be always around him a-plagu'n' of 'im. She don't never let 'im be: for ever a-play'n' some trick on 'im or a-giv'n' 'im a bump in pass'n' like: only t'other day, when he's a-setting' on a stool, she whips it from under him an' down 'e goes full length on the ground. 'Pon my word, that's the way folk do behave when they do be in love, but 'ee don't never throw me so much as a word like. Same as a block o' wood, 'ee be: a score o' times I might pass along of 'ee and never get a touch or a word out of 'ee. Lor' lumme! 'Tain't good enough! 'ee don't give a fellow no encouragement at all.

CHARLOTTE. An' what do 'ee expect me to do? 'Tis the way I be made. I can't do no other.

PETER. I don't give a rap for the way 'ee be made. When folk be in love they did ought to show it some ways or other.

CHARLOTTE. Well then, I do love 'ee all I know how. If 'ee bain't satisfied, 'ee mun go love somewheres else.

PETER. Well, now ain't that just what I said! Blow me!—if 'ee loved me proper 'ee couldn't say such things.

CHARLOTTE. Why must 'ee come a-worriting me so?

PETER. Oh lor', I bain't meanin' no harm. I bain't want'n' no more than a bit o' love.

CHARLOTTE. Then why won't 'ee leave me alone and not be always a troubl'n'? Perhaps one o' these days 'twill come over me all of a sudden.

PETER. Give me thy hand on that then, Lottie.

CHARLOTTE. Very well, there 'tis then.

PETER. Promise 'ee'll try for to love me a little bit more.

CHARLOTTE. All as I can do, I will, but love mun come of its own accord. Be this the gentleman, Peter?

PETER. Ay, that be him.

CHARLOTTE. Lor', bain't 'e a pretty man! 'Twould ha' been a shame had he been a-drownded.

PETER. I'll be back again soon. I mun go have a drop for to set me up again after all that I been through.

Enter DON JUAN *and* SGANARELLE.

DON JUAN. Well, Sganarelle, our scheme misfired. That unexpected squall upset both ship and plans, but to tell the truth that little peasant girl I have just left makes up for the mishap. She is so charming that I can almost forget our failure in the other affair. She mustn't slip through my fingers. I think I have already paved the way so that I shan't be kept sighing too long.

SGANARELLE. I must say you astonish me, master. Here we have just

465

escaped from peril of our lives, and, instead of thanking Heaven for its mercy, you are starting all over again, running the risk of its wrath with your usual goings on. These love affairs of yours are disgraceful and dis—Shut up, you fool! You don't know what you are talking about! The master knows what he is doing—get along with you!

DON JUAN (*noticing* CHARLOTTE). Ha, ha! Where did this one come from, Sganarelle? Did you ever see anything so charming? She's even prettier than the other. Don't you think so?

SGANARELLE. Oh, of course! (*Aside*) Off we go again!

DON JUAN. To what do I owe the pleasure of this charming encounter? Can there really be lovely creatures like you among these wild rocks and trees?

CHARLOTTE. Just as you see, sir.

DON JUAN. Do you belong to this village?

CHARLOTTE. Yes, sir.

DON JUAN. And you live here?

CHARLOTTE. Yes sir.

DON JUAN. And your name is?

CHARLOTTE. Charlotte, at your service, sir.

DON JUAN. What a lovely girl. What fire in her eyes.

CHARLOTTE. You be making me blush, sir.

DON JUAN. But why blush at hearing the truth? What do you say, Sganarelle? Did you ever see anything more delightful? Turn a little, if you please. Ah, what a charming figure! Look up a little, please. What a dear little face! Open your eyes wide. Aren't they beautiful? Now a glimpse of your teeth. Delicious!—and what inviting lips! She is really enchanting. I've never met such a charming girl.

CHARLOTTE. You be pleased to say so, sir, but I don't know whether you are making fun of me or not.

DON JUAN. Making fun of you. Heaven forbid! I am too much in love with you. I do really mean it.

CHARLOTTE. If that is so, I'm much obliged to you, sir.

DON JUAN. Not at all. There's no need to be obliged at anything I'm saying. It's no more than what is due to your beauty.

CHARLOTTE. Fine talk like this be too much for me, sir. I don't know how to answer you.

DON JUAN. Just look at her hands, Sganarelle.

SGANARELLE. Tch, sir. They are as black as I don't know what.

DON JUAN. What are you talking about? They are the loveliest hands in the world. Permit me to kiss them.

CHARLOTTE. Oh, sir! You do me too much honour. If I'd known it afore, I would have washed them in bran.

DON JUAN. Tell me just one thing, my dear Charlotte—you are not married, by any chance?

CHARLOTTE. No, sir, but I be a-promised to Peter, neighbour Simonetta's lad.

466

DON JUAN. What! A girl like you marrying a mere peasant! Never! It's a profanation of beauty—you weren't born to live in a village. You are worth something far better. Heaven itself knows it and has sent me here for the very purpose of preventing the marriage and doing justice to your charms. In short, my beautiful Charlotte, I love you with all my heart. You only need say the word and I will take you away from this wretched place and give you the position in the world that you deserve. This declaration no doubt sounds rather sudden, but what of it? It all comes of your being so beautiful, Charlotte. You have made me fall as deeply in love with you in a quarter of an hour as in six months with anyone else.

CHARLOTTE. Truly, sir, when you talk like that I just don't know what to do. I love to hear you talk so and I'd like to believe you, but I've always heard tell as how a maid should never believe fine gentlemen's talk and as how ye all be deceivers as come from the court and only want to lead girls astray.

DON JUAN. I am not that sort of man!

SGANARELLE (aside). No! Not he!

CHARLOTTE. You see, sir, it's not right for a maid to let herself be led astray. I be only a simple country maid, but I set store by my virtue. I'd die sooner than lose my reputation.

DON JUAN. And do you think I could be so wicked as to deceive a girl like you? Do you think that I could ever be so base as to betray you? No, I could never do such a thing. I love you, Charlotte, truly and honourably, and to show you that I am speaking the truth, let me tell you that I have nothing but marriage in mind. I am ready whenever you wish, and I call my man here to witness my promise.

SGANARELLE. No, no, have no fear! He'll marry you to your heart's content.

DON JUAN. I see that you don't know me yet, Charlotte. You wrong me when you judge me by other men. There may be scoundrels in the world who make love to girls only to deceive them, but don't include me among their number. Never doubt my word. Surely your beauty should give you confidence. You need fear nothing. Believe me, no one could dream of deceiving a woman like you. As for myself, I declare I would die a thousand deaths rather than harbour the slightest thought of betraying you.

CHARLOTTE. Oh lor'! I don't know whether you are speaking the truth or no, but you have such a way with you I would fain believe you.

DON JUAN. Only put your faith in me. You won't be disappointed. Let me repeat my promise to you once again. Won't you accept my word and consent to be my wife?

CHARLOTTE. Yes, if Auntie agrees.

DON JUAN. Then, Charlotte, since you yourself are willing, give me your hand.

CHARLOTTE. You won't deceive me, sir, will you? It would be a wicked thing to do when you see how I trust you.

DON JUAN. What! Do you still doubt my sincerity? Then I'll swear the most solemn oaths. May Heaven—

CHARLOTTE. Oh lor', please don't swear! I believe you.

DON JUAN. Then give me a little kiss as a pledge of your promise.

CHARLOTTE. Nay sir, wait till we be married and then I will kiss you as much as you like.

DON JUAN. Very well, then, my dear Charlotte, just as you like. Only give me your hand and let me cover it with kisses to show how delighted I am by your—

Enter PETER.

PETER (*interposing between them and pushing* DON JUAN). Easy, maister, steady on, if ye don't mind—if ye be wax'n' that warm ye'll be a gett'n' 'eartburn.

DON JUAN (*pushing him roughly*). Where did this lout come from?

PETER. I tell 'ee to keep off—'ee bain't go'n' to be a-kiss'n' my intended.

DON JUAN (*pushing him again*). What are you making a fuss about?

PETER. Lumme! Don't 'ee be a-shov'n' folk like that.

CHARLOTTE. Let him be, Peter.

PETER. How do 'ee mean, let 'un be. I bain't nowise for lett'n' 'un be.

DON JUAN. Ah!

PETER. Confound 'ee! Because 'ee be a gen'l'man do 'ee think 'ee can come kiss'n' our women under our very noses? Why can't 'e go kiss 'is own women?

DON JUAN. Heh?

PETER. Heh! (DON JUAN *gives him a box on the ear.*) Lord help us! Don't 'ee be a hitt'n' me. (DON JUAN *gives him another blow.*) Hey! What the . . . (*Another blow.*) Lor' lumme! (*Another.*) Hang it! that ain't no way to behave. That ain't no way to repay a feller that's saved 'ee from drown'n'.

CHARLOTTE. Now don't 'ee get mad, Peter.

PETER. I will get mad if I want to and it bain't nowise right of 'ee to be a-let t'n' un cajole 'ee so.

CHARLOTTE. Oh, Peter, things bain't the way 'ee be thinking. This gentleman be a-goin' to marry me and there ain't no call for 'ee to get mad.

PETER. Dang it! Bain't 'ee a-promised to me?

CHARLOTTE. That don't make no matter, Peter. If 'ee do love me 'ee ought to be main glad to see me a-goin'· to be a lady.

PETER. Lor' lumme! I'd as soon see 'ee dead as married to another feller.

CHARLOTTE. Go on now, Peter—don't 'ee be a-frett'n'. When I be a fine lady I'll see 'ee don't lose by it. I'll have 'ee bring butter and cheese to the house.

PETER. Criminy! I won't never bring 'ee noth'n', not if 'ee pay twice over, I won't. Be that why 'ee 'ave 'earkened to him? Lumme! If I'd have knowed that I wouldn't never have pulled 'im out o' the water—I'd have fetched 'un one over the 'ead with the oar, I would.

DON JUAN (*threatening to strike him*). What's that you say?

PETER (*getting behind* CHARLOTTE). Lumme! I bain't frightened o' no-body—

DON JUAN (*going round after him*). You wait a minute.

PETER (*dodging round* CHARLOTTE). I don't care noth'n' for nobody.

DON JUAN (*following him*). We'll see about that.

PETER (*taking refuge again behind* CHARLOTTE). I seen many a better man than—

DON JUAN. Hah!

SGANARELLE. Now, master, let the poor beggar alone! It's too bad to knock him about. Listen to me, my lad—get out and don't say another word to him.

PETER (*comes in front of* SGANARELLE *and looks defiantly at* DON JUAN). I'll say what I want to 'un. I will . . .

DON JUAN. I'll teach you. (*Strikes at* PETER *who ducks and* SGANARELLE *gets the blow.*)

SGANARELLE (*looking at* PETER). Confound the fool!

DON JUAN. That's what you get for your kindness.

PETER. Lor'! I mun go tell her auntie about these 'ere goings on.   *Exit.*

DON JUAN. And now I'm going to be the happiest of men. I would not exchange my good fortune for all the world could offer. What pleasures we shall enjoy once you are my wife!

Enter MATHURINE.

SGANARELLE (*seeing* MATHURINE). Ha, ha!

MATHURINE. What are you doing with Charlotte, sir? You are not a-court'n' her too?

DON JUAN (*to* MATHURINE). No, on the contrary. It was she was suggesting she would like to be my wife and I was telling her that I was engaged to you.

CHARLOTTE. What does Mathurine want with you?

DON JUAN (*to* CHARLOTTE, *aside*). She is jealous at seeing me talking to you. She wants me to marry her, but I was telling her that you are the one I want.

MATHURINE. Why—Charlotte—!

DON JUAN (*to* MATHURINE, *aside*). It's no use trying to talk to her, she's got the idea firmly fixed in her head.

CHARLOTTE. Why, Mathurine!

DON JUAN. It's a waste of time talking to her. You will never make her see sense.

MATHURINE. Can she really—

DON JUAN (*aside to* MATHURINE). She just won't listen to reason.

CHARLOTTE. I would like to—

DON JUAN (*to* CHARLOTTE *aside*). She is as obstinate as the very Devil!

MATHURINE. Really—

DON JUAN (*to* MATHURINE *aside*). Don't say a word to her—she's crazy.

CHARLOTTE. I think I—

DON JUAN (*to* CHARLOTTE *aside*). No, leave her alone. She's out of her mind.

MATHURINE. No, no, I must speak to her.

CHARLOTTE. I must hear why she—

MATHURINE. What's that?

DON JUAN (*to* MATHURINE, *aside*). I bet she tells you I have promised to marry her.

CHARLOTTE. I—

DON JUAN (*to* CHARLOTTE, *aside*). What do you bet she will make out I have promised to make her my wife?

MATHURINE. Hark 'ee Charlotte! It's not fair to be a-queer'n' other people's pitches.

CHARLOTTE. It's not right of you, Mathurine, to be jealous because the gentleman is talking to me.

MATHURINE. Well, 'twas me the gentleman seen first!

CHARLOTTE. If 'twas you he seen first 'twas me he seen second and 'tis me he's a-promised to marry.

DON JUAN (*aside to* MATHURINE). There you are! What did I tell you?

MATHURINE. Get away with you, 'tis me, not you, he be a-taking to wife.

DON JUAN (*aside to* CHARLOTTE). Didn't I just guess as much?

CHARLOTTE. Tell that tale somewhere else—'tis me he be promised to—

MATHURINE. Ye be trying to fool me—'tis me he be going to wed.

CHARLOTTE. Well, let him speak for himself. Let him say if I be not in the right.

MATHURINE. Ay, let him say if I don't speak honest truth.

CHARLOTTE. Be it she you have promised to marry, sir?

DON JUAN (*aside to* CHARLOTTE). Are you trying to tease me?

MATHURINE. Be it true, sir, that you have promised to wed her?

DON JUAN (*aside to* MATHURINE). How could you believe such a thing!

CHARLOTTE. Hark, how she be stick'n' to it.

DON JUAN (*aside to* CHARLOTTE). Let her talk as she pleases.

MATHURINE. You are a witness how she will have it 'tis so.

DON JUAN. Let her say what she likes.

CHARLOTTE. No, no. We must know the truth.

MATHURINE. Yes. 'Tis a thing must be settled.

CHARLOTTE. Ay, Mathurine, I'll have this gentleman show 'ee what a young silly 'ee be.

MATHURINE. Ay, Charlotte, I'll have him bring 'ee down a peg.

CHARLOTTE. Please to put an end to the quarrel, sir.

MATHURINE. Please to decide for us, sir.

CHARLOTTE (*to* MATHURINE). Now 'ee'll soon see!

MATHURINE (*to* CHARLOTTE). 'Ee'll see, right enough!

CHARLOTTE (*to* DON JUAN). Tell her how 'tis.

MATHURINE (*to* DON JUAN). Speak to her now.

470

DON JUAN (*embarrassed, speaking to both of them*). What do you want me to say? You both claim that I have promised to marry you, but don't you each know the truth without any need for me to explain? Why make me go over it once more? Surely the one I have really given my promise to can afford to laugh at the other. Why need she worry so long as I keep my promise to her? All the explanations in the world won't get us any further. We must do things, not talk about them. Deeds speak louder than words. There's only one way I can hope to reconcile you. When I do marry, you will see which one I love. (*Aside to* MATHURINE) Let her think what she pleases! (*Aside to* CHARLOTTE) Let her amuse herself with her fancies! (*Aside to* MATHURINE) I adore *you*. (*Aside to* CHARLOTTE) I am devoted to *you*. (*Aside to* MATHURINE) There is no beauty like yours. (*Aside to* CHARLOTTE) Since I have seen you I have no eyes for anyone else. (*To both*) I have some business I must attend to. I will be back in a quarter of an hour. (*He goes out.*)

CHARLOTTE. There now, I be the one that he really loves.

MATHURINE. But 'tis me he be a-goin' to marry.

SGANARELLE. My poor girls! I pity your simplicity. I can't bear to see you rushing to your ruin. Take notice of me, both of you. Don't be deceived by his stories, but stay at home in your village.

DON JUAN (*coming back*). I should very much like to know why Sganarelle isn't following me.

SGANARELLE. My master's a rogue. His only intention is to deceive you as he has deceived many another. He marries any woman he comes across and—(*seeing* DON JUAN) That's not true! You can tell anyone who says so he's a liar! My master doesn't marry every woman he comes across, not a bit of it. He isn't a rogue. He doesn't intend to deceive. He has never deceived a woman in his life. Hold on, here he is. You can ask him yourselves.

DON JUAN (*to himself*). Yes.

SGANARELLE. Master—there is so much slander in the world, I thought I would take precautions. I was just telling them that if anyone were to come and say anything to your discredit they were not to believe it and they shouldn't hesitate to tell him he was a liar.

DON JUAN. Sganarelle!

SGANARELLE. Yes! The master's a man of honour, you can take my word for that.

DON JUAN. Hum!

SGANARELLE. Such people are just a lot of good-for-nothings.

Enter LA RAMÉE.

LA RAMÉE. Sir, I must warn you that it's not safe for you here.

DON JUAN. What's that?

LA RAMÉE. There are a dozen horsemen coming in search of you. They'll be here any moment. I don't know how they've managed to follow you, but I got the information from a peasant they had been questioning. They gave him your description. You must be quick. The sooner you get out of here the better.

DON JUAN (*to* CHARLOTTE *and* MATHURINE). I'm called away on urgent business, but remember my promise and be sure that you shall hear from me before to-morrow evening. (MATHURINE *and* CHARLOTTE *go out.*) Since the odds are against us I must find some stratagem to avert the danger that threatens me. Sganarelle, you had better put on my clothes and I—

SGANARELLE. You can't mean that, master! Would you have me risk being killed in your clothes—it's—

DON JUAN. Come along! Be quick! You should take it as an honour. A servant should be happy to have the privilege of dying for his master.

SGANARELLE. Thank you very much for the honour! Oh Lord, if I must die, grant that I may not die in mistake for somebody else.

ACT THREE

DON JUAN *dressed for the country and* SGANARELLE *dressed as a doctor.*

SGANARELLE. Upon my word, master, you must admit that I was right. We are properly disguised now. That first idea of yours wouldn't have done at all. This will hide our identity much better than what you wanted to do.

DON JUAN. You certainly look well. I can't imagine where you dug out that ridiculous get-up.

SGANARELLE. They are the robes of some old doctor. I picked them up at a pawnshop. They cost me good money too! But would you believe it, master, I'm already treated with respect because of my clothes? People I meet salute me with deference and some are coming to consult me as a learned man.

DON JUAN. What do you mean.

SGANARELLE. Five or six country people who saw me on the road came to seek my advice about their various ailments.

DON JUAN. And you admitted your ignorance, I suppose?

SGANARELLE. Me? Not likely! I had to maintain the honour of the cloth. I held forth to them about their complaints and gave them each a prescription.

DON JUAN. And what remedies did you prescribe?

SGANARELLE. Upon my word, master, I just took whatever came into my head and gave my prescriptions at random. It would be a joke if they got better and came back to thank me!

DON JUAN. And why not? Why shouldn't you enjoy the same prerogatives as other doctors? They are no more responsible for curing their patients than you are. Their skill is sheer make-believe. All they do is take the credit when things turn out well. You can take advantage of the

472

patient's good luck just as they do, and see your remedies given the credit for whatever chance and the workings of nature achieve.

SGANARELLE. Why, master! Are you a heretic where medicine's concerned too?

DON JUAN. It is one of the greatest errors of mankind.

SGANARELLE. What—you don't believe in senna then, nor in cassia, nor in antimony?

DON JUAN. Why should I believe in them?

SGANARELLE. You are a real unbeliever! But you must have seen what a stir there has been lately about antimony. Its miraculous cures have convinced the most sceptical folk. Only three weeks ago I saw a wonderful case with my own eyes.

DON JUAN. What was that?

SGANARELLE. There was a man who had been a week at death's door. No one knew what to do for him. All remedies were useless. In the end they decided to give him antimony.

DON JUAN. And he got better, eh?

SGANARELLE. Oh, no, he died.

DON JUAN. Remarkably effective, I must say!

SGANARELLE. How d'ye mean? He had been dying a whole week and couldn't manage it, and this stuff finished him off right away. What could you want better than that?

DON JUAN. Oh nothing, of course!

SGANARELLE. Well, supposing we leave medicine, since you have no faith in it, and discuss something else. This get-up gives me confidence and I feel in the mood for arguing with you. You remember I am allowed to argue so long as I don't preach at you.

DON JUAN. Very well, then.

SGANARELLE. I'd like to find out what your ideas are. Do you really not believe in Heaven at all?

DON JUAN. Suppose we leave that alone.

SGANARELLE. That means that you don't. And Hell?

DON JUAN. Eh?

SGANARELLE. No again! And the Devil, may I ask?

DON JUAN. Yes, yes.

SGANARELLE. No more than the rest! And don't you believe in a life after this?

DON JUAN. Ha! Ha! Ha!

SGANARELLE (aside). This chap will take some converting! (To DON JUAN) Now just tell me this—the Bogy Man—what do you think about him?

DON JUAN. Don't be a fool!

SGANARELLE. Now I can't allow that. There's nothing truer than the Bogy Man. I'd go to the stake for that. A man must believe in something. What do you believe?

DON JUAN. What do I believe?

SGANARELLE. Yes.

DON JUAN. I believe that two and two make four, Sganarelle, and that two fours are eight.

SGANARELLE. Now that *is* a fine sort of faith. As far as I can see then, your religion's arithmetic. What queer ideas folk do get into their heads! And, often enough, the more they have studied the less sense they have! Not that I've studied myself, master, not like you have, thank the Lord! Nobody can boast that he ever taught me anything, but with my own common sense and using my own judgement I can see things better than books, and I know very well that this world we see around us didn't spring up of its own accord overnight—like a mushroom! I ask you who made these trees, these rocks, the earth and sky above, or did it all come of its own accord? Take yourself, for example! You exist! Are you a thing of your own making or was it necessary for your father to beget you, and for your mother to bring you into the world? Can you look on all the parts of this machine which make up a man and not wonder at the way one part is fashioned with another, nerves, bones, veins, arteries, lungs, heart, liver, and all the other things which go to—Oh, for goodness' sake do interrupt me! I can't argue if I'm not interrupted. You are keeping quiet on purpose and letting me run on out of sheer mischief.

DON JUAN. I am waiting until you have finished what you are trying to say.

SGANARELLE. What I'm trying to say is that there's something wonderful in man, say what you like, and something that all your learned men can't explain. Isn't it remarkable that here am I with something in my head that can think of a hundred different things in a moment and make my body do whatever it wants; for example, clap my hands, lift my arms, raise my eyes to heaven, bow my head, move my feet, go to the right or the left, forward or backward, turn round—(*In turning round he tumbles over.*)

DON JUAN. Good! And so your argument falls to the ground!

SGANARELLE. Oh, what a fool I am to waste time arguing with you! Believe what you like, then! What does it matter to me if you go to damnation!

DON JUAN. I think we have gone astray in the course of discussion. Give that fellow down there a hail and ask him the way.

SGANARELLE. Hello! You there! Hello! Just a word, friend, if you don't mind.

Enter a poor man.

SGANARELLE. Can you show us the way to the town?

POOR MAN. Just follow this road, gentlemen, and turn to the right when you come to the end of the wood, but I warn you, be on your guard; there have been robbers about here lately.

DON JUAN. I am very grateful to you, friend. Thank you very much.

POOR MAN. Would you care to help me, sir, with a little something?

DON JUAN. So your advice wasn't disinterested!

POOR MAN. I'm a poor man, sir. I have lived alone in this wood for the last ten years. I will pray to Heaven for your good fortune.

DON JUAN. Hm! Pray for a coat to your back and don't worry about other people's affairs.

SGANARELLE. My good man, you don't know my master. All he believes in is that two and two make four and two fours are eight.

DON JUAN. How do you employ yourself here in the forest?

POOR MAN. I spend my days in praying for the prosperity of the good people who show me charity.

DON JUAN. You must live very comfortably then.

POOR MAN. Alas, sir, I live in great penury.

DON JUAN. Surely not? A man who spends his days in prayer cannot fail to be well provided for.

POOR MAN. Believe me, sir, I often haven't a crust of bread to eat.

DON JUAN. Strange that you are so ill repaid for your pains! Well, I'll give you a gold piece here and now if you'll curse your fate and blaspheme.

POOR MAN. Ah, sir, would you have me commit a sin like that?

DON JUAN. Make up your mind. Do you want to earn a gold piece or not? There is one here for you provided you swear. Wait—you must swear.

POOR MAN. Oh, sir!

DON JUAN. You don't get it unless you do.

SGANARELLE. Go on, curse a bit. There isn't any harm in it.

DON JUAN. Hear, take it, I tell you, but you must swear first.

POOR MAN. No, sir, I'd rather starve.

DON JUAN. Very well, then, I give it to you for humanity's sake. But what's happening over there? One man attacked by three others. That isn't fair odds. I can't allow that! (*He runs towards the fight.*)

SGANARELLE. The master's completely mad. Fancy rushing into danger when he could well avoid it! Upon my word, though, he has turned the scale! The two of them have put the three to flight.

Enter DON CARLOS.

DON CARLOS (*sword in hand*). They have taken to their heels thanks to your valuable help. Permit me to thank you, sir, for your noble and—

DON JUAN (*sheathing his sword*). I have done nothing, sir, that you would not have done in my place. One is in honour bound to intervene on such an occasion. The scoundrels' behaviour was so cowardly that to have kept out would have amounted to taking their side. But how did you come to fall into their clutches?

DON CARLOS. I happened to become separated from my brother and the rest of our company. I was trying to find them when I encountered these robbers. They killed my horse, and, but for your valour, would have killed me too.

DON JUAN. Are you making towards the town?

DON CARLOS. Yes, but I don't mean to enter it: my brother and I are compelled to stay without because of one of those troublesome affairs which oblige gentlemen to sacrifice themselves and their families to their rigorous code of honour, and must, even at the best, end disastrously, since if one does not lose one's life one must quit the realm. It is, to my way of thinking, an unhappy obligation of a gentleman that he can never be certain, however discreet and honourable his own conduct, that he will not become involved, in observance of the laws of honour, in someone else's unruliness and so find his life, his peace of mind, his property, at the mercy of the first rash fool that takes it into his head to put upon him one of those affronts for which an honourable man must imperil his life.

DON JUAN. We have this satisfaction, that we can make those who wantonly offend us run the same risks and face the same discomforts as we ourselves do. But would it be indiscreet to ask what your own trouble might be?

DON CARLOS. It can hardly remain secret much longer, and once the insult is publicly known we are not in honour bound to keep our shame secret. On the contrary, it rather behoves us to proclaim our desire for vengeance and publish our plans for achieving it. Therefore I need not scruple to tell you, sir, that we are seeking to avenge our sister, who has been seduced and carried off from a convent. The author of this foul crime is a certain Don Juan Tenorio, son of Don Luis of that name. We have been seeking him for several days and followed him this morning on the report of a servant, who told us that he set out on horseback with four or five others and passed along this coast. But all our efforts have been in vain. We have not been able to find what has become of him.

DON JUAN. And do you know him, sir, this Don Juan of whom you speak?

DON CARLOS. I have never seen him myself. I have only my brother's description of him, but one hears little to his credit. He is a man whose life—

DON JUAN. Say no more, sir, if you please. He is, in a way, my friend, and it would not become me to hear him ill spoken of.

DON CARLOS. In consideration for you, sir, I will say nothing at all. The least I can do for you after your having saved my life is to keep silent about him in your presence, for if I did speak of him at all I could say nothing good. But though you are his friend I should hope that you would not condone what he has done, and that you will understand why we seek revenge upon him.

DON JUAN. On the contrary, I am willing to help you and spare you unnecessary trouble. I am a friend of Don Juan. I cannot well be otherwise, but there is no reason why he should offend gentlemen with impunity, and I undertake that he shall give you satisfaction.

DON CARLOS. But what satisfaction can one offer for an outrage of this kind?

476

DON JUAN. Whatever you can in honour require, and to save you the trouble of seeking Don Juan I undertake to produce him when and where you wish.

DON CARLOS. I should look forward to such a meeting with pleasure, sir, because of the injury I have suffered, but in view of my obligation to you I should hate to have you involved in the affair.

DON JUAN. My connexion with Don Juan is so close that he could hardly fight without my fighting too. Indeed I answer for him as for myself. You need only say when you want him to appear and give you satisfaction.

Enter DON ALONSO *and three followers.*

DON ALONSO. Have the horses watered and bring them along after us. I will go on foot a little. Heavens! What is this? You, brother, with our mortal enemy?

DON CARLOS. Our mortal enemy?

DON JUAN (*withdrawing two or three paces and proudly putting his hand on the hilt of his sword*). Yes, I am Don Juan. The disparity of numbers shall not make me disown my name.

DON ALONSO. Ah, miscreant! You shall die—

DON CARLOS. Stay, brother! I owe my life to him. Had it not been for his help I should have been killed by robbers.

DON ALONSO. And would you let this consideration stand between us and our revenge? No services received at an enemy's hand could be sufficient to justify such scruple in us. If the obligation is to be measured against the injury, your gratitude is absurd. Honour is more precious than life. What obligation can one owe, then, for one's life, to a man who has already robbed one of honour?

DON CARLOS. I know the distinction a gentleman must make between the two and I do not cease to resent the injury because I remember the obligation. Nevertheless I ask you to let me render back to him what he gave me. I owe him my life. Let me requite him. Let us postpone our vengeance and allow him a few more days to enjoy the fruits of his good deed.

DON ALONSO. No, no. To defer revenge is to risk losing it. The opportunity may never recur. Heaven offers it here and now, and we should take advantage of it. It is no time to think of acting with moderation when honour has received a deadly wound. If you shrink from taking part in the deed you need only withdraw and leave the honour of the sacrifice to me.

DON CARLOS. I beseech you, brother—

DON ALONSO. This talk is superfluous. He must die.

DON CARLOS. Stop! I warn you, brother. I will not permit any attack upon his life. I swear to Heaven I will defend him against anyone who attacks him. I will offer in his defence the life he saved. If you would strike at him, your blows must first fall on me.

DON ALONSO. What! You take our enemy's part against me! So far from sharing my rage at the sight of him, you extend him your sympathy!

DON CARLOS. Brother, our purpose is a legitimate one. Let us show moderation in achieving it. In avenging our honour let us not give way to the unbridled fury which you now betray. Let us master our feelings and show that our valour is free from any element of ferocity, and that reason, not blind rage, inspires us. I have no wish to remain indebted to my enemy. I must first of all repay my obligation to him, but our vengeance will not be less but more effective because it is deferred. To have an opportunity and refrain from taking it will make our vengeance appear more just in the eyes of the world.

DON ALONSO. Oh! Strange weakness! What dreadful blindness to endanger the requirements of honour because of a ridiculous notion of some imaginary obligation.

DON CARLOS. No, brother, you need have no concern. If I prove wrong, I shall make amends. I take full responsibility for our honour and I know the obligations it imposes upon us. The day of grace which my sense of gratitude demands for him will only make me the more determined that honour shall be satisfied. Don Juan, you see that I am at pains to repay your boon. You can judge from that what manner of man I am and rest assured that I am not less eager to fulfil obligations of another kind, not less scrupulous in repaying an injury than in returning a benefit. I ask no explanations from you now, but I offer you an opportunity to consider at leisure what decision you must take. You know the enormity of the injury you have done to us: I leave you to judge for yourself what reparation it demands. There are peaceful means of satisfying us and others which are violent and bloody. Whatever choice you make, remember you have promised me satisfaction from Don Juan. Bear that in mind, and remember that henceforward I own no obligations save to honour.

DON JUAN. I have asked nothing of you. I will do for you what I have promised.

DON CARLOS. Let us go, brother: a moment of restraint will not blunt the edge of our resolution. *Exeunt.*

DON JUAN. Hello there, Sganarelle!

SGANARELLE. At your service, master.

DON JUAN. So! You scoundrel! You run away when I'm attacked, do you?

SGANARELLE. Pardon me, sir, I was close at hand. I think these doctor's clothes must have a purgative effect. They are as good as a dose of medicine.

DON JUAN. Confound your impudence! Can't you think of a more decent excuse for your cowardice? Do you know who he is, this fellow whose life I saved?

SGANARELLE. No, I don't know.

DON JUAN. One of Elvira's brothers—

SGANARELLE. One of—

478

DON JUAN. Yes, and he's a very good fellow. He has behaved well, and I am sorry to have any quarrel with him.

SGANARELLE. You could settle everything easily enough.

DON JUAN. Yes, but my passion for Dona Elvira is spent. The connexion has become irksome. I must have freedom in love, as you know. I cannot resign myself to confining my heart within four walls. I have often told you that my natural propensity is to follow my fancy wherever it may lead. My heart belongs to all womankind. It is theirs to take in turn and keep as long as they can. But what is this noble edifice I see among the trees?

SGANARELLE. Don't you know?

DON JUAN. Indeed I don't.

SGANARELLE. Why! It's the tomb the Commander was having built at the time when you killed him.

DON JUAN. So it is. I didn't know it was here. I have heard wonderful accounts of it and of the statue of the Commander. I should like to have a look at it.

SGANARELLE. Don't go in there, master!

DON JUAN. Why not?

SGANARELLE. It's not the thing, to go calling on a man that you've killed.

DON JUAN. On the contrary, I wish to pay him the courtesy of a visit. He should take it in good part if he's a gentleman. Come! Let us go in.

The tomb opens, revealing a superb mausoleum and the STATUE *of the Commander.*

SGANARELLE. Ah, isn't that beautiful? Beautiful statues, beautiful marble, beautiful pillars. It really is beautiful. What do you say, master?

DON JUAN. I should think that a dead man's ambition could hardly go further. What is most remarkable to me is that a man who in his lifetime was content with quite a modest dwelling should want to have such a magnificent one for the time when he could no longer have any use for it.

SGANARELLE. This is the statue of the Commander.

DON JUAN. By Jove! Doesn't he look well in his Roman toga!

SGANARELLE. Goodness, master. It's a beautiful piece of work. You would think he was alive and just going to speak. I should be frightened of the way he looks at us if I were alone. I don't think he is at all pleased to see us.

DON JUAN. Well, that's very wrong of him. It's a poor return for the compliment I am paying him. Ask him if he would like to come and sup with me.

SGANARELLE. I should think that is one thing he hasn't any need for.

DON JUAN. Ask him, I tell you!

SGANARELLE. You must be joking! It would be idiotic to talk to a statue.

DON JUAN. Do as I tell you.

SGANARELLE. Your Excellency the Commander! (*Aside*) I'm laughing at my own silliness, but it's my master who's making me do it. Your Excellency! My master, Don Juan, asks if you would do him the honour of coming to sup with him. (*The* STATUE *nods.*) Oh!

DON JUAN. What is it? What's wrong with you? Come on. Speak, will you!

SGANARELLE (*nodding his head as the* STATUE *did*). The statue—

DON JUAN. Well, what is it? Speak up—you scoundrel!

SGANARELLE. I tell you the statue—

DON JUAN. The statue? Well what about the statue? I'll brain you if you don't speak up.

SGANARELLE. The statue—it nodded its head to me.

DON JUAN. Confound the fellow!

SGANARELLE. It nodded to me, I tell you. It's true! You go talk to him yourself and you'll see. Perhaps—

DON JUAN. Come on—you rascal—come on! I'll show you what a coward you are. Watch me! Would your Excellency the Commander care to take supper with me?

The STATUE *nods again.*

SGANARELLE. I wouldn't have missed that for ten pounds. Well, master?

DON JUAN. Come on. Let us get out of here!

SGANARELLE. So much for your freethinkers who won't believe in anything.

ACT FOUR

SCENE ONE

DON JUAN, SGANARELLE, RAGOTIN.

DON JUAN. Whatever it was, we will leave it at that. It is of no importance. We may have been deceived by a trick of light or overcome by some momentary giddiness which affected our vision.

SGANARELLE. Ah, master, don't attempt to deny what we both saw with our own eyes. Nothing could be more unmistakable than that nod of the head. I haven't the least doubt that Heaven is outraged by your way of life and wrought this miracle to convince you and to restrain you from—

DON JUAN. Listen! If you pester me any more with your idiotic moralizing, if I hear a single word more from you on the matter, I shall send for a whip and have you held down while I flog you within an inch of your life. Do you understand?

SGANARELLE. Completely, sir—absolutely! You've made your meaning quite clear. That's one good thing about you—there's no beating about the bush. You do put things plainly!

DON JUAN. Come along. Get them to prepare my supper as soon as possible. (*To* RAGOTIN) A chair for me, boy.

Enter LA VIOLETTE.

LA VIOLETTE. Sir, there's a tradesman, Mr Dimanche, wants to speak to you.

SGANARELLE. Good! We only needed a creditor to call on us! What business does he think he has, to come asking for money? Why didn't you tell him the master was out?

LA VIOLETTE. I've been telling him that for the last half-hour, but he doesn't believe it. He's sitting there waiting.

SGANARELLE. Let him wait to his heart's content!

DON JUAN. On the contrary. Ask him to come in. It's always bad policy to hide from one's creditors. It's well to pay them with something and I know how to send them away satisfied without giving a farthing.

Enter MR DIMANCHE.

DON JUAN (*very polite*). Ah! Mr Dimanche! Do come in. I am delighted to see you and I'm most displeased with my servants for not showing you in at once. I had said I would see no one, but that wasn't intended for you. My door should never be shut against you.

MR DIMANCHE. Sir, I am very much obliged to you.

DON JUAN (*to his lackeys*). Ah, you rascals! I'll teach you to keep Mr Dimanche waiting in the ante-chamber. I'll teach you to know who's who.

MR DIMANCHE. It is of no consequence, sir.

DON JUAN. Fancy saying I was out to Mr Dimanche, and he one of my very best friends!

MR DIMANCHE. Your servant, sir. What I came for was—

DON JUAN. Quick. A seat for Mr Dimanche.

MR DIMANCHE. I'm quite all right as I am, sir.

DON JUAN. Not at all. Not at all. I want you to come and sit near me.

MR DIMANCHE. There is really no need, sir.

DON JUAN. Take this stool away and bring an arm-chair.

MR DIMANCHE. Sir—you can't really mean it—

DON JUAN. No, I know what is due to you. I won't have them make any difference between us.

MR DIMANCHE. Sir!

DON JUAN. Come! be seated.

MR DIMANCHE. There's really no need, sir. There's only one thing I wanted to say to you—I just came to—

DON JUAN. Come and sit here.

MR DIMANCHE. No—I'm quite all right, sir. I just came to—

DON JUAN. No, I won't hear a word unless you sit down.

MR DIMANCHE. As you wish, sir. I just—

DON JUAN. By Jove, Mr Dimanche, you are looking well.

MR DIMANCHE. Yes, sir, at your service. I just came to—

DON JUAN. You are the very picture of health: ruby lips, fresh colour, and a sparkle in your eyes.

MR DIMANCHE. I really wanted to—

DON JUAN. And how is your good lady, Mrs Dimanche?

MR DIMANCHE. She's very well, sir, Heaven be praised!

DON JUAN. What a splendid woman she is!

MR DIMANCHE. She's your humble servant, sir—I just came to—

DON JUAN. And your little girl—Claudine, how is she getting on?

MR DIMANCHE. Very well indeed.

DON JUAN. Such a pretty child. I am really fond of her.

MR DIMANCHE. You are too kind, sir, I just wanted to—

DON JUAN. And little Colin—does he make as much noise as ever with his drum?

MR DIMANCHE. Yes. He's still the same, sir. I—I—

DON JUAN. And your little dog, Brusquet. Does he still growl as fiercely as ever? Does he still get his teeth into your visitors' legs?

MR DIMANCHE. He's worse than ever, sir. We just can't break him of it.

DON JUAN. Don't be surprised that I want news of all the family. I take a real interest in them.

MR DIMANCHE. We are all very much honoured, sir, I just—

DON JUAN (*offering his hand*). Give me your hand on it, Mr Dimanche. You really feel you are one of my friends?

MR DIMANCHE. I'm your humble servant, sir.

DON JUAN. Dash it! You know I am genuinely fond of you.

MR DIMANCHE. You do me too much honour—I—

DON JUAN. There's nothing I wouldn't do for you.

MR DIMANCHE. You are too kind, sir . . .

DON JUAN. And for no other reason than the regard I have for you, believe me!

MR DIMANCHE. I've done nothing to deserve such a favour, sir, but—

DON JUAN. Oh come now, Mr Dimanche. Don't stand on ceremony! Won't you stay and have supper with me?

MR DIMANCHE. No, sir. I really must go back at once. I only came—

DON JUAN (*getting up*). Quickly, there. A torch for Mr Dimanche. Four or five of you take your muskets and escort him on his way.

MR DIMANCHE (*rising*). Sir. There's no need. I shall get along quite well on my own. But—I just—

SGANARELLE *quickly takes away the chairs.*

DON JUAN. Come! I insist that you have an escort. I am concerned for your welfare, you know. I'm your humble servant, and, what's more, I'm your debtor—

MR DIMANCHE. Ah, Sir!

DON JUAN. I make no secret of it. I let everyone know it!

MR DIMANCHE. If—

DON JUAN. Would you like me to see you home myself?

MR DIMANCHE. Ah sir—you are joking, sir—I only—

DON JUAN. Well, then, give me your hand. Once again, do please consider me your friend. There's nothing in the world I wouldn't do for you. (*Goes out.*)

SGANARELLE. I must say the master's very fond of you.

MR DIMANCHE. So it seems. He shows me such politeness and civility that I never managed to ask for my money.

SGANARELLE. I assure you everybody here would do anything in the world for you. I only wish something would happen to you, someone try to beat you up, for example—you'd see how we should all—

MR DIMANCHE. I don't doubt it, but I wish you would have a word to him about my money, Sganarelle.

SGANARELLE. Oh don't you worry. He'll pay you, all right.

MR DIMANCHE. But you yourself, Sganarelle, you owe me something on your own account.

SGANARELLE. Come, come! Don't let us talk about that.

MR DIMANCHE. Why not—I—

SGANARELLE. Do you think I don't know very well what I owe you?

MR DIMANCHE. Yes, but—

SGANARELLE. Come then, Mr Dimanche. I shall have to explain to you.

MR DIMANCHE. But my money. . . .

SGANARELLE (*taking his arm*). Surely you can't be serious?

MR DIMANCHE. I want—

SGANARELLE (*pulling him*). Eh?

MR DIMANCHE. I mean—

SGANARELLE (*pushing him*). Oh, nonsense!

MR DIMANCHE. But—

SGANARELLE (*pushing*). Go on with you!

MR DIMANCHE. But I—

SGANARELLE (*pushing him off the stage*). Get on with you—I say.

SCENE TWO

DON JUAN, SGANARELLE.

Enter LA VIOLETTE.

LA VIOLETTE. Your father is here, sir.

DON JUAN. Ha! Isn't that nice for me. It only needed that to complete my annoyance.

DON LUIS (*entering*). I can see that I embarrass you. No doubt you could well do without my coming here. The truth is we are the curse of each other's existence. If you are tired of the sight of me, I am equally weary of your goings-on. Ah! how little we know what we are doing when, instead of being content to leave it to the Lord to decide what is good for us we must needs know better than he does and be importuning him in our blindness for this, that, and the other. Nobody ever wanted a son more than I did, no one ever prayed for one more ardently than I, and now the son for whom I wearied Heaven with my prayers and thought would be my joy and consolation, turns out to be the bane of my life. What am I to think of your accumulation of villainies? What excuse can I offer for them in the eyes of the world? Your never-ending succession of crimes has reduced me to wearying the King's indulgence until I have exhausted the goodwill won by my own services and the credit of my friends. What depths of infamy you have sunk to! Don't you blush to be so little worthy of your birth? What right do you think you have to be proud of it still? What have you ever done to deserve the name of gentleman? Or do you think it is enough to bear the title and the arms of one? What credit is it to be born of noble blood if one lives in infamy? Birth is nothing without virtue, and we have no claim to share in the glory of our ancestors unless we strive to resemble them. The renown which their deeds shed upon us imposes an obligation to be worthy of them, to follow in the paths they marked out for us, and, if we wish to be esteemed true descendants, never to fall short of their virtues. You claim descent from your ancestors in vain. They disown you. Their illustrious deeds reflect no credit upon you. On the contrary, they throw your dishonour into greater relief; their glory is a torch which lights your shame for all the world to see. Finally, you can take it from me that a gentleman who lives an evil life is an offence against nature, a monster, and that virtue is the first title to nobility. For my part, I have more regard for a man's deeds than for the title he can subscribe to his name: I should feel more respect to a labourer's son if he were an honest man than to a prince of the blood who lives the life you do.

DON JUAN. You would talk more comfortably sitting down, sir.

DON LUIS. No, insolent wretch! I will neither sit down nor speak further, for I see that nothing I say makes any impression upon you. But I would have you know, unworthy son that you are, that you have exhausted your father's love by your misdeeds and that I shall find means, and sooner than you think, to set bounds to your evil ways, to anticipate the wrath of Heaven and, in punishing you, wipe out the disgrace of having begotten you.   *Exit* DON LUIS.

DON JUAN. Ay, well, the sooner you die the better. Every dog has his day, and I have no use for fathers who live as long as their sons. (*Sits down in his arm-chair.*)

SGANARELLE. Ah, master—that was wrong of you!

DON JUAN. Wrong? *I* was wrong?

SGANARELLE. Master—

DON JUAN (*rising*). *I* was wrong?

SGANARELLE. Yes, master, you were wrong—to let him talk as he did; you should have pitched him out neck and crop. Did you ever hear

484

such nonsense! Fancy a father coming and remonstrating with his son, calling him to mend his ways and remember what's due to his birth, lead a decent life, and a score of similar absurdities. How could you put up with it—a man like you, who knows the way of the world? I am surprised at your patience. If I'd been in your place, I'd have sent him packing. (*Aside*) Oh cursed subservience! To what depths do you reduce me.

DON JUAN. Will that supper never be ready?

Enter RAGOTIN.

RAGOTIN. There is a veiled lady, sir, wishes to speak to you.

DON JUAN. Who can she be?

SGANARELLE. We must see.

Enter DONA ELVIRA.

DONA ELVIRA. Do not be surprised to see me, Don Juan, at this hour and in this dress. Reasons of great urgency impel me to come to see you, and what I have to tell you will brook no delay. I no longer come in anger—the anger which I recently showed: indeed, you will find me greatly changed from what I was this morning. I am no longer the Dona Elvira who heaped reproaches on you, whose wounded heart could think of nothing but menaces and threats of vengeance. God has purged my soul of my unworthy passion for you, the tumultuous emotions of a sinful relationship, the vain transports of an earthly and sensual love. There remains in my heart nothing but a love purged of sensuality, a holy tenderness, an affection which is dispassionate, disinterested, concerned now only for your good.

DON JUAN (*to* SGANARELLE). You weep, I fancy!

SGANARELLE. Forgive me!

DONA ELVIRA. In this pure and perfect love I have come to you for your good, to bring you a warning from Heaven above and to snatch you back from the abyss for which you are heading. Yes, Don Juan, I well know all the irregularities of your life, but God, who has touched my conscience and opened my eyes to my own wrong-doing, has inspired me to seek you out and warn you that your offences have overtaxed his mercy; that his dread anger is about to be loosed upon you and that only immediate repentance can save you now. Perhaps only a single day still stands between you and the most dreadful of all misfortunes. As for myself, I am freed from all earthly ties which bound me to you: I have turned my back, thanks be to Heaven, on all my foolish fancies: I have made up my mind to withdraw from the world and I ask for nothing more than to live long enough to expiate my fault and by strict repentance to earn pardon for my blind attachment to a guilty passion. But in my retirement from the world I should grieve to see one whom I have loved tenderly become an awful example of the justice of Heaven: it would be joy unspeakable for me could I but bring you to avoid the dreadful fate which threatens you.

I beg you, Don Juan, as a last favour, grant me this great consolation. Do not deny me your salvation. I implore you with my tears. If you have no consideration for your own well-being, at least let my prayers move you and spare me the horror of seeing you condemned to eternal torment.

SGANARELLE. Poor lady!

DONA ELVIRA. I loved you tenderly. You were dearer to me than all the world; for your sake I forsook my duty and gave you everything. All the recompense I ask is that you should amend your way of life and save yourself from eternal ruin. Save yourself, I beg you, whether for love of yourself or love of me. Once again I implore you with my tears, Don Juan, and, if the tears of one whom you once loved do not suffice, I ask it in the name of whatever is most dear to you.

SGANARELLE (*aside*). Cruel! Cruel! Tiger-hearted!

DONA ELVIRA. I am going now. That is all I have to say.

DON JUAN. It is late. Stay here to-night. You shall have the best accommodation the house affords.

DONA ELVIRA. No, Don Juan, do not detain me further.

DON JUAN. I assure you it would afford me great pleasure if you would stay.

DONA ELVIRA. No, let us not waste time in unnecessary conversation. Let me go at once. Do not seek to accompany me. Think only of profiting from my message. *Exit* DONA ELVIRA.

DON JUAN. You know, I found I had still some slight feeling for her— there was something rather pleasant in the novelty of the situation! Her disordered dress, her tenderness, and her tears stirred the last embers of my extinguished passion.

SGANARELLE. So what she said had no effect on you at all?

DON JUAN. Quick, to supper!

SGANARELLE. Very well.

DON JUAN (*sitting at the table*). All the same, Sganarelle, we shall have to mend our ways.

SGANARELLE. We shall indeed!

DON JUAN. Upon my word, yes! We shall have to mend our ways. Another twenty or thirty years of this present life and then we'll look to ourselves.

SGANARELLE. Oh!

DON JUAN. What have you to say to that?

SGANARELLE. Nothing. Here comes the supper. (*He takes a morsel from one of the dishes which are brought in and puts it in his mouth.*)

DON JUAN. You seem to have something in your cheek. What is it? Speak up! What have you got in your mouth?

SGANARELLE. Nothing.

DON JUAN. Let me see! Good Lord! He has a swelling in his cheek! Quick, something to lance it! The poor fellow can't bear it—the abscess may choke him! Steady! See how ripe it was—ah, you rascal!

486

SGANARELLE. I only wanted to make sure that the cook hadn't put in too much salt or pepper, master.

DON JUAN. Come along. Sit yourself down there and eat. I need you when you have eaten. You are hungry, it seems.

SGANARELLE (*sitting at table*). I should think I am, master. I have eaten nothing since morning. Try some of this. It's excellent. (*Servant takes* SGANARELLE's *plate away as soon as he puts food on it.*) Eh! My plate! My plate! Go easy, please! Goodness me, lad, you are pretty good at dealing out clean plates. As for you, La Violette, you certainly know how to serve wine at the right moment. (*While one lackey is serving* SGANARELLE *with wine the other takes his plate away.*)

DON JUAN. Who can be knocking like that?

SGANARELLE. Who the devil comes disturbing us at mealtime?

DON JUAN. I will at least finish my meal in peace. Let no one come in.

SGANARELLE. Leave it to me. I'll go myself.

DON JUAN. What is it? Who is there?

SGANARELLE. The (*nodding his head as the* STATUE *did*)—it's come!

DON JUAN. Let us go and see. I'll show that nothing can shake me!

SGANARELLE. Poor Sganarelle, where can you hide yourself!

The STATUE *of the Commander comes forward and sits at the table.*

DON JUAN. Come, a chair. Lay a place. Quickly! (*To* SGANARELLE) Come along. Sit down at the table.

SGANARELLE. I've lost my appetite, master.

DON JUAN. Sit down, I tell you. Bring wine. I give you the Commander's health. Sganarelle. Fill his glass, somebody.

SGANARELLE. I'm not thirsty, master.

DON JUAN. Drink, and give us a song to entertain the Commander.

SGANARELLE. I've got a cold, master.

DON JUAN. Never mind that. You others come along and play an accompaniment.

STATUE. Enough, Don Juan. I invite you to come and sup with me to-morrow. Dare you come?

DON JUAN. Yes. I will come—with Sganarelle alone.

SGANARELLE. Thank you very much. I am fasting to-morrow.

DON JUAN (*to* SGANARELLE). Take this torch.

STATUE. No need for light when Heaven shows the way.

ACT FIVE

DON LUIS, DON JUAN, SGANARELLE.

DON LUIS. What! My son! Has Heaven in its mercy heard my prayers? Is this the truth you are telling me? You are not deluding me with false hopes? Can I really believe in this sudden and surprising conversion?

DON JUAN (*playing the hypocrite*). Yes, I have turned from the error of my ways. I am a new man since last night; the Lord has wrought a sudden change in me which will astonish everyone. He has touched my heart and removed the scales from my eyes; I look back with horror on the blindness in which I dwelt so long and the wickedness of my past life. When I go over in my mind the tally of my abominable deeds I wonder that Heaven has suffered them so long and not loosed its dreadful vengeance upon me twenty times over. My eyes are open now to the favour and mercy vouchsafed me in withholding the punishment of my crimes. I mean to take advantage of it and offer the world the spectacle of a sudden change in my way of life. Thus I shall make amends for the evil example of my former actions and endeavour to earn pardon for my sins. That is what I intend, and I ask you, sir, to assist me in this design by yourself choosing me a mentor under whose guidance I may safely follow the course I am about to embark upon.

DON LUIS. Ah, my son, how easily can a father's love revive, and filial offences be forgotten at the first word of repentance! What you have told me wipes from my memory every sorrow you have occasioned me. Oh, what overwhelming happiness! I weep for joy, for all my prayers are answered, and I have nothing more to ask of Heaven. Kiss me, my son, and do not falter, I conjure you, in your laudable intentions. I must go at once and take the good news to your mother, share my happiness with her and render thanks to God for the holy purpose he has deigned to inspire you with. *Exit* DON LUIS.

SGANARELLE. Ah, master, what a joy it is to see you converted. I have waited for this a long time, and now, thanks be to God, my hopes are realized.

DON JUAN. Confound you! You blockhead!

SGANARELLE. Blockhead! Me?

DON JUAN. Do you mean to say you take my words at their face value? You think that I meant them?

SGANARELLE. Then it isn't—You're not—Oh, what a man! What a man! What a man!

DON JUAN. I have not changed in the least. I'm just the same as I always was.

SGANARELLE. You won't even yield to the miracle of a statue that moves and speaks?

DON JUAN. There is certainly something there that I do not understand, but, whatever it is, it shall neither change my convictions nor shake my courage. When I talked of mending my ways and living an exemplary life it was a calculated hypocrisy, a necessary pretence, which I had to assume for my father's benefit because I need his help, and as a protection against society and the hundred-and-one tiresome things that may happen to me. I take you into my confidence deliberately, Sganarelle, because I like to have one witness to my real feelings and my motives for acting as I do.

SGANARELLE. What! You don't believe in anything, and yet you want to set yourself up as a man of principle!

DON JUAN. And why not? There are plenty of others like me who ply the same trade and use the same mask to deceive the world.

SGANARELLE. What a man! What a man!

DON JUAN. Such conduct carries no stigma nowadays, for hypocrisy is a fashionable vice, and all vices pass for virtues once they become fashionable. The role of a man of principle is the best of all parts to play, for the professional hypocrite enjoys remarkable advantages. Hypocrisy is an art, the practice of which always commands respect, and though people may see through it they dare say nothing against it. All other vices of mankind are exposed to censure and anyone may attack them with impunity. Hypocrisy alone is privileged. It stills the voice of criticism and enjoys a sovereign immunity. Humbug binds together in close fellowship all those who practise it, and whoever attacks one brings down the whole pack upon him. Moreover, men whom one knows to be acting in good faith, men of integrity, are always taken in by the humbugs and caught in their snares, and blindly lend their support to men who only ape their virtues. How many men have I seen contrive to repair the disorders of their youth in this way, making religion a cloak under which they continued to live as wickedly as they pleased! People may be aware of their machinations, they may even recognize them for what they are, but they are not held in less regard on that account. They bow their heads from time to time, heave an occasional sigh of mortification, roll their eyes to Heaven now and again, and that atones, in the eyes of the world, for anything they may do. It is under shelter of this pretence I intend to take refuge and secure my own position. I shall not abandon my pleasures, but I shall be at pains to conceal them and amuse myself with all circumspection. So, if by any chance I am discovered, the whole fraternity will make my cause their own and defend me against every criticism. By this means I shall contrive to do whatever I choose with impunity. I shall set up as a censor of the behaviour of others, condemn everyone, and hold a good opinion of no one, myself alone excepted. Let anyone offend me in however slight a degree, I shall never forgive, but steadfastly nurse an implacable enmity. I shall constitute myself the avenger and servant of the Lord and use that convenient pretext as a means of harassing my enemies. I shall accuse them of impiety and find means to turn loose on them the officious zealots who will raise a public outcry against them without even knowing what it is about, overwhelm them with recriminations and damn them roundly on their own private authority. Thus one may profit from human frailty; thus a wise man may accommodate himself to the vices of the age.

SGANARELLE. Oh Lord! What do I hear? You only needed to turn hypocrite to become the complete villain. This is the final abomination! This is more than I can stand, master. I can keep quiet no longer. You can do what you like to me: beat me, knock me down, kill me, if you like, but I must open my heart to you and tell you what I think, as a faithful servant should. You know, master, the pitcher can go to the well once too often, and, as some writer very truly said—who he was I don't know—men in this world are like the bird on the bough, the bough is part of the tree and whoever holds on to the tree is following sound precepts; sound precepts are better than fine words; the court is the place for fine words; at the court you find courtiers, and courtiers do whatever's the fashion; fashion springs from the imagination and imagination springs from the soul; the soul is what gives us life, and life ends in death; death sets us thinking of Heaven; Heaven is above the earth; the earth's different from the ocean; the ocean's subject to tempests, and tempests are a terror to ships; a ship needs a good pilot and a good pilot needs prudence; young men have no prudence, so the young should be obedient to the old; old men love riches; riches make men rich; the rich aren't poor; poor men know necessity and necessity knows no law. Without law men live like animals, which all goes to prove that you'll be damned to all eternity!

DON JUAN. Fine reasoning, I must say!

SGANARELLE. If you don't admit you are wrong after that, so much the worse for you.

Enter DON CARLOS.

DON CARLOS. This is an opportune meeting, Don Juan. I am glad to be able to speak with you and ask you for your decision here rather than at your own house. You know what my obligation is. I assumed it in your presence. For my own part I admit that I would like to see things settled amicably. I would give anything in the world to induce you to choose that alternative and see you publicly acknowledge my sister as your wife.

DON JUAN (*putting on the hypocritical tone*). I only wish I could give you that satisfaction, but Heaven itself has set its face against it and inspired me to reform my way of life. Now I am filled with one desire only—to renounce all earthly ties, divest myself forthwith of all vain attachments and henceforward atone by a life of austerity for all the wickedness into which the blindness of youth has led me.

DON CARLOS. But that intention does not run counter to my own suggestion, Don Juan. Lawful marriage is not incompatible with the good intentions heaven has implanted in you.

DON JUAN. Alas, you are mistaken. Your sister has herself taken a like decision. She has decided to retire into a convent. The spirit moved us both at the same time.

DON CARLOS. Her taking the veil does not satisfy us, since it might be imputed to your affront to her and our family. Our honour demands that you acknowledge her as your wife.

DON JUAN. That, I assure you, cannot be. For myself, I could wish for nothing better. Only to-day I sought Heaven's approval for such a course, but after I had prayed I heard a voice that said I should think no more of your sister for I should never find salvation with her.

DON CARLOS. And do you think that you can put us off with these fine excuses, Don Juan?

DON JUAN. I obey the voice of Heaven.

DON CARLOS. Do you expect me to be taken in by this sort of talk?

DON JUAN. Heaven wills it so.

DON CARLOS. You think you can carry off my sister from a convent and then abandon her?

DON JUAN. Such is Heaven's command.

DON CARLOS. And we are to bear this stain on our family honour?

DON JUAN. You must blame Heaven for that.

DON CARLOS. What! Heaven again!

DON JUAN. Heaven so ordains.

DON CARLOS. Enough, Don Juan! I understand you. This is not the place to deal with you, but before long I shall not fail to find you.

DON JUAN. As you please. You know I am no coward and that I can use my sword when need arises. I shall pass directly along the narrow lane that leads to the convent, but I would have you know that if we fight it is by no wish of mine. Heaven forbids me to think of such things. But if you attack me we shall see what will happen.

DON CARLOS. We shall! We shall indeed. (*Exit.*)

SGANARELLE. Master, what on earth are you up to? This is worse than ever. I'd much rather have you as you were before. I have always had hopes for your salvation, but now I begin to despair. Heaven has borne with you till now, but it will never suffer this latest outrage.

DON JUAN. Oh, come now! Heaven isn't as exacting as you think. If every time men—

SGANARELLE. Ah, master (*seeing the* SPECTRE). It's a warning from Heaven.

DON JUAN. If Heaven wishes to warn me it must speak a little more plainly, if I am to be expected to hear.

Enter a SPECTRE *in the form of a veiled woman.*

SPECTRE. Don Juan has but one moment left to profit from the mercy of Heaven: if he repent not now his end is certain.

SGANARELLE. Master, do you hear?

DON JUAN. Who dares speak thus to me? I fancy I know that voice.

SGANARELLE. Ah, master. It's a spirit. I can tell by its walk!

DON JUAN. Spirit, apparition, devil. I will see what it is.

The SPECTRE *changes to Time with a scythe in his hand.*

SGANARELLE. Oh Heavens! Look, master, how its shape changes.

DON JUAN. Nothing can frighten me. I will test with my sword whether it be flesh or spirit.

The SPECTRE *disappears as* DON JUAN *makes to strike it.*

SGANARELLE. Ah, master, yield to these proofs and repent quickly.

DON JUAN. No, come what may it shall never be said that I am the repenting sort. Come, follow me.

Enter the STATUE.

STATUE. You gave me your word yesterday to come and sup with me.

DON JUAN. Yes, where do we go?

STATUE. Give me your hand.

DON JUAN. There.

STATUE. Don Juan, those who persist in their wickedness come to dreadful ends: those who reject Heaven's mercy bring down its wrath.

DON JUAN. Oh God! What is happening to me? Unseen fires consume me. I cannot bear it. My body is aflame—ah . . .

Rolls of thunder, flashes of lightning. The earth opens and swallows him up. Flames rise from the pit into which he has vanished.

SCANARELLE. Ah, my wages! My wages! Everybody gets satisfaction from his death: the Heaven he offended, the laws he violated, the girls he seduced, the families he dishonoured, the parents he disgraced, the wives he led astray, the husbands he drove to despair. Every one is satisfied but me! I'm the only unlucky one! After all my years of service the only reward I get is to see my master punished for his impiety with my own eyes and in the most dreadful way possible. My wages, my wages—my wages!

■

The first page of the *Confessions* of Jean-Jacques Rousseau (1712–78), given here, could be called the prime source of the peculiarly modern search for complete understanding and articulation of the innermost self. In his assertion that his *Confessions* explain and justify his moral being, Rousseau implies that any ethics must be based on total fidelity to the inner self and must tend to foster the free development of that self. The individual, the needs and potential of his personality, has been placed at the center of the universe. In the "Ode to the West Wind," Percy Bysshe Shelley (1792–1822) appears to have accepted this premise. Self stands at the center of a grandiose natural world, relating everything to itself and also investing itself into everything—which may be the underlying cause of the anguish that the earth-bound, mortal persona of the poem experiences. Finally, the very brief play by August Strindberg (1849–1912) printed in this section suggests with great economy and power our modern conception of character as force of personality and implies how in turn this definition presides over the creation of memorable literary characters.

FROM # Confessions

Jean-Jacques Rousseau

I have formed an enterprise which has no precedent and, completed, will have no imitator. I wish to display to my fellow men a man in all the truth of nature; and that man will be myself.

Myself alone. I feel my heart and I know men. I am not made like any of those I have seen; I dare to believe that I am not like any that exist. If I am not any better, at least I am different. Whether nature did well or ill in breaking the mould in which she formed me is a question that can be answered only after having read me.

Let the trumpet of the Last Judgment sound when it will; I shall come forward with this book in my hand to present myself before the Sovereign Judge. I shall proclaim aloud: this is what I have done, what I have thought, what I was. I have stated the good and the ill with the same frankness. I have omitted nothing bad, and added nothing good, and if I have chanced to use some indifferent ornament, this has never been but to fill some gap caused by a defect of memory. I may have taken for true what I thought might be true, never what I knew to be false. I have shown myself as I was, despicable and vile when I was so, good, generous, sublime when I was that. I have uncovered my inner self as Thou Thyself have seen it. Eternal Being, gather around me the innumerable host of my fellow men; let them hear my confessions; let them groan at my unworthy acts, let them blush at my petty ones. Let each of them in his turn bare his heart at the foot of Thy throne with the same sincerity; and then let anyone say, if he dares, "I was better than this man."

(Trans. P. B.)

Ode to the West Wind

Percy Bysshe Shelley

I

O wild West Wind, thou breath of Autumn's being,
Thou, from whose unseen presence the leaves dead
Are driven, like ghosts from an enchanter fleeing,

Yellow, and black, and pale, and hectic red,
Pestilence-stricken multitudes: O thou,
Who chariotest to their dark wintry bed

The wingèd seeds, where they lie cold and low,
Each like a corpse within its grave, until
Thine azure sister of the spring shall blow

Her clarion o'er the dreaming earth, and fill   10
(Driving sweet buds like flocks to feed in air)
With living hues and odours plain and hill;

Wild Spirit, which art moving everywhere;
Destroyer and preserver; hear, Oh hear!

II

Thou on whose stream, 'mid the steep sky's commotion,
Loose clouds like earth's decaying leaves are shed,
Shook from the tangled boughs of Heaven and Ocean,

Angels of rain and lightning: there are spread
On the blue surface of thine airy surge,
Like the bright hair uplifted from the head   20

Of some fierce Mænad, even from the dim verge
Of the horizon to the zenith's height
The locks of the approaching storm. Thou dirge

Of the dying year, to which this closing night
Will be the dome of a vast sepulchre,
Vaulted with all thy congregated might

Of vapours, from whose solid atmosphere
Black rain, and fire, and hail will burst: Oh hear!

III

Thou who didst waken from his summer dreams
The blue Mediterranean, where he lay,   30
Lulled by the coil of his crystalline streams,

Beside a pumice isle in Baiæ's bay,
And saw in sleep old palaces and towers
Quivering within the wave's intenser day,

All overgrown with azure moss and flowers
So sweet, the sense faints picturing them! Thou
For whose path the Atlantic's level powers

Cleave themselves into chasms, while far below
The sea-blooms and the oozy woods which wear
The sapless foliage of the ocean, know   40

Thy voice, and suddenly grow gray with fear,
And tremble and despoil themselves: Oh hear!

IV

If I were a dead leaf thou mightest bear;
If I were a swift cloud to fly with thee;
A wave to pant beneath thy power, and share

The impulse of thy strength, only less free
Than thou, O uncontrollable! If even
I were as in my boyhood, and could be

The comrade of thy wanderings over heaven,
As then, when to outstrip thy skiey speed   50
Scarce seemed a vision; I would ne'er have striven

As thus with thee in prayer in my sore need.
Oh! lift me as a wave, a leaf, a cloud!
I fall upon the thorns of life! I bleed!

A heavy weight of hours has chained and bowed
One too like thee; tameless, and swift, and proud.

V

Make me thy lyre, even as the forest is:
What if my leaves are falling like its own!
The tumult of thy mighty harmonies

Will take from both a deep, autumnal tone,   60
Sweet though in sadness. Be thou, spirit fierce,
My spirit! Be thou me, impetuous one!

Drive my dead thoughts over the universe
Like withered leaves to quicken a new birth!
And, by the incantation of this verse,

Scatter, as from an unextinguished hearth
Ashes and sparks, my words among mankind!
Be through my lips to unawakened earth

The trumpet of a prophecy! O, wind,
If Winter comes, can Spring be far behind?   70

The Stronger

August Strindberg

Translated by Elizabeth Sprigge

CHARACTERS

MRS. X, *actress, married*
MISS Y, *actress, unmarried*
A WAITRESS

Scene: A corner of a ladies' café (in Stockholm in the 1880's). Two small wrought-iron tables, a red plush settee and a few chairs.

MISS Y. is sitting with a half-empty bottle of beer on the table before her, reading an illustrated weekly which from time to time she exchanges for another.

MRS. X. enters, wearing a winter hat and coat and carrying a decorative Japanese basket.

MRS. X. Why, Millie, my dear, how are you? Sitting here all alone on Christmas Eve like some poor bachelor.

(MISS Y. *looks up from her magazine, nods, and continues to read.*)

MRS. X. You know it makes me feel really sad to see you. Alone. Alone in a café and on Christmas Eve of all times. It makes me feel as sad as when once in Paris I saw a wedding party at a restaurant. The bride was reading a comic paper and the bridegroom playing billiards with the witnesses. Ah me, I said to myself, with such a beginning how will it go, and how will it end? He was playing billiards on his wedding day! And she, you were going to say, was reading a comic paper on hers. But that's not quite the same.

(A WAITRESS *brings a cup of chocolate to* MRS. X. *and goes out.*)

MRS. X. Do you know, Amelia, I really believe now you would have done better to stick to him. Don't forget I was the first who told you to forgive him. Do you remember? Then you would be married now and have a home. Think how happy you were that Christmas when you stayed with your fiancé's people in the country. How warmly you spoke of domestic happiness! You really quite longed to be out of the theatre. Yes, Amelia dear, home is best—next best to the stage, and as for children—but you couldn't know anything about that.

496

(MISS Y.'s *expression is disdainful.* MRS. X. *sips a few spoonfuls of* *chocolate, then opens her basket and displays some Christmas* *presents.*)

MRS. X. Now you must see what I have bought for my little chicks. (*Takes* *out a doll.*) Look at this. That's for Liza. Do you see how she can roll her eyes and turn her head. Isn't she lovely? And here's a toy pistol for Maja. (*She loads the pistol and shoots it at* MISS Y., *who appears* *frightened.*)

MRS. X. Were you scared? Did you think I was going to shoot you? Really, I didn't think you'd believe that of me. Now if *you* were to shoot *me* it wouldn't be so surprising, for after all I did get in your way, and I know you never forget it—although I was entirely innocent. You still think I intrigued to get you out of the Grand Theatre, but I didn't. I didn't, however much you think I did. Well, it's no good talking, you will believe it was me . . . (*Takes out a pair of embroidered slippers.*) And these are for my old man, with tulips on them that I embroidered myself. As a matter of fact I hate tulips, but he has to have tulips on everything.

(MISS Y. *looks up, irony and curiosity in her face.*)

MRS. X. (*putting one hand in each slipper*). Look what small feet Bob has, hasn't he? And you ought to see the charming way he walks— you've never seen him in slippers, have you?

(MISS Y. *laughs.*)

MRS. X. Look, I'll show you. (*She makes the slippers walk across the table,* *and* MISS Y. *laughs again.*)

MRS. X. But when he gets angry, look, he stamps his foot like this. "Those damn girls who can never learn how to make coffee! Blast! That silly idiot hasn't trimmed the lamp properly!" Then there's a draught under the door and his feet get cold. "Hell, it's freezing, and the damn fools can't even keep the stove going!" (*She rubs the sole of one slipper* *against the instep of the other.* MISS Y. *roars with laughter.*)

MRS. X. And then he comes home and has to hunt for his slippers, which Mary has pushed under the bureau . . . Well, perhaps it's not right to make fun of one's husband like this. He's sweet anyhow, and a good, dear husband. You ought to have had a husband like him, Amelia. What are you laughing at? What is it? Eh? And, you see, I know he is faithful to me. Yes, I know it. He told me himself—what *are* you giggling at?—that while I was on tour in Norway that horrible Frederica came and tried to seduce him. Can you imagine anything more abominable? (*Pause*) I'd have scratched her eyes out if she had come around while I was at home. (*Pause*) I'm glad Bob told me about it himself, so I didn't just hear it from gossip. (*Pause*) And as a matter of fact, Frederica wasn't the only one. I can't think why, but all the women in the Company seem to be crazy about my husband. They must think his position gives him some say in who is engaged at the Theatre. Perhaps you have run after him yourself? I don't trust you very far, but I know he has never been attracted by you, and you always seemed to have some sort of grudge against him, or so I felt. (*Pause. They look at one another guardedly.*)

MRS. X. Do come and spend Christmas Eve with us tonight, Amelia— just to show that you're not offended with us, or anyhow not with me. I don't know why, but it seems specially unpleasant not to be friends with you. Perhaps it's because I did get in your way that time . . . (*slowly*) or—I don't know—really, I don't know at all why it is.

(*Pause.* MISS Y. *gazes curiously at* MRS. X.)

MRS. X. (*thoughtfully*). It was so strange when we were getting to know one another. Do you know, when we first met, I was frightened of you, so frightened I didn't dare let you out of my sight. I arranged all my goings and comings to be near you. I dared not be your enemy, so I became your friend. But when you came to our home, I always had an uneasy feeling, because I saw my husband didn't like you, and that irritated me—like when a dress doesn't fit. I did all I could to make him be nice to you, but it was no good—until you went and got engaged. Then you became such tremendous friends that at first it looked as if you only dared show your real feelings then—when you were safe. And then, let me see, how was it after that? I wasn't jealous— that's queer. And I remember at the christening, when you were the godmother, I told him to kiss you. He did, and you were so upset . . . As a matter of fact I didn't notice that then . . . I didn't think about it afterwards either . . . I've never thought about it—until *now!* (*Rises abruptly.*) Why don't you say something? You haven't said a word all this time. You've just let me go on talking. You have sat there with your eyes drawing all these thoughts out of me—they were there in me like silk in a cocoon—thoughts . . . Mistaken thoughts? Let me think. Why did you break off your engagement? Why did you never come to our house after that? Why don't you want to come to us tonight?

(MISS Y. *makes a motion, as if about to speak.*)

MRS. X. No. You don't need to say anything, for now I see it all. That was why—and why—and why. Yes. Yes, that's why it was. Yes, yes, all the pieces fit together now. That's it. I won't sit at the same table as you. (*Moves her things to the other table.*) That's why I have to embroider tulips, which I loathe, on his slippers—because you liked tulips. (*Throws the slippers on the floor.*) That's why we have to spend the summer on the lake—because you couldn't bear the seaside. That's why my son had to be called Eskil—because it was your father's name. That's why I had to wear your colours, read your books, eat the dishes you liked, drink your drinks—your chocolate, for instance. That's why —oh my God, it's terrible to think of, terrible! Everything, everything came to me from you—even your passions. Your soul bored into mine like a worm into an apple, and ate and ate and burrowed and bur-

498

rowed, till nothing was left but the skin and a little black mould. I wanted to fly from you, but I couldn't. You were there like a snake, your black eyes fascinating me. When I spread my wings, they only dragged me down. I lay in the water with my feet tied together, and the harder I worked my arms, the deeper I sank—down, down, till I reached the bottom, where you lay in waiting like a giant crab to catch me in your claws—and now here I am. Oh how I hate you! I hate you, I hate you! And you just go on sitting there, silent, calm, indifferent, not caring whether the moon is new or full, if it's Christmas or New Year, if other people are happy or unhappy. You don't know how to hate or to love. You just sit there without moving—like a cat at a mouse hole. You can't drag your prey out, you can't chase it, but you can outstay it. Here you sit in your corner—you know they call it the rattrap after you—reading the papers to see if anyone's ruined or wretched or been thrown out of the Company. Here you sit sizing up your victims and weighing your chances—like a pilot his shipwrecks for the salvage. (*Pause*) Poor Amelia! Do you know, I couldn't be more sorry for you. I know you are miserable, miserable like some wounded creature, and vicious because you are wounded. I can't be angry with you. I should like to be, but after all you are the small one—and as for your affair with Bob, that doesn't worry me in the least. Why should it matter to me? And if you, or somebody else taught me to drink chocolate, what's the difference? (*Drinks a spoonful. Smugly.*) Chocolate is very wholesome anyhow. And if I learnt from you how to dress, *tant mieux!*—that only gave me a stronger hold over my husband, and you have lost what I gained. Yes, to judge from various signs, I think you have now lost him. Of course, you meant me to walk out, as you once did, and which you're now regretting. But I won't do that, you may be sure. One shouldn't be narrow-minded, you know. And why should nobody else want what I have? (*Pause*) Perhaps, my dear, taking everything into consideration, at this moment it is I who am the stronger. You never got anything from me, you just gave away—from yourself. And now, like the thief in the night, when you woke up I had what you had lost. Why was it then that everything you touched became worthless and sterile? You couldn't keep a man's love—for all your tulips and your passions—but I could. You couldn't learn the art of living from your books—but I learnt it. You bore no little Eskil, although that was your father's name. (*Pause*) And why is it you are silent—everywhere, always silent? Yes, I used to think this was strength, but perhaps it was because you hadn't anything to say, because you couldn't think of anything. (*Rises and picks up the slippers.*) Now I am going home, taking the tulips with me—*your* tulips. You couldn't learn from others, you couldn't bend, and so you broke like a dry stick. I did not. Thank you, Amelia, for all your good lessons. Thank you for teaching my husband how to love. Now I am going home—to love him. (*Exit.*)

Self Against Role

In the first section of Part IV we saw how men seek to differentiate themselves from other animals, from nature; in the second section we saw how after becoming a distinct species, men sought to become distinct individuals. More often than not, such a process involves the ability to maintain an existential balance between the expectations of a given society on the one hand and the impulses of the self on the other. In the degree to which we "belong" to society, we are typical of it. In France, for instance, adult males who wear berets and ride bicycles are immediately recognized as workers by other Frenchmen. But in the United States we would probably suppose a man wearing a beret and riding a bicycle to be an intellectual. But beyond these aspects of one's social "uniform"-ity—and others less superficial—there are obviously traits of character that are not available to sociological typification. This French worker may be typical of other French workers in his dress, his eating and drinking habits, where he lives, and how he votes, but his biography will in certain crucial aspects differ from that of others in his sociological category: his family was a particularly unhappy one, perhaps, or he may have grown up in the country, surrounded by trees and sunsets unknown to his fellow workers raised in the city. And insofar as his memories differ from those of his fellows, he will be different. There is no sociology so refined it can contain all the contingency that ensures that each man will have a unique life, that his character will not be completely subsumed by mere institutional categories.

The enormous variety of individual biographies is both a blessing and a curse. It confers the gift of distinctiveness—and it would seem that all men, at least in Western society, have a need to feel themselves unique, no matter how "typical" they appear to others. Some years ago, *Life* magazine attempted to dramatize what certain socio-economic

500

categories ("upper-upper," "lower-middle class," etc.) were by choosing actual families from a typical Midwestern city (Rockford, Illinois) to represent them. The magazine was flooded with letters from the families chosen, each of which indignantly maintained it was *not* typical, although sociologists, on the basis of exhaustive research, claimed they were. To be typical is in some sense to be determined, and although most of us are shaped in important ways by our society, we prefer to feel free and unique. It is the role of chance in all our lives that provides the opportunity for such freedom. As such, it would seem beneficial and even necessary to the project of shaping our character.

But such freedom is also a burden. Insofar as we are not typical of our society, insofar as we cannot blame or praise it for making us what we are, *we* must accept the responsibility for what we are, a situation Kierkegaard has called "the vertigo of liberty." In the past it was felt that character was a function of forces exterior to men, forces more often than not identified with religion. If someone performed in a way considered by the rest of his fellows to be deviant, he was said to be "possessed": *he* was not in control, evil spirits were. The Christian doctrine of free will immensely complicated this process, but its finer points were beyond the ken of most, so the majority of men continued to operate as if their lives were determined by extrahuman agencies.

In the last few hundred years religion has for many lost much of its power so to determine lives. But the impulse to ascribe character to exterior forces seems as strong as it was in the Middle Ages, only now the forces have been secularized and given different names. Medicine suggests physical or, since Freud, psychological reasons that determine how men act. The recent popularity of the social sciences has had its effects in the courts, and increasingly attempts are made to assess the degree to which a criminal's behavior grows directly out of his environment.

These tendencies have raised in a new and disturbing way the question of how—and how much—our actions (the sum of which is often called character) are determined from the outside or willed by an irreducible core of uniqueness. The texts of the preceding section confronted the problem of distinguishing the individual from the others around him. Here we will be concerned with the ways in which the individual, once identified, asserts himself with respect to the society in which he lives. One of the more common ways in which the dilemma has presented itself is in a metaphor taken from the theater: role-playing. Just as an actor may play Hamlet one night and Falstaff the next, so, many have assumed, do men in real life play various parts—lover, citizen, student, and so on. The theatrical metaphor may be extended. Two schools of acting have developed that make contradictory claims as to whether a player should identify himself with his role. One maintains that a successful performance demands that an actor "become" his role; that, for the duration of the play, he forget he is an actor. The Russian director Stanislavsky developed special techniques and exercises to help his actors "live into" their parts. If he were doing *Julius Caesar*, he would have the actors wear togas for weeks before opening night, in the belief that they would therefore move more naturally in this uncustomary clothing; thus one more element would be eliminated that might remind the actor he was merely a twentieth-century Russian imitating a pre-Christian Roman as imagined by a seventeenth-century Englishman.

Another school, associated with the German playwright Bertolt Brecht, contends just the opposite: it is only by keeping at a distance from his role that an actor will maintain the critical insight necessary to carry it off convincingly. In order to play Caesar well you must remember you are *not* Caesar.

These two theories define fairly well the possibilities open to us as we act out the drama of our own lives. We may *become* our roles, or we may *play* them. Most of us shift between these possibilities: we may be sons and soldiers, believing we are the one and acting as if we were the other. But as society grows more complex it reaches into heretofore untouched aspects of our lives, and it is increasingly difficult to find an area that we may convincingly call our "selves" when so much of our existence is consigned to credit card, telephone, social security, and other numbers. Where are we to find the self that must choose which of our roles we shall believe and which we shall merely act? More and more of us are confronted with the responsibility for either assuming responsibility for our own selves or being swallowed up by the prepackaged identities society would assign us.

The Diary of a Madman

Nikolai Gogol

Translated by Priscilla Meyer

This is a story about a man who is unable either to play *or* believe the role society has assigned him. Like many other characters in the short stories of Gogol (1809–52), Poprishchin is a low-grade civil servant. As such he has a clearly defined (if very lowly) place in nineteenth-century Russian society, which was organized according to a table of fourteen ranks, each of which had its title, uniform, and other identifying insignia. One always knew where he was in this hierarchy. Why then does Poprishchin experience difficulties? Precisely because his social status *is* clear: he is so much the petty bureaucrat in the eyes of his co-workers and of society that no one ever sees in him anything else. He is only his rank; he has no individuality. If he is treated inhumanly it is because no one perceives him as a human being, but only as a category in the system of ranks. Initially, there is no conflict of the self and the others: the others deny the possibility of Poprishchin's having a unique self.

But Poprishchin, as it turns out, *does* have a self, which, when it finds the role of civil servant incommensurate, creates a new role, that of the king of Spain.

In the final pages of the story we are confronted by some of the same questions raised in "The Case of Miss Lucy R." in Part I: whose is the fiction, the therapist's or the patient's? Why can't the patient convince others (society) that his "story" is the correct one? Society redefines Poprishchin's category from civil servant to madman. But as king of Spain Poprishchin can believe his new role. The country he rules in his mind becomes a home for a new self. He exists not only in a different space but in a different time from the others at the end of the story, when we see him slip completely into himself. The movement of the story, then, is from a self completely dominated by society (Poprishchin as clerk) to a self that completely excludes society (Poprishchin as king).

■

October 3rd

An extraordinary incident occurred today. I got up rather late in the morning, and when Mavra brought me my cleaned boots I asked what time it was. Hearing that it had already long ago struck ten, I hurried to dress as quickly as possible. I confess, I wouldn't have gone to the department at all, knowing in advance what a sour face the chief of our division would make. For a long time he's been saying to me: "How come, brother, your head's always in such a muddle? Sometimes you run around like a lunatic, you get your work so tangled up that Satan himself couldn't make it out, you write a small letter in the heading, you don't put in either the date or the number." The damn heron! He probably envies me for sitting in the director's study and sharpening quills for his Excellency. In a word, I wouldn't have gone to the department if it weren't in the hope of seeing the treasurer and somehow getting even a little of my salary in advance out of that Jew. What a creature! For him ever to give money a month in advance—my God, the Judgment Day will come sooner. Beg him, tear your hair, be desperate—he won't give it, the grey-haired devil. But at home his own cook slaps him in the face. The whole world knows that. I don't understand the advantages of serving in my department. There are absolutely no benefits. In the provincial civil and treasury offices it's a completely different matter: there, you look, someone is squeezed into a tiny corner and writing. His wretched frockcoat is vile, his snout makes you want to spit, but just look at the dacha he rents! Don't bring him a porcelain gilded cup: "That," he'll say, "is a present for a doctor," but give him a pair of trotters, or a drozhky, or a beaver coat at three hundred rubles. He looks so quiet, speaks so tactfully: "Lend me your little knife to sharpen my little quill," and then he'll so clean out a petitioner that he'll leave him only his shirt. True, our work on the other hand is respectable, there is such cleanliness everywhere as a provincial office will never see, the tables are mahogany, and all the superiors use the formal form of address to us. Yes, I confess, if it weren't for the respectability of the work, I would have long ago left the department.

I put on my old overcoat and took my umbrella because it was pouring rain. There was no one on the streets; I saw only peasant women covering their heads with their skirts and Russian merchants under umbrellas, and coachmen. As for the respectable classes, only a fellow clerk was plodding along. I saw him at the intersection. As soon as I saw him I said to myself: "Aha! No, my dear, you're not going to the department, you're hurrying after that woman who's running along ahead of you and looking at her legs." What a beast our fellow clerk is! I swear to God, he's worse than any officer: some female goes by in a little hat and he's bound to attach himself. While I was thinking this, I saw a carriage drive up to the store I was passing. I recognized it at once. It was our director's carriage. But he has no reason to go to the store, I thought: "Probably it's his daughter." I pressed myself against the wall. A footman opened the doors, and she fluttered out of the carriage like a little bird. How she glanced left and right, how her brows and eyes flashed . . . My God! I was lost, completely lost. And why did she have to go out at such a rainy time. Now try to tell me women don't have a great passion for all those rags. She didn't recognize me, and anyway I deliberately tried to wrap myself up as much as possible, because I had on a very dirty overcoat, and an old-fashioned one at that. Now they wear cloaks with long collars but mine were little short ones one on top of the other; besides the cloth wasn't at all rainproof. Her little dog, not managing to leap in the door of the store, remained on the street. I know that little dog. Her name is Madgie. I hadn't been there a minute when I suddenly heard a thin little voice: "Hello, Madgie!" How do you like that! Who's speaking? I looked around and saw two ladies walking under umbrellas: one an old lady, the other a young one; but they had already passed, while near me again sounded: "Shame on you Madgie!" What the Devil! I saw that Madgie was exchanging sniffs with the little dog which had been following the ladies. "Aha!" I said to myself, "hang on, am I drunk? Only that, it seems, rarely happens to me." "No Fidèle, you're wrong to think that," I myself saw Madgie say "I was bow wow! I was bow wow wow! very sick." Oh you little dog! I confess, I was very surprised to hear her speaking human language. But later, when I thought this all out thoroughly, I stopped being surprised. Actually, a great number of such things have already happened in the world. They say that in England a fish swam up which said two words in such a strange language that scholars have been trying to identify it for three years already and still to this day haven't discovered a thing. I also read in the papers about two cows that came into a shop and asked for a pound of tea. But, I confess, I was much more surprised when Madgie said: "I did write to you, Fidèle; Polkan probably didn't bring you my letter!" Well I'll forfeit my salary! Never yet in my life have I heard of a dog that could write. Only a nobleman can write correctly. Of course, some shopkeeper–book-keepers and even serfs do a little writing sometimes, but their writing is mostly mechanical: no commas, no periods, no style.

This surprised me. I confess, recently I've begun to hear and see such things sometimes as no one has seen or heard before. "I think," I said to myself, "I'll follow that little dog and find out what she is and what she thinks." I folded up my umbrella and set off after the two ladies. They crossed to Gorokhovoy, turned into Meshchansky, then to Stolyarny, finally to Kokushkin Bridge, and stopped in front of a large house. "I know this house," I said to myself. "This is the Zverkov house." What a thing! What people live in it: how many cooks, how many Poles! and our fellows, the clerks, sit one on top of the other like dogs. I have a friend there who plays the trumpet well. The ladies went up to the fifth floor. "Good," I thought, "I won't go in now, but I'll remember the place and won't fail to make use of it at the first opportunity."

October 4th

Today is Wednesday, and therefore I was in our chief's study. I deliberately arrived a bit early and, having sat down, sharpened all the quills. Our director must be a very intelligent man. His whole study is lined with books. I read the titles of some of them: all scholarliness, such scholarliness that for one of my ilk there's no approaching it: it's all either in French or in German. And when you look him in the face: foo, what importance glows in his eyes! I have never yet heard him say a super-fluous word. Only perhaps when you give him a paper, he'll ask: "What's it like out?" "Damp, your Excellency." Yes, not a match for our ilk! A statesman. I've noticed though that he particularly likes me. If only the daughter too . . . ekh, rascalry! . . . Never mind, never mind, silence! I read the *Bee*. What a stupid people the French are! Well what do they want? I'd take them all, I swear to God, and birch them! There I also read a very pleasant description of a ball written by a Kursk landowner. Kursk landowners write well. After that I noticed that it had already struck twelve-thirty but our man hadn't come out of his bedroom. But around one-thirty an incident occurred which no pen can describe. The door opened, I thought it was the director, and I leapt from my chair with some papers; but it was she, she herself! Holy fathers, how she was dressed! Her dress was white as a swan: foo, how luxurious! And how she gazed: the sun! I swear to God, the sun! She bowed and said "Has Papa been here?" Ai yai yai! What a voice! A canary, really, a canary!

"Your Excellency," I wanted to say, "Don't command me to be executed, but if you want me executed, execute me with your little aristocratic hand." Yes, the devil take it, somehow my tongue wouldn't obey and I only said: "No, Miss." She looked at me, at the books, and dropped her handkerchief. I rushed after it, slipped on the damn parquet and almost knocked my nose off; however, I recovered myself and got the handkerchief. Saints, what a handkerchief! the most delicate, batiste—ambergris, absolute ambergris! It simply exudes aristocracy. She thanked me and smiled slightly so that her sweet little lips almost didn't move, and after that she went out. I sat for another hour when suddenly a footman came in and said: "Go home, Aksenty Ivanovich, the master has already gone out." I can't stand the footman set; they're always lounging around the front hall and won't even make the effort to nod to you. As if that weren't enough, once one of these beasts took it into his head, without even getting up from his place, to offer me some snuff. Do you know, you stupid serf, that I'm a clerk, I'm of noble origin. However I took my hat and put on my coat myself, because these gentlemen will never help you on with it, and went out. At home I mostly lay on my bed. Then I copied out some very good little verses:

> Not having seen my love an hour,
> I thought at least a year had passed;
> And finding that my life'd grown sour,
> Do I not live in vain, I asked.

Must be Pushkin's work.[1] In the evening, wrapped up in my overcoat, I walked to the entrance of her Excellency's house and waited for a long time to see if she wouldn't come out to get into her carriage so that I could have another little look at her,—but no, she didn't come out.

November 6th

The chief of the division was furious today. When I arrived at the department he called me in and began to talk to me like this: "Well, tell me please, what are you doing?" "What do you mean what? I'm not doing anything," I answered. "Well, think it over carefully! After all, you're over forty, it's time you got smart. Who do you think you are? You think I don't know all your tricks? You're chasing the director's daughter! Well, look at yourself, just think a bit, what are you? You're a zero, nothing more. You don't have a cent to your name. Just take a look in the mirror at your face, how can you think about that!" The devil take it, just because he has a face that looks a little like a druggist's bottle, and a clump of hair on his head curled into a pompadour, holds his head in the air and smears it with some kind of rosette oil, he thinks

---

[1] In fact by N. P. Nikolev (1758–1815). [The notes to this story are the translator's.]

that only he can do anything he wants. I understand, I understand why he's angry at me. He's jealous; maybe he's seen the preferential signs of approbation shown me. Well I spit on him! So what if he is a court councillor! He gets a gold chain for his watch, orders boots at thirty rubles—and the devil take him! Am I some plebian, some tailor or subaltern's child? I'm a nobleman. I can rise in the service too. I'm still forty-two—the time when service only really begins. Just wait, friend! We too will become a colonel, or maybe, if God's willing, something a little higher. We too will get ourselves a reputation even better than yours. How did you get it into your head that except for you there just isn't a single decent person? Just give me a fashionably tailored frock-coat, and let me put on a tie just like yours,—then you won't hold a candle to me. I have no means—that's the problem.

November 8th

Was at the theater. They did the Russian fool Filatka. Laughed a lot. There was also some vaudeville with amusing verses about clerks, especially about a certain collegiate registrar, quite freely written, so that I was surprised that the censorship let it through, and they say right out about merchants that they deceive the people and that their sons are debauched and climb into the nobility. There was also a very amusing couplet about journalists: that they love to rail against everything and that the author requests protection from the audience. Very funny plays authors are writing nowadays. I love going to the theater. As soon as there's a penny in your pocket—you can't keep from going. But among our fellow clerks there are such swine: he absolutely won't go to the theater, the peasant; only maybe if you gave him a ticket free. One actress sang very well. I remembered the one who . . . ekh, rascalry! . . . never mind, never mind . . . silence.

November 9th

At eight o'clock I set off for the department. The head of the division pretended he hadn't noticed my arrival. I too for my part, as if there had been nothing between us. I looked over and folded some papers. Went out at four o'clock. Passed the director's apartment but no one was in sight. After dinner mostly lay on my bed.

November 11th

Today I sat in our director's study, sharpened 23 quills for him, and for her, ai! ai . . . for her Excellency four quills. He really likes a lot of quills around. Ooh! What a brain he must be! Always silent, but in his head, I bet, always deliberating. I would like to find out what he thinks about most; what's going on in that head. I would like to have a closer look at the life of these gentlemen, all these equivoques and court doings, what they're like, what they do in their set—that's what I'd like to find out! Several times I've thought of starting a conversation with his Excellency, only, the devil take it, my tongue just doesn't obey: you only say it's cold or hot out, and you absolutely won't get out anything more. I would like to get a glimpse of the livingroom, which you only sometimes see through into still another room. Ekh, what rich decor! What mirrors and porcelain. I'd like to get a glimpse of the half where her Excellency is, that's what I'd like to see! The boudoir, how all those little jars and bottles are arranged, such flowers that it's terrifying even to breathe on them, how her dress lies thrown down there, looking more like air than a dress. I'd like to get a glimpse of the bedroom . . . there, I bet, are marvels, there, I bet, is a paradise such as is not even to be found in the heavens. To have a look at the little stool she stands on getting out of bed, at her little foot, at how she puts on her little stocking white as snow on her little foot . . . ai! ai! ai! never mind, never mind . . . silence.

Today however it came to me in a flash. I remembered that conversation between the two dogs that I heard on Nevsky Prospect. "Fine," I thought to myself. "Now I'll find out everything. I have to seize the correspondence those rotten little dogs were carrying on. There I'll probably find out something." I confess, I once even called Madgie over and said: "Listen, Madgie, here we are alone now, if you want, I'll even lock the door so no one will see, tell me everything you know about your mistress, what's she like? I swear to you I won't tell anyone." But the sly dog tucked her tail under her, doubled up and quietly went out the door as if she hadn't heard a thing. I have long suspected that dogs are much smarter than people; I was even sure that they can talk, but that they have a kind of stubbornness in them. They're exceptional politicians: they notice everything, a person's every step. No, no matter what, tomorrow I'll go to the Zverkov house, interrogate Fidèle and, if possible, seize all the letters Madgie wrote her.

November 12th

At two o'clock in the afternoon I set out to see Fidèle without fail and to interrogate her. I can't stand cabbage, the smell of which pours out of all the small shops on Meshchansky; furthermore such hellishness wafts out from under the gates of every house that I wrapped up my nose and ran as fast as I could. What's more, the foul craftsmen let out such a quantity of soot and smoke from their workshops that it's absolutely impossible for a respectable person to take a walk here. When I made my way up to the sixth floor and rang the bell, a not completely bad-looking girl with little freckles came out. I recognized her. It was the same one who had been walking with the old lady. She blushed a bit, and I suspected at once: you, dearie, want a fiancé. "What do you want?" said she. "I need to speak with your dog." The girl was stupid! I knew at once she was stupid! At that moment the dog ran up with a bark; I wanted to grab her but, the vile thing, she almost grabbed me by the nose with her teeth. However I saw her basket in the corner. Ah, that's just what I need! I went up to it, rummaged in the straw in the wooden box and, to my singular satisfaction, pulled out a small packet of little papers. The loathsome dog, seeing this, first bit me on the calf and then when she had sniffed out that I'd taken the papers, began to whine and fawn, but I said: "No, dearie, goodbye!" and ran off. I think the girl took me for a madman, because she was extraordinarily frightened. Having come home, I wanted to get to work at once and decipher those letters because I see a little badly by candlelight. But Mavra decided to clean the floor. These stupid Finns are always inappropriately cleanly. And therefore I went to take a walk and think over this occurrence. Now I'll finally find out all their affairs, designs, all those springs, and I'll finally get to the bottom of everything. These letters will reveal everything to me. Dogs are an intelligent lot, they know all the political relationships and therefore probably everything will be in there: a portrait and all the affairs of that husband. There'll also be something about her . . . never mind, silence! Towards evening I came home. Mostly lay on my bed.

November 13th

Well, let's see: the letter is pretty clear. However there's something sort of doggy in the handwriting. Let's read it:

> Dear Fidèle, I just can't get used to your bourgeois name. Couldn't they have given you a better one? Fidèle, Rose—what vulgar taste, however that's beside the point. I'm very glad we decided to write to each other.

The letter is very correctly written. The punctuation and even the spelling is right everywhere. Even our division chief couldn't write that simply, though he says he studied in a university somewhere. Let's look further:

> I think that sharing one's thoughts, feelings, and impressions with another is one of the great blessings in the world.

Hm! The thought is taken from some composition translated from the German. I don't recall the title.

I say this from experience, although I haven't been around in the world further than the gates of our house. Doesn't my life flow pleasurably? My mistress, whom Papa calls Sophie, loves me madly.

Ai, ai! . . . never mind, never mind. Silence!

Papa also pets me very often. I drink tea and coffee with cream. Akh, ma chère, I should tell you that I just don't see the pleasure of the big gnawed bones which our Polkan gobbles in the kitchen. The only good bones are from gamebirds, and then only when no one has sucked the marrow out of them yet. It's very good to mix several sauces together, only without capers and without greens; but I don't know of anything worse than the custom of giving dogs little balls rolled out of bread. Some gentleman or other sitting at the table who's held all sorts of trash in his hands will start mashing bread with these hands, call you over and shove a little ball in your teeth. To decline is somewhat impolite, so you eat it; with disgust, but you eat it . . .

The devil knows what that is. What nonsense! As if there weren't a better subject to write about. Let's look on another page. Maybe there'll be something a bit more sensible.

I'm quite ready and willing to inform you about all the events going on at our house. I've already told you something about the chief gentleman, whom Sophie calls Papa. He's a very strange person.

Ah! At last! Yes, I knew it: they have a political view of every subject. Let's see what Papa is like:

. . . a very strange person. Mostly he is silent. He speaks very seldom; but a week ago he talked to himself incessantly: "Will I get it or won't I get it?" He would take a paper in one hand, close the other empty one and say: "Will I get it or won't I get it?" Once he even turned to me with the question: "What do you think, Madgie? Will I get it, or won't I get it?" I couldn't understand anything at all, I sniffed his boot and went away. Then, ma chère, a week later Papa came home overjoyed. All morning gentlemen in uniforms came to see him and congratulated him for something. At the table he was merrier than I've ever seen him, told anecdotes, and after dinner held me up to his neck and said: "Look, Madgie, what's this?" I saw some little ribbon. I sniffed it, but found absolutely no aroma; finally, on the sly, I licked it: a little salty.

Hm! That little dog, I think, is a bit too . . . she ought to be whipped! Ah! So he's ambitious! This must be taken into account.

Farewell, ma chère! I must run and so on . . . and so on . . . Tomorrow I'll finish the letter. Well, hello! Now I'm back again. Today my mistress Sophie . . .

510

Ah! well, let's see what Sophie is like. Ekh, rascalry! Never mind, never mind . . . we will continue.

> . . . my mistress Sophie was in an extraordinary flurry. She was going to a ball and I was delighted that I could write to you in her absence. My Sophie is always extraordinarily glad to go to a ball, although she almost always gets angry getting dressed. I simply can't understand, ma chère, the pleasure of going to balls. Sophie comes home from balls at 6 A.M., and I almost always deduce from her pale and exhausted face that they haven't given her anything to eat there, the poor dear. I confess, I could never live like that. If they didn't give me gravy with grouse or hot chicken wings . . . I don't know what would become of me. Gravy with kasha's good too. But carrots, or turnips, or artichokes will never be any good . . .

Extraordinarily uneven style. It's immediately clear that a person didn't write it. She'll begin properly but end in dogginess. Let's have a look at another little letter. A bit longish. Hm! The date's not even given.

> Akh! My dear, how one senses the approach of spring! My heart beats as if it kept waiting for something. There's a perpetual noise in my ears. So that I often stand several minutes with lifted foot listening at the doors. I'll confide to you that I have many suitors. I often watch them as I sit on the window sill. Akh, if you knew what freaks there are among them. One coarse mongrel, terribly stupid, stupidity is written on his face, goes along the street importantly and imagines that he is the most distinguished individual, he thinks that everyone will turn to look at him. Not at all. I didn't even pay any attention, as if I hadn't even seen him. And what a terrifying great Dane keeps stopping in front of my window! If he were to stand on his hind legs, which, the boor, he probably can't do, he would be a whole head taller than my Sophie's Papa, who is also rather tall and fat. That blockhead must be awfully arrogant. I growled at him but he couldn't have cared less. If he'd at least frowned! He stuck out his tongue, hung his huge ears and looks in the window—such a peasant! But do you really think, ma chère, that my heart is indifferent to all seekers—akh, no . . . if you were to see one cavalier named Trésor climbing over the fence of the next house. Akh, ma chère, what a dear little snout he has!

Foo, the devil with it! . . . What trash! . . . And how can one fill letters with such stupidities? Give me a person! I want to see a person; I demand food of the kind that would nourish and delight my soul; but instead such trivia . . . Let's skip a page, maybe it'll be better:

> . . . Sophie was sitting at the table and sewing something. I was looking out the window because I like to watch the passersby. Suddenly the footman came in and said "Teplov!" "Ask him in" cried Sophie and ran to hug me. "Akh, Madgie, Madgie! If you only knew who that is: dark-haired, a court chamberlain, and what eyes! Black and bright as

511

fire!" And Sophie ran to her room. A minute later a young court chamberlain with black sidewhiskers walked in; he went up to the mirror, arranged his hair and looked around the room. I growled and sat down in my place. Sophie soon come out and gaily bowed to his heel clicking; but I continued looking out the window as if not noticing anything; however I bent my head slightly to the side and tried to hear what they were talking about. Akh, ma chère, what nonsense they were talking about! They were talking about how some lady did one figure instead of another in a dance; also about how some Bobov looked very much like a stork in his ruffled shirt and had almost fallen down; that some Lidina thinks she has blue eyes, whereas they're green,—and the like. What, I thought to myself, if you compared the court chamberlain with Trésor! Heavens! What a difference! First of all, the court chamberlain has sidewhiskers all around a completely smooth broad face as if he had tied it up in a black handkerchief; but Trésor has a slender little snout and a white patch on his forehead. And there's no comparing Trésor's waist with the court chamberlain's. And his eyes, ways, manners are completely different. Oh, what a difference! I don't know what she finds in her court chamberlain. Why is she so enraptured by him? . . .

It seems to me too that there's something wrong here. It's impossible that a court chamberlain could so fascinate her. Let's look further:

> It seems to me, if she likes that court chamberlain, she'll soon start liking that clerk who sits in papa's study. Akh, ma chère, if you knew what a freak he is. A real turtle in a sack . . .

What clerk could that be? . . .

> He has the strangest name. He always sits and sharpens quills. The hair on his head looks a lot like hay. Papa always sends him out instead of a servant . . .

It seems to me that this vile cur is alluding to me. Since when is my hair like hay?

> Sophie just can't keep from laughing when she looks at him.

You lie, you damn dog! What a vile tongue! As if I didn't know that it's a matter of envy. As if I didn't know whose doings these are. These are the doings of the division chief. After all, the man's sworn himself to unbending hatred—and so he attacks and attacks, at every step he attacks. Let's look, however, at another letter. Perhaps the matter will become clear by itself.

> Ma chère Fidèle, forgive me for not writing for so long. I have been in utter ecstasy. Truly did some writer say that love is a second life.

Furthermore there are big changes at our house. The court chamberlain is here every day now. Sophie is madly in love with him. Papa is very gay. I even heard from our Grigory who sweeps the floor and almost always has conversations with himself, that soon there'll be a wedding; because papa absolutely wants to see Sophie marry either a general or a court chamberlain, or a colonel . . .

The devil take it! I can't read any more . . . Everything's either a court chamberlain or a general. Everything that's best in the world, everything goes to court chamberlains or generals. You find yourself some poor treasure, you think it's within arm's reach,—and a court chamberlain or a general grabs it from you. The devil take it! I'd like to become a general myself, not to win her hand and so on. No; I'd like to be a general only in order to see how they dangle around doing all these various court routines and equivoques, and then tell them I spit on both of you. The devil take it. It's irritating! I tore the stupid dog's letters to bits.

December 3rd

It can't be. Rumors! There won't be a wedding! What if he is a court chamberlain? After all that's nothing more than a position; not some visible thing you could hold in your hands. After all, just because you're a court chamberlain you don't get a third eye in your forehead. After all, his nose isn't made of gold, but it's just like mine, like everyone's; after all, he uses it to smell with, and not to eat with, to sneeze with, not to cough with. I've wanted several times to figure out where all these differences come from. Why am I a titular councillor and why should I be a titular councillor? Maybe I'm some court or general, and only seem to be a titular councillor? Maybe I don't know myself who I am. After all, there are so many examples in history: there's some simple guy, not quite a noble, but simply some bourgeois or even a peasant —and suddenly it's discovered he's some magnate, and sometimes even a ruler. When a peasant sometimes turns out like that what might a noble turn out to be? Suddenly for example, I come in in a general's uniform: an epaulette on my right shoulder and an epaulette on my left shoulder, a blue ribbon across my chest—what'll happen? What tune will my beauty sing then? What will Papa himself say, our director? Oh, what an ambitious man! A mason, certainly a mason, although he pretends to be this and that, but I noticed at once that he's a mason: if he gives someone his hand, he only sticks out two fingers. And can't I this very minute be appointed governor general or commissary or some other thing? I'd like to know why I'm a titular councillor? Why precisely a titular councillor?

December 5th

Today I read the newspapers all morning. Strange things are going on in Spain. I couldn't even really figure them out. They write that the throne is vacant and that they are having difficulty trying to choose a successor and therefore insurrections are taking place. This seems extraordinarily strange to me. How can a throne be vacant? They say that some donna is supposed to ascend the throne. A donna can't ascend the throne. She just can't. A king should be on the throne. But they say there is no king.—It can't be that there is no king. A government can't be without a king. There is a king, only he's incognito somewhere. It might be that he's right there, but either some family reasons or threats on the part of neighboring powers, France and other lands, are somehow forcing him to hide, or there are some other reasons.

December 8th

I was quite ready to go to the department, but various reasons and considerations kept me. I just can't get the Spanish affairs out of my head. How can it be that a donna should become a queen? They won't permit that. And, in the first place, England won't permit it. And furthermore political affairs of all Europe: the Austrian emperor, our sovereign . . . . I confess, these events have so exhausted and shaken me that I absolutely couldn't do anything all day. Mavra kept remarking to me that I was exceptionally distracted at the table. And actually, it seems I threw two plates on the floor out of absentmindedness which instantly broke. After dinner I walked up to the hills. Couldn't get anything instructive out of it. Mostly lay on my bed and thought about the Spanish affairs.

Year 2000 43rd of April

Today is a day of the greatest jubilation! There is a king in Spain. He has been found. I am this king. Only just today did I find out about this. I confess, it struck me suddenly like lightning. I don't understand how I could think and imagine that I was a titular councillor. How could this mad thought get into my head. It's a good thing no one thought of putting me in the mad house at the time. Now everything has been revealed to me. Now I see everything clear as day. But before, I don't understand, before everything was in a kind of fog before me. And it all, I think, comes from the fact that people imagine that the human brain is located in the head; not at all: it is brought by the wind from the direction of the Caspian Sea. At first I revealed who I am to Mavra. When she heard that the king of Spain was standing before her, she threw up her hands and almost died of fright. The stupid woman had never seen a king of Spain before. However, I tried to calm her and tried to assure her in gracious words of my good favor, and that I wasn't the least angry that she sometimes cleaned my boots badly. After all they're a benighted lot. They can't talk about elevated subjects. She was frightened because she is convinced that all kings in Spain look like Philip II.[2] But I explained to her that there is no resemblance between me and Philip and that I don't have a single Capuchin . . . Didn't go to the department. The devil with it! No, friends, you won't entice me now; I'm not about to copy your foul papers!

Marchtober the 86th
Between day and night

Today our messenger came to get me to go to the department since I haven't been going to work for more than three weeks already. I went to the department just for kicks. The division chief thought that I'd bow to him and start apologizing but I looked at him indifferently, not too angrily and not too graciously, and sat down in my place as if not noticing anyone. I gazed at the whole office scum and thought: "What if you knew who's sitting among you . . . My god! What a hubbub you'd raise, and the division chief himself would start bowing low to me the way he now bows to the director." They put some papers before me for me to do an extract of them. But I didn't even lift a finger to them. After a few minutes everything flew into a flurry. They said the director was coming. Many clerks ran up and vied with each other to show themselves to him. But I didn't budge. When he passed through our division everyone buttoned up their frock coats; but I didn't do a thing! What's a director! I'm supposed to stand up for him—never! What kind of director is he? He's a cork, not a director. An ordinary cork, a simple cork, nothing more. The kind they stop bottles with. What amused me most was when they thrust a paper at me to sign. They thought that I'd write on the very bottom of the sheet: clerk so-and-so, what else? But in the most important place where the director of the department signs, I wrote: "Ferdinand VIII." You should've seen what an awed silence reigned; but I just waved my hand, saying: "No signs of allegiance are necessary!"—and went out. From there I went straight to the director's apartment. He wasn't home. A footman didn't want to let me in, but I said such things to him that he simply gave up. I made my way straight to her dressingroom. She was sitting before a mirror; she leapt up and retreated from me. However, I didn't tell her that I was the King of

---

[2] King of Spain during the peak of the Inquisition.

Spain. I only said that such happiness awaited her as she couldn't even imagine and that, despite the machinations of our enemies, we would be together. I didn't want to say anything more and went out. Oh, what a perfidious creature is woman! Only now have I comprehended what woman is. Until now no one has yet discovered who she's in love with: I'm the first to discover it. Woman is in love with the Devil. Yes, no joking. Physicists write stupidities, that she's this and that—she loves only the Devil. You see over there, in the first tier of boxes, she's focusing her lorgnette. You think she's looking at that fat man with the medal? Not at all, she's looking at the Devil who's standing behind his back. Now he's hiding in his medal. Now he's beckoning to her with his finger! And she'll marry him. She will. And all those people, all their high-ranking fathers, all these who fawn in all directions and climb into court circles, and say they're patriots and this and that: rents, rents are what these patriots want! They'd sell their mother, father, God for money, ambitious creatures, Christ-sellers! It's all ambition and ambition comes from a little bubble under the tongue and in it there's a small worm the size of the head of a pin, and it's all done by some barber who lives on Gorokhovaya. I don't remember his name; but it's certainly true that he and a certain midwife want to spread Mohammedanism throughout the whole world and therefore, they say, the majority of the people in France already profess the faith of Mahomet.

No date at all.
The day was dateless.

I walked incognito along Nevsky Prospect. The imperial sovereign drove by. The whole city took off their hats and I did too; however I gave no sign whatsoever that I was the king of Spain. I considered it indecorous to reveal myself right there in front of everyone because my tall confrère would probably have asked why the king of Spain had not yet been presented at court. And indeed one should present oneself at court first. The only thing that stopped me was that I still don't have a king's raiment. At least if I could get a royal mantle. I wanted to order it from the tailor, but they're complete asses, besides they're utterly careless with their work, they're addicted to fraud and mostly cobble stones on the street. I decided to sew myself a royal mantle out of my new uniform which I'd only worn twice. But so that those scoundrels couldn't ruin it, I decided to sew it myself, locking the door so that no one would see. I cut it all up with the scissors because it was necessary to redo it entirely and give the whole cloth the appearance of ermine tails.

Don't remember the date.
There was no month either.
The devil knows what there was.

The royal mantle is completely ready and sewn. Mavra screamed when I put it on. However I still haven't decided to present myself at court. There's still no delegation from Spain. It's improper without deputies. There'll be no weight to my dignity. I expect them any hour.

The 1st date

The extraordinary slowness of the deputies surprises me. What reasons could be detaining them? Not France? Yes, that's the most unfavorably disposed power. I went to the post office to find out if the Spanish deputies hadn't arrived. But the postmaster was extraordinarily stupid, he doesn't know anything: no, he says, there aren't any Spanish deputies here, but if you want to write letters, we'll take them at the established rate.—The devil take it! What's a letter? A letter's nonsense. Druggists write letters . . .

Madrid. Februarius the thirtieth

And so I'm in Spain, and it happened so quickly that I could hardly regain my senses. This morning the Spanish deputies came to me and I got into a carriage with them. The extraordinary speed seemed strange to me. We drove so fast that in half an hour we reached the Spanish border. However, there are now cast iron roads all over Europe and steamboats go extraordinarily fast. Spain is a strange land: when we entered the first room I saw a number of people with shaved heads. However I guessed that these must be either Dominicans or Capuchins because they shave their heads. The conduct of the State Chancellor who led me by the arm seemed extraordinarily strange to me; he pushed me into a small room and said: "Sit here and if you keep calling yourself King Ferdinand I'll beat that whim out of you." But, knowing this was nothing more than a test, I answered negatively, for which the Chancellor hit me twice with a stick on the back so painfully that I almost screamed, but I restrained myself, remembering that this was a custom of the knights on entering high rank, because in Spain even to this day knightly customs are maintained. Remaining alone, I decided to occupy myself with government affairs. I discovered that China and Spain are absolutely one and the same country, and it's only from ignorance that they're considered different nations. I advise everyone to write down Spain on paper, and it'll come out China. But I was exceptionally grieved by an event which will take place tomorrow. Tomorrow at 7 o'clock a terrible phenomenon will be accomplished: the earth will mount the moon. The famous English chemist Wellington writes about it. I confess, I felt real anxiety when I imagined the unusual delicacy and frailty of the moon. The moon after all is usually made in Hamburg; and is most poorly made. I'm surprised that England pays no attention to this. A lame cooper makes it, and it's clear the fool hasn't the least conception of a moon. He used tarred rope and part olive oil; and therefore there's a terrible stench all over the earth so that you have to hold your nose. And therefore the moon itself is such a delicate sphere that people simply can't live there and now only noses live there. And that's why we can't see our own noses, for they're all on the moon. And when I realized that the earth is a heavy substance and by mounting could grind our noses into flour, such anxiety possessed me that, putting on my shoes and socks, I hurried into the State Council hall in order to give an order to the police not to let the earth mount the moon. The Capuchins of whom I found a great number in the State Council hall were a very intelligent lot and when I said: "Gentlemen, let us save the moon; because the earth wants to mount it," everyone at once ran to carry out my monarchal will and many climbed the wall in order to get the moon; but at that time the great Chancellor came in. Seeing him, everyone scattered. I, as the king, remained alone. But the Chancellor, to my surprise, struck me with a stick and chased me into my room. Such power do folk customs have in Spain!

January of the same year,
occurring after February

I still don't understand what kind of a country Spain is. The folk customs and court etiquette are quite unusual. I don't understand, I don't understand, I absolutely don't understand anything. Today they shaved my head, despite the fact that I shouted with all my might about my unwillingness to be a monk. But I can't even remember anymore what happened to me when they began to drip cold water on my head. I have never felt such hell. I was ready to fly into a frenzy, so that they could hardly restrain me. I just don't understand the significance of that strange custom. The custom is stupid, senseless! The folly of the kings who haven't yet abolished it is incomprehensible to me. Judging by all probabilities, I wonder: haven't I fallen into the hands of the Inquisition, and the one I took for the Chancellor, isn't he the Grand Inquisitor himself? Only I still can't understand how a king could be subject to the Inquisition. It's possible, true, on France's part and especially Polignac's.[3] Oh, that beast Polignac! He's sworn to harm me to the death. And now he

[3] Reactionary prime minister of France in 1830.

518

pursues and pursues me; but I know, friend, that you're being led by the Englishman. The Englishman is a great politician. He bustles about everywhere. It's already known to the whole world that when England takes snuff France sneezes.

date 25th

Today the Grand Inquisitor came to my room but, hearing his steps when he was still at a distance, I hid under the chair. Seeing that I wasn't there, he began to call me. At first he shouted: "Poprishchin!" I didn't say a word. Then: "Aksenty Ivanov! Titular councillor! Nobleman!" I keep silent. "Ferdinand VIII, King of Spain!" I was about to stick out my head, but then I thought: "No, brother, you won't find me! What do we need you for: you're going to pour cold water on my head again." However he saw me and chased me out from under the chair with a stick. The damn stick hits extraordinarily painfully. However, today's discovery rewarded me for all that: I found out that every rooster has a Spain, that it is found under his feathers. The Grand Inquisitor however left me in a rage and threatening me with some punishment. But I completely disregarded his impotent malice, knowing that he is acting like a machine, as a tool of the Englishman.

Da 34 te Mth gdao. ɟɹɐnɹqǝℲ 349

No, I have no more strength to endure it. God! What they're doing to me! They pour cold water on my head! They don't listen to, don't see, don't hear me. What did I do to them? Why are they tormenting me? What do they want·from poor me? What·can I give them? I don't have anything. I don't have the strength, I can't bear all their torments, my head burns and everything whirls before me. Save me! Take me away! Give me a troika with horses swift as a whirlwind! Take your seat, my coachman, ring, my bells, soar up, steeds, and bear me away from this world! Further, further, so that nothing, nothing is visible. There the heavens swirl before me; a little star twinkles in the distance; the forest rushes past with dark trees and the moon; a blue-grey fog spreads out beneath my feet; a chord rings in the fog; on one side the sea, on the other—Italy; over there Russian huts can be seen. Is that my house showing blue in the distance? Is that my mother sitting at the window? Mother, save your poor son! Shed a tear on his sick head! Look how they torment him! Press your poor orphan to your bosom! There is no place for him in the world! They're chasing him away!—Mother! Have pity on your sick child! . . . And did you know that the Bey of Algiers has a bump right under his nose?

Lady Lazarus

Sylvia Plath

This powerful poem works on several levels. It is perhaps most obviously autobiographical, the "story" of how Sylvia Plath (1932–63) came close to death three times: accidentally when she was ten years old, and as a near suicide at the ages of twenty and thirty. The text seems to be saying at this level that the poet has gone through three selves: the thirty-year-old who wrote it is living on the ashes of the ten- and twenty-year-old "selves" she has lived through. No longer a child or young girl, she is yet "the same, identical woman." On another level this pattern of emerging anew at various ages suggests mythic parallels, Lazarus and the Phoenix. Like Lazarus, the poet rises living out of the dead past. Also present is the suggestion of the Phoenix, the legendary bird that every five hundred years would burn itself on a pyre and be regenerated. The flame imagery is tied in with the poem's third level, which mediates between the personal and the mythic: history. The poet identifies fire with the ovens in which the Nazis burned their Jewish victims (of course Lazarus was also a Jew). Just as her individual self has arisen anew out of the pyre of her former identities, so, the poet asserts, will the Jewish "selves" be purified and be regenerated. Life will arise out of death.

■

I have done it again.
One year in every ten
I manage it——

A sort of walking miracle, my skin
Bright as a Nazi lampshade,
My right foot

A paperweight,
My face a featureless, fine
Jew linen.

Peel off the napkin   10
O my enemy.
Do I terrify?——

The nose, the eye pits, the full set of teeth?
The sour breath
Will vanish in a day.

Soon, soon the flesh
The grave cave ate will be
At home on me

And I a smiling woman.
I am only thirty.   20
And like the cat I have nine times to die.

This is Number Three.
What a trash
To annihilate each decade.

What a million filaments.
The peanut-crunching crowd
Shoves in to see

Them unwrap me hand and foot——
The big strip tease.
Gentleman, ladies,   30

These are my hands,
My knees.
I may be skin and bone,

Nevertheless, I am the same, identical woman.
The first time it happened I was ten.
It was an accident.

The second time I meant
To last it out and not come back at all.
I rocked shut

As a seashell.   40
They had to call and call
And pick the worms off me like sticky pearls.

Dying
Is an art, like everything else.
I do it exceptionally well.

I do it so it feels like hell.
I do it so it feels real.
I guess you could say I've a call.

It's easy enough to do it in a cell.
It's easy enough to do it and stay put.   50
It's the theatrical

Comeback in broad day
To the same place, the same face, the same brute
Amused shout:

"A miracle!"
That knocks me out.
There is a charge

For the eyeing of my scars, there is a charge
For the hearing of my heart——
It really goes.   60

And there is a charge, a very large charge,
For a word or a touch
Or a bit of blood

Or a piece of my hair or my clothes.
So, so, Herr Doktor.
So, Herr Enemy.

I am your opus,
I am your valuable,
The pure gold baby

That melts to a shriek.   70
I turn and burn.
Do not think I underestimate your great concern.

Ash, ash—
You poke and stir.
Flesh, bone, there is nothing there——

A cake of soap,
A wedding ring,
A gold filling.

Herr God, Herr Lucifer,
Beware
Beware.   80

Out of the ash
I rise with my red hair
And I eat men like air.

The Theater of Cruelty

Antonin Artaud

Translated by Mary C. Richards

Artaud (1896–1947) was a great dreamer who led a tortured life as poet, mental patient, screen star, experimenter with drugs, director, and actor on the French stage. But he is best remembered for his revolutionary theories about the future of the theater. Artaud's ideas are rooted in an attempt to break away from the artificiality of the theatrical experience in the West. He sought to bridge the distance between actors and audience, the drama and "real life." The theater should not be mere entertainment, escape from reality: rather, it should take on a higher reality of its own.

The concepts of self and role constitute a metaphor derived from the theater, as we have seen. But it is taken from the kind of theater that Artaud wants abandoned because it implies "play-acting," "pretending" —separations. Western theater has traditionally depended on words. Artaud, however, envisions a total theater in which "living heiroglyphs" will replace the centrality of the word. Such a theater "ultimately breaks away from the intellectual subjugation of the language, by conveying the sense of a new and deeper intellectuality which hides itself beneath the gestures and signs."

We saw in the introduction to Part IV how literary characters from Achilles to Tarzan discover they cannot express their essential selves in words. If the theater ever succeeds in realizing Artaud's dream for it, the distinctions between self and role that find their analogue in traditional drama will fall away. Perhaps the drama will then provide a new metaphor for identity, a metaphor not of division, but of unity.

■

We cannot go on prostituting the idea of theater whose only value is in its excruciating, magical relation to reality and danger.

Put in this way, the question of the theater ought to arouse general attention, the implication being that theater, through its physical aspect, since it requires *expression in space* (the only real expression, in fact), allows the magical means of art and speech to be exercised organically and altogether, like renewed exorcisms. The upshot of all this is that theater will not be given its specific powers of action until it is given its language.

That is to say: instead of continuing to rely upon texts considered definitive and sacred, it is essential to put an end to the subjugation of the theater to the text, and to recover the notion of a kind of unique language half-way between gesture and thought.

This language cannot be defined except by its possibilities for dynamic expression in space as opposed to the expressive possibilities of spoken dialogue. And what the theater can still take over from speech are its possibilities for extension beyond words, for development in space, for dissociative and vibratory action upon the sensibility. This is the hour of intonations, of a word's particular pronunciation. Here too intervenes (besides the auditory language of sounds) the visual language of objects, movements, attitudes, and gestures, but on condition that their meanings, their physiognomies, their combinations be carried to the point of becoming signs, making a kind of alphabet out of these signs. Once aware of this language in space, language of sounds, cries, lights, onomatopoeia, the theater must organize it into veritable hieroglyphs, with the help of characters and objects, and make use of their symbolism and interconnections in relation to all organs and on all levels.

The question, then, for the theater, is to create a metaphysics of speech, gesture, and expression, in order to rescue it from its servitude to psychology and "human interest." But all this can be of no use unless behind such an effort there is some kind of real metaphysical inclination, an appeal to certain unhabitual ideas, which by their very nature cannot be limited or even formally depicted. These ideas, which touch on Creation, Becoming, and Chaos, are all of a cosmic order and furnish a primary notion of a domain from which the theater is now entirely alien. They are able to create a kind of passionate equation between Man, Society, Nature, and Objects.

It is not, moreover, a question of bringing metaphysical ideas directly onto the stage, but of creating what you might call temptations, indraughts of air around these ideas. And humor with its anarchy, poetry with its symbolism and its images, furnish a basic notion of ways to channel the temptation of these ideas.

We must speak now about the uniquely material side of this language—that is, about all the ways and means it has of acting upon the sensibility.

It would be meaningless to say that it includes music, dance, pantomime, or mimicry. Obviously it uses movement, harmonies, rhythms, but only to the point that they can concur in a sort of central expression without advantage for any one particular art. This does not at all mean that it does not use ordinary actions, ordinary passions, but like a springboard uses them in the same way that HUMOR AS DESTRUCTION can serve to reconcile the corrosive nature of laughter to the habits of reason.

But by an altogether Oriental means of expression, this objective and concrete language of the theater can fascinate and ensnare the organs. It flows into the sensibility. Abandoning Occidental usages of speech, it turns words into incantations. It extends the voice. It utilizes the vibra-

524

tions and qualities of the voice. It wildly tramples rhythms underfoot. It pile-drives sounds. It seeks to exalt, to benumb, to charm, to arrest the sensibility. It liberates a new lyricism of gesture which, by its precipitation or its amplitude in the air, ends by surpassing the lyricism of words. It ultimately breaks away from the intellectual subjugation of the language, by conveying the sense of a new and deeper intellectuality which hides itself beneath the gestures and signs, raised to the dignity of particular exorcisms.

For all this magnetism, all this poetry, and all these direct means of spellbinding would be nothing if they were not used to put the spirit physically on the track of something else, if the true theater could not give us the sense of a creation of which we possess only one face, but which is completed on other levels.

And it is of little importance whether these other levels are really conquered by the mind or not, i.e., by the intelligence; it would diminish them, and that has neither interest nor sense. What is important is that, by positive means, the sensitivity is put in a state of deepened and keener perception, and this is the very object of the magic and the rites of which the theater is only a reflection.

Technique

It is a question then of making the theater, in the proper sense of the word, a function; something as localized and as precise as the circulation of the blood in the arteries or the apparently chaotic development of dream images in the brain, and this is to be accomplished by a thorough involvement, a genuine enslavement of the attention.

The theater will never find itself again—i.e., constitute a means of true illusion—except by furnishing the spectator with the truthful precipitates of dreams, in which his taste for crime, his erotic obsessions, his savagery, his chimeras, his utopian sense of life and matter, even his cannibalism, pour out, on a level not counterfeit and illusory, but interior.

In other terms, the theater must pursue by all its means a reassertion not only of all the aspects of the objective and descriptive external world, but of the internal world, that is, of man considered metaphysically. It is only thus, we believe, that we shall be able to speak again in the theater about the rights of the imagination. Neither humor, nor poetry, nor imagination means anything unless, by an anarchistic destruction generating a prodigious flight of forms which will constitute the whole spectacle, they succeed in organically re-involving man, his ideas about reality, and his poetic place in reality.

To consider the theater as a second-hand psychological or moral function, and to believe that dreams themselves have only a substitute function, is to diminish the profound poetic bearing of dreams as well as of the theater. If the theater, like dreams, is bloody and inhuman, it is, more than just that, to manifest and unforgettably root within us the idea of a perpetual conflict, a spasm in which life is continually lacerated, in which everything in creation rises up and exerts itself against our appointed rank; it is in order to perpetuate in a concrete and immediate way the metaphysical ideas of certain Fables whose very atrocity and energy suffice to show their origin and continuity in essential principles.

This being so, one sees that, by its proximity to principles which transfer their energy to it poetically, this naked language of the theater (not a virtual but a real language) must permit, by its use of man's nervous magnetism, the transgression of the ordinary limits of art and speech, in order to realize actively, that is to say magically, *in real terms,* a kind of total creation in which man must reassume his place between dream and events.

The Themes

It is not a matter of boring the public to death with transcendent cosmic preoccupations. That there may be profound keys to thought and action with which to interpret the whole spectacle, does not in general concern the spectator, who is simply not interested. But still they must be there; and that concerns us.

The Spectacle. Every spectacle will contain a physical and objective element, perceptible to all. Cries, groans, apparitions, surprises, theatricalities of all kinds, magic beauty of costumes taken from certain ritual models; resplendent lighting, incantational beauty of voices, the charms of harmony, rare notes of music, colors of objects, physical rhythm of movements whose crescendo and decrescendo will accord exactly with the pulsation of movements familiar to everyone, concrete appearances of new and surprising objects, masks, effigies yards high, sudden changes of light, the physical action of light which arouses sensations of heat and cold, etc.

The Mise en Scène. The typical language of the theater will be constituted around the *mise en scène* considered not simply as the degree of refraction of a text upon the stage, but as the point of departure for all theatrical creation. And it is in the use and handling of this language that the old duality between author and director will be dissolved, replaced by a sort of unique Creator upon whom will devolve the double responsibility of the spectacle and the plot.

The Language of the Stage. It is not a question of suppressing the spoken language, but of giving words approximately the importance they have in dreams.

526

Meanwhile new means of recording this language must be found, whether these means belong to musical transcription or to some kind of code.

As for ordinary objects, or even the human body, raised to the dignity of signs, it is evident that one can draw one's inspiration from hieroglyphic characters, not only in order to record these signs in a readable fashion which permits them to be reproduced at will, but in order to compose on the stage precise and immediately readable symbols.

On the other hand, this code language and musical transcription will be valuable as a means of transcribing voices.

Since it is fundamental to this language to make a particular use of intonations, these intonations will constitute a kind of harmonic balance, a secondary deformation of speech which must be reproducible at will.

Similarly the ten thousand and one expressions of the face caught in the form of masks can be labeled and catalogued, so they may eventually participate directly and symbolically in this concrete language of the stage, independently of their particular psychological use.

Moreover, these symbolical gestures, masks, and attitudes, these individual or group movements whose innumerable meanings constitute an important part of the concrete language of the theater, evocative gestures, emotive or arbitrary attitudes, excited pounding out of rhythms and sounds, will be doubled, will be multiplied by reflections, as it were, of the gestures and attitudes consisting of the mass of all the impulsive gestures, all the abortive attitudes, all the lapses of mind and tongue, by which are revealed what might be called the impotences of speech, and in which is a prodigious wealth of expressions, to which we shall not fail to have recourse on occasion.

There is, besides, a concrete idea of music in which the sounds make their entrance like characters, where harmonies are coupled together and lose themselves in the precise entrances of words.

From one means of expression to another, correspondences and levels of development are created—even light can have a precise intellectual meaning.

Musical Instruments. They will be treated as objects and as part of the set.

Also, the need to act directly and profoundly upon the sensibility through the organs invites research, from the point of view of sound, into qualities and vibrations of absolutely new sounds, qualities which present-day musical instruments do not possess and which require the revival of ancient and forgotten instruments or the invention of new ones. Research is also required, apart from music, into instruments and appliances which, based upon special combinations or new alloys of metal, can attain a new range and compass, producing sounds or noises that are unbearably piercing.

527

Lights, Lighting. The lighting equipment now in use in theaters is no longer adequate. The particular action of light upon the mind, the effects of all kinds of luminous vibration must be investigated, along with new ways of spreading the light in waves, in sheets, in fusillades of fiery arrows. The color gamut of the equipment now in use is to be revised from beginning to end. In order to produce the qualities of particular musical tones, light must recover an element of thinness, density, and opaqueness, with a view to producing the sensations of heat, cold, anger, fear, etc.

Costumes. Where costumes are concerned, modern dress will be avoided as much as possible without at the same time assuming a uniform theatrical costuming that would be the same for every play—not from a fetishist and superstitious reverence for the past, but because it seems absolutely evident that certain age-old costumes, of ritual intent, though they existed at a given moment of time, preserve a beauty and a revelational appearance from their closeness to the traditions that gave them birth.

The Stage—The Auditorium. We abolish the stage and the auditorium and replace them by a single site, without partition or barrier of any kind, which will become the theater of the action. A direct communication will be re-established between the spectator and the spectacle, between the actor and the spectator, from the fact that the spectator, placed in the middle of the action, is engulfed and physically affected by it. This envelopment results, in part, from the very configuration of the room itself.

Thus, abandoning the architecture of present-day theaters, we shall take some hangar or barn, which we shall have reconstructed according to processes which have culminated in the architecture of certain churches or holy places, and of certain temples in Tibet.

In the interior of this construction special proportions of height and depth will prevail. The hall will be enclosed by four walls, without any kind of ornament, and the public will be seated in the middle of the room, on the ground floor, on mobile chairs which will allow them to follow the spectacle which will take place all around them. In effect, the absence of a stage in the usual sense of the word will provide for the deployment of the action in the four corners of the room. Particular positions will be reserved for actors and action at the four cardinal points of the room. The scenes will be played in front of whitewashed wall-backgrounds designed to absorb the light. In addition, galleries overhead will run around the periphery of the hall as in certain primitive paintings. These galleries will permit the actors, whenever the action makes it necessary, to be pursued from one point in the room to another, and the action to be deployed on all levels and in all perspectives of height and depth. A cry uttered at one end of the room can be transmitted from

528

mouth to mouth with amplifications and successive modulations all the way to the other. The action will unfold, will extend its trajectory from level to level, point to point; paroxysms will suddenly burst forth, will flare up likes fires in different spots. And to speak of the spectacle's character as true illusion or of the direct and immediate influence of the action on the spectator will not be hollow words. For this diffusion of action over an immense space will oblige the lighting of a scene and the varied lighting of a performance to fall upon the public as much as upon the actors—and to the several simultaneous actions or several phases of an identical action in which the characters, swarming over each other like bees, will endure all the onslaughts of the situations and the external assaults of the tempestuous elements, will correspond the physical means of lighting, of producing thunder or wind, whose repercussions the spectator will undergo.

However, a central position will be reserved which, without serving, properly speaking, as a stage, will permit the bulk of the action to be concentrated and brought to a climax whenever necessary.

Objects—Masks—Accessories. Manikins, enormous masks, objects of strange proportions will appear with the same sanction as verbal images, will enforce the concrete aspect of every image and every expression—with the corollary that all objects requiring a stereotyped physical representation will be discarded or disguised.

The Set. There will not be any set. This function will be sufficiently undertaken by hieroglyphic characters, ritual costumes, manikins ten feet high representing the beard of King Lear in the storm, musical instruments tall as men, objects of unknown shape and purpose.

Immediacy. But, people will say, a theater so divorced from life, from facts, from immediate interests . . . . From the present and its events, yes! From whatever preoccupations have any of that profundity which is the prerogative of some men, no! In the *Zohar*, the story of Rabbi Simeon who burns like fire is as immediate as fire itself.

Works. We shall not act a written play, but we shall make attempts at direct staging, around themes, facts, or known works. The very nature and disposition of the room suggest this treatment, and there is no theme, however vast, that can be denied us.

Spectacle. There is an idea of integral spectacles which must be regenerated. The problem is to make space speak, to feed and furnish it; like mines laid in a wall of rock which all of a sudden turns into geysers and bouquets of stone.

The Actor. The actor is both an element of first importance, since it is upon the effectiveness of his work that the success of the spectacle

529

depends, and a kind of passive and neutral element, since he is rigorously denied all personal initiative. It is a domain in which there is no precise rule; and between the actor of whom is required the mere quality of a sob and the actor who must deliver an oration with all his personal qualities of persuasiveness, there is the whole margin which separates a man from an instrument.

The Interpretation. The spectacle will be calculated from one end to the other, like a code (*un langage*). Thus there will be no lost movements, all movements will obey a rhythm; and each character being merely a type, his gesticulation, physiognomy, and costume will appear like so many rays of light.

The Cinema. To the crude visualization of what is, the theater through poetry opposes images of what is not. However, from the point of view of action, one cannot compare a cinematic image which, however poetic it may be, is limited by the film to a theatrical image which obeys all the exigencies of life.

Cruelty. Without an element of cruelty at the root of every spectacle, the theater is not possible. In our present state of degeneration it is through the skin that metaphysics must be made to re-enter our minds.

The Public. First of all this theater must exist.

The Program. We shall stage, without regard for text:
1. An adaptation of a work from the time of Shakespeare, a work entirely consistent with our present troubled state of mind, whether one of the apocryphal plays of Shakespeare, such as *Arden of Feversham,* or an entirely different play from the same period.
2. A play of extreme poetic freedom by Leon-Paul Fargue.
3. An extract from the *Zohar:* The Story of Rabbi Simeon, which has the ever present violence and force of a conflagration.
4. The story of Bluebeard reconstructed according to the historical records and with a new idea of eroticism and cruelty.
5. The Fall of Jerusalem, according to the Bible and history; with the blood-red color that trickles from it and the people's feeling of abandon and panic visible even in the light; and on the other hand the metaphysical disputes of the prophets, the frightful intellectual agitation they create and the repercussions of which physically affect the King, the Temple, the People, and Events themselves.
6. A Tale by the Marquis de Sade, in which the eroticism will be transposed, allegorically mounted and figured, to create a violent exteriorization of cruelty, and a dissimulation of the remainder.
7. One or more romantic melodramas in which the improbability will become an active and concrete element of poetry.

530

8. Büchner's *Wozzek,* in a spirit of reaction against our principles and as an example of what can be drawn from a formal text in terms of the stage.

9. Works from the Elizabethan theater stripped of their text and retaining only the accouterments of period, situations, characters, and action.

Author-Title Index

B 4
C 5
D 6
E 7
F 8
G 9
H 0
I 1
J 2